MYANMAR IN THE FIFTEENTH CENTURY

Myanmar in the Fifteenth Century

A TALE OF TWO KINGDOMS

Michael A. Aung-Thwin

University of Hawai'i Press ◈ Honolulu

Paperback edition 2021

Printed in the United States of America

26 25 24 23 22 21 6 5 4 3 2 1

Library of Congress Cataloging-in-Publication Data

Names: Aung-Thwin, Michael, author.
Title: Myanmar in the fifteenth century : a tale of two kingdoms / Michael A. Aung-Thwin.
Description: Honolulu : University of Hawai'i Press, [2017] | Includes bibliographical references and index.
Identifiers: LCCN 2016055815 | ISBN 9780824867836 (cloth ; alk. paper)
Subjects: LCSH: Burma—History—To 1824.
Classification: LCC DS529.3 .A88 2017 | DDC 959.1/02—dc23 LC record available at https://lccn.loc.gov/2016055815

ISBN 978-0-8248-8942-5 (paperback)

University of Hawai'i Press books are printed on acid-free paper and meet the guidelines for permanence and durability of the Council on Library Resources.

To Maria

CONTENTS

ACKNOWLEDGMENTS

The people to whom I am really indebted for this book are those whose works are listed in the bibliography. Yet, there are those whose works are not listed—with whom I have worked out in the gym, corresponded via email, talked on the phone, had meals in places my wife would never go near, and travelled to remote parts of Myanmar despite our best judgments—who have stimulated my thinking in no inconsiderable way but are not acknowledged here. Of course, I cannot remember them all here but wish to convey my heartfelt thanks to them just the same.

As for institutions, I owe much to the University of Hawai'i at Mānoa, my home institution, and the Asian Studies Program, my department—not least my academic position, which allows me to conduct research of this nature. But I would also like to thank other institutions for this particular work: both the National University of Singapore and Nanyang Technological University, also in Singapore, for their generous support. The former, in 2009, saw the germ of this manuscript, and the latter, in the summer of 2015, allowed me to "fine tune" it. Thanks to family usually conclude one's acknowledgments, so in addition to my immediate family here in Hawai'i, thanks are also due to my extended *'ohana,* here as well as in other areas of the world, especially Myanmar, Singapore, and the Philippines.

SOURCES AND ROMANIZATION

The contemporary stone inscriptions (*kyauksa*) erected during the period under study are the most crucial to the reconstruction of the institutional history of Ava and Pegu and to the verification of the narrative history found in later chronicles (*yazawin*). More than four hundred inscriptions erected at Ava and approximately a hundred at Pegu survive, counting those that belong to the period of time just prior to, during, and shortly after each dynasty.

Unlike Ava, reconstructing Pegu's institutional history from contemporary and original evidence is problematic because of its scarcity; the kingdom simply produced far less original and contemporary source materials than Ava did. Moreover, the most abundant sources about Pegu are actually in Burmese, with a few English translations of original Middle Mon inscriptions and a smattering of short, but firsthand, European accounts of its later stages. Indeed, this paucity of contemporary sources regarding Pegu may be the reason there is not a single scholarly book on its history published in English or Burmese heretofore, especially one that has been reconstructed from original data. Nonetheless, and having been dealt that hand, one does the best one can with it.

In terms of narrative history, I have depended on the standard chronicles called *yazawin.* But here as well, nearly all of the earliest and most comprehensive ones were written in Upper Myanmar and in Burmese (even those about Pegu and the Mon), supplemented by others that are more focused on individual kings, dynasties, and regions. Similarly verse: whereas many genres were produced by the Ava court in Burmese, I know of none that were produced by Pegu in Mon. Few *sittan* (revenue, demographic, and cadastral surveys of a statistical nature), *thamaing* (histories of important events and sites both sacred and secular), and what were then called *sayin* and/or *mawgun* (lists, records, censuses) have also survived. Most of them, and the earliest of them, were products of Ava and written in Burmese. All *ayedawpon* (stories of important people and events) that have survived are in Burmese, and written well after the Ava and Pegu periods, of which the most famous is about King Yazadarit of Pegu and his relations with Ava. Although *dhammathat* (civil law codes) were said to have been written during the Pagan period, those that have survived appear to be later products, written in Burmese, Pali, or in *nissaya* (a combination of Pali and Burmese). At least one *yazathat* (criminal law code) survives today, along with dozens of *ameindaw* (royal edicts or orders that were used as legal precedents, all of them in Burmese). But since most of these were issued during the eighteenth century, they have only a tangential bearing on this study.

Two things should become clear from the above: the bulk of these sources are in Burmese, nearly all products of Ava rather than Pegu, and for the most part, none of the original and contemporary epigraphs is new to Myanmar historians.

They are in large measure the same as those I used in *Mists* (2005) and *Myth* (1998), although about forty new inscriptions have been discovered since *Myth* was published and only one since *Mists*.[1] Some of these have added information to Ava's history but none to Pegu's. So also the chronicles and other similar literary sources written on more perishable media; they have been known for quite a while even though some of their translations have been done only recently, which I deal with in their respective sections.

I have also used a small, select group of unpublished secondary sources that are close to being primary or important to the present topic in other ways. These include dissertations that touch on this period of Myanmar's history or address some of the issues important to this book, as well as several expository articles that have used primary sources or are pertinent to this study in other important ways. These are cited where appropriate and are included in the bibliography.

In terms of published secondary works, there is very little written on Ava and Pegu, hence the paucity of "engagement" with these. Certainly, none has invalidated the central conclusions I had previously made on Ava or Pegu, so that both conventions—that Ava was a "Shan period" and that Pegu's foundations lay in a Mon kingdom called "Ramannadesa" that existed in Lower Myanmar prior to the decline of Pagan—must remain in the realm of mythology and hagiography until proved otherwise by original evidence.[2] A synopsis of each convention and its critique is given in its respective section in the present study.

I have kept to a minimum citations of primary—that is, original and contemporary—sources. I do not note every page and line number of every inscription every time I make a reference to "the inscriptions" unless it is a remark about a specific event, date, or individual. Similarly when I refer to "the chronicles," unless it is a reference to a specific event or individual, it is left without a citation. Of course, information obtained from published secondary works and quotes from them are noted in the usual manner following standard stylistic practices.

One reason for reducing the number of references with regard to the primary sources is that the basis for the bulk of my scholarship rests on essentially the same corpus of material that I (and others studying early Myanmar) know well, having already cited them over many years in various published works; so there is no need to repeat it all, and the current bibliography is quite extensive. Apart from exceptions such as the forty-odd inscriptions discovered in recent decades noted above, these primary sources are not new to any of us working on early Myanmar. For those who are not privy to them, or who do not read Old and Chronicle Burmese, citing the volume, page, and line number of the pertinent inscription or chronicle should make no difference.

There is another reason for this "limited citation approach." Quite apart from the sheer tedium involved in dealing with such minutiae, it distracts from other more important aspects of the study. Thus, for instance, the significance of the inscriptions for this study lays not so much with each and every donation recorded, but with the totality of the donations, so that the entire corpus listed in the bibliography is the more valuable reference, the sum being greater than the parts.

Similarly with the chronicles—they already rely heavily on each other, whereby later ones took large sections (often verbatim) from earlier ones, so that the particular page number in U Kala's chronicle (as opposed to, say, Twinthin's) regarding a particular story is not what is important, but rather the information obtained from this particular genre of sources, particularly its importance for narrative history. Of course, it might be interesting to know why and how the narrative of a story or event in U Kala might differ from (or might be exactly the same as) Twinthin's, as well as the probable reasons for these similarities and differences. For those who read Chronicle Burmese, those answers are easy enough to find, even just by surveying their table of contents, while for those who do not read the language, what page something is on should make no difference.

Also, I see my contribution to Myanmar scholarship as one that has more to do with new and different ways of looking at these old sources and scrutinizing them to determine if long-held conventions are in fact supported by them, rather than with discovering "lost" inscriptions or chronicles that might make a dramatic "splash" in the field of Myanmar studies. There is more than enough to do just getting the story straight from the existing primary sources. For all the above reasons, I have kept the citations in this book to a minimum. All the data I have used in this book can be found in the works listed in the bibliography. Although it might make it less convenient for some Myanmar scholars to find the information of a period or topic about which he or she is less familiar, if they are so inclined, and if they already know the language, given my bibliography and references, it should not be all that difficult.

I have decided to use the popular way of spelling Burmese words in English, against my own inclination. But they will be more easily recognizable for the English reader interested in Myanmar and Southeast Asia, especially the generalist. Words spelled in this popular fashion, of course, cannot satisfactorily reproduce the original Burmese for the specialist, an annoyance especially for linguists and historians who may want to know how they were spelled. Nonetheless, because this book is meant for both the specialist and the generalist, and the specialist is already familiar with the numerous ways in which Burmese is romanized (transcribed), the reader will see that Aniruddha is Anawrahta, Kalancacsa is Kyanzittha, Pugam is Pagan, Aloncansu is Alaungsithu, and so on. In terms of the most familiar place names, I have used mainly the indigenous versions unless their anglicized forms seem more appropriate in context. So Yangon is used for Rangoon, Muttama for Martaban, and Myanmar for Burma, unless they are found in a British context or in a quote. But Arakan retains its anglicized form, rather than Rakhaing or Yakhaing, since it is better known in that form. I have also deliberately left out diacritics, as they create more problems than they solve for both the author and the reader. (Specialists know that the word *sangha* should have a dot over the "n" but generalists know what the word means without that dot.) When I use the term "T'ai," it is a reference to all speakers of that language, including Shan and Lao. In the end, romanization should not be a contentious issue for either the specialist or nonspecialist of Myanmar, and my intent here is to help rather than confuse the reader.

MYANMAR IN THE FIFTEENTH CENTURY

Introduction

The Study of Ava and Pegu

Objectives and Description of the Book

When the great kingdom of Pagan, the "classical" state and "golden age" of Myanmar, declined politically in the late thirteenth and early fourteenth centuries, largely as a consequence of internal structural factors, Upper Myanmar[1] reconstituted itself into three main centers of power, each controlled by a member of the old court. Lower Myanmar, on the other hand, began the process of state formation for the first time, finally independent of Upper Myanmar's political and military hegemony.

For approximately the next half century, this transitional situation continued until two new dynasties and kingdoms arose. In Upper Myanmar, it was the First Ava Dynasty and kingdom in 1364, and in Lower Myanmar, the First Pegu Dynasty and kingdom in 1349.[2] Both had their immediate origins around the second half of the fourteenth century, reached their pinnacles in the fifteenth, and declined before the first half of the sixteenth century was over. The period they occupied is the only gap left in Myanmar's mainstream historiography, which this book intends to fill.

The likely reason for this neglect, particularly in the English-language historiography of Myanmar, is that both Ava and Pegu were situated between the two most exemplary kingdoms in the country's history: Pagan and Toungoo.[3] The first ruled between the ninth and fourteenth century and the second occupied most of the sixteenth century. While Pagan was to last more than four hundred years,[4] the Second Pegu/Toungoo Dynasty, although the shortest-lived,[5] was the most territorially extensive and militarily accomplished, having conquered nearly all of Western and Central Mainland Southeast Asia during the sixteenth century.[6]

Sandwiched between these two exemplary models, the First Ava and First Pegu kingdoms were characterized as "medieval" in the European sense—situated, as it were, between the "Classical" and "Renaissance" periods—with all the negative judgments appertaining thereto. This image has only been exacerbated, as historical research on Pagan and the Second Pegu/Toungoo Dynasties continued to receive more and more attention, while Ava and Pegu, less and less. Imagine an account of Europe following Rome's decline that skips to the

Renaissance (attractive though that may be), without first having dealt with the early and late medieval periods.[7]

Certainly in terms of wealth and territory, political and military power, and administrative efficiency—perhaps also in terms of artistic, religious, and legal achievements—neither Ava nor Pegu could match either Pagan or the Second Pegu/Toungoo Dynasties, while the image of the fifteenth century as a "barbarous" and "fragmented age" (at least in Upper Myanmar) did not encourage enthusiastic scholarship for that period. Although not entirely unfounded, the notion that fifteenth-century Upper Myanmar was a "dark age" is still unwarranted, and will receive more in-depth scrutiny than it has had heretofore, hopefully shedding more and different light on an otherwise much-neglected period in Myanmar's history.

I have already published a short article on the relationship between Ava and Pegu with nearly the same title as this book.[8] But it gave only a glimpse of the much greater detail found in sixteen chapters here, in terms of historical narrative and data, as well as analysis of broader themes and patterns affecting the country and region's history. I have also published an article on the events of the late thirteenth and early fourteenth centuries that ushered in the decline of Pagan, but their consequences, which led to the rise of the kingdom of Ava, and some of the broad patterns they generated, are only now described in eight chapters in the present work.[9] As for Pegu, there is no book-length study published in English (as of this writing) that has been based on original and contemporary indigenous sources, especially one that has addressed historiographic and other social science concerns of a conceptual nature.

To reiterate, then, my primary purpose here is to fill the nearly two-hundred-year gap in the country's mainstream historiography, using largely primary sources while redressing important historiographic and other academic issues and problems created by that gap. The current manuscript is mainly a *narrative* history of these two kingdoms and their relationship (hence its subtitle, *A Tale of Two Kingdoms*), although it also provides some information on some of their institutions wherever possible. Admittedly, the present work could be two separate studies, one on Ava and another on Pegu; but it is their *relationship* that I feel defines fifteenth-century Myanmar—hence, their integration here.

This book revolves around and is anchored by "the state." It is a deliberate choice, for without that focus, I feel no viable history of Myanmar during that period can be reconstructed honestly, since all the primary evidence (epigraphic and chronicle) are largely products of that state (or its provincial centers), even when describing areas outside its direct rule. The so-called (often wistful) "periphery," comprised of nonstate regions, had no original and contemporary written information about itself that was not center-derived, for center purposes, or recorded in the language of the center by center-appointed agents. One may lament this, but it is a fact: In early Myanmar, there simply is no written, primary evidence genuinely representing the "voices" of the "periphery" except in the languages (and perspectives) of its centers, the most dominant of which, Burmese, represented the state.

Attempting to write the early history of such a region without using center-derived sources becomes an exercise in anachronistic methodology, for one is compelled to use much later colonial and postcolonial ethnographies or even more recent anthropological accounts as one's primary source material. That means the description of the "periphery" is invariably a projection backward of modern, mainly Western data and conceptualizations, as if they applied to indigenous situations and people several centuries earlier. Even near-contemporary Chinese sources close to the period in question are also state-centered, so they do not truly reflect the "voice" of the "periphery" either. Although not a focus of this study, these comments are nonetheless meant to address a currently popular exercise in producing "stateless" histories of Myanmar (and Southeast Asia) without the use of original and contemporary evidence.[10]

Besides, why would a "stateless" history of Southeast Asia be intrinsically more desirable or valuable anyway? Imagine what "classical" Southeast Asian history would look like without Pagan, Angkor, Sukhotai-Ayuthaya, Dai Viet, Sri Vijaya, Champa, and Mataram/Majapahit? Similarly, with the "post-classical" period: Why would a history of Southeast Asia that did not include Ava/Pegu, Ayuthaya, Phnom Penh, Vien Chiang, Dai Viet, Melaka, and "Later Mataram" be more desirable or valuable intrinsically? It would be equally impoverished, tantamount to accounts of early Japan without Kyoto, Greece without Athens, or Italy without Rome. Thus, I consider a "stateless" history of Southeast Asia to have little or no merit—perhaps except for the kinds of tangential, theoretical questions it raises—especially since empirically, such a history does not represent the lives of the vast majority of the people in the region, their institutions and values, or the historical events that have had the most impact on those people and the region. I also find such a perspective to be highly conjectural, certainly anachronistic, and designed to be commensurate with currently popular political and/or philosophical positions.[11]

Apart from the introduction and the conclusion, the bulk of the present book is divided into two parts: Ava (part 1) and Pegu (part 2). Both are organized chronologically around three circumscribing topics: origins, development, and decline. In the "origins" sections, both the legendary and historical beginnings of each kingdom are discussed, separating (as much as possible) known historical fact from fiction (especially of a hagiographic nature), while analyzing the historical and historiographic significance of those origins and their impact on the political and/or academic issues of today.

The "development" sections, focused on the entire fifteenth century, are straightforward narratives of known kings and queens, their lives and activities, their contributions to each kingdom and to the country's history. This part of the reconstruction was particularly enjoyable: the Burmese chroniclers are not without their sense of irony, humor, and satire, and the narrative here is more that of a historical novel than heavy social science analysis. As Ava and Pegu interacted most intimately during this phase, their relationship is of primary concern here, as important to the history of the country as a whole as to the individual histories of each.

Finally, the "decline" sections trace both the remote and immediate factors—institutions as well as events, domestic as well as "international"—that were responsible for the political "end" to both Ava and Pegu. They also attempt to recapture some of the legacies each kingdom may have left for posterity, both in Myanmar and (less often) also Mainland Southeast Asia. The study ends with the conclusion, which seeks to place Ava and Pegu's relationship and its historical significance in the broader and longer context of the country and region's history until today.

Importance of the Period

The presence of a nearly two-hundred-year gap in the English-language histories published on the country—from approximately the first several decades of the fourteenth century to beyond the first quarter of the sixteenth—is one of the most important problems in the mainstream historiography of Myanmar.[12] Filling it will finally make available the individual histories of the First Ava and the First Pegu kingdoms for the first time, heretofore no more than short chapters in outdated books. Perhaps nearly as important, and certainly for the first time as well, filling such a gap will enable the reassessment of their significance to the history of the country and region.

We will be able to ask, finally, what the historical significance of Ava and Pegu was on the "post-classical" (or "early modern") period in Myanmar's history and the broader region of Southeast Asia. Did Ava and Pegu affect, or were they affected by, the famed "Age of Commerce,"[13] said to have made its mark during this period on the maritime world of South, Southeast, and East Asia? Were Ava and Pegu in any way part of that famous age, and if so, how exactly were they connected? Or, did the famous age arrive a little too late, and was its reach a little too maritime, to have significantly affected the rise, development, and decline of these two kingdoms? Heretofore, such questions (even if asked) could not have been answered properly because neither Ava nor Pegu's histories had been reconstructed in any depth.[14] I attempt, therefore, in parts 1 and 2, to not only reconstruct their histories but also provide an analysis of their historical significance to the larger history of Myanmar and the region as a whole.

Filling the gap also means a reexamination of some important issues heretofore accepted as "true" in the historiography of Myanmar for over a century now. Thus, for example, precisely because the Ava-Pegu period appeared to have been the "poor cousin" of the Pagan and Second Pegu/Toungoo periods, its importance in the larger history of Myanmar has been minimized if not denigrated. While Ava was characterized as a European-like medieval "dark age" of "fragmentation," "anarchy," and "barbarism," Pegu was considered a mere shadow of the great Second Pegu/Toungoo Dynasty of Tabinshwehti and Bayinnaung that succeeded it.

Much of this image of Ava and Pegu originated with early colonial scholars, particularly Arthur Phayre, G. E. Harvey, and, to a lesser extent, D. G. E. Hall (who depended on the former two for his narrative of indigenous history).[15]

Being the most authoritative English-language histories of the country during the late nineteenth and much of the twentieth century, these conventions of Ava and Pegu persisted into the early twenty-first century without being critically assessed in detail.[16] To be sure, while this view presented by colonial scholars is not entirely without merit, the present study will demonstrate that the situation is far more complicated than characterized heretofore.

Of course, not all historians depicted this period in Southeast Asia as one of "darkness" and "barbarism." Those who were not specialists of Myanmar, such as the late Harry Benda, actually considered the period itself to have been a continuity of the "classical era," calling it the "post-classical" period,[17] while recent generations of historians portray it as one of substantive transformation underlying its label—the early modern period.[18]

Although both the adjectives "post" and "early" are more or less neutral in themselves, they nevertheless take on additional meaning when attached to the words "classical" and "modern." Thus, Benda did not explicitly suggest a "dark age" when he used the term "post-classical," but one of continuity and equilibrium. However, once attached to the word "classical," the word "post" hints of "darkness" or "decline," for it seems to lament the passing of the celebrated "classical" age. Similarly, the phrase "early modern": although the word "early" is more or less neutral, when attached to the word "modern," it takes on a meaning that suggests a certain qualitative level of development and movement toward "modernity," a term loaded with historical significance in both European historiography (whence it came) and Asian historiography (whence it went).

By accepting these characterizations to categorize this period of Southeast Asian history, its scholars are acknowledging, de facto, that the region at this time experienced, like Europe, either a medieval-like stasis cum decline or an irrevocably progressive period of change that was a transition to "early modernity" (thence, to "modernity"). While Pegu might fit the latter characterization to a certain extent, Ava certainly cannot, along with several other successors of the "classical" kingdoms in Southeast Asia such as Angkor. In other words, the totality of historical evidence in Southeast Asia suggests that the situation during this period is far more mixed than either decline from "classicalness" or progressive transformation toward modernity.[19]

Be that as it may, simply framing Southeast Asian history in such exogenous categories raises another serious conceptual issue: whether the period should be characterized at all with these externally conceived notions. Not only do they stem from a historiography derived from European history, but it is one that has been imposed on a quite different part of the world and its history, thereby making etic (European) concerns rather than emic (Southeast Asian) ones the underlying framework of analysis for the region's history. Even if only for heuristic purposes, meant to enhance our understanding of history, they nevertheless shape and affect that understanding.

To use one example from Myanmar's historiography: the indigenous chronicles do not divide the country's history into Western categories of "classical," "medieval," and "modern" periods.[20] So right off the bat, the terms (and therefore conceptualizations) are inappropriate. Instead, Burmese chronicles follow a straightforward chronological approach that records individuals and events, focused mainly on royalty and their activities: hence, the formal term for "history" (*yazawin*, literally, royal genealogy).[21] And even when only two (out of many) chronicles in Myanmar contained "periods," called *khit* (literally, age or era), these were not named for their particular historical character (such as Renaissance or Enlightenment) or for their dynasties (such as Tudor or Tokugawa). Rather, they were named after the capital city (or location) from which each dynasty ruled: hence, the Sri Ksetra, Pagan, Inwa (Ava), Bago (Pegu), and Konbaung Dynasties or eras. Consequently, Myanmar's history is organized according to a set of criteria that belies certain indigenous, not Western, assumptions.

One of the most important of these criteria is the all-important Buddha prophecy, which states that during such and such a time, the location will become a center that will promote the religion. Each city from which a major dynasty ruled was said to have received this honor, thereby designating the place as an exemplary center and its dynasty as a legitimate one. Names of dynasties in Myanmar, then, were not derived from the family names of their rulers, but from centers designated by the Buddha as fittingly exemplary. Thus, neither the *function* for periodizing history (a heuristic tool for organizing it) nor the *reasons* for characterizing a period (its achievements or failures to help us better understand it), was a concern for Myanmar's precolonial historiography.

Yet, trained and teaching in the West, I am invariably part of the Western discipline of history and its discourse on historiography. And although respecting indigenous episteme and conscious of other societies' priorities, I still find that, at least professionally, creating "periods" in Myanmar's history around their "character"—especially for heuristic purposes—furthers understanding better than not doing it. Notwithstanding, and regardless of how carefully and sensitively one uses exogenous terms, criteria, and priorities to organize and assess Myanmar's history, such an approach nonetheless raises an old historiographic issue that continues to haunt Southeast Asian studies today: namely, the late John Smail's plea for an "autonomous history" of Southeast Asia.[22]

Myanmar's history, especially of the fifteenth century, has not been conceived from an "autonomous" perspective. That is to say, approached from an "angle of vision" that looks outward from its courts and capitals, kings and queens, monks and scholars, lawyers and plaintiffs, provincial centers and rural villages, monasteries and convents, ports and *padi* fields. Rather, the perspective from which most of Myanmar's history has been written, especially in the English language, has been an external one, with much weight given to, and importance placed on, what are essentially external (in today's terms, "global") issues and concerns.

For Smail, the essential difference lay between "perspective" and "moral viewpoint," a distinction he had painstakingly and methodically made, dissecting and separating them into two very different issues. At the time, his effort was very much appreciated by students and scholars of Southeast Asian studies. But recent and popular trends in Southeast Asian historiography—especially among some who appear not to know his work or fully appreciate its value (and with a tendency to regard older scholarship as passé in any case)—suggest that this distinction between perspective and moral viewpoint has been recombined, passing off as matters of perspective what are really (political) moral points of view.[23] Despite Smail's best efforts, then, perspective and moral viewpoint have once again become conflated. Using history as a political tool is, of course, not new. And that is precisely the reason we historians have to reinstate that distinction between perspective and moral viewpoint in the current discourse on Southeast Asian historiography.

But the problem is more than analytical clarity; the methodology for implementing that recombination is also flawed, particularly its "ahistoricism" and "acontextualism." As noted above, some recent and popular attempts to conceptualize the history of early Southeast Asia are not only exogenously derived but are in fact projections backward on situations far distant in time and space, the modus operandi of this new "recombinant" school of thought.[24] As a result, there are ex post facto rationalizations for using late colonial and postcolonial data as "evidence" for earlier periods, celebrating minority causes, and framing analyses in twentieth- and twenty-first-century contesting ethnic scenarios that are dichotomous and binary.

I attempt to redress these issues of "ahistoricism" and "acontextualism" by simply returning Ava and Pegu to their rightful historical contexts, and ensuring (as far as possible) that the data used to reconstruct them are not only true to their respective (chronological) periods, but also that the evidence is of a primary and contemporary (or near-contemporary) nature, rather than of a secondary kind and anachronistically very late. This study thus attempts to use period-correct evidence that also represents internal (autonomous) values, so that Ava and Pegu are viewed not only from the fifteenth century but also from the inside out, rather than from the twentieth century and from the outside in. Myanmar should be the foreground, not the background.

Admittedly, and in the end, it matters less what the particular moral viewpoint being espoused is—pro-center or pro-periphery—it is more serious when one is used as if it were a genuine, academic perspective, when in fact it is really a disguised moral point of view. Such moralizing leads to other problems of creating false dichotomies and then privileging ones that we like. Views from or about the periphery are more often favored in conceptualizations of Southeast Asia and its history than in those from or about the center.

While both are legitimate perspectives, the center is more likely to be regarded in a negative or undesirable way by academia—especially in recent years, as the notion of "the center" becomes more and more associated with the much-maligned nation-state, characterizing it as an invention (and therefore somehow "untrue"). In contrast, the "periphery"—equally an invention (for it cannot by definition exist without a "center," otherwise what would it be "peripheral" to?)—is usually celebrated and its emphasis considered more desirable and politically and academically more "correct." In other words, in the field of Southeast Asian studies, the periphery is seldom considered in the same disparaging manner as the center is. In order to rectify this, I have attempted to replace the dichotomous, binary framework of analysis with a dualistic one, so that the periphery is placed *in terms of* the center rather than *in opposition to* it.[25]

Thus, this study (a) characterizes the Ava/Pegu period in a modern, interdisciplinary way to better understand it, but uses autonomous rather than external criteria; (b) returns Ava and Pegu to their rightful chronological period to address the problems of "ahistoricism" and "acontextualism"; and (c) integrates center and periphery in defining "the state" by arguing that one does not have to *live* at the center to be *part* of the center. As to the related issue of how best to characterize the Ava/Pegu period—as a "dark age," a "post-classical medieval continuity," or part of an "early modern transformation"—my answer is that it contained elements of all three.

Reified Ethnicity as Historical Causation

Another problem in the historiography of precolonial (as well as colonial and modern Myanmar) is the assumption that Burmese history was invariably *caused by* ethnicity: that is, a history of ethnic struggles, competition between and among its main ethnic groups, particularly Burman, Mon, Arakanese, and Shan. Although since approximately the 1960s such reification of ethnic and resulting ethnic interpretations of history have been shown to be theoretically and empirically untenable,[26] the case for Ava and Pegu has yet to be made. This study shows that there is no evidence to support the notion that reified ethnicity in general, or (even more specifically) that a sense of Shan ethnic identity versus a Burman one, was responsible for the conquest of Ava in 1526–1527, or that a sense of Burman ethnic identity versus a Mon ethnic identity was the basis of wars between Ava and Pegu. In fact, the data show that the history of Ava and Pegu during this period had little (if anything) to do with reified ethnicity or ethnic identity, but with geopolitical, military, economic, and even personal factors.

Part of this "reified ethnicity paradigm" includes the belief that certain ethnolinguistic groups were superior to others, so that the Mon were labeled the "Greeks of Southeast Asia" by early colonial scholars. This imagined and celebrated image of the Mon has also been demonstrated to be without any merit in recent scholarship,[27] although unfortunately, it continues today in disciplines that remain ignorant of the direction in which Myanmar's historiography is headed.[28] In fact, it is precisely because no primary evidence exists to confirm the above image of the Mon that rationalizations depicting them as "victims" of Burman oppression have continued to this day. That contention was best represented by the works of influential nineteenth-century colonial scholar Emil Forchhammer.[29]

While the Mon were glorified as the "Greeks of Southeast Asia," the Shan, in contrast, were disparaged as barbaric, and their role in Myanmar's history was depicted largely as one of spoilers and only incidental to the main (Burmese-Mon) story. In fact, however, the present study demonstrates that the Shan (or more appropriately in the current framework of analysis, the "highlanders") were as important to the dominant Burmese speakers (the "lowlanders") in the interior of the country, as the Mon (the "downstreamers") were on the coasts, especially in the fifteenth century.

But if that were the case, one could legitimately ask why, then, is this study focused on Ava and Pegu instead of (say) Ava and Mohnyin or Ava and Onbaung (a major Shan center in Upper Myanmar at the time)? The answer is that, precisely *because* the history of fifteenth-century Myanmar was not an ethnic story but a geopolitical one in which Ava and Pegu were the dominant geopolitical and socioeconomic players in the history of fifteenth-century Myanmar, they and their relationship have been chosen to represent the period.

The methodology used in this study for mitigating the ethnic interpretation of Myanmar's history is to simply stop using an ethnic framework of analysis and replace it with a geopolitical and socioeconomic one. Once that is done, the arguments for reified ethnicity as historical causation almost immediately disappears. Data suggesting probable causes of conflict (or cooperation) can now be assessed without attributing them to ethnicity, which had heretofore led to speculations about vague and unproven beliefs of "natural" animosity and antagonisms between and among "races" since "time immemorial." Such reification of ethnicity, assumed to be self-evident by the colonial (and subsequent) intellectual and political contexts of the time, can now be discarded with aplomb.

In short, military conquests, peace treaties, patron-client relations, court intrigue, marriage alliances, and diplomatic maneuvers should be taken at face value, based on geopolitical, economic, and even personal factors, rather than on abstract notions of ethnicity or ethnic identity. The whole convention that claimed reified ethnicity as the main causal factor in the making of Ava and Pegu's history should no longer be considered viable, and discarded.

Issues of "Agency"

Next there is the methodological problem of giving "agency" to the conventions mentioned above—"dark ages," "early modernity," reified ethnicity—that have also affected the historiography of Ava and Pegu. Giving "agency" is, of course, a prerogative taken by the scholar conducting the study; we all give weight to things we consider important. A hard scientist choosing to study one chemical rather than another gives "agency" to that chemical, which is no different from a journalist choosing to report on one incident and not another, or a historian focusing on the history of "the state" (as I do here), rather than on another sector or aspect of society. The issue of agency affects even the choice one makes of the sources used, beyond the usual problems that plague historical sources (a topic discussed below).

Deciding what is interesting in Burmese history and what is not—hence, what to include and what to exclude in one's reconstruction of history (therefore what to privilege and what not to)—often depends on assumptions that give weight to certain things and not to others. I found it interesting that one of the most important "histories" of the Myanmar Mon credits the founding of their first political center in the country to a Burmese king of Pagan. But when I asked myself why that was interesting to me, I realized it was because I did not expect the Mon to attribute their origins to a Burmese king. And why did I not expect this? Because the field has so ingrained in us that the Burmese and Mon were quintessential enemies, oppressor and oppressed, that such an admission should not have been made by the Mon. In other words, it was interesting only because of the assumptions and expectations of the field, not because of what the evidence actually had to say. Indeed, the indigenous chroniclers themselves never suggested that the founding of the first Mon capital in Myanmar by a Burmese king was in any way extraordinary (hence, interesting), nor did each group see the other in the manner we think they did.

Similarly, when I reflect upon why some events recorded in the indigenous chronicles surprised me, again it was because of the same assumptions, held by the field as true. Since it has long been assumed that Mon and Burmese hated each other, it was surprising to find Mon king Yazadarit of Pegu treating the Burmese crown prince of Ava in the gracious manner he did when the lad was captured after a battle. Or to take another case, it was surprising that the Onbaung *Sawbwa* fought alongside the king of Ava against his own "brethren" Shan *Sawbwa* when he "should have" (according to the field) allied with his own ethnic and cultural group against the Burmese, revealing our assumptions (not theirs) about how he "should have" behaved because of notions of (reified) ethnicity we have attributed to him, a major concern of ours, not necessarily theirs. Thus, modern Myanmar historiography's privileging of reified ethnicity as the paramount, motivating factor of political behavior is largely the result of projecting our own modern sentiments onto people who did not necessarily feel that way, and who lived at a totally different time and space.

In yet another example, I found it surprising that, in one of the most celebrated Mon-language chronicles, Yazadarit was not given as many words as other Mon kings less important than he. Here, I was surprised because we in twenty-first-century America hold in high regard "secular" political leadership, whereas the author (a Mon monk) of the *Slapat* (in which the story appeared) considered religious history (and behavior) far more important. To him, Yazadarit's political actions were only *incidental* to his religious behavior, hence the trivializing of his political importance, which we applaud.

These issues that we find interesting and surprising, then, are essentially the result of having given agency to certain things that we (not they) considered valuable and important, ultimately leading to self-fulfilling analyses and foregone conclusions. To be sure—and to bring it into the present—the opposite is also true. Most Myanmar scholars residing in the country pay scant attention to scholarship published by those outside the country, as if it did not exist, focusing instead on topics *they* find more interesting, revealing their assumptions and concerns. Consequently, the works of overseas Myanmar scholars are often not read, some clearly for political reasons, but some for personal ones as well (such as inaccessibility or prohibitive costs), while others, for a lack of language skills or paucity of theoretical training in a country that tends to foster a disinclination for such concerns. Of course, it is not all a matter of political agendas, personal preferences and priorities, costs, language skills, or types of training; some are simply the result of bad scholarship.

Less obvious and more difficult to deal with is the *inadvertent* giving of agency, quite apart from personal and other identifiable biases inherent in the discipline and field. Simply using a particular kind of source—in the present case mainly chronicles (*yazawin*) and inscriptions (*kyauksa*)—gives agency to certain perspectives and not to others, shaping the way Burmese history is interpreted and written. Indeed, the mere use of sources affects even larger historiographic issues such as change and continuity. In other words, objective differences between *kyauksa* and *yazawin* have a direct bearing on the subjective historiography their use produces.

Let me be more precise. There are a variety of contemporary and near-contemporary sources for the reconstruction of Ava and Pegu, the best of which are original and contemporary (or near-contemporary) stone inscriptions recorded at the time of erection.[30] Supplementing the stone records are numerous other kinds of (usually later) data that range from a variety of religious texts to, in the case of Ava, romantic and other kinds of poetry.[31] And as noted above, Ava also used administrative records called *sittan* (revenue, demographic, and cadastral surveys of a statistical nature), *thamaing* (histories of important events and sites both sacred and secular), and what were then called *sayin* and/or *mawgun* (records, lists, censuses).[32] Most of these are statistical in nature and represent Ava's public institutions.

Of these, the stone inscriptions, especially, reflect public values best, and are tantamount to today's bronze plaques encased in important buildings, names of fallen national heroes inscribed on granite walls, faces of presidents carved on mountainsides, even paper or (more permanent) microfilm and digitized records of title deeds, birth certificates, and marriage licenses in county and state ledgers. As crucial repositories of public memory, these kinds of sources not only represent the dominant social values of society, but their use also influences a perspective of institutional continuity.

In contrast are *yazawin,* often glossed over as chronicles.[33] They are another genre of evidence, both in terms of content and raison d'être. *Yazawin* can be official or unofficial, with no legal (but moral) standing, written by private individuals (religious and secular) at their own volition and expense, or by ministers and monks close to the court at its expense, or, less often, by those without portfolio quite distant from the inner circles of the court. The subject matter normally concerns the lives of kings and those with whom they dealt, so are essentially historical narratives about royalty and their activities, not the general public. As texts with moral standing, they tend to include dialogue and narratives of a didactic nature, most often pertaining to this fleeting human world and its impermanency, especially of royalty. In other words, they are by nature change-oriented, so that their use invariably produces a change-oriented narrative.

For example, the convention that the Ava period after the decline of the Pagan kingdom was one of war and anarchy, fragmentation and decentralism, is essentially a chronicle view of things, not that of the inscriptions. The latter, in contrast, shows the same old (Pagan) institutions and processes of integration at work: descendants of the same royal family protecting the traditional social and political hierarchy, still in charge, and still attempting to entrench their power even further with the usual marriage alliances with other elites; the same agrarian economy of redistribution in which the same religion was deeply embedded in the same way using the same rituals; the same religious values that continued the flow of wealth to the *sangha*; the same Theravada Buddhist ideologies of political legitimation; the same entrenched patron-client structures that held society together.

Thus, while the inscriptions represent what are considered eternal universal principles and are evidence of permanent institutions whose use results in a *synchronic* perspective of society, the chronicles are more representative of the ideology of impermanence, particularly of people and events, whose use results in a *diachronic* view of society.

But their use produces more than that; it also privileges the scale and scope of one's subject matter. Historians who use chronicles often extrapolate what is in fact elite, political activity at court to project it on society below it, as if the masses also experienced a similar dynamism, when they really did not. Similarly, historians using the inscriptions often privilege the religious intent and function of these stones—for the vast majority are records of religious donations—thereby focusing less on the economic and political factors affecting state and society.

However, one cannot assume that the combined use of both chronicles and inscriptions, therefore, balances and equalizes the problem; it is still imbalanced. Because the elite political history of the chronicles is more sensational and memorable, "interesting" and "exciting," it and its use are more popular, monopolizing most of the "national narrative," while the repetitive and boring religious donations do not. Institutional history (represented largely by inscriptions) thus takes a backseat to narrative history (represented mainly by chronicles). That gives agency to *yazawin* as a genre of evidence, further skewing one's analysis to favor events and individuals over institutions and organizations—and, in the process, also to change rather than continuity.

Even if some of these "interesting" and "exciting" political events found in the chronicles are shown to have been important in their own right, to support the contention that change indeed occurred, the only real claim that can be made in such cases is that change was of a political nature and it occurred in elite society, the predominant subject matter and class, respectively, about which most chroniclers wrote. There is no reason to suppose that substantive ("deep" structural) changes must have also taken place in the social, religious, economic, and cultural lives of most of the people in that society because of what happened at court among a few individuals. Even massive mobilization for war involved mainly crown troops, who did the actual fighting, not the majority of the population, who were farmers. (Myanmar did not have private or peasant armies as in Europe and China.)

Yet, although "boring" and "mundane," inscriptions better represent the general population and its values, while their contemporaneousness and relative neutrality make them more intrinsically valuable as historical sources. Not a single *yazawin* was written from the perspective of the people at large, and not a single one that has survived can claim to be contemporary to the events it describes or, if copies, to represent in their entirety actual firsthand, neutral descriptions representing most of society. But nearly every inscription can. As a genre of source material, then, the more valuable inscriptions are not given the significance they deserve but are relegated to the dustbin of antiquarians.

Having said all that, this contrast between *yazawin* and *kyauksa* cannot be construed to imply that therefore it represents "contesting narratives," the type of binary analysis so eagerly embraced by more recent, postmodern generations of scholars, where agency is given to competition and contrast. Rather, I see chronicles and inscriptions as different kinds of evidence about the same society, and therefore, complementary: both genres of evidence are necessary, indeed crucial, for reconstructing a more complete and accurate picture of Burmese society at large, even if they are not "equal" in terms of either their value or the weight given to them as sources.

Once that is recognized, the artificial divisions we ourselves had created, along with their binary features, disappear, revealing instead a dualism, in which the discontinuity of events and individuals are found to operate within a continuity of institutions and structure. The chronicles and inscriptions together are repositories that reflect and represent the bulk of Myanmar's mainstream history.

But problems of agency do not end there: they are further exacerbated by (Western) heuristic concerns for organizing history. Relegating Pagan and Ava into two distinct "periods" has rendered evidence found in one inadmissible for assessing the other. It is true that the Old Burmese stone inscriptions belonging to Pagan and Ava so far published are not labeled as such (that is, as "Pagan Inscriptions" and "Ava Inscriptions," respectively) but are chronologically arranged into a series of sequential volumes. Nevertheless, scholars using them have invariably operated as if these volumes represent distinct and inviolable periods, thereby adopting a self-fulfilling and tautological methodology wherein one's premise about Pagan and Ava (as distinct periods) is "affirmed" by the data one uses. The result is that inscriptions dating to the Ava period are considered inadmissible evidence when dealing with Pagan society and vice versa, even though it is not the information in them that disqualifies them, but our own pre-analysis categorization of periods with dates we consider correct, as well as assumptions of change that lead to such periodization in the first place.

The famous European medievalist Marc Bloch warned us long ago in his reconstruction of feudal society that it is acceptable to carve up the creature of flesh and blood into *Homo economicus, juridicus*, and *philosophicus*, as long as we are not deceived by it.[34] Put another way, as long as the categories we as historians have created for the sake of organization do not deceive us into thinking they also exist independently of, and outside, our analyses, this should not be a problem. But that is precisely what we have done when data from the Pagan period is disallowed to reconstruct (or even understand) the Ava period, projecting our categories of analysis as if they exist "out there" as well. Worse, this methodology ends up privileging technical concerns of writing and publishing over the intrinsic value of the evidence, giving agency less to the accurate reconstruction of history than to its organizational schemes that appeal to the publisher, reader, teacher, and student.

Indeed, the distinctions created between the Pagan and Ava periods are quite artificial. If one were to bring back to life a literate person from the Pagan period and show him or her an inscription of Ava, he or she could easily read it, and if it did not have a date on it, would conclude that it belonged to the Pagan period—they are that similar. The medium (hence, stature), function, content, format, vocabulary, language, methodology, style, and legal intent of Ava *kyauksa* are virtually identical to those of Pagan. This suggests more than mere linguistic continuity between Pagan and Ava epigraphs; it reveals a more profound, overall structural continuity between the two societies than is implied by the distinct periods into which we have divided them.

Early in this study, therefore, I decided to read and use the Old Burmese inscriptions without being inhibited by the conventional organization of discrete periods created by colonial period scholars of early Myanmar. That does not mean Ava and Pagan were not different, or that dates are unimportant in institutional history. On the contrary, without dates, one cannot tell when an institution (or an entity, such as Ramannadesa) might or might not have actually existed at a particular time. Dates are also crucial in determining when (say) the accumulation of religious donations made to the *sangha* finally becomes a critical mass to have an effect on the state. What I am saying is that the evidence should not be considered admissible or inadmissible a priori, determined by conventional periodization schemes and preconceived notions of change that we created in the first place. Rather, one should allow the data to speak for itself.

As part of the effort to rectify these kinds of historiographic problems, my approach to the reconstruction of both the Ava and Pegu kingdoms is similar to the one I took in *Mists*: namely, to reassess the primary sources independently of the presuppositions and conceptualizations of the conventional view. For only when the evidence is examined outside of such underlying premises can a picture emerge requiring no lengthy rationalizations and/or qualifications, no elaborate and labyrinthine explanations why the evidence contradicts the convention, and no parrying the evidence as being "ironic," "surprising," "puzzling," or "paradoxical." Even if this methodology does not resolve all the problems, at least it removes the shackles heretofore imposed by convention on new ways to analyze and interpret Myanmar's history.

The Ava and Pegu Conventions

In the study of Ava and Pegu, the above problems and issues have coalesced into two circumscribing conventions: namely, that Ava was a new kingdom led by new Shan speakers, and Pegu was an old one led by old Mon speakers, skewing nearly all subsequent interpretations and analyses of Myanmar history to fit those conventions. In fact, as this study will show, it was just the opposite: Ava was actually a continuation of an old kingdom (Pagan) led by (old) Burmese speakers, while Pegu was essentially a new (and later) kingdom led by new Mon speakers. These I have called the "Ava Convention" and the "Pegu Convention," dealt with in greater detail in parts 1 and 2, respectively.

The study ends with a concluding chapter that places the significance of both the Ava and Pegu kingdoms and their relationship in a broader historical context, bringing the discussion up to today's Myanmar. In brief, it describes the history of Myanmar during the late fourteenth century and the whole of the fifteenth, as basically a tale of two kingdoms and their relationship: one old and one new, one upstream and one downstream, one inland and one coastal, one agricultural and one commercial, one led largely by Burmese speakers and one by mainly Mon speakers, both Buddhists, and both the immediate beneficiaries of the legacy of Pagan. Indeed, this symbiotic relationship between "upstream and downstream" did not end with Ava and Pegu; it continues today with Naypyidaw and Yangon.

PART I

The Kingdom of Ava (1364–1527)

The First Ava Dynasty (1364–1527)

Thadominbya (1364–1367)

Minkyiswa Sawkai (1367–1400)

Mingaung the First (1400–1423)

Hsinphyushin Thihathu (1423–1425/1426?)

Mohnyin Min (1426–1438)

Hsinphyushin Minye Kyawswa (1438–1441)

Narapati the Great (1441/1442?–1467)

Mahathihathuya (1467–1479)

Mingaung the Second (1479/1480?–1501)

Narapati the Second (1501–1526)

1

Prelude to Ava

The Decline of Pagan

Having integrated much of the territory known today as Myanmar for the first time in its history between the eleventh and thirteenth centuries, the great Kingdom of Pagan—the "golden age" of Myanmar and its "classical" state—began to decline at the very end of the thirteenth and beginning of the fourteenth century for a variety of structural and historical reasons discussed in greater detail elsewhere.[1] Its political decline was a relatively slow process that involved at least two types of causal factors.

The first comprises what historians refer to as "remote" causes, the "kindling" or "smoldering material" (so to speak)—long-term structural trends and patterns operating within a geopolitical and demographic equilibrium that lasts many decades (perhaps centuries). It is the kind of situation found in medieval France, which the famous French historian of the Annales School, Emmanuel LeRoy Ladurie, called "l'histoire immobile" or "history that stands still."[2] The second type of historical causes are the "immediate" ones, especially events closer to the crisis being studied and other "incidents of the moment" (to use the late Clifford Geertz's apt phrase) that ignite the "remote" causes (the "smoldering material"), either bringing those long-term trends and patterns to fruition or preventing them from doing so.

Remote Causes

THE FLOW OF WEALTH TO THE *SANGHA*

The most important remote cause responsible for the decline of Pagan is, in my view, the unceasing and permanent transfer of taxable wealth from state and society to the tax-exempt *sangha*, a process that over several hundred years slowly drained the economic wherewithal, hence also the political foundations, of the kingdom.[3]

Initially, however, patronage of the religion and *sangha* was not a problem—just the opposite. Theravada Buddhism's merit-path to salvation stimulated the socioeconomic, demographic, and political development of the state during its inchoate years rather than inhibiting it. At the height of the Pagan period, peace and stability, spectacular religious and secular festivities, and the prestige of belonging to one of two "superpowers" in the region (the other was Angkor) were surely attractive, hence, not only retaining established residents but also encouraging the emigration of newcomers from outside the kingdom. Without these kinds of demographic increases of the general population, along with natural population growth as a result of favorable economic conditions, it is inconceivable how else Pagan (and Angkor as well) could have sustained themselves at such productive levels for over four centuries each.

In the case of Pagan, after several hundred years of wealth moving from the taxable to the tax-exempt sector, what was once an asset increasingly became a liability. Moreover, because donations to the *sangha* are usually permanent and irrevocable, the process is cumulative, so that by the late thirteenth century, the tax-exempt sector had reduced the state's "treasury" significantly, particularly in terms of ownership of, and/or rights to, productive lands and labor. This shifting of wealth (or the rights to that wealth) between state and *sangha* from the eleventh to the beginning of the fourteenth century, is demonstrated in figure 1, reconstructed from original epigraphs.

Yet, neither state nor society could (or would) simply cease patronage of the *sangha*, for the legitimacy (indeed raison d'être) of both depended on such behavior. To be sure, the kings of Pagan must have been aware of the problem, so they attempted to regularize, or in other ways mitigate, the process by better controlling it to manageable proportions and, in certain cases, even recouping some of the wealth. Most legitimate of these strategies was *sasana* reform (or reform of the religion), a traditionally sanctioned and orthodox ritual used to reform both the *sangha* and the scriptures, for Buddhist doctrine declares that both will decay with time and need to be purified periodically. It was also justifiable because the *sangha* being gorged with wealth obviously contradicted its own vows of poverty, thereby raising questions regarding its purity. But such attempts were temporary measures, in part because the purer the *sangha* was (as a result of the reform), the more donations it would attract, since the quality of the merit accruing to the donor is directly related to the purity of the religion and *sangha*.

Such a scenario had more than ideological consequences. While the dwindling of state resources would have weakened the state's wherewithal for political patronage internally, the *sangha*'s opulence displayed in the thousands of temples and monasteries on the plains of Pagan further attracted the attention of external forces, especially the Mongols, who not only thrived on conquest and plunder but were, in the thirteenth century, at the peak of their military might.

OTHER REMOTE CAUSES

There were likely other remote causes, such as court factionalism, an endemic structural weakness that in part stemmed from the *myosa* (to eat) system based on patron-client principles. But since these principles were also the most effective means of governance and a source of strength, the system was retained. The slow migration of the Syam (Shan) into the river valleys of central Mainland Southeast Asia from the north, including the Irrawaddy and Chindwin Rivers by the early to mid-thirteenth century, and the Mon speakers into Lower Myanmar, eventually cutting off the coastal trade and commercial revenues for the interior, should also

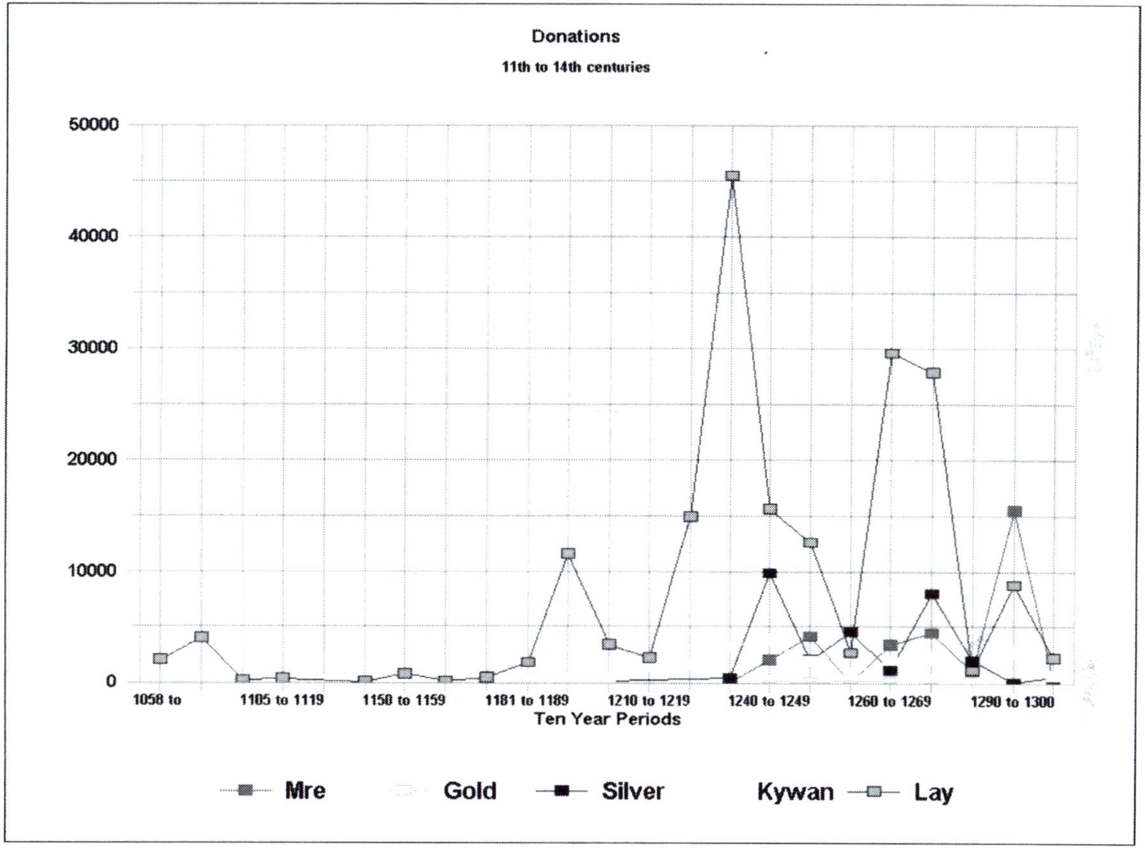

Figure 1. Chart of Religious Donations at Pagan

be considered remote factors affecting the decline of Pagan. But direct contemporary evidence is simply not available to unequivocally demonstrate that either factor weakened the kingdom of Pagan; certainly it is not as abundant, detailed, or quantifiable as the flow of wealth to the *sangha* is.

In recent years, climate change as an explanation for the decline of some of these "medieval" states and societies in Southeast Asia has also received attention. In this regard, Victor Lieberman has been one of the most active among Southeast Asia historians in assessing the situation for the region.[4] Among archaeologists, Roland Fletcher, director of the Greater Angkor Project, and his colleagues, have been most convincing in attributing Angkor's decline to climate change. They show that severe climatic instability between the fourteenth and sixteenth century in central Mainland Southeast Asia brought oscillations of mega-monsoons and mega-droughts that had serious effects on Angkor's survival. To address this problem, Khmer engineers used short-term methods to rectify the situation, so that when higher than normal rainfall returned, it was disastrous for the city (and kingdom). Using devices such as LIDAR (Light Detection and Ranging) and other scientific methods such as AIRSAR (Airborne Synthetic Aperture Radar), old-fashioned ground surveys and excavations, dendrochronology, palynology and sedimentology, Fletcher et al. have pieced together the natural and human factors that demonstrate how climate was responsible for Angkor's decline.[5] (It is certainly more convincing than the old theories attributing it to the Thais and the "superbolshevism" of Theravada Buddhism.)

Yet, what happened to Angkor could not have happened to Pagan for a variety of reasons. Pagan's three main irrigation systems, on which its rice supply depended, lay eighty to one hundred miles away from the capital, fed by perennial rivers that arose in surrounding areas with much heavier rainfall, while the survival of the already arid capital city itself would have been little affected (if at all) by either mega-drought or mega-rainfall. In other words, its rice fields and population (hence, wealth) was spread out over the kingdom and not concentrated at the capital as it was at Angkor. Pagan also did not depend symbolically, ideologically, and materially on the kind of massive water-engineering works located right at the capital the way Angkor did as a mega-city; indeed, Pagan's royal enceinte, in which mainly the royalty and some members of court resided, was only a half-mile square, while most of the population was distributed much more widely. And finally, by the time the effects of the extreme fluctuations of the monsoons hit central and eastern Mainland Southeast Asia—beginning in the fourteenth century—Pagan had already long declined, the result of the remote factors mentioned above. Thus, the story of the decline of the two largest and virtually contemporary superpowers on Mainland Southeast Asia is more one of contrast than of similarity.[6]

Immediate Causes

The conventional interpretation for the "fall" of Pagan—that it was conquered by the Mongols in 1287—is a notion still prevalent in some of the most recent books on Myanmar, and certainly among the popular literature. Yet, we have known for three decades that the Mongol invasions did not cause the end of the Pagan kingdom, and that there simply is no contemporary evidence that any of their three invasions even reached the capital city of Pagan as claimed.[7] Rather, it was their incursions into the northern reaches of the kingdom that created a sense of urgency and crisis at the capital, accelerating certain remote causes to come to fruition. This includes long-term structural factors, such as political factionalism invariably coalesced around "natural" adversarial groups within the court and, in the thirteenth century, exacerbated by the loss of wealth to the *sangha* that could have been used instead for political patronage.

In other words, crises (such as the Mongol invasions) often lay bare long-standing domestic problems of a structural nature; the invasions themselves did not create those problems or cause the decline.[8] What the Mongol invasions did was expose the underlying fissures, stresses, and tensions that already existed in Burmese society.[9] One of the surest indicators of such social disorder and/or disruption of central authority in Myanmar's history is the sudden and unexplained cessation of religious donations, especially at the capital. This is precisely what the record shows—after two and a half centuries of continuous donations, none was recorded at Pagan between 1285 and 1290, coinciding approximately with the arrival and departure of two of the three Mongol invasions.

The first Mongol invasion was of little consequence to the capital itself, as it did not advance farther south than Tagaung, about 150 miles north of Pagan. It was the second Mongol invasion, in 1287, that ultimately led to King Narathihapade's flight and subsequent death, because this time, it penetrated much farther than the earlier invasion of 1284, creating the kinds of conditions that drove the Pagan court to flee the capital and seek shelter in places that the Mongols were not likely to follow on horseback. This was probably the occasion that inspired posterity to give the hapless Pagan king the epithet "Tayok Pye Min" (King who fled the Tayok). The Mongols did not reach the city of Pagan this (second) time either, much less destroy it, as is so often erroneously claimed by even very recent references to the event. The original evidence suggests they may have advanced to within fifty miles north of the capital. Eventually, and according to the Mongol's own (Yuan) source, they had to retreat with heavy losses of over seven thousand soldiers.[10]

Nevertheless, the sense of crisis and perhaps even panic created by the second invasion was what allowed Narathihapade's younger son, Thihathu, lord of Prome, to depose the king.[11] And it was this occasion that provided the chroniclers an opportunity for Queen Saw to admonish the king with her famous royal scolding, about not "boring thy country's belly" and other improper acts of royal behavior thought to lead to such disasters.

Narathihapade's death opened the doors to a struggle for the throne by the usual contenders: his many offspring. Epigraphic evidence suggests that an older son of Narathihapade, Kyawswa, lord of Tala (a town close to present day Yangon),[12] was the one who finally took the throne; at least, he is the one recorded in contemporary inscriptions as the next king to be crowned. Thereafter, the struggle moved to one between two major factions of the court: on the one hand, the legal heirs, and on the other, those who had the military power. Normally, legal heirs also had military power, but in this particular case, the famous Three Brothers of Myanmar history (Athinkhaya, Yazathingyan, and Thihathu) had the military power but may not have been legal heirs, as they were of ministerial rather than princely rank (unless the Thihathu of the Three Brothers was, in fact, Narathihapade's son, as suggested by the Chinese sources).

Even under these unstable conditions of the late 1280s, the "fall" of Pagan was not inevitable. Had able leaders arisen and reunified the scattered resources of the kingdom, as was often the case time and again in Myanmar's long history, the Pagan Dynasty, if not the kingdom, might have been saved. And for a while, at least until the mid-1290s, King Kyawswa, who seemed to have had considerable administrative experience, appeared to have done precisely that: he restored some of the authority of the Pagan monarchy.

In an inscription found at Kyaukse prior to Kyawswa's formal coronation, dated February 1289 and recorded by the Three Brothers, they requested his consent to dedicate land to the *sangha*, thereby publicly acknowledging his authority, legitimacy, and suzerainty. By July of 1289, several months after that event, Kyawswa was formally anointed king.[13] Known as Shwenanshin (Lord of the Golden Palace), he adopted the standard regnal title of Pagan kings: Siri Tri Bhuvanaditaya Pavara Dhammaraja. As late as March 1290, the brothers were present in Pagan at another royal dedication.

But only three years after Kyawswa was crowned king, the Three Brothers declared publicly in an inscription that it was they who had defeated the Mongols and saved the dynasty from collapse, and by inference, that it was a result of their efforts that Kyawswa even had a throne on which to sit.[14] It was a harbinger of things to come, as Kyawswa's authority was not to last. In fact, power had already (and irreparably) shifted from the court and king to Athinkhaya, Yazathingyan, and Thihathu,[15] "the three great ministers," as the Three Brothers are referred to in contemporary inscriptions.[16] That meant the seat of power had shifted geographically as well, from Pagan to Kyaukse, where the best irrigated lands in the kingdom lay, the rice bowl of the kingdom. It was also the place where the fiefs of the Three Brothers—strategically placed fortified cities—were located.

This shift in power, however, was not one that went from center to periphery, since Kyaukse, located about eighty miles from Pagan, had always been (structurally, administratively, economically, and conceptually) very much a crucial component of the center. And even though contestants, the Three Brothers were still very much part of the center's establishment. Rather, the shift was of the same kind that occurred between the state's resources and the *sangha*: that is, within the state itself, not to loci outside it.

The claim by the Three Brothers that it was they, not the king, who had saved the kingdom, subsequently set the stage for a struggle between the relatively weak king and the older, established military power of the successful and popular Three Brothers. By January of 1295, Athinkhaya, the eldest of the

Three Brothers, who appeared to be the most loyal to the king (at least publicly), attended a third ceremony held by Kyawswa in Pagan. However, neither of his two younger brothers was present on this occasion, considered by one Myanmar scholar as a deliberate slight. That same year, Thihathu, the youngest (and brashest) of the Three Brothers assumed the title of Hsinphyushin, "lord of the white elephant," in obvious defiance and public challenge of the king. The following year, Thihathu again asserted himself, using the title of *mankri* (*mingyi*), "great king."[17]

Although he did this on his own turf and not at Pagan, his behavior nevertheless reveals his confidence and daring to publicly announce who he thought should be king, challenging the established authority to prove it otherwise. On the other hand, his elder brother Athinkhaya was married into the royal family[18] and therefore supported Kyawswa almost to the end, while attempting to counterbalance the impatience of his younger brother.[19]

Kyawswa and Pagan were not totally effete yet, for an inscription of 1296 stated that Anantajeyyapikram, a general of the crown, recaptured the Lower Myanmar port city of Tala (the king's old fief), which had rebelled.[20] By mid-decade, then, although the influence of the Three Brothers (especially Thihathu's) had obviously grown in Upper Myanmar, King Kyawswa still managed to control some of the critical centers of Lower Myanmar that had been part of the Kingdom of Pagan. The king also had the correct genealogy, the prestige of the throne, and the exemplary center in hand.

However, as noted, Pagan was at least eighty miles from Kyaukse, equally far from the Mu Valley, and nearly as far from Minbu, the three most heavily populated and intensively irrigated regions under the crown. The king may have held Minbu and the Mu Valley, but without Kyaukse he could not hold the entire kingdom. Two hundred and fifty years earlier, it was King Anawrahta's development and control of Kyaukse in the eleventh century that ultimately enabled the Kingdom of Pagan to expand beyond the Dry Zone of Upper Myanmar. Now, during the last decade of the kingdom, it was again Kyaukse that would determine the dynasty's fate; the conditions were remarkably similar to those more than two centuries before.

By the late thirteenth century, then, the geopolitical center of gravity had shifted farther to the northeast, from Pagan to the confluence of the Irrawaddy and Myitnge Rivers where the Mandalay-Ava-Sagaing region is located, the nucleus that was to become the center of the Burmese monarchy intermittently for the next seven hundred years. Along with this geographic shift was a parallel one in the source and structure of power—from the capital to its satellite cities, the monarch to his ministers/generals, and the royal palace to the battlefield. The city of Pagan itself would soon become more a symbol than the actual source of patronage, which dissipated with each acre of crown *padi* land and with each battle it lost to its ministers, the Three Brothers.

Thus, the Three Brothers who had once been Kyawswa's source of support and strength now became his nemesis. They had played a major role in the kingdom's successful resistance to the Mongols that had put Kyawswa on the throne; yet that same success had enhanced their power until they became rivals of the Pagan monarch, with whom he now had to contend.

Partly because of this competition at home and the need to strengthen his domestic power, and partly because China's approval was in the larger interest of the Pagan throne as a regional power, Kyawswa courted external support.[21] In early 1297, the king sent his son, Singhapati, to Peking to obtain official recognition from China as legitimate heir to the Burmese throne. Invariably, the Chinese considered most established authorities in Southeast Asia legitimate and almost always supported such candidates for the throne; once again, they complied. In the customary fashion of Myanmar (and other Southeast Asian) kings, who either had internal problems with domestic rivals or already had the power but wished to have it formally recognized by the strongest power in Asia, Kyawswa paid tribute.

It worked, for in March of 1297, Kyawswa was officially recognized as "king" and Singhapati as "heir-apparent of Mien Kingdom."[22] The Chinese also referred to Kyawswa by his royal title of Ti-li-p'u-wa-na-ti-t'i-ya (Tri Bhuvanaditaya). It appears that the eldest of the Three Brothers, Athinkhaya (called "Athin" by the Chinese), was on that mission as well, and received a "tiger tally" in the process, a high badge of honor. Kyawswa now had prestigious external support for his position as king, and for his son's position as heir to the throne.

But courting China's support, instead of stabilizing the domestic political struggle, complicated and destabilized it even more. The strategy may have helped Kyawswa's prestige initially, but since there was no military or financial support, it could not be sustained. China under the Yuan had weakened after Kubilai Khan's death in 1294, so it could not exert the kind of military pressure it was once able to, even had it wanted. Other than token tribute missions to China to help legitimize authority at home, domestic conditions, individuals, and events continued to have a greater impact than external ones.

Not until the mid-fourteenth century, with the rise of the Ming and a return to the kind of commercial activity and military power in the region (as witnessed earlier in the eleventh and twelfth centuries with the Cholas and Sri Lanka), could external forces once again reassert a larger role in domestic Myanmar politics. This time, it came from the Lower Myanmar coasts. (That is part of the story of "Teng-lung," a newly created kingdom centered at Pegu, the subject of part 2.)

An inscription found in Myin Saing, dated only ten months after the abovementioned mission to China, described Kyawswa pouring the water of consecration for a donation, usually a function reserved for the king or a close representative. The stone records the date as the month of Pyatho, thirteenth-day waxing, fifth-day of the week: that is, December 17, 1297. In it, Kyawswa was called Nankya Min, "the King who fell from the throne [or palace]." For complicated reasons described fully elsewhere, which include evidence from six more contemporary inscriptions, the earlier Burmese chronicles, and the contemporary Chinese sources, it seems far more likely that Kyawswa was not dethroned until 1298 and not killed until, at earliest, 1299.[23]

In fact, in June and July of 1298 (six to seven months after the above donation), the Three Brothers attacked Pagan and arrested the king, his eldest son Singhapati, and younger sons (recorded in the Chinese sources as Chao Chi-li and Chao P'u, neither of whom can be positively identified in Burmese sources but could have been the Saw Mun Nit and Saw Nit respectively of the chronicles) and imprisoned them all "for 11 months" in Myin Saing. "Ever since you submitted to China," they told Kyawswa, "you have not ceased to load us with shame."[24]

Clearly, therefore, the inscription dated to 1297 in which Kyawswa was called "the dethroned king" must have been inscribed only later, the date on it referring to his royal activities performed earlier in 1297, not to the date when the stone was erected (as convention has it), and should therefore be regarded as a statement made in a later context.[25] In other words, only after 1298 when, indeed, he had been dethroned, would he have been referred to as "the dethroned king," not before. Subsequently, Sawnit, his sixteen-year-old son, was placed on the Pagan throne as puppet.

According to a Myanmar scholar, the dethronement was said to have triggered another Mongol invasion in the winter of 1300–1301. I have some doubts about this interpretation, for it suggests that the Mongols were motivated by some moral or political principle (or both), and willing to spend the kind of time, money, and energy, and risk the inevitable deaths of many of their soldiers, on such an invasion for the sake of those principles. More likely, they may have wanted some revenge for their earlier failure of 1287, as well as to show the "world" that the rumors about their demise were premature. Lord Dalhousie's remark five hundred years later, that no one in the East was going to show the British to the door, must have been the same way the Mongols felt about the Burmese in the fourteenth century. As it turns out, both the British and the Mongols were shown to the door, the British perhaps less ignominiously.

The Three Brothers were said to have held their ground at Myin Saing, east-southeast of Kyaukse, to which the Mongols marched directly, rather than to Pagan, revealing that they knew that at Myin Saing lay the real power. It was a smart move on the part of the Three Brothers (if the identification of Myin Saing by Myanmar scholars is correct), for not only would the location have diverted attention away from Pagan, but Myin Saing was well fortified with three continuous and interconnected walls and lay in one of the hottest areas of the Dry Zone. All the Three Brothers had to do was hold the siege until the "cold" weather was over.

By the time of the invasion, Kyaukse's first (and largest) rice crop would have already been harvested and stored within fortified towns, while adequate water supply from perennial streams ran close to almost every one of these forts, including Myin Saing. Further, because the city was one of the southernmost among the major towns in Kyaukse, the Mongols had been drawn far into the interior, the southeast corner of Kyaukse, with most of its fortified towns now at their rear and on their flanks.

This Mongol siege of 1300–1301 apparently generated a Burmese poem (in hindsight), which was embellished by Harvey's translation to promote his perspective of the situation. It read,

The Chinks came down the passes
Roaring boys roaring;
The rain of their arrows
Pouring boys pouring

Notwithstanding poetic license, the Burmese original Harvey also provides actually reads,

The Taruk Came
Many as can be
Arrows Rained
Many as can be

The original has no "boys," "roaring," "pouring," "Chinks," or "passes." More important, the arrows that "rained" were not referring to those of the Mongols but the Burmese. The Yuan's own contemporary report of the event stated that, "on the 19th day (February 28th), arrows, stone, timber were shot from the top of the city and 500 government troops were killed."[26]

The late Burmese chronicles claimed that only during that siege was King Kyawswa actually killed by the Three Brothers, his head then shown to the Mongols to inform them that the alleged reason for their invasion (to reinstate the king) no longer applied. Since that was probably not the reason the Mongols invaded in the first place, they were not impressed or persuaded by this dramatic act of bravado (if it even occurred). What most likely persuaded them to withdraw were Myin Saing's unique fortifications (triple adjoining ramparts), its defenders (who were militarily tested and led by experienced generals, the Three Brothers), the fact that those within Myin Saing were defending their homeland (while for the Mongols it was just another of many military forays), and, of course, the weather.

By April of 1301, as the hot weather was already near its peak in that region, the Mongols, who were used to the cool climate of the high Yunnan plateau, began their second retreat within living memory of both parties, shedding their heavy coats, armor, and felt boots until they finally reached Yunnan. There, the generals responsible for the defeat were said to have been publicly strangled for allegedly having taken bribes from the Burmese. That was the last time the Mongols attacked Myanmar, and by 1303, Cheng-Mien, the "Chinese" province of Myanmar, created when the Mongols first entered the country in the 1270s, was formally abolished "forever."

In summary, by the first decade of the fourteenth century, the last invasion of "Myanmar" by the Mongols, even though unsuccessful, nevertheless weakened whatever centripetal forces were left that had held Pagan together, and ushered in the always present centrifugal ones, so that the whole, once again, began to unravel and revert to its parts. More precisely, a tripartite pattern of power ensued during the next sixty years under the tutelage of the Three Brothers and their descendants, as Myin Saing, Mekkhaya, and Pinle (their fiefs) filled the power vacuum, replacing Pagan as the center of Upper Myanmar.

The Legacy of the Three Brothers

Once again the Three Brothers had saved the country from complete disintegration, further enhancing their prestige and power. Sawnit, the sixteen-year-old king and son of Kyawswa, placed on the Pagan throne by the Three Brothers, became even more of a figurehead than his father had been. From his reign onward, the now politically effete kingdom of Pagan was no longer the real center of authority. The balance of power had shifted from Pagan to Kyaukse and the fortified towns of Myin Saing, Mekkhaya, and Pinle.

Although the Three Brothers initially continued to pay formal deference to the lad in public, they clearly held the reins behind the Pagan throne. In time, even that formality ceased when Sawnit died, and claims to the throne by the youngest of the Three Brothers, Thihathu, grew more brazen and public. In 1306, he took the title Anantasihasurajeyyadeva, and by October of 1309 held his coronation, at which event Thihathu not only adopted a typically Pagan royal title, but also donated lands to the *sangha*, a bold and unequivocal statement of his role as protector and patron of the religion. There was little Sawnit's successor at Pagan, Sawmunit, could do.

Meanwhile, the eldest of the Three Brothers, Athinkhaya, moved to a more strategic location, Sagaing, across the Irrawaddy from present day Mandalay, and east of the mouth of the Mu River where it empties into the Irrawaddy. Sagaing was not a new city and is mentioned in Pagan inscriptions. It controlled the Mu Valley, where Pagan kings Alaungsithu and Narapatisithu built many irrigation works during the twelfth century. By controlling Sagaing, Athinkhaya commanded a sizeable portion of the agricultural revenues of central Myanmar, rivaled only by Kyaukse, which Thihathu controlled from Pinle. In effect, then, there were now two centers of power left: Pinle and Sagaing. Myin Saing had served its purpose during the Mongol siege, but, mainly for geographic reasons, it could not serve as the center of a united Upper Myanmar the way Sagaing could: it had no direct access to the Irrawaddy, a sine qua non of any Myanmar capital during precolonial times.

Subsequently, an inscription of 1310 stated that "the exalted Asankhya [Athinkhaya], the elder brother . . . who had firmly controlled the country and capital without timidity and fear, died." Thereafter, it continued, "Rajasankyan [Yazathingyan], the middle brother and Thihathu shared power from their respective places. They together continued to control the great country [*pyi gyi*]."[27]

Two years later, when Yazathingyan also died, Thihathu was the only one left of the famous Three Brothers who had "saved" the kingdom, with few (or no) viable opponents to the throne of Upper Myanmar. He left Pinle and made Pinya, farther north, his capital, naming it Wijayapura, "City of Victory." The *Mahayazawingyi* gives the usual omens and prophecies for the founding of Pinya, adding that Thihathu followed tradition in building "the seven requisites" of a legitimate capital city: the palace and enclosure, a clock tower, the golden *zigon* (*stupa*), a new cave-temple, a long supporting tank, a royal lake, and the moat.[28] This kind of palace architecture not only made Pinya the exemplary center of Upper Myanmar, but it symbolized, as did the Pyu capitals and Pagan before it, the center of the Buddhist universe.

Pinya was located south of the future site of Ava, and the choice of its location revealed economic and military concerns. It was strongly built, with a large brick wall, close enough to Myin Saing (if the need should arise to take refuge there again) and right on the western fringe of the rich Kyaukse Valley, with easy access not only to the Irrawaddy River, but also the rest of the fortified towns that controlled the most important rice-producing region of Myanmar at the time. From here, Thihathu attempted to reestablish and resurrect the traditional relationships within his own *dhamma*-realm that were once part of the integrated structure of Pagan.

Thihathu married the chief queen of deceased Pagan king Kyawswa, thereby establishing, unequivocally and directly, royal credentials for himself and his offspring. By now, Pagan under Sawmunit was reduced to a governorship, so that he had become a mere de facto *myosa* (town eater). Patronage and reform of the *sangha* was another state ritual performed by Thihathu. This was absolutely necessary for any new king, as the well-being of the *sangha* was a sure sign of his legitimacy, particularly one whose genealogical credentials were not unequivocal and could be contested.

After that came the regularizing of succession, whereby Thihathu gave the office of heir apparent to his eldest son, Uzana, making him *Einshemin*, literally, "lord of the eastern [or front] palace,"[29] the same title used by Pagan's heirs apparent. With that office, Uzana was said to have received one hundred war elephants, eight hundred cavalry, and ten thousand infantry. Thihathu's middle son, he made lord of Pinle, his old fief in Kyaukse, along with eighty war elephants, six hundred cavalry, and ten thousand soldiers. His youngest son, he made *myosa* of another important town.

Thihathu thus reestablished the principle of the *sa* (to eat) administrative system, whose fiefs he bestowed on his closest kin and supporters, while demanding oaths of loyalty from leaders of more distant towns that were only nominally under his authority. He harnessed his economic resources by repairing and improving the Kyaukse irrigation works close to his capital, while establishing marriage alliances farther away in Taungdwingyi by giving in marriage his daughter, Saw Pulay, born of his northern queen, to the "eater" of that city.

The chronicles also described the extent of his dominions by listing the major towns he controlled, including Prome farther south, Toungoo on the southeast, and up to Pinya, his capital, in the north. If accurate, this means the king had control, mainly, of the territory from Pinya southward, including several places on the west bank of the Irrawaddy north of Prome, but not much more, as Athinkhaya's descendants held Sagaing and the valuable Mu Valley to its north.

Thihathu, also called Tasishin, "lord of one" (elephant) in his epigraphs, probably died around 1324. In indigenous historiography, he is one of the more conspicuous rulers of early Myanmar, and the Pinya years today are considered and celebrated as a distinct and legitimate era called Pinya Khit (Pinya Era) with some standing. But he and his dynasty are largely unknown to Western historians and therefore ignored, for not only was he considered a Shan—hence, not part of the centralist's story—but little has been written about him in English.

In summary, at a crucial time in the history of Upper Myanmar, when the first integrated kingdom in the country (Pagan) had been weakened by both long-term internal structural factors and more immediate external pressures, the Three Brothers rose to the occasion to provide some order to the embattled state and society for nearly a quarter century. They continued Pagan's most cherished beliefs, rituals, and customs, preserving them as institutions during what must have been trying times.

The Three Brothers also acted as regents and guardians of the religion, the monarchy, the court, and the kingdom, initially, to subsequently take the throne for themselves and marry into the ex-royal family to become part of the royal lineage. The political unity they established in the heart of Upper Myanmar—the Sagaing-Mandalay-Ava region—provided the wherewithal for the rise of a new dynasty there, and it was their political, if not genealogical, offspring who created the next dynasty that was to last another century and a half.

Conclusion

The decline of the Kingdom of Pagan triggered certain coping mechanisms in Burmese state and society that became historical patterns in subsequent centuries. When the kingdom was still strong, individuals were compelled to operate within a context of state institutions. But when these weakened, strong individuals and their clients began to replace them, in effect, "becoming" the "structure" of society. That was precisely the case in the late thirteenth and early fourteenth centuries, when strong individuals emerged to preempt and circumvent weak institutions that had once been dominant and stabilized society. We would see this pattern recur periodically throughout precolonial Burmese society.

Ava arose in such a context, where individuals were paramount over, and preempted, weakened institutions. Indeed, Pagan had arisen in the ninth century in much the same way: when the Pyu Kingdom had been invaded by Nanzhao, rendering its institutions effete. It was then that individuals such as Nyaung-U Sawrahan and Kyaung Phyu Min (Anawrahta's grandfather and father, respectively) and Anawrahta himself seized the moment to assert their primacy, which led to the founding of the Pagan Dynasty. During the first several decades of the fourteenth century as well, men of action, such as Kyawswa, the Three Brothers, and Thihathu, rescued Upper Myanmar society from total disintegration from the Mongols.

Yet, even such men of action could not maintain a viable state indefinitely, and would have had to eventually create new or rebuild old institutions that would be more permanent and stable, ones that could outlast them and their charismatic, personal leadership. And in that rebuilding, it is no surprise that they chose the only system they, and the society at large, knew instinctively well—Pagan's. But in so doing, they once again set in motion the beginning of a process that would end in a similar fate over a century and a half later.

The Ava Convention

Historical Background

For about a century, and well before Pagan had declined in the late thirteenth and beginning of the fourteenth centuries, the T'ai speakers—known as, and spelled, "Syam" in Old Burmese inscriptions (and pronounced Shan)—had been moving down several river valleys in Western and Central Mainland Southeast Asia, including the Irrawaddy. Some had been migrating across northern Myanmar into what is now Assam. As early as the late twelfth century, it appears the Shan[1] were already inhabiting the northern and eastern hills that abut the plains of the Irrawaddy in Upper Myanmar and by the thirteenth century had become an important demographic, if not also military, factor there.

Although the waning of the Kingdom of Pagan overlapped with the growth and political development of the Syam in both Myanmar and Thailand, particularly with regard to one of their earliest states, Sukhotai, there is no evidence that those Syam migrations were directly or indirectly responsible for the decline of Pagan. Subsequently, by the mid-fourteenth century, the Syam (and other T'ai speakers) had forged several discrete polities in central Mainland Southeast Asia that eventually crystallized into a T'ai kingdom called Ayuthaya, which became the conceptual, demographic, and political basis for the future nation of Thailand.

In Myanmar, however these T'ai/Shan speakers (as a community) never united into a pan-Shan kingdom. Indeed, the first time they were integrated as an ethno-cultural group in the country (and then, only administratively) occurred during the colonial period when the British created the "Shan States" after the annexation of Myanmar in 1886. Why the Shan in Myanmar, as a distinct ethno-linguistic and cultural group, were not able or did not want to forge an integrated kingdom of their own in Myanmar, as they did in Thailand, is interesting since they had (at least) the demographic means to do so, as the largest minority. Consider the Arakanese and Mon, two much smaller minority groups in Myanmar, without the kind of demographic advantage that the Shan had, who still managed to forge kingdoms for themselves, with an impact on the history of Ava. However, such questions were seldom (if ever) raised about Shan history even by Shan historians, so that its historiography remains static in a time warp.[2]

One of the reasons, surely, is the fact that Upper Myanmar was already the "heartland" of the Burmese speakers, where the bulk of the country's population resided. By the time the Shan speakers entered the scene, Myanmar had long been politically, militarily, and administratively integrated as a kingdom, especially under the Pagan Dynasty, with established social, economic, cultural, religious, and legal institutions, whose structure circumscribed hundreds of settlements of cultivators working vast agricultural resources (weirs, canals, sluices, reservoirs), the likes of which the new Shan-speaking migrants probably had not yet encountered. It was thus much easier and more realistic for the Shan in Myanmar to integrate into preexisting Burmese state and society than attempt to overthrow it or seriously try to create a new one to compete with it. Indeed, that is precisely what the evidence shows they did.

Whatever the reasons, the fact that the Shan did not create their own kingdom is directly pertinent to the history of Ava. It allowed Ava to emerge without much (if any) competition initially, and thereafter to maintain its momentum and strength. Instead of a three-kingdom scenario with another (northern) front for Ava to contend with, the divided Shan vied for positions as allies of Ava, thereby allowing Ava to focus most of its energies on Pegu and the south. And when colonial historiography attributed the kingdom of Ava to the Shan—resulting in the Ava Convention—the question of Shan unification appeared moot.

The Ava Convention

Essentially, the Ava Convention contends that the Kingdom of Ava was an ethnic Shan polity from its very inception, led and ruled by the Shan for over a century and a half; and the period, a tumultuous one largely of decentralism and fragmentation, paradoxically also witnessed the "birth" and apogee of Burmese literature. Although the basis for the convention has been demonstrated to be erroneous,[3] some reiteration and more recent information and thoughts on the subject are warranted to address concerns directly related to the present study.

It is virtually certain that the locus classicus of the Ava Convention is Sir Arthur Phayre's 1883 *History of Burma*, the first comprehensive history of the country published in English. He had followed the traditional narrative on the "fall" of Pagan and "rise" of Ava found in U Kala's eighteenth-century Burmese-language chronicle, the *Mahayazawingyi*, and had interpreted a sentence in it to conclude that the lineage of the famous Three Brothers who saved the kingdom of Pagan from the Mongols was Shan. This effectively transformed the Three Brothers of indigenous history and historiography into the "Three *Shan* Brothers" of colonial historiography.[4] From Phayre's work onward, all historians of colonial Myanmar and their Burmese protégés, who were part of that academic lineage, invariably and uncritically accepted the notion of, and referred to, the Three Brothers as the "Three Shan Brothers." Indeed, in one case, the word "Shan" was inserted between the words "Three Brothers," even when not found in the original.[5] Their "Shan-ness" was therefore never questioned by colonial historiography, and so never problematized.

The link between the Three Brothers alleged to be Shan and the Kingdom of Ava lay in the assumption that the founder of the Ava Dynasty in 1364 and governor of Tagaung, Thadominbya, was a descendant of the "Three Shan Brothers." Hence, the Ava Dynasty he created, and the entire Ava kingdom and period thereafter, also "became" Shan in Myanmar's English-language historiography. In effect, what the Ava Convention did was to create an ethnic kingdom ruled by an ethnic dynasty whose life span defined and marked an ethnic period. These ethnic categories, in turn, became the criteria for conceptualizing and organizing precolonial Myanmar's history subsequently. The pieces of this three-layered analysis (of kingdom, dynasty, and period) are so enmeshed in one another that to address or critique one also requires addressing and critiquing the other two, as I shall do.

PROBLEMS OF EVIDENCE

The most serious problem for the Ava Convention is that there is not a shred of original and contemporary evidence to support it. None of it refers to the Three Brothers as Shan; none suggests they were perceived (either by themselves or by others) to have been Shan; and none supports either their reification or their identification as Shan. Thus, not a single contemporary stone inscription of the late Pagan and Ava periods erected by the Three Brothers themselves, or by their contemporaries who knew them, or by anyone else that mentioned them, ever stated they were, or were perceived to have been, Shan. In these contemporary stone inscriptions, they were simply known as *amatkyi thon yauk* (the three great ministers). Similarly, there is not a single indigenous chronicle or Chinese record that stated they were Shan. In the former, they were simply referred to as *min nyi naung thon pa* (the three royal brothers), while the latter never mentioned their ethnicity and considered them part of the Burmese court.

Indeed, in later indigenous sources, the ethnic background of the Three Brothers (reified or not) is never an issue. It is only in colonial historiography that they "became" Shan, hence, also there that their "ethnicity" became an issue. And that is precisely the reason the Ava Convention cannot be found anywhere in the precolonial indigenous historiography of Myanmar: it exists only in the English language. When I asked Burmese educated in the country's history but not familiar with its English-language historiography what the "Shan period" was, or who the "Three Shan Brothers" were, their response was invariably one of sheer bewilderment; they had never heard of either! The Ava Convention was never a part of indigenous epistemology and, by and large, is still not. Rather, it belongs mainly (or only) to the colonial epistemology of Myanmar.[6]

Since the attributed ethnicity of the Three Brothers is the linchpin of the whole "Ava is Shan" thesis—on which, in turn, are based the notions of an "ethnic kingdom," "ethnic dynasty," and "ethnic period"—it means the latter are also untenable, prima facie. Yet, disproving these characterizations with original and contemporary evidence poses a methodological problem, for the Ava Convention never explained what a "Shan Ava" meant, nor did it describe what it might have looked like had it been "Shan." Its advocates simply made the assertion and left it at that. In other words, if we are to disprove the "Ava is Shan" thesis empirically with original evidence, then a "Shan Ava" needs to be reconstructed first before it is deconstructed.

I have therefore reconstructed what a "Shan Ava" might have looked like, using the arguments of the Ava Convention and its notions of ethnicity. If Ava had been a Shan kingdom, it should have been one where (a) the majority of the people at least identified themselves as Shan, (b) most of the people in it dressed in what is considered Shan clothing, (c) the food eaten was recognizable as Shan, (d) everyone (or many) worshipped "Shan" deities and spirits, (e) people obeyed (or disobeyed) Shan law and custom, (f) Shan marriage rules and birth and death rituals were followed, (g) its architects built palaces of Shan design and temples based on Shan cosmology, (h) the government was organized according to Shan principles of administration and conceptions of leadership, (i) the public enjoyed music, dance, theatre, poetry, and literature that can be identified as Shan, and, (j) perhaps most important, the language of state was Shan (T'ai), written in a Shan script. If the above reasonably portrays what a "Shan Ava" might have looked like, then *that* Ava does not exist in Myanmar's history. There is nothing in the original and contemporary sources to support any of it.

Perhaps the most telling evidence—with or without reconstructing a "Shan Ava"—is linguistic. Not a single stone inscription that has been recovered, erected by royalty or commoner; not a single stanza of verse (of many) composed; and not a single sentence in any royal edict proclaimed, administrative and provincial record submitted, legal code compiled, cadastral survey taken, political or religious treatise produced, or religious donation made during the Ava period, *is written in the Shan (or T'ai) language.* All genres of writing at all levels of society throughout the entire kingdom during its life (and beyond)—poems, *dhammathat,* chronicles, edicts, and so on—were in Old Burmese (except for a few written in either Pali or Pali-Burmese *nissaya*).

Burmese, not Shan then, was Ava's lingua franca and the written language of state and society. And because written inscriptions were public, legal records meant for the general population, the language on them undoubtedly represents the language of the general public also, not just that of an elite. Clearly, Ava, both elite and masses, must have consisted predominantly of Burmese speakers,[7] to the extent that the polite word for male in Burmese at Ava (*amyo tha*) literally meant "son of the race," and the word for female (*amyo thami*), "daughter of the race." (These are still the polite words in Burmese used for males and females today.) Furthermore, the same scholars who created the Ava Convention are agreed that the "birth" and "apogee" of Burmese literature occurred at Ava. Yet, at the same time, they continued to maintain that Ava was Shan, providing no explanation for this incongruity. One is therefore compelled to ask how did, how could, and why would a "Shan Ava" produce the birth and apogee of Burmese literature, especially if the Ava kingdom was considered a "dark age" of "fragmentation" and "decentralization" ruled by "barbarous" Shan people?[8] Were these historians of Myanmar not even curious about that dissonance? Perhaps they were, but they parried the issue by declaring that the development of Burmese literature during a "Shan period" was a "puzzle," "paradox," or "surprise."

In other words, they accepted Ava's literary accomplishments—since they could not refute the incontrovertible evidence—but still refused to give up their thesis of a "Shan Ava." What needs correcting at this point is not the evidence regarding the place of Burmese literature at Ava (discussed in greater detail in another chapter) but the assertion that the phenomenon is "surprising," "puzzling," or "paradoxical." It is none of that.

First, note that it was only at Ava's fall, in 1526–1527, that a Shan *sawbwa* for the first time took the center and, with his two successors, reigned there until overthrown in 1551 by a member of the old Ava royal family. If there were a "Shan period" in Myanmar's history at all, this was it, amounting to a total of twenty-four years! Even then, of those three *sawbwa,* only the first, Thohanbwa (1527–1543), was reported to have purged Burmese culture, whereas his two successors promoted and patronized it as part of their efforts at legitimation. Effectively, then, it was only Thohanbwa's reign that can be claimed to have been a "Shan Period" in Myanmar's history: a mere seventeen years. (Even this was two hundred years too late, well after the date given by the Ava Convention as the beginning of Shan rule in 1364.)

Besides, and second, by the time Thohanbwa conquered Ava in 1526–1527, the kingdom had already attained the achievements in Burmese literature for which it has been acclaimed. In other words, during the entire twenty-four years Ava was ruled by Shan *sawbwa,* no Burmese literature of note (that I am aware of) was produced at Ava itself, but at other centers that previously had been under Ava, such as Prome, Toungoo, and Shwebo, to which the most prominent literary figures that had been producing at Ava fled when the capital was taken. Thus, the literary achievements of the Kingdom of Ava and the period of "Shan rule" had nothing to do with each other—it is a false issue—so that there is no reason for "surprise" or for declaring "paradoxes." To the advocates of the Ava Convention, however, because this achievement in Burmese literature occurred during what they thought was a long "Shan period" beginning with the fictitious "Three Shan Brothers" at Pagan, of course, it was a "surprise" and "paradox."

None of this is meant to suggest that there were no Shan cultural influences on Ava at all. Certain titles of queens of both Pagan and Ava often used the term *saw* (as in Queen Saw), thought to be a Shan honorific.[9] This is not surprising, given the marriage alliances between Ava royalty and the Shan *sawbwa* during the Ava period. There is also evidence of people with Shan background having integrated into Ava society, particularly in the military and political sectors. Art historians might also find "Shan influences" in (say) Buddha statues produced during the Ava period, although that conclusion may stem from a retrospective interpretation: they are thought to reflect "Shan influences" because Ava was *already presumed* to be Shan in the historiography of Myanmar.

Whatever the cultural exchanges were, they need not imply anything more than that, and certainly do not prove (or even suggest) that the Kingdom of Ava was therefore politically, culturally, and demographically Shan. Indeed, I would argue that most of the cultural influences during that period went in the opposite direction in any case. It was Ava's that radiated outward from the central plains of the Dry Zone's Irrawaddy River valley to the hills, not the other way around. These would include literacy in the Burmese language and script; "localized" Burmese Theravada Buddhism and all its accouterments; Indianized (Pagan) conceptions of state and king, of legitimacy and authority; Burmese Buddhist cosmological underpinnings in the designs of palace architecture;[10] Burmese Buddhist codified law; high wrought techniques in the arts and crafts; even important annual cereals based on irrigation (such as *sawah* or wet-rice) and other Upper Myanmar river-valley crops such as the variety of pulses.[11]

Indeed, it is far more likely that periphery peoples were drawn toward Ava physically and culturally, participated in and adopted the center's norms and characteristics (as the two *sawbwa* after Thohanbwa did), than vice versa. After all, Ava, not Hsiphaw or Momeit, was the exemplary center in Upper Myanmar; it was the former's culture being emulated, not the latter's. Certainly no historian of Myanmar has ever demonstrated (or even suggested) that Ava's social customs, laws, conceptual system, and religious and political institutions came from, and resembled, those of Momeit and Hsiphaw or, for that matter, of Chiang Mai, Chiang Rai, or Ayuthaya. On the contrary, and as we shall see, Ava looked very much like a small Pagan, hence my phrase, "Ava was Pagan writ small."

PROBLEMS OF CONCEPTUALIZATION, METHODOLOGY, AND ANALYSIS

In addition to the absence of evidence, the conceptual, methodological, and analytical basis for the Ava Convention, beginning with the famous Three Brothers, is seriously flawed. It ultimately stems from the *reification of ethnicity*; that is, turning a relative, abstract perception of ethnic identity into an "objective" and concrete trait and then attributing it to a particular ethno-linguistic group (or "race"). Had ethnicity not been reified, the Ava Convention might not have emerged at all. Although such reification of ethnicity has been soundly criticized in recent decades, as noted above, during Phayre's time and before, it was unquestioned truth. There was thus little reason for his generation not to have accepted notions of ethnic identity as concrete reality, especially since one could clearly see that certain "objective" cultural traits were practiced by particular ethno-linguistic groups and not by others.

People who considered themselves Shan, for example, spoke Shan as their "mother tongue," dressed in ways different from other ethno-linguistic groups, ate certain foods others might not, worshipped particular deities, practiced their own marriage rituals, celebrated certain customs, and preserved origin myths that were sui generis. And one could actually see that these traits were distinct from (say) the language spoken by the Padaung, the dress of their women (with their famous neck rings), their religious beliefs, their burial rituals, their marriage customs, and so on. As these traits were not trivial but considered representative of a particular culture, one can understand how these "objective" factors shaped other peoples' image of particular groups as well as the way members of these same groups identified themselves. Thus, "ethnic traits" were not entirely attributions by someone else, but "reality" based on clearly observable features.

But that is different from saying that these cultural traits must therefore be synonymous with the ethnicity (or "race") that practiced them.

Still, it was not entirely unreasonable for administrator/scholars such as Phayre, writing in the late nineteenth century, to have embraced such beliefs. Modern anthropological analyses and conceptions of ethnicity were still nearly a hundred years in the future, while anthropology itself, as a modern discipline, was in its infancy, especially in the study of Myanmar. In fact, as late as the first decade of the twentieth century, colonial "anthropologists" of Myanmar were measuring the size and shape of people's heads they considered to be "pure Mon specimens" in Lower Myanmar to distinguish them from those they thought were "pure Burman." Such beliefs regarding ethnicity were very much part of Phayre's intellectual context, from which he devised his conceptual framework. It should come as no surprise then, that he interpreted the "ethnicity" of the Three Brothers in a similar (reified) way.

These physical attributes of "race" were then linked to political behavior by the next generation of Myanmar historians. G. E. Harvey wrote that decentralism was a characteristic of the Shan qua Shan, for they were "a hill-race with a congenital incapacity for combined action." In other words, "Shan-ness" itself was thought to have been a factor in decentralism helped by geography. That belief led to his assertions that the Ava period was a "marked decline" from Pagan with "half a dozen squabbling little courts, all of them, even when not positively barbarous, busily engaged in degrading the country with civil war."[12] Harvey was also said to have described Upper Myanmar during the last days of the Ava Dynasty as a "bedlam of snarling Shan states" by D. G. E. Hall, who depended on both Phayre and Harvey for the indigenous components of his own history. Hall therefore agreed that it was a period of Shan penetration and a "welter of barbarism,"[13] interpretations that secured agreement even from a colonially trained Shan historian, the late Sao Saimong Mangrai.[14]

The "Ava is Shan" thesis fostered the notion of "ethnic periods" and "ethnic kingdoms," perhaps even more so than before, for by the time of Harvey and Hall, reified ethnicity had become a public, political issue in nation-building. Harvey's *History* had been written during the thick of the nationalistic period in Myanmar, when ethnicity was being reified in public debate and had become an important part of the agenda in the political process of forming a modern nation, as had Hall's, only later. The political atmosphere in which Harvey, Hall, and many of their contemporaries wrote surely helped make the myth of the "Three Shan Brothers" and a "Shan period" at Ava not only believable and desirable (in some quarters) but also more "relevant."

However ethnicity may have been perceived and understood, and whatever the prevailing intellectual context might have been, there were other, more basic problems of methodological analysis among those advocating the "Ava is Shan" thesis. At least colonial scholars should have explained what they meant by that phrase. How could such a claim that "Ava is Shan" even be made without explaining what "Shan-ness" is, in comparison to, say, their notions of "Chinese-ness" or "Burmese-ness"? Equally important, they also did not explain *how* that "Shan-ness" was passed down from the (erroneous) reified ethnicity of the Three Brothers to that of an entire kingdom, like some congenital trait passed down from one generation to the next by DNA. Even had the Three Brothers been Shan, the advocates of the Ava Convention never indicated what concrete links there might have been between them and the institutions and characteristics of the Ava kingdom itself,[15] since the first two brothers had died by 1312, and the third in 1324, whereas the Kingdom of Ava was not founded until thirty years later—1364! (To reiterate, the problem in chronology lay in Phayre's confusion between the Shan who conquered Ava in 1526–1527 and the Three Brothers of late thirteenth- and early fourteenth-century Pagan.)[16]

Problems of a practical and personal nature also plagued the "Ava is Shan" thesis. To be sure, when the earliest pioneers such as Phayre were writing, the bulk of the epigraphic evidence was not yet available; most of the Ava inscriptions (and other textual sources) on which current information is based had not been discovered, so that none of the epigraphs with which we are now familiar had yet been collated or otherwise organized for research. (And Phayre's book reflects that paucity.) Indeed, the latest five-volume edition of Old Burmese inscriptions, with three of them having a direct bearing on the Ava period, appeared only in the 1970s and subsequently, and they saw limited distribution even among those who read Old Burmese. On the other hand, with or without the inscriptions, had Phayre used only U Kala's chronicle and nothing else, but without reifying ethnicity to the extent his context led him to, the entire "Ava is Shan" thesis might not have emerged at all, and hence, no Ava Convention to deconstruct today.

At the time Harvey and Hall wrote their histories, many of the Old Burmese inscriptions to which Phayre did not have access had been collected and/or published in one form or another. Chronicles not available in print during Phayre's day had also been published, or at least were accessible in manuscript form. Thus, by then, it was no longer a case of the unavailability of primary sources, but one of not having the ability to read them, as well as, of course, the uncomfortable and daunting task of rejecting an already established historiography. Although I cannot assess Harvey's reading knowledge of Burmese fairly,[17] rejecting an established historiography presupposes good cause, and without a sound reading knowledge of Burmese, finding such good cause would have been unlikely. As for Hall, I do have personal knowledge that he could not speak or read Burmese, certainly not well enough to have conducted research in it,[18] and was therefore properly cautious about the Shan-period thesis. Indeed, perhaps precisely because of that problem, he showed greater circumspection than did some of the others.

Unlike Phayre's generation, then, by the time the subsequent generation of Myanmar historians appeared, most of the pertinent sources (primary as well as secondary, in Burmese as well as in English) were available in some sort of researchable form. That means these scholars should have at least asked why, if Ava were a Shan kingdom, virtually everything was written in Old Burmese? Should they not have wondered something was amiss with the "Ava is

Shan" thesis when not a single line of a single contemporary and original text had been written in the Shan language during a period of 226 years they thought had been a Shan period?[19] That Myanmar historians still did not ask that question (or those kinds of questions) even after they had the best sources available suggests several other problems of context still prevalent.

First, and ultimately, they believed they already had the "truth" about Ava, so never seriously sought to challenge it. Even had they done so, it would have required a paradigm shift, a major revision of Myanmar's English-language historiography, at whose foundations lay a most tenacious belief, with huge cultural, social, and political (if not also personal) implications—namely, reified ethnicity and its role in the making of Myanmar's history. So it was far more reasonable (and easier) that Ava "remain" Shan than to find an alternative explanation for it, particularly given the political context of the time.

It is also likely, second, that the evidence was not scrutinized very carefully, for the mere raising of such probing questions regarding an accepted truth presupposes in-depth research into (what were to most) difficult sources. Even had some of them known the language well enough, much of the rich literature available on the Ava period is in verse and extremely difficult to understand even for native speakers of the language. And the few immersed and competent in Ava verse have shown little interest in the kinds of historiographic issues with which historians were concerned.

Moreover, as Ava was believed to have been a "decadent" period, most historians of Myanmar were not particularly interested in it, overshadowed as it was by both the Pagan and Second Pegu/Toungoo kingdoms. Even today, no historian of early Myanmar in the West has conducted original research on the Ava period in any depth before the present study, and among the handful of students and scholars in Myanmar itself who have shown an interest in the country's history, the First Ava period has not been a favorite focus of research.

To these contextual problems can be added the social, psychological, and cultural factors that prevented (or inhibited) subsequent generations from seriously challenging their mentors to whom the Ava Convention belonged. In British and independent Myanmar, not only does one not challenge the wisdom of one's teachers, there were few acceptable (and comfortable) mechanisms with which to do so even if one were so inclined. This was particularly true of native Burmese historians whose mentors were Westerners; in the context of colonialism and its enduring aftermath, that simply did not happen very often, if at all.

At a more individual level, that the late G. H. Luce did not ask such questions of the Ava Convention appears to have been mainly a matter of personal and professional research preference; he focused on the first half of the Pagan period, not Ava. Also, as he considered the Burmese chronicles to be largely unreliable as history, he did not pay much attention to them, particularly those sections dealing with the Ava period. Yet, it is precisely an analysis of these parts of the chronicles and inscriptions—not so much the earlier (Pagan) period—that led me to the myth of the "Three Shan Brothers." Besides, Luce had little reason to question their reified ethnicity, for it "confirmed" their usurper role that he espoused.

One of Luce's most famous disciples was Dr. Than Tun, whose scholarship followed and overlapped with his teacher's. Certainly he was not about to challenge Luce in public even had he disagreed (and he did on several issues). With regard to the present topic, it is clear from his publications (and my personal contact with him) that neither the ancestry of the Three Brothers nor Ava's "Shan-ness" was particularly an urgent issue (or much of a problem) for him, perhaps because both were already considered part of convention and he felt he had more important subjects to address, which he did. Moreover, he belonged to the traditional school of Burmese-colonial history, where verifying dates and events was far more important than interpreting them in the context of the kinds of broader historiographic issues being raised here. Indeed, he and a colleague, Tin Hla Thaw, published two seminal articles on the Ava period in English in the late 1950s that should have once and for all ended the Ava Convention. But neither challenged the "Ava is Shan" thesis directly or implicitly. In fact, they actually perpetuated a related component of it—Ava's decentralism—by calling the period "a century of unrest" and "the most troubled [in] Burmese history."[20]

In contrast to both Luce and Than Tun, Htin Aung's view on the Ava thesis was not only a knee-jerk reaction to Luce's (admittedly, often wild) assertions, but an attempt to accommodate the "contradiction" between a "Shan Ava" and his belief (correctly, it turns out) that Ava was ruled by Burmese speakers. That suggests he was at least thinking about the various dissonant factors discussed above; either that or, as an ardent Burmese nationalist, he could not accept the notion of a "Shan Ava." But because he seldom cited original evidence as support, it is difficult to know what he actually knew in terms of the data, and what, in fact, was personal sentiment. Nonetheless, he was correct (perhaps for the wrong reasons) that Ava was Burmese in everything but name, endorsed by Sao Saimong Mangrai, descendant of a prominent Shan *sawbwa*.

By the mid-twentieth century, then, all of Myanmar's English-language historiography had placed the country's history in a framework of reified ethnicity. The earliest, the era between the first two centuries BC and approximately the ninth century AD, was called the "Pyu period," an ethnic designation of a people about whom we still know very little. The Pagan period was considered to be the "Burmese cum Mon" period, while Ava was, of course, Shan. The First Pegu period (thirteenth to the beginning of the sixteenth century) was also known as a "Mon period," while the Second Ava (also called the Restored Toungoo) period (seventeenth to the mid-eighteenth century) was designated a "Burmese period." The Konbaung period of the mid-eighteenth to the late nineteenth century remained a "Burmese period," followed by the "British" and "Japanese" periods. Thus, reified ethnicity was the ultimate basis for organizing the history of Myanmar.

But the conceptualization of ethnic periods goes beyond an abstract notion of "race"; it is also deeply embedded in the idea of a "bloodline" that continues via individuals and groups, illustrated by the following example. The dynasty of

"Burmese" king Tabinshwehti, after he had conquered the "Mon Dynasty" of Pegu in 1539, is named the "Toungoo" Dynasty by Western historians. Why? Because the "Burmese ethnicity" of Toungoo's "bloodline," had replaced the "Mon ethnicity" of Pegu's, even though the capital remained at Pegu. And when this so-called Toungoo Dynasty centered at Pegu was ended in 1599 by the kingdoms of Mrauk-U (in Arakan) and Ayuthaya (in Siam), and a new dynasty established in Upper Myanmar by one of its royal descendants, it was named the "Later Toungoo" Dynasty (by one historian) and the "Restored Toungoo" Dynasty (by another), again demonstrating that the criterion for retaining the name "Toungoo" was the perceived continuation of its (reified) ethnicity in the bloodline of its leadership. Yet, in the precolonial *indigenous* historiography of Myanmar, no such name as the "Toungoo Dynasty," much less, the "Later" and "Restored," exists. In other words, this appellation—"Later" or "Restored" Toungoo—is found only in the Western historiography of Myanmar. The reason is that indigenous historiography used an entirely different criterion for the identification, organization, and naming of its dynasties. And that had much more to do with the city from which these dynasties ruled rather than the attributed ethnicity of their leadership's bloodline. As long as these cities had received a Buddha prophecy, their exemplary status and function were confirmed. Hence, as noted above, dynasties in Myanmar were named after the cities (or locations) from which they ruled: Tagaung, Sri Ksetra, Pagan, First Ava, Pegu, Second Ava, and Konbaung. To the indigenous chroniclers, the continuity of reified ethnicity through the dynasty's bloodline had little or nothing to do with identifying, naming, or organizing Myanmar's history and its dynasties; that was colonial historiography's obsession.

And precisely because there was no necessary connection between the organization of Myanmar's history and changes in a dynasty's (reified) ethnicity, the beginnings and ends of dynasties did not follow the periodization scheme of Western historiography either. Whereas conventional English-language historiography "ends" the Pagan Dynasty in 1287 because its "Burmese line" of kings was (about to be) replaced by (what it erroneously thought was) a Shan line of kings (in the Three Brothers) indigenous historiography "ends" it when Pagan ceased being an exemplary Buddhist center when Saw Mun Nit died in the fourteenth century.

Similarly, the English-language historiography of Myanmar "ends" the First Ava Dynasty in 1526–1527 because a Shan *sawbwa* had taken the capital—thereby changing its (reified) "ethnic" bloodline from Burman to Shan—*even though this interpretation was directly contradictory to its own "Shan is Ava" thesis.* And by so doing, colonial historiography gave Ava a mere 163 years, whereas indigenous historiography ends Ava's role as exemplary center only in 1752, giving it 388 years, including both the First and Second Ava Dynasties. Ava as an exemplary Buddhist capital did not end simply because its bloodline of Burmese kings was replaced by that of Shan leaders between 1527 and 1551.[21]

To put it another way, the chronicles did not end Ava's role as a Buddha-prophesied city simply because the Burmese *min set* (list of kings, that is, dynasty) ended and a Shan *min set* replaced it temporarily. In fact, the chronicles included the three *sawbwa* who reigned at Ava in its list of kings, until the city no longer fulfilled its function as exemplary center for the religion in 1752. For the same reasons, Tabinshwehti is included in the list of kings of Pegu even though he belonged to a "Burmese" center (Toungoo) and took the "Mon" capital in 1539, even after overthrowing the founding Wareru Dynasty and its kings.[22] For, as long as Tabinshwehti ruled from and made Pegu his capital, which was also a Buddha-prophesied city, the chronicles considered him part of that dynasty.

Thus, to modern Myanmar historians trained in Western historiographic traditions, whether or not a city received a Buddha prophecy had nothing to do with identifying a dynasty or allotting it with a particular span of time. For the indigenous chronicles, however, it had everything to do with it. Labeling a dynasty or age by the ethnicity of its founders is an entirely exogenous and nonautonomous colonial reconstruction, not found in indigenous epistemology. And which criterion we use—indigenous or colonial—affects, in no small way, the writing of Myanmar's history.[23] This stark disjuncture between the etic and emic epistemologies of the country continues to plague Myanmar studies today.

There *is* a solution of sorts to all this. One need not accept either criterion in toto for periodizing Myanmar's history. Instead, one can choose what was suggested by Harry Benda a half century ago: namely, organize history according to evidence of *structural change* in society. Although that gives agency to change and to structures, it still allows continuity a place in the schema, while eliminating both reified ethnicity and sacred prophecy as criteria for periodization.

Thus, for example, the end of the kingdom and dynasty of Pagan would not date to 1287 when King Narathihapade fled the capital, as convention has it, but to the first decade of the fourteenth century, when the Mongols left, when the Pagan throne was no longer in charge, and when the Three Brothers assumed real power in Upper Myanmar. Or, Pagan's end could be placed in 1364, when Ava clearly and unambiguously became the political capital of Upper Myanmar, centered at a new location with new leadership. In either case, one could argue that structural change had taken place at least at the elite level, although the bulk of society's institutions and people remained much the same. Admittedly, and in both cases, politics would be clearly privileged over (say) religious beliefs, for if religion were given agency, no period markers would be needed at all, since little or no substantive structural or ideological transformation occurred in religion during the Pagan and Ava periods.

And as noted above, Ava's "end" need not be dated to 1526–1527 when the Shan took the capital—they were gone in twenty-four years anyway—but to 1752, when the city of Ava as the center of political, economic, legal, and religious power of (at least) Upper Myanmar (and much of the country for a significant amount of time) ceased being such. So also the First Pegu period: it need not have to "end" in 1539, when Tabinshwehti took it and made it its capital thereafter, but in 1599, when the city was burnt to the ground and was no longer the center of things, especially the religion.

The latter event changed conditions considerably for both elite and commoner in Lower Myanmar. Among other things, the leadership and center of the state returned to an in-land agrarian environment instead of remaining in a commercial maritime location. And since the criterion for deciding whether or not structural change had taken place is not a matter only of elite politics but also of an entire way of life for the bulk of society, a period marker is certainly justified after 1599. In any case, it is structural change (following Benda), not reified ethnicity or sacredness of centers, that would determine the organization (periodization) of Myanmar's history in this book.

The English-language historiography of Ava remained dormant until around 1971, when the late Paul Bennett, as part of a master's thesis at Yale, finally questioned the issue of Ava's cultural discontinuity with Pagan.[24] Still, neither Ava's "troubled" nature, the ancestry of the Three Brothers, the notion of reified ethnicity and Ava's "Shan-ness," nor the other historiographic and evidentiary issues crucial to the Ava Convention raised herein was addressed by him, so that all remained basically intact. And because of that, a decade and a half later, in 1984, a distinguished historian of Myanmar and Southeast Asia (now also world history), Victor Lieberman, focusing on another period of Myanmar's history and other issues, continued part of the Ava Convention when he characterized the period as one of "fragmentation lasting 260 years."[25]

By the 1980s, then, the above historiography of Ava was over a century old (1883–1984), and had become an accepted convention, within whose framework, all (or nearly all) early and modern Myanmar history was being analyzed and interpreted. Admittedly, I was also very much part of that convention, although I did express some skepticism about the ethnicity of the Three Brothers by the time *Pagan* was published in 1985.[26] Yet, at the time, that particular doubt did not result in a challenge of the prevailing paradigm, since I also did not ask the kinds of questions that should have been asked.

It was not until 1996, well over a century after Sir Arthur Phayre began what later became known as the "Ava is Shan" thesis, that I finally published "The Myth of the 'Three Shan Brothers' and the Ava Period in Burmese History."[27] It demonstrated that there was no empirical basis whatsoever for attributing Shan ethnicity to the Three Brothers, thereby disputing the very heart of the myth. In 1998, that article was slightly revised and published as a chapter in *Myth and History in the Historiography of Early Burma* along with several other myths about early Myanmar's history. What these publications did was lay the foundations for the present dismantling of the entire Ava Convention, seeking not only to set the record straight in terms of empirical evidence but also to address the historiographic issues and problems in it.

I had hoped, when the above two works were published, that at least the Shan ethnicity attributed to the Three Brothers would no longer stand, and not continue beyond the present (especially) younger generation of Myanmar scholars. And although established senior scholars of Myanmar and Southeast Asia have made such acknowledgment,[28] conventions die hard and their staying power is uncanny, so that in at least two cases, Ava and the Three Brothers remained Shan.[29]

Aside from ignoring new research in the field, it is also the sheer "power" of academic conventions, along with their fairly long-term political and economic support—and some bad timing—that perpetuated the "Ava is Shan" thesis. The literature in the field of Southeast Asian studies had long favored minority ethnic groups over majority ruling ones, so that contrary sentiments are often regarded as "politically incorrect," something I have elsewhere called "privileging the periphery."[30] Depriving the minority Shan of their only major claim to fame in Myanmar history (as founders of the Kingdom of Ava) was not welcomed with open arms in Myanmar and Southeast Asian studies, especially at a time when the country's government—regarded as dominated by majority "ethnic Burmans"—was being castigated and pummeled by the most powerful Western powers and their media. Because the latter also shared the anti-centrist perspectives of academia, virtually anything that enhanced minority ethnic autonomy in Myanmar was celebrated in their vast and unequaled worldwide communications networks. And not least, the "staying power" of both these academic and political/journalistic exercises had extensive financial backing by Western governments and semiprivate organizations whose outlays averaged over $10 million a year over three decades, especially for promoting populist ideas of political decentralization such as democratic federalism.[31]

That is not to say, of course, that reified ethnicity and/or framing it as an adversarial majority-minority relationship was a new idea; indeed it goes back to earlier colonial days when it fostered, on the one hand, the political strategy of "divide and rule" and, on the other, the academic convention of organizing Myanmar's history into ethnic kingdoms, dynasties, and periods. Ironically, these ideas of "ascribed ethnicity" did not end when independence was attained and power was handed back to an indigenous government. Rather, those colonial notions were actually adopted and continued by the new political and academic leadership,[32] not only impeding the quest to build a nation based on citizenship but also perpetuating their place in Myanmar historiography. The ensuing nearly half century of civil war, characterized as being essentially a struggle between majority and minority ethnic groups, further tended to confirm the interpretation of the country's past (since time immemorial) as an irrevocably adversarial and hostile contest between and among majority and minority ethnic groups at the national level.

Thus, instead of the more complicated and fluid modus vivendi that existed between the majority ethnic group and the prominent minority ones for centuries—a far more accurate picture of the way "ethnic politics" worked in precolonial Myanmar[33] (and probably the rest of Southeast Asia)—the adversarial framework of analysis prevailed, ensconcing majority-minority (reified) ethnic relations in a binary and synchronous straitjacket. This, in turn, was fodder for the "anti-nation" discourse increasingly heard in academia during the same decades. It is this kind of modern, politically and economically shaped historiography of Ava and Pegu that I have attempted to change in this book, by returning it to a chronologically correct time, and to the academic arena.

A New Approach to the Study of Ava

Dispelling the "Ava is Shan" thesis means the current study has discarded the conceptual, methodological, and analytical foundations that underlay it. That is accomplished largely by analyzing the primary evidence independently of the assumptions of the Ava Convention and, in general, working outside the intellectual contexts that spawned it. This has allowed me to reconstruct the Ava period afresh, so that it begins and ends "outside the box," so to speak. Particularly important in this approach is the present reconstruction of the narrative and institutional history of Ava from sources contemporary to it without placing it in a framework of reified ethnicity and its assumed role in the making of Myanmar's history. Admittedly, it is difficult to avoid using ethnic terms and categories altogether, especially when the society being studied also did the same. Nonetheless, and in any case, the focus of this book is not reified ethnic groups or their contributions as such, but the way in which individuals and events operated within a certain Upper Myanmar geopolitical, sociocultural, ideological-conceptual, and historical contexts in the making of Ava.

The present study is also more narrative history—the "l'histoire evenementeille" of Ladurie of the Annales School—than institutional history, admittedly, more a matter of necessity than of preference. The reason is that the available data privileges narrative history better for this period than (say) the Pagan period, when it was the other way around. There is more in-depth information about Ava's narrative history in later chronicles and other texts not readily found for earlier periods, so the historian is compelled to write more of a diachronic than a synchronous history.

Conceptually too, narrative history can be challenging, for my historiographic position is that although events and individuals may have an immediate impact on history, they must nevertheless be placed in a longer and larger institutional context for their significance to be fully appreciated. It is an approach that has always been part of my concerns as a historian, having contended that while individuals do shape and create events of importance, events themselves have a meaningful consequence only (or mainly) within the cultural and material contexts in which they occur. In other words, although narrative history may take center stage in this particular book because of the quantity and quality of the data that "privileges" it, its primacy is not being advocated. Indeed, in Myanmar's premodern history, events by themselves rarely preempted institutions.

In any case, as my framework for reconstructing Myanmar's history uses neither ethnic lineage nor religious rationalization, but geopolitics, like the colonial historians mentioned above, I also place the First Ava period between approximately 1364 and 1527, although it is done for entirely different reasons. It is not because the lineage of Burmese rulers ended and Shan rulers ascended the throne of Ava, but because the First Ava kingdom became (in 1364), and ceased being (in 1527), the exemplary religious, political, economic, administrative, social, and cultural center of Upper Myanmar, thereby meeting the criterion used by indigenous chronicles for defining dynasties. By doing this, I am also suggesting that structural change had taken place, thereby adopting Harry Benda's criterion for periodization.

Because the main framework for reconstructing Ava's (and in general, Myanmar's) history should be geopolitics rather than ethnic kingdoms, periods, or dynasties, the story of fifteenth-century Myanmar invariably becomes one of a relationship between "upstream" and "downstream," inland and coastal, agrarian and commercial, plains and hills, new and old. To be sure, both ethnic identity and Buddhist ideology remained important and involved in this framework of analysis, but they are not considered the main causes or underlying factors responsible for such a relationship or such a history.

The above approach has allowed me to offer some fresh suggestions in terms of Ava's historical significance to the history of Myanmar (and Southeast Asia). Rather than projecting backward modern academic (and in some cases, political) concerns that "confirm" those prejudices—that the Ava period was a dark age of "Shan barbarism" or that its history was an endless ethnic conflict—I consider the Ava period to have been a "mini-renaissance" that resurrected most of the institutions of "classical" Pagan and some of its splendor for at least another century and a half; hence, to reiterate, my phrase, "Ava was Pagan writ small."

In virtually every way, Ava, especially at its zenith, was Pagan, only smaller. This is manifest most clearly in its possession of the same (or nearly the same) material and human resources in Upper Myanmar that had been Pagan's. Ava kept intact Pagan's economic, social, conceptual, political, and legal institutions, along with the principles underlying them. Most of the evidence for this continuity can be found in the approximately 431 Old Burmese inscriptions that were recorded between the "end" of the Pagan period in the first decade of the fourteenth century and the end of the Kingdom of Ava before the first half of the sixteenth century.[34] At the root of this continuity is the eco-demographic context; and since that did not change, it had an overwhelming bearing on the rest of state and society, which also did not change in a structurally fundamental manner, to be demonstrated more fully in subsequent chapters.

The above conclusion stems from the initial, simple question I asked myself regarding the Kingdom of Ava when I began the research: namely, what was it like? The answer was found in its structure. States and societies "remember" the conditions under which they were formed and store the secrets in their institutional composition and cultural characteristics. Ava's tell us that the fundamental principles and patterns, mentality and values, traditions and rituals that underlay state and society at Pagan were resurrected, and that resurrection occurred within the same geopolitical, socioreligious, and eco-demographic environment. Thus, even though events and individuals were new and different, developmental patterns, forms of social action, and types of religious, political, and economic behavior did not change fundamentally.

Yet, this assertion—that Ava was Pagan writ small—raises at least one crucial question that requires some discussion. I had concluded earlier in *Pagan: The Origins of Modern Burma* that by the end of the thirteenth century, nearly 63 percent of good, cultivated state lands, large amounts of silver, and much hereditary labor had shifted to the tax-exempt *sangha* over several hundred years, subsequently weakening the kingdom of Pagan and ushering in its decline. But if Ava were an agrarian kingdom like Pagan was, and dependent on the same material and human environment, how could it have even arisen in the first place? What would have been its material basis if the state had already lost much of it to the *sangha*?

The Ava data suggests at least two answers. First, Ava "downsized." It simply had less of everything, and as a result, was a smaller kingdom in almost every way. Downsizing was not only easier to accomplish but necessary, since there were virtually no other viable options. Fewer resources were available to Ava since Lower Myanmar and the maritime provinces were now in the hands of a newly formed kingdom centered at Pegu (called Ramannadesa in later hagiography); Upper Myanmar's resources in the northeast sector were also much more difficult to access now, with the increased migration of the Shan speakers into this region; and Arakan was beginning to grow in terms of maritime economic and political power that would soon coalesce into an independent kingdom called Mrauk-U in the sixteenth century. And, to reiterate, much of the productive land in Upper Myanmar and its agricultural labor—the most crucial material basis of the Upper Myanmar state—were sequestered in tax-exempt *sangha* hands, while a small amount had turned into jungle or was left fallow. Thus, Ava had fewer resources than Pagan to begin with, so that downsizing was the only viable option.

However, and second, Pagan's loss of material resources to the *sangha*, to the jungle, to newly created (or resurrected) centers, and to various non-state sectors of society does not mean that these resources had evaporated into thin air after its "fall"—*they had only changed hands*. The economic foundations of Pagan—its population, irrigated lands, natural resources, central and regional administrative structure (and in many cases, their personnel or their descendants), its fighting men and materiel (along with their descendants and their holdings), its monasteries and monks (along with their descendants and their temples and glebe lands)—remained intact in Upper Myanmar. Only, they were no longer integrated under the control of one center; and in that sense, had *dis-integrated*.

Similarly, the resources of the maritime and mountain provinces that Pagan once held (or at least from which it received tax and/or tribute), also had not disappeared but only changed hands. Indeed, in some cases, such as the maritime regions, wealth had actually increased. But this wealth had either reverted to its original local sectors, or had gone into the creation of new polities. Thus, recently arisen Martaban and Pegu in Lower Myanmar and, although less significant, the emerging Arakanese entity in western, coastal Myanmar, now enjoyed the resources that Pagan had once commanded, while the Shan principalities in the far reaches of Upper Myanmar's hills and mountains regained their economic and political autonomy. In other words, it was the *relationships* regarding the country's wealth that had changed; the wealth itself had not disappeared.

What Ava had to do, then, was to reconstitute those relationships. It was not a matter of securing an absolute acreage of irrigated lands, tons of *padi*, chests of silver cash, or large numbers of people, but one of rebuilding and then regaining control of the apparatus (physical and conceptual) that held the rights to those resources that Pagan had lost. And that was precisely what Ava did, and it did it by resurrecting and/or maintaining Pagan institutions.

One of the advantages Ava had in this process of recovery vis á vis other would-be contenders was that it was created and led by close as well as remote, real as well as fictive, descendants of Pagan's royal family. And because Pagan's old elite, their descendants, and/or their allies were, in essence, also Ava's new leadership, they consciously chose to resurrect polities that emulated Pagan, the only exemplary model they had and the only one they knew how to operate. Thus, the knowledge, as well as some of the personnel (and/or their descendants) who could be harnessed for participating in the creation of the new kingdom were not only available (particularly in the earlier stages), but were willing and able. That not only legitimated and enhanced their own privileged past but also served their current social, economic, and political positions and interests.

What all this means is that the kingdom of Ava did not require entirely new personnel, new legitimation schemes, a new conceptual system, or new ideologies of state and society to make it work; the old ones not only sufficed but were also desirable and actually more advantageous. At the same time, it disadvantaged those who had not been part of the Pagan elite, in terms of political and economic power, genealogy, language and culture, and notions of Burmese identity. Also, because Ava was downsizing, it did not even need new wealth in creating this new kingdom; old wealth also sufficed.

Ava did this by remaining in the "heartland," the Dry Zone of Myanmar, rather than moving to the coasts (as Ayuthaya did around the same time). Besides, as noted, Ava could not simply move to Lower Myanmar at will, for a new polity centered at Pegu led by Mon speakers had arisen there to prevent it, whereas, in Thailand, there was nothing of consequence to stop the T'ai speakers from creating their new polity on the coasts.

By remaining in Upper Myanmar, then, Ava continued a situation that geographers call "constancy of place," which had certain advantages and disadvantages. It provided economic equilibrium to the kingdom, particularly in terms of a predictable and dependable agricultural resource base that it knew how to operate. Furthermore, it was a spatial environment that was not only familiar but culturally, economically, and psychologically more comfortable; it still is today, as the move in 2005–2006 of the country's capital to Naypyidaw, next to Pyinmana in the Dry Zone, attests. "Constancy of place" creates a self-perpetuating and self-regulating system.

Ava must have looked like medieval France between the fourteenth and eighteenth century, in the sense that both appeared to "stand still"—"l'histoire immobile," the famous phrase coined by Ladurie. "L'histoire immobile" does not mean France did not change at all; rather it means that state and society were at equilibrium because its population between 1350 and 1750 saw little net rise. The reason for that lay in what Ladurie called internal "braking mechanisms"—social mores, disease, war, and famine. In other words, because demography was the engine for fundamental change in society—the "master" and not "servant" of the economy, as he put it—society remained at equilibrium.[35]

I find a kind of "l'histoire immobile" to have been operating at Ava as well, whereby the stability of its agrarian population and economy remained at equilibrium. Although we do not have the kinds of demographic data for Ava that we do for France, I know of no historical demographer or historian of Myanmar who has demonstrated (or even suggested) that the Ava period saw a net increase in either population or agriculture/economic production compared with the Pagan period. Indeed, from what we know of the size, power, and wealth of Ava, there was a marked decline in all three components relative to Pagan. And from what we know of Ava, the same sort of internal "braking mechanisms" that France experienced—especially war (and presumably, the resulting famines caused more by war than by the weather)—plagued Ava as well.

Such demographic and material stability in society was both cause and consequence of the continuity of the dominant institutions and beliefs of the Ava kingdom. Notions and practices regarding legitimate leadership and authority, symbolism of the state, patron-client relations, sociopolitical hierarchy, the economy of redistribution, the merit-path to salvation, rules of royal succession, the always important symbiotic relationship between state and *sangha*, all remained intact during, and well beyond, the Ava period.

Yet, resurrecting old institutions with old personnel while occupying more or less the same old habitat, rather than creating a new one or moving to a different material environment, meant that the same (or nearly the same) historical trends and patterns that Pagan experienced recurred, including the same (or nearly the same) problems, which were addressed in much the same (or nearly the same) ways. Thus, although "constancy of place" provides civilizations certain advantages, it also creates analogous problems, usually resolved by the same (or nearly the same) solutions.

To reiterate, Ava was able to rise, on the one hand by being smaller, and on the other by reconstituting the institutions and resources that had made Pagan what it was, institutions and resources that had not disappeared with Pagan but had only lost the integrative mechanism holding them together: the state. The parts that made the whole still existed; Ava simply recombined and reunified those parts to create itself.

Ava's "resurrection" of Pagan, in turn, gave posterity the wherewithal and necessary ingredients to preserve and perpetuate the fundamental institutions of Pagan. Thereafter, the most endearing and enduring features of this classical Burmese tradition (along with whatever had been localized by succeeding dynasties) continued into the postcolonial and modern periods, at least among the vast majority of the population who remained rural and agrarian.

To put it more succinctly, at a very crucial time and place, and in an important and critical way, the Kingdom of Ava was extremely important in the process that made modern Myanmar, in whose fabric and memory Pagan's classical traditions to this day are very much interwoven. For that contribution to Myanmar's history, Ava's leaders should be given credit, individually and collectively. I consider them to be the ones responsible for creating and establishing a guardianship over Pagan's classical tradition—in effect, of preserving Burmese civilization. As Burmese speakers, they had a huge advantage not only in terms of numbers but also as bona fide "owners" and "guardians" of the "classical" Burmese tradition. They maintained their advantage over their keenest competitors—the later-arriving (mainly Mon) populations in Lower Myanmar, the Shan in the northern hills surrounding the Irrawaddy and Chindwin River valleys, and the Arakanese on the west coasts—and by various means: demographic, political, military, and ideological.

Part of the reason for this success of the Burmese speakers was that none of the three minority groups mentioned above had, or a desire to have, a political, cultural, genealogical, or historical claim to Pagan or its tradition (real or imagined). They also did not have a numerical superiority over the Burmese speakers, even when combined and multiplied several times over, so that the Burmese speakers could not only make such claims of a guardianship of the country's "classical" traditions legitimately, but also had the wherewithal to actually implement them with their better-endowed demographic, political, and military resources.

In sum, because what was once Pagan's material environment, core population, and belief system had been subsumed by Ava, the character and principles of state and society in Upper Myanmar remained essentially the same. Ava remained in the Dry Zone of Upper Myanmar, the capital shifting only eighty miles northward, with its agrarian economy intact. There were also no major shifts in population from the "heartland" of Upper Myanmar to areas outside it after the "decline" of Pagan, while the indigenized Theravada Buddhism of Pagan remained the central belief system of Ava. The political system and the military-administrative structure were also replicas of Pagan's. But it was not just a matter of Ava retaining Pagan institutions; the *relationships* of these institutions to each other also remained intact, as we shall see.

3

Ava's Founding Fathers

Thadominbya and Minkyiswa Sawkai

Thihathu, the last of the famous Three Brothers, was succeeded by Uzana, his eldest son and heir apparent, who reaped the benefits of his father's efforts, particularly the consolidation of agricultural resources. Uzana apparently had enough of a surplus to continue in the tradition of earlier kings, building two large pagodas in 1332 and a third at Myinkhondaing in 1335. He also built a large *gu* (cave-temple) in 1340 in his home town. But we know little more of him, and in 1340, on September 1, Myin Saing Sithu, another nonentity (except that he was lord of Myin Saing) became king. (Indeed, the chronicles do not even mention him; he is found only in the inscriptions.) His nephew, known as Sinphyu Ngasishin (lord of the five white elephants) in contemporary inscriptions, and as Ngasishin Kyawswa (Kyawswa, lord of the five [white elephants]) in the chronicles, became king in 1342 or 1344.[1]

Sinphyu Ngasishin's son, also taking the tile of Kyawswa, succeeded in 1351. It was this king who, in 1359, collected stone inscriptions to check the bona fides of religious lands, as Pagan king Kyaswa had done earlier in the thirteenth century and King Bodawhpaya would do more than four hundred years later, in 1793. It is worth noting that the consequences of wealth flow to the *sangha* were already being felt again, this soon, only fifty years since the end of the Pagan kingdom. Thereafter, Pinya as a center declined in influence and power, while Sagaing, held by Athinkhaya's branch of the royal family, increased its leadership role.

Finally, inscriptions record that in 1359, and again in 1362, "the Syam [Shan] . . . came to disturb the country . . . ,[2] families were broken up on both sides as there was much disturbances [sic] within the capital [or, kingdom]." In 1364, Sagaing, the stronghold of Athinkhaya's family, "was destroyed by the northern Syam."[3] The story of this destruction of Sagaing in the inscriptions is fleshed out by U Kala's chronicle, but written almost four hundred years later. It was instigated, he claimed, by one Narathu, who was not of royal line and therefore had no hope for legitimate ascension. He was called Hsinphyu Thonsishin (lord of three white elephants) in the inscriptions and supposedly encouraged the younger brother of the powerful Shan chieftain, Tho Han Bwa, named Tho Khyin Bwa, to take Sagaing, saying, "I will take only the outer shell [*akhun*], I will give [you] the inner core [*ahsi*],"[4] a standard literary device used at different, appropriate places in the chronicles. But when the *sawbwa* took Sagaing, Narathu remained at

Pinya, providing no aid, so the former decided to cross over to Pinya, attacked and took it, along with Narathu.

The Syam apparently left after taking the city of Pinya, desiring not to keep, destroy, kill, or haul its population back with them, for the chronicle continued by saying that the ministers met together after the Syam had left to select the appointed heir, Uzana Pyaung, as king, after marrying him to Queen Saw Umma. But Thadominbya, who held Tagaung (in the north) as fief decided to show his displeasure at the decision. He came down and defeated the new king, raised Saw Umma as his own chief queen and made himself king at Pinya (1364–1367). He was said to have descended through his father from one of the Three Brothers. Some say his lineage came through Thihathu of Pinya; others, Athinkhaya of Sagaing. All this only reinforced colonial historiography's erroneous conclusion that the Ava Dynasty was Shan.

Shortly thereafter, Thadominbya gathered his advisers to discuss the city's location. He said that it, along with Sagaing, was vulnerable to attack, as attested by recent events. To illustrate his point, Thadominbya filled a tray with water, took a chalice and placed it upside down in the middle of it, and said, "Like the chalice which becomes an island, enemies cannot easily take Inwa." So he decided to erect a new city where Ava stands today.

Various omens, prophecies, and dreams accompanied this essentially strategic decision to move the capital to Ava. One of the dreams included six events, which were interpreted by Thadominbya's *sangharaja* (the head of the *sangha*) to confirm the king's decision that Ava was the right place. Then, on the most auspicious day of the month, time of day, and proper alignment of the constellations, in the year 1364 AD, Thadominbya consecrated Ava, formally naming it Ratanapura, "City of Gems." By that act, not only did he establish the seat of Burmese (and Myanmar's) power intermittently for the next five centuries, he also founded what is known in indigenous history as the First Inwa Dynasty, which, in many ways, perpetuated the Kingdom of Pagan for another 163 years.

U Kala's chronicle includes a section on Thadominbya's ascension that honored his city with a standard Buddha prophecy, essentially legitimating its dynasty, not so much in a secular, genealogical sense, but in terms of a circumscribing Buddhist ideology. Considerable prestige and honor were usually given ex post facto to capital cities that became centers of dynasties, which, in the opinion of these indigenous authors, perpetuated the Buddha's religion. That kind of recognition, in turn, marked the Ava period as a valid "conjuncture" (in Braudel's sense of the term) with the Pagan period in the organization of Burmese history by both indigenous and modern historians.

The account of the Buddha's journey to Myanmar with Ananda, his premier disciple and brother, also tells us something about the state of affairs during the Ava period as understood by U Kala. He wrote that it began at Ngasaungkyan, an important northern frontier fortress under the Kingdom of Pagan—now inside the Chinese border—which was probably still under Burmese control at the time of U Kala. The journey of the Buddha and Ananda next took them to Kaungsin, another important fortified city during the Pagan period (and obviously

U Kala's time as well), that lay at the confluence of three rivers in the north, also near the China border. From there they went south to the district in which were located Sri Ksetra, Pagan, and Tagaung, three extremely important cities in Myanmar's history, major centers of the Upper Myanmar Dry Zone. Subsequently, the Buddha and Ananda visited the Mandalay area, which became (over a hundred years after U Kala wrote) Myanmar's last capital. U Kala also mentions Taungthaman, where Amarapura (the capital that preceded Mandalay) was built (and recently excavated to expose a Bronze and Iron Age urban site), as well as Sagaing, well known in Myanmar's history. Finally, they reached the place where Ava was to be built.

There, the standard story about the Buddha and Ananda is told. Ananda asked the Buddha why he was smiling, and the Buddha replied that in this place, a great city will be founded that will promote and perpetuate his religion.[5] Thus was Ava given a Buddha prophecy and provided with Buddhist legitimacy, while the journey taken by the Buddha and Ananda "mapped" the Burmese kingdom as U Kala knew it.

Ava, especially as Thadominbya had rebuilt it, lay on what became a makeshift island. On its north and west was the Irrawaddy River, on its east was the Myitnge (Little River), which flowed north into the Irrawaddy, and on its south was the Myittha Stream, a tributary of the Irrawaddy running east–west (see figure 2). To the latter was joined a canal likely built by Thadominbya, linking it to the Myitnge on its east and the Irrawaddy on its southwest, thereby surrounding the larger metropolitan area of Ava on all sides by a mostly natural moat.

Satellite pictures today also reveal that the walled city within that larger metropolitan area had another moat around it, the water diverted from the Irrawaddy on one side and the Myitnge on the other. Obviously, security and defense were on the mind of the new king when he made Ava capital and built it in this fashion.

In Old Burmese, Inwa means "mouth" (of a lake or other body of water). But it can also mean "replete with *in*" (supernatural power), although I am skeptical of the latter interpretation in this case. Whatever the supernatural prowess of Ava may have been, it certainly made much better military, political, and economic sense to move the center of the new kingdom to the "mouth" of the confluence of the Irrawaddy and Myitnge, where Ava stood.

Militarily, the shift northeast from Pagan to Ava, over eighty miles away, addressed an important concern that all Upper Myanmar capitals theretofore had faced: invasion from the north. For it was from that direction that hostile forces could drive right down to the heart of the most important economic centers of Upper Myanmar via the Chindwin, Irrawaddy, and/or the Shweli River valleys. The Pyu kingdom in the ninth century had been invaded from the north by the Kingdom of Nanzhao, probably via the Irrawaddy route, and Pagan had to fight unknown forces from the north in the early twelfth century, only to be invaded again (on three separate occasions) from the north in the thirteenth century by the Mongols using basically the same route.

The leadership that unified the Kingdom of Pagan seemed to have recognized this problem early, so that by King Anawrahta's reign (1044–1077), if not earlier,

Figure 2. City of Ava

it had been addressed by building a line of forty-three forts along that invasion path. (The Yuan sources actually mentioned three hundred stockades.) The largest standing army was also located in the north, while the ablest generals were stationed in the north. Ava was obviously chosen to most effectively defend that direction.

There were other reasons that made the location of Ava more appealing, especially during the fourteenth century. During the eleventh and twelfth centuries, Nanzhao had closed off the north from the Chinese (and perhaps, in part, the Shan) threat. And as long as the Nanzhao buffer remained where it was, Pagan could also remain where it was. Indeed, it was an ideal location for the time. Not only did it give the city the geographical wherewithal to manage all three irrigated areas of the Dry Zone most effectively, but also to move downriver to the coasts quickly where its commercial resources lay and, hence, the enormous wealth Pagan enjoyed when both the north and south were controlled. But once the Nanzhao buffer between China and Pagan was broken in 1253 by the Mongols, Pagan's location increasingly became less an asset and more a liability. In fact, Pagan's distance from Kyaukse was responsible, in part, for its loss to regional governors (the Three Brothers) in the years following the Mongol raids, as we have seen in an earlier chapter.

By the second half of thirteenth century, then, the capital city of Pagan had less of the administrative and military reach that it had enjoyed during the twelfth and first half of the thirteenth centuries, and had become too far removed from its economic resources; neither Kyaukse, nor the Mu Valley or Minbu, could be held as securely as they once had been. Thus, under late thirteenth-century conditions of growing decentralization, Pagan, as capital, had become more and more strategically impotent, even if it retained its prestige as a cultural, religious, and historic center.

By the early fourteenth century, after the Mongol threat had ended and was no longer a factor, first the Shan, and subsequently Ming China, became concerns. The new Burmese monarchy was compelled not to return to Pagan but to find an alternative place, so that Ava, right on the edge of the Kyaukse Valley on its east and the Mu Valley on its west across the Irrawaddy River, became ideal, controlling at least two of the three most productive areas and mainstays of any Upper Myanmar kingdom. And since Ava could not hold the Lower Myanmar coasts in any case—because the new kingdom of Pegu (Ramannadesa) had arisen there—it did not have to concern itself (as Pagan had to) with going too far inland and losing the coasts in the process.

Whereas Pagan needed these Lower Myanmar ports to maintain the level of power, status, and wealth it enjoyed, Ava did not, for it was already smaller, less powerful, and less wealthy. The choice of Ava's location, then, was in large part dictated and limited by the then current geopolitical, military, and socioeconomic conditions and needs, whose scheme did not include Lower Myanmar as a high priority, only the north. Thus, the decision by Thadominbya to build the new capital at Ava next to its main economic resources revealed mainly military and economic concerns, hardly supernatural ones.

However, that does not mean there was no Buddhist cosmology associated with the decision. Some have suggested that the style and configuration of the capital city of Ava drawn in old manuscripts represents a sitting lion in profile. Yet, the city was not called Sihapura or Singhapura (Lion City) in original and contemporary sources, but Ratanapura, "City of Gems," so that the "sitting lion" configuration may have been the result of someone's twentieth-century imagination and association with the ubiquitous Burmese *chinthe* (lion) profile. Indeed, that configuration (nose and mouth of the lion) may actually be later extensions of defensive walls, as suggested by satellite photography. Besides, it is clear that the palace placed at city-center, within another square fortification (of teak logs), shows traditional concentric cosmological concerns of a mandala. Ava, like other Burmese capitals, represented "heaven on earth" and was designed to suggest that the king, while in this city, was the intermediary between this world and the heavenly realm.

More practically, Ava was located at the mouth of the Myitnge River (literally, little river, but in fact, it is quite sizeable). It watered and also drained the Kyaukse rice plains and its river systems that flowed northward into the Irrawaddy. That means Ava controlled this most important path to and from Kyaukse and the Irrawaddy, whence to distribution points elsewhere. The *Mahayazawingyi* stated that Thadominbya filled up four lakes to build Ava, perhaps using the earth from the canal he had dug to link the Myittha stream with the Myitnge, as described above.

From Ava, one could also cross over relatively easily to Sagaing, which lay near one of the narrowest sections on the Irrawaddy. Sagaing, in turn, was the southern entrance to the entire Mu Valley and its vast irrigated fields (see figure 3). In fact, about a hundred years later, King Narapati of Ava recorded in an original inscription that he built a bridge across the Irrawaddy from Ava to Sagaing where the "four forces of the army" could pass abreast.

Not surprisingly, Thadominbya rebuilt and consolidated the triangle consisting of Pinya, Sagaing, and Ava, cities that were key to the control of the "bend" in the Irrawaddy along with the Kyaukse and Mu Valleys. That triangle was defended by the northern cities he already held, particularly Tagaung (which was his old fief). With direct control of both Kyaukse and the Mu Valley, Ava had enough human and material resources to exert more direct control of Minbu, farther south, the third most productive agricultural region of Upper Myanmar. Indeed, as noted above, these three were the most reliable and productive *padi* growing regions of Upper Myanmar, which, for centuries (until the British drained the swamps of Lower Myanmar), constituted the bulk of the "GNP" of precolonial Myanmar. Only after they were secured could any designs on Lower Myanmar even be considered.

But barely had Thadominbya secured his capital than the lords of Toungoo, Pyinmana, and Sagu rebelled and attacked nearby Yamethin (another rich rice-growing area considered part of the royal domain). In response, Thadominbya went on the offensive. He marched on Bhayakyawthu, the lord of Sagu, who was already at Yamethin and was said to have killed him with his own hands. Then the king was said to have placed his royal tray of food on the corpse's chest and eaten his meal there. That frightened all his ministers and officers and brought many of them in line. (It is this story that Harvey used to "prove," in part, that Thadominbya was a barbarous Shan, "confirming" the "Ava is Shan" thesis.)

The following year, Thadominbya continued to march south to subdue Sagu, the key to controlling the rich Minbu rice lands that were now probably under Bhayakyawthu's offspring. Thadominbya's contemporary inscription, written in good Old Burmese, which commemorated the event, stated, "When the great king Satuiw [Thado] returned from subduing Caku [Sagu] he stopped at a *sima* [ordination hall] built by General Asankhya [eldest of the Three Brothers] at a place called Kukhan. He was given one ox, one pig, a total of 5 fowls [*sic*], ten jars of liquor, ten pots of rice and ten pots of curry."[6]

The king continued his "pacification" and unification of the southern Dry Zone by next marching on Taungdwingyi in 1366. When he arrived at the city of Pagan on the way, he paid his respects at the Shwezigon, the palladium of the Burmese state during Pagan times. There, Sawmunit, the last of the Pagan royalty, swore allegiance to Thadominbya and paid tribute, confirming Pagan's de facto status as subordinate rather than leader, an event that had begun over a half century earlier.

Taungdwingyi at the time was held by another descendant of the royal family of Pagan, Thihapate, who therefore had legitimate, genealogical claims to the throne. He repaired his defenses to await Thadominbya's arrival, but once surrounded and with his major minister assassinated, U Kala wrote that Thihapate sent "happy and pleasant words" and gave his allegiance to Thadominbya. Taungdwingyi was now a vassal city of Ava, at least formally.

But before Thadominbya could complete unifying other important places in Upper Myanmar, he contracted smallpox and fell ill. Knowing he would not make it, he instructed a trusted servant named Nga Nu Nge to go back to Ava and kill his queen, for otherwise, he said, someone else will marry her when he died, and "that's really a waste."[7] Shortly after Nga Nu Nge hurried off to Ava, Thadominbya died, at age twenty-five.

When Nga Nu Nge reached Ava, instead of killing the queen, he informed her of Thadominbya's instructions, hearing which the queen asked, "Well, Nga Nu Nge, aren't you a man?" In other words, "What are you waiting for?" suggesting he take her as queen. He did, but after half a month, both had to flee to Sagaing, where Nga Nu Nge became lord, as the ministers at court would not recognize them as rightful heirs to the throne at Ava.

In fact, upon receiving the news that Thadominbya had died in the field, his ministers had already deliberated and decided to ask Thilawa, governor of Yamethin, to be king. He replied that he barely spoke three, maybe four, words a day. "I have no desire to be king." But, Thilawa suggested, "Sawkai, the lord of Amyint is brother-in-law of the king and replete with the right characteristics." Agreeing, the ministers asked Sawkai to be king. His full name thus became Minkyiswa Sawkai, or "Exalted King Sawkai."[8] Just as Pagan king Sawnit was placed on the throne by the Three Brothers, and others before him, the chief ministers of the court had once again selected the king. This kind of ministerial influence at court would remain a key pattern in Myanmar's history well into the nineteenth century.

U Kala, writing three hundred years later, had strident words for Thadominbya. He "was uncivilized and barbaric, and he did not respect the Three Gems."[9] Yet, importantly, U Kala never called him a Shan nor suggested that he was uncivilized *because* he was Shan. He was considered uncivilized because he did not promote the religion as U Kala thought he should have. Notwithstanding U Kala's eighteenth-century Buddhist standards of what "uncivilized" and "barbaric" meant, from the vantage point of greater hindsight and twenty-first-century Western social science (and Burmese) secular political criteria regarding effective leadership, Thadominbya's historical legacy was very important.

After all, he was a warrior-king, perfectly suited for those unstable conditions when society was in need of strong leadership that could resurrect central authority and provide some law and order. Given the situation, it is understandable that he paid less attention to religious pursuits and more to military and political concerns. Similar to the kind of cultural continuity and politically unifying hub that the Three Brothers had provided Upper Myanmar society during the time of the Mongol invasions, Thadominbya had done much the same during a time of uncertainty and insecurity created by Syam attacks.

He had seized the moment, and although building on the work of the Three Brothers and other such individuals and their own moments in history, his actions reestablished the political power and leadership position of the majority Burmese speakers. In other words, Thadominbya created and preserved the sort of environment that more easily allowed the perpetuation of what we know today as the country and culture of Myanmar.

In the tradition of Anawrahta more than two hundred years earlier, of Bayinnaung two hundred years later, and Alaunghpaya nearly four hundred years after him, Thadominbya, in the middle of the fourteenth century, not only reunified the Dry Zone for the first time since the Pagan Dynasty came to an effective political end, but also founded the city and dynasty of Ava. These actions set the foundations that subsequently sequestered the legacy of Pagan, allowing that tradition to be perpetuated for another one hundred and sixty years. Without Thadominbya's leadership at the right time and place, there might never have emerged a Kingdom of Ava, and the history of Myanmar today would have been vastly different.

After Thadominbya's untimely death, this inchoate kingdom could have collapsed, but it did not, surely a testimony to the strength remaining in its social and political institutions, but also to his leadership, especially given the mere three or four years he had had to accomplish what he did. At the right time emerged another strong leader, Minkyiswa Sawkai, who, also seizing his moment, rose to the occasion as his predecessor had done.

Minkyiswa Sawkai: "Savior" of the Kingdom

Minkyiswa Sawkai went to Ava in 1367 from his fief of Amyint after the ministers were persuaded to select him king over the man who barely spoke four words a day. After consulting with them, he officially ascended the throne the following year (according to the *Zatatawpon* [Chronicle of Royal Horoscopes] and confirmed by the *Yazawinkyaw*).[10] Parts of the *Zatatawpon* were written in the late thirteenth century (and therefore quite reliable in terms of certain contemporary information), while the *Yazawinkyaw*, also an Ava-period text and one of the two earliest extant *yazawin* of Myanmar to have survived, was written in the early 1500s. Yet, a contemporary inscription of Ava states that Minkyiswa ascended the throne on September 5, 1367, one year earlier. U Kala and the *Maniyadanyabon*, two later texts, corroborate the inscription, giving Maniyadanyabon Thadominbya only three years of reign before he died of smallpox. In any case, the usual, auspicious events were provided at Minkyiswa Sawkai's ascension to the throne. They were interpreted to suggest that the king will have a long life and his kingdom will be wealthy, peaceful, and pleasant.

Sawkai secured his genealogy by marrying both the elder and younger sisters of his predecessor, raising them as chief queens. The elder sister of Thilawa, lord of Yamethin, the king also made into a queen, with whom he had several children. He also inherited the patronage system left by his predecessors, which meant he had to get rid of his most serious rivals, at least at court.

He began with Nga Nu Nge, the confidant of Thadominbya who had betrayed Thadominbya by running off with his queen. As it turned out, the minister of

Sawkai, Yazathingyan, was Nge Nu Nge's elder brother. Sawkai commanded Yazathingyan to capture his younger brother for what he had done. And for his efforts, Yazathingyan was promised the fiefs of Wayindok and Taungbyongyi as well as Saw Umma, Sawkai's sister (?), the one who had ran off with Nge Nu Nge. Yazathingyan captured his younger brother by guile, playing upon their kinship, thereafter admonishing him by saying, "you are not of royal line, your father is also not of royal line," and placed him in irons. But Nge Nu Nge escaped to a place called Lahu, which, U Kala wrote, is known "today" as Mya Taung (Emerald Mountain).[11]

Shortly thereafter, Minkyiswa Sawkai began the work left undone by Thadominbya: namely, the pacification of his new kingdom. More specifically, he continued the economic and political vision of Thadominbya, which had been to establish Ava's complete control of the Dry Zone of Myanmar. Sawkai did this by astute marriage alliances and careful parceling of the most important cities to his closest relatives.[12]

After giving Sagaing to Yazathingyan as promised (even though Nge Nu Nge had escaped), the king reconfirmed Thilawa, the one who had nominated Minkyiswa Sawkai and spoke no more than four words a day, as lord of Yamethin. Sawkai then gave Pyi to his own elder brother, while Thindwe, an important center in Arakan, was given to Saw Yin Naung, and Toungoo, to Pyankhi Gyi. Taungdwingyi was reconfirmed as Thihapate's fief, while Pagan was "eaten" by Sithu, as Sawmunit, the last in the royal line of Pagan kings, had passed away. Talop was given to Yazathu "to eat" and Sagu was given to one Thihathu. Bhayakyaw received Nyaungyan, and Pakhangyi went to Tayaphya. The important "Khayaing of five sluices" was eaten by Sithu Thambhawa, while Mekkhaya was "eaten" by Saw Hnaung. Min Pulay obtained Pauk Myaing, Wati (an old Pyu site) was given to Thinkhaya "to eat," Myedu went to Thek She Kyauw Htin, Tagaung was "eaten" by Nga Nauk Sin, while Tipeyin was "eaten" by Thado Thingathu.

I have deliberately gone through this list of rewards, typically presented or reconfirmed at the formal ascension of new kings, for it likely reveals the actual extent of Ava's dominions during Sawkai's time. If U Kala had used an original source for this information, it probably reflects genuine Ava period personalities and place-names. It hardly needs saying that this kind of data is unlikely to be invented or to be the kind of fodder ordinarily used for purposes of ex post facto legitimation.

If accurate, the Kingdom of Ava probably extended to and included the major fortified towns in the Dry Zone, and had hegemony over nearly all of Upper Myanmar, from Pyi in the south to at least Tagaung in the north; southeast as far as Toungoo; northwest as far as Myedu, including the three most important irrigated regions of Upper Myanmar; and west as far as Arakan's Thindwe.[13]

Min Yaza: The King's Minister

In 1368, the great irrigation tank of Meikhtila broke its banks. So with his troops, Sawkai marched and dammed it up once more. At the time of repair, he discovered an inscription that mentioned statues made of the lords of Linzin (Vien Chiang) and Ayuthaya, as well as those of their sons and daughters. So the king asked the headman of Winsin, a nearby village, about it, who said he didn't know. But, he added, an *athi*[14] of the village might know, as he carries along a book in his lap while plowing and is knowledgeable about these things. The king summoned him, and when asked, the latter replied that he has heard of the story surrounding the inscription.

"It was during the time of your great ancestor, Alaungsithu" (of Pagan) the young man said, "when those kings [of Linzin and Ayuthaya, an anachronism during Pagan times] swore allegiance and had their sons and daughters live with the king at the palace." Subsequently, so that later kings will know of these sons and daughters after they died, their images were made and buried. "That's what I've heard."[15]

The king was excited about the story and told the young man, "When I get back to the palace, I'll call for you," which he did. The *athi* was said to be so wise and eloquent that the king gave him the title of Sitapyit, and gave him the fief of Taungpyongyi and Wayindok "to eat," along with a tusker, and ten measures of gold. Sitapyit eventually became the chief adviser to Sawkai, and subsequently to two successive kings of Ava, holding that office for fifty-three years. He was later given the title Min Yaza, also affectionately known as Hpo Yaza ("grandfather" yaza).

His career and rise to fame is important for several reasons, not least because he left at least two very important records.[16] Although none survives in its original form, one of them, a genre of texts called "submissions," has been incorporated (apparently in toto) into a late eighteenth-century treatise.[17] The Indic model for this genre was probably the *Milinda Pannha*, where the king would ask questions on moral, ethical, political, and historical issues, and they would be answered by a wise minister. Both the questions and answers had didactic functions thought to be universal and timeless. At the same time, the text touched upon actual problems and events of the time, and so revealed the kinds of issues and concerns then current, while corroborating certain historical events. Some of Min Yaza's answers were given as parables taken from the *Jataka*, some from *yazawin* then in existence, while others were the result of his own creativity.

These "submissions" of Min Yaza survive today in a later manuscript written in 1781 by Shin Sandalinka, who stated that he "finished writing his *Min Yaza Shaukhtonkhaw Maniyadanyabon Kyan* [The Maniyadanyabon: Min Yaza's so-called Submissions] on the seventh day of the waxing moon of Thadingyut in the year 1143 of the Burmese era." Sandalinka also stated that the compilation had used "various books of chronicles," although he was most faithful to Min Yaza's "submissions," especially those parts that more or less followed the same structure of the "submissions" genre.[18]

One of the questions asked of Min Yaza by the son of Sawkai, while still a prince, had to do with the country's history, particularly the establishment of authority in the land and the origins of the Ava Dynasty. Min Yaza's answer shows (at least) what the then-current "discourse" and sentiments were on such subjects at Ava during that particular time. In this case, there was no doubt in Min Yaza's mind that the kingdom of Ava and its leaders were direct successors and descendants of the kingdom of Pagan and its kings. Pagan's ancestors, in turn, were thought to have gone back to the royalty of Sri Ksetra and Tagaung: hence, the rhyme and metered proverb, "Myanma asa, Tagaung ka" (Myanma Origins, Tagaung at) still recited today by people in the country.

In other words, whatever we have that was written by Min Yaza, even if copied and preserved in later works, deserves serious consideration, for his stature and responsibilities at the Ava court ensures a unique and valuable perspective on fourteenth-century Ava.

Apart from leaving us a most important record, Min Yaza's career and rise to prominence is important in itself, for it tells us certain things about Ava society. First, there was some mobility for rural people with intellect (or other kinds of talent) who climbed from village to court, from the plough to the pen, ending up as chief minister to three successive kings. And it is not the only example of such mobility, for another person of the Ava period, Shin Thilawuntha (discussed below), accomplished the same feat with his religious talents and knowledge. Second, such cases also suggest that rural monastic education, at least in terms of literacy, must have been relatively effective, as their literary talents were achieved and recognized *before* they went to the capital. And third, Min Yaza's career illustrates the important roles ministers played in serving several kings in succession. This invariably provided balance and continuity to the flux and instability caused by factionalism among the princes and their allies at court. And in this respect, Min Yaza's example is not the only one, for another most famous minister, Disapramok of Pagan, similarly served three successive kings, while Kinwun Mingyi of the last (Konbaung) dynasty served at least two kings (Mindon and Thibaw) in succession.

Competition From Lower Myanmar

Meanwhile, a new kingdom had been forged in Lower Myanmar by the late thirteenth century, after the power of the Pagan Dynasty had waned, a story to be told in greater detail in part 2. It was led by Mon king Binnya U, whose dynasty was centered at Hamsavati (Pegu) by the mid-fourteenth-century. Clearly nervous about Minkyiswa Sawkai's growing power, Binnya U sent a *yazathan* (literally, royal sound), a diplomatic communiqué written on gold requesting a peace treaty. The two kings met "at the border," exchanged presents and colors, "swore an oath" of peace, ate together, and afterward returned to their respective places.

Having dealt with his southern borders, at least temporarily, Sawkai next took Kale and Mohnyin in the north, and gave them to two of his trusted lieutenants. His kingdom now stretched from Kale in the northwest to Tagaung on the northeast and at least down to Pyi in the south and Toungoo on the southeast. All he needed was the northern parts of Arakan to secure the window to the Bay of Bengal—as Ava was then landlocked, with Pegu holding the Lower Myanmar coasts—and to better protect his southwest flank. He did this in 1373, taking Arakan after its king died, giving it to his uncle, Saw Mun Gyi, to govern.

When Binnya U of Pegu died in 1383, he was succeeded by his son, the famous Yazadarit (or formally, Yazadhiyaza, King of Kings), who would become a "problem" for Ava for several decades to come. Lauk Phya, the "eater" of Myaungmya in the Lower Myanmar delta during Yazadarit's father's reign and uncle of Yazadarit, did not approve of the succession and so conspired with Minkyiswa Sawkai to take Pegu, saying, "You can take the inner core, bestow upon me only the outer shell."

While conferring with his ministers, the brash son of Minkyiswa Sawkai, then only eighteen years old, boasted he could take Pegu. Appointing his son (and heir apparent) as commander in chief, the king led the "*myosa* of nine cities," each with a force of two hundred war elephants, five thousand cavalry, and seventeen thousand infantry to march on Pegu. The king's younger son, then only fourteen years old, was also appointed commander of another force of nine *myosa* consisting of two hundred war elephants, five thousand horses, and sixteen thousand infantry.[19]

U Kala's figures with regard to the strength of Ava's military capability do not seem exaggerated and are probably accurate. (An original inscription of Pagan recorded some thirty thousand cavalry under Narapatisithu in the twelfth century.) The organization and structure of Ava's army (and in another campaign, navy) is also consistent with what we know of it earlier during the Pagan period and later during the Konbaung period. It is further supported by another, partially earlier source, the *Zatatawpon*, which had a variety of miscellaneous data, including the number of towns designated to provide a certain number of troops as part of their crown obligations.

The direction and paths taken by Ava's troops on campaigns in Lower Myanmar, and the general nature of warfare in the country at the time, also rings true. It is clear that Upper Myanmar was a polity consisting of fortified urban areas under crown appointees who were mainly blood relatives of the king, or those related by (carefully arranged) marriages, and supported by crown troops. There were no private armies held by private lords, as in medieval Europe or Japan; all the armed forces belonged to the crown, which in large part contributes to the absence of a true feudal system (and the consequences therefrom).

The commander in chief took the Toungoo route (that is, straight south, down the Sittaung River valley) while his younger brother took the Tharawaddy route (that is, down the Irrawaddy River valley) in a pincher movement. But for a variety of reasons, including, said the chronicle, three hundred foreigners with guns (it may have been too early for them to have been Portuguese),[20] Yazadarit could not be defeated and Ava's forces had to return before the monsoons broke. Two months after they returned to Upper Myanmar, Yazadarit, realizing that Ava had nearly succeeded in taking Pegu, had it not been for a few mishaps and had the Ava king himself come down with a larger force, decided to send a peace treaty, a royal communiqué written on *shwe pe* (gold [palm] leaf), along with various presents to Ava.

U Kala quotes directly from this alleged communiqué, so may either have had access to it, or simply, like Herodotus and Thucydides, invented a "dialogue" appropriate to the occasion. The language was respectful, Yazadarit addressing Minkyiswa Sawkai as *bagyidaw* (royal father, or uncle) and himself as *kywanup* (an abbreviated respectful "I," literally, thy royal *kyun*, that is, subject). In it, he said that the *myosa* of Myaungmya, his uncle, had conspired to create a rift between them, violating the accord between Minkyiswa Sawkai and Binnya U, Yazadarit's father.

Unfortunately, Yazadarit's two ambassadors had apparently added uncomplimentary innuendoes to the communiqué, saying that because the two princes (Sawkai's sons) did not stay long when they came to the city, they could not be received properly with food and presents, language that inflamed the situation, for it insinuated in no uncertain terms that the two princes were defeated quickly and easily. At this point, Minkyiswa Sawkai recited a proverb to the ambassadors, saying, "It does not hurt when you pound, it hurts when you grind," and then reportedly referred to Yazadarit as the "Talaing kale" (the little Talaing).[21]

The *myosa* of Myaungmya, upon hearing of Yazadarit's communiqué (and perhaps Sawkai's response), attempted to further sow seeds of enmity by laying out a better battle plan for Ava to take Pegu. It provides insight into the way in which Lower Myanmar was most vulnerable. He said, first you must take Hlaing, then Hmawbi, then Tala, then Dagon (modern Yangon), only after that, Pegu. It was a movement that went from west to east, once the delta was reached via the Irrawaddy River and its valley. It also confirms a bane in Burmese society: the personal nature of "national" crises.

Accordingly, Ava prepared to take Pegu with all the forces it had, with the heir apparent as commander in chief leading the land forces, numbering eleven battalions, while the water forces amounted to ten battalions, led by Minkyiswa Sawkai. He left four battalions with his younger son to guard Ava. The land forces were said to have numbered four hundred elephantry, six thousand cavalry, and 120,000 infantry while the "navy" totaled one thousand boats and 1,200 war boats, along with 170,000 soldiers.[22]

The water route reveals the names and number of riverine towns that were responsible for providing boats and troops in times of war, presumably in lieu of taxes. These towns located on the Irrawaddy River are some of the most well-known in Burmese history: Pyi, Sagu, Salin, Talop, Pakhangyi, and Sagaing. Two Shan battalions also participated on Ava's side. Minkyiswa Sawkai, riding the "Golden Jewel Barge," came down the river and was joined by the *myosa* of Myaungmya (Yazadarit's uncle) with five *thinbaw* (the word for oceangoing ship in Burmese, ostensibly taken from the Malay *sanphaw*), seventy *yai hle* (war boats, a not-unreasonable figure for a coastal city), and two hundred *hlawga* (ceremonial boats of state).

But Ava's forces were not successful in taking the major towns that could have led to Pegu, as outlined in the plan by the lord of Myaungmya, and because the rains were approaching, while many had become sick, wounded, and ready to desert, Minkyiswa Sawkai decided to return to Ava. Although unsuccessful in taking Pegu, Ava's ability to harness large numbers for campaigns must have motivated the Shan *sawbwa*, Tho Ngan Bwa, lord of Maw, to bring his daughter, "replete with all the necessary virtues," to Ava for a marriage alliance. After some consultation with his most trusted adviser, Min Yaza, the king married his younger son, lord of Pyinsi, named Min Shwe, born of the northern queen, to the Shan princess.

In 1389, in retaliation for his uncle's intrigue that had instigated the Ava-Pegu campaigns, Yazadarit attacked Myaungmya. This suggests that Pegu's hegemony was not very extensive, as Myaungmya was right in the delta, just southeast of Pathein (Bassein) and west of Dagon (now Yangon). Thus, even in the reign of Yazadarit, one of the most powerful and militarily successful kings of Pegu, his "dominions" did not extend much beyond Yangon on the west and Muttama on the east.

With two of his sons, Byakyun and Byakyan (probably Mon names), and most of his elephants and horses, Lauk Phya fled to Ava, where Minkyiswa Sawkai received him well. The king bestowed Burmese titles on the two sons and gave them valuable fiefs "to eat," particularly Byakyan, the younger son, who received Pyi, since its *myosa* had died. This must have incurred some jealousies at the Ava court, since Pyi, although far from the center of things, was still an important fief. Minkyiswa Sawkai must have taken into consideration the lad's Lower Myanmar background and knowledge of the Mon language and culture when he did this, as Pyi was the gateway to Lower Myanmar (and Arakan).

In 1390, Yazadarit attacked and took the town of Guhtwet, just south of Pyi and considered part of Ava's dominions, which he then fortified under the charge of one of its officers. When Minkyiswa Sawkai heard of the event, he gathered all his troops and marched on the city. Yazadarit sent a large force to reinforce the city and, with another, set up defenses at a nearby town. The Ava king attacked Guhtwet by land and water without success. Later, joined by his eldest son and heir, they finally took it, left a governor there with support troops, and returned to Ava.

The next year, word that a white elephant was seen in Tharawaddy south of Pyi and north of Dagon sent Minkyiswa Sawkai and about twenty thousand of his troops looking for it. However, Yazadarit heard of the troop movements south, and gathered his own troops to meet them. Minkyiswa Sawkai was said to have said, "I did not come down here to fight the Talaing, only to catch a white elephant." But with only a skeleton force, Sawkai had to retreat to Pyi without his prize.

Competition in the North

Ava's periodic preoccupation with Lower Myanmar left its northern frontier vulnerable. In 1392, Tho Han Bwa, brother-in-law of the lord of Mohnyin, Tho Khan Bwa, attacked Myedu, which lay at the head of the rich Mu Valley, considered by Ava a part of its dominions. Minkyiswa Sawkai commanded his northern *myosa* with their troops to march by land. The king himself went by water up to Tagaung with one thousand war boats and eight hundred state barges. The land forces suffered a defeat, chased by the Shan, who, when they reached Sagaing, set fire to houses that lay outside the city. Minkyiswa Sawkai rapidly returned to Ava and prepared to defend the city. He then called the southern *myosa* to make haste and come to Ava. The *myosa* of Yamethin got there and joined up with the land forces that had retreated. His forces soundly defeated the Shan troops, after which he gathered his own troops and, without entering Ava, returned to Yamethin.

The king, rather annoyed that the Yamethin *myosa* did not enter Ava and pay his respects after their victory, asked his adviser, Min Yaza, why the Yamethin *myosa* did that. The minister said the *myosa* did not have very good *lu mhu* (human affairs, what today we might call people skills) and that he meant no insult, at which the king sent the *myosa* many rewards. When the Yamethin *myosa* died in 1394, his fief, along with sixty war elephants, eight hundred horses, and ten thousand soldiers were bestowed upon his elder brother.

In the *Maniyadanabon*, published about fifty years after U Kala's account, the same incident is recalled with much elaboration and loquaciousness that included many parables. At the end of it, its author was said to have said, "Kings who wish their affairs to go well must know when to forgive. My lord King, you must never think of your own irritation with your ministers or officers or generals or others of this sort; you must not think of your personal friendship with them; you must not treat them as close, you must not treat them as distant. Even if their behavior ignores the niceties of their position, you forgive them and support them and cherish them."[23]

U Kala's account of Minkyiswa Sawkai is long and detailed,[24] the general character of whose reign is confirmed by the few inscriptions we have. He also gave an excruciatingly detailed genealogy of the king, his queens, and his princesses, including one Chinese personal attendant with whom he had two children. It appears that U Kala obtained his information from the daily court records kept by scribes, now lost to us. And there seems to be no political reason for him to have invented any of this, writing as he did several hundred years later as a private individual, not commissioned by the king, and during the reign of a different king and dynasty.

U Kala bestowed the following judgment on the king. He wrote that Minkyiswa Sawkai was generous, his heart was good and clear, he loved knowledge, and throughout the city, he encouraged intelligent talk. He then provided a list of the king's works of merit, which seemed to have been much of the reason for U Kala's favorable assessment of the king. It included the Ava Shwezigon (*zigon*, a solid pagoda) that still stands today, to which was attached a royal monastery; the Shwethikyi Zigon, with its royal monastery; the Nyaungyan Zigon and its royal monastery; the Ngapaukwa Zigon and its royal monastery; and a fifth *zigon* on "the north side lake" and its royal monastery. At Amyint city, his old fief he had held as a prince before becoming king, Minkyiswa erected a big monastery and bestowed it with a white umbrella, calling it the king's monastery. It was built for the head of the *sangha*, whose appointment followed the usual practice of making one's teacher head of the church when one became king. He also built the Ava Thandaw Zigon and royal monastery, and the Myinmi (?) Zigon and royal monastery. An inscription also records a religious revival the king held which was attended by Brahmins and Sinhalese teachers, on which occasion, Ava, "the capital of the Mranma . . . [was considered] as pleasant as Tavatimsa,"[25] the most important of Buddhist heavens which was also Pagan's celestial model for its earthly domain.

U Kala ended his account on the king by writing that Minkyiswa Sawkai was thirty-seven years in the Nether House, ruled for thirty-three years, and lived to be seventy years until he attained *anissa* (impermanence). At that time, a vulture alighted on the Shwezigon, and a crocodile was seen in the Myitnge River. He was a Sunday-born son.

In my twenty-first-century view, Minkyiswa Sawkai's historical legacy lies with his timely pacification of Upper Myanmar, which his predecessor Thadominbya had begun without (or before) losing precious momentum. Geographically, politically, and ideologically, Sawkai also added to the foundations of the kingdom of Ava laid by his predecessor, on which posterity could build further. His long reign of thirty-three years (until 1400) suggests a stability that is hardly characteristic of an alleged anarchic and decentralized "Shan period," which conventional historiography had so long proclaimed for that early portion of the Ava period.

Another convention that needs rectifying is the name Tryaphya III, given to Minkyiswa Sawkai by modern Myanmar historians, as if that clarified things. The adding of Roman numerals to the names of kings is an approach I prefer not to adopt in general, unless it is also found in the original sources and their identities are clear in both the inscriptions and chronicles. Otherwise, it just adds another layer of confusion to the current one between inscriptional and chronicle names. Adding these numerals to a king's name also assumes the list is definitive and fixes their existence in a set sequence that can create problems later.[26] With a few very well-known exceptions, I prefer to use the names given to these kings in the chronicles, which are not only well known to Burmese society at large but also much better known to Western historians.

After Minkyiswa Sawkai's death, all the chronicles state that his son, "lord of the white elephant," ascended the throne in 1400 AD. However, as he ruled for only five months (confirmed by the *Zatatawpon*, although given only one month by the *Yazawinkyaw*, and seven months by U Kala),[27] he had no time to perform an *abhiseka* (ceremony of coronation), whose recording is normally reserved for stone—hence, the silence of epigraphy regarding him. In any case, the chronicles attribute his short reign to his interests in hunting and fishing only, not in affairs of state. He was said to have been killed by the *myosa* of Tagaung, who then took the throne for himself. But the ministers overthrew him, and asked the younger brother of the deceased king, the lord of Pyin Si, named Min Swe, to take the throne. Min Swe replied that he really did not have the military and political acumen to be king, although he would support his uncle, the *myosa* of Yamethin to be king: the successor of the one without good "people skills," who had helped defeat the Shan earlier.

At that, the younger brother of Pyin Si, Shin Thidat, asked his older brother if it were true he was stepping down in favor of their uncle. When his brother replied in the affirmative, Shin Thidat in disbelief admonished him: "You can offer your food to someone, but not the throne!" With that, he said he was going to resist.[28] He did, and in the ensuing battle, the lord of Yamethin was killed. The ministers then placed Pyin Si on the throne, most likely with Shin Thidat, his younger brother, holding the real reins of power behind the scenes. And with Pyin Si, although not by him, began the more than one hundred years of literary achievements at Ava that are still being celebrated and, in some cases, emulated today.

Conclusion

Thadominbya and Minkyiswa Sawkai, much like Pagan's famous Three Brothers, were also men of action who seized their moments without much hesitation. Whereas the Three Brothers had rescued Upper Myanmar from total disintegration, Thadominbya and Sawkai had taken that valuable respite and built upon it the foundations of a new kingdom and dynasty. Their particular age called for strong, charismatic (sometimes ruthless) personal leadership, replacing some of the inoperative institutions of society. At the same time, they knew that society would eventually need more permanent institutions to survive them, so began the process of building these.

The first, invariably, was ensuring that the *sangha* was provided for, which, in addition to meeting the spiritual and psychosocial needs of the majority of the population, would have had a pacifying effect on the kingdom at large, while keeping the economy stimulated with temple construction and land endowments. Those activities not only increased (or reclaimed) cultivated land but also pumped money into the arts and crafts industry, whose links to other sectors of the economy are innumerable. As in Pagan days, promotion of the *sangha* and religion had political, economic, and demographic consequences far beyond the spiritual realm.

Reestablishing the *myosa* (town eater) system of patronage was also important, particularly since capable regional leaders were already entrenched in their respective localities, without whose allegiance and acquiescence the king and center had little hope of genuine consolidation. At the same time, giving loyalty to the center was also in the interests of these regional leaders, for, as descendants of those who had been appointed by previous center leaders, they had good reason to continue support of the center, perhaps even with some hope of future eligibility to the throne itself. Not only would they enjoy extended tenure of their fiefs without pecuniary and other interruptions, but their support of the center promised better sociopolitical mobility for their kinfolk, as princesses or queens at court, and thereby genealogical links to royalty (or perceived royalty).

As for those who resisted, they were ultimately subdued by either Thadominbya or Minkyiswa Sawkai, with their fiefs confiscated and given to those who did not. With each success by the center, more would find it in their interests to pledge loyalty to the king, so that those who were undecided initially would find it increasingly difficult to remain so as time passed. After such personal loyalties were secured by oaths of allegiance, marriage ties, rewards, and threats of punishment, the business of regularizing and enhancing the kingdom's agricultural resources was the next step. Virgin as well as abandoned land was developed and reclaimed, irrigation works repaired, taxes reinstated, social rank and occupations reconstituted, religious and folk festivals rejuvenated, the palace refurbished: in other words, all the kinds of activities that a legitimate Buddhist kingdom in agrarian Upper Myanmar was wont to (and must) do.

Only after the heartland was secured militarily, politically, administratively, and economically were attempts made to conquer parts of Lower Myanmar once again, to reestablish the kind of rule Pagan had over it and to secure its lucrative commercial revenues. But here, for the most part, Ava was unsuccessful, for Yazadarit, one of the most famous and able of Lower Myanmar's kings, controlled that region. Although Pegu, like Ava, was Pagan's creation as well, built as it was on the Pagan's physical and conceptual infrastructure, neither one could unite both parts to become, in essence, another Pagan.

The Consolidation of Ava

As shown in the last chapter, two strong leaders, Thadominbya and Minkyiswa Sawkai, were instrumental in the creation and early development of the Kingdom of Ava, despite the trying conditions that could have reversed the process and returned the situation to what it was during the earlier decades of the fourteenth century. It is also fortunate for the Burmese speakers and their culture (and, ultimately, the modern Union of Myanmar) that these two founding fathers were followed by four equally strong kings who continued their predecessors' work and consolidated what they had done. In so doing, these kings who lived and reigned during the first half of the fifteenth century not only set the stage for but also began the process of Ava's efflorescence, which reached fruition during the second half of the fabulous fifteenth century, making Ava look like a small Pagan (the topic of chapter 5).

Mingaung the First

The second son of Minkyiswa Sawkai ascended the throne on November 25, 1400, at the age of twenty-eight, with the title Anawrahta Min Saw.[1] (This must have been the prince Pyin Si, who had offered the kingdom to his uncle but was chastised by his younger brother for doing so.) If so, he was popularly known as Pathama Mingaung (Mingaung the First) in the chronicles, reigning for a long quarter century and raising the kingdom of Ava to heights theretofore unattained. Most of the primary sources seem to agree that he ascended the throne after Minkyiswa Sawkai's first son and heir, Tayaphya, reigned for a short five (or seven, depending on the source one reads) months, before he was killed by his uncle, the lord of Yamethin, who was in turn killed by Pyin Si's younger brother, as described in the previous chapter. (The uncle-nephew struggles continued to haunt Burmese succession thereafter, well into the nineteenth century.)

At, or shortly after, his formal ascension, Mingaung the First claimed in the same inscription noted above that "Myanma Pyi" extended on the east to "Shan Pyi," on the northwest to "Timmasala" (Assam?), on the west to "Kula Pyi," and on the south to "Talaing Pyi."[2] What these entities might have been depends on the word *pyi*. Since Pagan times, the Old Burmese word *pran* (*pyi*) has been used in both a concrete, geopolitical and cultural sense (as it is here), as well as in an abstract way, such as in the phrase *nibban pyi* (the state of *nirvana*). It is very much like the word "state" in English—the "state of things in American politics" and "the state of Iran." And because the "states" mentioned above were in fact monarchies (or perceived as such), the word "kingdom" might be the closest English equivalent for the word *pyi* at the time. Note also that the word *pyi* is preceded by an ethno-linguistic cum cultural adjective—Myanma, Shan, Talaing, Kula—indicating that these "kingdoms" were being perceived and identified as distinct ethno-linguistic entities. Mingaung's sentence can thus be translated as the "kingdoms of" the Myanma, Shan, Kula, and Talaing.

Whether or not the latter ethno-linguistic terms represent a reification of ethnicity, long attributed to colonial scholars, is an issue scholars can debate further. But what is important for us here is that the inscription reveals the physical extent of Mingaung's kingdom and political/military reach. The king made more explicit in another part of the inscription the extent of his "Myanma Pyi," in which he included known towns during Pagan and Ava times, such as Lower Myanmar's Dagon and Dala (Yangon and Tala), even Winka (an old Pyu site) near Thaton, Khanti and Khun Kyaw in the far north, and Danu and Paunglaung Amyauk (probably on the southeast of Ava).[3] Although some sites in the claim (such as Winka, Tala, and Yangon) were likely exaggerated, the totality of the evidence does suggest that by about 1400 AD, Ava controlled and/or had hegemony over much of the Upper Irrawaddy River valley—particularly the Dry Zone of Myanmar—although more in a north–south than an east–west direction.

It was at formal and public ceremonies, such as the royal *abhiseka* (coronation) recorded on stone, that fiefs, titles, ranks, positions, and the rewards that went with them were announced and granted. With great pomp and ceremony, the heir apparent and chief queens were appointed, the head of the *sangha* officially designated, and *myosa*-ships awarded. The latter, particularly, were pointedly given as part of "the royal compassion" (*thana daw*), that is, at the pleasure of the king. They were not technically hereditary, although in practice were usually regarded as such, especially by the recipient. These public ceremonies are also useful for information about the king's allies, as well as the towns and cities most important in the kingdom. They also tell us the degree to which the center's authority had expanded or contracted since his predecessor conducted the same ceremony.

Thus, for example, Yamethin had been difficult to bring under Ava's control since its inception, but because the lord of that city had recently died, at Mingaung's coronation, another who was a supporter of the king was given the city instead, along with fifty war elephants. Altogether sixteen important towns and cities were awarded as fiefs by Mingaung to his clients, including Salin, given to one of the sons of Lauk Phya, uncle of King Yazadarit of Pegu and lord of Myaungmya (in the Lower Myanmar Delta), who had instigated the Ava-Pegu wars and stood on Ava's side. Another supporter, Saw Nit, was given a princess to marry along with command of the "Northern Cavalry's Nine regiments." This information suggests Ava's authority had expanded, for the list included several cities not mentioned previously, such as Badon and Dipeyin on the northwest side of the Irrawaddy.[4]

The ceremony also revealed who and what the king considered "uncivilized," that is, un-Buddhist. The killing of human beings to make them *nat* (spirits) by "the naked Naga . . . [of] Timmasala"[5] (thought to be Nagaland), where people were said to have been killed alive under city gates and other powerful spots to ensure their malevolent spirits thereafter remain to protect that location—long claimed by colonial historians to have been a Burmese practice later called *myosade*—was clearly frowned upon at Buddhist Ava. That means Burmese society did not have to wait another century and a half for King Bayinnaung to give similar orders prohibiting such practices, heretofore cited as evidence to suggest that Burmese Theravada Buddhism increased in orthodoxy during the "Early Modern Period" until it reached a pinnacle of orthodoxy with the last, Konbaung, dynasty. On the contrary, the above evidence suggests that orthodoxy was not a linear process that increased with the passage of time.

As in the Pagan period, Mingaung's queens were placed in the four cardinal directions while the title Saw, also as in Pagan times, was given to the chief (southern) queen. This particular chief queen seemed to have been a direct descendent of Somin Kodawgyi, daughter of Athinkhaya, the eldest of the famous Three Brothers. The chronicles provided a list of the queens (most confirmed by contemporary epigraphs),[6] one of whom was the Shan princess who was given to Mingaung in marriage while he was still a prince. She was the only one who bore him four children who were to play important roles later.

The inscriptions confirm that his queens also received certain towns "to eat." In 1402, the king "gave the golden capital of Pukam [Pagan] known as Arimattanapura, where the strength of [the] three precious gems abounds, to (his) grandmother."[7] Although Pagan had lost its role as political center, it had clearly retained its stature as an exemplary religious center, and remained an important *myosa*-ship.

It was also on occasions such as the coronation that leaders of tributary states formally and publicly expressed their loyalty to the king, as the ruler of Kathe (Manipur?) did, by sending a daughter along with other kinds of tributary gifts. None, of course, came from Lower Myanmar, which had proved difficult (if not impossible) to conquer. As a result of being partially blocked from the commercial revenues of Lower Myanmar, Arakan, Chiang Mai, and the Shan states had become alternative political and economic resources for Ava. The inscriptions confirm that Arakan was (again) conquered, around 1407 or 1408, and one of the king's daughters was sent to govern it.[8] She may have been the famous Yakhaing Mibaya (Queen of Arakan), and if so, is well remembered in verse, as a ballad in her honor was composed called "Yakhaing Minthami Egyin" (The Ballad of the Princess of Arakan), still read in schools today.

U Kala provided additional details of the Arakan conquest. Ava blamed the Bayin (King) of Arakan, Thoyagyi, for "touching" and "destroying" parts of what were considered Ava's "royal dominions" on the west bank of the Irrawaddy, across the mountain passes from Arakan. When the king heard of that "intrusion," he consulted with his ministers and generals, appointed his son Minye Kyawswa commander—then only thirteen years old—and called upon select regional *myosa* to provide ten battalions of soldiers (*tat*). The *tatmadaw* (literally, main royal force) numbered four hundred war elephants, five thousand cavalry, and ten thousand infantry.

The king of Arakan came out to meet them with his troops at Nge Nun Taung and was soundly defeated, mainly by elephantry and cavalry, with Sawnit, the commander of the Northern Cavalry, cutting off the head of the Arakanese king. The Arakanese troops fled with the fall of their king, and Ava's forces overcame the remaining troops defending the capital, entered, and took the city. When the king of Ava heard of the capture, he appointed the Kale *myosa,* named Anawrahta Minsaw (whose fief was probably the closest, located on the Upper Chindwin River), to also govern Arakan, after raising him to the rank of prince with the requisite five insignia, suggesting that practical considerations, not just genealogy, guided *myosa* appointments and conferred royal status.

The detailed narrative given by U Kala on the battle with Arakan further provides insight into military strategies used by Ava. It is clear that Ava fought best on hard ground with cavalry and elephantry, but was not as successful in marshy, coastal areas such as the Lower Myanmar Delta, where many streams had to be crossed and war boats put to effective use, as campaigns there proved. The battle against the Arakanese king also revealed what seems to be a tried and true military tactic of separating the flanks by going down the middle, focusing on the leader's elephant, knowing that charismatic and personal leadership, along with military ability, held the force together and that, once the leader falls, his support also crumbles.

Taking advantage of Ava's preoccupation in Arakan, the *sawbwa* of Onbaung, Tho Kyaung Bwa, "touched" an area considered part of Ava's "royal dominions." But this time, instead of troops, Mingaung sent his minister, Min Yaza, to discuss the matter with the *sawbwa,* who subsequently accepted Ava's overlordship. The *sawbwa* was given the king's niece in marriage, and also a house at Ava, where he was made a vassal (*kyun*) of the king, who then "bore the royal burden" (*amhudan*) in a military capacity.[9]

In 1405, Hto Hmain Gyi, the *sawbwa* of Nyaungshwe, located at the north end of Inle Lake, sent a message that he also wished to give allegiance to Mingaung and "bear the royal burden" like the *sawbwa* of Onbaung, who had recently come to Ava with many presents "to live under the sole of the king's foot." Perhaps his behavior was motivated by Ming pressure in the north to pacify Yunnan, or he wanted to be considered equals in the eyes of Ava and other *sawbwa.* He too was given a military post with cavalry and elephants to lead. Thus, it was Ava's patronage that was being sought by the Shan leaders, not the other way around, demonstrating its position as exemplary center in Upper Myanmar and giving it the kind of advantage it needed to keep the *sawbwa* divided.

That same year, Yazadarit, king of Pegu, again "marching by land and water" with his elephants and horses, attacked a town that was considered part of the Ava kingdom. Not able to withstand the attack, the *myosa,* his troops, and the people fled to Hlaing, a nearby town in Lower Myanmar under Ava. Yazadarit surrounded the town "by land and water" and attacked, but could not take it because of the barrage from guns and cannon. So they decided to attack Pyi, hoping that, if it fell, it would be easier to take Hlaing. Pyi also had prepared its defenses with guns and cannon, so could not be taken either. Yazadarit had to lay siege to the city instead, which, invariably resulted in Ava sending reinforcements.

Mingaung's order to particular *myosa* to join the march south shows that the principle on which the *myosa* system was based made a great deal of practical sense. Since distances were long, and in emergencies, travel had to be faster than normal,[10] dispatching *myosa* who were closest to the troubled spot meant royal troops could be placed anywhere in the kingdom in a relatively short span of time: that is, as long as it took to get the message sent and implemented. In other words, royal *myosa*-ships were strategically arranged in such a way throughout the kingdom so that each one was within a day or two's march of another.

This *myosa* arrangement also meant that the king did not have to use the troops guarding the capital for every emergency. In this particular case, the Northern Division stayed where it was (to defend against any attack from the north), and Mingaung called up only the *myosa* of the Southern Division to deal with the problem at Pyi.[11] Only when the Southern Division could not defeat Yazadarit and Pyi's food supplies began to dwindle did Mingaung sent another *myosa* with two thousand horses laden with *padi*, each horse carrying two *tin* (each *tin* was a basket weighing approximately fifty-six pounds), while the king, riding on his elephant, broke the siege.

In other ways also, the *myosa* system served a polity like Ava well. It was based largely on personal relationships, and enforced with rewards and punishment that were designed to serve both the center's interests and those of each *myosa*. At the same time, the military, economic, and political independence of each *myosa* provided the incentive and military wherewithal for challenging the center, thus the reason virtually every "rebellion" in precolonial Myanmar's history was among elites rather than between peasants and elite.

In 1407, the king's younger brother, who was lord of Sagaing, showed signs of rebellion and subsequently challenged Mingaung to single combat on elephants. The king won, said the chronicle, because his opponent's elephant, being "younger," dared not show his face to (confront) his "elder" and fled. (That incident allowed U Kala to insert a ballad [*egyin*] about a lion and a pig.) After being placed under house arrest, the ex-lord of Sagaing fled to Lower Myanmar to serve Yazadarit, who welcomed him as a "brother-in-law." He was received with great honor and given a good fief, which, of course, not only incurred jealousies in the Pegu court, but also broke the peace accord with Mingaung and stopped the flow of annual revenues of Pathein (Bassein) to Ava.

This kind of manipulation by ambitious leaders of each center was another component of the picture, a situation that often drew in other centers such as Arakan and, occasionally, Chiang Mai which harbored hard feelings for years to come. Personal jealousies and vindictiveness accounted for several battles between Ava and Pegu, far more frequently than did perceptions of reified ethnicity.

Either U Kala made everything up or he must have had some detailed information, for he mentions the names, fiefs, and relationships of virtually all the important individuals in the above incident, including the names of the "Talaing" generals who were involved. Some of his information is corroborated by other histories, but we must be careful here, for most chronicles based their information on U Kala's. Some contemporary inscriptions do confirm the general pattern of patron-client relationships and especially the place-names of important towns likely to have been fiefs, while the narrative itself is consistent with the general sequence of events, dates, and other facts.

Having said that, however, dialogues of a didactic nature, prophecies, and omens were also very much part of U Kala's narrative. Prophecies were usually used to legitimize places, individuals, and events that were extraordinary, while omens were meant to demonstrate the link between the supernatural and the natural, the terrestrial and the celestial. In such cases, one can virtually predict when they are about to appear, before and after which "history," as we know it, normally resumes.[12]

While standard prophecies and omens were inserted whenever and wherever the situation warranted, dialogues required a bit more literary skill, imagination, and knowledge of the culture's political, social, and religious values. Like prophecies and omens, they too were used in the narrative at places and times U Kala thought the situation warranted. So, in the tradition of Herodotus and Thucydides—whereby the "speeches" of their characters (such as Creosus' public oration in support of the Peloponnesian Wars) represented the prevalent and important issues of the time or that of the authors—U Kala did likewise. These revealed certain "universal" Buddhist principles and beliefs concerning leadership, kingship, loyalty, greed, and impermanence of things.

For example, in the battle over Pyi mentioned above, Pegu's soldiers had retreated by crossing the river, at which Yazadarit was said to have ordered those fleeing to be killed. At that, one of his ministers said, "Only the three commanders are responsible to your highness. The soldiers themselves are faultless. Killing them is like burning down the whole house to get the mouse. You are the king who asked for the boon of Buddhahood," at which, Yazadarit relented.[13]

There are other similar occasions in which unsolicited advice was given to the king in subtle (therefore, not so embarrassing) ways. On one occasion, King Mingaung was said to have requested the trusted old adviser of his father to counsel him on kingship, whose reply became the basis for the *Zambu* text mentioned in an earlier chapter.[14] The counseling took up several long paragraphs in the published version of U Kala's chronicle and is probably regarded as the "dialogue" par excellence for representing such advice. The model for each category of royal behavior was a deity: Yama, Sakra, Suriya, Pannarasa, Mahasamuddara, Mahapathiwi, and Pajjuna Nat. (Here, of course, *nat* referred to the celestial Brahmanic deities, not the chthonic indigenous spirits of nature also called *nat*.)

The long reply of the adviser not only expounded on kingship, it also became a standard literary device with which subsequent chroniclers created the kind of atmosphere needed for certain occasions, then inserting didactic messages at the appropriate places. It was different from Queen Saw's famous admonishment of King Narathihapade for his role in the "fall" of the Pagan kingdom, in that, here, the wise old adviser preempted such disaster by telling the king what he should and should not do rather than chastising him after the fact.

The advice recommended both secular and practical, as well as ritualistic and symbolic, action, stating that the king has the duty to always consult with his wise counselors, to be in agreement with his military commanders, to be upright when dealing with taxes and meting out justice, to give to the guardian *nats* of the capital and other cities their due, and to observe, guard, and protect the well-being of the *sangha*. Only if these things were done, would all the creatures in the kingdom be exceedingly happy. For this, the king bestowed upon his wise adviser the title of Min Yaza.[15]

Yet, there are other direct quotes in U Kala's work that are not literary devices used for didactic purposes, particularly those found in the communiqués issued among kings. Their content cannot be confirmed with any degree of certainty, of course, but U Kala appears to have had access to some of the records that no longer survive today, although the categories of sources called *yazahtan* (literally, royal sound, but more like, royal voice) we know did exist. In one of these communiqués between Mingaung and Yazadarit, the parties were cordial, the classifiers and "hierarchic" verbs correct, and the euphemisms appropriate; indeed they were like real communiqués between kings.

At the same time, their content often revealed the extent to which personal grudges were involved. Mingaung's conciliatory gesture for instituting a lasting peace treaty that their respective fathers signed and honored—"as long as fire burns and water quenches"—was met with a cold reply by Yazadarit, who reminded Mingaung of his attack some years ago at the instigation of one of Yazadarit's own disaffected *myosa* (his uncle), which caused much suffering in his kingdom.

Finally, after some intrigue and hostage-taking of messengers, a peace accord was signed so that "the happiness of all creatures, on which rests the king's buddhahood when Maitreya returns," may be attained. Many presents were exchanged, listing each item, providing clues to the kinds of goods each region considered special to it (and difficult for the other to obtain).[16] The oath was sworn at the Sandawshin Pagoda (The Temple of the Hair Relic, that is, the present Shwedagon), so that the entire ceremony was on hallowed ground with the highest religious sanction. They also agreed on the political border between "Myanma Naingnan" and "Talaing Naingnan" (probably best translated for the time as the Dominion of the Myanma and the Dominion of the Talaing), marked by a post, "upward" of which was the former and "downward" of which was the latter, west and east of which were "other" places.[17] Marriage alliances were then made to seal the treaty, whereby Mingaung gave his son in marriage to Yazadarit's daughter in return for the annual revenues taken from ships that docked at Pathein harbor and thirty war elephants every year. Mingaung also offered his elder sister as a queen for Yazadarit.

No sooner had the treaty been signed than Yazadarit took Arakan, placing one Nayameikhla on the Arakanese throne who had earlier fled to Pegu when Ava conquered Arakan. Ava's governor of Arakan, Mingaung's daughter, and her husband were taken prisoner to Pegu. Yazadarit killed the husband and raised the wife (Mingaung's daughter) to be his own queen.

That brazen insult resulted in the mobilization, in 1408, of a large number of troops by Ava. According to U Kala, the army consisted of eight hundred war elephants, twelve thousand cavalry, and two hundred thousand infantry, which included two Shan *myosa* (of Onbaung and Nyaungshwe) and their regiments.[18] Once again, the reason for this retaliatory invasion by Ava was primarily a personal one, where slights and insults played a far larger role than did (if at all) reified ethnicity as convention has it. Arakan became a battleground, and even the king (*bayin*) of Chiang Mai was drawn into the fracas. The latter, not considered Syam (T'ai) but Yun (Lao) by U Kala, was enticed to pinch Pegu on its opposite flank via the Sittaung route.[19] But as usual, Pegu could not be taken, while Ava's troops had to return at the onset of the monsoons, after a peace treaty was signed at a pagoda.

Arakan was the only major center in Myanmar that Ava could conquer relatively easily, which it did the following year once again. Ava also took Thindwe (Anglicized as Sandaway), one of Arakan's coastal cities. The governor who had been placed there by Yazadarit fled to "India" (Kala Pyi), and Ava replaced him with its own governor, attaching a nearby Ava *myosa*-ship to Arakan as reinforcement. Of course, that meant Yazadarit had to take Arakan once more, which he did, first taking Thindwe, then moving up to the capital of Arakan to take it, after which he took back to Pegu as hostages the new governors recently placed there by Ava.

During such times when Ava was preoccupied in Lower Myanmar, certain Shan *sawbwa* would attack its northern cities. In 1411, the *sawbwa* of Theinni actually came down with many soldiers to attack Ava. But the *sawbwa* of Onbaung, Tho Kyaung Bwa, loyal to Mingaung rather than to his ethnic brethren, warned him of the march, so that Ava's cavalry easily defeated the Theinni *sawbwa*. From the battle, Ava obtained six elephants, two hundred horses, and over eight hundred prisoners of war. The king's son, Minye, in command, continued to Theinni itself to take it, but since it was defended by "the Chinese" (probably Yunnanese) for some reason, he did not succeed.

Minye then heard that the Chinese were sending reinforcements, so stole away at night to lay in ambush in the forests. When the Chinese arrived on the scene, he split his troops into three columns and attacked at different points and "destroyed them," said the chronicle. (This victory appears to be supported by a contemporary inscription of Ava.)[20] Along with five Chinese ministers (*amat*), one thousand horses and two thousand people were taken. Over five hundred horses died, lamented U Kala.

When Yazadarit heard of Minye's siege of Theinni and Ava's preoccupation in the north, he attacked Pyi "by land and water." Once again, because Pyi was defended by cannon and guns, Yazadarit failed. On Yazadarit's southeastern flank was Ayuthaya, which now got into the act once Yazadarit was preoccupied at Pyi, by attacking Ye, a suburb of Muttama (Martaban), which Yazadarit considered part of his domain. So he had to march back to Muttama, leaving a contingent at Pyi to continue the siege. Hearing of Yazadarit's plight of having to fight on two fronts, Mingaung marched south with seven battalions, as Minye had another seven with him at Theinni, although some had to guard Ava. Eventually Minye joined Mingaung at Pyi and chased Yazadarit back to Pegu.

Upon their return to Ava, Minye was formally given the title of heir apparent, *Einshemin.* A "shake-up" at court followed, as positions, titles, and fiefs were redistributed. Toungoo was given to Sawlu Thinkhaya, while Min Letyagyi, formerly lord of Toungoo, was given Pyinsi Myo instead. Pagan was given to Pakhan Tayaphya, while his former fief of Pakhan was given to Mingaung's middle son, Minye Kyaw Htin. His youngest, Thihathu, was given Pyi, while Sagaing was given to minister Yazathingyan. Myedu, which guarded the northern entrance to the Mu Valley and its valuable irrigation works, was given to Thettawshe (Royal Long Life), while Sagu was given to Nga Khin Nyo, apparently not royalty. Paukmyaing was given to the commander in chief's son, Sithu Nge.

Then the *myosa* of Moke (?) presumably in the northern Shan territories and apparently not under Ava, "touched the royal dominion of Myedu," which had just been given to Thettawshe. Minye was sent with some troops that successfully repelled the invaders who were said to have fled to "China" (Tayok Pyi). Minye returned with some elephants, horses, people, and the sons and wives of the rebellious *myosa.* Eventually, the latter returned with "Chinese" troops and all the *sawbwa* they could gather to demand the return of his sons and wives or else they would attack. It was an inopportune time for Mingaung, for his son and heir had most of the troops down in Lower Myanmar fighting Yazadarit. Ava held out for a month until the "Chinese" presented Mingaung with a challenge for single combat on horseback.

Mingaung called his officers of elephants and horses and asked for a champion. No one volunteered. Finally, one of the ministers asked Mingaung to let the challenge be known to Yazadarit's son-in-law, Thamein Payin; he had been captured earlier and was at the time in the stockade at Ava. He agreed to take up the challenge and spent some time selecting the right horse, a "red" one. Thamein was well cared for, and given the personal sword of the king and other weapons. The narrative by U Kala of this battle was vivid, horses dashing back and forth, the champions sizing each other up, making feints, attacking and tactically retreating.

Predictably, Ava's champion won, but only with much luck, for the cord that kept the sword in the hand of the Chinese champion, Kamani, broke, cutting his opposite hand. At that point, Thamein Payin hooked Kamani with his pike, cut off his head with his sword, put it in a basket, and took it into Ava fort. The Chinese, wrote U Kala, were full of awe and wonder, saying this could not be human but a *nat.* Pleased with all this, Mingaung arranged Thamein Payin's marriage to the daughter of a prominent *myosa,* awarded him with the colors and trappings of a prince, and gave him Lakaing Myo as fief. People loaded him with many gifts, while the Chinese, as agreed, left. Such stories may sound corny to those of us in the twenty-first century, the stuff of action movies. But battle of champions, especially in labor-scarce Southeast Asia, where fighting men were extremely valuable, was in the interests of both parties. Whether or not it was historical, the motif itself must have had some appeal to U Kala's readers as a plausible rather than fantastic story.

Every winter (dry) season, the movement of troops between Upper and Lower Myanmar, was predictable, wherein the two primary kingdoms, and occasionally, four other contiguous polities, were involved. The struggle between Ava and Pegu, or perhaps even more correctly, between Mingaung and Yazadarit, continued unabated for at least two decades. There were more than twelve major campaigns between the two that neither won. In each case, Ava, if the chronicles are correct, had the superior number of troops, elephants, and horses; but in each case, Yazadarit could not be defeated. Indeed, Halliday's translation of the Mon-language *Slapat Rajawan Datow Smin Ron* (A History of Kings), states that the story of Yazadarit's wars with Burma is "used as a school book by the Siamese" as a lesson on how to deal with the Burmese.[21]

True or not, what is interesting is the treatment of Yazadarit by U Kala, who was from "Burmese" Ava. He spent nearly 141 manuscript "paragraphs" (close to 121 published pages) on the Mon king, whereas the Mon author who wrote the later *Slapat* had only a single paragraph on the king, saying he "had made friends with enemies, [and therefore] gained a knowledge of the customs of war. . . . Because he was great in war always, he had no opportunity to enshrine pagodas."[22] U Kala had preserved in the Burmese language the history of important Mon kings in Myanmar much better than the Mon themselves had done of their own royalty.

In 1416, the son and heir apparent of Mingaung, Minye Kyawswa, died. He died as he had lived—on the battlefield—when his elephant fell on his leg (gored, said another chronicle). He had initially hidden, but was subsequently discovered by Yazadarit's forces. He refused aid, medicine, food, and even Yazadarit's own daughter, along with an ostensible offer to make him heir. Instead, he replied that he would not return to Ava without taking Hamsavati (Pegu), and he would never be someone else's subject (*kyun*). He died from his wounds the following day just before dawn. Yazadarit gave him a splendid funeral,[23] which involved placing his cremated remains in a golden pot and, according to the *Yazawinthit,* burying it "*in the Mon fashion.*"[24]

In 1421, after many more battles had been fought in Lower Myanmar, the old minister, Min Yaza, died. He had been promoted from a young, talented *athi* lad of a rural area to one of the longest-lasting chief ministers of Ava. According to U Kala, his death created a serious change of heart in Mingaung, who gave up warlike things and intelligently focused on domestic issues, honored those with knowledge, did good deeds accruing merit, built several pagodas, notably the Yan Aung Myin and the Kyaungdaw Thein. He died after twenty-one years of reign at the royal age of fifty.

Inexplicably, after hearing of Mingaung's death, Yazadarit was also said to have died within a few months, U Kala insinuating in no uncertain terms that although contestants, they were soulmates and worthy opponents.[25] Some of the descriptions of this event used by U Kala are found almost verbatim in the *Yazadhiyaza Ayedawpon,* whose original is thought to have preceded U Kala's work by several hundred years (more on this in part 2). U Kala also refers to Yazadarit as "Shin Bayin Alaung" (Lord King, imminent Buddha), which honored him with *bodhisatta* status. Yet, and probably unlike Mingaung, who was presumably cremated, U Kala wrote that Yazadarit's cremated remains were placed in a gold vase and buried within the wood stockade when the new city was erected,[26] reminiscent of Pyu practices of almost 1,600 years ago.

Despite, or perhaps because of, regular threats from numerous quarters, there may have been a greater consciousness of, and need for, unity at the Ava court, at least during most of the fifteenth century. During this period, Ava followed the rules of succession more often than not, which were, for the most part, uncontested militarily. Of the approximately twelve kings of Ava mentioned in the contemporary inscriptions (there were two more mentioned in some chronicles, but they did not last more than a year each), all came from the legitimate pool of candidates, since almost everyone in that group was either the son or brother of the previous king—in principle, the most eligible—and almost all had been formally appointed heir apparent. And if someone violated the rules—some tried—almost always, someone closer to the throne used his power to counteract such acts. The long-held convention in Myanmar studies that there were no rules of succession in monarchical Myanmar—with, of course, implications for the modern period—is simply not true.

Hsinphyushin Thihathu

The inscriptions state that in 1423, Mingaung's son and crown prince, Thihathu, succeeded. He is also known as Sinphyushin Thihathu (Thihathu, lord of the white elephant) in the *Zatatawpon,* and as Awa Hsinphyu Ashin (Ava's Lord of the White Elephant) and Minye Kyawswa Thihathuya in the inscriptions.[27] U Kala agreed on the successor, but puts the date of ascension in 1422,[28] while the *Zatatawpon* confirms the inscriptional date,[29] with the eighteenth-century *Yazawinthit* dating it to 1421.[30] At the coronation, the new king made the usual appointments, including that of naming his younger brother crown prince.

But, alas, the new king enjoyed physical pleasures only with Queen Bome, and not with Queen Saw Min Hla, who, complaining that the king had forgotten that she was also a queen, decided not to stay in the palace. Building a Tazaung (four-cornered edifice) west of the Golden Zedi, she moved there. Thenceforth, she was called the "Lady of the Tazaung."

Meanwhile, Lower Myanmar after Yazadarit's death had split into three factions around his three sons. The eldest, and king, held Pegu, the second held Dagon (modern Yangon), and the third held Muttama. The fractured nature of the situation was ripe for Ava to strike. King Thihathu of Ava appointed Mohnyin

Thado as commander of the land forces and Kale Kye Taung Nyo as commander of the navy and sent them down with a large force of five battalions in 1423. They attacked Dagon but could not take it, so laid siege, which was finally broken when Princess Shin Saw Bu, Yazadarit's daughter by his queen Suddhamaya, was offered as consort to the Burmese king. Her husband had died earlier, leaving her at age twenty-eight with one son. Shin Saw Bu, a most famous and unique woman in Myanmar's history, was taken back to Ava with great pomp and ceremony. (Her story, brief as it is, will be told in greater detail in part 2.)

Now that the king had Shin Saw Bu, he no longer paid attention to his previous favorite, Queen Bome. Her "heart was pained," so she went to the lord of Onbaung, Le Thin Bwa, a Shan chieftain, and told him that Thihathu was at Aung Pinle (Victorious Ocean), a large irrigation tank near Shwebo, working on a canal used in the production of *padi.* She told him that while he is enjoying sensual pleasures with his female personal attendants, "look to see that his guard is down and attack, and take the throne." Le Thin Bwa came with his forces and attacked Thihathu. The latter defended himself while on his elephant, called Ye Khet Hsin Hla (attractive elephant, difficult to battle). But when his elephant got stuck in mud, he was hit with three arrows.[31] His young attendant fled the scene and made it back to Ava with the news. The ministers organized the troops and attacked the *sawbwa*'s forces and defeated them.

U Kala's judgment of Thihathu was that although the king was attractive and had a good heart with an appetite for women, he did build a *zigon* (solid pagoda) and royal monastery, and donated lands for their permanent upkeep. He ruled for only three years, according to both U Kala and the *Zatatawpon*'s calculations, although each gave different beginning and ending dates.

In 1425,[32] during the month of Tawthalin, Min Hla Nge became king. He was a son of the deceased king and Queen Tazaung, the "lady of the Tazaung" whom the late king had allegedly rejected physically, although apparently not entirely. However, Queen Bome, whom the late king also rejected when he brought back Shin Saw Bu from Lower Myanmar, had previously arranged with another powerful *myosa,* Kale Kye Taung Nyo, for precisely such a situation. Now she instructed him to hurry up and get there with his troops, which he did. He subsequently poisoned the king and took the throne. Min Hla Nge was to last a mere four months.

But the lord of Mohnyin, who controlled the Mu Valley from his fief, would have nothing of the sort and marched on Ava. Kale Kye Taung Nyo had parceled out the spoils to his supporters—the lord of Taungoo, Sawlu Athinkhaya, Taungdwin Thihapate, Bhayakamani, and Yazathingyan—and had given Shin Saw Bu to Pakhan Tayaphya. He also gave Le Thin Bwa, the *myosa* of Onbaung and the one who had killed Thihathu, presents and weapons. Then with a large force, he went to meet Mohnyin forces.

Mohnyin's sons, *myosa* of two towns, destroyed the fleet that was sent up, taking more than two thousand men. Mohnyin himself defeated the land troops, which retreated to Ava. The four lords who had received rewards then went out with their troops to meet Mohnyin, who, as he came down from the north, made local officers swear oaths of allegiance to him. He destroyed the naval forces defending Wet Khet and gained more than one hundred war boats and more than one thousand fighting men. Then he set up camp south of Sagaing at Yan Aung Myin district (District where Victory over enemies can be seen). He then sent a message to the Onbaung *sawbwa*: "You take the presents given by Kye Taung Nyo, but neither help him nor me; are you going to sit around ignoring the crisis?" Without replying, the Onbaung *sawbwa* took his rewards and troops and returned to his fief.

With the Onbaung *sawbwa* out of the picture, Mohnyin's two sons were sent to cross the Myitnge and set up camp east of Ava. Mohnyin then stretched his war boats around Ava from Mintha Island to Londawpauk. The four lords who had been supporting Kale Taung Nyo decided to take their troops and return to their fiefs as well, the lord of Pakhan taking the Mon princess Shin Saw Bu with him.

This slow, methodical, and deliberate strategy by Mohnyin, of waiting for the invariable disaffection among opportunists such as the four lords, was successful. By not attacking immediately, it allowed opponents to reconsider their decisions made under duress or on the spur of the moment, size up the situation, change their minds, and return to their fiefs if they wished. Mohnyin's goal was to dethrone Kale Taung Nyo, who had set himself up illegitimately, and either take the throne himself or put someone else legitimate on it. Fighting four lords simultaneously was not in Mohnyin's interests or part of his immediate objectives. Besides, the lords may not have been entirely supportive of Kale and were just being opportunistic, fearing for themselves, or had been persuaded during the heat of the moment to take his side. Mohnyin must have felt he could always deal with them later, and he did. But for the present, Kale was the focus.

Mohnyin's actions suggest that, again, ethnicity—if indeed he was a Shan *sawbwa* as his title and location of his fief suggest—had little or nothing to do with his decision not to support the coup (as was the Onbaung *sawbwa*'s decision to do so), and that conceptions of legitimacy were more than just the center's exclusive ideology, but one that was shared by many of the kingdom's leaders, whether Shan, Mon, or Burmese.

With the four lords now back at their fiefs, the coup leaders at Ava no longer had the strength to defend against Mohnyin. Kale and his supporters decided to flee to Arakan by sneaking out at night, and when they reached Tayok, got on boats and went to Salin, thence to Arakan. But before he could make it there, Kale died. Queen Bome, the one who was rejected for Shin Saw Bu and had enticed the Onbaung *sawbwa* to kill Thihathu earlier (instigating this whole chain of events), instead of going to Arakan, fled to Lower Myanmar, a move that had far more serious repercussions subsequently. Although Kale had usurped the throne (as he was not designated heir), and "ruled" for only seven months, he was still included on the list of the kings of Ava by the chronicles, probably because he was of royal stock.[33]

Mohnyin Min

The *Mahayazawingyi* states that on the waxing moon of Nayon, in 788 (1426), Mohnyin took the golden umbrella and the golden throne with the title of Siri Sudhammaraja. Later inscriptions confirm the date of ascension: "After subduing the city of Muiwnan [Mohnyin], [he] ascended the golden palace of Ava as a result of his diligence, power, character, industriousness, thought, and wisdom on 20 May 1426."[34] Since Mohnyin had not been appointed heir, he also was not directly or immediately in line for the throne. But like many others, he was part of the large pool of eligible candidates, being a cousin of Mingaung and uncle of Thihathu.[35] More important, he had proved his worth (and *karma*) by winning the throne with his military abilities while removing an obviously undesirable and illegitimate usurper.

At his coronation, his elder son, the *myosa* of Mo Shwe, was awarded with the title Minye Kyawswa, traditionally reserved for the heir apparent, and "given the eastern [front] residence," making him *Einshemin*. His fief encompassed the important rice production centers—Sagu, Salin, and Lagaing—of the Three Khayaing district. The king's younger son, Thihathuya, was given Pyi, which was still called "Pyu Pyi" (the city, or capital, of the Pyu) even though it had been seven hundred years since the end of the Pyu kingdom. The daughter of the lord of Pakhan was made consort of the heir apparent with the title Tabintaing Princess (Princess of the Single Post). The elder sister of Mohnyin was married to the lord of Pyinsi, Thihapate, who was nephew of the queen dowager. Mohnyin himself had only one queen, the daughter of the lord of Taungdwin, Shin Mi Myat. Perhaps he realized that the recent problems began with the jealousies among two of the queens for the king's attention, as well as their ambitions to have their sons become king.

At this point, U Kala meticulously traced the genealogy of Mohnyin back to King Narapatisithu of Pagan, naming, in sequence, each and every person pertinent to it, including marriage relationships, their ranks, and their titles. The information does not appear to have been simply invented by U Kala—it could have been checked by others at the time if they so desired, since it was so precise and detailed—but taken from the royal archives available to him. To bolster this claim, U Kala also inserted into his narrative a dream Mohnyin allegedly had, which included a prophecy that clinched his ascension ex post facto.

Because the old palace was "wilted" and "dull," U Kala records, Mohnyin decided to build a new palace in 789 (1427 AD).[36] However, we cannot find this event recorded on stone, as it surely would have been. Rather, the building of a new palace by one of his successors, much later, in 1509–1510, is recorded on stone, taking up eighty-eight lines. U Kala may have confused the two, or Mohnyin may have simply done some repairs to the upper parts (*ahtek*) of the palace.

The first order of business after the formalities ended was to find out who was loyal to the king and who was not, who was to serve as example for resisting his authority and how they were to be treated. In general, Mohnyin was much too conciliatory toward the four lords who had supported Kale, the usurper, but he probably realized that without their support, which was important, he would remain only primus inter pares, not sovereign. He also must have understood that one's current opponent may be one's future ally and that sides are often taken under duress or on the spur of the moment and that, if given time to reflect, most will act in ways that serve their long-term interests, which usually coincide with that of the center. He must have realized too that he was taking a risk with some of them by being too generous, but he chose, nevertheless, to persuade rather than kill the powerful lords, and must have felt that they would see it was more in their interests to swear loyalty to him than to fight him.

But he needed a test case, an opportunity for those who would to show their loyalty to him, as well as to make them realize what it meant to resist him. The first in line was Yazathingyan, minister to the previous king. But, as most ministers, he was too valuable to be eliminated. The king next summoned the lord of Toungoo, Sawlu Thinkhaya, who came hesitantly but ended up "eating betel" with the king, a formality that sealed their partnership. When that happened, the rest also came to swear oaths of allegiance.

However, once back in their fiefs, with the exception of Yazathingyan who, as minister, remained at court, they threw off their allegiance. Both Min Nge Kyaw Htin, who was given Thet Sein, and Thihapate, *myosa* of Taungdwin, threw off their allegiance as well. All had supported Kale when he took the throne and resisted Mohnyin until he showed up in force, forcing them to steal away in the night to their fiefs. Their behavior now suggested to the king that they were self-serving "spoilers" with little or no larger vision than their own power and success, and that they swore oaths of allegiance only to suit their immediate needs.

The king therefore ordered his eldest son, the heir apparent, to command the troops to attack Tayaphya, the lord of Pakhan (Gyi?), a major center, one flank going by the southern route overland to Tayok, then crossing over to Mingun port, and the other, via the northern route and led by the king's younger son, first going to Amyint and crossing over at Anein. Mohnyin also summoned his *myosa* of Pagan, Sale, Pakhan Nge, Salin, and Pyi to join the attack, thus forcing them to demonstrate their loyalty. The heir took Pakhan Gyi, thereby also Tayaphya and Min Nge Kyaw Htin. Tayaphya was placed under "house arrest" of sorts. Pakhan Gyi was given to one of his supporters, Thiyi Zeyathuya.

Mohnyin also obtained the allegiance of the Mogaung *sawbwa* located in the far north, near his old fief of Mohnyin, who would "watch Ava's back" from there. Mohnyin city itself he gave to the son of the lord of Mo Thit. He then sent his son and nephew to Sagu to intercept Queen Bome, who had fled with Bhayakamani, one of the ministers who had opposed Mohnyin. She was brought back with pomp and ceremony and given a residence within the palace at Ava. These conciliatory gestures were lost on those who continued to resist him, making them actually more desperate. The advice of his counselor, Yazathingyan, was not to deal with them directly, but with those who supported them, without whom they could not survive. Mohnyin followed that advice.

Mohnyin, wanting to create the kind of unity Pagan had enjoyed, summoned all his ministers for a council to deliberate on "the state of the kingdom and affairs of villages" (*pyi ye ywa mhu*). Yazathingyan, his chief minister, began by saying that internally, the country is not yet calm. Toungoo, Taungdwin, Yamethin, and Pinle were still autonomous and not part of the integration. Pyi (an extremely strategic place) was close to Toungoo, Taungdwin, Yamethin, as well as the "Talaing kingdom" while Arakan's *myosa* was getting old. He advised giving the *myosa* another town as fief, and Pyi to the younger son of the king, Thihathu. Then the minister said, "Give your son-in-law Thihapate, lord of Pyin Si, to govern Pakhan instead. In the north, put Myedu in charge of your younger brother, Anawrahta, commander of the Northern Cavalry." The king did as he was advised, adding his own solutions to Yazathingyan's suggestions.[37]

Power, under the circumstances found at Ava, was based not only on what was perceived to be legitimate genealogy, but also on the personal ability of the king to maintain kinship ties and relationships. That allowed control of the kingdom's material and human resources, which were invariably parceled out to kin and loyal allies as fiefs on coronation day. Instilling fear or granting favors to those assigned to administer strategic regions was key under the *myosa* system. And although institutionalized, it was essentially patron-client and ad hoc, meant to spread the authority of the center via such individuals farther than the center could extend by itself. The system best served those with the kinds of leadership skills most effective in dealing with other strong (and often difficult) personalities; but therein also lay its curse.

To reiterate, this is particularly the case since no rebellion at Pagan or Ava—indeed in all of precolonial Myanmar's history—ever occurred between peasants and lords, but between lords and lords, and usually over the throne.[38] The primary reason appears to be that, while *myosa* came and *myosa* went according to the demands of the political situation, the daily social, economic, and religious lives of the ordinary people whose produce they "ate" were hardly affected by the political vicissitudes of court and capital.

Mohnyin, thinking that he was well-prepared now, ordered the heir apparent, with five battalions, to march on the first three recalcitrant *myosa* and their cities: Pinle, Yamethin, and Taungdwin. Pinle, an old Pagan stockade, peculiarly (horseshoe) shaped, with solid brick walls, could not be taken; neither could Yamethin, because it was, said U Kala, defended by Shans. This means there were Shans fighting both for and against the Burmese crown. Next, the heir went to Taungdwin, but because the city walls, moats, and defenses were very strong, he could not take it either. So he laid siege but, after three months, was recalled to Ava. Curiously, whereas the *myosa* of these cities had been loyal to Ava under Mingaung the First, they were no longer so under Mohnyin; the problem must have been personal.

Realizing that Ava was not strong enough to take the recalcitrant *myosa*, the lord of Toungoo and his younger brother, the lord of Tharawaddy, gave the former's daughter to Bannya Ram, the king of Pegu, and asked him to attack Pyi. They convinced him that it was also in his own interest, so Bannya Ram marched by land and water to Pyi. But Pyi had gotten wind of it, and had stocked up on provisions and strengthened its defenses. As a consequence, Bannya Ram did not attack but surrounded the city at a distance and waited to see what Ava would do.

Yazathingyan advised Mohnyin not to attack but undercut the support of the two *myosa* by negotiating directly with Bannya Ram, which he did. Mohnyin marched to Pyi to negotiate with Bannya Ram who was laying siege to it. After the usual conciliatory as well as accusatory remarks, a peace accord of sorts was reached when Mohnyin agreed to take as wife one of Pegu's princesses, a niece of Bannya Ram. So a marriage alliance settled the immediate crisis once more; but these alliances were also what often precipitated and perpetuated the longer-lasting hostilities. Part of the bargain included sending an ambassador to Ava to see if the Mon queen, Shin Saw Bu, was still alive and well. The ambassador, after being kept waiting for three months, finally received an audience and saw her, after which he returned downstream. Satisfied, Bannya Ram returned with his troops to his capital, Pegu. Minister Yazathingyan's advice had worked; Toungoo's plot had been undermined, leaving it isolated, forcing Sawlu to return to his base.

Around 1429, after numerous attempts, Shin Saw Bu finally escaped with the help of two undercover monks, whose colorful story is recounted in the chronicles with great embellishment (and discussed more fully in part 2). When she reached the Mon kingdom, Bannya Ram, her younger brother, welcomed her with a great deal of overcompensatory fuss (since it was he who had offered her up to Ava in the first place to break an earlier siege). Her son, Banna Pha Ru, said he did not know her since she had been gone for so long in Upper Myanmar. Her escape, in hindsight, was one of the most important events in the history of Lower Myanmar, allowing her to become the only (documented) woman sovereign in the country's history.[39]

During that same year, 1429, two famous monks, Siri Saddhamma Lankara and Siha Mahathera, originally from Ava, who had spent time in Sri Lanka, returned to Myanmar.[40] When they landed at Pathein, the main entry port for traffic emanating from the west, the king of Pegu urged them to remain in Lower Myanmar. They chose to go to Ava instead, which revealed their perception of its superior religious stature compared with the Mon kingdom of Pegu at the time. Nevertheless, the Mon king, Bannya Ram, escorted them as far as Pyi, the recognized political cum military border between the two kingdoms, from where forty boats sent from Ava took them back with great fanfare. When they reached the vicinity of Ywa Thit Gyi (Great New Village), queens, ministers, and officers all came to meet them with the royal golden barge. When they finally docked at Ava, there was an earthquake, which, in this case, was interpreted as a good omen. The five bodily relics of the Buddha brought back by the two monks were enshrined in the Yadana Zedi at Sagaing in 1430, on Saturday the full moon day of Tabaung. On the west, a golden monastery of brick was built for the monks, and three storehouses with seventy-eight doors and windows.

That Pegu escorted the monks to Pyi, even though they chose Ava over Pegu in which to reside, demonstrates not only that both Ava and Pegu acknowledged the same religious orthodoxy, but that monks of such repute and religious activities of such importance put "on hold" the political and military activities even between these two competing kingdoms. Indeed, a common religious system encompassed most of the country in precolonial (and I would add, postcolonial) Myanmar that was taken for granted by indigenous *yazawin*. Religion and religious activities often preempted not only political and secular concerns, but also whatever reified ethnic issues that Ava and Pegu may have had, or were attributed to have had, according to colonial historiography.

Like his legitimate predecessor Mingaung, Mohnyin also spent much time and money on works of merit. A total of twenty-seven new temples and monasteries were built during his twelve-year reign, including one at Rajagriha in India. All of these probably cost him some 1,620,000 *kyats* of silver, according to my preliminary calculations, not including the usual endowments of people and land for their subsequent upkeep. On average, that comes to 2.25 complexes built annually, in addition to repairing ruined or decaying religious buildings, which he was said to have also done.[41]

In 1436–1437, Mohnyin was persuaded by "knowledgeable persons" to change the old era warning him that if he did not, the instability in the country would continue and all creatures would become unhappy. Minister Yazathingyan, a practical, experienced adviser to at least two kings, however, counseled against it, saying that earlier kings who had tried to change cosmology did not last long. The king replied that he could not be afraid of death if it meant making all creatures happy. So he consulted people knowledgeable about such things, who decided that when the year *sakkaraj* 800 [1438] was complete, two years would be subtracted to make *sakkaraj* 798, and then everything could begin again with year two. An inscription of 798 recorded the event.

> At the completion of Sakarac 800 . . . wise men from all over the Mranmma kingdom, well versed in the pitakas and vedas debated and discussed . . . [the era]. After the discussion a big and spacious pavilion was erected on the open ground at the silver market on the right of the Palace, south of Ava and north of Tonpilu. In the company of princes, princesses, royal grand-children, royal friends, royal relatives, king's governors, ministers and military commanders, monks, brahmins, after giving away . . . gold, silver, precious gems, elephants, horses, servants, land, buffaloes, bulls, cows, clothes . . . padi . . . nothing lacking, in great quantities, the king eliminated the notorious, difficult and extraordinary era.[42]

Not only did the king die within the year, the new era did not take hold and everyone continued to use the old era. The king was sixty when he died, having reigned for nearly thirteen years. U Kala's opinion of Mohnyin was a favorable one. He wrote that the king respected the Three Gems and guarded the truth, was replete with the ten laws (probably "kingly virtues"), cognizant of state affairs, correct about the past and future, diligent and determined in warfare, and full of courage, ability, and physical strength. Then U Kala listed his twenty-seven works of merit all over the kingdom, revealing to us the extent, at least, of the areas under Ava's direct rule.[43]

Hsinphyushin Minye Kyawswa

According to some chronicles, Mohnyin was succeeded by his eldest son and heir apparent, Minye Kyawswa, in *sakkaraj* 800 (1438), although according to U Kala and an inscription, it was in 801 (1439).[44] The late king had left many religious edifices but also political opposition. The first order of business, then, was to pacify Toungoo, Taungdwin, Yamethin, and Pinle, the same four centers whose lords had given his father the most trouble. Minye Kyawswa attacked Pinle first but failed to take it. He then attacked Yamethin but could not take it either. So he marched on Taungdwin and took the entire city, giving it to his brother-in-law, Thiyi Zeyathuya, whose queen was the daughter of a previous king, Thihathu, the one who was killed by three arrows at Aung Pinle. As for Toungoo, its *myosa*, Sawlu, had died several years earlier, so had been succeeded by his son-in-law, Uzana. But he was attacked and killed by Pegu king Bannya Ram, who placed Sawlu's son, Min Saw U, instead as *myosa*. (One might recall that his father had not supported Ava and was Bannya Ram's ally temporarily.)

In *sakkaraj* 803 (1441 AD), two *myosa* were sent to take Mogaung to pacify the north, then under the Shan *sawbwa*, Tho Ngan Bwa. The operation was successful, and Mogaung came under Ava's hegemony. But it was during that battle that the king, Minye Kyawswa, died from wounds (or disease, it is not clear), at the age of forty. U Kala wrote of Minye Kyawswa that he suffered from what we today refer to as "anger management problems," although, physically, he was replete with good martial qualities. He donated several temples and monasteries and endowed them with glebe lands.

Even with the king gone, chief minister Yazathingyan, with Bhayakamani (apparently now forgiven), marched on recalcitrant Toungoo from Taungdwin. After a duel on elephants, Yazathingyan defeated and killed Min Saw U and took the city. It was given as a fief to the son of Pakhan Tayaphya, even though he had also been an opponent of Mohnyin. Thus, for the first time since Mohnyin ascended the throne in 1426, Toungoo and Taungdwin were finally under Ava. That left only Yamethin and Pinle, both surrounded by Ava and its allies. This whole incident suggests, incidentally, that even without a king, the court continued to function with able ministers.

After the most immediate problems had been resolved, and the most defiant regions of the kingdom were now under Ava, the ministers gathered and discussed who should be nominated as king, revealing a process we seldom hear about regarding the Burmese monarchy. The following is a paraphrase of the deliberations as recorded by U Kala. The ministers said, the younger son of the king, Thihathuya (or Thihathu), is in Pyi; his son-in-law, Thihapate, is still fighting in Mogaung. We should not remain long without our king. So they decided to ask Thihapate (who was lord of Mohnyin) to be king. But he refused, saying, "I am neither the younger brother nor the son of the king.[45] I also do not have a desire to reign. Let us support our lord's younger son, Thihathu, lord of Pyi and make him king." The ministers agreed to this suggestion, and with a mighty entourage of cavalry, elephants, war boats, and soldiers descended the river to Pyi. Upon reaching it, they offered the crown to Thihathu, who accepted, made his brother-in-law lord of Pyi, and ascended the river to Ava with his mighty host. (It is likely that the reason the ministers did not consider him initially was their desire to keep control of power at court, knowing that Thihathu was a stronger leader than Thihapate.)

Thihathu formally ascended the throne in *sakkaraj* 803 (1441) according to the *Zatatawpon* (1442, according to U Kala[46] and the inscriptions).[47] His regnal name in the chronicles is "Narapati the Great." Ever since Mohnyin's ascension in 1426, Ava's authority had been slowly expanding. However, it had not completely subdued the rebellious regions. It was under Narapati that the Kingdom of Ava finally reached its apogee, especially after capturing the grandson of Tho Khin Bwa, known as Tho Ngan Bwa, "Lord of the nine levels, the great King of Mo [Maw], who is lord of twenty one umbrellas" (that is, twenty-one *sawbwa*-ships, called *maing*), each of which was named.[48]

Even before then, an inscription of 1440 used, perhaps for the first time, the term *amyo tha* (sons of the race, or countrymen) as a reference to the people in the Kingdom of Ava.[49] Although it was likely a reference mainly to the dominant Burmese speakers in his kingdom (the Myanma), the context also suggests that it included many who were not originally born Burmese speakers, but belonged to other ethno-linguistic groups, who had become "citizens" of the kingdom. Thus, Ava once again began to resemble not only its earlier years under Minkyiswa Sawkai and Mingaung the First, but went well beyond that period to become, in essence, a miniature Pagan during Narapati's reign and subsequently, until Ava was conquered in 1526–1527.

5

The Fifteenth Century and the Apogee of Ava

At least three exceptional leaders had consolidated the kingdom of Ava during the first half of the fifteenth century; three more extraordinary kings succeeded them to take Ava to even greater heights during the rest of the century. Indeed, it was during the second half of the fifteenth century that Ava made its greatest contribution to the country, especially in terms of Burmese literature; its achievements were rarely again equaled. But since that subject requires a treatment of its own, it is discussed in chapter 8 as part of Ava's legacy to the country's history. The present chapter describes and analyzes the reigns of these last three kings of the fifteenth century—Narapati the Great, Mahathihathuya, and Mingaung the Second, best representing the leadership of the Ava kingdom at its apogee. That zenith is characterized largely in terms of political integration, military prowess, social order, religious stature, economic self-sufficiency, and overall well-being of the state. Although much of the fifteenth century can be regarded as the height of the Ava Dynasty and period (see figure 3), the second half of that century particularly stood out.

Narapati the Great

Known as "Narapati the Great, donor of the Htupayon Pagoda," two long inscriptions of his, dated to 1442 and 1444, described his ascension in 1442.[1] It fell on the day after the full moon of Kason (corresponding to May), Friday, when the twenty-six Nakkha (lunar mansions) were aligned. There, he was anointed with his formal and complete title: Siri Tri Bhavanadityapavara Narapati Mahadhammarajadhirajadhipati. His chief (and southern) queen was titled Atula Siri Mahadhammadevi, while his senior son was appointed crown prince with the title Mahathihathuya, which included, ex officio, the position of commander of the armed forces, as in the Pagan period. But probably for the first time, instead of the usual Burmese term *Einshemin* for the heir apparent, the Pali term *Uparaja* was used on the appropriate medium for such declarations: stone. The chronicles, however, preserving local tradition, preferred (and therefore continued) to use the Burmese term *Einshemin* on palm leaf.

According to the above sources, by the time Narapati ascended the throne, his brother-in-law Thihapate (who had refused the crown earlier, as he was neither son nor brother of the deceased king) had already conquered Mogaung far in the north, above the twenty-fifth parallel, a few miles southwest of today's Myitkyina. With great pomp and ceremony, Thihapate brought back down to

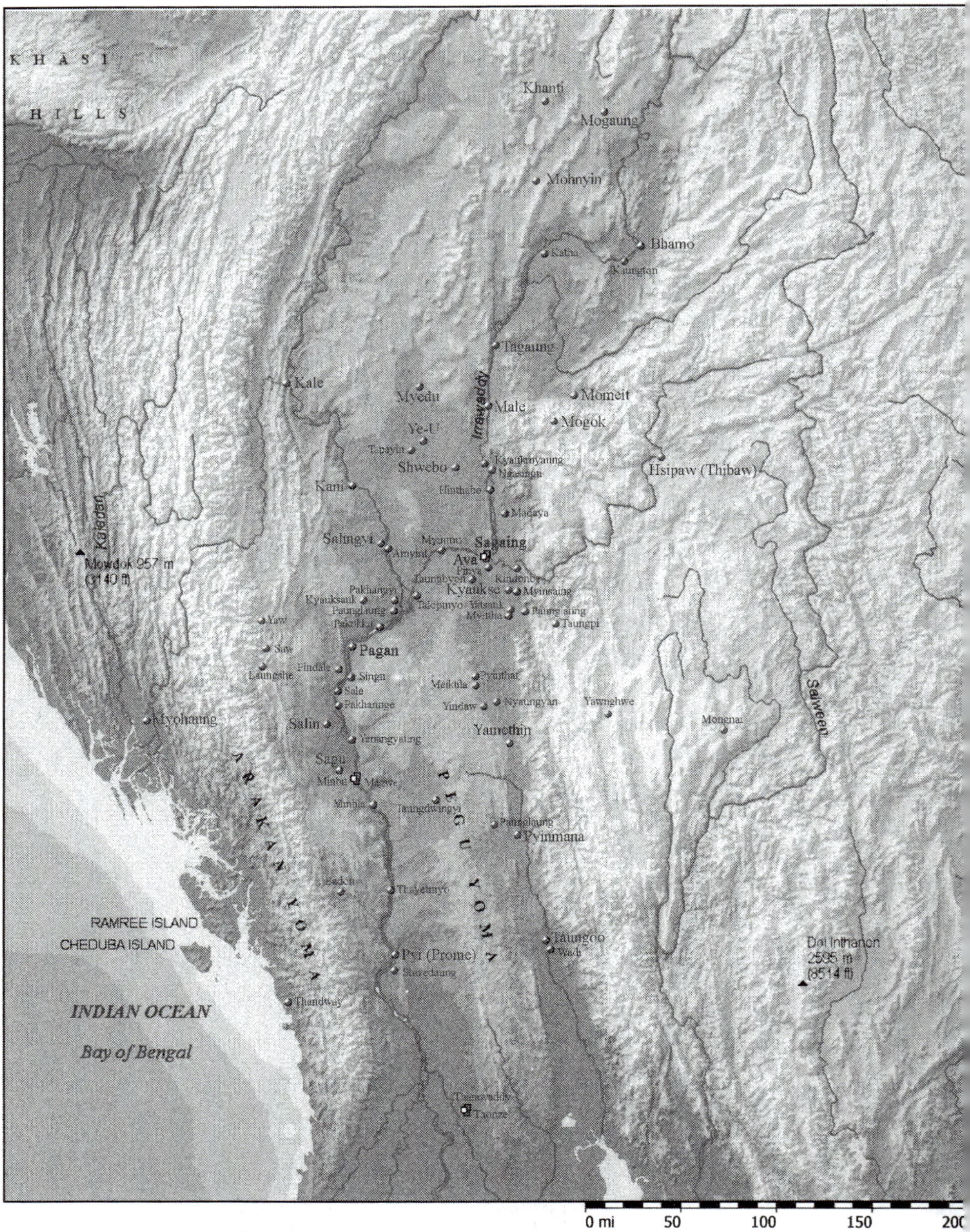

Figure 3. Kingdom of Ava at its height

Ava its chief, Tho Ngan Bwa, head of the Maw Shan, along with his sons, wives, and the *myosa* of a nearby city, to pay respects to Narapati at his ascension and to retain them as hostages at the capital. This event is confirmed by the 1442 inscription noted above.[2]

Another son of the king was made governor of Salin, an important city south of Ava, while a younger one was made lord of Taungdwin, also south of Ava and west of the present capital of Naypyidaw. One of the king's daughters by the chief queen enjoyed Pinya as fief while the brothers of the chief queen were made *myosa* of select towns in the Minbu irrigated region. The chief queen's genealogy and descendants commanded two whole pages in U Kala.[3] Much of this information is confirmed by the long inscription of 1442 mentioned above.[4] The chief queen's brothers were also rewarded with fiefs: Tharawaddy, a place called Taungphet (south, or mountain side), and Sagu.[5]

The year following the building of the Htupayon Pagoda, whose long inscription of 1444 reveals much about state and society at Ava, Narapati subdued two more *sawbwa,* who, with presents, offered themselves "to the royal feet." In return, he bestowed them with many favors and rewards. In an inscription of 1446, the king stated that he gave the responsibility of running the kingdom to the crown prince,[6] which U Kala qualified, saying the crown prince was left to guard the capital while the king himself roamed up and down the river with his royal barge to receive tribute and oaths of loyalty from specific lords, such as the "eater" of Thonze, a Shan chieftain by the name of Tho Khin Bwa.[7] At the same time, Ava also managed to obtain allegiance from two other important centers in Upper Myanmar not secured earlier: Yamethin and Pinle. The former's *myosa* came with his wives and sons to Ava to demonstrate his loyalty, and after the oath was taken, Yamethin was given back to him as his fief.

Pinle was more problematic. It was one of the original "Eleven Khayaing" of Pagan days and well defended, surrounded by high brick walls, and could not be taken by force, so a siege had to be laid. (U Kala's narrative suggests it was eventually taken.) It was also during Narapati's reign that the *sawbwa* of Onbaung "came with presents and offered them at the royal feet." In Lower Myanmar, Bannya Ram had died, and Shin Saw Bu's son, Bannya Baru, had ascended the throne, for which Narapati's endorsement was requested (and given). An inscription of Ava actually confirmed this event, stating that Narapati attended the funeral of "the [previous] Tanluin king."[8] Narapati's 1444 inscription also confirmed Ayuthaya's hold on Tenasserim, which Ava did not contest.[9]

By 1448, Narapati's power was described as exceeding those of all the "thrones that had prospered at Arimaddana, Punnagama, Jeyyapura, Pran, Panya, and Awa-Cackuin," claiming that his rule extended to all the regions of the *naingnan* (dominion, at the time, now nation) as far north as Mohnyin and as far northwest as Kale, as far west as Yakhaing and Thindwe (Arakan and Sandaway), and as far south as Pathein and Myaungmya. Even the "great king of Maw," it claimed, became a subject of Narapati. Hamsavati (Pegu) was conspicuously not on the list.[10]

But Ava's political and military growth had other unintended consequences. Perhaps it was getting too powerful for its own good, for a 1448 inscription noted that the Tayok (the [Ming] Chinese) invaded Myanmar with five hundred thousand soldiers.[11] The inscription stated that Tayok soldiers under the command of General Hsin Thwe invaded, and, "due to their foolish pride, touched the domain of [General Anantasuriya] . . . [whose inscription this was]. He claimed to have killed . . . [hundreds of thousands] of generals beginning with General Hsin Thwe."[12]

U Kala confirms the attack by the Ming (commanding three and a half printed pages in his history), but qualifies it by stating that the Chinese, led by four generals (whose individual names he also cites) came with three hundred thousand soldiers. The heir apparent was recalled from Pinle, defenses for Ava were prepared and, with Minister Bhayakamani, were ordered to hold the capital. The king took five hundred elephantry, eight thousand cavalry, and two hundred thousand infantry, organizing them in twelve battalions, and waited at a site called Mandalay.[13] The Chinese, then camped at Maingmaw in the Shan States, asked why, as in the time of Anawrahta (four hundred years ago!), tribute had not been forthcoming? Narapati replied that "since the building of Ava, in no reign was this request ever made. Only now have I heard this talk." After the Chinese ambassador returned to Maingmaw and relayed Narapati's response, the Chinese generals marched to Bamo and built a bridge on the Irrawaddy. The *sawbwa* of Mogaung, Kaungton, and Mone all supported Narapati against the Ming.

As it turns out, the Chinese really wanted one particular Shan chieftain, Tho Ngan Bwa, whom Narapati had captured a decade earlier, and with whose people the Chinese had been fighting, apparently without any results. The preoccupation of the Shan with the Chinese may also explain why Ava could take and keep northern Myanmar and most of the *sawbwa* under its sway relatively easily. Tho Ngan Bwa's confinement at Ava as hostage to keep the loyalty of the other *sawbwa* may also explain why they joined Ava against the Ming so readily. In any case, some curious bargaining reminiscent of the negotiations with the Mongols in 1301 ensued. But before Tho Ngan Bwa could be given up, he allegedly took poison and died. Narapati wrapped his body splendidly and sent it to the Chinese. However, according to U Kala, they gutted, impaled, and roasted him over a fire, spread him out to dry, then took back the remains.[14]

The following year the Ming appeared again in force and built a bridge across the Irrawaddy at a point from where they prepared to attack Mogaung and Mohnyin. They were met by the two *sawbwa* brothers of Mogaung, who defeated them and got the city of Nattaung in the process. When the news arrived in Ava, Narapati rewarded the brothers with ten thousand *kyat* of royal silver. Fortunately for Narapati, the *sawbwa* were successful, for while the north was occupied, Thindwe (in Arakan) had taken advantage of the situation and was being "disrespectful." So Ava marched and took it, giving it as fief to a minister, along with the usual garrisoned troops. Also luckily for Narapati, Lower Myanmar during these years was having internal problems. Its king, Bannya

Baru, had been killed by relatives in a struggle for the throne. But an impasse at court had caused the ministers of Pegu to once again request aid from Narapati to support Bannya Kyam as the new king. Narapati sent down a force that successfully backed the former's claim to the throne. Bannya Kyam, wrote U Kala, "sent many presents" to Ava for its support.[15] Thus, the north, the west, and now the south were under either the control or influence of Ava.

The relationship with most of the Shan *sawbwa,* although in Ava's favor generally, oscillated from time to time. In 1450, when Thihapate, lord of Mohnyin and brother-in-law of the king, died, the Uti (the usual term for the governor of Yunnan), along with the two *sawbwa* brothers of Mogaung who had earlier helped Ava, Tho Kyi Bwa and Tho Pauk Bwa, decided to rebel. When Narapati heard of that, he sent his son and heir apparent to head seven battalions and himself marched on Mohnyin. He destroyed the forces led by the Uti and captured him, who was holding hostage the sons and wives of the *sawbwa* brothers. The latter went to meet Narapati to explain that the Uti had come to Mogaung and demanded military help, which they had refused. But when they were absent, their wives and sons had been taken. Narapati made them swear an oath of allegiance, gave Mohnyin to Tho Pauk Bwa's son to govern, and released them. The following year, Narapati sent his son and heir north to Kaungton to test the loyalty of Tho Pauk Bwa's son and collect Ava's share of the taxes of Mohnyin. He was well received and also obtained three hundred *viss* of good silver.[16]

In Pegu, Bannya Kyam, whose ascension Narapati had endorsed previously, had died. His successor also needed and requested Narapati's support, which was given. But within the year, the new king had also died, at which time, the ministers and officers raised Shin Saw Bu as sovereign with the title of Bannya Thau at age fifty-three, approximately between 1451 and 1453 AD. It was the first time in the country's history that a woman had become sovereign.

In the western part of the country, the king (Bayin) of Arakan, Ali Khan, "desiring to be friends with" and to meet Narapati, sent an ambassador to Ava. Narapati convened his council to discuss the matter. Again, the old minister Yazathingyan's advice was conciliatory; he stated that it was in Ava's interest to be on good terms with Arakan, as it had many knowledgeable ministers and officers with many good elephants, horses, and troops.

The results of the detente are interesting, for the situation again raises important questions in Myanmar and Southeast Asian studies about indigenous concepts of territory and political boundaries. After meeting at a place called Bo Khaung Nwe Daw with the usual protocols, the two kings swore an oath on which to agree, and marked the respective territories of the two kingdoms. That demarcation, according to U Kala, was the following: "The Kingdom of Ratanapura [Ava] lies to the east of the spine [that is, ridge] of the Bo Khaung Mountain; the Kingdom of Dhannyawadi [Arakan] lies to the west of the spine of the Bo Khaung Mountain."[17] After demarcating their respective territories, with their entourages, they returned home.

Although the actual demarcation of these boundaries were general and vague ("east" and "west of the spine"), the *principle* of sovereign, political boundaries that belonged to a particular kingdom and not to another, was quite clear, demonstrating that even at that time, or at least when U Kala wrote, so-called Western conceptions of boundaries and territories, said to be unfamiliar in Southeast Asia, were already practiced, although obviously not according to precisely calculated latitudes and longitudes. In fact, even abstract notions regarding "air space" and "underground space" that are also part of Western notions of boundaries can be found—but mainly with regard to religious property. When marking the boundaries of ordination halls, for example, all roots "transgressing" the boundary underneath it were cut, while all branches "transgressing" the "air space" overhead the boundary were also cut. Thus, conceptions of planes above and below surface boundaries were not only understood but applied. Such sacred space, of course, had to be more precise and important than broader geopolitical space.

The *sangha* during Narapati's reign also appears to have been fairly well integrated with the state. His primate, Pitu Sangharaja, was referred to in an inscription of 1516 as *sasana asyan sangharaja,* "lord of the *sasana,*" that is, supreme patriarch of the religion. Under him were subordinate *sangharaja* (lords of the *sangha*) such as Pinya Hsinga Sangharaja and Pagan Hsin Phyu Shin Sangharaja, presumably with religious jurisdiction over the major cities of Pinya and Pagan. It appears that each of the important secular fiefs held by royal governors had its ecclesiastical counterparts. Indeed, these *sangharaja* were also said to "ascend golden monasteries," the same terms used for kings when they ascended the throne called "the golden mountain." None of this is meant to imply that "forest-dwelling" monks did not exist or were unimportant. They were also patronized, particularly one belonging to the descendants of the famous Mahakassapa of Pagan, who was honored with a white umbrella called the Kanakkatan, as insignia of prestige and rank, whose followers were referred to as *arannawasi taw klon* monks (forest monastery dwelling monks) associated not with degeneracy but with purity in their asceticism.

Without sending a religious mission to Sri Lanka, traditionally believed in Myanmar to be the source of orthodox Theravada Buddhism, Narapati's reign would not have been completely legitimate. In 1455, therefore, he sent two high ministers with many gold and silver valuables to make offerings to Sri Lanka's tooth relic. They were given two hundred *kyat* (?) of silver by the king for building a rest house and a tiered edifice. After giving the presents to the king of Sri Lanka and making the offerings to the glorious tooth relic, "at the harbor called Valikarama, in the village called Girima, after the tiered edifice was built, so that the *sangha*'s needs were met during their renunciation at the rest house, land was bought from the Sri Lankan king whose produce and revenue were allocated to the feeding of the monks."

Narapati was also fortunate that, during his reign, Min Nge Kyaw Htin, lord of Pinya (and recently with control over Toungoo), who had resisted Ava's domination throughout his political life, died in 1458 when killed by one of his own subjects. That left the door open for Narapati to give Toungoo to his brother-in-law, Thiyi Zeyathuya, lord of Taungdwin, who as a result enjoyed both fiefs. In return, the younger daughter of Min Nge Kyaw Htin was brought to Ava and married to the son of the lord of Pyi. In the same year, the *sawbwa* of Kale came to Ava to pay homage and swear an oath of allegiance.

When the Onbaung *sawbwa* died that same year (1458), the decision to make his son lord of Onbaung was not supported by its ministers. The *sawbwas* of Yauk Hsauk and Htaw Hmaing (located relatively close to Ava) were also "not of the same mind" about the new successor of Onbaung. The son therefore requested Narapati's support. The king sent a force of four hundred war elephantry, six thousand cavalry, and eighteen thousand infantry as military support. When they got to Yaunk Hsauk, they were joined by a combined force from Mone, Nyaung Shwe, and Nyaung Mun, so that there was no more resistance to the appointment of the son of the departed lord as *myosa* of Onbaung. This act once again confirms Ava's influence and power as the dominant center, as the Shan *sawbwa* looked to Narapati to settle their differences.[18] It also showed how the center's political will was implemented in areas quite distant from it.

Narapati also conducted some reorganization and shuffling of fiefs, strengthening his position even further. He gave his brother-in-law, Minye Kyawswa and lord of Tharawaddy, the fief of Paungtin Myo, while Tharawaddy was given to his son, along with the title Thado Min Saw. Narapati's old minister Yazathingyan, who had also been his father's adviser, was given Bagyi Hse Taik (a Pagan period fief), along with ten war boats and the splendidly walled town of Amyint. Sagaing, also extremely important, was given to his nephew, Min Hpyu, along with ten other northern towns. And to his younger brother-in-law, Athinkhaya, went Sagu. All these were strategic urban areas. Then something happened at Toungoo in 1466, for, said the chronicle, the king no longer believed his uncle, the *myosa* of Toungoo, so he withdrew the appointment and gave it instead to Lek Mya Zeya Thingyan.

By midcentury, then, the Kingdom of Ava controlled and/or had hegemony over much of the most important and populated regions and urban areas of Upper Myanmar. To reiterate, in terms of economic, political, and military power, administrative and social stability, religious stature at home and abroad, and relations with external neighbors, Ava during Narapati's reign probably reached a pinnacle that was not again reached during the remainder of the kingdom's life. Upper Myanmar in the mid-fifteenth century once more began to resemble Pagan of the eleventh and twelfth centuries, not only in terms of structure but nearly also in terms of the territory controlled and/or under its hegemony.

For all his accomplishments, Narapati left the throne in a most unbecoming manner. His grandson, named Thado Kyaw, son of the heir apparent, was having a love affair with the daughter of the king's aunt, who held Sagaing as fief. The aunt told the chief queen about it, and she and the king were extremely angry with the grandson, so "grounded" the young woman to the palace. Thado Kyaw had told his grandparents many times that he would marry her. But before the marriage, he would sneak into the palace at night, about which the king knew. And when the king caught him at it, he beat the grandson thoroughly.

Hurt, Thado Kyaw and his three hundred retainers set fire to his father's (the heir's) residence. When the fire was well along, they rushed into the palace and hacked Narapati with swords, but did not kill him. Wounded, the king managed to escape with his queen to the docks, where Yazathingyan, who was on his way over when he saw the fire and heard the commotion, told him not to worry, he would capture Thado Kyaw and kill him. Narapati said, "I will not stay here. Please take me to Pyi to my middle son."[19] So Yazathingyan, recorded the chronicle, in 1468, on the twelfth waxing day of the month of Waso, took the king from Ava to Pyi.

Jealous of Yazathingyan and his son's reputation, the lord of Pyi challenged the son to a duel, which ended with both father and son fleeing back to Ava. There, the eldest son of the king, the heir apparent, saying he would support his parents, descended the river with his troops and two other sons of the king. When they arrived, they left their weapons and, wearing clean white clothes, worshiped together at the Hsandawshin pagoda. The king swore an oath of allegiance with them, after which all five ate together. When asked by the heir to return to Ava and take the throne, Narapati told him he was not returning to Ava, just ensure that only the heir apparent with the ten laws of kings become king. He then gave each of his sons a ring. After paying homage and showing respect to his parents, the heir apparent returned to Ava by land and water.

According to an inscription, on the fifth waxing day of the month of Wagaung (Sunday, July 24), in 1468, Narapati the Great "ascended to the abode of the nats,"[20] apparently from the wounds inflicted by his grandson. (The *Zatatawpon* put the event at 1467.)[21] His son enshrined the "bodily relics" of his father in a Zedi,[22] an act technically reserved only for *cakkavatti* and *arahat*, once again raising the issue of "funerary temples" in early Southeast Asian studies.

Narapati's major works of merit included a temple-monastery complex that had at least nine satellite religious edifices attached to it, spread all over the major cities of his kingdom, the most famous being the Htupayon, which still draws many pilgrims today. In terms of secular constructions of importance, in 1444 or 1456, Narapati built a bridge across the Irrawaddy from Ava to the Sagaing side, something apparently never done before or since, until the British built one in the twentieth century. His inscription commemorating the event stated, "A big bridge strong enough to let the four forces of the army pass was made across the river called Erawati."[23] U Kala confirmed the inscription, saying that in the Sagaing district where the king built the Htupayon Pagoda, Narapati built a bridge on the Irrawaddy River where the fourfold army, along with many people and monks, could cross.[24] It must have been a pontoon bridge, as excavations so far have revealed no permanent foundations for it.

Mahathihathuya

When the heir apparent and senior son of the Chief Queen Atula Siri Mahadhammadevi reached Ava from his fief, he consulted with the wise men versed in the *Vẹdas,* and in 1468 (1467 according to the *Zatatawpon*), took over the golden umbrella and golden throne. He assumed the title of Bayin Mahathihathuya. His chief queen received the *abhiseka* as Amitta Siri Mahadhammadevi. The eldest son Nawyahta was also given the title of Mahathihathuya and placed in the Front [East] Palace as heir, with important Dipeyin as his fief.[25] Appointing him heir apparent, of course, immediately cut off the lineage of Narapati's younger brother, lord of Pyi, from the throne, once again generating the uncle-nephew struggle so common in the history of the Myanmar monarchy.

The king's middle son, Thado Kyaw, the one who had set the palace on fire and hacked his grandfather, was given the title of Thado Dhammaraja and married to the young woman with whom he had been intimate. He was given the fief of Salin with its eleven cities as fief, perhaps to keep him busy, so that he would not have similar designs on his father. The youngest son was given the title of Siri Dhammasoka and married to the younger sister of his elder brother (Thado's) wife. His fief was Myedu, although he was later given other fiefs with additional titles. The king's eldest daughter was given in marriage to the son of the younger brother of Mohnyin Min Taya (her grand-uncle and previous king). She was also given Myedu (perhaps after her elder brother received other fiefs) and a place called Paukthit.

The queen mother, Atula Siri Maharaja Devi, wife of deceased king Narapati, said she would not bow down to Ava (and her own son) and sent the message to the lord of Toungoo, Letya Zeyathinkyan, who, like the queen, also belonged to the older generation of rulers. Angered by his mother's action, Mahathihathuya, sent a large force to Toungoo. The lord of Toungoo requested help from the Mon sovereign, Shin Saw Bu, who halfheartedly sent a force to Toungoo. It was defeated, with many killed and many elephants and men taken by Ava. The lord of Toungoo then pleaded for his life, which was granted by the king, but gave Toungoo to the *myosa* of Nyaung Yan, Sithu Kyaw Htin, giving the former a militarily insignificant fief. Soon thereafter, in 1470, Shin Saw Bu died. She was followed by the famous monk Dhammazedi, who had been her minister, ascending the throne of Pegu. (Their stories follow in part 2.)

The next year, the family and clients of the lord of Pyi, uncle of the king whose path to the throne was eliminated with the appointment of the king's son as heir, had some rude words for Ava. The king put a stop to it with pleasant and happy words, said U Kala. After the crisis was over, the king, with his queen mother and all his uncles and aunts, worshiped at the temple of the hair relic (at Pyi), reciting the verses dealing with suffering. After regilding the temple and making various other donations in Pyi, and paying respectful homage to his mother, the entourage returned to Ava. Other public acts of largesse were heaped upon the religion by various members of the royal family, including pilgrimages to and donations in Sri Lanka by two of the queens, who took as presents for its king Chinese cloth of wool and musk. One of the high points of religious and diplomatic relations with Sri Lanka must have been the return visit of the king of Sri Lanka to Ava in the same year, 1473, who was received with a great deal of ceremony.[26]

In 1475, the *sawbwa* of Onbaung requested help from Ava because the *myosa* of Nyaungshwe and Yauk Hhsauk were being "disobedient." The heir apparent and his younger brother were sent with seven battalions, which were combined with the forces of the Onbaung *sawbwa*. They marched and attacked Yauk Hsauk and Nyaungshwe. All three cities (including Nyaungshwe) were taken, along with the *sawbwa*, their sons and wives, elephants, horses, and soldiers. The *sawbwa* were made to swear oaths of allegiance and the three were placed under the single authority of the Onbaung *sawbwa*, who sent many presents and gifts for Ava's help.

The next year, the Shan requested Ava's help again. This time, the *sawbwa* of Mohnyin was fighting the *sawbwa* of Mogaung, and since they were both considered *myosa* under Ava, each requested aid from Ava. The king sailed upriver with his navy on his golden barge, while the forces under the command of his youngest son marched by land. He stopped at Katha port with his navy, where he presumably met the land forces, thence marched to Mohnyin. Neither *myosa* dared oppose him and both received him respectfully with the usual presents and protocol. The king then removed the Mohnyin *sawbwa* from Mohnyin and gave him Tagaung instead, while Mohnyin was given to the younger brother of the Mogaung *sawbwa*, after which the king returned to Ava. These events and several others like them during this period make clear that ethnicity was less of a factor, with Shan fighting other Shan and requesting help from the Burmese king, than were geopolitical concerns.

The relations with Lower Myanmar were also cordial, partly because Dhammazedi, who succeeded Shin Saw Bu, was a strong king who had been a monk of repute at Ava and knew how to publicly and intelligently deal with the deleterious economic consequences of religious donations that continuously drained revenues from the state. The congenial relations with Ava, however, had a curious story that sounds like a variation on the *asvamedha* theme, particularly since U Kala wrote that he had gotten the story from the *Hanthawaddy Ayedawpon* (literally, The Royal Crisis Account of Hanthawaddy).

In this story, the younger brother of Dhammazedi was given the title Samin Param and given the city of Sittaung, northeast of Pegu on the Sittaung River, protecting Pegu's northern flank from invasion down the Sittaung Valley. He promised Dhammazedi that he would march up to the China border with only fourteen thousand soldiers and erect iron boundary posts (*mye khya than taing*) demarcating Pegu's territory. But on his way up, he marched only through the jungles and therefore met no resistance until he reached the border town of Khanti, where he erected an iron boundary post, an act to which the *myosa* of Khanti dared not object. But when the Utibwa (the governor of Yunnan) heard of this, he marched with his troops and started removing the boundary markers. Samin Param, after having erected these iron posts, boasted of the feat, and returned.

When King Mahathihathuya realized the deception, he attacked Samin Param's forces. They were defeated and Samin Param was captured, becoming a vassal of the king of Ava. The Chinese governor sent one of his ministers with ten thousand cavalry, demanding the "usual" tribute of gold and silver vases (?) that Pagan, since King Aniruddha's time, had given to China, and which the present king's predecessor also gave. Here, the narrative returns to an almost identical story found earlier when a similar confrontation occurred with the Chinese.

The Ava king said no such tribute was given during his father's reign and that Ava owed nothing. When this message was delivered to the Chinese general, he replied that a great battle would take place. However, it could be decided by champions on horseback to avoid killing many people. "If we win, you have to make good on our demand; if you win, we will leave," said the Chinese general.

The king called together his heir apparent and his ministers and officers. The heir said that the Chinese are very good on horseback and would probably win; they could not compete with whoever was named. Only someone experienced in aggressive riding would be suitable. "Let us inquire of the captured Mon, Samin Param, if he is willing." The latter, when asked, replied that there was no one on or outside of Jambudipa of whom he was afraid with regard to battle on elephant, horse, or foot. "Just allow me to choose the horse I like. I will bear the royal burden favorably."

Of more than two hundred horses belonging to ministers and officers that were shown, he did not like any. Then, as he circled the entire city still looking, he saw one red horse near the moat that belonged to a widow who had let it roam free since she did not dare ride it. He said he must capture and ride that red horse. The ministers said this horse bites and no one dares capture him. Samin Param captured and managed to ride the horse until it was exhausted, and said he would like to ride him for a week more. "Which day do you want me to fight on horseback," he asked? King Mahathihathuya, with gratitude, said that if he won over the Chinese, Salon Kyaw Khaung (its champion), together with the rank and colors of the ministers and officers, under the feet of the king, along with all the trappings, he would give Arakan to him.

When the appointed day arrived, the king gave Samin Param his personal sword, studded with rubies, and armor covered with gold, and made other arrangements. Bowing three times to the king, Samin Param went out to the battlefield with a person who spoke Chinese. The Chinese champion, holding a spear that weighed three *viss* (around ten pounds), came out from among the troops. When Samin Param saw him, he said "Elder brother is a champion. I am also a champion. Let us ride the horses three times then begin the battle." Having done that, the Chinese champion showed the palm of his hands to signal the beginning of battle. Samin Param, after having said "Let's do battle," let his horse go. When they got close, Salon Kyaw Khaung, holding a sword whose blade was one hand's breadth wide, raised it to strike. Samin Param saw that there were breaks in his opponent's iron mail and pierced him with his lance. After Salon Kyaw Khaung fell from his horse, Samin Param took his head and rode back into the city.

Everyone—people, monks—praised him and were in high spirits. The king, extremely satisfied, said that "during the reign of Bayin Mingaung, the son-in-law of Yazadarit (also) called Samin Param, fought in single combat on horseback. At that time, when he took the Chinese champion Kamani's head,

I heard about it, but did not see it. Only now, am I able to see Samin Param the champion take the head of Salon Kyaw Khaung. I will make you a noble. If you desire to return to Hamsavati, I will send you there in my barge." Samin Param replied that "he has many sons and daughters; only if you show compassion and release me will I be able to see the faces of my children." The king, filling a boat with all the colors and trappings, sent Samin Param to Pegu. When he arrived there, King Dhammazedi was pleased and rewarded those who had brought him and sent back to King Mahathihathuya many diverse cloths and books.

At first glance, one might suspect that U Kala had repeated one event as two different ones. But in both Mingaung's reign and Mahathihathuya's reign, the contemporary sources on stone claimed two intrusions by the troops of the Chinese Utibwa, which they claimed were defeated. Moreover, the names for both Chinese champions were different, and U Kala explicitly named the most recent Ava champion, "Samin Param the Second,"[27] so clearly knew the difference between the two events.

As noted, for those of us living in the twenty-first century, single combat by champions deciding the fate of nations seems to be a bit too romantic to take seriously. But given the numerous times that this kind of contest is said to have actually happened and been documented in original sources, not only in Asia but elsewhere, and given the shortage of labor in general, and economic value of trained soldiers in Southeast Asia, along with the esteem with which individual military skills were regarded in societies where warriors are honored, I see no good reason presently to dismiss either story as total fabrication. Embellishment and mythologizing there probably was, although not necessarily by U Kala, who seemed to have been faithful to his sources, but perhaps by those whose records he used.

According to the *Zatatawpon,* King Mahathihathuya died after reigning twelve years, at the age of fifty-four in 1479 (U Kala does not give the date).[28] He was said to have built nine works of merit throughout the kingdom, and donated many glebe lands for their upkeep. Before he died, while still ill, he called the lord of Toungoo, Sithu Kyaw Htin and said, "If my sons are disobedient, help out the eldest son and discipline the others. If, however, the middle and youngest sons are obedient, but the eldest and heir apparent does not heed my orders and suppress them, help out the other two." With that he died. And when he ascended the abode of the *nat,* the lord of Toungoo, saying he would carry the (cremated) bones of his lord and cast them in the water, took them on the golden barge and carried out the rites, a custom that the *Yazawinthit* attributes to the Mon. That the lord of Toungoo was selected to keep a guardianship over the king's sons reveals the personal trust the king had for his abilities, and most likely, the military strength and political influence he had.

Dutiya Mingaung (Mingaung the Second)

According to U Kala, in 1480 the eldest son of Mahathihathuya, the crown prince, became king with the title Siri Sudhammarajadhipati, popularly known as Dutiya Mingaung (Mingaung the Second). The *Zatatawpon* gives 1479 as the date of his ascension. An inscription mentions this king (sometimes also called Anawrahta Mingaung) in 1482 but does not give his ascension date.[29] His chief queen was crowned with the title of Atula Siri Dhamma Devi, a title once held by the king's grandmother.

Even though the eldest son of the new king was only seven years old, he was given the title of Mahathihathuya and placed in the Front Palace as heir apparent. This, as usual, immediately prevented the brothers of the deceased king (uncles of the new king) and their sons, as well as the new king's younger brothers, from inheriting the throne, unless they took it by force. However, because after a few generations there would be so many eligible princes in the pool of candidates, officially appointing one's eldest son as heir apparent was probably a more prudent option for any new king than leaving the position of heir open, and therefore "up for grabs." Dutiya Mingaung also appointed the lord of Toungoo, Agga Maha Senapati (commander in chief) of the entire state.

The first rebellion against the new king was begun by his younger brothers who had been cut off from the throne. In 1481, the *myosa* of "Salin Ten Cities," the middle brother of the present king (the one who set fire to the palace and chased his grandfather Narapati out of Ava), along with the "eater" of Yamethin and the "Five-Canal Khayaing," and also the youngest brother, Minye Kyawswa, all rebelled. When Sithu Kyaw Htin, the commander in chief whose fief was at Toungoo, heard of this, he sent word to them that this was not in keeping with their (late) father's order, and that he was going to send "long-life" Yazathingyan with cavalry and elephantry. He also moved on Yamethin from Toungoo with his own forces to quell the rebellion.[30]

Not waiting for the forces from Ava that were led by Yazathingyan, Sithu Kyaw Htin arrived at Yamethin earlier. Seeing this, Minye Kyawswa moved out of the city and met Sithu Kyaw Htin, who defeated Minye Kyawswa, but apparently did not capture him. When the Ava troops reached Yamethin, Minye had no strength left to meet them outside, so defended from within the city. Because the city had guns and cannon, noted the chronicle, Yazathingyan "did not dare" come close but remained at a distance. After two months, they were recalled and returned to Ava. When Sithu Kyaw Htin died (it was not explained how it happened), Toungoo was given to his son, Sithu Nge (Sithu the Younger, or Young Sithu).

In 1482, when the uncle of the king and lord of Pyi died, a younger uncle by the name of Thado Min Saw made himself lord (*min*), came upriver as far as Magwe with his troops, and "touched the royal dominions." Because he was not formally appointed by Ava and had usurped the position, his "touching" Magwe was regarded as a challenge to Ava's authority. When Dutiya Mingaung heard of it, he consulted with his ministers and officers, listened to their counsel, selected a number of cavalry, elephantry, and infantry from the "Downriver Fifteenth Battalion," and chose Mingyi Theingathu as commander to descend by land and water. When they reach a place called Manun, they made camp. Thado Min Saw also made camp, and for a month they remained that way without attacking each other. Having cooled down, "they sent each other presents and the king returned to Naypyidaw" (literally, the royal city of the sun, but also translatable as royal abode, or capital).

The next year, the *myosa* of "Salin Ten Cities," held by the younger brother of the king, died. His seconds came to the king and requested that the king take back all the elephants, horses, and soldiers of the deceased. Dutiya Mingaung, riding on the Golden Barge followed by all his troops, went to Salin. The eldest daughter of his deceased brother and another who had received a title as "royal poetess," also urged the king to confiscate his younger brother's fief. The king raised the two women in the palace as if they were his own daughters, while giving Salin to another relative with the tile of Thiri Zeyya Noyahta. That same year, the old minister Yazathingyan was given Myedu, an important garrisoned town in the Mu Valley, together with its forces.

By 1484, the intransigent younger brother of the king, Minye Kyawswa, lord of Yamethin, said he would attack Nyaung Yan city and Yemet, for the latter had begun to shore up its defenses, a "sure sign of rebellion." But before Minye reached Nyaung Yan, the king sent a royal order to Bhaya Kyaw Htin, another *myosa* nearby, to attack Nyaung Yan, while he himself marched rapidly to the same objective. As Bhaya Kyaw Htin was successful in taking the city, all its human and material resources were given to him by the king, who then returned to his capital.

It appears that the king was out to prevent his younger brother from obtaining any more men and materiel, since the real competition for the throne after the king dies would normally lie between this younger brother and the king's very young son (only twelve years old at this time) already appointed heir. But in a system like Ava's, there was always a refuge for those who got into trouble with the center. Minister Caturanga, whose title reveals his military portfolio, in the very next year, 1485, was "disobedient" and had to flee. Where did he go but to the fief of the king's younger brother, where he was sheltered. Dutiya Mingaung marched on Yamethin and tried several times to take the city, but because it was defended with guns and cannon, he could not and had to lay siege instead. But, typically, the siege was lifted after three months, when the rains came. Ava's troops returned to the capital.

While this was going on, in Toungoo, its *myosa*, Sithu Nge, was overthrown by the king's nephew, Minkyinyo, who made himself lord of Toungoo. This is the first time the important name of Minkyinyo appears; he was to become the founder of the great Second Pegu/Toungoo Dynasty. At the time, however, he was just another usurper who had successfully wrestled away the Toungoo seat from the officially appointed *myosa*. But instead of marching to Toungoo to reinstall his appointee, Dutiya Mingaung actually sent presents of two elephants and weapons and officially gave Toungoo to Minkyinyo. The reasons for not objecting to Minkyinyo's coup are not entirely clear, for nephews are invariably opponents of the king, but in this case, it appears that there was little the king could do about Minkyinyo's coup.

Whatever the reasons, in hindsight, this decision proved to be a most important one, not only for Myanmar's history, but for the history of Western and

Central Mainland Southeast Asia, because it provided Minkyinyo a power base that laid the foundations for the Second Pegu/Toungoo Empire that subsequently conquered most of Western and Central Mainland Southeast Asia, particularly what is now Thailand and Laos, to become (even if for a short time) the largest in Mainland Southeast Asian history, a feat never to be repeated by any other state on Mainland Southeast Asia.

Dutiya Mingaung continued to secure supporters with well-calculated marriage alliances. When, in 1486, his uncle Thiri Zeyya Noyahta, *myosa* of Salin, died, he gave the fief to his brother-in-law, *myosa* of Singu, Min Thingathu, along with the men and materiel that came with the appointment. Four years later, he secured the link by marrying the eldest daughter of Thingathu with his son and heir, Mahathihathuya. That was a highly significant marriage, since it meant their offspring were certain to be in direct line for the throne if not guaranteed the office of heir apparent. Two years later, in 1492, the king gave his younger son, Min Swe, in marriage to Thingathu's younger daughter, along with the fief of Singu.

A glance at the geography of Upper Myanmar reveals the reason Dutiya Mingaung did all this. Salin is on the southwest of the "Y" where the Irrawaddy and Chindwin meet, while Toungoo, where Minkyinyo had recently staged a coup that the king approved, is straight south of Yamethin. East of the latter are the Shan hills and the fief of Nyaung Shwe, governed by its *sawbwa* whom Ava had helped previously and to whom the *sawbwa* owed allegiance. Thus, Yamethin, held by the king's strongest competitor, his younger brother, with clear rights to the throne and a city that Dutiya Mingaung had tried to but could not take, would be now encircled.

That same year, word arrived that King Dhammazedi of Hamsavati had died, succeeded by his son, Bannya Ram. When the lord of Toungoo, located directly on the Sittaung route to Pegu, heard that, he decided to attack the outlying areas of Pegu. One of these was Kyaung Pya, held by its Shan *myosa* Tho Taing Bwa, who, however, lost in single combat, giving Toungoo much men and materiel. When Dutiya Mingaung heard of this victory, he was extremely satisfied and heaped largesse on Minkyinyo. Although "Minister Long Life" warned him that Minkyinyo had built another fortified town called Dwarawati and had obtained many men, elephants, and horses, and that he would break away from Ava, Dutiya Mingaung replied that he would not dare to be an equal.

Meanwhile, Bannya Ram of Pegu marched on Dwarawati with a large force and surrounded it. The lord of Toungoo requested the king of Ava to send as strong a force as fast as he could. Dutiya Mingaung planned to send military aid, but before that happened, Toungoo had defeated the Lower Myanmar forces, obtaining over three thousand men and seventy elephants. Upon hearing of this victory, Dutiya Mingaung gave Minkyinyo the title Maha Thiri Zeyyathuya with the five insignia of princely rank and allowed him to wield the white umbrella.

Dutiya Mingaung was now ready to take Yamethin and test Toungoo's loyalty at the same time. In 1495, he sent orders to Toungoo to destroy the areas surrounding Yamethin. Toungoo complied but, deliberately perhaps, sent a relatively small force of fifty war elephants, three hundred cavalry, and twelve thousand soldiers. Much *padi* from Yamethin was taken, along with many cattle, water buffalo, and people, all sent back to Toungoo. The lord of Yamethin, Minye Kyawswa, came out with his troops to do battle with great force, forcing Minkyinyo to retreat. When Dutiya Mingaung heard of the *padi* and produce that had been taken, he gave Minkyinyo the rings and bracelets he wore on both hands. The struggle between the king and his younger brother, therefore, had priority over the inevitable struggle that would later materialize between the king and his nephew.

This struggle between king and younger brother only benefited the nephew, Minkyinyo. Dutiya Mingaung did not live long enough to see any of it materialize, for he died between the fifth day after the full moon in the month of Tagu (April) in the year 862 (1500), according to U Kala, and 863 (1501), according to the *Zatatawpon* (and a contemporary inscription).[31] Before he died, his young son and heir had also died, so the throne was "up for grabs," even more so than normal. U Kala states that Dutiya Mingaung ruled for twenty-one years, was a Saturday son, and died at age fifty-four, to which we should add one more year if the *Zatatawpon* and the inscription are correct.

The judgment by U Kala of Dutiya Mingaung, based on eighteenth-century Burmese Buddhist (and other, to us unknown) criteria, was highly favorable. There was nothing he was not skilled in, and a long list of physical and athletic abilities are described, largely pertinent to single combat techniques and feats performed at full gallop. U Kala praised him for his scholarly activities as well, saying he was well-versed in a variety of subjects, religious as well as secular. He supported scholarship, especially the works of Maha Thilawuntha, who came from Taungdwin to become one of the most famous literary figures in Burmese history. And, of course, Dutiya Mingaung built the expected works of merit (although far fewer than either Mohnyin or Narapati had done), and endowed them with lands that were tax-exempt.

If ever there was a period during the First Ava Dynasty that could be considered the most powerful politically, the most stable socially, the strongest militarily, the most self-sufficient economically (even wealthy), and the most "orthodox" religiously, it was the hundred years from 1400 to 1500, especially the last half of the fifteenth century, between Narapati and Dutiya Mingaung's reigns. That, unfortunately, was not to last.

In 1501, Dutiya Mingaung was succeeded by his inexperienced twenty-five-year-old son, later known as Narapati the Second. Although he was able to delay the final "fall" of Ava as the exemplary center of Upper Myanmar because of the solid foundations built by the above three kings and their predecessors, the kingdom began to unravel toward the end of his reign. It was the beginning of the end.

Ava
Pagan Writ Small

As demonstrated in the previous chapter, Ava reached its zenith in many categories of achievement during the fifteenth century. As we will see, however, throughout its life, as a state and society—economically, socially, conceptually, politically, administratively, and legally—Ava was essentially Pagan, only on a smaller scale.

The Economy of Redistribution

The Dry Zone of Upper Myanmar, the "heartland" of Pagan, was also the "heartland" of Ava, based on the same three irrigated regions that served Pagan: Kyaukse, Minbu, and the Mu Valley. As during Pagan times, the average annual production of *padi* in these three areas—more or less the same, more or less consistent—provided the economic wherewithal for the foundations of the state.

Land remained divided into the same three major legal categories as at Pagan—crown (*myedaw*), glebe (*wutmye*), and ancestral (*bobabaing mye*)—reflecting the general organization of people as well (discussed below), while the administration of that land depended on the same patron-client based *myosa* (to eat) principles. Although there was private ownership and alienation of land,[1] the lion's share of the total irrigated and/or cultivable land clearly belonged to the state and *sangha*. And, as at Pagan, the most important was *lay* (irrigated *padi* land), as *padi* remained the state's economic mainstay, and hence, the commodity by which the value of nearly everything else was measured. The price of gold and silver surely seemed to have been pegged to it, rather than the other way around. Even the yields of *padi* at Ava appeared to be similar to if not the same as at Pagan, for after all, the same plots of land were being worked with the same implements and methods, in a region with the same climate watered by the same major irrigation works—and without any evidence of an increase in the cultivator population.

As at Pagan, the agrarian economy was also vital to Ava, while maritime trade (if accessible) was "only" important. Admittedly, the contemporary and original stone inscriptions are primarily religious in nature and deal mainly with land and labor endowments, so that information on overseas maritime trade is rarely, if ever, mentioned, even had it been more prominent. And the regular attempts to take control of the major economic and political centers of Lower Myanmar during the Ava period suggests that at least the *acquisition* of trade revenues in that region must have been an important motivating factor in Ava's relationship with Pegu.

Notwithstanding, since Ava's access to the Lower Myanmar coasts, and thence to other parts of maritime South and Southeast Asia, was restricted if not obstructed almost entirely by the rise and establishment of the new kingdom of Pegu that had emerged at the very end of the thirteenth century, Ava turned its focus on Arakan on the west coast instead, and more often than not had control of it. But Ava never once managed to take Pegu (Lower Myanmar's political and economic center) or Muttama (its trade and commercial center), although it had influence on some of their activities some of the time. That means it is doubtful that maritime commerce was ever a realistic factor in, or a large part of, Ava's economy except on an irregular and ad hoc basis.

That, however, does not preclude active internal overland trade, especially between and among various regions of Upper Myanmar. The temple construction industry, the maintenance of society at the level Ava managed, and the existence of a capital where most of the elite and people of the kingdom resided presume the presence of such local trade, to where most nonagricultural products moved. There is even an inscription of Ava that mentions "the main merchant road." But it was not just a matter of retaining the same geographic, economic, and demographic contexts; continuity of the economy was also a matter of retaining the same kinds of relationships between and among state institutions. Thus, as at Pagan, the economy was also very much embedded in religion and politics, so that those structural relationships continued to operate in much the same way as before, in general and specific ways, in name as well as function. Religious endowments at Ava continued to stimulate the economy by creating jobs, generating related economic activities, and redistributing wealth.

By donating scarce labor to work cultivable land, religious endowments remained a major mechanism for increasing productivity, not only of *padi,* but also of other cash crops such as fruit and vegetable gardens and toddy palms. When applied to virgin land (*mye sein,* literally, unripe or green land), they affected the clearing, cultivating, and irrigating of otherwise fallow areas. And, of course, donations include the hiring of skilled craftsmen for the building, repair, and upkeep of religious edifices. Very important also, religious endowments provided for the education of the young (discussed below). Such activities also had similar social and political consequences as they had at Pagan, by "pacifying" newly settled areas and providing rural society with monasteries and monks who met Ava's psychological and spiritual needs—the "fields of merit" for society's predominant concern with better rebirths on their way to *nirvana.*

The specific ways in which goods and services were redistributed are also similar to those practiced at Pagan. Absolute amounts of *padi* were often allotted to the *sangha* (and to individuals performing services for the monks), using the standard unit for measuring *padi* (*tin*) at Pagan. A donor in 1378 stipulated that each member of the *sangha* be given, on a daily basis, one *pyi* (one-sixteenth of a *tin,* or about three pounds) of rice, and two *pyi* of *padi* for his curry (that is, used as payment for his curry). Similarly, in a donation of 1342, the abbot received a fixed eleven *tin* of *padi* (about fifty pounds per *tin*, so, 550 pounds per month. (As this is too much for the daily intake of any single person, particularly monks who are not supposed to eat after noon, the rest was presumably exchanged for cash or services or perhaps given to relatives.) In other words, absolute allotments suggest that one did not normally expect any changes in yields, which, in turn, suggests a certain amount of stability or equilibrium in the production of *padi*.

That assumption of stable yields was probably also the reason produce taxes were calculated according to presumed yields rather than actual yields. A rule-of-thumb formula (as true in nineteenth-century Myanmar as in the Ava period) was to calculate produce taxes according to "the area of *lay* that can be plowed by one water buffalo," as an inscription of 1503 stated. Since this was obviously a per-harvest tax, the formula itself assumed a constant average yield, anticipating and presupposing a stable human and animal energy output each time, along with a sustained fertility of the soil and water supply. Perhaps such practices applied to areas where the soil was always fertile, watered by perennial streams and rivers, such as in the three irrigated regions mentioned above.

Sometimes, however, instead of absolute amounts of *padi*, donors allotted relative shares of land and/or its annual yield to the monks, based on their stature or rank. In other words, it was status, not yields, that determined shares. In 1342, a donor provided some *lay* as an endowment for the monks of a monastery, dividing it into three shares: one for the *mahathera* "to eat" and the other two for the rest of the ordinary monks (*arya*). In another endowment of 1350, shares were allotted to the caretakers of *sangha* property, stipulating who received how much *pay* of *lay* (to a fraction) for services rendered on behalf of the monks and their property. In such cases, perhaps the value placed on the caretakers' particular function as well as their rank determined the size of the share. In 1365, a donor determined his allotment not only according to the spiritual rank of the recipients but also the performance of particular activities and the upkeep of specific edifices. The inscription states that of the total 175 *pay* of land dedicated, ten shares were allotted for (preaching) the law (*taya*), the temple received five, the "humans" (ordinary people) thirty-five, and the monks, 125. Another donation in 1374 stated that the yield was to be divided into three parts, two of which were reserved for the *arya* (monks) and one for the "humans."

The lord of Taungdwin, who made a large donation in 1442, divided his endowment into five parts, the first of which was reserved for his teacher (the abbot of the monastery to whom he was making this donation), while the other four parts were given to the rest of the monks. He also stipulated the amounts allotted to specific maintenance and repair work, such as lighting the oil lamps, repairing the monastery, washing the white umbrellas when they became dirty, and so on, and donated specific garden lands whose products were payment for the work performed. Similarly, when the king built his major work of merit in 1444, of the thirty allotted measures of *lay*, he designated the revenue obtained from twenty-five *pay* of that *lay* for the preaching of the law, while the revenue from ten *pay* obtained from another fifteen measures of *lay* was to be used as food for the head monk of the temple.

Along with status, perhaps allotting relative shares rather than absolute amounts of *padi* might suggest that these were in areas where yields were less predictable, where the land was more dependent on rainfall, without the presence of perennial rivers and nearby streams to replenish the soil with silt.

An *athi* commoner in 1446 used the Pali term *bhaga* (share) to describe his allotments, stating that a fifth of his total endowment goes to the monks, of which the chief monk (*thera*) gets two parts, the rest of the monks (*arya*), three. The other shares from the endowment went toward the (upkeep) of the monastery, the food (presumably for the workers), and the oil lamps for the temple and monastery. Another donor in 1454 also divided his endowment according to fifths. Of the five parts, two shares were allotted to the "humans" and two to the monks, while the fifth was earmarked for the maintenance of the monastery and the oil lamps.

Some endowments were divided into ten parts, subdivided into three main shares. The first of the three main shares went to the head monk, the second to the rest of the monks who lived in the monastery, while the third was subdivided into another five shares and allotted to those who were in charge of feeding the monks, lighting the oil lamps, preaching the law, taking care of the temple, and the last to musicians (who presumably performed for certain religious ceremonies).

Sometimes, the amount allotted was in a form of sharecropping, in which practical concerns determined the type of services performed. A donor in 1485 planted thousands of *htan* (toddy palm trees) and commissioned *athi* villagers to take care of them. Each person who took care of ten trees was allotted the produce of one; of one hundred trees, the produce of ten; of a thousand, the produce of one hundred. (This rule of thumb, one-tenth, was used for the collection of taxes well into the eighteenth century.) And each of the craftsmen assigned to provide services for the upkeep of the donation—mason, sculptor, stone carver, carpenter, and blacksmith—was given a hundred shares (of what, it is not stated and therefore must have been some standard produce obvious to everyone living there).

Thus, as at Pagan, the criterion for determining the size of one's share probably had less to do with the annual supply and demand of labor (or produce) than with religious and social concerns, one of the principles in economies of redistribution, whereby religion and other nonmonetary factors were embedded in the economy.[2] At the same time that this practice acknowledged spiritual hierarchy, it also showed concern for community demands of goodwill and harmony, for larger annual yields meant everyone received a larger share, while a smaller annual yield, a smaller share.

These nonmonetary factors affected (indeed, often offset) the natural supply-demand-price mechanisms at Ava to the extent that economic value was not independent of religion, politics, social status, and community concerns, as it might have been in a true market economy. Indeed, there is no mention in Ava inscriptions of higher or lower prices of *padi* attributed to fluctuating supply and/or demand, nor is there any objective data that suggests such a cause-and-effect economic relationship.

Equilibrium in prices of *padi,* of course, does not mean there were no differences in the *value* of *padi* land. Although there is some data on the price of *padi,* the best information we have on Ava concerns the price of *lay* itself. In general, that remained stable over the long run, during not only the Ava but the Pagan period as well, so that the few differences that existed in the price of *lay* at both Pagan and Ava, upon closer scrutiny, reveal that they were not necessarily the result of market principles of supply and demand but were apparently determined by the quality of the *lay* being bought or sold.

For example, in exceptionally well-watered areas, the price of *lay* could go up as high as fifteen or sixteen *kyats* per *pay.* In 1341, one inscription records the purchase of one *pay* of *lay* at a place called On Lay Gyi, for fifteen *kyats,* while another the same year commanded a price of sixteen *kyats.* The latter appears to be land where cavalry and other crown troops lived, and if so, they were not supposed to be selling that land, as it had been allotted to them as inalienable fiefs in return for their duties. Selling it illegally, therefore, involved risks, and perhaps was part of the reason for the slightly higher price. The buyers were referred to as *athi ala* (people not attached to the crown or *sangha*), who apparently lived nearby and acted as (eager) witnesses to the transactions.

In another case, in 1399, the price for one *pay* of *lay* was again an unusually high seventeen *kyats* of silver. (In contrast, "green jungle" land sold for only 1.32 *kyats* of silver per *pay* of land.) On average, however—and during both the Pagan and Ava periods—*lay* hovered between eight and ten *kyats* of silver per *pay.* Prior to the founding of Ava, in 1364, the price of *lay* at Pinya (south of Ava) was 8.50 *kyats* per *pay.* By the time Ava was founded a few years later, *lay* sold for 11.18 *kyats* per *pay,* where the buyers were a high-ranking minister and his wife, perhaps part of the reason for the increase in price. In 1439, 4.5 *pay* of *lay* was bought for forty-seven *kyats* of silver, coming to 10.4 *kyats* per *pay.* In the same year, by the same person, for the same donation, but for another piece of land, the donor paid fifty *kyats* of silver for five *pay* of *lay,* also amounting to ten *kyats* per pay. Again in 1439, a couple bought six *pay* of land at Kyun Pin Yin village for sixty *kyats* of silver, averaging ten *kyats* per *pay.*

In 1441, the head of the *sangha* himself bought and donated lands to endow the temple he had just built. He paid, in one case, thirty-seven *kyats* of silver for two *pay* of *lay* (which amounts to an extremely high 18.5 *kyats* per *pay*). Although this is nearly double the average price, upon closer scrutiny of the inscription, it turns out that this price was not just for the *lay,* since in the same purchase he also received two *ya* (dry fields, that is, fields for crops such as *Sesamum*), along with twenty-four toddy palm trees. The total price he paid, therefore, included these other items.

Toddy palms at another place cost the same monk one *kyat* per tree, and *ya* prices were similar. That would put the price of the two *pay* of *lay* at about seven or eight *kyats* of silver per *pay,* within the average price range of *lay* for the Ava period. By way of comparison with other lands, millet (or corn, we cannot be certain, as the word *pyaung* is the same for both) cost five *kyats* of silver per *pay*, while "green jungle" land, that is, virgin land, was cheap, approximately 1.3 to three *kyats* per *pay*, almost the same price as a toddy palm.

A few lines down in the inscription, the donor recorded the price of *lay* that he bought elsewhere, uncomplicated by other purchases and unambiguously noted, amounting to ten *kyats* per *pay*, nearly the same as another piece of *lay* he bought at Pinle (in Kyaukse) for which he paid 10.9 *kyats* per *pay*, a price normally expected for *lay* in that rich irrigated valley.

There were other nonmonetary factors that affected these calculations, although not by much. The real cost of *lay*, especially when it involved a religious donation, was not just the price paid for it. It included certain customary costs, what the inscriptions called "closing feasts," that included food and liquor consumed at the time of closing and incurred by the purchaser. In one case, it was 1.75 *kyats*, in another two *kyats*, comparable in price to a toddy palm tree. Considering that food and drink were consumed, with nothing to show for it afterward, one could argue that the value was not that good. In 1439 once again, the costs were about the same: the meat cost two *kyats* and a pot of liquor was one *kyat*. These clearly did not affect the price of *lay* by much. In general, then, the price of *lay* saw little or no increase at Ava, which, in turn must have been the reason for stable *padi* prices over the long run, similar to what they had been at Pagan well over a century earlier.

That the price of *lay* and *padi* was stable, created by the eco-demographic conditions in which both Pagan and Ava lay, as well as by religious and social concerns embedded in their costs, accounts in part for the equilibrium of the economy as well as for the assumptions held by people for the continuation of such equilibrium based on the general predictability of the annual output of *padi*. It was not just wishful thinking, as production was based on a system of sophisticated irrigation works that were well-maintained and built around perennial streams and rivers that guaranteed at least two, sometimes three, crops of *padi* per year. In general, there seemed to have been few problems in terms of the supply of *padi*, as clearly evident in the existence of huge annual surpluses, without which none of the immense temple construction projects, which continued for the nearly seven hundred years of the combined Pagan and Ava periods, could have been undertaken.

The "objective" reason for this stability in the prices of *lay* (and *padi*) may have been the stable relationship between population and land; more precisely, between the cultivator classes and cultivated land, especially of *lay*. Land per se was plentiful, but unless there was a large increase in labor, particularly of cultivators to work it, it was only dirt and of no value. And as there is no evidence for any large influx in population (especially of cultivators) during the Ava period, the kingdom must have been in a demographic equilibrium, affecting its production and keeping its economy also at equilibrium.[3] To reiterate, then, the stable price of *lay* accounts for the stable price of *padi*, and because the economy as a whole depended on both, everything else was affected by this equilibrium.

Thus, the best explanation I have for the differences in the price of *lay*, as indicated by the evidence, is its quality. During the Pagan period, such stability in the price of *lay* (bought and sold with silver) was reflected in the ratio of silver to gold, which remained the same for four hundred years (always ten to one, with one unusual exception of twelve to one). At Ava, however, there may have been an inflation in the value of silver for unknown reasons, for an inscription of 1407 seemed to imply that five *kyats* of gold was obtained from cutting 150 (units) of silver, making the ratio one to thirty. This is an unusually large increase and is the only case I have seen, but may be suggestive of a temporary inflation in silver prices.

The cash economy of Ava also seemed to have been fairly well developed, as at Pagan. Although to date no coins have been found datable to either Pagan or Ava, silver and gold *kyats* were used, which were based on the weight of the metal. (In the nineteenth century, a silver *kyat* was said to be approximately half an ounce in weight, but we have no information of that during the Ava period). Each *kyat* had smaller denominations. For example, an inscription of 1360 (among many others) showed that the land purchased totaled "62 *kyats* and a quarter," while payments that used "three-quarters" and "half *kyats*" were also mentioned. And like Pagan, *khwet* (cup-shaped pieces of lead and/or copper found throughout Southeast Asia) continued to be used at Ava, although silver and gold were still the favorite metals.

There were other equivalencies, such as elephants, horses, and goats, that appear to be at least as valuable at Ava as they were at Pagan. (One and a half *pay* of good *lay* was bought with one "chief bull" in 1329, one female elephant was worth about a thousand *kyats* of silver, and one horse was easily worth thirty *kyats* of silver, if not more.) The above suggests barter was also part of the economic scheme, although it is not found very often for purchases of *lay* or for payment of craftsmen, where silver was the most common medium, hence likely preferred.

Some items such as *htan* (toddy palms), mentioned only rarely as donated items during the Pagan period, became ubiquitous in Ava donations. These *htan* produced a sweet syrup that was boiled down to make jaggery (brown sugar) or fermented into a form of liquor said to be called *the*. (The Middle Eastern term *arak* [Old Burmese *ayet*] was also used for liquor during the Ava period, so *the* might have been the local term for the brew.)

There also appears to have been an unprecedented increase in cash donations to the *sangha* during the Ava period, especially in gold and silver. Not surprisingly, however, the number of donations in *lay* was recognizably much lower relative to these other items. I suspect this was due in part, by then, to the large amounts of *lay* already sequestered as *sangha* property, the consequence of Pagan society having made large donations to the *sangha* continuously during the previous four hundred years, all inviolable, and all in perpetuity. Not only did the absolute amount of *lay* donated to the *sangha* decline at Ava, the total area of irrigated land the state controlled in the first place was already smaller than what Pagan had controlled. At the same time, access to the cash revenues of Lower Myanmar that Pagan had enjoyed—which might have helped balance the reduction in *lay*—no longer existed as supplementary wealth at Ava, since that region was now in the hands of an independent polity, Pegu.

Had market principles been dominant, such a decrease in the total supply of *lay* with a continued demand should have resulted in an increase in its price. Yet the price of *lay* did not increase appreciably between the Pagan and Ava periods, even though there was clearly a shortage of *lay*. That the Ava period saw an increase in amounts of virgin land being turned into cultivable plots is also very much overstated; there is evidence of only two (at most three) such cases recorded, which amounted to a very small total. Again, part of this exaggeration has to do with the notion of Ava as a "century of unrest."

Because of the relative scarcity of *lay* at Ava compared with Pagan (in terms of its availability for donations), a donor had to go through a difficult and costly process to make his/her donation legally valid. As at Pagan, only the king (or a high-ranking representative) could grant such permission, and in most cases regarding large donations, only his personal appearance and performance of the water-consecration ritual would legally and officially "release" donations from the human (taxable) to the sacred (tax-exempt) world. It was a regulatory device for the crown to help mitigate the runaway flow of wealth (especially of *lay*) into the church's tax-exempt coffers, while holding on to one of its prerogatives, which the crown was unlikely to relinquish easily. It was also a means to ensure that the king (and his queens) accrue some of the merit (and fees) accumulated from such donations.

Thus, in 1347, two high-ranking military officials, wishing to donate and endow land to their monastery and *zedi*, had to present the queen mother with "a gift" of two hundred *kyats* of silver in order to obtain some royal land. Another donor had to give one hundred *kyats* of gold to secure permission to legally dedicate the lands and villages he wanted to donate as endowment for the maintenance of the temple and library he had built, while another (the crown prince and his princess at that), had to give "the royal present" (Let Hsaung Daw) of gold, silver ornaments, two horses, lacquer, forty *kyats* of silver, and another ten *kyats* of silver and one *kyat* of gold to the queen, among other gifts. A high ranking official in 1350 gave "a horse with white hoofs" as "the royal present" to either secure permission (or purchase thirty *pay* of *lay*) with which to endow three temples (or Buddha statues, it is not clear) and one monastery. In 1358, a donor asked the king for some land to donate, giving him an elephant for the twenty-five *pay* of *lay* he received in return.

Even during the height of the Ava period, when resources were presumably more abundant (or at least under better central control and therefore more easily accessible) and the kingdom more politically stable and peaceful, this trend continued. In 1416, the great minister of the king (and one of his grandsons) Nayathinkha, having built a great brick monastery, offered the king an "exceedingly good horse" and a golden chalice of ten *kyats* weight for three hundred *pay* of land with which to endow his monastery. Subsequently, he requested permission from the king to donate another 110 *pay* of dry land (*mye chauk*), for which he presented him with an "exceedingly healthy horse" and three hundred *kyats* of silver and a boat. Even high-ranking monks such as the *sangharaja* (literally, lord of the *sangha*) had to provide royal presents, in this case of twenty-six *kyats* of gold and four hundred *kyats* of silver.

In 1440, a Shan officer of the elephantry, desiring that the *sasana* (religion) lasts five thousand years, built a monastery. But like everyone else, he needed land to endow it, for which he applied to the king. He received either the permission and/or the land itself, the inscription is not clear. For that, he had to present the king with a ruby bracelet and ten *kyats* (in weight) of smelted gold. In 1462, even though the land being donated was already the donor's, inherited from his ancestors, he still needed to pay "the royal present" for having the king perform the ritual of water consecration, the only ceremony that made his donation legally religious and tax-exempt, as at Pagan.

In another case, a man of high rank, probably a general who had served the state well, still had to pay "the royal present" of three hundred silver *kyats,* one silver chalice worth twelve *kyats,* and one horse for having the ceremony performed. In this particular case, the symbolism of releasing property from the secular (and taxable) world to the spiritual (and tax-exempt) realm as inviolable, was made most poignant, for the (clay?) pot holding the water of consecration was broken upon completion. The ritual of water consecration was found in nearly every religious dedication during both the Pagan and Ava periods; only, during the latter, the requests were far more frequent and carried with them expensive royal presents, which was not very common, if it occurred at all, during the Pagan period, when there apparently was little shortage of good land, until the late thirteenth century.

Although this procedure suggests pecuniary and political motives of the king and royalty, it also speaks to how important religious motives were to the donors, for most of "the royal presents" were greater in value than the *lay* purchased and donated. But they had little recourse, especially if they wanted to make sure that their donations were legally tax-exempt and remained so in perpetuity, particularly if it were a *sanghikha* donation, in which legal title is transferred to the *sangha* as an institution rather than to individual abbots of monasteries.

At the same time, however, some economic motives were surely involved on the part of the donors. For, if their donation were not *sanghikha* but *puggalikha,* donors and their descendants would retain legal title to the donated property. That means the revenues from the land and the services of people donated, ordinarily liable for taxes to the state, would be sheltered as tax-exempt. The donor "ate his cake and had it too"—that is, obtained merit while keeping legal title to his or her property.

There are other indications of a scarcity of *lay* at Ava. The precision with which even a few acres of *lay* was marked by stone boundary posts, seldom done during the Pagan period, was commonplace at Ava. An inscription of 1364 took thirteen lines on the stone to describe the boundaries of its donation marked by stone pillars. In another case, the person responsible for erecting the many stone boundaries did it on elephant-back, revealing the large number of stone posts he must have carried and used. In still another, a donation in 1526, made the same year as the beginning of Ava's "fall," 245 stone markers were erected to mark off a measly ten *pay* of *lay*.

In other instances, part of the produce of land already given to crown cavalry for their service did "double duty" by also being donated to the *sangha*. (I am not sure how the two parties involved handled this illegal activity.) In another case, in 1338, 1,634 *kyats* of silver and 1.50 *kyats* of gold were spent by the donors for constructing a very nice brick temple and a monastery. But when it came time to provide an endowment of land and labor for their maintenance, the donors managed only a paltry 38.25 *pay* of *lay*, and no labor. Sometimes, people from different walks of life would pool their resources to endow *lay* to a temple or monastery built by someone else. Indeed, one inscription of 1430 actually stated that there was no cultivated land left to donate.

Yet, this sustained demand on a low supply of *lay*, rather than increasing its price (as it should have in a true market economy), only caused a decrease in the amount of *lay* donated, while prices remained relatively stable and donations in cash (silver and gold) and other liquid assets increased by large amounts. There was also a marked increase in the donation of other items not ordinarily recorded in the donations of Pagan as noted above, such as *htan* (toddy palms), along with a few donations of "green forest land" (*taw sein*) after clearing and plowing it.

To reiterate, the absolute amount of *lay* and *kyun* donated to the *sangha* at Ava was well below Pagan totals. But that does not mean the relative amount of total wealth that flowed to the *sangha* at Ava was any less. In fact, the reduction in the donation of *lay* and *kyun* was easily outstripped by donations in cash (silver and gold particularly) and other items such as toddy palms. Even though Ava was less wealthy than Pagan, and even though it did not have access to Lower Myanmar's cash revenues, its use of silver and gold in donations exceeded, even absolutely, that used at Pagan. There was simply less *lay* and fewer people left by the Ava period to donate, since both had been heavily committed in perpetuity during the Pagan period, so more donations were made in cash.

Where this cash came from is not clear: perhaps from domestic silver and gold mines (for which there is some evidence), perhaps from inland trade with China and with coastal and maritime Myanmar, whose economy by then was booming, linked to the global economy via Vijayanagara, the Ming (both of whom are mentioned in Ava inscriptions), and perhaps the Portuguese. And since there is no evidence that the Lower Myanmar delta was cleared, drained, settled, and cultivated until the nineteenth century under colonialism, Upper Myanmar likely supplied its rice and other interior products in exchange for that silver and gold.

Moreover, during the Pagan period, cash donations per se to the *sangha* appear to have been smaller since much of the money was spent in the actual building of the temples. Pagan temples were far more complicated in design and individually much larger than their Ava counterparts, demanding more skilled labor and materiel, and were therefore far more expensive to build. Also, the total number of temples (especially in terms of size) built during the Pagan period far surpassed those built at Ava. That means during the Pagan period, most of the money went into the cost of construction itself, particularly since land was plentiful and labor in good supply (from immigration and conquest), whereas during the Ava period, since the temples were mainly solid *stupas*, simpler and smaller and far less costly, most of the money went into the creation of their (temples') landed endowments.

Along with fewer acres of cultivated land available to the state, like much of early Southeast Asia, Ava also seems to have been susceptible to the scarcity of labor. Unlike Pagan, however, this affected Ava more severely, for the former could, and did, increase its supply by attracting significant amounts of labor by both conquest and voluntary immigration, the result of its military power and its booming economy generating enormous employment opportunities that were based on its vast temple-construction industry. Pagan probably offered the highest wages at the time in the region (a feat Ava could not match), while its incomparable stature as a superpower and exemplary Buddhist kingdom in Western Mainland Southeast Asia must have provided additional incentives for migrating there. In Ava's case, there is no evidence that a large number of people migrated there who could have replenished the cultivator pool and enhanced the economy.

To be sure, there was some movement of Shan (T'ai) speakers into the river valleys of Upper Myanmar (the Chindwin and Irrawaddy) already inhabited by Burmese speakers during the Ava period. But the few Shan mentioned in the contemporary epigraphs of Ava were nearly all military personnel, so not only was this movement selective and sparse, it did not necessarily include cultivators. In other words, there is no evidence of migration by a large number of cultivators or artisans into Upper Myanmar during the Ava period to significantly alter that demographic segment of the population, and hence, the economy. The principles that underlay the economy of redistribution remained intact at Ava despite an overall shrinkage.

Patron-Client Social Organization

As at Pagan, virtually everyone in Ava society, from court to village, was officially organized into two main categories: attachment and non-attachment. Attachment was to the crown, *sangha*, or private individuals, designated as *kyun-daw*, *hpaya kyun*, and *kyun*, respectively. Indeed, the term *kyun phyit* (to become *kyun*) illustrates poignantly the fact of *becoming* attached. Those not attached were referred to as *athi* (sometimes, *athi ala*). All indications are that attachment rather than non-attachment was the preferred situation for the vast majority of the population.

KYUN-SHIP (ATTACHMENT)

One of the most egregious errors made by colonial scholarship about attached people at Pagan and Ava, whether *kyun-daw*, *hpaya kyun*, or *kyun*, is that they were slaves. The definition of what constitutes a slave as we understand the term—especially in its worst form, where they were considered less than human, whose lives could be taken at will—simply does not apply to the situation of attachment (*kyun*-ship) at either Pagan or Ava.

As neither Pagan nor Ava was tribal any longer, outsiders could enter without necessarily becoming slaves—the general rule in genuine tribal societies. Rather, attachment and non-attachment were the legal categories that distinguished people who owed services and/or taxes from those who were exempt. When used outside this more narrow legal context, the word *kyun* broadly meant "subject" or "vassal."

The most comprehensive Burmese-English dictionary that recaptures the oldest meanings in Burmese is the 1891(?) edition of *Judson's Burmese-English Dictionary.* Reflecting the most common usage by then, its first definition for the word *kyun* was still "subject," followed by "servant," and only last by "slave"—the last definition reflecting the least common and most recent, rather than the most common or oldest, usage of the word.

Indeed, equating the Burmese word *kyun* for the English word "slave" is a modern attempt to find a Burmese equivalent to the English word "slave" rather than vice versa, much like the Burmese phrase *kyezu tin ba de* was developed to approximate the English "thank you." Neither the concept of "thank you" nor the phrase that expressed it existed in the Burmese language prior to the introduction of the English concept of it. It is similar to words like *sawaddi* in T'ai and *mingalaba* in Burmese, both very recent attempts (the latter invented only in the late 1960s) to find equivalents for the modern, English greeting.

The socioeconomic status of people who were attached (especially *hpaya kyun*), during the Pagan and Ava periods, is best illustrated in a four-face inscription of 1442 recording a large donation made by the lord of Taungdwin and his wife. Taking up 182 lines of text, it includes the building of at least one monastery at Pagan's Wek Kyi In district to which was donated approximately 386 (mainly) religious texts. The donation also mentioned irrigated *padi* and other cultivated lands on which were grown a variety of crops, thousands of toddy palms, along with fruit gardens that produced mangoes, pomelos, betel, coconuts, and bananas. This endowment of valuable agricultural land provided the permanent, material wherewithal for at least twenty-eight caretakers of the monastery, called *kyun,* each of them listed by name and all donated as families, not as individuals. Some of them were responsible for menial tasks such as fetching bathing water for the monks, taking care of the gardens, and so on. But a large segment of this group of *kyun* consisted of five families of scribes who copied the above-mentioned texts. They were literate not only in Burmese but also in Pali, revealed by the names of the majority of the texts they copied in that language. They were paid in cash for this task, the total coming to 7,679.25 *kyats* of silver, an incredibly large amount, hardly the kind of pay scale of ordinary scribes, and even less of "slaves." And this was not an atypical situation of *hpaya kyun* at either Ava or Pagan.

In another inscription (at Pagan), a high-ranking minister of the court deliberately and willingly donated himself and his daughters to the *sangha*, with the expressed intention of gaining merit for all of them. Similarly at Ava, in 1392, another relatively well-off person donated his entire family and himself as *hpaya kyun.* In 1526, in another inscription, the king's personal guardians (husband and wife) were referred to as *kyun.* Yet the husband was a general in the armed forces who had just won a major battle. (Obviously, the meaning of the word *kyun* in this case was "vassal" or "subject," the first of two definitions found in Judson's 1891 *Dictionary.*) There was also a *kyun sa ye* mentioned in an Ava inscription of 1509, that is, a *kyun* whose occupation was that of a scribe—a group of literate specialists that earned good wages, as shown above.

Several parents at Ava gladly gave their sons to the monastery and "released" (*hlut*) them to the monks, a practice that continues in Myanmar today, as late as 2006, which I have witnessed personally. Although in the United States this kind of situation would have brought the wrath of Child Protective Services and the full power of the law upon the parents, the monks, and the monastery, in Myanmar, not only much merit accrued to the parents for their act, but they also received public congratulations and blessings.

It is true that the lot of most *hpaya kyun* was hereditary. At first glance, and to those brought up to celebrate modern democracy, this would be undesirable. But the importance placed on their *lineage* as servants of the religion was desirable, valued, and considered very important in Burmese society. In other words, while we (today) may disparage their hereditary situation, it provided security, while the profession itself was regarded as honorable, and served the religion for generations, very much like those (in England) who were in service "downstairs" to nobility "upstairs" also considered as quite an honorable profession.

There were also other *kyun* (usually *kyun-daw* if they were skilled in military occupations) who might have been obtained as prisoners of war and later settled in various parts of the kingdom of Ava, as suggested by one inscription that records lands called *kyun naingnan lay.* The meaning is not entirely clear but it sounds as if these were *lay* (irrigated *padi* lands) worked by and set aside for subjects brought back from a conquest (*naing*), in which case, the term "slave," even for prisoners of war would be inappropriate.

It is true that money was used to "purchase" *kyun*, who were then donated to the *sangha.* Thus, in 1345, ten couples who were already attached to the crown as *kyun-daw* were "bought" and donated to the *sangha.* However, upon closer scrutiny, their status as *kyun-daw* was actually *redeemed* (rather than "bought") for four hundred *kyats* of royal silver, after which they were redonated to the *sangha*, thus becoming *hpaya kyun.* In other words, their contract to the crown as *kyun-daw* was being "bought out" and transferred to the *sangha*, not they themselves. ("Buying-out" contracts is, of course, commonplace today in societies without any implications of slavery attached to the practice.)

Bought or redeemed, one could still argue that such people probably had little or no choice in the matter. Yet, the very issue of choice is laden with modern sentiments about individual political freedom in *this* life. Becoming *hpaya kyun* at Ava was quite an entirely different situation, connected to one's rebirth as a higher being in the next life, hence a step on one's path toward *nirvana*. One cannot, then, use today's Western political values about freedom and individual rights to assess a situation in fifteenth-century Ava or thirteenth-century Pagan in which both the goals and means were entirely different. It is true, of course, that even in such a religious context, there probably was no doubt at Pagan and Ava as to who was higher in rank: those who *were kyun* or those who *donated kyun*. But hierarchy per se need not imply slavery. Lest I be accused of romanticizing (worse, of advocating the "happy slaves" theory), it needs to be made clear that the issue here is not whether slaves were happy or sad, but whether the *kyun* of Ava (and Pagan) were slaves at all.

Hierarchy also had to do with closeness to spirituality as well as to political, social, and economic power. The inscriptions made a clear distinction between the word used for ordinary humans (*pu kuiw*) and monks (*arya*), for elder and younger, and for ordinary *athi* and *athi-daw* (that is, unattached people who worked for the religion or state and received the honorific *daw*). Such sentiments are revealed by the use of classifiers, so that "low" objects were classified with "low" classifiers and "high" objects, with "high" classifiers. The classifier *khu* (used today for inanimate things) was, at Ava and Pagan, used with "low" animals such as buffalo and cows, while "high" animals such as elephants and horses were given functional classifiers (*si*) denoting their ability to be ridden. Inanimate but holy objects such as Buddha statues were given high classifiers such as *hsu*, although some religious edifices (such as *cetiyas*) continued to be classified by their shape (*lon* for round objects).

NON-*KYUN*-SHIP (NON-ATTACHMENT)

Linking attachment to Western notions of slavery has led to another erroneous (but logical) conclusion: that *non*-attachment therefore, must have meant freedom, or "free born," as most early Western scholars of Myanmar have put it. Yet, the word *athi* (the word used for those unattached people) has nothing in its etymology to suggest political freedom or being "free born," while the function and condition of *athi* also implies no such thing.

The modern, colonial definition given to *athi* stems ultimately from a binary and dichotomous analysis whereby its (contrived) opposition to *kyun*-ship (presumed to be slavery) suggested that *athi* (its assumed counterpart) "must have been" free born, resulting in a neat package of free versus unfree people at Pagan and Ava, tautologically reconfirming our view of ourselves and "the Other."

By insisting that Western, twentieth-century sentiments regarding individual political freedom also applied to Myanmar, the true nature and significance of attachment and non-attachment in precolonial Burmese society was not only overlooked but also misunderstood and reversed. To reiterate, in a society such as Myanmar, people generally *preferred* attachment to non-attachment. But such indigenous values were something colonial historians did not (or could not) understand, having equated attachment with slavery and non-attachment with individual freedom, values underlying their own twentieth-century societies.

It is thus an egregious mistake not only to use the word "slave" for the indigenous term *kyun* (and its related categories of *kyun-daw* and *hpaya kyun*), but to use the term "free" or "freeborn" for unattached *athi*. Not only does it perpetuate a myth that has misinformed the field for over a century, it also imposes a cultural-centric, binary framework of analysis ("freedom" versus "slavery") as the only, or most important, yardstick by which to measure such institutions in Southeast Asia, further perpetuating—even if inadvertent and unintentional—the kind of academic and "intellectual imperialism" we as scholars have tried hard to avoid and undo. In short, *kyun*-ship was the best mechanism that allowed society to organize itself around patron-client principles.

Important to one of the themes in the book, one should note that, as at Pagan, the criterion for one's social rank at Ava had little to do with reified ethnicity. It certainly had little or nothing to do with *kyun*-ship (or *athi*-ship) either, as implied by past scholarship (probably including my own). Attachment and non-attachment were applied with little or no regard for ethnic background; all who were not attached were considered *athi* and all who were attached were *kyun* (of one version or another). An inscription mentioned a *kala athi kyi* (the "big" Indian *athi*, or the headman of the Indian *athi*), while another records a group of Palaung people selling land who were also *athi*. In 1445, the king himself bought toddy-palm and mango land from four Chin *athi* for four hundred *kyats* (?) of silver, which was witnessed by several people including monks and headmen.

Most minorities must have become culturally Burmese after one or two generations. One striking example is that of a Khmer harpist with a Burmese name. If my reading is correct, these Khmer artists included female musicians, a nose-flute player, drummer, and two (what appears to be) sculptors. As the inscription is dated to 1444, these people may have been Khmer refugees from the slow decline of Angkor during this century. Although some of their names are clearly Burmese (suggesting that they had apparently integrated into Ava society by that time), others still sound "foreign," perhaps Khmer or Tai. In any case, at Ava, they had been given a village "to eat" called little Kyauk Hsauk village (little village built of stone?).

There is also evidence of intermarriage between Burmese speakers and minority ethnic groups. The father-in-law of a headman of a place called Thindwe was a Shan, who himself was a headman of bodyguards, while another headman of a place called Pe-nwe was either related to or had close associations with several people with obvious Shan names. In another case, a woman with a typical Burmese name was the wife of a Mr. Pan Siy (that is, Panthe, Chinese Muslim). The Pyu people, who dominated the country during the first millennium and said to have disappeared by the mid-ninth-century, were apparently not all gone. There is mention of a Pyu firewood dealer (Pyu Htin-the) and "Pyu maidens" during a palace building ceremony.

In any case, it was not ethnicity that made people *athi, kyun-daw, hpaya kyun,* or *kyun* since we find people of different ethnic groups in these categories. With the above general principles in mind, I now scrutinize each category of attachment and non-attachment in greater detail to see how close the Ava institution was to that of Pagan.

KYUN-DAW

As at Pagan, those attached to the crown at Ava were also referred to as *kyun-daw,* although a new term, *ahmudan,* had emerged as a close approximation by the Ava period (and was still in use in the twentieth-century). These *kyun-daw* or *ahmudan* were provided with land to "live on" (*ne mye*), "work on" (*lok mye*), and "to eat" (*sa mye*). Ideally, they would be grouped together according to their occupations, so that villages of shield bearers or cavalry can be found living on lands allotted to them under their own leaders. One such group mentioned in the Ava inscriptions was the Paung Laung Myin (Palaung Horse, that is, Palaung cavalry) who lived on lands in Kyaukse. Another group of war boat (*hlawga*) rowers were given lands "to eat" called *hlawga sa* in 1374. *Lamaing* (crown cultivators) were also mentioned as early as 1338.

If these crown subjects performed military functions, their group names retained their Pagan terms *sitha* (soldiers); *thuye* (braves), a reference to ordinary soldiers; and *bhopa*, the designation for officers. More specific terms that denote the particular branch of the military to which they belonged also continued to be used. Thus, cavalry were called *myin-si sitha* (literally, horse riding soldiers), and their leaders were *myin thugyi* (head persons of cavalry), exactly the terms used during the Pagan period.

These groups might have had administrative functions on the crown lands assigned to them when not on duty at the capital or on actual campaigns. In one such case, for instance, two cavalry officers measured out a piece of land donated by a high-ranking minister and placed boundary posts to mark it, normally a job performed by *athi,* suggesting that the latter had no such functions or jurisdiction on crown lands. Police duties were also assigned to crown soldiers, who already had the training and weapons needed to enforce criminal law, whose headmen were called *kin thugyi* (head person of police), while a *htaung thugyi* (head person of jails) is mentioned, perhaps with authority over both *kyun-daw* and *athi.*

Over *kyun-daw* were crown officials with both administrative and military functions called *kalan* and *thanbyin,* as ubiquitous in the inscriptions of Ava as they were in those of Pagan. And it appears that at Ava, crown service groups seemed to have grown stronger politically, or at least remained as strong as they had been in Pagan, further entrenching or retaining their status in society.

HPAYA KYUN

Like *kyun-daw* attached to the crown, *hpaya kyun* were attached to the *sangha.* People could become *hpaya kyun* in a variety of ways. The most common method was to be included in religious donations, in some cases to redeem debt and in others volunteering to be *hpaya kyun* for spiritual and socioeconomic reasons. *Hpaya kyun* performed a variety of functions related to the maintenance of religious property, including copying religious texts housed in monastic libraries and archives, writing and preserving the title deeds of religious property, managing the finances of that property, repairing (or overseeing the repair) of the temples and monasteries as they deteriorated, ensuring that the daily food was cooked for the resident monks, students who were taught the rudiments of literacy at monastic schools, those performing music and dance when required, others keeping the religious complex clean and doing basic housework. In other words, *hpaya kyun* were the lay guardians of the complex in many ways, as monks were technically forbidden to do such worldly work.

Normally, these *hpaya kyun* did not have corvee obligations to the state, since they had been legally "released" (*hlut*) to the tax-exempt, religious sphere. They were also most likely exempt from per capita tax, as were *kyun-daw*, who, in lieu of such taxes, paid in service to the crown. An important point to be made regarding *hpaya kyun* is that, contrary to convention that they could not become monks, one inscription of 1430 explicitly described a person as *phondaw phyit kyun* (a *kyun* who had become a *pongyi*, the common word for monk).

KYUN

The last category of attachment was the ordinary *kyun*, those beholden to individuals and not to larger institutions of state and society, and distinguished in numerous ways from other kinds of attachments. Their status appears to be well below that of the previous two categories, and they likely became *kyun* for reasons ranging from debt to poverty, although the majority appear to have volunteered to serve their patrons in return for protection and security, both highly desirable in a patron-client–based society where attachment (of any kind) meant one had a place in society rather than none. Most *kyun* were probably ordinary household servants (*ein htaung kyun)* without the special skills needed to become crown and *hpaya kyun*. At Ava, as at Pagan, this last category of ordinary *kyun* was clearly not a significant factor in the economy as a whole, for their numbers appear to be relatively minuscule.

ATHI

As noted above, those who were not attached were usually referred to as *athi*. Both the etymology and the actual functions of *athi* as found in the contemporary inscriptions show that they were often owners of property and practitioners of the crafts, so much so that when the word *thi* is attached to their craft, it is equivalent, in English, to the "er" attached to certain occupations (such as baker, fletcher, fish seller, carpenter).

Many *athi* had occupations as artists, craftsmen, scribes, bankers, and moneylenders, as well as other nonmilitary professions, and probably paid per capita tax in lieu of corvee service. They also appear to have been organized into guild-like organizations based on their professions, led by crafts foremen, so that the "cellular" organization of society based on occupation (such as the goldsmiths at Pagan) also remained intact and functional at Ava.

Athi could attach themselves voluntarily to either the state or *sangha*, or involuntarily through debt or some other reason, such as war, although there is no contemporary and direct evidence of the latter during the Ava period. As the king was considered "lord of land and water" and had authority over everyone, he could transfer *athi* tax obligations to the state and give them to the *sangha* instead, such as when an entire village of *athi* was donated to a particular monastery by the king, although this ordinarily occurred with *kyun-daw* rather than *athi,* as during King Kyanzittha's reign, around 1112, when his son Rajakumar dedicated three villages of *kyun* to a particular temple. In an inscription of 1374, a donor listed blacksmiths, masons, and sedan-chair carriers as part of the donation, referred to them as *kyun,* and gave them lands "to eat" for their services. One long inscription of 1378 lists *athi* who had become *kyun,* but whose original status as *athi* is revealed by their suffix *thi,* such as the tailor (*po khin thi*), the laundry woman (*ku ha thi*), the carver (*pan put thi*), and the potter (*o htein thi*). In other inscriptions, one dated to 1388, weavers (normally *athi*) were considered *kyun* once they became attached. This suggests that they could also become *kyun-daw* or *hpaya kyun,* depending on their skills and the patron to which they became attached, and also serves as proof that the word *kyun* was itself the legal term that stipulated attachment.

Athi appear to have been paid in cash most often but sometimes also in kind. Craftsmen were well paid, even during the alleged "troubled years" between the fall of Pagan and the rise of Ava, when donations and building of religious edifices continued. A donation made by a husband and wife around 1338 reveals the following relative wage levels of *athi* who plied the arts and crafts. The wages (*lek kha ngwe*) for building two religious edifices (a temple and a brick monastery) came to 342.50 *kyats* of silver for the masons, not counting the five hundred *tin* of *padi* baskets (each weighing approximately fifty-six pounds) used to pay for their meals during the construction project. In addition to wages and food, the donors paid sixty *kyats* of silver for the bricks and another sixty for the brick makers, thirty-one *kyats* of silver to clothe them, and another hundred *tin* of *padi* for the cost of their food. The inscription recorded that the craftsmen finished the job in a month and a half.

After the temple was completed, the donors had to make a Buddha statue for it. Wages for the sculptor who made one cross-legged Buddha of four *taung* (each *taung* was about a cubit or eighteen inches) came to twenty *kyats* of silver, plus another thirty-one *kyats* to clothe him (the sculptor). The wages for the *cankram* (plinth) alone (on top of which was the statue) cost the donors another sixteen *kyats,* while carpenters were paid with sixty *tin* of *padi.* Wood-carvers were also involved and were paid ten *kyats* of silver for making throne ornaments (?) for the Buddha statue. The gold leaf itself cost 1.50 *kyats* of gold, while ten *kyats* of silver was paid for the painters who pasted it on. The latter also received another fifty *kyats* of silver for "painting" the finial of the temple. The cost of the "paint" itself (which must have been gold leaf) was a substantial 263 *kyats* of silver. And, of course, the painters had to be clothed as well, which cost the donors another 8.50 *kyats* of silver.

The wages for the people who plastered the walls were sixty-nine *kyats* of silver. The wages for plastering the monastery (since it was also brick) cost another eighty *kyats* of silver. Once all the buildings were done, the donors gave the abbot on whose behalf these buildings were built a cow, two goats, and one hundred *tin* of *padi,* along with personal effects including a *puso* (male *sarong*), face towel, and items for the room, all of which cost ninety *kyats* of silver.

The wages for the firewood cutter and his wood were one hundred *kyats* of silver, relatively expensive compared with wages of expert craftsmen, although the amount of wood is not known. (By way of comparison, wages commanded by scribes appear rather high. In one case in 1344, a scribe received thirty *kyats* of silver for his written reports.) Then the roof that was put on top of the *cankram* cost twenty-five *kyats* of silver. When the time came to "release" these offerings formally, the *Vessantara Jataka* was recited (a favorite not only at Pagan and Ava but also today), people were fed, and so on, which cost another seventy-three *tin* of *padi.* The donors also gave away 150 *puso,* twenty-two goats, one boat, one horse, one elephant (?), one cow, and one ruby ring, and fed 250 monks. That was not all, for the couple donated more the very next year.

These wages for craftsmen appear to have remained relatively high a hundred years later. In 1421, a group of craftsmen were paid 984 *kyats* of silver along with *padi* and other in-kind payments for a temple and its plinth, which used 387,000 bricks. In 1445, a donor built a *cetiya* (solid *stupa*) and paid 383 *kyats* of silver and 766 *tin* of *padi* for the bricks and brick-makers (we are not told how many bricks were used), 163 *kyats* and 516 *tin* of *padi* for the mortar, and ninety-eight *kyats* and 196 *tin* of *padi* for the water haulers. Wages for the masons came to one hundred *kyats* of silver, fifty *tin* of *padi,* and ten pieces of cloth; wages for the sculptors came to 150 *kyats* of silver, fifty *tin* of *padi,* and ten pieces of cloth. The cost of the cloths altogether came to forty *kyats* of silver. Approximately a decade later, in 1462, a husband and wife team spent twenty thousand *kyats* of silver, thirty *kyats* of gold, and more on building a monastery. That represented their total costs, including wages for the carpenters, wood-carvers, sculptors, masons, gold-leaf pounders, and others listed as having been involved in the building process.

Athi were also mentioned in the inscriptions as officials who measured land (*lay taing*), charging fees for both measuring and assessing the value of the land. In areas distant from the capital, it made sense to leave the administration of such tasks to resident *athi* instead of extending the state apparatus there with valuable *kyun-daw.* The title of *pyiso* (one with authority over the *pyi*), was conferred on those whose function was to *taing hsauk* (guard the *taing*). But there were also *pyiso* who had authority over cities, such as the Sagaing *pyiso,* or the Salin (*pyi*) *so. Pyiso,* then, appears to be a generic term for those with authority over a particular place, rural or urban.

Even if many *athi* craftsmen were well paid, the status and conditions of attachment in general appear to have been more desirable than those of non-attachment, for several reasons. As argued above, attachment provided economic, social, and personal security. If attached to the *sangha,* one was not only exempt from military and other more dangerous duties, but held a relatively high spiritual status as well. If attached to the crown, it is true that soldiers would face the dangers of war also, but they would be compensated with high sociopolitical status and economic security.[4] Moreover, *athi* did not ordinarily have protection of a patron and were more or less left to their own devices, whereas attached people had patrons all the way to the royal family. Besides, skilled craftsmen who were attached could still ply their trade and work for the good of the religion; but now, their lives would be far more secure than if they were not attached at all. It was tantamount to being part of a large firm compared with going on one's own as a small businessman in today's world.

In short, it was crucial for most people to be attached rather than unattached, especially in precolonial Myanmar society. Having no niche by not belonging to one of society's major institutions was probably the worst situation for any individual or family to be in. Indeed, those not attached in early Myanmar could be compared with faculty in American academia today who are not tenured, while those attached, to those who are tenured. Which situation would one prefer?

THUGYI AND *THINGYI*

Attached or unattached, villages were sometimes settled according to craft specialty, often taking the name of that craft, as in "salt-making village," "potters' land," "artists village." Other villages adopted the ethnic identity of their inhabitants, such as Talaing Ywa (Talaing Village), while some were named for a particular sexual proclivity or condition, such as Lin Ma Lo Ywa (village that does not need husbands—or spouses, as the word *lin* was a reference to both "spouse" and "husband" at the time). Perhaps it was a village of avowed spinsters, bachelors, or homosexuals. There is no indication that this village was ostracized or stigmatized; rather, its name appears to have been an identifier, much like Panthe In (Chinese Muslim tank), referring to a reservoir that was presumably near or belonging to a village of Chinese Muslims (Panthe).

The majority of the people at the village level appear to have been under the immediate authority of people titled *thugyi* (literally, head persons, often translated into English as headmen). Thus, the head person of *athi* artists (*pagyi*) in 1341 was called *pagyi thugyi,* while the *yetthi thugyi* (head person of the weavers) was said explicitly to have authority over the *taik* (district?) of the *yetthu* (weavers). The head person of *kyun-daw* who rowed war boats (*hlawga*) was called *hlawga thugyi,* that of the bodyguards was called a *koyan thugyi,* and that of *hpaya kyun* was referred to as the *hpaya kyun thugyi* (head person of *hpaya kyun*).

Heads of ethnic groups, whether attached or unattached, and regardless of occupation, were also called *thugyi,* so that, for example, one finds a Lawa *thugyi* and a Palaung *thugyi* in the inscriptions, presumably with authority over their respective ethnic groups. (Either that or it was a reference to *thugyi* who were ethnically Lawa and Palaung.) In the case of the Lawa *thugyi,* he also happened to be a military officer, so was a *kyun-daw.* In one case, a *ywa thugyi* (village head person) of the Pyo (?) people, a less well known ethnic (?) group, is mentioned, and in another, of a *kala thugyi* (head person of Indians). Thus, the title *thugyi* appears to have been a generic term, not reserved for any specific category (attached or unattached), occupation, ethnic group, or gender (although most appear to have been male).

We also find *athi* living under the authority of *myo* and *ywa thugyi* (town and village head persons, respectively). This was a territorial designation, whose offices, at least in later Burmese history, were hereditary. In one particular case, a *thugyi* was called the *hsinke ywa thugyi* (village head person of the elephantry officers), which could mean he was head of a group of elephantry officers or that he was head of that particular village, suggesting both a territorial as well as demographic jurisdiction.

Mention is also made in Ava inscriptions of *thingyi,* which, depending on the tone, can mean either head of an organization or "great teacher," ubiquitous figures at Pagan and still around and active during Ava times. If the tone marker for the word *thin* in *thingyi* makes this person head of an organization, then the term may have been a generic one for a person who was head of any organization (rather than of people), secular or religious. Whether or not this title was related to the suffix *thin* included in names of rather well-off people (somewhat like the "von" in German), and found in both in Pagan and Ava times, is not clear.

On the other hand, an inscription of Ava dated to 1345 describes a *thingyi* as chief teacher at a particular monastery, among generations of teachers, suggesting that the meaning of *thingyi* in this case (with a different tone for *thin*) was "great teacher." Another inscription of 1372 explicitly states that *thingyi* lived in monasteries and had the title *thakin,* at the time reserved only for monks. Society at Ava was much like Pagan's.

The Conceptual System

All the most important Theravada Buddhist beliefs found at Pagan were also found at Ava. These ranged from general notions of the Buddhist universe to the specific ideologies concerning the Four Buddhas of this Kalpa and Maitreya, the fifth and future Buddha. They include the knowledge of, and reverence given to, the *Tipitakas* as well as the *Jatakas,* both of which were as much a part of Ava society as Pagan's.

Although not nearly as well-regarded "internationally" in the Buddhist ecumene as Pagan had been, Ava was nonetheless far from being considered a provincial "backwater" as a Theravada Buddhist state. There was continuous contact since the Pagan period with Sri Lanka and India with regard to religious missions, as preceding chapters have shown.

But most important for most ordinary people most of the time, as recorded in their daily religious activities, was the desire for a better rebirth, particularly as a human when Maitreya returns to earth to preach the Ultimate Sermon, which virtually guaranteed *nirvana*. This desire for a better rebirth is what Melford Spiro has called *kammatic* Buddhism, the practice of acquiring merit to affect that goal, as distinct from *nibbanic* Buddhism, attaining *nirvana* by meditation, which was mostly the domain of monks. Donors at Ava invariably ended their gifts with prayers to the effect that they be reborn as humans when Maitreya returns, a concern repeatedly heard at Pagan and throughout the centuries in Myanmar until today. Indeed, even a high-ranking member of the *sangha* donated goods to the religion in order to obtain merit, a belief and practice not unknown at Pagan either.

This relentless pursuit of merit was as equally consuming an activity at Ava society as it was in Pagan, while the socio-legal procedures for making merit were identical, from the giving of sundries to establishing permanent endowments of land and labor for the religion to the king's role in legally turning taxable crown and private property into tax-exempt glebe property. In other words, the ideology, the procedures, and the structure of *kammatic* Buddhism at Ava was identical to those at Pagan.

What this tells us is that the social, economic, and political *consequences* of the merit-path to salvation also continued to be important at Ava, as they had been at Pagan, stimulating economic development initially and depleting state resources subsequently. It also means that state-*sangha* relations at Ava mirrored those at Pagan, with all that the relationship implies. In other words, because the merit-path to salvation continued to be the central legitimating ideology of state and society, the economic and political consequences of that ideology, not surprisingly, also continued.

Perhaps as important, the persistence of the above ideologies and processes also assured the physical preservation at Ava of religious establishments (monasteries, temples, landed estates, and their human resources), which in turn were the repositories for those ideologies. The turbulent years that have been characterized as "a century of unrest," after the decline of Pagan, clearly did not appreciably affect the survival of religious estates, precisely because the ideologies and processes that were their foundation could not be eliminated by mere crises. We cannot assume, rather must prove, that crises, even major ones, destroyed everything, including intangibles such as abstract beliefs that were the foundations of these religious estates. Similarly, the legal title to these establishments remained inviolate, even if religious property in a few cases might have been taken illegally, or fallen into disuse.

Indeed, the evidence shows that many of the same monasteries and temples built and endowed during the Pagan period continued to exist and function during the Ava period. They retained legal title to properties well after the original personnel had long died and been replaced by new, surviving the turbulent political events of the first several decades following Pagan's decline. The ultimate reason this could happen was the existence of a literate society, which kept written records of ownership. In addition, these titles were recorded on nonperishable stone—difficult to dispose of, especially when encased in the brickwork of a temple or monastery—while duplicates were preserved on palm-leaf manuscripts by the state, the recipient, and the donor. Thus, providing proof of ownership of *sanghikha* property was not a difficult task, even if a great deal of time has passed and the original recipient had passed away.

That legal titles remained inviolable despite political crises is borne out by the epigraphic evidence. One of the earliest donations made at Pagan, dated to

1051 during the reign of King Anawrahta, was still considered valid glebe property by 1346, nearly three hundred years later. Another endowment of land made in 1139 by King Alaungsithu to the Taing Khyut pagoda, consisting of 750 *pay* of *lay*, was rededicated as legally valid glebe, to which was added thirty new *pay* of *lay* and eight more *kyun* and recorded in an inscription of 1344, 205 years later. The record dedicating the Mahabodhi Temple and its endowed lands, made during the mid-thirteenth century, remained in the care of one old couple, who, as an act of merit, had a new inscription made of the earlier one in excruciatingly precise detail; clearly the kind of activity that preserved the integrity of the original gift subsequently (and one obviously in their interests). Another donation made in 1261 during King Narathihapade's reign was duly rededicated in 1341. One more example, an inscription of 1363, erected one year before Ava was formally made capital of the new dynasty, stated that (the descendants) of the monks of the Anantathu monastery, built and donated during the Pagan period in the thirteenth century, still occupied it.

Indeed, in 1992 when the late U Nyein Maung, compiler of the several volumes of Old Burmese inscriptions I use here, checked on some identifiable villages to which glebe lands were donated and named in an inscription of 1335, they (and the glebe lands) were still intact and legally valid, while others donated during the Pagan period that I personally investigated in 2005 were also still legally religious property. To put it another way, that legal title to religious property dedicated three centuries ago remained valid, that the same temple and monastery existed to make the claim with proof of clear title, and that the names and locations of those endowed lands remained unchanged after nearly three hundred years, is part of the reason for, and testimony to the structural continuity of, the society in which this happened. For, it is largely in those religious establishments that the ideas and values of society were preserved. The physical and legal survival of religious endowments was, in part, responsible for the continuity of Ava society as a whole, despite political events that may have brought changes at the court and county levels.

It is true, of course, that some of these title holders or their descendants, either as individuals or as corporations, did not necessarily survive the early decades of the alleged disorder at the end of the Pagan dynasty. In the few cases we have on record, the state probably claimed possession of such property. But such illegal acquisitions were almost always successfully challenged subsequently by their owners (usually members of the *sangha*), so that many ultimately reverted to being religious property, although a very few cases exist where relatives, friends, and neighbors appropriated this property without being challenged.

Often, new donations of land and labor were made during the Ava period to old temples and monasteries built during the Pagan period, some located at Pagan, some at Ava, and some elsewhere. Most people probably could not afford to build new religious edifices every time they wanted to donate to the religion, yet had enough resources to endow land and labor to, or repair, already existing temples and monasteries. In 1363, a donor gave land and labor at Myin Mu, across the Irrawaddy from Ava and west of Sagaing, to a monastery that was physically located at Pagan. When Ava donors added to previous donations whose stone records no longer existed, they would normally precede their own narrative with information regarding the previous donation (presumably) taken from palm-leaf or other duplicate records. The information is so precise—date, location, boundaries, names of people, amount donated, and so on—that the new donor must have had a written record in hand.

Of course, it was also in the interest of the new donor to make sure that the property being currently donated remained distinct from the earlier one, not only for calculating the merit one accrued but for legal purposes as well. Thus, a donation made in 1368 for a temple built in 1237 reiterated the data contained on the original donation, separating the property of that earlier donation from the current one in great detail, while another in 1397 made certain that his donation of (even a paltry) five *pay* of *lay* was distinct from earlier donations made in 1299.

Sometimes, religious land fell into disuse during periods of disorder, and the jungle took over. Even if subsequently cleared and cultivated by the state or private individuals, most were invariably rededicated to the *sangha*. When a donor in 1386 rededicated old and new glebe lands to a particular monastery, he recorded on the new stone that the Chinese in 1255 had destroyed some lands, which had turned into jungle. In time, these had been usurped by crown troops, but subsequently, under protest by the descendants of the monks who laid claims to those lands, the king ordered (on a stone pillar where his command was inscribed) that the property be declared glebe once more, giving it back to the current abbot of the monastery to which the title originally belonged. A similar incident occurred with a donation of 1398. In this case, crown troops had not usurped the land but the jungle had taken over; the property was then cleared and plowed and rededicated to the *sangha*.

In a few cases, unencumbered virgin land was cleared and cultivated. However, this kind of development constituted only a very small portion or component of the total economy of the kingdom, due mainly, I suspect, to the shortage of labor. By and large, such examples did not represent a significant amount of wealth, with only a handful of examples that can be securely documented and whose total acreage is minimal. Thus, although there probably was some recycling and reclamation of land and labor, the evidence for it is meagre and could not have amounted to much.

In short, not only did the most important ideologies of Burmese Theravada Buddhism continue at Ava, the institutions that upheld, supported, and financed them, the physical establishments themselves (the temples, the monasteries, the endowments), as well as the legal apparatus and processes that upheld their titles of ownership (the stone inscriptions, the palm-leaf manuscripts, the archives) also survived. Despite this continuity, convention has it that Ava was religiously unorthodox, no doubt influenced by the thesis that "Ava is Shan," positing a major discontinuity. Historians of Myanmar have asserted that certain incidents of eating meat and drinking liquor by monks, allegedly found in the inscriptions of Ava, suggest unorthodox practices of at least some members of the *sangha*, in turn confirming the broader notion of political and religious decline at Ava. Leaving aside the issue of what constitutes orthodoxy and unorthodoxy, there is an even more basic problem regarding the evidence. So far, the data at Ava directly contradicts the conventional view.

It is true that when a legal transaction surrounding a religious donation was complete, at closing (*pyi*), the donor customarily also paid for meat and liquor, called "closing eats" (as one inscription put it) and "closing feasts" (as another called it). On one such occasion, in 1430, there were many *athi* present, with an endless flow of liquor, while musical instruments were played all day under the big Ma-U tree until it was dark. However, in not a single one of these Ava inscriptions that recorded such closing feasts (and there were dozens) is there evidence that monks actually participated in the eating and drinking of this meat and liquor. Nor is there any evidence that monks were even present, with two exceptions. The first is a donation made in 1431 by the head of the *sangha*, the *mahasangharaja*, so of course he would have to be present as the purchaser and donor of the land, and equally obliged to provide for the customary closing feasts as other donors were. That, however, does not mean he partook of the meat and liquor, nor is there any evidence that he did.

In the second exception, several monks were indeed mentioned as part of the group of legal witnesses for the closing ceremonies. But in this case, there is no mention of liquor or beef being offered, although there was music performed. Apparently, the inscription had not been read very carefully by previous scholars, for it continues to state that, subsequently, in October–November, stone posts were erected to mark off the boundaries of the glebe lands donated, which was not completed until June-July of the following year. Only by the ensuing September-October was it finally completed, and only then was a cow butchered for a headman and scribe who came to inspect and make the official inventory. The monks who were present during the initial ceremony of closing nearly a year earlier (where music was played) were not mentioned and presumably no longer present at the time the meat and liquor were served. These were two separate phases of the same donation, nearly a year apart, but recorded on the same stone.

In other words, closing feasts where meat and liquor were served were meant only for lay people and officials who had been involved in the legal transactions, not monks. Besides, even if monks participated in closing feasts where meat and liquor were served (although there is no evidence of it), that does not necessarily imply that the entire Theravada Buddhist *sangha* in Ava and its doctrines were therefore unorthodox, no more than a few Roman Catholic priests convicted of sexual abuse in certain parishes in the United States necessarily signaled the decline of orthodoxy in the US Roman Catholic Church. Besides, I am not certain we can ever agree on what constitutes orthodoxy and what does not; and how we would go about proving one or the other? I know of no religion without unorthodox components, especially in practice, even if we agree that following of orthodox texts constitutes orthodoxy, which, of course, is a tautology.

One thing for certain that is sorely needed, as demonstrated by the above cases, is that we must make sure the evidence is far more carefully scrutinized than has heretofore been done before rushing to judgment. Ava, for all intents and purposes, was no more and no less orthodox than Pagan was, even if Pagan enjoys the prestige of being the exemplary model of Myanmar's Theravada Buddhist orthodoxy. Neither the Pagan and Ava evidence nor that of subsequent periods supports a linear and progressive development toward religious orthodoxy in Myanmar's history. Instead, I believe orthodoxy and unorthodoxy (even if one could define them) went in cycles, a process that is still going on today.

To be sure, despite this obvious and overall continuity in religious beliefs and institutions, Ava *did* break with Pagan religious traditions in several ways, particularly in terms of religious art and architecture. The city of Sagaing, across the Irrawaddy from Ava, represents its "field of merit" where most of its temples and other religious edifices were built. The majority of the monuments at Sagaing reflect a preference for the solid *stupa* rather than what art historians call the *stupa*-temple, which represents a *gu* (cave), a style ubiquitous at Pagan. Although the solid *stupa* was also important at Pagan, it was not as spectacularly dominating a style as the *stupa*-temple was, with its large interior spaces; exquisite keystone arching; magnificent, robust, and breathtaking barrel vaults; and soaring double and triple stories, ingeniously constructed interior stairways, and distinctive floor plans.

Part of the reason Ava's religious architecture was clearly inferior may have been that it had lost the engineering technique of vaulting, the architectural principle so fundamental to the design, shape, size, and integrity of the *stupa*-temple. Even the few Pagan-style *stupa*-temples built during the immediate post-Pagan period at the city of Pinya, brief predecessor of Ava, already showed signs of flawed and tired design in their vaulting, so that by the time the Kingdom of Ava emerged, most, if not all of the royal temples were solid *stupas.* All this is clearly related to economic resources; Ava did not and could not recapture the wealth needed for this kind of technically demanding and extremely expensive temple construction on the size and scale enjoyed by Pagan. But all this was not the result of unorthodoxy; it was a question of money and expertise.

In any case, when the Kingdom of Ava became a fully developed entity by the early fifteenth century, its religious system as a whole had not been transformed into something substantively new and different from Pagan's. Unlike maritime Southeast Asia, which went through a major transformation during approximately the same period of Ava's rise and decline—the introduction and growth of Islam that eventually (after several centuries) replaced (and then, not entirely) the earlier belief systems in much of maritime Southeast Asia, while Catholicism in the Philippines did much the same thing there, along with, some would argue, "Confucianism" in Vietnam—for the most part, agrarian, interior Myanmar preserved and perpetuated its classical system.

The Political and Administrative Structure of the Kingdom

In actual size, the Kingdom of Ava was not nearly as large as the Kingdom of Pagan had been. But in terms of structure—both principles and actual governance—Ava was nearly identical to Pagan. Whereas Pagan stretched from inside the borders of China today (Ngasaungkyan fortress) in the north to what is today Mergui (Myeik or Byeik) in the far south, Arakan in the West to (at least) Inle on the East, Ava's authority was confined largely to Upper Myanmar, its influence and hegemony extending to certain centers in Lower Myanmar only occasionally. At its height in the mid-fifteenth century, Ava's reach did extend as far north as Momeit, Mogaung, and Bhamo, as far east as Nyaung Shwe and Mone, as far west as Thindwe in Arakan (most of the time), and as far south as Pyi, although sometimes also to Pathein and Myaung Mya in the Myanmar Delta (as shown in figure 3, chapter 5).

Yet, its smaller size and interior focus did not mean Ava was isolated from its neighbors. Distant Vietnam (as Annam), especially its conquest by what Ava inscriptions referred to as "Maha Cina" (Great China), Peking (as Taitu), and Yunnan, were all well known and often mentioned. An inscription of 1364 referred to Kubilai Khan as "the great Chinese [Tayok] king, Cakravatiy Khan [world conqueror Khan] whose strength is given by Sakra." Ava knew of and considered Sukhotai a *pyi* (kingdom, polity, state). Ayuthaya was mentioned several times, and in one context, Ava conceded the King of Ayuthaya's hegemony over Tenasserim, while his grandson was referred to as Muttama Hsinphyushin (lord of the white elephant of Muttama). Lower Myanmar, usually called Ussa Pegu, along with a list of its Mon kings, was also well known. One inscription mentioned the great Yazadarit who once ruled Hanthawaddy Pyi (or, the kingdom of Hanthawaddy). His elder sister Mahadevi and his uncle, both enemies of Yazadarit (the uncle was Ava's ally) were also mentioned in Ava inscriptions, information later reiterated in late Mon and Burmese chronicles.

In terms of political and administrative principles and institutions, as well as actual implementation, Pagan and Ava were very similar. Anyone who belonged to the Pagan court two hundred years earlier would have been familiar with the structure of the Ava court. Not only did virtually all its members retain the official titles of their counterparts in Pagan, but they also appear to have exercised the same functions.

Thus, for example, the office of crown prince (heir apparent) continued to be called *Einshemin* (Lord of the Eastern [Front] Palace). The most legitimate principle with regard to this office was that he be the eldest son of the king and his chief queen, followed by the king's brothers. Although the office of heir and rules of succession were created (at Pagan) to institutionalize and stabilize such events, it also created an in-built and ongoing contest between the son(s) and the brother(s) of the king, both legitimate heirs. If the son were officially appointed heir, that would have eliminated the claim of the king's brother and his lineage forever (and vice versa). As we have seen, it became the basis for the invariable uncle-nephew struggle of monarchical Myanmar well into the Konbaung period.

Yet, and despite that problem, of the sixteen kings of Pagan who succeeded to the throne and whose historicity can be confirmed by epigraphy, twelve had been designated heir apparent. At Ava, of the thirteen or fourteen Burmese kings that succeeded the founder until the toppling of the dynasty by three Shan *sawbwa,* at least nine had been designated heir, while the rest had legal claims to the throne. Thus, the rule of succession, even with inherent problems, managed to function as it was designed to function most of the time.

The king's adviser and head of the *sangha* at Ava, as at Pagan, was also called the *mahasangharaja* (great lord of the *sangha*), and the religious hierarchy found at Pagan was similarly found at Ava. The old descending organization of the *sangha* from the *mahasangharaja,* the *sangharaja* (lord of the *sangha,* probably a provincial head), *mahathera* (great monk, an elder of a prominent monastery), *thera* (monk, or elder, the ordinary ordained cleric) to the *samanera* (novice) remained essentially unchanged. That suggests both the hierarchy as well as the administration of the *sangha* remained operative, while its unifying role in society that crossed ethno-linguistic, cultural, political, economic, and geographic boundaries continued as well.

The southern queen retained her title of *saw* and remained chief queen, while the chief minister who usually assumed the title Yazathingyan continued as well, along with those of ministers, who, as a group kept their Sanskrit title of Amataya. As in Pagan, one of these ministers was the Mahathaman, still in charge of royal donations at Ava. The officers under the ministers who had military portfolios, as in Pagan, retained their titles of Sithugyi (head of military), under whom were officers called Bhopa and Kalan.

Members of the Ava court, indeed the court itself, also behaved in similar ways. It conducted royal coronations, built at least one new palace, intrigued for the throne, enhanced its political power through marriage alliances and patronage, made war and peace, and consolidated its military strength in traditional ways. Members of the court also built, repaired, and maintained temples, monasteries, and libraries, and donated land, people, money, and (sometimes) themselves to the *sangha.* The court cleared, irrigated, and cultivated land, conducted cadastral and demographic surveys, ordered revenue inquests, and collected taxes.

The Ava king was probably as often primus inter pares as he was sovereign, depending on the particular reign or period. Especially during the first sixty years after the fall of Pagan and the rise of Ava, that is, between 1300 and 1360, he was clearly primus inter pares rather than sovereign. Thereafter, with the exception of few brief lapses, he became more sovereign, especially as he garnered more wealth, hence power and influence, as indicated by the increasing length of his reign and scope of his influence. In contrast, at Pagan, once established, the king was more often sovereign than he was primus inter pares. But both features (as ends of a spectrum) existed in both kingdoms.

This means that at Ava, the ever-present disintegrative factors—particularly underlying court factionalism—often strained the integrative factors more often than they did at Pagan. The political groups that coalesced around the southern (chief) queen and crown prince, the familiar tensions between brothers of the king and sons of the king, and the endless personal jealousies that triggered disastrous events were all too familiar. At the same time, loyal and experienced ministers whose tenure would often last well beyond a single reign, and whose "national" interests extended well beyond the immediate concerns of princely intrigues, provided the balance and stability the court needed at both Pagan and Ava.

At virtually all levels—"national," provincial, township, and village—the *myosa* (town eater) system remained the modus operandi of administrative organization, whose principle of patron-clientelism was euphemistically termed "at the royal compassion" (*thanadaw*). It was essentially an administrative expression of *kyun*-ship. Lucrative fiefs were given to kinfolk, friends, and followers, based on personal and close sociopolitical relationships, so that both near and distant provinces continued to be governed and administered by *myosa*. Fiefs were given both to favorites of the king, simply as favors, and to competent administrators, as payment for their services.

The "to eat" principle underlay the religious sector as well, as the *sangha* applied the same principles regarding its own clients. Indeed, one could argue that Ava depended more on this principle than did Pagan, for the latter was wealthier, militarily stronger, and far better integrated administratively, making it institutionally more stable and therefore less in need of the *myosa* principle, whereas Ava could not have done without it. But the principle itself underlay both Pagan and Ava's systems and geographically stretched to the far reaches of both kingdoms while it structurally affected every level of society.

Political Ideology: Conceptions of Kingship

It should not be surprising that Ava also adopted and expressed the same ideas of kingship found at Pagan: the *kammaraja, devarajika, dhammaraja, bodhisatta,* and *cakkavatti* notions of the king. Among historical monarchs, Asoka remained, as at Pagan, the quintessential model for Ava kings. Even two women, one a commoner, the other of high rank, made donations and invoked the image of Asoka. The bones of one Ava king were enshrined in a *cetiya,* a ritual meant to be reserved only for *arahat* and *cakkavatti.* Another Ava king enshrined the bodily relics of his ancestors, implying that they too were *cakkavatti.* These acts surely would have also underscored the *devarajika* (and supernatural) components of kingship.

The conceptions of a *dhammaraja* certainly continued at Ava as well. Legitimacy and authority of the king are found in his role as patron, preserver, and promoter of Buddhist state and society. Many Ava inscriptions state, as at Pagan, that the material well-being and happiness of soldiers, monks, and people rest on the king. One of the ways in which the *dhammaraja* accomplished this was *dhammavijaya* (righteous victory), directly related to the material and spiritual development of his kingdom. Not only would the king acquire labor from conquered areas, but military victories resulted in material rewards to military officers, much of which ended up as donations to the *sangha.* Thus, the growth of state, society, and the *sangha,* the preservation of the conceptions surrounding the *dhammaraja* and the implementation of *dhammavijaya,* were all importantly and closely linked, as they were at Pagan.

Like the Pagan king, and apart from Buddhist notions of kingship, the Ava king was commonly also perceived as "lord of land and water." This was more than mere rhetoric, as we have seen in previous chapters, although it needed ritual to institutionalize and confirm it. The king therefore often used his personal gold drinking cup to pour the water of consecration that released land donations from secular ties (and taxes) to the spiritual (and tax-exempt) realm.[5] Using his own personal drinking cup symbolized the patriarch quenching the thirst of his children, much like Kyanzittha of Pagan, who stated that he was like "the father who wipes away the nasal mucus from the noses of his children."

Other forms of non-Indic, local perceptions of kingship were best expressed in the king's jurisdiction over (especially) urban society, in the same way spirits and other forces of nature had jurisdiction over their natural domains. Thus, one inscription stated that whosoever violates his donation, besides suffering in hell, if he travels by water, may the dangers inherent in water befall him, if he takes a mountain path, may the dangers inherent in mountains befall him, *if he enters a village, may the dangers of kings befall him,* may the earth swallow him, may lightning strike him, may tigers and crocodiles eat him, may he vomit clots of blood. In other words, the king was part of the natural order of things, and had jurisdiction over settled society (represented by the village) in the same way animals, water, mountains, the earth, and lightning have jurisdiction over unsettled society.

The kinds of integrative state activities found during the Pagan period did not disappear with Pagan but remained at Ava, especially the "national" rituals performed with great pomp and ceremony, spectacles (to paraphrase the late Clifford Geertz) that displayed, in ritual form, the dominant themes of one's culture. One of the most compelling pieces of evidence that demonstrates the continuity of such "national" rituals is found in an inscription dated to 1510 that commemorated, in excruciating detail, the building of a new palace by King Narapati.[6] It is a virtual replica (hence, reenactment) of the building of King Kyanzittha's palace, dated to around 1102, four hundred years earlier! Interestingly also, Narapati's inscription of 1510 was placed in a temple called the Htihlaingshin, the name by which Kyanzittha was allegedly known to posterity. The new palace at Ava, like Kyanzittha's, had the usual auspicious twelve gates, each representing a zodiac sign, and was therefore, among other things, a symbol of heaven on earth and the Indic cosmos.

Both Pagan and Ava palace-building rituals were clearly Brahmanic, with some indigenous and Buddhist elements integrated therein, overall revealing much about the principles and patterns of king and state, society and religion, earth and cosmos. I summarize and paraphrase the Ava palace-building ceremony from the Old Burmese inscription of 1510 that took up eighty-nine lines of the stone. Perhaps better than any other single source, this inscription reveals and articulates the various notions of kingship. Unfortunately, many parts have been flaked off, but enough remains to provide the gist (and in some cases, details) of the ceremony, which are extremely important and revealing. The reader can easily compare this to King Kyanzittha's, which had been translated into English earlier. (U Kala also has a description of it in as much detail, except had the date wrong.)

The king, "Shwenan Kyauk [*sic*] Shin Narapati, gathered all the wise men in the great centers beginning with Sagaing, Pinya, Pagan, and Ava who were knowledgeable about the *Pitakas* and astrology. When the constellations were aligned properly, offerings were made of cow's milk, butter [ghee], curds, cream"—all the foodstuffs familiar to and favorites of Brahmanic India, but not necessarily of Upper Myanmar, Burmese culture. There were several magnificent parades "beginning with riders holding weapons, sheathed lances, gold masks, many decorated elephants, infantry and all the 'braves' [soldiers], followed by all the resplendently attired ministers surrounding and moving gracefully around the king, who wielded a white umbrella."

On another day, "the king rode on an elephant decorated with gold ornaments holding up white umbrellas," while crown soldiers (*kyun-daw thuye,* literally, royal servants, braves) "pulled the special wood that was to become the palace, with the root sides facing west and the top sides facing east.[7] The wood was placed northeast of the palace site and with butter, honey, yogurt [and presumably some of the same ingredients mentioned above, as the inscription is flaked off here], offerings were made." After that, "water was fetched from a special confluence of the river," people carrying more than a hundred earthen, brass, silver, and gold jars, probably to wash down the selected wood (inscription flaked here as well) and offerings made to deities of certain trees. At that northeast corner where the selected wood for the palace was placed, offerings were made to the "Paramesvara *nat* king who ruled over all the creatures of that region" to act as guardian. The ceremony included those "wielding golden shields, bows and arrows, ceremonial lances, followed by those playing drums, wind instruments and clappers, along with 126 people wearing silver hats and carrying brass jars, followed by people wearing good *paso* [male *sarong*] who carried [?] a covering [?] made of white cloths."

They were followed by (their?) "beautiful daughters, carrying golden vases, in which were banana and sugar cane plants, coconut shells, and betel leaves. Members of the clergy, replete with various qualities, followed them." Then came the astrologers, Brahmins, architects, rich men, giving us a glimpse of society's hierarchy and priorities.

When they reached the edge of the river, "the king ascended his royal golden barge surrounded by many golden barges to perform the water retrieving ritual where the various vases and jars were filled." This water was used, on another day and ceremony, to wash and clean the main posts of the palace using the king's own golden cup and conch, moving clockwise (literally, right-wise, or sunwise, in Burmese). Then the astrologers, Brahmins, and architects made offerings of cow's milk, clarified butter (ghee), curds, yogurt (?), honey, and jaggery (palm sugar). Musicians performed at a specific time when the constellations were correct.

The next day, the site where the royal temple was to be built was marked off with much ceremony again. Using gold and silver spades, the site for building a temple called the royal area was leveled and its dirt stirred. The *paritta* was recited, after which the monks were fed.

Several days later, when the constellations were again aligned correctly, the wood specifically selected was used to build various buildings of the palace. On the Sabbath, eighth waxing day of the month of Tagu (approximately answering to April), the royal teacher named Mahadhammagutta and his forty-four disciples were fed.

On Saturday, full moon of Tagu, the palace ground was rubbed smooth with *durba* grass, cow dung, cow's milk, curds, yogurt, ghee, jaggery, and glue to cleanse it. Earthen jars in which water fetched from select confluence of rivers had many flowers placed in them. Seeds and sprouts of flower baskets, including orchids were placed there. Fish, with their tails on, were placed there as food.

The one hundred and eight *nats* were placed in their appropriate locations. The Moon Nat, Sakra with his thunderbolt, and Sujata were placed on top of the white elephant Eravana, while Galon was placed on top of Naga, on top of which rode the image of Sunday. The fire *nat,* color coded and wearing red, with red cloths and umbrellas, and red flowers, was also placed in its proper pavilion. The zodiac figure of Friday was put in its proper place with the checkered (?) umbrella.

In the fourth pavilion, on the south side, with black cloths, black flowers, and black umbrella was placed the buffalo riding Yama *nat* [Vedic god of the dead]. The inscription continues with each of the week days and their representative zodiac figures, their placements, colors and insignia, including Rahu (the inauspicious planet residing in the second half of Wednesday), Varuna with a lasso, Saturday zodiac, and Monday zodiac riding on a tiger. Ganesha was placed in the jeweled, celestial mansion with all his accouterments. In the ninth pavilion, on its western part, was placed Paramesvara on a white cow. Brahma's statue was also included. Twenty other *nat* represented by twenty pillows and beds, were offered a variety of foods.

The king then circumambulated these figures "right-wise" and propitiated them. "So that all the people in the entire kingdom can also worship these *nat* and celebrate this ritual, all big and small villages were visited with bronze gongs announcing it. After the pagoda was finished, the scaffold was removed and prisoners were released."

The palace itself was called *rajathani* (king's place), which was circumambulated three times and sprinkled with water taken from the confluence of select rivers. Other parades and rituals followed, including an interesting remark made by the inscription about daughters of Brahmins and daughters of the Pyu who wove a spread of some sort with 108 threads to be placed atop a finial of some structure that was illegible. Toward the end, horoscopes written on gold, silver, lead, iron, and copper sheets were buried with a stone slab that held the main post of the palace. The inscription then stated that this is the ritual of the earth. (The palace in Myanmar is, of course, called the *mye nan,* palace of the earth.) The ceremony began sometime in November-December and ended in July-August. Someone from Pagan who had witnessed King Kyanzittha's palace-building ritual four hundred years earlier would have easily recognized this one of 1510.

The Legal System

Colonial scholars of Myanmar have been reconstructing the subject of law and legal institutions of the precolonial period since the late nineteenth century; many of their conclusions, however, have been challenged in recent years by twentieth-century students of the subject. The topic is immense, and I leave it to those more competent than I, both established scholars and a younger generation with a great deal of promise in filling this gap.[8] What I *can* do here, however, is show from original inscriptions that Ava, like Pagan, also used codified law, and how the former's traditions were likely based on the foundations built by the latter. Some scholars feel that the earliest *dhammathat* (civil code of laws dealing with marriage, divorce, inheritance, and so on) in Myanmar may go back to the Pyu period, between the first century BC and the ninth century AD. Although there is no unequivocal proof of it, one of the *hpyathon* (compilation of legal precedents) is called the *Duttabaung Hpyathon,* named for a king who was said to have ruled Old Pyi, one of the centers of the Pyu dated between the second century BC and ninth century AD. Another, the *Pyumin Dhammathat,* named after Pyuminhti, legendary founder of Pagan, was said to have been compiled in 727 AD. It is listed in the *Pitakat Thamaing* (a nineteenth-century bibliography) and other chronicles, while the king who was said to have compiled it, Pyuminhti, might actually have been a historical figure.

Moreover, the complex society that the Pyus had—urban settlements of walled cities; a kingdom ruled by a monarchy of at least two known dynasties that was to last approximately a millennium; a relatively uniform culture in terms of language, writing, art, and architecture; a coinage system linked to the trade and commerce of the "international" world; an agrarian economy with at least tank, if not canal, irrigation; several ethnic and social groups plying a variety of occupations; a conceptual system grounded on Theravada and other older forms of Buddhism—suggests that some codified uniform law was probably present. And although there is no conclusive evidence that *dhammathats* per se existed at the time, the conditions suggest the presence at least of uniform, codified civil laws.

By the Pagan period, it is clear that civil law codified in *dhammathats* existed. One of these may have been the much-celebrated *Dhammavilasa Dhammathat* recalled by legal scholars in subsequent periods. If so, the title of the work suggests that the jurist with the title *Dhammavilasa* probably compiled it, who may have been the famous monk Sariputta, mentioned in contemporary Pagan inscriptions. One dated to 1216 AD, referring back to 1187 AD, called him "our lord Dhammavilasa," who donated two temples and other sundries to the Buddha. If this were the noted jurist, it places him during King Narapatisithu's reign, which later chronicles also contend was the period in which Dhammavilasa lived.[9]

Furthermore, contemporary stone inscriptions of Pagan that described incidents of civil law being practiced echo important principles expressed in the *dhammathats.* For example, even the cost of attachment and/or redeeming *kyun* in Pagan was the same as that found in the *dhammathat.* Some of the practices of becoming a servant of the *sangha* (thereby releasing oneself from secular service obligation) are confirmed by principles in the *dhammathat.*[10] There are other indications that legal practices in Pagan reflected codified law, for even the orthography and vocabulary used in the inscriptions are retained in later copies of *dhammathat.* Prima facie as well, it would be difficult to imagine a society with the size, wealth, complexity, and power of Pagan not to have had a codified system of laws. Although there is surely some debate over some of these issues, that a *dhammathat* was actually used for civil law seems likely enough.

There also existed at Pagan a legal code called *amunwan ca* that was distinct from the civil *dhammathat.* It dealt with what appears to have been criminal law, including theft, arson, and murder. King Kyaswa's inscription of 1249, a royal order, whose copies were said to have been dispersed throughout the kingdom, stated, "In the *amunwan* it says that a thief, if he has committed such and such a transgression, must pay such and such a penalty. [Then] the King matches the thief's transgression in the *amunwan* and exacts the penalty incurred by that crime."[11] That, in fact, describes a code of law, the crime, its punishment, and the procedure for its implementation. And in this case, that code was a criminal code, since theft fell under that category. Note also that the king himself determined the sentence and exacted the penalty, unlike the *dhammathat* left to the civil courts and their judges. Because the Burmese term for "criminal punishment" is *mindan* or *yazadan* (king's punishment), it clearly ties criminal law with crimes against the authority of the king, and by extrapolation, the state. Theft and arson directly challenges the king's role as *dhammaraja* who provides law and order. Even if the etymology of *amunwan ca* is obscure, its function was clear: it served as a collection of explicit punishments for explicit crimes. All of this leads me to believe that the *amunwan ca* was likely the prototype for the later *rajathat* (king's law). Neither *dhammathat* nor *rajathat* were mere regalia of kings, as often suggested, but actually used as basis for meting out justice.

At least the *dhammathat* tradition can be documented to have continued into the Ava period, although it would be reasonable to assume that the *rajathat* tradition did as well. A *dhammathat* is mentioned in the contemporary sources of Ava, although it was found among a list of texts dedicated to a monastery, so it is quite possible that the text was not a current or active legal code in use. But because *dhammathat* had long been the written basis for civil law at Pagan, one could also argue that, even if this particular one were not, it does not preclude the actual use of *dhammathat* in Ava society. Including it in a donation is not unusual, for such texts were held in high esteem, close to sacredness.

Later sources also speak of a *Kungya Dhammathat,* said to have been written in 1426 during the Ava period, but I have not found that particular text mentioned in contemporary Ava sources. That another text with the word "*Kungya*" in the title exists is clear, written by the famous minister mentioned earlier who served several kings, Hpo Yaza or Minyaza. He may have also been the author of the *Kungya Dhammathat.* Another monk of high stature, also with the title of Dhammaraja Vilasa, was mentioned in an inscription erected in 1347 by the queen. And an inscription of 1442 (noted above) records a donation made by a governor and his wife that included several hundred books in which was mentioned a *dhammasatta.* To which particular *dhammathat* it was referring, we do not know. The latest version of the *Pitakat Thamaing,* compiled in the nineteenth century, also claims that the *Pasadha Dhammathat* was written in 1468 AD. Indeed, *dhammathat,* as written texts, had attained such a stature that several verses were composed that extolled their virtues.

As for codified criminal law, I have not seen explicit evidence of its practice at Ava, either referred to as *amunwan ca* or by another name. That there was crime and punishment, of course, is reasonable to assume. After Ava, especially in the Second Ava and Konbaung periods, there seems to have been an explosion in the writing of legal texts, although that abundance of evidence may be just a matter of document survival. Whatever the situation may have been at Ava regarding the likely use of *dhammathat,* what is more striking and conspicuous, especially compared with Pagan, is the total absence of lawsuits over land and labor in the Ava inscriptions. Also conspicuously missing is any mention of the components of a legal apparatus, such as attorneys (*shene,* except for one ambiguous case); judges (*thinphama*); reference to plaintiffs, defendants, and witnesses in such disputes; judicial decisions from "the bench"; civil suits won and lost; and other pertinent legal jargon found in the inscriptions of Pagan. In the Ava inscriptions, there is mention of one local arbitrator called *taya thugyi* (literally, headmen of the law), who was involved as a witness in a legal transaction over land, but that is it.

This paucity of original evidence regarding litigation over land suggests several things. First, laws regarding land ownership by then had been better established and understood, so that there were fewer reasons for dispute than there had been previously, particularly with regard to establishing clear title to religions holdings, because ownership had been secured in writing, both on stone and palm leaf, and securely kept in monasteries. It could also mean, second, that society had fewer occasions (or the luxury) for such litigation, for Ava was less wealthy than Pagan and certainly with much less legally unencumbered land to donate (hence also to dispute). To be sure, there appears to have been a large increase of donations in cash, but that kind of unambiguous and straightforward, one-time gift hardly invites disputes, which land donations given in perpetuity long ago to overlapping jurisdictions and requiring proof of title, and other such requirements, can. Third, because the *sangha* invariably had written title to its property on palm leaf and stone, and because most lawsuits during the Pagan period were contestations not among members of the *sangha* but among lay individuals (or between individuals and the state) over the bona fides of donated property rather than over ownership per se, legal title to *sangha* holdings by the Ava period was probably no longer much of an issue, providing little or no reason for that kind of litigation.

In summary, although the Kingdom of Ava by the fifteenth century was not as large, powerful, wealthy, and magnificent as Pagan had been, it was probably as close to a (miniature) Pagan as one could expect, both in context and content. Ava was physically smaller in size, less powerful, less grand, with less stature in the region and the Buddhist world, and with fewer resources coming in from Lower Myanmar in terms of revenues and people. Yet, as shown in this chapter, its structure—institutions and their relationships—as well as the ingredients that went into them—the material resources, the behavior, values, sentiments, and beliefs of its people—were still the same. One of the most important of these was the relentless pursuit of merit-making, so that the reason for and actual flow of wealth from the taxable to the tax-exempt sector continued unabated. Because of this, from its inception Ava was already doomed, but not before it made a significant impact on the future of the country.

7

The Last Decades and the Decline of Ava

The kingdom that was Ava came to an end in 1526–1527. It can be attributed to both long-term structural (institutional) causes as well as "incidents of the moment," events that set afire the former "kindling." These events often accelerate but can also slow down (sometimes, actually reverse) long-term patterns and trends. In Ava's case, they accelerated its decline.

As previous chapters have shown, the Kingdom of Ava's remote origins go back to the Mongol invasions of 1301; thereafter Ava developed in political, military, economic, administrative, religious, and cultural ways during the second half of the fourteenth and the first half of the fifteenth centuries, finally reaching its zenith during the second half of the fifteenth century. The foundations built by Narapati the Great, Mahasihasura, and Mingaung the Second enabled the kingdom to remain strong and relatively vibrant for more than another two decades. Then, during the beginning of the third decade, toward the end of the reign of Narapati the Second, things began to unravel until the capital was taken twice, once in 1524 and finally in 1526, by one of its Shan vassals, Salon, governor of Mohnyin, ending the First Ava Dynasty by 1527.

Thereafter, Ava became an ordinary *myosa*-ship and ceased being an exemplary center of Upper Myanmar, until raised once again as capital of the Second Ava Dynasty in 1600. However, that story belongs to the seventeenth century and is not within the scope of the present study.[1] Here, the focus is on the factors responsible for the decline of the First Ava Dynasty. What were those long-term structural causes that were brought to fruition by "incidents of the moment"?

The Decline of Ava: The Remote Causes

THE MERIT-PATH TO SALVATION

First, one of the most persistent structural factors in Myanmar's history—and Ava was no exception—has to do with the flow of wealth to the tax-exempt *sangha*. As long as the merit-path to salvation remained the primary ideology of the Ava kingdom and society, donations to the *sangha* and religion continued. And, as at Pagan, such activity initially enhanced the socioeconomic and political development of Ava, especially since it was recovering from the disruptions of the late thirteenth and early fourteenth centuries created by Pagan's decline. However, in time, after the process continued unabated for over two centuries, in Ava's case (in Pagan's, four centuries), what once was an asset had become a liability. Thus, in both situations, whereas the merit-path to salvation initially provided the economic, cultural, social, and political stimulant to growth and integration, it subsequently led to decay and disintegration. In other words, religious donations should be regarded as both a factor in development and a factor in decay. Combined, therefore, they created an oscillation between growth and decay, rather than a one-time, linear process never to be repeated again.

The original and contemporary data that tells this story comes from approximately 431 inscriptions that have been recovered from the period between 1284, when the Mongols first attacked the Kingdom of Pagan, and 1526–1527, when Ava was taken. These 431, however, represent approximately 531 distinct donations made to the *sangha*, so that the number of actual donations exceeds the number of stones on which they are recorded, because more than one donation is recorded on each stone, sometimes just below the first, but more often on the reverse side of the stone.

This kind of discrepancy also exists between the actual number of inscriptions that record each religious edifice built and the number of actual temples that survive. The latter exceeds "their" stone records by a ratio of almost six to one, so that for each stone record that survives, there are five temples that stand today. (In other words, although there are a total of nearly three thousand religious edifices that stand at Pagan today—most built during the Pagan period—only about five hundred *original* inscriptions that record their construction actually survive, when there should be as many stone inscriptions as there are temples.) One must therefore assume that many of the original stone records are lost. And if we depend solely on the data that survives (although we must), it means the figures derived from them are very much underrepresented.

They are so in yet another way. Sometimes the donor would simply record that a temple, monastery, and library were built and donated without revealing the costs of construction involved. This was also true regarding the costs incurred for the daily offerings of food, oil lamps, fruits, and so on, or those made periodically during the year such as robes and other items. In addition, land that was obviously donated but for which the donor did not give any figures, or figures that are either partially or totally flaked off, have not been counted in this study. The same is true of records of labor and cash donated, or costs of the donations, that are now illegible.

Moreover, if only the inscriptions between 1364 (when Ava was officially founded) and 1526–1527 (when the Shan *sawbwa* took over) are counted, we have only 173 inscriptions with which to work. Yet, during the previous decades—from the "fall" of Pagan (say 1301–1302) to the "rise" of Ava in 1364—another 218 inscriptions survive, so that there is actually a total of 391 inscriptions for the period between Pagan's "fall" and the rise of Ava as capital city. This means more inscriptions have survived from the period leading up to the rise of Ava—conventionally labeled as one of "fragmentation," "troubled," and "barbaric"—than from the Ava period proper (1364 to 1526–1527).

This supports my contention that serious doubts exist about the "anarchic" nature of that interim period, especially since donations to the *sangha* tend to decrease significantly (or totally disappear) during periods of real disorder and/or anarchy. Here, in contrast, it shows that even when Upper Myanmar was ruled by three centers of power, considered a period of fragmentation and anarchy, it produced approximately 55 percent of the total religious donations, whereas when it was ruled by one center, Ava, only 44 percent.[2] Perhaps more serious in terms of the issue of inadmissibility or admissibility of evidence, this demonstrates how unsound our fetish for creating "inviolable" periods can be, which would have rejected the majority of the primary evidence as "inadmissible."

It also means—and unlike the pattern found at Pagan—donations to the *sangha* decreased as the Ava kingdom became more integrated and grew in power and wealth, although in terms of the *value* of the donations, like Pagan, it increased. The reason for this decrease in the absolute number of donations is likely the result of the limited amount of productive land and labor that Ava possessed to begin with, unlike Pagan, whose material and human resources were virtually limitless until the end of the thirteenth and beginning of the fourteenth centuries. Nonetheless, and to reiterate, as at Pagan there was also at Ava a close relationship between the decline and "fall" of the kingdom and the flow of wealth from the taxable state and society to the tax-exempt *sangha*.

In table 1, I have combined the data taken from the Pagan period (whose "end" I have dated to 1301) with the above two periods (the "interim period," 1302–1363, and the "official" Ava period, 1364–1527) because donations to the *sangha* were given in perpetuity. That means their *cumulative* results are what we should be considering. The land area is given in *pay*, each of which equals approximately 1.75 acres, which I have converted to acres in the last row.

Thus, we see a total of 253,315 *pay* of *lay* (443,301 acres), another 171,002 *pay* of *mye* (299,253 acres); 28,728 *hpaya kyun;* along with 1,040,907 *kyats* of silver and 103,894 *kyats* of gold flowed from the state and society to the tax-exempt, religious sector during the period 1301 to 1527, approximately from the "end" of the Pagan Dynasty to the "end" of the First Ava Dynasty, representing 226 years.

During the interim period, that is, between the "fall" of Pagan around 1301 (when its authority yielded to the Three Brothers) and 1363, the year prior to the official founding of Ava in 1364, 20,618.91 *pay* of *lay* (36,083.09 acres), 37,587.5 *pay* of *mye* (65,778.12 acres), 12,177.75 *kyats* of silver and 541.5 *kyats* of gold were donated to the *sangha*. Although relatively small compared with the Pagan period and somewhat less than the "official" Ava period in terms of value, one should remember that these figures, to reiterate, are very much underrepresented. Remember too that this was a period of relative uncertainty, during which three centers ruled Upper Myanmar and at least two invasions by Shan forces occurred, creating problems for the inchoate kingdom. Indeed, it is surprising that these religious donations occurred at all; or, perhaps it was precisely these unsettling conditions that motivated the desire for some celestial intervention.

One should also note that virtually all the figures that have been calculated for both the interim and Ava periods represent new donations that had not been

Table 1. Wealth flow to *sangha* (Pagan and Ava)

DATE	LAY (in *pay*)	HPAYA KYUN	SILVER (in *kyat*)	GOLD (in *kyat*)	MYE (in *pay*)
Pagan period (to 1301)	194,238.75	22,511	29,094.25	976.15	45,475.91
Interim period (1302–1363)	20,618.91	1,397	12,177.75	451.5	37,587.5
Ava period (1364–1527)	38,457.4	4,820.00	999,635	102,466.50	87,938.75
Pagan/Ava cumulative	253,315.06	28,728	1,040,907	103,894.15	171,002.16
In Acres	443,301.355				299,253.78

Note:
1 *pay*=1.75 acres
1 *kyat*=0.56 ounces

made previously, and when added to Pagan donations made in perpetuity, the total amount of wealth shifting to the tax-exempt *sangha* by the first quarter of the sixteenth century, when Ava "fell," is quite significant. What "recycling" there was in religious wealth was miniscule, as we have seen (and shall see).

Table 1, then, represents the *cumulative* results of this wealth flow to the *sangha* in all three periods—Pagan (to 1301), "interim" (1302–1363), and Ava (1364–1527).[3] To reiterate, that totaled 443,301.355 acres of *lay* and 299,253.78 acres of *mye* which had shifted from the taxable sectors of state and society to the tax-exempt religious sector between the eleventh and sixteenth-centuries.

The acreage figure is underrepresented in yet another way: I have used the "general *pay*" of 1.75 acres for the calculations rather than the "royal *pay*" of 3.75 acres, which would have more than doubled the total. In other words, over a million acres would have shifted to the *sangha* if the royal *pay* rather than the general *pay* were used in our calculations. Similarly, the 28,728 *phaya kyun* donated does not count the many generations and their descendants, just the original outlay, as most would remain *phaya kyun* since their lot was largely hereditary. In terms of cash, it was huge: 1,040,907 *kyats* of silver and 103,894 *kyats* of gold approximately,[4] and again, representing just the original donation, not the economic impact it surely would have had.

Moreover, the four major categories of wealth I have used—*lay, mye, kyat* (of gold and silver), and *hpaya kyun*—were not all that were donated: many more items were given to the *sangha* that cannot be calculated. There was copper cash (*kye*), valuable animals (such as elephants, cows, sheep, horses), toddy palms, mango trees, betel nut trees, and boats, costs I have not included in the calculations above. How many *kyats* of silver should be equivalent to a boat, a goat, a cow, or a bale of good cloth? Such valuable items were invariably parts of donations. We do know that the price of a female elephant at Ava was approximately one thousand *kyats* of silver, but how does one calculate the long-term value of mango trees, betel nut trees, vegetable gardens (many of which fetched a premium in silver), sesame, and other dry weather crops grown on *mye* over two centuries?

Also important, and apart from the immediate wages paid to artisans and craftsmen, how does one calculate the cost of labor "lost to the state," for *hpaya kyun* were hereditary and remained in the tax-exempt sector more or less forever? Thus, table 1 represents only a part of the *initial* value of items that shifted from the taxable to the tax-exempt sector, not their long-term economic impact on the economy as a whole, although these figures probably represent the majority, as well as the most important categories, of wealth that moved.

One of the facts in the above data that is conspicuous is the huge increase in cash donations (silver and gold), for which I have not found a good explanation from the available evidence. But clearly the kingdom had much gold and silver to spend—unless the figures on stone are incorrect. Another is the decline in donations of good *lay*, although the answer for this is not difficult to find. Since over 63 percent of the state's good irrigated rice lands in Upper Myanmar had already been donated to the *sangha* during the Pagan period, by the end of the Pagan period, there was simply less good *lay* left to donate, particularly in the amounts common during the Pagan period, especially since Ava also depended on the same productive rice lands as Pagan did.

Even if there were "unlimited" amounts of land, that would not necessarily translate into more *lay*, for a proportionate increase in the population of the state, especially of cultivators, would also be needed. But there is little or no evidence for that during the post-Pagan period. And even if some religious lands that had lapsed into jungle over the years reverted to the taxable sector (by reclamation or other means) it happened so seldom (fewer than four recorded cases) that it would hardly affect the figures given above adversely. In other words, unless there was a huge influx in population of cultivators, the amount of *lay* in Upper Myanmar society would tend to remain "fixed" relative to the population of cultivators available.

This stable or fixed supply of *lay* is suggested by the relatively small amounts donated to the *sangha* during the Ava period. Indeed, my first reaction to these, especially donations made by royalty and high-placed, presumably wealthy, elites was, "Is that all?" Many of their *lay* donations were far below those made even by commoners during the Pagan period. Of course, one could donate uncultivated land to the *sangha*, but not only would it be just dirt—hence, useless, for members of the *sangha* who were not supposed to plow and plant or do other types of manual labor—the size and quality of one's merit depended on the size and quality of one's donation. So only in a very few instances was uncultivated land donated to the *sangha*.

In terms of reliability of the data, since my earlier book, *Pagan*, was published, I have gone over this data of wealth-flow to the *sangha* many times with the help of new software that has helped enhance its accuracy. That process has allowed me to make a distinction not previously made between *lay* and *mye*: that is, between irrigated padi land and cultivated land in general. This has reduced the total acreage of *lay* donated to the *sangha* as published in *Pagan*. But it is more than made up by what went into the new category of *mye*. And although a bit of a discrepancy still exists between the current figures on Pagan and my earlier ones, it is a minor one, without serious ramifications. Certainly, the new figures in the present work on both Pagan and Ava should be taken as the most accurate and up-to-date, albeit, as noted above, as seriously underrepresented.

The issue of inadvertently duplicating data is another concern, about which I am quite aware and always on my guard. But since each legible inscription almost always contains the name of the donor, the date of the donation (including the year, the day of the week, sometimes even the hour and exact position of the constellations at the time of offering), along with a unique narrative, duplicate records are easy to spot. And once placed in a computerized data base, it is even easier, for one can instantly call up a record (say) with its date to make sure no duplication has occurred. In terms of duplication "in the field" (that is, at Ava itself by its donors), I have not found a single *original* inscription that is duplicated.[5] Sometimes, when a donor is making a donation, he or she would refer, on the same stone, to an earlier dedication that contains detailed information regarding it, suggesting that the donor had a written record in-hand. This kind of record can indeed be duplicated.

But in most such cases, the donor makes clear what is being donated currently and what had been donated earlier, usually providing exact dates, precise objects donated, the names of each individual *hpaya kyun*, names of villages and/or location of lands pertinent to the donation, and often, also the totals of each category donated. That makes it easy enough to distinguish past figures with present ones; and they are never the same. In fact, I regard such "duplicated" information less as a problem and more as a viable, though partial, solution to another problem. That is, if I find that these earlier donations cannot be found among any of the original records contained in the master list of all Old Burmese inscriptions recovered so far in the country, it means the original stone on which the earlier donation was inscribed is lost. Therefore, the reiteration of older information on newer donations is a very good way to recover data from lost stones that otherwise would never be part of the historical record, its analysis, and its calculations.

In any case, because state legitimation and society's salvation depended on promoting and perpetuating the religion, the merit-path to salvation remained the central ideology of state and society at Ava as much as at Pagan, indeed, until today. That means wealth, especially in the form of productive land, people, and money, continued to flow to the religious sector throughout Burmese history, and the Ava period was no exception. The relative impact on the state was also almost as important to Ava as it was to Pagan.

The mere presence of donations tells yet another story, already alluded to above. It is a good indication of social and political order, inasmuch as a lapse in religious donations during a particular period of time can tell us that society was in disarray, when the promotion and perpetuation of Buddhism (and hence, salvation itself) was being "put on hold." Thus, whereas no donations were recorded for six years after 1285 (during the first of three Mongol invasions that began in 1284), the years between the origins of Ava (late 1290s and early 1300s) and its conquest in 1526–1527 show a relatively vibrant period of religious activity, when state and society were being enthusiastically reconstructed and donations abound.

Then, after 1526–1527, when Ava was taken by the Shan, donations stopped almost totally again. Between 1527 and 1555, when Ava was recovered by King Bayinnaung of the Second Pegu/Toungoo Dynasty, whose center was at Pegu, there were a total of only five recorded donations on stone found in all of Upper Myanmar. Thereafter, when the Burmese royal family returned to the heartland for good by reestablishing Ava as the seat of the new dynasty, religious donations increased once more. Yet, for the next eighty-one years, between 1555 and 1636, when King Thalun built his famous Kaungmhudaw in Sagaing, only eight Burmese stone inscriptions have been recovered in the entire country.[6] Not surprisingly, the Second Ava Dynasty was also affected by wealth flow to the *sangha* until it too was destroyed over a century later, giving rise to the last dynasty, the Konbaung, which was conquered in 1885–1886, also after much spending on the religion, especially during King Mindon's reign.

THE NATURE OF THE BURMESE MONARCHY

Another long-term structural factor responsible for Ava's decline is the built-in factionalism at court that was very much part of the nature of the Burmese monarchy. And although inherent in the system, it was exacerbated by the growing scarcity of material resources moving toward the tax-exempt sectors. The primary contenders of this factionalism, around whom other subfactions coalesced, were (usually) the eldest sons and younger brothers of the king, the ever-present uncle-nephew struggle that we have witnessed time and again throughout Myanmar's history.

To briefly reiterate, at the *abhiseka* ceremony commemorating the royal coronation, the king appoints his "cabinet." There, he formally designates the heir apparent, the chief queen, the Tabintaing princess (Princess of the Single Post, a formal title for the unmarried consort of the heir), and awards fiefs, names the head of the *sangha* (usually his teacher when he was a prince), and so forth. Thus, it is not the absence of a law of succession, or of clearly defined succession procedures, that was the problem in Burmese history—as often contended—but their violation.

In the majority of cases, the appointment of the eldest son of the king as heir apparent meant that and he and his future sons would effectively replace the younger brother of the king and his sons from the crown forever. Thus, the interest of the heir would be in supporting the king, his benefactor, not in overthrowing him, whereas the opposite would be true for the younger brother of the king, the heir's uncle. Indeed, modern social science tells us that eldest sons in general tend to cast their lot with parental authority, while younger brothers, having to compete against the odds, were, as one interesting study has it, "born to rebel."[7] And in Myanmar, cut off from the throne formally, younger brothers had very few options but to accept the status quo or rebel. And even if they had no intention of seizing the throne, they would, nonetheless, be prime suspects every time an attempt was made on the throne by anyone. Some Ava kings knew this and therefore assigned competent younger brothers to distant fiefs.

Complicating these two primary factions were those centered on the four main queens, all of whose sons were eligible for the throne as well. Moreover, the queens had their own positions to protect, which were often dependent on the outcome of the struggles between the main uncles and nephews. There were other minor queens whose sons were also eligible, but usually only if the formal and established procedures went awry. Thus, it was in their interest to make sure that things *did* go awry, or at least be prepared to capitalize on such situations. For such contingencies, they made sure their sons' eligibility matched their military talent.

Balancing all this were the ministers. As they had no moral or legal access to succession, they were probably one of the most stabilizing components of the Burmese court, the best examples of whom were Min Yaza, minister of Minkyiswa Sawkai who counseled several kings for over fifty years, and "Long Life" Yazathingyan who, beginning before Mohnyin Mintaya's ascension, served four different kings in Ava, including even the "barbaric" Shan *sawbwa*, Thohanbwa. Ministers were pillars of continuity that preserved, operated, and maintained the country's administration in the midst of ever-changing political winds.

THE PATRON-CLIENT (*MYOSA*) SYSTEM

A third structural factor in the decline of Ava (and other Burmese kingdoms) was the *myosa* system itself, although (similar to the merit-path to salvation) it contributed to *both* stability and disorder. Under normal conditions, the kingdom was too large and the "bureaucracy" too small to ensure the center's direct presence everywhere. In order to govern this large territory, it made perfectly good sense to assign royal favorites and other supporters "to eat" strategic towns and cities that were widely, but more or less evenly, distributed over the kingdom. This means that from any one of these centers, crown troops assigned to individual governorships could reach any other one relatively quickly.

In times of crisis, this arrangement was even more important. When approximately only twenty miles a day could be covered by a large contingent of troops moving by land (about twice that much by water), problem areas could be reached relatively quickly by crown troops stationed at each *myosa*-ship. There was no need to wait for troops to arrive from the capital itself, for it would take not much more than one, at most two, days for troops from each of the fifty-odd *myosa*-ships in the country to reach any other *myosa*-ship, invariably the nucleus of rebellion.

But that advantage was also a disadvantage: every single internal rebellion against the throne during the Ava period (indeed during *all* of precolonial Burmese history) was an elite affair. Until the Saya San Rebellion of 1930–1932 against the colonial system and regime, there was not a single true peasant rebellion in Burmese history (where peasants rose up against the center).[8] They were all elite rebellions. And in these, the throne was the ultimate prize, not an imagined independence of the periphery against the center, or an inchoate struggle for "freedom" against tyranny, the underlying assumptions of most modern treatments of Burmese history projected backward to include its premodern period. In each case, the leader of the rebellion either wanted the throne for himself or herself (or for someone else he or she supported), or wanted to deny it to the holder or heir. Such resistance was not conducted on behalf of the presumed downtrodden masses, but on behalf of certain elites against other elites.

Thus, while the *myosa* system helped central authority under both normal and crisis conditions, it also provided the nuclei for resisting the throne, as each royal fief included a sizeable number of crown troops under the authority of each *myosa,* most of whom were members of the royal family, hence, eligible for the throne. Thus, the *myosa* system provided as much opportunity for weakening the state as for strengthening it, as much for decentralism as for centralism.

Yet even if the position of *myosa* were unstable (since appointed at the pleasure of the king), positions below it such as the *ywathugyi* and *myothugyi* (village and township headman, respectively), being hereditary, were quite stable. *Myosa* came and went, but the fief they "ate"—the people, produce, revenues, crops, and the hereditary leaders under him—remained intact. A large part of the reason was that wars were fought primarily, if not exclusively, by hereditary crown troops, not peasant armies (since there were none), so that outside the battlefield, which was usually focused on the walled city of a *myosa*-ship or a militarily strategic zone, few if any peasants would have been involved or affected. The actual combatants and victims were mainly crown soldiers. Indeed, one village near the Three Pagodas Pass, upon making its ten-year cadastral survey report, made no mention whatever—as if it did not even know—that Ayuthaya had been invaded and destroyed during those ten years, even though the armies passed within a few miles of it.

SHAN COMMERCIAL ASCENDANCY

Finally, the growth in wealth of several Shan polities—particularly Mohnyin and Mongmit, as a result of their trade in gems with Ming China, a process that went back to the Yuan Dynasty—was, according to Myanmar-China historian Sun Laichen, an important factor in the political and military ascendancy of these two Shan polities.[9] Indeed, it explains how one of them (Mohnyin) was able to take Ava at all, especially considering the absence of any agricultural surplus or evidence of population growth in Mohnyin, almost invariably needed for such military success. It was the development of the gem trade with Ming China over a matter of several decades that provided the economic wherewithal for Mohnyin to overthrow its overlord, Ava.[10]

In summary, the flow of wealth from state and society to the *sangha*, the fractious nature of the court, the weaknesses in the *myosa* system that, at the time, overpowered its strengths, and the growth in economic power of certain Shan centers, were the long-term (institutional) contexts in which more immediate events operated. To be sure, these "incidents of the moment" were always present but could not effect substantive political change unless they appeared at times of institutional weakness. And although that ebbed and flowed and was addressed by strong leadership, serious weaknesses did not begin to appear until the last few years of the otherwise long and strong reign of Narapati the Second.

The Decline of Ava: The Immediate Causes

THE REIGN OF NARAPATI THE SECOND (1501–1526)

A young, relatively inexperienced monarch, who in hindsight turned out quite capable, followed the three stalwart kings mentioned in the last chapter. On April 12, 1501, Dutiya Mingaung's younger son, only twenty-five, taking the old Pagan title of Siri Tri Bhavanaditya Narapati Pawara Maharaja Dhipati ascended "the golden palace of Awa known as Ratanapura" (City of Gems).[11] In the *Zatatawpon,* he is called Shwenan Kyaw Shin Narapati (Narapati, lord of the famous Golden Palace) and, sometimes, "Narapati the Younger" or "Second." That same year, in the month of Waso (answering to nearly July), his father's unrelenting competitor, the lord of Yamethin, Minye Kyawswa (and Narapati's uncle) died.

The Ava throne was finally rid of its most ardent detractor, who had been a thorn in its side for many years, so that the path now seemed clear for completing the consolidation of the center. Upon the death of Minye Kyawswa, his daughter (perhaps to save her own skin) requested confiscation of all his men, horses, elephants, armaments, and gold and silver, rather than assigning them to his male successor (as was customary), her brother. The king readily agreed, brought the princess back on a state palanquin, and, when she reached Ava, raised her to be queen.

But Minye Kyawswa's death was as much a blessing as it was a curse, for it left a power vacuum. In the month of Nadaw (corresponding to December), in the same year, a servant of the son of the king's deceased elder brother (a natural competitor) named Nga Thauk Kya (Mr. Friday), attacked the king with a sword at a time when his guard was down. He missed and inadvertently struck the post of the white umbrella instead, bringing it down over his own body (clearly, a symbolism U Kala did not want the reader to miss). The son of the king's personal attendant, the *myosa* of Yenantha, ran up and grasped Mr. Friday, who dropped his sword. He said to the king, "Strike us both." But Narapati surgically struck only Mr. Friday "without touching a hair on the other," recorded the chronicle. Upon the throne itself the assassin died—a harbinger of things to come, and an inauspicious event in the eyes of the chroniclers who wrote later.

The king ordered the *myosa* of Yenantha to capture Shwe Nawyahta, the son of the king's deceased elder brother. At the time, Shwe Nawyahta was only twelve years old and living with his mother within the palace, so was easily captured and sent to the king. Narapati investigated the matter and eliminated those related to his nephew. The son, who was probably not even aware of what had happened, was drowned, to ensure no future competition from that sector. Five vassals of the deceased prince who feared for their lives fled to Toungoo with over seven hundred of their retainers and became the vassals of its lord, enhancing his power even more.

Narapati then married off the son of the younger sister of the southern (chief) queen to a younger sister and gave them the fief of Yamethin, finally vacated by the death of Minye Kyawswa, the nemesis of the king's father for over two decades. He also raised one of the daughters of the lord of Pakhan Gyi, another important fief, to be one of his queens, as he did with the daughter of the lord of Taungdwin, thereby creating alliances with those families as well. The son of the lord of Taungdwin he gave in marriage to a princess born of one of his aunts, also a queen. His younger brother was married off to the daughter of the lord of Toungoo. The king may have hoped that with these marriage alliances, he was creating a "divide and rule" situation that would better ensure his own safety.

In 1502, the king convened a council of his ministers to determine the state of the state. As usual, Minister Long Life (a portfolio given to a minister who could theoretically speak with impunity) addressed the king first. He said, "Myedu, currently part of the royal dominions is under the influence of Mohnyin Salon, the *Sawbwa* of Mohnyin. Moreover, your highness does not believe the Lord of Pyi, thy grandfather Thadominsaw, has any affection for thee. Toungoo's Lord, Maha Thiyi Zeyathuya [Minkyinyo, who became the founder of the famous Second Pegu/Toungoo Dynasty] has many elephantry and cavalry. He can remain independent without honoring the oath of loyalty." Because of this situation, Minister Long Life advised the king to establish further marriage alliances with other royal kinfolk producing good descendants so that the long-term interests of the monarchy could be served.

The king took Minister Long Life's advice and proceeded to establish additional marriage alliances. One of the most important was giving in marriage the daughter of one of his uncles who held "Salin and the Ten Cities" (south of Ava), with the lord of Toungoo, Minkyinyo, issuing a royal edict that conferred on him the title of crown governor with royal status. This only recognized and confirmed Minkyinyo's power, more than bestowing on him something he did not already have, strengthening his hand even more.

That same year, Salon, the *sawbwa* of Mohnyin, with an army of elephants and horses, attacked Myedu, a highly strategic town guarding the northern entrance to the Mu Valley, the second most important irrigated region in Upper Myanmar. The *myosa* of Myedu (Yazathingyan, who enjoyed the title of Minister Long Life) could not sustain the attack, even with reinforcements sent to defend the city, and so retreated with his troops at night. Only when they reached Debeyin, another important garrisoned town farther south, did they combine forces with its *myosa* to regroup. But by then, Myedu was already in the hands of the Salon *sawbwa*.

Unfortunately for Ava, the *myosa* of Salin, Thingathu, with whom the king had made important marriage alliances earlier, died. Instead of supporting the king, Thingathu's successor (a son-in-law), sensing the king's vulnerability at the time, threw off his allegiance to the king, at which many of his own retainers, not desiring to incur the royal wrath also, fled to a major royal governorship, Pyi. The king, leading the naval and land troops, riding on the golden royal barge, went down to Salin, took his mother-in-law, confiscated the elephants, horses, and men given her and, when he got back to Ava, placed her in the inner palace. As for the fief of Salin, the king gave it, along with the usual troops, to Sithu, the younger of his personal attendants.

In 1503, another one of the king's supporters, the *myosa* of Yamethin, Bayakyawhtin, died. His son Mindonta and others gave their allegiance to the lord of Toungoo instead and rebelled against Ava. Emboldened, Mindonta and the princes who had rebelled, with the support of the lord of Toungoo and Pyi, surrounded Sale in 1505, an important city guarding the entrance to the third most important irrigated region under the kingdom, Minbu.

King Narapati called together his ministers and officers and said that the lord of Pyi and the lord of Toungoo together had surrounded Sale city. He told the group he had heard they were strong. One of the ministers said "this is not the work of Mindonta and the princes. It is that of the lords of Pyi and Toungoo, and hence the many troops. Separate the northern towns of the Kingdom like Dibeyin and Hsintha, and do not order them to come, since they are close to the Mohnyin Shans. However, call upon the Onbaung *sawbwa* for military help." This advice was taken.

The latter quickly came down with sixty war elephants, three thousand cavalry, and fourteen thousand soldiers. When he got to Ava, Narapati, with a large force, riding on his royal barge, called the Ratana Rhwe Bhon (Jewelled Golden Barge), with three hundred large boats (*kattu,* of the kind seen in Mergui and Tavoy), two hundred *hlawga* (war boats) and *thin lhe* (another kind of boat), and seventeen thousand "braves," led the naval forces. The land forces were considerable, commanded by the *myosa* of Pagan.

The Onbaung *sawbwa*'s son also marched on the king's side. When they got to Sale, the boats docked, and riding on his elephant named Saw Yin, Narapati himself led the battle. The forces belonging to the lords of Pyi and Toungoo were defeated and fled; many died. The troops of Mindonta were destroyed by the son of the Onbaung *sawbwa.* Many elephants, horses, and men were obtained, including Mindonta himself and his elephant. From then on, the lords of Pyi and Toungoo "had more respect [for Ava] and became loathsome [contrite?]," wrote U Kala.[12]

With the south "pacified," the problem in the north could be more easily addressed. The following year, Mohnyin Salon attacked Dibeyin with a large force and took it. When the king heard of the news, he ordered Pagan Thado (the *myosa* of Pagan) to march quickly with an army. Although they attacked and got back nearby Myedu, "Our lord," wrote U Kala, "did not want to extend the offensive and stayed there instead." He asked Salon if he wished to give up the city of Dibeyin or do battle. Salon replied that he had many troops and "is not afraid to fight or to negotiate. I'll do what I like. Only when 'elder brother' replies will I know." Narapati and his ministers deliberated and said, "Let the region from Myedu up to Ngayanai be the kingdom of the Shan *sawbwa.* From there downwards, let it be our kingdom." The Mohnyin *sawbwa* said let the agreement as stated by "elder brother" be affirmed and gave back the city of Dibeyin to the king.

Although Dibeyin was important, this "treaty" was actually a major blow to the Kingdom of Ava, for Myedu was even more important. It was one of the "gateways" controlling the Mu River valley and its irrigation works from the north, and had always been (since Pagan times) a historically and economically important area for all Dry Zone powers. Narapati may have considered the compromise a calculated risk, since he did not control Myedu anyway, perhaps hoping that he would later retake it. Moreover, he may have been worried about spending too much time and effort on this particular battle in the north when Pyi and Toungoo, though recently beaten, were equally (if not more) important and not out of the picture yet. In fact, they just might capitalize on precisely such attention given to the north.

In 1507, another one of the king's staunch and able supporters, "royal grandfather" Thihapati, the *myosa* of Pakhangyi, died. Several younger brothers of the king and their supporters entered Pakhangyi and proceeded to rebel against Narapati. When the king heard of that, he marched with his troops by land and water. When he got to Myaungdu, he combined forces with those of Yemek, both under Ava, all of them surrounding Pakhangyi city. "Within seven days it was taken, as the weapons were few inside the city," wrote U Kala. The three brothers were summoned to court, and in front of the ministers, the king chastised them, saying that instead of helping out in running the affairs of the country, they had instead rebelled without any respect for the office of heir apparent, just pursuing their own selfish agenda "come hell or high water." He then executed all three, along with all the leaders.

In 1508, the *myosa* of Pyi, Thadominsaw, attacked Magwe which was under Ava, took it, and stockaded himself inside. The king ordered Minister Long Life to go by land, while he went by water. When they got to Magwe, they attacked the naval forces that had come up from Pyi, defeating them and sending them fleeing downriver. After that, Magwe was surrounded by land and water, and attacked. The city was taken, along with thirty war elephants, sixty horses, and over two thousand people, after which it was given to a Mon Prince from Pegu staying at Ava as fief, along with the forces obtained from it.

It had taken nearly a decade to quell these contests for the throne, a not irregular occurrence at succession. But for now, they were over, giving Narapati a respite. In order to symbolize that unchallenged power, he built a new palace on a grand scale (described in the previous chapter). It was a virtual duplicate of the procedures and ceremonies held 407 years earlier at Pagan. Here at Ava as well, Brahmins led in reciting the rituals in which "Pyu dancing girls" also took part. (This may be the last mention of the "Pyu people," who had been absorbed into the Pagan kingdom more than eight hundred years before.)[13]

Narapati did not have too much time to enjoy his new palace, for the Burmese elite competing with each other and creating problems for the center were not the only ones: there were also Shan *sawbwa* competing with each other for Ava's favor, invariably dragging it into their affairs. Harboring resentment because Narapati and the Onbaung *sawbwa* were related (by marriage) and close friends and allies, Salon, the *sawbwa* of Mohnyin, in 1511, decided to take

Bhamo, a most important city in the north, whose revenues had been given to the Onbaung *sawbwa*.

Bhamo was a crucial and most important center for the trade with China.[14] The Onbaung *sawbwa* requested Narapati to move on Myedu, at the time defended by Mohnyin's sons. Narapati wanted Myedu back at some point anyway, after having been compelled to give it up for Dipeyin earlier. When the king arrived at Myedu with his troops, he attacked the city but could not take it because of its guns and cannon. He retreated to a safe distance and set up an offensive perimeter. That night, at two in the morning when it was very dark, Mohnyin's supporters, the *myosa* of Twin Thin, Min Khin, and Kale attacked and destroyed the forces of Narapati, who had to escape to Sipottaya city near Dibeyin.

That defeat triggered a host of other rebellions. In 1513, the Sagu *myosa* rebelled. It was taken back by Narapati eventually, but two years later, he had to march on Myede, near Pyi. However, its *myosa,* who was the son of the lord of Pyi, came out and greeted the king with presents instead, so that crisis was, for the time being, over. Next, it was the *myosa* of Hpyinda, again located around the environs of Pyi. But it was well defended and could not be taken. This preoccupation with Ava's southern flank encouraged the *sawbwa* of Mohnyin in 1517 to once again march with an army and attack the suburbs of Myedu. Hearing that, the king marched with his forces and stopped at Sitha district. From there he marched to Ngayane, where some of Mohnyin's forces were defeated, who then retreated into the city. When Narapati took the city, U Kala wrote, "the Shans fled." It was placed in the charge of old minister Yazathingyan, whose fief was nearby. He set up defenses at Myedu, and gave the town of Ngayane to another officer with troops to defend it.[15]

The following year, Salon provoked a fight with the *sawbwa* of Kale. The king assembled his court to discuss these never-ending crises. One of the ministers, Nandathuriya said that "the *sawbwa* had fought each other now for about eight months and no one has won. If the king took a large force, and ordered the Heir to do likewise, we may be able to take both cities." So, the king marched. When they arrived at Min Khin (king's fields), the *sawbwa* of Kale sent his son to the heir with many presents and said he would submit to him. That year, several other cities in what is now the "Shan states" once again became part of the Ava kingdom.

With these gains, the king called his court together in 1520 and said that the disintegration of the kingdom could now be reversed. So that in future governance would be stable, he asked his ministers what they thought should be done. At that, Pagan Thado (the *myosa* of Pagan) said, "Mohnyin Salon has a large force. He also has many means with which to fight. There is no doubt that later he will march again. For that reason, Min Khin's moat and walls must be made strong and many elephants, horses, and men must be placed there. Ngayane, Sipottaya, Dibeyin, the defenses of these cities must also be strengthened." The king followed the advice and implemented the recommendations, giving Yazathaman to guard Min Khin. Myedu was also strengthened with Sithugamani in charge. Sipottaya was put in Yazathingyan's charge along with additional soldiers. Dipeyin was placed in Bhayakamani's charge. The *sawbwa* of Kale was given Amyint.

Thus, by 1520, the Kingdom of Ava had reconsolidated its hold of the Mu Valley once again, and appeared strong, with governors placed in refortified strategic towns and cities. In hindsight, however, it turned out to be actually the lull before the storm, for just six years later Ava was taken by Salon. What happened?

THE LAST DECADE AND THE END OF THE FIRST AVA DYNASTY

Once again, it was Mohnyin Salon. In 1523, he marched with a large force down the Mu Valley and surrounded Min Khin. When the king heard about it, he mobilized fifteen battalions to meet him. When they arrived at Myedu, Salon had already taken Min Khin. From there he marched to Myedu. The advance guard of the king's cavalry, upon meeting them, attacked. "The Shan retreated," wrote U Kala, but "regrouped and sent in the elephants, which forced the Burmese cavalry to retreat." When Salon saw "the Burmese retreating," he gathered all his troops and attacked in full force. Many of the fifteen battalions of Narapati, out of formation, were defeated.

That success made another important city of the Mu Valley, Sipottaya, held by "wise minister" Yazathingyan, even more vulnerable. Salon attacked it, and the whole city, along with Yazathingyan and his troops, were captured. Unable to get his officers to regroup, the king's forces were now seriously divided. Salon's forces pursued Ava's forces up to In Hpe Tayaing, another important garrisoned town, capturing many horses and elephants. Bhayakamani, the commander of Dibeyin, the other major stronghold, was unable to defend it and fled with the king. The people, cows, and buffalo of the entire northern region of the Mu Valley were taken by Salon's forces. The path straight down to Sagaing now lay open, across the river from which was Ava.

Mohnyin Salon stayed at Myedu for the rainy season to regroup and reorganize and, in 1524, marched down to Sagaing. When he got there, he set fire to the houses and monasteries in the suburbs first. (This was a virtual repeat of the mid-fourteenth century, when Sagaing was taken twice by the "Syam" [Shan] who came down the same route from the north.) Salon then attacked the nearby garrisoned towns of Kani, Kane, Nat Taung, Badon, and Amyint, and got them all. From there he crossed over to Pakhangyi and took it, along with many towns around it. From there, he marched west. But all the *myosa* of Sagu, Salin, Legaing, and Paunglin fled, not "daring to defend their cities under his onslaught." Now there was general panic in Upper Myanmar, as all the most important and strategic cities west and north of Ava had been taken. Only Ava lay ahead.

But instead of going straight to Ava, Salon decided to deal with Pyi first, for it would have been at his rear if he were to attack Ava. The lord of Pyi, thinking only of his own interests, said he would help in the attack of Ava if he were placed on the throne, and would "bear the burden" of Salon (that is, "be his vassal"). Mohnyin replied that if his request were genuine, Ava would be attacked, "and *thwethauk* will be placed on the throne." (This reference to the lord of Pyi as *thwethauk* was likely a deliberate slight inserted by U Kala, for the title was used for a mere military officer.) The lord of Pyi then went personally to meet with Salon. They exchanged pleasantries, and after swearing the oath of loyalty, Salon led the land forces while the lord of Pyi went by water.

Thus, until the very end, the lord of Pyi would rather fight Ava—his own kith and kin, source of strength, culture, salvation, and birth—than join with it to resist people who were a threat to (his own) Burmese civilization. For those of us brought up in the twentieth century in a modern nation-state, that kind of pure self-interest is sometimes difficult to fathom. But remove the concept of the nation-state in the analysis, and it is quite understandable. In any case, all the *myosa* on the south, such as Taungdwingyi and Yamethin, not daring to resist, also fled and hid, wrote U Kala. Eventually, Salon's forces arrived on the outskirts of Ava. And when he found out that most dared not resist, he marched rapidly, taking everything in his path until he reached the capital city.

Earlier, when Salon was crossing over to take Pakhangyi and the other cities on the west, Narapati had called together his ministers and officers to discuss the situation. Nandathuriya said that "Mohnyin Salon has destroyed and taken our entire kingdom. They are men, we are men. We cannot just stay and hope. With the whole army, without regard for one's life, only if we, with courage, fight, will the crisis be addressed." All the ministers then took an oath of loyalty and stated that "in this time of difficult crisis, we must stick with our lord, our benefactor, without regarding our lives as one piece of *hinywet*" (vegetable leaf).

But another said, "Those are brave words but what we really need to do is get word to the Onbaung *Sawbwa* to help us out." The king liked the second suggestion better and sent a liaison to the Onbaung *sawbwa* for military aid. When he got there, the Onbaung *sawbwa* said, "So, Salon, while I'm still alive, is going to destroy the realm [*naingnan*] to which I have drunk the blood oath of loyalty, eh?" He then came down with his army. When he reached Ava, he constructed a bridge on the Myitnge (?) and, after crossing it, made camp at Taungbilu ward. The king invited Onbaung to the palace and provided him with a feast. Narapati told him how grateful he was for his coming to help. He then told him of Salon and the lord of Pyi marching on Ava even though they had also taken the oath of loyalty to Narapati. They then discussed defensive strategies.

When Mohnyin Salon arrived at Ava, he made camp. After five days, Mohnyin's son, Thohanbwa, riding on an elephant, attacked the force stationed at Taungbilu. Salon showed his sword to every one of his officers, so that they only attacked and dared not retreat. The defensive forces of the outer city of Ava were destroyed, so they all retreated into the inner city. "Many soldiers died," wrote U Kala. As Narapati and the Onbaung *sawbwa* dared not resist from within the city, they escaped when night fell. The other ministers also fled and caught up with the king.

After three days, Salon, taking horses, elephants and men from Ava, crossed over to Sagaing and returned home. Once Salon had left and showed no interest in creating a new dynasty at Ava (hence, playing only the role of "spoiler") the lord of Pyi must have known he could not resist Narapati and the Onbaung *sawbwa* by himself, and therefore went back to his own stronghold as well. He gathered all the leaders and elders left in Ava and descended the river to Pyi. By 1524, then, Mohnyin Salon had under his authority all the cities northwest of Ava—that is, virtually the entire Mu Valley.

As it turned out, both Narapati and the Onbaung *sawbwa* had some fighting men left. The former had some 250 war elephants, four thousand cavalry, and eighteen thousand infantry. Onbaung had, not counting the Yun forces, eighty war elephants, five hundred horses, and seventeen thousand infantry. When the lord of Pyi left, Narapati and the Onbaung *sawbwa* reentered Ava. This part of the narrative by U Kala is a bit puzzling at first, but it appears that only the experienced administrators and military men who stayed, along with war materiel that was left, were taken when the city fell. As most civilians did not have their residences in the inner city in any case—even Yazathingyan, the king's minister, had to cross the river from his house and did not live in the walled city—few noncombatants actually lost life and limb during such battles. Even combatants who were defeated, I suspect, were taken prisoner rather than killed wantonly, as labor, especially skilled soldiers, was still extremely valuable.

The lord of Toungoo, Maha Thiri Zeyyathuya was waiting for just such a moment. When he first heard about Mohnyin Salon's taking of Ava, he immediately capitalized on the situation and began taking the human and material resources of the towns and villages south of Ava. The lord of Yamethin, brother-in-law of the king, informed Narapati and the Onbaung *sawbwa*, who marched down rapidly to Yamethin. The lord of Toungoo retreated without resisting. Both Narapati and the Onbaung *sawbwa* continued to chase him all the way to Toungoo itself. But it was too well defended. Numerous times they attempted to take the city but were repelled by guns and cannon. After a month, as Ava was still not quiet, Narapati and the Onbaung *sawbwa* returned to the capital. When they arrived, the latter told Narapati to let him know if there were any more crises, but because the rains were near, he would return home. Not forgetting the help provided by the Onbaung *sawbwa*, Narapati presented him with five *viss* (nearly twenty pounds) of gold, thirty of silver (about a hundred pounds), ten elephants, and many other valuable articles. The Onbaung *sawbwa* said, "I owed you. I will not take these presents." Narapati then insisted that the *sawbwa* ride his own horse, which had a ruby harness, and gave him two silver match-locks. The Onbaung *sawbwa* accepted these and returned to his fief, the heir accompanying him up to the Shwesiyin pagoda. Narapati then called on all the kingdom's *myosa* to take the oath of allegiance as forever binding, after which many rewards were given.

That formality did not change the fact that the entire Mu Valley (and its vast irrigation systems and rice fields) was now lost to Salon. It would be only a matter of time before Ava would be attacked once again, and Narapati knew it. But at the present time, with the monsoons on, he could wait for the planting and harvesting season to be over before it became a reality that had to be faced.

As anticipated, in 1526, Thohanbwa, the son of Mohnyin Salon, marched down the Mu Valley with his troops until he reached Halin, near Shwebo, where he called upon all the *myosa* in the region. Ava's heir apparent was ordered to defend at Pakhangyi and sent there with an army. He reached Pakhangyi, crossed the river, and took Amyint, which had been defended by Salon's forces. After staying two days at Amyint, he marched to and attacked Badon, which he also took. From there he crossed to Kinne, attacked it, and won there as well. The tide was beginning to turn for Ava.

While staying at a place called Kanni, however, the heir apparent contracted a fever at night and died. Just when it seemed that Ava had once again regained the upper hand and momentum, an accident, an "incident of the moment," reversed it all. One wonders what might have happened had the heir lived to become king, with the Mu Valley back in Ava's hands. But that was not to be, and his death was the fatal blow for Ava. His officers, without their heir and commander in chief, gathered their troops and returned to Pakhangyi. That retreat left the Mu Valley wide open again, which Mohnyin Salon took advantage of immediately: he simply marched down the valley and went straight to Sagaing as he had done the previous year. This time, without securing his flanks, he made rafts, crossed over to the Ava side with his army, and surrounded it.

Since the Onbaung *sawbwa*, who had been informed, had not yet arrived, the king did not come out of the city to attack Salon. He placed cannon and guns around the top of the city walls and set up his defenses. After eight days of surrounding the city, Salon said, "Tomorrow, we will attack the city. Those who do not climb properly, I will kill with my sword." The officers, wrote U Kala, were more afraid of Salon's sword than the guns on top of the city walls, so together planted ladders on the walls and climbed up. They died as guns mowed them down from atop the walls. Many also died from mace (?) and lance. Despite the toll, and not regarding death, they managed to scale the walls.

DEATH OF NARAPATI AND THE END OF THE FIRST AVA DYNASTY

Narapati, riding the elephant named Shwe Sadaik (Golden Library), opened the city gate and exited. He rode toward the east, in order to cross from the head of the island on that side that was held by Thohanbwa, who resisted him with his elephant. But a ball fired from a cannon hit the head of Narapati's elephant and also killed the king—on the twelfth waxing day of the month of Tagu (April), 1526. (Harvey has 1527.) With his death, and the subsequent "ascension" of Thohanbwa to the Ava throne in 1527, the First Ava Dynasty came to an end, ushering in the brief (and only) "Shan period" in Myanmar's history.

U Kala wrote that the *min set* (royal lineage) of fourteen kings from Thadominbya to Narapati had been broken by Thohanbwa, making clear the distinction between the former fourteen and the latter's genealogy.[16] The *Zatatawpon* also made clear the distinction between the Ava *min set* and that of the three Shan *sawbwa* who followed, by noting that "beginning with Thadominbya to Narapati, the Myanma *min set* [numbered] 13 [*sic*]" followed by a "Shan lineage [*set*]."[17] Thus, although neither U Kala nor the *Zatatawpon* gave the three *sawbwa* royal Burmese credentials, the three were not expunged from the "master list" of Ava kings either. This confirms my contention that the ultimate criterion used by both chronicles for inclusion on Ava's "master-list" of kings was whether or not one reigned at Ava—a Buddha-prophesied city—rather than one's ethnicity or even royal genealogy. Indeed, what is most interesting (and "surprising" to us in the twenty-first century) is that both Burmese chronicles included Shan *sawbwa* on the official list of Ava kings at all![18]

After Salon had placed his crude and brash young son Thohanbwa on the Ava throne (whom Harvey called a "full-blooded savage"),[19] he again chose not to stay at Ava, as in 1524, and returned home. Before leaving, however, knowing his son's proclivities, Salon requested Narapati's nephew, Yan Naung, probably an official at the Ava court who remained, to counsel his son while on the throne of Ava, since he was not "clever in Myanma affairs."[20] Thohanbwa, of course, did not listen and did as he pleased. And when Salon was later killed by one of his vassals, Thohanbwa not only lost a powerful ally in his father, but someone who might have been able to restrain his worst behavior.

U Kala had little good to say about Thohanbwa. He was said to have killed monks, suppressed the Burmese people, and openly insulted them in many ways. He also treated holy temples as if they were places to be looted. U Kala wrote that Thohanbwa "did not know the difference between good and bad . . . [and] had no respect for the religion."[21] He goes on to recount the story of how, in 1540 at Taungbilu, southeast of Ava, Thohanbwa held a public ceremony to feed monks. When they were all in the pavilions erected, he surrounded them with his soldiers and massacred them. It is said that out of 1,300 monks in Ava, Sagaing, and Pinya, he killed 360, of whom thirty were eminent for their learning. For the feast itself, Thohanbwa had slaughtered buffalo, cows, pigs, and fowl—not the usual foods offered to, or eaten by, orthodox Buddhist monks, who are supposed to be vegetarian—and therefore, perhaps a statement by U Kala about their "just desserts." Thohanbwa subsequently seized manuscripts in the monasteries and burned all of them.

Because of Thohanbwa's cruel rule, ministers of the (conquered) Ava court, who had remained to serve the new rulers, appealed to Yan Naung to do something, and eventually in 1542, after a dramatic and ingenious plan, Yan Naung was able to kill Thohanbwa, at which point, wrote U Kala, "the Shan ran away."[22] Thohanbwa was only twenty-two years old when he took the throne of Ava, and after ruling for about fifteen years, died at age thirty-seven. U Kala wrote that Thohanbwa only "ate" Ava, rather than ruled or reigned, implying that he was nothing more than a *myosa*.[23]

Although pressed by the court's ministers, Yan Naung refused the throne, saying he had no desire to be king. Meanwhile, the old and reliable ally of Ava, the Onbaung *sawbwa*, had also died. So, his son and successor, Hkonmaing, came down to Ava and pleaded with Yan Naung to take the throne. Yan Naung, however, supported Hkonmaing, for after all, he was the son of the Onbaung *sawbwa* (so was part of Ava royalty by marriage), who had been a staunch ally and friend of Ava's last king, Narapati. After repeating that he had no desire to be king, Yan Naung entered the forest and became an ascetic. Hkonmaing thus became king of Ava in 1542, the second *sawbwa* in Myanmar's history to reign there. In contrast to his assessment of Thohanbwa, U Kala did not disparage

Hkonmaing; instead, he was said to have patronized rather than vilified Burmese culture.

For someone who was said to have pleaded with Yan Naung to take the throne, Hkonmaing acted very much the ambitious king. Allied with seven other *sawbwa,* he forged a formidable land and water force to take Pyi, one of only two major centers left (along with Toungoo) ruled by descendants of Ava's royalty but disloyal to Ava. Pyi prove to be too strong and could not be taken, so the *sawbwa* surrounded the city and laid siege to it. That led Mintaya Shwehti (the famous Tabinshwehti) to march from Pegu (which had, in 1539, become the seat of the Second Pegu/Toungoo Dynasty) to lift the siege. Apparently, he must have felt that if Pyi fell to the *sawbwa,* Pegu was next, and he would rather take the fight to them.[24]

Mintaya Shwehti had cannon with him on his war boats and used them with great effectiveness, which finally broke the ranks of the *sawbwa* and destroyed much of their fleet. Many soldiers were killed, while many, along with their war boats, were captured by his forces. After a council of war, all the *sawbwa* decided to retreat and return to Upper Myanmar. Mintaya did not let them go in peace but gave chase and did battle with them, destroying the "*sawbwa* seven." Pegu now had the territory up to and beyond Pyi. Hkonmaing was succeeded by the Mobye *sawbwa* in 1547, after which, in 1551, Ava was retaken by a member of the old Ava court.

After that, the country was once again reintegrated around three centers, as it had been in 1300; only now, it was Ava, Pyi, and Pegu that dominated, with none powerful enough to unify all. So they reached an accord and swore oaths of loyalty with each other to keep the status quo. It remained this way until 1555, when, under the famous and militarily brilliant kings Tabinshwehti and Bayinnaung, the country was reunified. By then, Ava had become just another *myosa*-ship, as Pegu had become the capital of the country. Within the next decade and a half, Pegu expanded into central Mainland Southeast Asia, taking at least two of the most important centers there, including Vientiane (once) and Ayuthaya (twice). Thus, Pegu had conquered nearly all the major centers still operational on Mainland Southeast Asia except Vietnam's Thang Long and Cambodia's Phnom Penh. That is an accomplishment never seen previously or ever to be seen again in Southeast Asian history.

Conclusion

Unique events ("incidents of the moment") operating within a given institutional context (structure) ultimately precipitated the "fall" of the kingdom and dynasty of Ava, giving some agency to the role of "chance" in history. Had the untimely deaths of several of Narapati's staunch allies or of the militarily talented heir apparent who caught a fever at precisely a time when Ava was recovering its losses from the Mohnyin *sawbwa* not occurred, the Ava Dynasty might have survived well beyond 1527. Had Minye Kyawswa, the young, brilliant military leader whose leg was crushed by his own elephant while on a Pegu campaign earlier, not died, it might have allowed Ava to recapture the coasts and resurrected, in effect, the Kingdom of Pagan. And there was the prince who was caught in the palace by the king for sneaking in to see his girlfriend, the consequences of which reversed (at least, disrupted) the direction in which Ava was headed—toward more stability at court.

Unpredictable events outside the capital also affected Ava's decline. It was often drawn into the personal and political rivalries between and among the most powerful Shan *sawbwa*, especially if they were allied with Ava, as most were. In addition, the two recorded Ming invasions earlier in midcentury kept Ava's focus on, and resources committed to, the north for a long time, disallowing it to take advantage of Lower Myanmar's burgeoning commercial revenues that eventually exploded during the sixteenth century with the so-called Age of Commerce. Had better firearms not been introduced by the Chinese and Portuguese to Lower Myanmar and Southeast Asia,[25] the outcome of several campaigns in the south might have turned in Ava's favor. Had Pegu (and also Ayuthaya) not arisen to become serious competitors for the growing trade and commerce in Lower Myanmar and other regions of coastal Southeast Asia during the early sixteenth century, Ava might have been successful in reunifying the country as Pagan had been.

Thus, unpredictable or predictable, events do have lives of their own that can either alter broader institutional structures and patterns, and history (which otherwise might have continued undisturbed), or conversely, accelerate their paths or change their trajectories. But to do so, institutions had to be weak or at least be at a weakened stage for these "incidents of the moment" to be effective. Important Ava institutions appeared to be weak precisely at those stages when some of these events occurred.

Of course, a system contains both weaknesses and strengths, and is more vulnerable at certain times than at others. When strong, it is difficult if not impossible to change structure simply with events, unless they turn into major revolutions such as the Protestant Reformation in late medieval Europe or the Chinese Communist Revolution in the twentieth century. When weak, much less is needed to effect such transformations.

In the case of Ava, by resurrecting Pagan institutions to provide itself with the wherewithal to initially emerge, it also resurrected Pagan's problems, and in the end suffered from some of the same weaknesses that Pagan had experienced. These internal, structural weaknesses were then overwhelmed by the effects of some of the immediate factors that erupted during the last few years of Ava's life, particularly from 1523 onward, bringing down the kingdom.

Yet, although events are certainly an important part of the story, they are on the whole mainly "sparks" that set off the combustible material: the long-term structural (institutional) factors that either trigger those events in the first place or make them so consequential. In other words, had certain institutions been stronger, or at a stronger stage in their oscillation between strength and weakness, when these events occurred, they might have been withstood and might not have had the consequences they did.

What the above events make clear with regard to the "fall" of Ava is that it had little or nothing to do with ethnic rivalry between Shan and Burmese, the casus belli long attributed by colonial historiography to it, and to just about every major event in Myanmar's precolonial (and sometimes, colonial) history. Indeed, as we saw, the lord of Pyi (presumably Burmese) acted purely out of self-interest with no regard for the consequences of his actions, while the Onbaung *sawbwa*, a Shan, was a principled man who kept his oath of loyalty to Narapati. In both cases, reified ethnicity had nothing to do with their behavior.

That is not to say, however, that no "we" versus "them" sentiment existed. U Kala's narrative about Thohanbwa and Yan Naung is illustrative, although perhaps it was more a characteristic of the "Early Modern Period" when U Kala was writing—and therefore representing the sentiments of his own time—than that of the Ava period itself. After ascending the Ava throne, Thohanbwa had wanted to attack Pyi and Toungoo, where relatives of the Ava court resided and were therefore potential centers of resistance. Yan Naung advised against it, saying it would only deplete and exhaust his army. Instead, he suggested Thohanbwa should satisfy himself fully at Ava.[26]

Although Thohanbwa did not listen to Yan Naung's advice, what is interesting about this account is the reason U Kala attributes to Yan Naung for his advice against attacking Pyi and Toungoo. He was said to have said that if Pyi and Toungoo had fallen to Thohanbwa, that would be the end of the Myanma Naingnan (Burmese realm) and "the Shan will rule all Myanma."[27] This suggests that U Kala appreciated the existence of a discreet Myanma Naingnan composed of, and ruled by, Myanma people, a culture with which he identified, as opposed to one composed of an "other" ruled by the Shan. It is all the more interesting since one of U Kala's parents was descended from a *sawbwa* (presumably Shan) and Burmanized Indian elite. Yet, he identified with neither Shan nor Indian culture, but with Burmese culture.

The term *naingnan* during the Pagan and Ava periods probably meant something like "conquered territory," "dominion," or "realm"—that is, a kingdom and its conquered peoples and areas composed of different ethnic groups and cultures. But in the early eighteenth century, when U Kala was writing, he appeared to have been cognizant of, and identified with, a cultural and political entity that had been under Burmese rule for nine hundred years, one that might, however, end if Thohanbwa had been successful and Shan people and culture had become dominant. That suggests that by U Kala's time, ethnic, cultural, and political identity had become more closely fused than it had been before.

At the same time, when U Kala wrote about Lower Myanmar and Yazadarit's advance on Ava, it did not produce similar emotions regarding the Myanma Naingnan being in danger or threatened with extinction. Perhaps it had something to do with U Kala's belief that whereas Yazadarit was a good Buddhist and therefore civilized and legitimate, Thohanbwa was not, and the thought of the Myanma Naingnan being ruled by such a person was very difficult to accept, and hence, U Kala's anxiety over the issue. Of course, he also knew it had not actually happened, but nevertheless may have been expressing a sigh of relief for what might have occurred.

Perhaps the most important historical consequence of Ava's "fall" for the state in Myanmar was the acceleration of Toungoo's rise. When Ava was taken in 1526–1527, many members of the royal family, ministers and other high officials of the court, military officers, monks, and scholars fled to Pyi and Toungoo. Apparently, many ordinary people not in agriculture also fled south, although some remained at Ava to serve the new patron. With much of the talented population of Ava swelling Toungoo, the latter grew both quantitatively and qualitatively. It was as much a demographic setback as it was a "brain drain" for Ava.

So, what was tragic for Ava was a boon for Toungoo, as the event allowed the latter's untrammeled rise in stature and strength, which, in turn, was the basis for the future reunification of the country, unrealized for about two and half centuries since the Pagan Dynasty. Ironically, however, the Shan *sawbwa,* by conquering Ava, created the conditions for their own conquest and absorption into the next unified Myanmar kingdom.

Ava's Legacy in Myanmar's History

Legacies can be obvious and tangible but also subtle and intangible. Ava produced both kinds. The most obvious and tangible legacy that Ava left to the country is in the area of Burmese language and literature. The least obvious and intangible legacy is the way Ava contributed to the making of modern Myanmar with Burmese language and literature, heretofore unrecognized by the field precisely because convention had it that the Ava period was a backward, Shan era. Both the tangible and intangible kinds of legacies are discussed in this chapter. But first, a summary of some of the particular problems this kind of issue raises might be in order.

In the absence of any serious scholarly study of Ava's art, architecture, iconography, music, and dance in the field of Myanmar studies, especially study based on original and contemporary sources, it would be premature to talk about an "Ava legacy" in these areas.[1] That is not to say, of course, that no art and architectural remains dated to the post-Pagan and First Ava periods have survived, that temples and Buddhist iconography were not produced during that time, or that there was no music or dance at Ava.

Rather, the problem lies in the scholarly neglect of the Ava period because of its characterization as a "barbaric" and "fragmented" medieval age, while encouraging scholarly attention on the Pagan and Second Pegu/Toungoo periods instead. Part of this neglect is justified; neither Ava nor Pegu can match the accomplishments of their predecessor or successor. In the political and military sphere, for example, while the Pagan Dynasty could claim a territory similar to present-day Myanmar's, the Second Pegu/Toungoo Dynasty went much farther, conquering most of Western and Central Mainland Southeast Asia. Whereas Ava, although successful in resisting the Ming two times and maintaining itself over two centuries, could not conquer Lower Myanmar even once.

Ava's artistic record also cannot match Pagan's, so that whatever was produced during the Ava period did not create any art historical legacy to speak of. In terms of quantity as well, one can hardly compare Pagan's construction output with Ava's, best represented by the remains at Sagaing, its "field of merit" that lay on the other side of the Irrawaddy River from Ava. Little or nothing survives in terms of secular architecture either. It is true that a new palace was built around 1510. However, because it followed King Kyanzittha's model of four hundred years earlier very closely, it does not appear to be original and was no more representative of Ava than of Pagan. Besides, not all that remains of the Ava palace today can be unequivocally attributed to the First Ava Dynasty in any case, for the Second Ava Dynasty built upon the ruins of the former, while archaeology has not made the remains of the two periods distinct.

There is one other secular engineering accomplishment worth reiterating: an original inscription belonging to Narapati the Great records the building of (what may have been a pontoon) bridge across the Irrawaddy from Ava to Sagaing, on which he claimed "the four-fold army" could cross abreast. We hear of nothing else of the kind built again that crossed the same span until the British built the Sagaing Bridge in the twentieth century.

The arts and crafts (painting, lacquerware, gold-leaf production, silver work, bronze casting, wood carving, marble sculpture), as well as some of the fine arts (dance, music, string puppetry) appear to have flourished at Ava and are mentioned in period inscriptions.[2] But the information available is hardly adequate to say much more about it. Since the Ava kingdom was much smaller and not nearly as wealthy as Pagan, the sheer demand for the arts and crafts could not have been at the level found in the latter, probably with a parallel decline in quantity and quality as well. In the area of religion, I know of no scholarship, in either Burmese or English, that claims Ava to have established a "legacy" that posterity regarded as a model. Perhaps in law, Ava may have established some sort of legacy, although none that can be supported by contemporary epigraphs so far.

In the area of Burmese literature, however, all Myanmar scholars are agreed that Ava was special, providing a lasting and extremely important legacy that, in some ways, has not been matched. As a historian, what I see as even more important than literature per se are the intangible consequences, especially in the preservation and use of the Burmese language as the lingua franca and "language of state," so that it became an invariable part of the "national tradition" and the modern Burmese nation.

Ava's Contribution to Burmese Literature

Scholars much more knowledgeable about the subject than I agree that Burmese language and especially literature in the country attained its zenith during the Ava period.[3] This is particularly evident during the fifteenth-century reign of Narapati the Great. Some of the most eminent literary figures of Myanmar lived, and some of the finest genres of secular and religious literature were produced, during the First Ava period even though their roots lay in the Kingdom of Pagan. After all, the Burmese script per se was invented at Pagan, while the kingdom's longevity, wealth, and sophistication only enhanced its development further. This is attested by the abundance of writing on religious and other subjects left on stone, terra cotta, and ceramic plaques, and as ink inscriptions on the interior walls of temples. Even though none apparently survives on palm leaf (the favored medium for literature), more than enough is recorded on stone itself and ample references are made to palm-leaf records to suggest that Pagan's achievements in writing likely established the standards and foundations for Ava's literary accomplishments.

To be sure, although Pagan was clearly a literate society that produced both religious literature of high quality in Pali that received accolades by the larger Buddhist world as well as sophisticated secular Old Burmese written by the non-religious sector, the largest number of verses, two of the earliest extant *yazawin,* and several of the most exemplary treatises on legal and religious matters that have survived belonged to Ava. Even ordinary persons there wrote inscriptions in verse, such as the headman of a place called Palaung in 1355, a decade before Ava was founded. But perhaps the most telling evidence of literacy at Pagan and Ava is the number of Old Burmese inscriptions erected by commoners as opposed to those erected by elite, whose ratio (at Pagan) was about three to one in favor of the commoners, and continued to be approximately the same (if not more) at Ava.

The strong tradition of copying religious texts (which accrued merit) assured that these were preserved from generation to generation. The practice of keeping palm-leaf duplicates of stone records dealing with land transactions is mentioned at Pagan, clearly the precursor of later *sittans* (lists, records). Pagan also produced what may have been the first written civil and criminal code, although strictly speaking, it might not be considered literature. Certainly in terms of producing religious and grammatical treatises, Ava did not surpass Pagan, especially those composed by and attributed to well-known religious and grammatical scholars who lived during the Pagan period.[4]

It may be that simply being two hundred years later, some copies of Ava's palm-leaf records survived while Pagan's did not; indeed, much of Pagan's literary achievements in that medium must have been resurrected by Ava's scholars. Certainly, some of Pagan's stone records are of a quality that no one will dispute is fine literature, particularly those from the early twelfth century. These include Rajakumar's Myinkaba Kubyaukgyi inscription (better known as the Myazedi Inscription) and Alaungsithu's prayer written in Pali on the twelfth-century Shwegugyi temple stone inscription (parts of it reproduced below). The latter is an example of exemplary literature that even Ava did not surpass. Certainly, its high level of sophistication is arguably still unsurpassed. Wrote G. H. Luce, "The poem consists of 100 verses, mostly in the *vatta* metre of 4 eight-syllable lines; varied at intervals by the *vamsattha* metre of 4 twelve-syllable lines, and the *vasantatilaka* metre of 4 fourteen-syllable lines." The following is a part of that inscription translated by Pe Maung Tin and G. H. Luce.[5]

By this my gift, whatever boon ensues,
Be it the best of boons, to profit all!
By this abundant merit I desire
Here nor hereafter no angelic pomp
Of Brahmas, Suras, Maras; nor the state
And splendour of a king; nay, nor the steps
Sublime of pupils of the conqueror.
But I would make my body a bridge athwart
The river of Samsara and all folk

Would speed across thereby until they reach
The Blessed City. I myself would cross
And drag the drowning over. Ay, myself
Tamed, I would tame the wilful; comforted,
Comfort the timid; wakened, wake the asleep;
Cooled, cool the burning; freed, set free the bound.
Tranquil, and led by the good doctrines, I
Would hatred calm. The three immoral states,
Greed, Hate, Delusion—rooted all in self—
O may they die, whenever born in me!

Apart from such fine examples of Pali verse, Pali scholarship per se was also at an advanced stage at Pagan, with at least several dozen works written in the language that received high acclaim at the time. Most of the subject matter was religious, including treatises on Buddhist philosophy, the *Vinaya* (text on monastic rules), and the *Abhidhamma* (commentaries on Buddhist philosophy). One particular treatise that stood out, written approximately around 1154 AD, was the *Saddaniti,* a Pali grammar that was acclaimed even by scholars from Sri Lanka, considered the supreme center for Pali scholarship at the time. The work is still considered a valuable contribution to Pali studies in general.

How fine works in Pali translate into fine works in Old Burmese literature is, of course, debatable. And when it comes to secular, vernacular Burmese verse, Ava seems to have eclipsed Pagan. Some of the most important literary figures at Ava include Ariyavamsa, Shin Uttamagyaw, Shin Thilawuntha, Shin Rattathara, Saddhammakitti, Shin Aggathamadhi, and Lady Yaweshinhtwe, not to mention two poetesses, Mi Nyo and Mi Phyu (Miss Brown and Miss White). This subject has seen very little scholarship in English, particularly research that has been derived from the primary sources. It could easily be a book-length monograph in itself, so what little is described here should be taken only as a very preliminary summary of what still needs to be done. My synopsis here is gleaned from both the primary sources, mainly the Ava inscriptions, in which verse abounds, as well as from secondary sources written by scholars on the subject, particularly the works of Mabel Bode, Anna Allott, John Okell, Dr. Hla Pe, Pe Maung Tin, U Kyaw Dun, and U Saw Tun.[6]

Shin Ariyavamsa was from Pagan and lived at Ava during the reign of Narapati the Great. He had studied at Sagaing earlier, showing how, even during times of military chaos, there were oases of peace, quiet, and learning. His training resulted in the writing of a treatise called the *Manisaramanjusa,* a commentary on the *Abhidhammatthavibhavani.* He wrote and taught at Sagaing, but moved to Ava, as it had become the kingdom's center of scholarship. According to Mabel Bode, one of his most important later works was the *Manidipa,* a treatise on the *Atthasalini* (a commentary) of Buddhaghosa, perhaps the most celebrated of all Buddhist monks in the Sinhalese tradition. Ariyavamsa also composed a grammatical treatise called the *Gandhabharana* and a study of the *Jatakas* called the *Jatakavisodhana.* He wrote mostly in Pali but also showed his talents in the vernacular, composing the first metaphysical work in Burmese, an *atthayojana* (interpretation) of a commentary, called the *Anutika*, on the *Abhidhamma.*

The next Buddhist scholar at Ava able to fill his shoes was Shin Thilawuntha. He and Shin Uttamagyaw were contemporaries, as monks who had entered the same monastery at Taungdwingyi, a provincial governorship under Ava (northwest of Naypyidaw, the present capital). The former wrote religious works in verse, such as of the *Sumedhakatha* (the story of the ascetic Sumedha, which was part of the introduction to the *Jataka* commentary), known as the *Buddhalamkara,* and another on his native Taungdwingyi, dignified with the Pali name *Pabbatabbhantara.*

Thilawuntha was apparently expelled from his monastery for writing "secular" poetry, the *Paraminganpyo*; but was nevertheless invited by Mingaung the Second to Ava at the relatively young age of thirty to continue his scholarship and teach the scriptures there. A grand monastery, the Yatanabiman, was subsequently built for him at Ava, an event recorded in a long and pedantic inscription.[7] He also wrote a grammatical work, and other "secular" verses such as *Hsutaungganpyo, Taungdwinlapyo* (on his home town), and *Tada-u-ti Mawgun,* an account of building the relatively well-known place called Tada-U (Head of the Bridge) a bit south of Ava. He is, of course, best known to historians for composing the *Yazawinkyaw* (Celebrated Chronicle) completed in 1520, ostensibly the earliest extant Burmese language *yazawin* found in Myanmar.[8]

Shin Uttamagyaw, who had entered the monastery together with Shin Thilawuntha in Taundwingyi at a young age, remained there for twenty years, and only after that moved to Ava to become a consultant in religious matters for the court. Yet his most famous work is called the *Tawla* (Forest Journey), which honored nature and was not strictly religious. Fortunately, it has been translated into English nearly in its entirety in the *Journal of the Burma Research Society* for those interested in Burmese literature.[9]

Shin Maharattathara (according to the author of the *Sasanavamsa*) was "equal in intelligence and power with the venerable Elder Silavamsa [Thilawuntha]. He composed 'metrical versions' of the *Bhuridattajataka, Hatthipalajataka,* and *Samvarajataka,*" and "also various other beautiful poems." Both scholars were "mildly censured" for writing poetry (considered a transgression of the religious rule concerning singing and dancing) by the author of the *Sasanavamsa,* a later (nineteenth-century) work compiled by a monk under King Mindon. Apparently, the court and capital of Ava at the time was more liberal and lenient, holding a less strict interpretation of the *Vinaya* than the provincial monastery from which Thilawuntha was expelled for writing secular verse.[10]

Saddhammakitti had it worse: he was a pupil of the famous Ariyavamsa but lived during the period after Ava had (finally) fallen and was being ruled by Thohanbwa, the Shan *sawbwa* whom Harvey called "a full-blooded savage,"[11] said to have cruelly persecuted the *sangha,* burning and looting monasteries and pagodas, which he considered repositories of wealth. Nevertheless, Saddhammakitti remained a scholar, doing the best he could under such trying circumstances, and compiled the famous vocabulary *Ekakkharakosa.* But it is unclear whether

Saddhammakitti remained at Ava and wrote the work there, for he died at Toungoo, which had become not only a refuge for people who had fled Ava with its fall, but also a haven for the religion and scholarship.

In terms of achievements in secular literature, the inscriptions and other records of the Ava period reflect an explosion in verbiage, particularly of verse. Especially between 1400 and 1500 AD, the exemplary center produced several lasting genres of Burmese poetry, establishing standards that later generations could only hope to imitate and emulate but, in most cases, not surpass.[12]

According to scholars of Burmese literature, elaborate use of simile, metaphor and other literary devices also abound in Burmese verse, especially in the works of Shin Maharattathara. One of these works rejects the comforts of marriage and secular life for that of a forest ascetic. The following is a translation by Dr. Hla Pe, John Okell, and Anna Allott.

> The maiden I marry shall be a forest dwelling, one that befits a hermit, far from the approach of men; she will tend to all my needs and will always keep me fed, with forest fruits for rice, and forest fruits for curry. I shall have Wisdom for my washing-water, for it cleanses the dirt of greed, hatred, and ignorance; and when I have neatly tied the ascetic's knot in my hair, I shall bedeck it with Faith for a garland; the fragrance of Meditation shall be my sandalwood, and I shall anoint myself with the sweet-smelling and cooling juice of aloes. . . . I shall wear the priceless and costly garment of the Law.[13]

The king is often the subject matter, and poems were written either by monks who were his preceptors and wrote on religious themes (often at the request of the monarchs) or by ministers and other court dignitaries who extolled the king's virtues, stature, achievements, and lineage. These poems were all written in the "four-syllable line," which, by the Ava period, can be categorized into at least three different forms: *pyo*, which dealt mainly with religious themes; *egyin*, with royal lineage; and *mawgun*, mostly with momentous and important events of the reign. While most *pyo* used one of the 550 *Jatakas* (stories of the previous lives of the Buddha) for their themes, others use Buddhist themes for didactic purposes (homilies and advice).

In addition to the literary scholars mentioned above, Shin Tejosara and Shin Aggathamadhi should also be mentioned as distinguished *pyo* writers of the Ava and post-Ava periods. *Pyo* continued to be written to the end of the nineteenth century, but in the opinion of the scholars (mentioned above), the best *pyo* of the Ava period has not been equaled.

Although *mawgun* by the Ava period had become a category of verse, its etymology suggests that it was initially used as "record" or "memorial." Typically, *mawgun* are records of important events. The large majority of *mawgun* dwell on subjects such as the building of pagodas, irrigation canals, reservoirs, or palaces; conquests of enemies; coronations of kings; visits by foreign dignitaries, and so on. The "four-syllable line" is used in writing *mawgun,* but unlike the *pyo,* written only (or mainly) by monks, and *egyin,* written only (or mainly) by lay courtiers, *mawgun* were written by both monks and laymen, although the former focused on religious themes and the latter on secular ones. One of the best-known *mawgun* was written by a military commander. It described a voyage made by the king down the Irrawaddy to Pyi (Prome), capturing a white elephant, one of the marks of a *cakkavatti.* Shin Thilawuntha's poem of the Yatanabeikman, a grand monastery built by the reigning king for him, was written as a *mawgun* on stone.

Egyin, written mainly if not exclusively by lay courtiers, are usually poems directed at royal offspring whose ancestors are extolled. It too allows many opportunities for praising the king in glorious terms. One of the most famous (and said to be the oldest to have survived) is called the "Yakhaing Minthami Egyin" (The *Egyin* of the Princess of Arakan) written in 1455 by a minister named Adu Min Nyo at the court of Arakan, where he had been appointed governor. Its high degree of development suggests that others were also produced at the time, although their originals seemed not to have survived.[14]

Another *egyin* by an Ava courtier named Shin Thuye, originally the term for a crown soldier, is a lullaby to a young royal princess, which in no uncertain terms makes clear her pedigree and status.

> In times gone by, and in a distant country, Duttabaung, the great-grandfather of your grandfather, by the power of Sakka from the heavens above and of Naga and Garuda . . . overpowered all who dwell on earth, in water and in the sky. Men of this generation, who saw it not, cherish the memory and repeat the story. But O how your father surpasses this! For him the Lord of the Raksas, the celestial ogre, came gliding down rushing and roaring, and said "If you need help to fight, I am your lordship's servant, bold and defiant." And you little Htwe great and noble blessing, desired of men and spirits, whose renown reverberates with wondrous clamor far and wide over the entire face of the earth–sleep, softly, sleep.[15]

Another genre of verse developed at Ava was called the *tawla* (forest journey), noted above, which was said to have become more popular subsequently (as more of them were discovered), although, as noted, that phenomenon might be a matter of record survival and not evidence of popularity. Using the four-syllable line, the *tawla* did not extol the virtues of kingship and royalty. Yet, it would have been written and read mainly at court, since its style and meaning, for the most part, would have been incomprehensible to common people. It is less grandiose than the other three genres and meant to describe the emotions one feels when one is with nature, particularly the forest.

Apparently the earliest *tawla* to have survived is one written by Shin Uttamagyaw, who recorded nature during his travel from Ava to Minbu, about 150 miles south of the capital. He describes the trees, the colors, the light and shade, the different birds and their calls, the sound of the wind. A mood of wistful sadness emanates from these sights and sounds, for it evokes ambivalence as to whether he should remain a monk or return to the life of a layman who can enjoy these simple pleasures. (These feelings evoked by nature remind one of the Japanese concept of *mono no aware,* found in the poetry of eleventh-century

Kyoto's Hean court society.) Below is a translation by Po Byu of a small section of Uttamagyaw's poem.

> In the three-fold region of Time and Place, the all-wise Sage stands without a peer. His endless glory reaches even the ringing rafters of the firmament. The blaze of majesty flashes free and cleaves clean the boundless space. The raying sun traces its path along the middle way. In this season of Thingyan showers, there is a rapture in the skies. Behold the elephant, the egret, the crab and the crow conserve their lustrous rays against the day for shining in brightest sheen. Scattered flocks of cloud land close and stand on Yugan's brow in motley-colored livery. The rainbow of the changeful clouds is tinted with sable and azure and purple and yellow and varied kindred hues. Pile upon pile of drifting columns vault their tricksome courses and clash together as the roc [*sic*] and the dragon met in a fierce contest. In Kason, Withakah appears and sheds its lucent beams. The fresh flame of the young new year quickens the scented sagawa from leaf to flower. The Nayon sun strikes the sweet jasmine branch into bloom. The ponnyet bursts in flower and loads Waso airs with a grateful odour. A gay-hearted noise announces the advent of the rains. In the bosom of Jove joy is lord. Celestial drums send forth a mighty roll and the fairy conch swells the pealing note. The lustre of the lusty sun is quenched in wreaths of cloud and the jocund sound rings into the azured vault like the thundrous rattle of arms. The god of the sky sends sheets of swift rain. Pools and lakes and woods, marshes and streams and springs brim over and form countless rivulets. Rivers and streams look ravishing in a thousand charms. In bold joyance, schools [of?] magans, crowds of turtles, shoals of fishes hold high festival and join the crabs that crouch at the mouths of their cozy holes in adoration before the man of men. With the fall of rain the gleesome hillman drives full hard his wonted harrow and sows his seed. When the palmyra casts its fleshy fruit, Atanada, Kuwera, Thatagiri and other fairy ogres duly bow before the Overman and clap their arms and show their snowy teeth with a liberal laugh.[16]

Poetry appears regularly in donative inscriptions, interspersed between the prose that record the contents of the donation. Some are rather long and composed entirely in verse. Many of them are esoteric and written mainly for the king and court, although most inscriptions should have been decipherable by the non-initiated as well. But then, virtually all high literature in Burmese, until the late nineteenth century, was produced by the center rather than the "periphery." Even works that praise the virtues of the rural farmer or the commoner were written by members of the court elite.

According to specialists on Burmese literature, what counts most in Burmese verse is rhyme and the number of syllables in a group less than vowel length and stress. The most basic, from which other forms of verse derive, is the four-syllable line verse, in which the rhyme is said to "climb" (actually it "descends") from the end of the line toward the beginning, the lines naturally falling into self-contained couplets, each linked to the previous or next with a rhymed word on the second syllable. And when the same tone and ending is necessary to rhyme, poetic license is taken and tones altered, rare or obsolete words are inserted, metatheses (that is, hysteron-proteron, as for example, using the word *matiketu* for *ketumati*) are used, suffixes are minimized or redundant ones inserted, and long Pali or Sanskrit words are abbreviated or shortened. All this allowed the poet to demonstrate his or her mastery of the language and genre, so that, for example, one particularly long poem used this form to list the accession and death of each king of each dynasty in Myanmar.[17]

Yadu is another form of poetry that probably originated at Ava, although it obtained greater popularity subsequently in the Second Ava period. Both Shin Maharattathara and Thilawuntha have been given credit for several *yadu*, which is also written in the four-syllable line but, unlike the others, is much shorter. The standard *yadu* has three stanzas, although some with one stanza exist. The latter can be used for poets to play games by writing only the first or first and second stanzas, leaving the third to be completed by the reader. Consequently, these are called "incomplete" and "completing" *yadu*. There is thus room for innovation, as one can play with rhyme, tones, content, and the like. The subject matter of *yadu* is varied and incorporates many components of the other genres: some are edifying, some didactic, but the main and greatest of the *yadu* express feelings of sadness and longing, somewhat like the *tawla*. Separation from a lover, being away from home, and contemplation on the beauty of the forests are all appropriate subject matter.

The king himself sometimes wrote *yadu*. In one case, Mingaung the Second wrote a poem called "Kyeze" (Parrot Messenger), which is considered by scholars of Burmese literature to be a fine example of *yadu*. In this poem, a parrot is sent with a message of longing to the poet's lover and returns with a reply in similar terms. It reminds one of the "Cloud Messenger" by famous Indian poet Kalidasa. Many later *yadu* used the king's "Kyeze" as model. In addition, Ava court society continued the writing of *linga*, a form of verse found earlier in the Pagan period,[18] along with, we are told, the *thachin*, a new genre of verse about which little has been published in English.[19]

Myitaza was apparently also developed at Ava during the fifteenth century. These were in the form of letters that give advice to the recipient. Written in verse in the usual format, they were used by monks who were advisers of kings, giving counsel on statesmanship and morality. One of these, written by the Kandaw Min Kyaung Sayadaw (1481–1527) was in mixed style: prose, rhyming prose and four-syllable line format. (One of the latest *myitaza* is "Letters to a Dictator," which ex-brigadier Aung Gyi sent to President Ne Win in the 1980s.)

Even *dhammathat*, generally a reference to codified civil law, were written in verse by monks such as Shin Saddhammapala. Others, such as Shin Jina Lankaradhaja produced a prose *dhammathat* called the "Manuvansa Pakasani" during the Ava period.[20] There is evidence of the existence of at least one *dhammathat linga*—that is, *dhammathat* that had been put into verse—during the Pagan period.[21]

Then came the conquest of Ava in 1526–1527 by the Shan, putting a virtual stop to all literary, religious, and artistic activities at the capital for the next two decades. As noted in earlier chapters, later Burmese language chronicles record that during this period, Buddhism was persecuted, monks murdered, books burned, and temples desecrated for their treasures. These accounts are supported indirectly by epigraphy, for during this period, there was a sudden end to religious donations at the capital, an unequivocal indicator of social disruption and political instability. Only a paltry three stone inscriptions are recorded during that period: two in the Mandalay area, one in a rural location, but importantly, none at Ava—and that, during a period of twenty-four years![22]

Also as noted in a previous chapter, many people of letters, skilled artists and craftsmen, merchants, crown service groups including elite soldiers, and, most importantly, monks—on whose presence the population depended for their accumulation of merit and "salvation"—were said to have fled to other centers such as Toungoo and Pyi. As a result, literature and the fine arts all but disappeared at Ava during this time. Certainly no self-contained and complete *yazawin* (chronicle) was written at Ava during those twenty-four years; at least none survives in Shan or Burmese of which I am aware.

However, at Toungoo and Pyi, and a few other oases of Burmese learning and culture, to where most of the renowned authors of Ava fled, Burmese literature continued to be written, albeit at a slower pace[23] and under the patronage of the governors of Toungoo and Pyi who were members of the ex-royal family of Ava. Indeed, some of the best "Ava period" literature that has survived was written not at Ava itself after its conquest but at Pyi and Toungoo. This may have been what prompted D. G. E. Hall to conclude (erroneously) that, despite Shan rule, the Ava period saw "the birth of Burmese vernacular literature."[24] Burmese vernacular literature there was, but not produced at Ava during the period of actual Shan rule—that is, from 1527 to 1551.

One such poet who wrote *yadu* during the Ava period but at Toungoo was Hlawga Thondaung Hmu (Commander of the 3000 War Boats), who had fled to Toungoo when Ava was conquered. He also wrote two well-known *egyin,* one of which was for the young prince of Toungoo, Tabinshwehti, who later became one of the greatest generals in Burmese history. In this particular *egyin,* Hlawga traced the prince's ancestry to the kings of Pagan, Myin Saing, Sagaing, and Pinya. It is from these kinds of verse that later historians writing *yazawin* might have obtained some of their ambiguous genealogical links.

Hlawga's *yadu,* however, were not very distinguished, according to scholars, whereas those of two other high officials, "Great" Nawade and Nat Shin Naung, were.[25] Nawade was a courtier and a soldier who carried the Ava tradition to Pyi[26] and wrote over three hundred *yadu* of very high quality, having written poetry since he was ten years old. He wrote *yadu* on numerous topics: the sky, the forest, flowers, the state, the throne, military campaigns, religious subjects, men, women, questions and answers, parrot messengers, and Sakka (or Indra), considered king of the *nats.* He also wrote *egyin,* even one on "the Queen of Ayuthaya."

Nat Shin Naung was a prince and general; he described his love for a princess who was given in marriage to another prince.

> I ached with longing, I knew not good from evil in my anguish. From that day I beheld her, allowing my eyes to rest where they would, I cannot forget. Stricken with an immense and uncontainable tenfold misery, I only wish to make her mistress of my life. Should even Sakka, King of the Gods, seeking her match in the Second Heaven, set beside her one chosen to compete, then would people say that my mistress shines like the bright moon beside a little star. In trying to tell of her glowing *brown smooth beauty* [my emphasis],[27] her fresh tender grace, her pure nature, he who sees her becomes bewildered and dizzy, he gropes for words, and tries to speak but cannot describe her. Again and again I gaze on her loveliness, far surpassing all rivals, and wherever I look I only have eyes for her face.[28]

Nat Shin Naung's love for his princess continued, and after she was widowed, he continued for another ten years writing *yadu* to her. She eventually married him, but in the same year he was executed for treason. According to literary scholars of Myanmar, the pathos of his *yadu* remains unsurpassed in Burmese literature and his *yadu* on unrequited love, a model for later generations. There were other *yadu* writers contemporary to Nat Shin Naung, such as Zeyayandameit and Shin Than Kho, about which I have little or no information.

After Narapati "the Third," of the old Ava royal family, recovered Ava around 1551 from the third Shan *sawbwa*, Burmese language and literature once again reappeared. Mi Nyo and Mi Phyu, the two court ladies mentioned above, wrote *yadu* during this period at Ava. Mi Nyo (Miss Brown, that is, Miss "Tan") was originally from Arakan, while her counterpart in *yadu* was Mi Phyu (Miss White). The subject matter of their *yadu* was mainly cosmological (about Mount Meru).[29] More important is the fact that these ladies were not only literate but excelled in poetry, for which they were recognized during their lifetimes. That speaks much for the accomplishment of women at the court of Ava,[30] perhaps giving some credence to the oft-repeated modern convention regarding the high status of Burmese women.

In sum, although politics and war were probably the main concerns of the court during the Ava period, there was room and time for the fine arts as well, especially literature of a high order. Such achievement in literature at Ava implies it could not have been accomplished without a genuine concern and support for the arts in general by the Ava monarchy. More important, these accomplishments were being produced right in the midst of the many struggles for the throne. Ava's literary achievements were being attained in the quiet of the capital's royal monasteries or royal archives by scholars (sometimes by the king himself), while the commander in chief and others were simultaneously fighting rebellious princes on the noisy battlefield. We sometimes forget that history and society are often full of such contradictions, and attempts to eliminate them mainly for the sake of consistency actually does a disservice to historical accuracy.

To reiterate my point from the introduction, narrative history, the stuff of which the Burmese chronicles are made, tends to be, by nature, tumultuous, whereas institutional history, represented largely by epigraphy, is by nature calm. But there is no reason these extremes cannot coexist, both in history as well as in the sources that speak about it. If we favor one extreme over the other (for whatever academic or political reasons we might be harboring), we will, in fact, be privileging not only that extreme and the sources it represents, but also what we sometimes consider sacred—consistency. Ava experienced both turmoil and peace, and did so at the same time. And the proof is in the poetry.

Burmese Language in the Making of Modern Myanmar

Even if the above description and discussion helps explain why the production of Burmese literature at Ava should not be considered a "surprise" or "paradox," as the Ava Convention claims, it still does not explain *how* Ava was able to accomplish such a feat in the first place. Although this issue was not even raised by followers of the Ava Convention, it still needs to be answered, even if preliminarily. The answer is that Ava had a long time in which to do it, with little or no competition from other languages and language speakers, and did not have to start from scratch. For approximately six hundred consecutive years (counting both the Pagan and Ava periods), Burmese was the lingua franca of state and society while the Burmese writing system enjoyed the same status of being the "script of state."

To be sure, local dialects and other languages must have been spoken in the kingdom, particularly in the areas where the minorities lived. But since Burmese was the lingua franca and language of state, if one wanted to move upward socially, economically, and politically at the capital and in the kingdom in general, or if one wanted to benefit from, rather than resist, the state's power, authority, and largesse, Burmese was the language of choice. Thus, other ethnolinguistic groups that wanted to get ahead in Burmese society would have learned the "national" language as well, in turn hastening their integration into mainstream society.

Thus, Shan speakers who had obviously learned to speak and write Burmese can be found at some of the highest levels of Ava society. The Minister of the Right (Hand) of the king was a Shan *sawbwa*, a relatively high officer of the elephantry corps (*hsinke*), and a *thugyi* (head person) of *myinsi* (cavalry, or literally, horse riders) were all Shan, while a Palaung cavalryman is also mentioned. We also find a Lawa as a high-ranking military officer (*sitke*) in the infantry. These people must have been able to speak, read, and write Burmese, for how else were they going to communicate with the majority of Burmese speakers over and under them? In fact, their situation demonstrates early integration of minority ethno-linguistic groups into mainstream Burmese society at a relatively high level.

The institution that was most clearly responsible for educating the Ava population at large—and indeed throughout precolonial history and well into the beginning of the twentieth century—was the *sangha* and its monastic school system. There, society's children were taught the "three Rs" in what were called *sa thin kyaung* (literally, monasteries where reading and writing are taught), as distinguished from ordinary monasteries (*kyaung*). One monastery that was donated during the Ava period included ten separate school buildings attached to it. Such donations would usually include endowments of land, part of whose revenues were specifically allotted to the teaching of children, especially boys. In another, fifty *pay* of land was donated in perpetuity as an endowment that provided for the education of children. And although, as at Pagan, Ava education was also likely to have been primarily religious in nature, in order to read the scriptures, one had to learn to read first. Indeed, that today the Burmese word for "monastery" and "school" are the same is an indication of their earlier dual function.

Ava's leadership had long realized that the Burmese language was a unifying mechanism for the kingdom, as it was at Pagan, so that it was very much in Ava's interest to develop and perpetuate the place of Burmese language in society. That was accomplished by using it exclusively for all official documents of state—donative inscriptions, *sittans*, chronicles, edicts, tax records, cadastral surveys, political appointments, religious treatises, and codified law. The medium that legally documented and permanently preserved society's memory of itself was theretofore (and thereafter) written Burmese. With that kind of history behind it, Ava's accomplishments in this endeavor are neither "surprising" nor "paradoxical." They were perfectly logical, understandable, and explainable.

Ava's achievements in written Burmese language went beyond the realm of the fine arts to become a major factor in the making of modern Myanmar. Resurrecting the Burmese tradition of Pagan, "archiving" it in the same language, and perpetuating it in writing for nearly another two hundred years not only ensconced Burmese as the lingua franca for a total of six hundred years, it also conferred on the majority Burmese speakers guardianship of the "national" language. Thenceforth, all attempts to secure the state came to be regarded as *their* role and responsibility, thereby linking not only the "ownership" but also the leadership of the state with the Burmese speakers. And if linguists like the late Pete (Alton) Becker are correct, that language *is* culture,[31] Ava was Burmese in terms of culture as well.

By the twentieth century, 1,200 years had passed with the Burmese speakers at the helm and Burmese culture considered mainstream, so that when the modern nation-state was being formulated before and during World War II, it was expected of the Burmese speakers to lead the way and carry the torch—which they did. In these twelve centuries of Burmese dominance, there were only two brief and unsuccessful interruptions: the seventeen years of Thohanbwa's reign, and a little over a half century of British rule.[32] Of course, neither could undo more than a millennium of history. Indeed, the structural and conceptual link established between the Burmese language and the modern Burmese state was reaffirmed by what actually happened. It is a matter of historical record that each time the state collapsed—from the Pagan period until today—it was always the Burmese speakers who resurrected and reunified it.[33] Nearly every dynasty and kingdom after the Pyu—Pagan, the First Ava Dynasty, the Second Pegu/Toungoo

Dynasty, the Second Ava Dynasty, and the Konbaung Dynasty—were led by Burmese speakers, so that each time, de facto and de jure leadership became synonymous, while *their* vision of state and society became "mainstream."

This is not a statement about the inevitability of history or a justification for Burmese rule, but an explanation, revealed only in hindsight, of that historical outcome. Unfortunately, explanation is often conflated or confused with political justification, particularly in recent years, when in fact, the present analysis is no different from one that explains the "making" of modern Germany, France, or Italy by German, French, and Italian speakers, or the "making" of modern Thailand, Cambodia, and Vietnam by the T'ai, Khmer, and Vietnamese speakers. That is not to say, of course, that Burmese assumption of leadership and vision of the state were uncontested or accepted by all without protest, no more than the fact of, and vision regarding, the "manifest destinies" of the Vietnamese, the Thai, the Khmers, and Americans were also accepted by all involved without dissension. But it *is* to say that during most of Myanmar's (especially precolonial) history, there were no other political groups with the necessary political and military power to successfully challenge the Burmese speakers and their vision of the state.[34]

The three groups with the best opportunity to have done that were the Shan, Mon, and Arakanese. The Shan, with the largest number among the minority groups, and about 9 percent of the population today; the Mon with the smallest, with less than 2 percent; and the Arakanese, with about 4 percent, had at least once each conquered and taken control of (what at the time) was the country's dominant political and eco-demographic center. The Shan took Ava in 1526–1527 ending the First Ava Dynasty, the Arakanese sacked Pegu in 1599 ending the Second Pegu/Toungoo Dynasty, and the Mon sacked Ava in 1752 ending the Second Ava Dynasty. Yet, none of the victors chose to reunify the country under their own aegis when they had the opportunity. Instead, each decided to return home with the loot, without any attempt to create, or showing any interest in creating, a unified political entity. As a result, none exercised leadership for any substantial amount of time on the "national" stage or offered alternative visions of the state, other than to destroy and plunder the spoils of war. Indeed, they were destructive rather than constructive, and invariably ended up being the "losers" in this contest for national supremacy, a quest that continued well into the twenty-first century.

There must have been compelling reasons the Shan, Mon, and Arakanese thought in these "local" rather than "national" terms. Why did the Shan speakers, especially with their larger numbers, not retain Ava, establish their own dynasty, and reunify the country? Why did the Mon speakers, after taking the Second Ava Dynasty, not stay in Upper Myanmar to also reunify the country under their aegis? Why did the Arakanese speakers return to the west coast of Myanmar and not stay at Pegu to resurrect the great empire of Bayinnaung?

The most obvious reason seems to be their vastly inferior numbers compared with that of the Burmese speakers, which, as a result, may have made such a leadership role appear unrealistic, and at best, temporary, although such a scenario is not unknown in history. They may also have been psychologically uncomfortable with agrarian life in the plains of the Dry Zone, for after all, the Arakanese and the Mon were coastal traders of multicultural commercial ports while the Shan seemed to have preferred life in the cooler, wetter, and less-congested hills. Yet, because the bulk of the country's population and its food supplies lay in the central plains, these material and human resources had to be taken first if all of Myanmar were to be controlled. And none of the three minority groups seem to have wanted to make that kind of long-term commitment when they all had the opportunity to do so.

But even had they wanted to, they did not have the "proper" credentials. None of the three could claim the country's "golden age" (Pagan) as theirs, since they had played only marginal roles in its establishment (if at all), nor offer any alternatives to it. In fact, we now know that Pegu and Lower Myanmar were legacies of Pagan, not the other way around, which was part of the reason the Mon never claimed Pagan as theirs—that claim was made *for* them by colonial scholars much later. Similarly, Mrauk-U was also partially a legacy of Pagan (and Bengal), and in any case appeared much too late to have been considered to be part of the "golden age" of the country. As for the Shan, they never managed to consolidate themselves as a unified polity representing any "national" tradition or exercise any leadership role, even during their twenty-four-year rule at Ava.

In other words, the polities of these three groups were too narrowly conceived and structured, more local than "national," with little or no conceptual attachment to the big picture. Their rejection of the plains areas of the Irrawaddy, especially the Dry Zone of Myanmar, as a long-term habitat, where the bulk of the country's resources lay and without which it could not be unified, is just one example of this parochialism. And even if, for the sake of argument, there had been a psychological disposition to live in, work, and control the Dry Zone, what mechanisms did the three minority groups have to unify the country?

What language, for example, would they have used as lingua franca—their own? Even combined, their languages were spoken by less than 15 percent of the country's population. How were they going to educate the other 85 percent of the population in their minority languages and convince the rest of the country to use them? What "national" script would they have used other than Burmese, the only one available to, and known by, the population at large? The Shan in Myanmar had none at the time, while Arakanese and Mon both used the Burmese script. And who was going to make all that happen? The only "teachers" in the country were the clergy, and they had already made Burmese the lingua franca of the country, while their monasteries were already established as "national schools." Were the members of the *sangha*, most of whom were surely Burmese speakers, about to voluntarily "retool" themselves in Mon, Shan, or Arakanese languages in order to teach the next generation those languages? What would have been their incentive? And who was going to force them to carry out such a plan?

In short, these three minority groups that had the best opportunity to unify the country under their own aegis would have had to create a new and viable "national" language with a "national" tradition that could compete with the Burmese language and tradition, and then "sell" it to the rest of the population. Thus, it was more than a matter of numbers; there were also many mental, social, institutional, and historical barriers that prevented the successful implementation of a unified polity led by any of these three minority groups.

None of the above, of course, means that the Shan, Mon, and Arakanese had no role on the "national" stage. Even as members of the "supporting cast," they established enduring relationships with the main actors, the Burmese speakers, during Ava's moment on the "national" stage. Ava, more so than Pagan, had more regular, intensive, and extensive political and military relations with the Shan of Upper Myanmar. Whereas they were very rarely mentioned in Pagan inscriptions, and then mainly as *kyun* (vassal, servant), in the Ava inscriptions, they are frequently found in various high-ranking military and political capacities, as we have seen. Some were forever linked to the royal family via marriage alliances, as daughters of Shan *sawbwa* were given as princesses to princes of the Ava court, whose offspring subsequently became part of Burmese royalty. Many of their centers were treated as important *myosa*-ships, hence, part of Ava's political universe. Some fought on Ava's side against the Ming and Pegu, and even against some of their own Shan brethren, as we have seen.[35]

There were also socioeconomic ties that brought highland Shan and lowland Burmese together in ways that preempted whatever ethno-linguistic factors there might have been. In terms of shared religious views, Shan who lived at Ava were as Theravada Buddhist as anyone else, and their donations on stone to the religion cannot be distinguished from those made by Burmans. Notions of royalty as reflected in Shan palace architecture—for example, that of the *sawbwa* of Nyaung Shwe—emulated Ava's rather than Ayuthaya's or Chiang Mai's palace architecture, so that Ava, rather than the latter two, was the model. If ever there was a period in Myanmar's history where Shan and Burmese culture interacted closely, it was the Ava, not the Pagan, period.

Ava's contacts with the Mon of Lower Myanmar were also important. Here too, whereas original Pagan epigraphy rarely mentioned Lower Myanmar except in very general terms, Ava inscriptions specifically recalled by name Yazadarit, Shin Saw Bu, and Dhammazedi (three of the most famous sovereigns of Pegu during the Ava period), as well as two princes of the Mon royal family. This is unprecedented. Marriage alliances between Ava and Lower Myanmar were not found in Ava epigraphy, perhaps because Lower Myanmar was nearly an equal in military strength and neither one needed the other in such an alliance. Pegu was also fairly well integrated as a kingdom, whereas the Shan never integrated into a consolidated polity in Myanmar, so needed to ally with one that was.

Economically, one surmises that the relations between Ava and Lower Myanmar served the interests of both parties, as Ava had the rice that Pegu, at the time, by and large did not. But Pegu did have access to the kinds of international luxury goods and other coastal products that Ava desired, which were traded not only for rice but also for other interior luxury products such as rubies. There are suggestions of this economic relationship and hints of what those products might have been in the chronicles as well as some of the European sources. And although the inscriptions are relatively silent on the subject per se, they are clear on the abundance of gold and silver Ava possessed, which, if not mined in the interior, probably came from the Ming and/or the coasts trading for precious stones.

As with the Shan, if ever there was a period in which cultural and other relations between Burmese speakers and the Mon speakers of Lower Myanmar were most intense and regular, it was the fifteenth century, not the eleventh as convention has it. In large part, that also explains some of the linguistic affinities between the Old Burmese of Ava and Middle Mon of Pegu.

Ava's association with Arakan during the same centuries was similar to what it had with northern and Lower Myanmar: largely political and military but also cultural, religious, and economic. Burmese and Arakanese are more or less the same language; indeed the Old Burmese script with which the contemporary stone inscriptions of Arakan are written is identical to that of Pagan and Ava.[36] And as shown above, some of the best Burmese literature was written in Arakan when it was a governorship under Ava (which was more often than not), or by those from Arakan (such as Miss Brown and Miss White) who resided at Ava.

Arakan was (and is) mostly Theravada Buddhist—even today, only about 12 percent of the people are Muslim, which is a later development in any case—and very much part of the Burmese Buddhist ecumene of Ava, and less of the Muslim experience of India and Southeast Asia. I suspect the economic relations between Ava and Arakan were also important, as European sources seem to demonstrate, but there is little contemporary and indigenous epigraphic evidence on that matter, particularly with regard to the fifteenth century.[37]

Thus, it was not just a matter of enmity; these three most important minority groups all shared a common history as part of the same geopolitical, socioeconomic, conceptual, and demographic universe. And within that universe, Ava had little or no competition in (a) establishing a "national" literature and lingua franca, (b) maintaining its demographic advantage, (c) providing a "universal" legitimation ideology concerning the state, (d) supplying leadership to the state, and (e) forging what was to become a "national" tradition and culture. Most of these advantages that Ava had, especially in the conceptual and ideological realm, were directly related to the monopoly it had on the Burmese language. But as demonstrated above, this legacy had gone well beyond its intrinsic (linguistic and literary) value to affect the more subtle legacy of laying other, related components of the foundations for the establishment of modern Myanmar.

Spatial Legacy

Apart from language and literature, one of the most important, concrete historical-cum-geographic legacies was Ava's sheer physical presence as the dominant power in the Dry Zone during the fourteenth to the sixteenth century. By recouping, retaining, and maintaining the human and material resources of the Pagan kingdom, Ava not only resurrected it (albeit writ small), but prevented its total physical dismemberment. The Kingdom of Ava was made up of the same demographic base inhabiting the same geo-economic region, especially the same three irrigated oases that were also Pagan's economic mainstay: Kyaukse, Minbu, and the Mu Valley. And by physically remaining in Upper Myanmar and reformulating its human and material resources there rather than starting anew on the coasts (as Ayuthaya had done), the wherewithal for the formation of a modern Myanmar and its legitimating principles were assured, in at least two ways.

First, as the kingdom straddled the traditional migration routes, it acted as a solid physical barrier that inhibited and blocked the southward movement of the T'ai speakers down the Irrawaddy, Chindwin, and Sittaung River valleys during their two-hundred-year "*drang nach suden*" into western Mainland Southeast Asia. If Ava had not been there and done that, the T'ai speakers might today have the largest nation on Mainland Southeast Asia, stretching from Assam on the west to Cambodia on the east, occupying the space that is now Myanmar, conceivably turning the Burmese speakers into a large minority in a predominantly T'ai nation. Not only did Ava prevent that from happening physically, it possessed the demographic, geographic, and institutional wherewithal for the formation of a Burmese nation, where a T'ai-speaking nation might have stood today.

Second, by remaining in the Dry Zone and resurrecting Myanmar's "classical" traditions, Ava reinforced the notion that the "heartland" of Burmese civilization lay there and not elsewhere. With only a single exception of sixty years out of a total millennium of Burmese history,[38] every single capital and every kingdom in precolonial Myanmar was located in the Dry Zone, reinforcing that notion of a "heartland." And by ruling from the Dry Zone, Ava reestablished the most dominant historical principle and pattern in Myanmar's history: Dry Zone Paramountcy. This, in turn, only reconfirmed the belief that guardianship of the country ultimately rests in the Dry Zone, so that location and legitimacy were invariably linked.

Indeed, it remained that way until the British broke the pattern in the nineteenth century by conquering the country and shifting its center of gravity to Yangon and the coasts. But that sojourn did not last, for the center of gravity moved back to the Dry Zone in 2005–2006 when Naypyidaw, Myanmar's new capital was built adjacent to Pyinmana, one of Upper Myanmar's important *myosa*-ships between Yamethin and Toungoo. That move not only reconfirmed and reinstituted the Dry Zone as the "heartland" of Myanmar, but reestablished the principle and pattern of Dry Zone Paramountcy.

One might say, then, that Ava, by resurrecting, maintaining, and retaining the most crucial components—spatial, human, and cultural—that made classical Pagan, provided the essential foundations in the future development of the Union of Myanmar five hundred years later, simply by being *what* it was *when* it was *where* it was.

PART II

The Kingdom of Pegu (1353–1538)

The First Pegu Dynasty (1353–1538)

Binnya U (1353–1383/1385?)

Yazadarit (1383/1385?–1423)

Bannya Dhamma Yaza (1423–1426)

Bannya Ram (1426–1446)

Bannya Barow (1446–1450)

Bana Kandau (1450–1453)

Shin Saw Bu (1453–1470/1472?)

Dhammazedi (1470/1472?–1492)

Bannya Ram (1492–1526)

Daka Rat Pi (1526–1538)

9

The Pegu Convention

While part 1 of this study dealt with the historiography and history of the Kingdom of Ava, part 2 will do much the same for the Kingdom of Pegu (or Hamsavati, its formal, Sanskrit, name). However, unlike the historiography of Ava, Pegu's is more problematic, as two distinct perspectives regarding the origins of the Lower Myanmar Mon are entangled in that historiography. One is the myth of Ramannadesa, a creation of fifteenth-century King Dhammazedi, and the other is what I call the "Mon Narrative," a collection of popular "histories" that post-dates Dhammazedi.[1] Their conflation produced the "Pegu Convention," a mish-mash of history, myth, anachronisms, contradictions, and hagiography regarding the origins and development of the Lower Myanmar Mon.

In part because of the "unruly" nature of the Pegu Convention, but also because the notion of Ramannadesa was unchallenged for two hundred years in the historiography of early Myanmar, until recently,[2] the Mon Narrative has not been noticed until now either, particularly as an alternate and "contesting" perspective to the myth of Ramannadesa, leaving the Pegu Convention more or less intact for the same two hundred years. Add to that, the paucity of reliable sources on the Kingdom of Pegu, reconstructing its history has been that much more challenging.

Despite all this confusion, one thing remained clear: Pegu, Thaton, and Muttama emerged as the three great centers of the Mon people of Lower Myanmar—in reality as well as in imagination, in history as well as in historiography. There is no doubt that they were historical entities. What is at issue here pertains to their chronology, sequence, and ethno-linguistic composition. When did they first appear in original sources, what was the order in which they developed, and who were their inhabitants? Answering these questions invariably requires dissecting and differentiating history from historiography, the modus operandi and focus of this chapter. As Thaton's historiography and history have been dealt with in detail in the *Mists of Ramanna*, Pegu and Muttama's are the focus of the present chapter.

The Hagiography of Ramannadesa

It all began when King Dhammazedi in 1479 linked Suvannabhumi (the land of gold, and the El Dorado of Buddhist Indian literature) with his own kingdom of Pegu, which he called Ramannadesa (the Realm of the Rman).[3] And because

Sona and Uttara, the two most famous Theravada Buddhist missionaries of the Third Buddhist Council of Asoka—whose reformed version of the scriptures was considered the ultimate in orthodox Theravada Buddhism of the time—were said to have travelled to Suvannabhumi to establish a community of believers there for the first time, in one stroke, King Dhammazedi had conflated the sacred geography, history, and orthodoxy of Buddhist India with Lower Myanmar, his kingdom, and its *sangha*. This conflation of an ideal past and actual history was subsequently resurrected by later colonial scholars, in their histories, to become the conceptual foundations for the historiography of early Myanmar in the English language.[4]

Not of royal stock but an ex-monk-turned-king, his kingdom too new for invoking the dignity of the past, his *sangha* too fissiparous and sectarian, and Lower Myanmar too heterogeneously, inhabited by a variety of peoples and cultures, Dhammazedi needed an integrating ideology with which to unite his kingdom, *sangha*, and Lower Myanmar society. What gave him the opportunity was a Hindu resurgence in South India, whose influences via the Vijayanagara Empire had reached the shores of Lower Myanmar, along with the efflorescence of an expanding Upper Myanmar kingdom of Ava led by Burmese speakers.

Dhammazedi used two strategies to address his political concerns: one religious (to countermand the Hindu resurgence) and one secular (to mitigate Ava's hegemony in Lower Myanmar). First, he reestablished the orthodoxy of Theravada Buddhism in Pegu by conducting a kingdom-wide reform of the *sangha*, a cause célèbre that followed the procedures of the Mahavihara school of Sri Lanka, considered to be the fount of Theravada Buddhism in Southeast Asia. As Sri Lanka was also being affected by the same Hindu resurgence in South India, both Buddhist societies were eager to renew their traditional religious alliances and provide a united Buddhist front.

The second, more secular, strategy was to formulate a political and social ideology to counterbalance the notion of Mranma Pran, "the Realm of the Mranma" established by Ava, while at the same time unifying his culturally and demographically diverse kingdom by using Rman culture and identity, representing Pegu's leadership. More specifically, he did this by creating the notion of an ancient Ramannadesa to which he traced his kingdom. After all, this was the first time a critical mass of Rman speakers and their culture had inhabited Lower Myanmar, crystallized around a discrete kingdom centered at Pegu and led by Rman speakers. Ramannadesa, therefore, was an "imagined community"[5] that served Dhammazedi's social and political needs to conceptually strengthen Pegu, in much the same way ideas of community unified the modern nation-state. In this sense, the king was quite prescient, and his vision of Ramannadesa, quite modern.

However, Dhammazedi's idea of a pan-Rman cultural and sociopolitical entity died with him, as his immediate successors apparently did not share his dream. Never once did they mention Ramannadesa in their epigraphs, while the later Mon-language histories written of him and his kingdom showed no appreciation of his vision either, suggesting that the public at large also did not share, or even knew of it.

Only four hundred years later was the notion of Ramannadesa as Dhammazedi had envisioned it resurrected by colonial administrators and scholars, not just as an idea but as if it were a concrete historical entity.[6] The colonial reifications of Ramannadesa, with the most effect on Myanmar's modern historiography, had roots going back at least to Michael Symes, then an important British military officer, who in his *Journal* of 1802 articulated the gist of it.[7] Two decades later, during the first quarter of the nineteenth century, when British India was poised to take Lower Myanmar with a plan called the Pegu Project, the notion that Lower Myanmar had long been an independent "realm of the Rman" and not part of Burmese Upper Myanmar was used as justification for Britain's conquest of Lower Myanmar.

The British wanted not only moral justification but also material support from the population of Lower Myanmar (at the time, part of the Burmese kingdom), believing that it comprised mainly Mon speakers who therefore would be eager and willing to comply.[8] Of course, that did not happen, as many of them had migrated to Thailand during the eighteenth-century unification efforts by King Alaunghpaya of the Konbaung Dynasty. The rest had integrated into Burmese society, so had no necessary knowledge of, or loyalty to, the idea of Ramannadesa, certainly not enough to risk life and limb to support British designs of conquering Upper Myanmar.

After the British annexed the entire country in 1886, the notion of an ancient Ramannadesa in Lower Myanmar (originally meant for wartime psychological contingencies of 1824), instead of disappearing after the wars, remained intact to become even more entrenched in the country's historiography, perpetuated by colonial scholars who also happened to be its officials and administrators and so were well attuned to the idea of a Ramannadesa. By the nineteenth century, then, the notion that Lower Myanmar was ancient Ramannadesa became central to the historiography of early Myanmar. And when colonial scholars discovered King Dhammazedi's Kalyani Inscriptions in the late nineteenth century, in which Ramannadesa was explicitly mentioned, its "historicity" was "confirmed" not realizing it was only the king's vision of an integrated realm.

The reasons for this oversight are not difficult to find. The earliest scholars most intimately involved in reifying Ramannadesa clearly wished it were true: not only did the notion of an ancient Mon "Camelot" support their belief that the Mon speakers were the "Greeks of Southeast Asia," who had enjoyed a flourishing civilization in Lower Myanmar until rudely usurped by the more "barbaric" and later arriving "Burmans," but also those indigenous and foreign scholars most instrumental in the conceptualization and writing of early Myanmar's history were of Mon background or intimately connected to it by marriage and other ties.[9] It was thus easy to accept Ramannadesa as historical—since they already believed it—turning what was a fifteenth-century socioreligious and political *strategy* of King Dhammazedi into a twentieth-century historical "fact"—hence, my phrase, "reified Ramannadesa."

Thus, instead of untangling a myth of earlier times, modern historians actually made it worse, for Ramannadesa was never considered anything but historical in the twentieth century English-language historiography of the country. Thereafter, the notion of Ramannadesa as historical became one of the most crucial components in the historiography of early Myanmar. By the mid-twentieth century, a much-embellished and full-blown thesis had emerged, which I have called the Mon Paradigm.

It alleged the following three essential components: (1) the existence of a Theravada Buddhist Mon kingdom called Ramannadesa in coastal Lower Myanmar approximately between the second half of the millennium BC and the eleventh century AD; (2) the existence and conquest of its putative capital, Thaton, in 1057 by King Anawrahta of Pagan; and (3) the removal and transportation of Thaton's entire population—the royal family and court, men of letters, artists and artisans—to Pagan, said to have led to the "civilizing" of Burmese Pagan by Mon Ramannadesa.

Subsequently, especially in the Western-dominated academic world, the Mon Paradigm became so ensconced in the study of early Myanmar that it was the only interpretation considered viable, shaping the academic environment to such an extent that it was difficult, if not virtually impossible, to challenge. It circumscribed and framed all scholarship on early Myanmar in terms of methodology, analysis, evidence, and conclusion. I too worked within this framework of analysis initially, believing that it was valid, as did every other Myanmar scholar.

And yet, one of the more interesting aspects of the Mon Paradigm is that, prior to the mid-twentieth century, ordinary Myanmar Mon themselves had no inkling of it, either as myth or as putative history. In part, that was because the theory existed only in the English-language historiography of colonial Myanmar, to which they had no access. But even by the second half of the twentieth century, when it did become known to a handful of Mon historians and one or two scholars who had learned of it from their colonial mentors, it still had no response from the Mon public, partly because they were still unaware of it but also because most had become Burmanized, with no particular interest in it, political, ideological, or financial.

In 1999, nearly two hundred years after Symes first articulated the basic components of the myth, an opportunity at the University of Leiden allowed me to scrutinize the history of Lower Myanmar in greater depth.[10] As I looked more closely at the primary evidence used to support the Mon Paradigm, I realized something was amiss between the theory and the history. So I discarded the sacrosanct convention altogether and reexamined the evidence independently of it. Methodologically, that meant not assuming *any relationship between the evidence found in Lower Myanmar and the Mon speakers.* When that was done, like magic, new options never before even imagined in early Myanmar's history almost immediately sprung up.

In 2001, I was given an opportunity to deliver a paper in Yangon at an annual international conference. I reworked the paper written earlier for the University of Leiden, calling it "The Legend That Was Lower Burma" and delivered it to the audience who knew Myanmar's history and its primary source materials best—scholars living and working in the country—and whose response I wanted most. The reaction was overwhelmingly positive, particularly from those Burmese scholars who mattered: that is, those who knew the language and culture firsthand.

By 2005, that paper had been expanded into a book, consisting of thirteen detailed chapters, titled *The Mists of Ramanna: The Legend That Was Lower Burma*, published by the University of Hawai'i Press. Along with the accolades[11] were also lukewarm responses from one or two Western academics, who either did not fully understand the book's import[12] and/or disliked its academic implications, partly because it had rendered erroneous or obsolete much of early Myanmar (and their own) scholarship.[13]

Understandably, destroying as it did sacrosanct conventions around which were built lifetime careers of scholarship, *Mists* was bound to be contested. Yet, it presented a dilemma to those who found themselves in that quandary. The book had raised serious issues regarding evidence and its interpretation, so that academics whose scholarship and reputations had depended on the viability of the Mon Paradigm were now faced with the choice of rejecting it (and their own scholarship) or accepting it (and rejecting the incontrovertible evidence). Not surprisingly, they decided to skirt the issue of evidence (which allowed them to maintain their positions) and instead, attack the assumed political motives for writing *Mists*, calling it "Myanmafication," which at the time the book appeared, appealed to activists and others attempting to support minorities against the military government of the country.[14]

Another (academic) reason for that kind of position was language incompetence, a "sticking point" in Southeast Asian studies that *Mists* had unintentionally raised. If my reading of the primary sources were to be challenged, proficiency in Old Burmese was necessary. If, usually when, that was not possible, the strategy of these critics followed two paths. One returned to the secondary sources that espoused the Mon Paradigm in the first place (Luce et al.), thereby reiterating the same old assertions being challenged by *Mists* rather than offering new responses to the new challenge; and the second veered off to other issues immaterial to the problem of being able to read the original evidence in Old Burmese.

Yet, it was more than just my reading knowledge of Old Burmese that initially led to questioning the Mon Paradigm; my predecessors could read it as well, if not better. And most wrote in English, so that much of the evidence was available for everyone to see, with or without language competence. Rather, it was more a willingness (perhaps eagerness) on my part to interpret the data "outside the box," invariably leading to fundamentally different conclusions. It was as much (perhaps more) the *interpretation* of the evidence as it was the evidence per se that led to my rejecting the convention, so that language incompetence was no excuse for missing something so obvious—an embarrassing situation for most (including myself earlier) who had unquestionably depended on the Mon Paradigm.

Mists also forced other Myanmar and Southeast Asia specialists into a position to support the convention even when they knew the evidence against it was compelling. The general inclination of Western-trained academics to support the "underdog" (in this case, the Mon people) and dislike of the recently "dissolved" military government were clearly related to assessments of *Mists.* Although the government had nothing to do with *Mists,* the book had nonetheless inadvertently removed the main justification for the creation of a separate Mon state in Lower Myanmar, so that Mon "nationalists" and other activists who were their supporters, were chagrined by the political implications of the thesis, irrespective of its academic merit even (especially when in many cases) they had not actually read the book. Most of those chagrined are actually T'ai in language and culture—having lived in that country for generations—and no longer even speak the Mon language. Nonetheless, the idea of an ancient homeland in Lower Myanmar that was once their "Camelot" was necessary to justify the creation of a separate Mon state there. Thus, the Mon Paradigm had become mired in the politics of minority identity and autonomy movements, relatively recent trends encouraged by (mainly Western) advocates and legitimated by the (mainly Western) crusade for establishing democracy worldwide: "Democracy Jihad," as I have called it elsewhere.[15]

Even though *Mists* was a study of the now academically "harmless" classical period, the politics of Myanmar's recent past invariably made that period and the book very much a part of the political discourse regarding the Union of Myanmar that is far from being benign. A case in point is the conference held in 2007 at Chulalongkorn University in Thailand, in direct response to *Mists,* with the stated goal of "Discovering Ramannadesa," whose very title and theme revealed its intent. It was really meant to defend, not discover, Ramannadesa, for it already assumed Ramannadesa was historical. Had such a resurrection of the myth been successful—there is nothing in the present academic literature to show that it was—the entire Mon Paradigm would have been regurgitated all over again! Instead of moving forward, then, the goals of the Chulalongkorn Conference harked backward: to the nineteenth- and twentieth-century historiography of Myanmar.

A colleague in Southeast Asian studies characterized the conference as an attempt "to preserve a particular reading of the past," similar to the contests over Jerusalem to determine whose "history" of it, Palestinian or Jew, will prevail. It "is an attempt to reassert a particular history for a particular political cause since *Mists* had disrupted that history." He saw it "as another chapter in the intellectual history of the Mon Paradigm," just the way *Mists* is, but which rescued rather than challenged it. To this colleague and his academic concerns, the Chulalongkorn Conference "provides an excellent ethnographic study in itself of how politicized the past has become in Myanmar Studies."[16]

Worse than politicizing the past was the dishonesty of the conference's intent, disguising its political motives as academic ones, mainly by allying with a few disgruntled ex-academics (whose scholarship had been dislodged by *Mists*), in order to garner some academic credibility (and funding) for it. So, into this (essentially) political rally were drawn certain philanthropic foundations that financially supported the conference since it was presented as an academic exercise, which in fact its thinly veiled political agenda made it obviously not. The political tail, unfortunately, continues to wag the academic dog.

Thus, as an attempt to set the historical record straight and free the scholarship of early Myanmar and Southeast Asia from the straitjacket of its past epistemology, *Mists* was more threatening than energizing, more insecurity-provoking than inspiring. Because the book was intended (and promised) to change the academic status quo, to open the door to new possibilities rather than fossilize old conventions, it went against the interests of those who wanted to preserve and protect the hagiography of Ramannadesa—mainly for professional, personal and political reasons.

I had ended *Mists* with a chapter meant to challenge the field into imagining what an early Myanmar (and, in part, Southeast Asia) might look like *without* the Mon Paradigm, suggesting that if such a scenario could not be conceived, the field had a serious problem. For it would be compelled to prove, using original and contemporary evidence that (a) an ancient Ramannadesa *did exist* in Lower Myanmar that *preceded* the Kingdom of Pagan; (b) a city called Thaton *did exist* prior to Pagan and *was conquered* in 1057; and (c) that Ramannadesa *already possessed* all the accoutrements of "civilization," which it then bestowed on Pagan. As of this writing, nothing has successfully challenged *Mists* on the basis of original evidence concerning these three points.

That means many studies of Myanmar dependent on the viability of the Mon Paradigm, some quite recent, would have to be reassessed, qualified, or, as the situation warrants, discarded. One notion to be discarded, but deeply embedded in Myanmar studies (and with a bearing on the origins of Pegu, the focus of the present chapter), is the importance heretofore given to ethnic identity and ethnic relations as major causal factors in the "making" of Myanmar (and Southeast Asian) history, both early and modern.[17] The evidence shows that Pegu's historical emergence was not caused by notions of, or behavior surrounding, ethnic identity, but by geopolitical, economic, historical, and cultural factors, as we shall see in greater detail in subsequent chapters.

That evidence, in turn, should eliminate another directly related and long-held convention: namely, the organization of the country's history into "ethnic periods." We should no longer accept the unqualified notion of a "Mon Pegu," a "Shan Ava," and a "Burman" (as opposed to a "Burmese") Pagan. Also to be thrown out are stereotypes of the Shan as "barbarous" and "snarling," the Mon as "civilized" and "learned," and the Burmese as "prosaic" and "down to earth," characteristics attributed to them by colonial historiography on the basis of (reified) ethnicity.

Another deeply embedded convention that must be discarded is the fantastical image of Lower Myanmar prior to the eleventh century as a fount of high civilization. It can no longer be regarded as anything but an undeveloped and largely inhospitable and sparsely populated "frontier" of Upper Myanmar, a recently formed delta that could have sustained only a few inhabitants, towns, and villages. The securely dated epigraphic and archaeological evidence shows nothing there resembling even the rudiments of a state or polity. That reality shifts the importance of Lower Myanmar in the history of maritime Myanmar and Southeast Asia to the fifteenth century and the so-called Early Modern period, not the "pre-classical" and "classical" periods to which it had been assigned as part of the myth of Ramannadesa. Thus, *Mists* returned Lower Myanmar to its correct historical context.

There were many other academic casualties of *Mists* that cannot be dealt with here in any detail: the origins of the national script, the evolution of the *stupa*-temple, the legend of Kyanzittha, an alleged "Mon period" in Pagan, the "downtrodden Talaing," and, most important to early Southeast Asian history, the origins of "civilization" in Myanmar and the direction in which state-formation "moved." Without the Mon Paradigm, in other words, the historiography of the early history of the country is indeed different, including that of Pegu, the subject of the rest of this chapter.

The Mon Narrative

The other component of the Pegu Convention, the Mon Narrative, immediately presents a problem upon closer scrutiny—the absence of any conflation with the myth of Ramannadesa. Indeed, neither the concept of, nor the term Ramannadesa itself, is mentioned.[18] The standard sources, all founts of Lower Myanmar Mon historiography that followed Dhammazedi's reign—the 1825 *Lik Smin Asah* (The Legend of Prince Asah),[19] the mid-eighteenth-century *Slapat Rajawan Datow Smin Ron* (History of Kings),[20] and the "Talaing Annals"[21] used by Arthur Phayre in his *History of Burma* (published in 1883)—never once mentioned Ramannadesa or invoked it as the ancient and exemplary origins of the Mon people.[22]

Such a glaring absence was very surprising to me at first, but the more closely these post-Dhammazedi sources were scrutinized, the more evident it became that the notion of Ramannadesa as an "imagined community" (to use the late Ben Anderson's famous phrase) was entirely Dhammazedi's own personal vision, not that of other kings, reigns, intellectuals, and society at large. Indeed, even his immediate successors failed to mention that vision of an ancient and resplendent "Camelot" the Mon in their epigraphs.

Moreover, and although quite prescient on the part of Dhammazedi to conceptualize what was in fact an embryonic form of nation-state, his message nonetheless reflects an elite and centrist ideology only he as head of state pursued, writing it in the Pali and Middle Mon of the Pegu court. In stark contrast, the authors of the Mon Narrative wrote from the perspective of society at large, often as private individuals, both monks and laymen, whose works reflected that society's priorities. After all, these authors lived and wrote after both the First Pegu and Second Pegu/Toungoo Dynasties had fallen, and well after the "last hurrah" of the Myanmar Mon had been vanquished, after 1757, when Pegu was conquered by King Alaunghpaya of Ava. By then, it had been approximately three centuries since Dhammazedi's notion of Ramannadesa was pronounced. Both the provenance and purpose of these two narratives, therefore, were fundamentally different.

Historical factors also set the two narratives apart. Although Dhammazedi's vision of Ramannadesa had died with him, Pegu continued as capital under the Second Pegu/Toungoo Dynasty. And because Kings Tabinshwehti and Bayinnaung of that dynasty were Burmese speakers from Upper Myanmar's Toungoo, they had little or no sentimental attachment to, or reason for perpetuating, Dhammazedi's vision of a Realm of the Rman—in fact, I suspect they would have been quite opposed to it. Then, when King Bayinnaung conquered Upper Myanmar in 1551, the country was once again reunified, but for the first time, with Pegu as the exemplary center.

Shortly thereafter, when all the most important centers of power in western and central Mainland Southeast Asia at the time were conquered by Bayinnaung—something never done before or since in Southeast Asian history—it only increased Pegu's stature. And as Pegu grew to greater heights, the concept that was Ramannadesa faded even more into the mists of Lower Myanmar. The dissonance in the narrative between the Kalyani Inscriptions of King Dhammazedi and the Mon Narrative—that is between mythical Ramannadesa and historical Pegu—is at least as pronounced as that in the history between the First and Second Pegu Dynasties; so much so that the Mon Narrative had forgotten (or chosen to forget) the notion of Ramannadesa entirely. After all, for most of the authors informing the Mon Narrative, approximately three hundred years had passed since Dhammazedi pronounced his idea. Besides, Ramannadesa was not *their* creation, while Pegu not only could be claimed as "theirs" but was also quite real, and whose recent glory was still part of public memory.

If the Ramannadesa and Pegu narratives were never really connected, when did the two become enmeshed and intertwined in the Pegu Convention, and why? Although the Mon Narrative gave some lip service to Thaton as the first capital of Lower Myanmar (without mentioning Ramannadesa by name), conflating Ramannadesa and Pegu was done much later, and by an entirely different source: colonial scholars and administrators. Ostensibly on behalf of the Mon people (their favorite, "downtrodden" ethnic minority), they found the notion of a combined Mon Ramannadesa and Pegu to be in their political and military interests, especially when they began planning to annex Lower Myanmar around 1824 in what was called "the Pegu Project."[23] Thus, the Ramannadesa and Pegu narratives had been conflated by the early nineteenth century, and by the late nineteenth and twentieth centuries, it had become sine qua non in the English language historiography of early Myanmar history.

Apart from the disjuncture with the Ramannadesa narrative per se, there are other, more subtle kinds of breaks within the Mon Narrative itself that bears investigation. These discontinuities I call "historiographic layers," somewhat akin to stratigraphy in archaeology, although not nearly as scientific or precise. Nonetheless, not only do these layers provide valuable information about breaks and tensions in the narrative, but also clues regarding the historical contexts in which Mon Narrative was written. All speak to the legendary and early historical origins of Pegu and Lower Myanmar.

One of the most interesting layers in the story of Lower Myanmar's origins and development is revealed more by what is omitted than by what is included: neither Dvaravati nor Haripunjaya, the historical homeland of the Mon speakers in Southeast Asia (currently in Thailand), is mentioned. Indeed, nothing in the entire written corpus of Mon-language records recovered in Myanmar to date has ever mentioned Dvaravati or Haripunjaya. Not a single Old Mon inscription erected by King Kyanzittha (in approximately forty-one separate faces), not a single Middle Mon inscription erected in Lower Myanmar (of approximately sixty-five), and not a single, standard Mon "chronicle" (or other kind of text) written subsequently recalled these two places.[24] Instead, Lower Myanmar's "gaze" (especially in the Mon Narrative) is always to the west (South Asia) and to the north (Upper Myanmar). Not only does the silence and direction of gaze mask what we know to be historical, it also implies that although the Mon Narrative was written in the Mon language, it did not exclusively reflect the history and legends of the Mon speakers themselves but included those of others who had migrated to, and lived among them in, Lower Myanmar.

It is understandable that Dvaravati was not remembered as the homeland of the Mon in any Myanmar Mon-language source, not only because it was said to have already declined by the ninth century or thereabouts, but because the Mon people of Dvaravati either stayed where they had been all along or migrated eastward rather than westward toward Myanmar.[25] If true, that means the Mon of Dvaravati never migrated to Myanmar, as alleged by Myanmar scholars, so there would be no reason for the Mon of Myanmar to have mentioned a place from which they had not come.

What then, about Haripunjaya, a later Mon center? Mon sources and scholars have claimed that Mon speakers migrated to Lower Myanmar from there, either in the tenth century, because of a cholera epidemic, or in the thirteenth century, when the T'ai conquered their kingdom, whose refugees then fled to Lower Myanmar. But if these events were historical, why was Haripunjaya also not remembered in any Mon-language record found in Myanmar?

If the Mon had migrated from Haripunjaya in the tenth century because of cholera (or any other disease), they may have simply forgotten their original homeland by the time the first Old Mon inscriptions appeared in Myanmar—a period of nearly two centuries. By the time their earliest *chronicles* were written—at earliest during the seventeenth but mostly during the late eighteenth and nineteenth centuries—it would have been approximately seven hundred to eight hundred years! That is a long time to remember anything, even had anyone *wanted* to remember, given the unpleasant reason attributed to the migration.

If, instead of the alleged epidemic, the conquest of Haripunjaya by the T'ai speakers in the thirteenth century is used as the marker for the exodus to Lower Myanmar, the distance in time from that thirteenth-century event to the first dated Middle Mon inscriptions of Pegu in the fifteenth century would still amount to two hundred years. By the time the Mon chronicles were written in

Modern Mon, the distance in time would have extended to approximately five hundred years. Whatever may have been the reasons for forgetting their homeland, the fact is that neither Dvaravati nor Haripunjaya is mentioned in the indigenous Mon sources of Myanmar, epigraphic or chronicle.

Even after colonial administrators and scholars had become aware by the middle of the nineteenth century that Dvaravati and Haripunjaya might possibly have been the original homeland of the Mon in central Mainland Southeast Asia, none of the Mon chronicles and texts produced in Myanmar subsequently made any mention of them.[26] Indeed, well after the "Paklat Talaing Chronicle" had been produced by the beginning of the twentieth century, and Mon national identity had become part of public discourse in a Myanmar seeking independence around the same time, there is still no mention of Dvaravati or Haripunjaya. Indeed, not until these two Mon centers were introduced by modern historians to Myanmar studies in the academic arena—by about the third decade of the twentieth century—did this information become known to Mon academics of Myanmar for the first time, much less to the Mon public at large. Thus, from the late eleventh century to the colonial and much of the postcolonial periods, not a word can be found about the actual, historical homeland of the Myanmar Mon in any of their primary records. It appears that most Mon of Myanmar even today still do not know where their original homeland was,[27] and some did not know until very recently, when Mon separatists (and their advocates hosting the Chulalongkorn Conference of 2007) made it a political issue.

The deafening silence regarding Dvaravati and Haripunjaya raises an important methodological issue. If the traditions of Lower Myanmar as represented by the totality of Mon language sources do not point toward Dvaravati and Haripunjaya, should we even consider these traditions to be Mon at all? In this case, although the language of these texts is in Mon, it appears that the contents do not exclusively (or necessarily) represent Mon history and culture as we know it. And the only viable reason that comes to mind for this phenomenon is that the Mon authors who wrote the texts in the Mon language had clearly forgotten whence they came. So, they had absorbed the "gaze" northward and westward *already present* in Lower Myanmar tradition and culture among the people living there, and wrote that down as if it were their own history. The language in which these texts were written, in other words, does not necessarily mean the people and culture associated with it wrote them.

Indeed, this gaze, westward and northward, is the main direction toward which the Mon Narrative looks for the origins of Pegu and Lower Myanmar. It is yet another historiographic layer, revealing the various influences that "made" Pegu and Lower Myanmar. Phayre's account, based on what he calls the "Talaing Annals"—by which he meant the Mon chronicles that were at his disposal—is the most precise regarding that gaze toward South India and Upper Myanmar. He wrote that in the traditions of Lower Myanmar then current, its origins began with migrations of people from the lower courses of the Krishna and Godavari Rivers in South India.[28] When they settled Lower Myanmar, they noted that it was inhabited by *raksha* (Sanskrit for demon, in Burmese, *bilu,* ogres), terms usually used as metaphors for "uncivilized" people who had not yet converted to Buddhism. The first of the settlers from India were two sons of a king named Tissa from Karanaka (Karnataka) in South India,[29] who was said to have died the same year the Buddha Gaudama attained *nirvana*, a date that was obviously a legitimacy marker.[30]

These two sons came to dwell as hermits in the "savage land" of Lower Myanmar, eventually raising a child born of a dragon from the seashore, who, when grown, built the city of Thaton and reigned as Siha Raja (Lion King). Phayre surmised this name was taken from Sihala, "fabled father of Vijaya, the first king of Ceylon." (However, the title Siha Raja also belongs to famous fourteenth- and fifteenth-century Mon king Yazadarit of Pegu.)[31] To whomever these legends were referring, obviously they were meant to link Buddhist India and Sri Lanka with the origins of Thaton, while invoking known and exemplary (although anachronistic) Lower Myanmar leaders in the founding of Thaton, which Dhammazedi (but not the later Mon texts), claimed was the capital of his Ramannadesa.

The Thaton "dynasty" given in Phayre's work is a mere list of fifty-nine kings, most of them famous figures from South Asian history (such as Dhammasoka, that is, Asoka), as well as anonymous ones, whose names ended in "yaza" (*raja*) interspersed with common names of Burmese kings. The fifty-ninth is the infamous Manuha, who (with another) is the "Judas" of Lower Myanmar Mon mythology, for he was said to have allowed Buddhism to decay in his kingdom, thereby bringing about his dynasty's end at the hands of King Anawrahta of Pagan (the quintessential "reformer") said to have conquered Thaton. In this (Thaton) segment of the "Talaing Annals" used by Phayre, we can see obvious influences from Upper Myanmar (in Anawrahta), Buddhist India and Sri Lanka (in Siharaja and Dhammasoka), and South India (in Tissa's two sons).

After the founding of Thaton, Phayre's "Talaing Annals" state that another center and dynasty emerged at Hamsavati (Pegu), named after the sacred swans (*hamsa*) living there.[32] This move from Thaton to Pegu is yet another layer in the narrative, although the attempt to link them is rather clumsy. Phayre's list of Pegu's kings, similar to that in the *Slapat* and *Lik Smin Asah*, begins with Samala and Wimala, conceived from a *naga* mother (mythological serpent representing the chthonic world) and the reigning king of Thaton (representing the celestial world), thereby linking not only heaven and earth, but also the genealogies of Thaton and Pegu, the Buddhist "universal" and the Lower Myanmar "local."

It was because of the mother's nonhuman status that all three were forced out of Thaton and settled at Pegu. Phayre notes that "there is [also] an obvious resemblance in this story to that of the two [blind] brothers who first reigned at Prome."[33] (Prome is ancient Sri Ksetra, dated scientifically to approximately the fourth or fifth century AD, and survived at least to the eighth or ninth—century.)[34] The "two brothers" motif—sometimes two male friends or two monks—as founders of dynasties, important cities, and sacred sites, is a common theme in the indigenous texts that merits further exploration.

The Pegu Dynasty thereafter was said to have continued until 781 AD, when eleventh-century (historical) King Anawrahta of Pagan destroyed Pegu, ending the reign of the "heretic" king (Tissaraja). The *Slapat* stated that after Pegu's conquest, it became a "desolate wilderness" and "a Burmese province" thereafter.[35] These years of desolation and annexation into a "Burmese province" might be another layer representing the period after 1599, when the Second Pegu Dynasty was utterly destroyed by Arakan (perhaps Vijayanagara's proxy) and Lower Myanmar did indeed become a "desolate wilderness," subsequently conquered by Upper Myanmar. In any case, from Tissaraja's death until the mid-eleventh century when Anawrahta conquered Thaton and took Manuha (its king) captive—the second king and city Anawrahta had conquered in a span of 269 years—Phayre wrote that there are no events recorded in the Talaing chronicles, so that Mon history is a blank.[36] Obviously, two legendary events—one on Pegu and the other on Thaton—had been garbled, while the dates are impossible.

Both Tissaraja and Manuha clearly symbolize kings who bring about the end of their dynasties as a result of their laxity in tending to the religion. That may be the reason both were said to have been conquered by King Anawrahta (even if the events and individuals are centuries apart), for the latter epitomizes the quintessential Buddhist reformer king who conducts *dhammavijaya* (righteous conquest) that ends the reigns of corrupt kings.

In contrast to the *Slapat*, the later *Lik Smin Asah* attributes the invasion of Pegu not to Anawrahta of Pagan but to mighty Vijayanagara instead, against whose assault, Asah, the hero of the poem, successfully defends. The text celebrates Asah's victory as a Lower Myanmar Theravada Buddhist triumph over Hindu South India, using the tale of the "steadfast Buddhist maiden" who stood up for orthodox Buddhism by refusing the machinations of the "heretic king" Tissaraja.[37] Either way, this is another layer that celebrates the defense and "saving" of Theravada Buddhism by Anawrahta, the "steadfast maiden," and Prince Asah, all living and performing in what the late Ben Anderson has called "Messianic Time."

The story about the invasion by Vijayanagara may be an allusion to its influence during the fifteenth century. If the *Writings of Nuniz*, compiled by the Persian Abdur Razzak, is correct, Pegu was said to have paid tribute to Vijayanagara.[38] That may account for the theme of resistance to, rather than voluntary acceptance of, Vijayanagara's culture and influence, emphasized in the story of Prince Asah defeating two invasions by "the Indians" along with their Goliath, the Indian Giant. The enmity may also be a reason there is little in Lower Myanmar art and architectural remains that suggest peaceful cultural exchanges between the two, especially when Vijayanagara is known (in India itself) for its magnificent Hindu iconography and spectacular architecture, celebrating South India's resurgent Hinduism.

Indeed, resistance to a Hindu revival at this particular time is historically consistent with the reigns of Shin Saw Bu and Dhammazedi (mostly contemporaneous with earlier Vijayanagara), for they represent Theravada Buddhism par excellence in Lower Myanmar. Whether or not Shin Saw Bu was the model for the "steadfast Buddhist maiden" who successfully resisted heretical Tissaraja and his attempts to impose Hinduism, Dhammazedi's reform of the *sangha* surely explains, at least in part, one of his strategies for counteracting the ideological threat of (or tension with) a resurgent Hindu South India.

Similarly, the story that attributes the founding of Pegu to the two princes, Samala and Wimala, expelled from Thaton because of their mother's demon status, might reflect another historical event in Southeast Asia alluded to above. The *Camadevivamsa,* a chronicle about the Mon of Thailand written in Pali, thought to have been composed in Thailand during the early fifteenth century (contemporary to the First Pegu Dynasty), attributes the move from Thaton to Pegu to a disease such as cholera, which was said to have been brought to Thaton from Haripunjaya earlier.[39] Disease, of course, is often interpreted as the work of supernatural beings, so that the mother's nonhuman demonic anger, described in vivid ways ("her eyes reddened and exuded . . . women died . . . if she but gazed on them . . . they died easily . . . many of them") may be an allegory regarding the effects of people struck by cholera or a similar disease.[40]

Finally, the Mon Narrative brings the story of Lower Myanmar's development to the "third dynasty," Muttama, clearly another historiographic layer. When the Thaton and Pegu texts are compared with that of Muttama (best represented by the *Yazadhiyaza Ayedawpon*), there are no genealogical links provided for Muttama that went back to either Thaton or Pegu, so that its dynastic list abruptly begins with a known historical king, Wareru, although he was said to have been a supernatural being previously, until the Buddha converted him into a human being—a standard transformation from barbarism to civilization, and a legitimating device found in most of these chronicles. Moreover, none on Muttama's list of kings is symbolic of some Buddhist principle or serves a didactic purpose; they all appear to be historical, as most (if not all) are corroborated by Burmese and other chronicles. In any case, all Myanmar historians consider the Muttama Dynasty to have been historical,[41] so that the disjuncture in the Mon Narrative with Muttama's beginning is likely to be emblematic of the break between history and mythology itself.

Although Muttama is relegated to "third place" in the sequence of state development in Lower Myanmar, it is historically the first. That position has confirmation in original inscriptions and other near-contemporary sources, as we shall see in the next chapter. Here, suffice it to say that whereas the sequence provided by the Mon Narrative begins with Thaton, continues with Pegu, and ends with Muttama,[42] original epigraphy has it *exactly the opposite*: Muttama appears first (in 1176), Pegu next (in 1212), and Thaton last (only in 1479 AD).[43] Thus, neither Thaton nor Pegu is the oldest urban site or the first center of "the state" in Lower Myanmar; it is actually Muttama.[44] This epigraphic evidence is supported by the *Yazadhiyaza Ayedawpon,* probably the earliest record of the Mon Narrative, which has nothing to say about Thaton or Pegu being Muttama's *precursors.* In fact, Pegu is explicitly said to have been its *successor,* while Thaton is not part of that story at all.

But why does the Mon Narrative place Muttama last rather than first? There may be many reasons, but I suspect one has to do with the fact that Muttama was relatively unremarkable at the time most of the Mon texts in the Mon Narrative were being written down. By that time, Muttama had been under Upper Myanmar's hegemony for a long time, as well as Pegu's and, for a while, even Ayuthaya's. For that reason, Muttama was not given a Buddha prophecy by the Mon Narrative, while Thaton and Pegu received that honor, and were therefore placed as legitimating foundations to Muttama. It may also be that Muttama, being the oldest historically, was the least well remembered, while Pegu and Thaton, being more recent and closer to the time some parts of the Mon Narrative were being written down, were better remembered, or had more sources that survived.

Notwithstanding Muttama's stature in "third place," there is a "silver lining" to this Muttama layer. With its advent, the Mon for the first time were recording what was in fact their own history, and not that of others. And it is a viable historical record of the origins of the first Mon state in Lower Myanmar. Not coincidentally, the Muttama story is focused on the region of which it was actually a part, and therefore much more a local history than an exogenous myth. There is also more on the region (Lower Myanmar) than outside it (Sri Lanka and Vijayanagara). The Muttama story even recalled some links to its east, particularly the T'ai kingdom of Sukhotai, its contemporary. Dvaravati and Haripunjaya, of course, are not mentioned, for by the time the original of the *Yazadhiyaza Ayedawpon* was probably compiled, both had long declined and had been largely forgotten.

Finally, we come to the most recent, colonial layer, also with its own mythology. By conflating the Ramannadesa and Pegu narratives, this layer took the historiography of Lower Myanmar down the wrong path for generations. Best represented by the Mon Paradigm, it claimed that Lower Myanmar had been composed of Mon speakers since ancient times, and that virtually everything there "belonged" to them. And even though the Mon Narrative was "looking" in other directions that made little sense to the Mon Paradigm (and so should not have been ignored), the theory had to be preserved at all cost. If one had simply removed the Mon speakers and their traditions as the earliest, near-exclusive culture of Lower Myanmar, and instead attributed the region to a variety of peoples and cultures (including the Mon) coming from different directions, the history of Pegu and Lower Myanmar immediately becomes more viable.

In short, these historiographic layers not only mark conjunctures in the Mon Narrative but also in the "real" history it records, whose patterns (even if vague) are recognizable. One reflects the earliest period of time that points to influences from Upper Myanmar ("Pyu" and Old Burmese), Sri Lanka, and Buddhist India. Another, later one, reflects a time when Pegu rose to heights never again attained, when Ramannadesa, if not forgotten, was contested. This is followed by a third period that includes all of the First and Second Pegu Dynasties, when contact with Hindu influences from Vijayanagara is apparent. Most of the accounts end after this, which is the "blank period" of Phayre and the "desolate wilderness" of the *Slapat,* likely portraying the time after the Second Pegu Dynasty was destroyed in 1599.

Among these historiographic layers, the gaze west toward South India needs some additional comment, since it makes much historical sense and has been sorely neglected. After all, it is for good reason that the Pegu region since the Pagan period (until today)[45] is called Ussa Pegu (Ussala or Orissa Pegu); that most scholars consider the etymology of "Talaing" (the general appellation for the people living in Lower Myanmar) to have come from Telingana (Telangana) in South India;[46] that Burmese words related to commerce and trade, such as "banker" (*bandha*), "rich man" (*thuhtay*), and *viss* (a primary unit of weight) go back to Tamil; that the Pyu, Burmese, and Mon scripts of Myanmar were likely derived originally from either South India's Kadamba of Kannada or Pallava of Tamilnad; and that we find late Hindu iconography of South India in Lower Myanmar.

If the gaze westward in the Mon Narrative is indeed reflective of some of Lower Myanmar's traditions, then the direction of research for the region should have been toward South India. But this perspective had been ignored precisely because an exclusive (and erroneous) relationship had been established between Lower Myanmar and the Mon speakers in the myth of Ramannadesa, while Burmese racism against Indians and their culture during the postcolonial period, as well as the field's long-time reluctance to accept (even in part) the general notion of "Indianization" as expounded by George Coedes, had discouraged such endeavors.

But now that South Asia's influence in the development of Lower Myanmar can be acknowledged as being part of the picture, future research directions should focus on the links between it and the major centers of South India: Nagarjunakonda, Vanavasi, Kancipuram, and Vijayanagara (among others). The degree to which especially the Kannada, Malayali, Tamil, and Telugu cultures affected the cultural development of Lower Myanmar should be taken much more seriously than they have been heretofore. This, of course, will add another historiographic layer to the previous ones.

Conclusion

Having dealt with the conflation of the myth of Ramannadesa and the Mon Narrative in the Pegu Convention, this conclusion—based mainly on verifiable epigraphic and other credible historical sources—provides a synopsis of how, when, and by whom Pegu and Lower Myanmar most likely developed, and therefore acts as a bridge to subsequent chapters.

Briefly, during the millennium between the last two centuries BC and the first several centuries AD, much of Upper Myanmar appears to have been under the hegemony of the so-called Pyu kingdom, consisting of approximately a dozen or more urban sites. Its reach also extended into Lower Myanmar, which at the time was a "backwater" of marshes and swamps (as the delta was still in its infancy), while its coastal areas were dotted by several small, obscure and nondescript settlements representing the "Pyu" kingdom's "frontier."[47]

Following this initial reach by the "Pyu" into Lower Myanmar, the expansions with the most impact on the latter's development came in the second half of the eleventh century and the entire twelfth century AD by the Kingdom of Pagan. The conquests made during the reigns of Kings Anawrahta, Sawlu, and Kyanzittha constituted the first phase.[48] It was followed by a second phase under Kings Alaungsithu and Narapatisithu, when Muttama was first mentioned. That phase penetrated as far south as the Tenasserim Peninsula, whereby Htaway (Tavoy), Mrik (Mergui), Thandok (Southeast of Mergui), and Thaninthayi (Tenasserim town) were also all mentioned for the first time in an original Old Burmese inscription dated to 1196 AD. It was erected by King Narapatisithu, who even claimed that the borders of his kingdom extended to Takwa (Takua Pa on the Kra Isthmus) and Negara (Nagara Sri Dharmaraja?).[49] Whether fact or hyperbole, it was only after these expansions by Pagan that original evidence for many of today's well-known urban sites in Lower Myanmar first appeared in Old Burmese, not Old Mon. This suggests that the foundational infrastructure for state formation in Lower Myanmar was being created for the first time during the eleventh and twelfth centuries AD, and as a consequence of Pagan's expansion.

As the thirteenth century progressed and Lower Myanmar became better integrated into the Pagan kingdom, Pegu and Muttama gained prominence as provincial governorships. As such, they must have supplied the center with trade revenues, likely the result of economic growth during an earlier "age of commerce"[50] that arose between the eleventh and thirteenth century in maritime South, Southeast, and East Asia.

When, in the late thirteenth century, Pagan had to loosen its hold over Lower Myanmar to defend against the Mongol incursions on its northern borders, Muttama struck out for independence. Pegu also chose to do the same around that time. Both then contested for regional supremacy, which Muttama won. Its first king, known by the name of Wagaru (1287–1296) and also by his regnal name, Wareru, was most probably a historical figure said to be of either Shan or Mon background. And when Muttama sought (and received) recognition from China as an independent kingdom in 1298, it was the first such political entity of Lower Myanmar in the country.

That Wareru Dynasty of Muttama remained the major power in Lower Myanmar until its leadership moved the center to Pegu by the mid-fourteenth century, therewith beginning the First Pegu kingdom. As a kingdom, then, Pegu did not emerge until then, even if its existence as provincial seat of the Pagan kingdom can be dated earlier. The Kingdom of Pegu, in other words, was a *new* entity, a product of Pagan's expansion, pacification, and "civilizing" of Lower Myanmar during the first and second millenniums AD. It was not an ancient center contemporary to either the Buddha's extinction or Asokan Buddhist India, as the mythology of Ramannadesa and the Pegu Convention had long contended.

Sources for the Reconstruction of Pegu

Although some of the sources used in the reconstruction of Pegu have been briefly described in the previous chapter, the present one analyzes all of them in greater detail. The sources under discussion are organized according to value, starting with the most "primary" (original and contemporary or near-contemporary) and moving to the least, including a few in European languages, which deal with the last few decades of the dynasty. The most important of all sources are the stone records in Middle Mon—the language of that era—nearly all of which are original and contemporary to the information they contain. Although also important but more problematic are those of the "chronicle" (*vamsa*) genre, all copies, none contemporaneous to the events or individuals they described except one contemporary Chinese source. As they contain the only information about the individuals and events of this particular period, and are based on a fairly sound oral and written tradition, we have little choice but to use them.

Mon-Language Inscriptions of Lower Myanmar

Nearly all original and contemporary Mon inscriptions of Myanmar—perhaps 98 percent of them—had been discovered by 1965. They were individually published in various places, but nearly all of them can be found together in U Chit Thein's compilation called *She Haung Mon Kyauksa Paung Chok* (Collection of Ancient Mon Stone Inscriptions).[1] He excluded King Dhammazedi's Kalyani Inscriptions, probably because they had already seen considerable scholarship and reproduction.[2] The rest, 106 of them, are contained in the above collection, the first part in Mon, and the second in Burmese translation, each line of the stone numbered sequentially in the compilation.[3]

Although the stone inscriptions in this work represent nearly all those written in Mon found in the entire country,[4] nearly half of them (forty-seven) are products of the Kingdom of Pagan and belong to the reign of one king, Kyanzittha, not the First Pegu Dynasty of Lower Myanmar. His inscriptions were written in Old Mon of the eleventh century, not Middle Mon of the fifteenth century, used at Pegu,[5] and therefore had little or nothing to do with (so can tell us little or nothing about) the history and culture of Pegu, which, in any case, was not to emerge for another two hundred years after his inscriptions were erected.

Thus, the epigraphy that best represents the fourteenth- and fifteenth-century Kingdom of Pegu are the remaining fifty-seven Middle Mon inscriptions. Although their dates vary somewhat, most belonged to the First Pegu Dynasty.[6] Approximately twenty-four to twenty-five of them are found in situ at Pegu, nearly all erected by members of the First Pegu Dynasty, most of them by King Dhammazedi. Two are found at Dagon (Yangon), six at (or have now been moved to) Thaton (not counting the three that belonged to Kyanzittha), five are at Pathein (Bassein), two at Kyaik Lat, and two at Kyaik Law. There are also two copper plate inscriptions housed at the National Museum in Bangkok, and one bell inscription each at or near Muttama and Maulamyaing (Moulmein). There is another set (of two faces by Shin Saw Bu?) called the Kawgun Cave inscriptions, and one brick slab inscription from the Kyundaw Kyun pagoda. Although most of the latter inscriptions found outside Pegu appear to be also products of the First Pegu Dynasty, the precise provenance of some is unknown. Thus, compared with the nearly 431 original Old Burmese inscriptions recorded at Ava, Pegu's stone records are, unfortunately, quite sparse, and their value quite mixed.

Part of the reason for this paucity, surely, is the fact that the Old Burmese writing system, from which written Old Mon of Myanmar is likely derived, had approximately a hundred years head start. And compared with Pegu's Middle Mon inscriptions, that head start was even more pronounced, amounting to nearly five hundred years. After all, the kingdom of Pegu was itself a late phenomenon, not to appear until after the mid-fourteenth century, while its foundations (at Muttama) went back to no earlier than the late thirteenth century. Thus, by the time the First Kingdom of Pegu emerged to record anything, Old Burmese at Pagan had already been written for half a millennium.

In addition, Pegu was a much smaller and certainly far more loosely organized polity in terms of both population and territory, so that central control was over a smaller area, and fewer people, most of whom were less dependent on land than on trade and commerce for their livelihood. That would have required fewer written records of a permanent nature by both the state and non-state sectors than would an extensive and demographically large agrarian polity, particularly where stone is invariably used to record title deeds concerning land ownership. In other words, when we compare the prevalence of written Old Burmese with written Middle Mon in terms of state administration, the latter's paucity and lateness are also understandable and explainable. Whatever the reasons, the fact remains that the number of contemporary inscriptions used for the reconstruction of the Pegu Dynasty and kingdom is, relatively speaking, late and few.[7] Even so, what these few, largely donative inscriptions of Pegu tell us is quite interesting and revealing.

One of the most striking features is the devotion of the donors to the ideology of the merit-path to salvation, as intense here as it was at Ava and Pagan. The behavior of the donors, the nature and costs of the gifts, the motives expressed, the prayers uttered, the wishes revealed, the curses invoked, are identical (or nearly so) to those of the devotees in Upper Myanmar. These donors could easily have been Burmese speakers living in Ava. As noted in a previous chapter, when it comes to religion, the two kingdoms behaved as if they were one.

There were other similarities of "deep culture" shared by the people in both Pegu and Ava regarding conceptions of, and principles undergirding, secular society. The meaning of the word *kyun* at Pegu, for example, is identical to that at Ava. Thus, the governor of Muttama, who enjoyed the title *min* (in context, lord), referred to himself in an inscription as the king's *kyun*: that is, not his "slave" but his "subject" or "vassal," exactly what it meant at Ava![8] In the Kawgun Cave inscription near Pha An, the "queen of Muttama" referred to herself as *kyun-up,* the (gender-less) personal pronoun "I" taken from the word *kyun* denoting her rank relative to the king.[9] It certainly did not mean "slave" here either.

Conceptions of kingship were also near-identical. Criteria for legitimating the authority of the king were derivatives of Pagan and Ava conceptions, embedded in certain Buddhist notions of the *bodhisatta, dhammaraja, cakkavatti,* and *devaraja,* coalescing in the *kammaraja.*[10] Correct genealogy, martial ability, and personal charisma were also very much part of the requisites demanded of leadership by secular society, principles that were integrated with the above Buddhist ones. If the situations had been reversed, Dhammazedi would have been considered just as legitimate at Ava as Mingaung the First would have been at Pegu. The exception, of course, would have been Shin Saw Bu, the only documented woman sovereign to have reigned in Myanmar. But even she would still have had the correct moral character and genealogy, along with religious devotion and meritorious works, that substituted for her lack of martial abilities compared with her male counterparts.

The Pegu court and kingdom were also considered symbolic representatives on earth of the Buddhist universe, particularly Tavatimsa, the abode of Sakra (Indra) with his thirty-two lords. Jambudipa, the Southern Island to which Maitreya will descend and in which *cakkavatti* rule, was equally important in Pegu's symbolism. The titles used by queens and kings and their arrangement at court were nearly identical to those found at Ava (and ultimately, Pagan).[11] The standard Buddha and Ananda story used at Pagan and Ava for ensuring Buddhist legitimacy for centers and their dynasties was also used for legitimizing Pegu (although at Pegu, Ananda was substituted with Gavampati). Even though relatively few in number, the Middle Mon inscriptions of fifteenth-century Pegu best represented the values, thoughts, and institutions of (at least) the court of Pegu.

A Contemporary Chinese Source

The only external and contemporary source that mentions the presence of any discrete kingdom (state, polity, "imagined community") in Lower Myanmar is the *Zhi-yuan Zhengmian Lu* (Records of the Expeditions against Mian during the Reign of the Zhi-yuan), a Yuan dynasty text of the thirteenth century.[12] It records an embassy sent in 1298 by a "*new* [my emphasis] Teng-lung Kingdom" from Lower Myanmar to China to seek recognition as an independent polity, invariably one of the first acts pursued by virtually every newly emerged political entity in Southeast Asia.[13] The only possible political entity in Lower Myanmar at that time that was new, referred to as "Teng-lung," and corroborated by indigenous epigraphy as well as later chronicles had to be Muttama (Martaban). If so, it represents the first phase in the rise and development of the Kingdom of Pegu subsequently, for its foundations go back to Muttama (as we have seen in the previous chapter, and shall see in a future chapter).

However, there are several issues with regard to the Yuan source that need discussion. What does the term "Teng-lung" actually mean? Professor Sun Laichen from the University of California at Fullerton translates it as "Talaing." Although most colonial scholarship considers it an exclusive term for the Mon people, in fact, it was used in Pagan and Ava inscriptions to refer to the people in Lower Myanmar *in general*, not to the Mon people specifically.[14] Mon or not, the relevant issue here is the presence of an independent polity, which the Chinese source confirms.

The Yuan source under discussion also mentions two of the leaders of this "Teng-lung" kingdom. They are currently unrecognizable but one could be interpreted to represent Wareru.[15] There is also no information in this Chinese account regarding the events and individuals that led to the creation of this kingdom; that must have been supplied by much later domestic chronicles. Although not ideal (since they are neither contemporary nor entirely historical in our sense of the term), without their information, a narrative history of a Mon Lower Myanmar for this era cannot be reconstructed at all. So, to these we must now turn.

Indigenous-Language Texts on the History of Lower Myanmar

BURMESE-LANGUAGE TEXTS

Apart from the thirteenth-century inscriptions of Pagan that mentioned Pegu (Payku) as a governorship under Pagan, in general, the earliest Upper Myanmar Burmese-language chronicles contemporary or near-contemporary to Pegu have little to say about that kingdom. The two, perhaps three, earliest extant copies of these, written in Burmese (or Pali-Burmese *nissaya*) about the origins and development of the First Pegu Dynasty, are the beginning sections of the *Zatatawpon Yazawin* (Chronicle of Royal Horoscopes), the last sections of the *Yazawinkyaw* (Celebrated Chronicle) and the *Taung-ngu Yazawin*[16] (said to have been near-contemporary to, or to have preceded, the above two), and the original of the *Zambu*, a treatise written by a famous minister who lived and worked at court during the height of the Ava period.[17] While the earlier parts of the *Zatatawpon* were likely written during the late thirteenth century, with much information added only later, the *Yazawinkyaw* was definitely written during the second decade of the Ava period (1520) by famous monk and author Shin Thilawuntha of Ava. As for the *Taung-ngu Yazawin* it is problematic in other ways, as we shall see below.

The *Zatatawpon Yazawin* does not have much narrative information even on Ava, not to mention Pegu. But it mentions the town of Dala,[18] located close to Dagon, now Yangon. It was under Pagan's suzerainty and an important fief then, and later under Pegu's, both confirmed by period epigraphy. The text mentions Hanthawaddy (Pegu), although one cannot tell when this information was inserted, as some of it reflects nineteenth-century people and events, so this reference could be a later interpolation.[19] But, and as noted in an earlier chapter, because Pegu (as "Hansabati") can be found in a near-contemporary external source—the 1292 Sukhotai inscription of Ram Kamhaeng—it is probable that the reference in the *Zatatawpon* was indeed a contemporary one and not a later interpolation.

The sixteenth-century date and provenance of the *Yazawinkyaw* is less ambiguous,[20] because its author, Shin Thilawuntha, is a well-known literary figure whose presence at Ava is documented by contemporary epigraphy and other texts. In this work, he stated that he had used even earlier chronicles.[21] But of the eighty-seven pages contained in the published version of the *Yazawinkyaw*, only ten are devoted to Myanmar; the rest deal with legendary Buddhist "history" beginning with Mahasammata, the "first king of the world." Nevertheless, the *Yazawinkyaw* is a contemporary text written by an eyewitness of exemplary stature, a rare phenomenon indeed. Unfortunately, it has nothing on the First Pegu Dynasty, an absence that is significant in itself.

The *Taung-ngu Yazawin* is less well known but might have been written around 1481. There is a microfilm copy of the manuscript by that name photographed by Kagoshima University in 1973,[22] whose palm-leaf version at the time was located at the Ministry of Culture in Yangon. The information it contains suggests its author lived in Taung-ngu (Toungoo) itself, during the reigns of "kings" Sithu and Minkyinyo. The latter was the founder of the "Toungoo Dynasty," so it places the source in the latter half of the fifteenth century. The spelling of many words in this manuscript is old, using Pagan and Ava norms, and although the copyist dated his copying to 1192 AD, because Ava, Pegu, and Toungoo's formal name, Ketumati, are mentioned, the copy date is more likely to be at least post-Ava and Ketumati, neither of which can be found that early. (However, the copyist might have simply copied the date found on the manuscript he was copying, rather than dating his copy to the time he did the copying.) This chronicle also had little or nothing to say of the First Pegu Dynasty, except referring to a Pegu.

What we can say with some confidence, however, is that at least two urban provincial seats of the Pagan kingdom (Muttama and Pegu) were mentioned in Burmese sources by the twelfth and thirteenth centuries, which in part supports the Chinese reference to a "new Teng-lung kingdom" in Lower Myanmar during approximately the same time.

MON-LANGUAGE TEXTS ON PEGU AND LOWER MYANMAR

Scholars have not found a single, original Mon-language chronicle dated prior to the mid-eighteenth century in Myanmar that deals with the origins of the Mon people in Myanmar or the First Pegu Dynasty. And it was not because their books were said to have been destroyed by the Burmans—"a favourite myth of the Mon historians" according to the (late) eminent Mon scholar H. L. Shorto[23]—but because the writing of Mon "history" (*rajavamsa* or *yazawin*) in the country in the Mon language by the Mon people is quite late.

Possibly the three earliest manuscripts (therefore closest in time to the First Pegu Dynasty) are the *Nidana Arambhakatha,* the "Mon Yazawin", and the *Yazadhiyaza Ayedawpon.*[24] Of these three, the earliest extant versions of the latter two are written in the Burmese language. Only the *Nidana Arambhakatha* is said to have been first found written in Mon. All three show signs of interpolations by much later hands. And since none of their originals exists, we do not know for certain in what language they were originally written, while none of the earliest extant versions of the three can be dated to earlier than the sixteenth century, if even that.

What the reader should also realize from the outset is that information in each extant manuscript of the three works can be found in every other one, so it is extremely difficult to distinguish provenance in any reliable way. But there are enough particulars omitted in some and included in others that an educated guess can be made as to their relative independence and interdependence. What we do know with some assurance is that all three texts are contained in the "Paklat Talaing Chronicle" described in the previous chapter. The latter work more or less represents the compendium of Lower Myanmar Mon history and myth, to be analyzed in greater detail below.[25]

Nidana Arambhakatha

According to H. L. Shorto, the manuscript from which the published version of the *Nidana* is derived comes from a manuscript found at the National Library in Bangkok, the main part of which was originally titled "Ramaññ'-uppatti-dipaka." From a Pali colophon "incorporated in the text" it appears to have been composed by a monk after the end of Dhammazedi's line in 1538, incidentally, the year before the First Pegu Dynasty fell to Tabinshwehti of the so-called Toungoo Dynasty in 1539, the significance of which will be discussed below. Shorto wrote that an analysis of the text suggests it is most probably derived from a historiographical tradition of Burmese origin.[26]

The *Nidana* begins with a very terse statement about legendary Thaton, its equally legendary king Manuha, and their (just as mythical) conquest by Anawrahta. It recounts the brief resurgence of the kingdom after the "conquest," which was led by the Burmese governor said to have been installed at Thaton by Anawrahta. The *Nidana* then records the founding of Pegu with the legendary brothers Samala and Wimala, and Prince Asah, ending with heretical king Tissaraja. After a lapse, the royal line was resumed in Wareru's dynasty of Muttama. From this point onward, wrote Shorto, "the *Nidana* generally followed the traditional account of Burmese history in so far as that relates to the rulers of Martaban and, after the establishment of the capital there in 1369, of Pegu."[27]

Thus, the original *Nidana* may not have contained much more material than what was needed (according to Shorto) to "supply a lacuna at the beginning of" an account on Dhammazedi.[28] This makes sense, as Dhammazedi is the focus of the main text of the *Nidana* (known as the "Ramaññ'-uppatti-dipaka"), in whose reign the term Ramanna was first used. Indeed, I would not be surprised if this text began as a "biography" of Dhammazedi, to which only later was added the parts of the *Nidana* dealing with Thaton and the infamous "conquest," with Anawrahta, Manuha, and the founding of Pegu with Samala and Wimala, thus giving Dhammazedi's lineage and the text some credentials of antiquity.

The *Nidana's* account of the famous Mon king Yazadarit (who preceded Dhammazedi) is extremely brief, with much more on his (Dhammazedi's) grandson Bannya Barow and his "stern justice."[29] Of course, Dhammazedi receives considerable attention, and the latest edition of the *Nidana* mentions Shin Saw Bu. Shorto wrote that after Dhammazedi, the text "carries the story rapidly" to the end of the dynasty in 1538. Even after the conquest by "Burmese" Toungoo, "the text continues the dynasty with Tabinshwehti's ascension in 1540. Thereafter, the entries get more precise; events are dated by years and by 1566, months and even days." It ends with Pyi Min of the Second Ava Dynasty in 1661,[30] showing that this information was added only in the mid-seventeenth century by writers of the Second Ava Dynasty. That also explains what Shorto meant earlier about the *Nidana* reflecting a Burmese historiographic tradition.

If the Pali colophon mentioned by Shorto regarding the date of the *Nidana* (1538) is correct, that means its earliest sections may represent one of the earliest non-epigraphic, Mon-language texts, as none earlier in the Mon language has so far been proven to exist. The date (1538) also corresponds with the end of the "golden years" of the First Pegu Dynasty, which was the first to create the idea of the Realm of the Rman to represent the "Camelot" of the Myanmar Mon. (Remember that the *Nidana*'s original title was "Ramaññ'-uppatti-dipaka," a reference to Ramannadesa.) If written at the end of Dhammazedi's reign as Shorto suggested, the original *Nidana* postdates (by about half a century) the most important place-names, individuals, and events found in the original epigraphy of Pegu belonging to the last quarter of the fifteenth century, precisely during King Dhammazedi's reign. In other words, the legends surrounding Suvannabhumi, Ramannadesa, Thaton, Anawrahta, and Manuha, all part of the hagiography of the Myanmar Mon, had already been constructed by Dhammazedi in his Kalyani Inscriptions nearly a half century before the *Nidana* was said to have been written. Thus, the date, original title, and information attributed to the earliest sections of the *Nidana* correspond well to that found in the original epigraphy of the First Pegu Dynasty.

At the same time, none of the legendary founders of Pegu (Samala, Wimala, Asah, Tissa) found in the later parts of the *Nidana* are corroborated by the epigraphic sources of the First Pegu Dynasty. Rather, such information could not have appeared until texts such as the *Lik Smin Asah* were written—in this case, 1825. Similarly, the *Nidana*'s cursory treatment of important kings such as Yazadarit is almost identical to the way the *Slapat* treated him, and the latter was written not before the mid- to late eighteenth century. To be sure, Dhammazedi was the main character of the *Nidana,* so it is not surprising that the focus of attention was on him and not Yazadarit.[31] Nonetheless, most of the information on the period before the First Pegu Dynasty, and contained in the later sections of the *Nidana,* very likely stemmed from the eighteenth century and later. Certainly, the narrative that continued, after the First Pegu Dynasty had ended, to 1661 and the reign of Pyi Min—a king who belonged to the (entirely different) Second Ava Dynasty of Upper Myanmar—was added much later.

But this raises some interesting questions, not only about the sources under scrutiny but their authors' notions of history. Why did the (alleged Mon) writers who lived during the Second Pegu/Toungoo Dynasty (that of Tabinshwehti and Bayinnaung, who succeeded Dhammazedi and Shin Saw Bu) add Burmese kings from the following Upper Myanmar Second Ava Dynasty to the First Pegu Dynasty of Lower Myanmar, as if they were of the same lineage, when they clearly were not? And why did these authors also include the leaders that came from Toungoo as part of the lineage of the First Pegu Dynasty, when it was they (Tabinshwehti and Bayinnaung) who actually destroyed that Pegu lineage? Does it suggest a subsequent attempt to write a reintegrated history of the country, part of the process of ideological integration by the above mentioned two kings who indeed successfully reunified "Myanmar" politically and militarily under their reigns?

Shorto, interested largely in the literary implications of this textual "integration," wrote that "the annalistic character of this later continuation, which appears to be without parallel elsewhere, clearly derives from an extraneous tradition, which is most likely to be Burmese; if so, it offers a most valuable opportunity for discriminating Mon and Burmese elements in the general historiographic tradition of the country."[32] In terms of our concerns in this chapter regarding historical sources, that integration of the Burmese historiographic tradition tells us something else that is important: it may well be that since the Second Pegu/Toungoo Dynasty was, in fact, led by Burmese kings ruling (presumably) a Mon area, and given that dynasty's demonstrated behavior for the relentless pursuit of unity, it is not at all surprising that a similar attempt was being made to textually unify the *historiography* of Lower and Upper Myanmar as well, thereby reinforcing and confirming something that was actually happening politically and militarily.

Such "historiographic integration" was very much within the religio-political ideology of the time. Toungoo kings were included in the First Pegu Dynasty in part because a legitimate dynasty was defined by its capital, which had been given a Buddha prophecy (as was the case with both Ava and Pegu), as much as (or more than) "blood" lineage per se. Thus, kings who reigned from such a city were considered part of the same dynasty regardless of their actual genealogy and, more importantly for this study, their ethnicity. In that way, both Burmese and Mon, or, better put, Ava and Pegu, eventually shared a similar if not the same historiographic tradition, particularly in organizing that tradition less around blood lineage (and reified ethnicity) than around Buddha-prophesied cities and their dynasties.

Whatever historiographic tensions there were lay not between Burmese and Mon histories, but between texts written by monks with a Buddhist ecumenical worldview, on the one hand, and those written by individuals more concerned with a domestic, secular kind of unity, on the other, although legitimated by Buddhist ideas. To be sure, both incorporated what were considered "universal" elements, so that most began with Buddhist world systems and/or Buddhist legitimation schemes and rationalizations, after which they would diverge, the former giving agency to things religious and "global," the latter to things secular and more parochial. When dealing with the same monarch, for example, the former would focus on his/her religious behavior and record, while the latter, on his military or political performance.

Then there is the issue of timing. Why was the *Nidana* written only a year before Pegu's final and successful conquest by Tabinshwehti, after two of his previous attempts had failed? Was there an atmosphere of impending doom prior to the conquest that triggered a sense of urgency to preserve in written form the memory of the first kingdom ever of the Lower Myanmar Mon? If so, not only does it suggest the *Nidana*'s place in the Mon *rajavamsa* tradition as the first, but also confirms what I have documented in *Mists*—that there was no Mon kingdom in Lower Myanmar called Ramannadesa prior to the First Pegu Dynasty. For, as shown above, it was only during that dynasty that even *the very idea of Ramannadesa* was first introduced by King Dhammazedi, in whose honor the *Nidana* was written. When we use data from the *Nidana* to reconstruct the First Pegu Dynasty, then, all these factors must be considered.

Yazadhiyaza Ayedawpon

This work is an account (*pon,* story)[33] of the great Mon king Yazadhiyaza (king of kings), popularly known as Yazadarit, who ruled between 1385 and 1423. In terms of subject matter, the *Yazadhiyaza Ayedawpon* should be considered a precursor of the *Nidana,* as the latter is focused on Dhammazedi, who succeeds Yazadarit chronologically. The text is different from the *Nidana* in other important ways as well. For example, the history of Pegu in the *Yazadhiyaza Ayedawpon* does not begin either with Thaton, or the legendary two brothers Wimala and Samala, but with Magadu and Muttama; thus, it is more historical. This distinction is important for another reason: as noted in the previous chapter, it suggests two contributing streams—one foreign (South India and Sri Lanka) and the other domestic (Upper Myanmar and Thailand). The *Yazadhiyaza Ayedawpon*'s narrative is also more detailed and chronologically coherent, particularly regarding the early years of Magadu's rise to power at Muttama, before its center shifted to Pegu, a sequence that is supported by epigraphy and the contemporary Chinese source mentioned above.

One could also say that the *Yazadhiyaza Ayedawpon* is much more "historical" in the Western sense of the term, focused on individuals and events, even if their importance is justified by the use of literary devices such as supernatural phenomena, prophecies, and omens. It is secular, down-to-earth, and largely concerned with the events of this world surrounding Yazadarit. Births and deaths of royal siblings, their political relationships, their achievements, their religious largesse, their childhood development, their supporters and enemies, their lovers, their ministers, and their personalities are all described in a rather matter-of-fact, believable narrative.

Nonetheless, as a source, the *Yazadhiyaza Ayedawpon* raises several important historiographic questions. Who wrote it? In what language and when was the original written? Is the final product (which is in Burmese) a translation of an earlier work in Mon, or was it written in Burmese from scratch? When was it completed? And finally, how is it important to the reconstruction of the First Pegu Dynasty and kingdom, the main concerns of this chapter?

For years, convention held that the original manuscript whose final product is the Burmese-language *Yazadhiyaza Ayedawpon* was a "biography" of King Yazadarit compiled and/or translated by Bannya Dala, a prominent minister at the court of King Bayinnaung of the succeeding Second Pegu/Toungoo Dynasty. He was thought to have either written it from scratch in Burmese or translated it into Burmese from an earlier manuscript written in Mon, thereby placing the work in the second half of the sixteenth century, before the minister died in about 1572. This convention, begun sometime in the early twentieth century, had remained gospel in the field of Myanmar studies, although its scholars had, off and on, attempted to resolve some "minor" disconcerting issues in it.

The late Nai Pan Hla, a Mon author on the history and culture of the Mon speakers in Myanmar, contended in the introduction of his edition to the *Yazadhiyaza Ayedawpon*, published in 1977, that there existed (at the time he wrote) nine different versions of the work, including palm-leaf and published items. All were in Burmese, all were copies from another source, and none was dated to earlier than the mid-eighteenth century. Most important, he claimed, there is no palm-leaf manuscript *written in Mon* called the *Yazadhiyaza Ayedawpon* per se. Rather, he stated, the *Yazadhiyaza Ayedawpon* (as such) is really the title of a Burmese *translation* by Bannya Dala of the third section found in another larger work written in Mon called the "Thaton-Hanthawaddy Chronicle."[34]

The claim that the *Yazadhiyaza Ayedawpon* was the third section of the Mon-language "Thaton-Hanthawaddy Chronicle" and translated by Bannya Dala in the sixteenth century implies that both sources are at least that old. In fact, however, the "Thaton-Hanthawaddy Chronicle" is part of the so-called "Paklat Talaing Chronicle," not compiled until the twentieth century in Thailand.[35] In other words, Nai Pan Hla's source has never existed *as such* in any of the palm-leaf records of the country or abroad prior to the twentieth century; it is a twentieth-century compilation.

Even the latest of the twelve stand-alone palm-leaf copies of the *Yazadhiyaza Ayedawpon* left in the country and written in Burmese are earlier than the "Thaton-Hanthawaddy Chronicle." The late Nai Pan Hla may be correct that there is no palm-leaf manuscript written in Mon called the *Yazadhiyaza Ayedawpon*, but to suggest that the "Thaton-Hanthawaddy Chronicle" is earlier than, and the original source of, the *Yazadhiyaza Ayedawpon* is surely mistaken.

To complicate matters, three Myanmar scholars, also following the convention that Bannya Dala was responsible for translating the *Yazadhiyaza Ayedawpon* into Burmese, stated in the preface of another book that the work Bannya

Dala allegedly translated was taken from a fourteenth- to fifteenth-century chronicle called the "Mon Yazawin," said to have been written in the Mon language.[36] However, they provided neither evidence nor analysis for their assertion.

As far as I know, the earliest (perhaps only) extant copy of the palm-leaf manuscript called the "Mon Yazawin" found in Myanmar is written in Burmese, not Mon.[37] Indeed, in general, that is what has happened in the country's historiography: the earliest extant accounts of the Mon in Myanmar have been written in Burmese. Our knowledge of the history of the Myanmar Mon is therefore largely found in Burmese-language sources; the Burmese, not the Mon, have preserved the history of the Mon in Myanmar. However, unlike the role played by Arab translations of Greek works, crucial to the reconstruction of ancient Greek thought, history, and society during the European Renaissance, in our case, Burmese works in most cases seemed to have preceded their Mon counterparts.

In any case, the "Mon Yazawin" under discussion and the *Yazadhiyaza Ayedawpon* are very different works. There is less than one palm leaf given to Yazadarit in the "Mon Yazawin," while the *Yazadhiyaza Ayedawpon* has approximately three hundred printed pages on him.[38] Furthermore, whereas the *Yazadhiyaza Ayedawpon* ends with Yazadarit, the "Mon Yazawin" includes his successors such as Shin Saw Bu and Dhammazedi, and does not end until nearly a century later, with Bannya Ram. Offhand, the "Mon Yazawin" looks very much like the later mid-eighteenth-century *Slapat Rajawan Datow Smin Ron* (History of Kings),[39] although a more thorough analysis by Mon- and Burmese-language scholars of their original palm-leaf manuscripts is needed to confirm this. (More on the *Slapat* below.)

Another theory is that of the well-known author Zawgyi (his pen name), who wrote the foreword to the third edition of the published *Yazadhiyaza Ayedawpon* that I use in this study. He believed that Bannya Dala did not write it but translated an earlier Mon-language work. However, that cannot be the "Mon Yazawin," as the three scholars above claimed, but a manuscript whose title was already the *Yazadhiyaza*,[40] but without the Burmese word *Ayedawpon* attached to it. This thesis has some promise, but Zawgyi, like the others, only states it; he provides no other information, analysis, or evidence for his case.

U Myint Swe, editor of volume 1 of the *Twinthin Myanma Yazawinthit* (Twinthin's New Chronicle of Myanma), written in the late eighteenth century by Twinthin Mahasithu, concurred with Zawgyi's assertion by "showing" that its author used the *Yazadhiyaza Ayedawpon* in *the Mon language itself,* without either demonstrating that Twinthin knew the Mon language or that the work he allegedly used existed.[41] To support his case, U Myint Swe provided a direct quote and page number (7) of a work edited by Nai Pan Hla in 1958, which U Myint Swe called the "Mon Yazadhiyaza Ayedawpon."[42] However, as noted above, because Nai Pan Hla himself had concluded that no work written in the Mon language with the title *Yazadhiyaza Ayedawpon* existed, U Myint Swe was likely referring to the "Thaton-Hanthawaddy Chronicle" that Nai Pan Hla had translated and taken from the third section of the late "Paklat Talaing Chronicle."

None of this means that no earlier manuscript in the Mon language existed (whatever its name) that was later translated into Burmese called the *Yazadhiyaza Ayedawpon*. In fact, there are internal clues in the narrative of the Burmese-language *Yazadhiyaza Ayedawpon* to suggest that the text may have been written first in Mon before it was translated into Burmese. For example, it would often quote proverbs or ditties (short, simple sayings) in Mon, then explain that when translated into Burmese, they mean such and such. Clearly, then, whoever compiled the work must have had a Mon text in hand. Thus, although the *Yazadhiyaza Ayedawpon* was most likely a translation, who the translator was, what the name of the Mon source was, and when it was translated remains unknown.

It does not help matters when the dates found in three of the only twelve extant manuscript versions of the *Yazadhiyaza Ayedawpon* found in the archives today are equally ambiguous. Each date has one missing digit, so that they are recorded as *sakkaraj* 115, 119, and 120. These could be, respectively, *sakkaraj* 1115, 1119, and 1120, corresponding to AD 1753, 1757, and 1758. Or, they could represent 1150, 1190, and 1200—that is, the missing digits are at the end, not the beginning—and correspond to AD 1788, 1828, and 1838.[43] Either way, all copies are no earlier than the mid-eighteenth century, and to reiterate, written in Burmese, not Mon.

Recently, the whole convention attributing the *Yazadhiyaza Ayedawpon* to Bannya Dala (as translator or author) has been questioned in a most convincing manner by Ko Shwe Thein Min.[44] After analyzing these twelve extant Burmese-language palm-leaf *copies* of the *Yazadhiyaza Ayedawpon* left in the country, he demonstrated that a misreading (and therefore, misinterpretation) of a word in three of those palm-leaf versions by several twentieth-century publications led to attributing the work to Bannya Dala erroneously, which was perpetuated by everyone else thereafter.[45] He shows that not a single one of the twelve palm-leaf records of the *Yazadhiyaza Ayedawpon* mentions Bannya Dala as author or translator. Instead, the mistake lay in one word that confused *pyinnya shi* (those "with knowledge") and *byinnya kyi* (those "with great stature") with Byinnya Dala (that is, Bannya Dala). After scrutinizing those sentences from copies of the three manuscripts, I must concur with Ko Shwe Thein Min's interpretation.

If not Bannya Dala, who, then, was responsible for the work? One normally finds such information at the "end statements" of most manuscripts. The published version of the *Yazadhiyaza Ayedawpon* that I use in this book—whose "end statement" is closest to those of palm-leaf manuscript numbers eleven and twelve—never mentioned Bannya Dala as author (except by the editors), and quite clearly states that it was compiled by a group of "wise men." The pertinent phrase, according to my own reading of the version I use, states that "men of intellect composed [and] wrote [this text]."[46] This is confirmed by other Burmese-language scholars whom I consulted. Eminent Burmese-language specialist John Okell translates the same phrase as "[Yazadarit] had wise men compile [a record]."[47] Another Burmese-language specialist, Dr. Than Than Win, translates the phrase as "wise men had composed" it.[48] U San Lwin, translator into English of the palm-leaf version of the published *Yazadhiyaza Ayedawpon* that

I use (although it is unclear whether the manuscript is number eleven or twelve), also translates the phrase as having been "chronicled by men of learning."[49] Dr. Pat McCormick, perhaps the only Myanmar-Mon scholar among the above list of scholars to have studied the work in the Mon language, read the phrase as "experts have composed [this narrative]."[50] And finally, Ko Shwe Thein Min writes that it was compiled by "men of intellect."[51] Thus, the consensus among Myanmar scholars who have scrutinized the relevant passage is that the *Yazadhiyaza Ayedawpon* was written or compiled by a *group* rather than a *single individual,* although the various copyists that came later could be single individuals. Whether they included Bannya Dala, as convention has it, or someone else, must be considered unknown.

Rejecting the convention that Bannya Dala wrote the work, however, creates another problem, not least, its date; because now, it means we can no longer attribute the original manuscript to the sixteenth century, when Bannya Dala lived. When was it written, then? John Okell's reading of the "end statement" provides a clue, for it makes Yazadarit the subject, "who had wise men compile" the work. This would mean the biography was commissioned during his reign, and since a monarch's order—especially someone like Yazadarit—is unlikely to be ignored, the date of completion might also have been during his reign: that is, the last quarter of the fourteenth and first half of the fifteenth centuries. If so, the original work was also probably written in Middle Mon rather than in Burmese, as the First Pegu Dynasty was led by Mon leaders who left nearly all their records in Middle Mon. This could possibly make the original manuscript that later came to be called the *Yazadhiyaza Ayedawpon* the earliest Mon-language "history" in the country, even earlier than the original *Nidana.*

If the original *Yazadhiyaza Ayedawpon* were in Middle Mon, and since all extant copies are in Burmese, it must have been translated at some point after the reign of Yazadarit. Although we cannot be certain when that happened, there are some clues to suggest that the Burmese-language version of the *Yazadhiyaza Ayedawpon* was already in existence before 1720 when the *Mahayazawingyi* was written. The editor of that work states in its preface that, U Kala, its author, used the *Yazadhiyaza Ayedawpon* as one of his sources, along with approximately seventy other texts.[52] The editor must have meant U Kala used the already translated Burmese-language version with the full title of *Yazadhiyaza Ayedawpon,* not the original Mon version (whatever its title was), particularly since there is no unequivocal evidence of its existence or that U Kala knew the Mon language.

U Kala himself did not corroborate the editor's statement that he used the *Yazadhiyaza Ayedawpon* in his history, but his account of Yazadarit suggests he did. His work gave approximately one hundred printed pages to the king, as much as, or more than, he gave any of the most famous Burmese kings. It is a quantity that cannot be found in any other single text on Yazadarit except the *Yazadhiyaza Ayedawpon* itself. There are other indirect suggestions that U Kala used the work: verbatim passages found in both works demonstrating some textual relationship,[53] as well as his criticism of the Mon authors for being "inconsistent" with their dating of events. This suggests that he was using the

Yazadhiyaza Ayedawpon not in a cursory fashion but scrutinizing it in some detail. Moreover, the *Yazadhiyaza Ayedawpon* must have been relatively well known and accessible to the public, since U Kala was not an official of the royal court of either Pegu or Ava, even though he was heir to the state records of his father, a *myosa* (provincial governor).

Yet, simply knowing which manuscript—the *Yazadhiyaza Ayedawpon* or the *Mahayazawingyi*—was written earlier does not resolve all the problems of provenance regarding certain stories contained in them. A case in point in the *Yazadhiyaza Ayedawpon* is the well-known account of King Asah defeating the "seven thousand Indians." According to Mon scholar Robert Halliday, the story about King Asah was not compiled until 1825, as noted above.[54] If true, that suggests the story was added to copies of the *Yazadhiyaza Ayedawpon* only in the nineteenth century.[55]

Another story closer to Yazadarit's reign records the relationship between the southern queen of Mingaung the First and his chief of elephantry, a story that only the inner court of the First Ava Dynasty in Upper Myanmar would likely have known in any detail. Yet, it is found in the *Yazadhiyaza Ayedawpon* as if its authors were also privy to such information. During one of the campaigns between Ava and Pegu, the queen (who was there "for the ride") fell off her elephant when it slipped in a stream. As the chief of elephantry was nearby, she called for his help. As he went to her rescue, he said to his *mahout* (elephant driver), "Mark my words, this is the day a death token has been given me."[56] Upon returning to Ava many days later, he was showered with gifts by the king and the queen's relatives for having saved her. However, the pair also aroused suspicions of having had an affair during the trip, when one day, nonplussed by dropping her betel-leaf holder, the queen instinctively cried out the chief's name. Even that startled cry, as written down in the *Yazadhiyaza Ayedawpon*, is virtually verbatim to that in U Kala's *Mahayazawingyi*.[57]

Since U Kala was said to have used the *Yazadhiyaza Ayedawpon* in his history, that the story appeared in his work creates no problems of chronology. But how could the authors of the *Yazadhiyaza Ayedawpon*, ostensibly writing in Lower Myanmar three hundred years before U Kala's work, have known this rather esoteric story that most likely circulated only within the Ava court, particularly the verbatim dialogues? One possibility is that there was an earlier Ava source from which the *Yazadhiyaza Ayedawpon* obtained this information. Yet, the most important chronicles of that period, whose originals likely preceded the *Yazadhiyaza Ayedawpon*—the *Zatatawpon, Yazawinkyaw*, and the *Taungngu Yazawin*—do not contain the story. That leaves only the "submissions" of Hpo Yaza preserved in the eighteenth century *Maniyadanabon* whose earliest sections were begun during Mingaung's reign.[58] Although it does not describe the story per se, Mingaung's questioning of his wise minister as to what to do about this (same) queen's "misbehavior," and the minister's response, alluded to his queen's love affair with an important follower of the king.[59] The details of that "misbehavior" is not made explicit but hinted, so that the story responsible for it was likely well known, and may have been written down in another text or passed down as oral history that the authors of the *Yazadhiyaza Ayedawpon* obtained. Indeed, Euan Bagshawe, translator of the *Maniyadanabon*, states that one of the daughters of Yazadarit's chief minister was given in marriage to Hpo Yaza, so there was a direct link between the author and Yazadarit's court.[60]

Another possibility is that texts and information were regularly exchanged between Ava and Pegu; Ava certainly knew the official Mon name of Shin Saw Bu (Bannya Thau), those of other Pegu kings, and events occurring at Pegu. Similarly, Pegu authors must have known of Burmese works produced by the First Ava Dynasty, especially with the explosion in Burmese literature at the time. It is also possible that when the future sovereigns of Pegu, Shin Saw Bu and Dhammazedi (both of whom had lived in Ava), later escaped to Pegu, they took such esoteric Ava court stories with them and subsequently relayed them to Pegu's historians, probably with some relish. As the authors of the *Yazadhiyaza Ayedawpon* were ministers and scholars—the "wise men" noted above—they likely had easy access to such records.

There might be yet another—and perhaps better—explanation for such "anachronistic" information. That is, stories from U Kala's *Mahayazawingyi* were inserted into later copies of the *Yazadhiyaza Ayedawpon*, just like the story of King Asah and the Indians, which actually belonged to a later age than the *Yazadhiyaza Ayedawpon*. Such late insertions are revealed by the following kind of blunder. In the *Yazadhiyaza Ayedawpon*'s narrative about one of the wars between Pegu and Ava, rather than regarding the Ava forces as "the enemy" (as it should have, since the speaker belonged to Yazadarit's troops), Pegu's forces were called "the enemy" instead.[61] This sounds as if the section regarding this event had been taken verbatim from U Kala (or somewhere else), but the compiler forgot to change the phrase "the enemy" to fit the correct speaker's perspective. Thus, even though the Burmese translation of the *Yazadhiyaza Ayedawpon* most probably preceded U Kala's work, stories from the latter found their way into the former's *later* copies. And it is from these copies that all published texts of the *Yazadhiyaza Ayedawpon* were derived and that scholars in Myanmar used. The date attributed to a text, by itself, cannot positively determine the date of all its contents, especially when we have only copies to analyze.

Whoever wrote or translated it, and whatever may have been the precise date of the original and/or translated version, the *Yazadhiyaza Ayedawpon* is nonetheless an important source, without which a detailed history of the early Pegu years cannot be reconstructed. The Burmese translation represents one of the earliest Mon-language manuscripts that we have today dealing with the origins and early years of the First Pegu Dynasty. The *Yazadhiyaza Ayedawpon* also has considerable detail not found elsewhere, particularly on Yazadarit. Virtually nothing else has been written from the perspective of the First Pegu Dynasty and kingdom prior to the colonial period, so that it provides "a voice" to that particular geopolitical entity during that particular time.

It also provides valuable information concerning Lower Myanmar's political organization, geography, spheres of influence, and the direction in which it "looked" most often. One of the most useful categories of such data are the names and general locations of the most important fiefs held by vassals of Pegu kings, which allow us to reconstruct a political map of Lower Myanmar's hegemony at that time. These places were mentioned without any hesitation or query, so that the composers of the *Yazadhiyaza Ayedawpon* not only appear to have been familiar with them, but indicated that they were still present, functioning, and important. Some of these places can be corroborated by epigraphy using Dhammazedi's contemporary Kalyani Inscriptions, which has a long list of over three hundred ordination halls (*sima*) built in towns and villages where his re-ordinations were held. Not surprisingly, these were important urban areas, the most important ones walled and fortified, commanding strategic locations at mouths of major rivers and tributaries or near mountain passes from or through which trade and commerce as well as troops could move, and so were "gateways" to valuable material resources such as forests of teak and homes of elephants and other valuable animals. Some were natural harbors and port cities on the then-current long-distance trade routes to and from maritime Southeast Asia.

Another kind of useful information found in the *Yazadhiyaza Ayedawpon* is of a cultural nature. Contrary to most assumptions held about how differently Upper and Lower Myanmar people must have thought, we often find that just the opposite is true. The text describes many important similarities between the major cultures of the two regions, particularly in terms of their overall conceptual system about man and his world (discussed above). It includes not only political values regarding conceptions of leadership, power, authority, legitimacy, and other Buddhist notions of karma and merit-making, but also the kinds of values that constitute "good society," values often confirmed by contemporary inscriptions. Some important customs, it turns out, were nearly identical. One of these is the cremation rituals concerning deceased royalty, whereby their ashes were placed in gold or silver urns and deposited in scared areas of the major rivers, a ritual that harks back to the first millennium AD "Pyu" people as well as other areas of Southeast Asia described by Chinese sources. Sometimes, the remains were interred in structures that resemble temples, to which obeisance was made in ways not different from those made to actual temples, raising once again the issue in Southeast Asian art history regarding "funerary temples."

And when one reads the *Yazadhiyaza Ayedawpon* and the *Mahayazawingyi* together, another picture emerges—the affinity of their historiographic tradition. This is particularly true of their narrative structure, which is nearly identical despite the geopolitical and cultural differences of the centers in which they were written. But then, they are *yazawin*, after all, a genre based ultimately on Sri Lanka's *vamsa* tradition. They dwell on certain kinds of behavior expected of royalty and ministers, anticipate certain kinds of responses from their readers for certain poignant stories, frame their narratives within a certain set of circumscribing parameters, and use certain literary devices (prophecies, omens, dialogue) to make didactic statements about certain truths considered to be self-evident and universal.

At the same time, it is clear that the historiography of Upper Myanmar (and Ava) was far more sophisticated and advanced than Lower Myanmar (and

Pegu's). The former's historians were more prolific, paid closer attention to dates and chronology, used a wider variety of literary and epigraphic sources, were considered to be more balanced and erudite on the whole, and seemed to have had a better education in "classical" (Indian) subjects. In contrast, the sometimes cavalier attitude in the *Yazadhiyaza Ayedawpon* regarding inconsistencies and general inattention to chronological precision prompted U Kala to criticize the "Mon chronicles' dates . . . [as] inconsistent." Shorto confirms such an assessment.[62]

In terms of quantity, the corpus of chronicles and other written texts in the Burmese language far exceeds that written in Mon.[63] Perhaps more important, the large number written in Burmese on various subjects, other than those dealing with Upper Myanmar history and about people other than Burmese kings, is rather impressive. It reveals a broader, "international" perspective of the authors, a shared notion of an integrated domestic society and polity, and specialization in a wide variety of subjects. There were chronicles written in Burmese about China, Sri Lanka, India, Chiang Mai, Ayuthaya, even Portugal and Iran; histories of a variety of political centers both within and outside the "heartland," such as Pagan, Toungoo, Thaton, Dhannyawadi (Arakan), and Pegu, along with some of their leaders (Yazadarit, Dhammazedi, Bayinnaung, Alaungmintaya, Nandabayin); accounts of specific ethno-linguistic groups that kept their ethnonyms; and other works written on a wide variety of topics such as religion, grammar, censuses, poetry, "national" as well as local history, biography, and bibliography. Ava and Upper Myanmar appear to have been most influenced by China's encyclopedic and South Asia's literary traditions.

Finally, we should remember that the *Yazadhiyaza Ayedawpon* gives "agency" to the role of loyal ministers and was written from their perspective, even while it was an *ayedawpon* to honor the king's important achievements. Part of the "end statement"—that Yazadarit achieved what he did because he followed "the words of royal ministers"—was also a comment about themselves, invoked in the story of Tein Nge, King Binnya U's (Yazadarit's father's) loyal minister, who was almost executed by Yazadarit for being loyal to his father, the then legitimately reigning king, and not initially to Yazadarit, who was not yet king.

Written from the perspective of court ministers, the work "privileges" their view of the world, advocating sympathy for misunderstood ministers, especially their difficult role in attempting to preserve and provide stability to the most important institutions of society—the state, *sangha*, and monarchy—when their leaders were sometimes impulsive, reckless, and stubborn but nonetheless were legitimate kings to whom loyalty had to be given almost unquestionably.[64] There is no equivocation in emphasizing the role of ministers being indispensable to the preservation of state and monarchy, suggesting in no uncertain terms that, had it not been for them, many kings would not have become what they became, or gone down in history in the positive way they did, a perception made clear in the *Yazadhiyaza Ayedawpon.*

Whatever the ambiguity surrounding its provenance and development, we are fortunate to have the *Yazadhiyaza Ayedawpon,* for, in the final analysis, it is its contents that matter most. It is still the best and (in some respects), only "chronicle" that describes a most important period during the crucial, developmental years of the First Dynasty of Pegu, so that despite the ambiguity surrounding its provenance, we are compelled to use it, especially for Yazadarit's rise and decline. What is not contained in the edition I use here (it ends with his death), I supplement with the *Nidana*, major Burmese-language chronicles, later Mon chronicles written in and/or translated into Burmese or English, and contemporary Mon epigraphy translated into English and/or Burmese. There are other miscellaneous sources that I considered but did not necessarily use, some of which are assessed below.

The "Mon Yazawin"

There appears to be only one, distinct palm-leaf text in the corpus of Mon and Burmese manuscripts actually called the "Mon Yazawin," whose title is written on its "cover page." This is the document in the National Library, number 2290,[65] microfilmed in the early 1970s by Kagoshima University and catalogued in reels 100–101.[66] According to the last leaf of the manuscript, it is a translation into Burmese of a Mon text of unknown date, made by or for the crown prince, the eldest son of the current king. But neither the king nor his dynasty is mentioned by name.[67] So, not only do we not know the name of the translator or date of translation, we also do not know when the original Mon text was written or copied.

However, there are some clues as to its provenance. First, the beginning sections contain an "origins" story regarding the patron saint of towns and cities in Myanmar, including that of the Lower Myanmar Mon, named Gavampati. In it, he is said to have come from one of two eggs laid by a female *naga,* a tale found as early as a late fifteenth-century Mon inscription.[68] Of course, that does not mean the "Mon Yazawin" was written then; only that some of its stories can be dated by original epigraphy that far back.

Moreover, the *Mon Yazawin* deals with the First Pegu Dynasty only, ending with Bannya Ram, as the most recent king of that dynasty, suggesting that it was probably written after his death in or around 1526, with no later interpolations in terms of subject matter. The manuscript contains some older spellings and usages found in both Pagan and Ava inscriptions (such as the use of consonants as tone markers)—therefore suggesting an even earlier Burmese original, as Mon is not a tonal language—although on the whole it uses "modern" tone markers generally found mainly after the seventeenth and eighteenth centuries. Thus, the translator's Burmese probably belonged to one of those later centuries. The section on King Dhammazedi appears to be the longest, and so the manuscript might have some connections to the *Nidana,* which, as noted above, focused on that king.

During the early twentieth century, a "*Mun Yazawin*" was said to have been published, which stimulated a brief discussion by J. A. Stewart in an early *Journal of the Burma Research Society* article.[69] He wrote that this small book of 110 pages (the "*Mun* Yazawin" is also small) was printed from an old manuscript found at the Mingun Pitaka Taik (Mingun Library) at Sagaing, across from Mandalay, the last capital of the Burmese monarchy. It contains a brief sketch of Thaton and Pegu, with a fuller account of Yazadarit and Dhammazedi. Stewart wrote that the author of this manuscript was one U Shwe Naw, who had based his work on old Mon manuscripts obtained by Sir Arthur Phayre from Thailand, on which his history of Pegu was based. That means the "Mon Yazawin" presently under discussion is clearly not the one on which U Shwe Naw's was based, since the former is not in the Mon language. Moreover, a survey of the Sir Arthur Phayre Collection in the British Library suggests that the only Mon history written in the Mon language found there is a palm-leaf manuscript, number OR 3414, listed by its cataloguer as "History of the Talaings."[70] Therefore, it also is not the "Mon Yazawin" under discussion here, as the latter is a translation in the Burmese language.

U Kala was said to have used a "Mon Yazawin" in writing his *Mahayazawingyi,* quite apart from the *Yazadhiyaza Ayedawpon.*[71] If that "Mon Yazawin" he used and the manuscript under discussion are the same, it would place it at least to the very early eighteenth century if not earlier. However, U Kala did not say whether the work he used was written in Mon or in Burmese, and there is no evidence that he read Mon. If not, and he used the translated version of it, then obviously, that text and its original must have gone back earlier than his writing of the *Mahayazawingyi.*

Presently, then, it looks as if the *Nidana,* the *Yazadhiyaza Ayedawpon,* and the *original Mon text* of the present Burmese-language translation called the "Mon Yazawin" appear to be the three urtexts for much of the information on the First Pegu Dynasty found in subsequent Mon documents.

Since the *Nidana* and *Yazadhiyaza Ayedawpon* that currently exist are likely the earliest representatives of Mon historical writing in Myanmar, and because they probably depended on earlier works, perhaps written during the First Pegu Dynasty, the earliest that can be reasonably claimed for the genesis of the chronicle tradition in the Mon language in Myanmar—at least as far as the evidence so far is concerned—is the late fourteenth and fifteenth centuries, precisely the time when the first Mon kingdom in Myanmar emerged. If ever there was a time for the Lower Myanmar Mon to celebrate their first kingdom in the country with written "histories," it would have been then, before which there would have been little or no reason (or wherewithal) for writing such "national" histories.

The "Gavampati"

There are later Mon-language sources that purport to deal with the origins of Pegu, although from what I understand from their translations (into Burmese or English), they more or less repeat what is found in the "Mon Yazawin," the *Yazadhiyaza Ayedawpon,* and/or the *Nidana.* One of these was translated by Shorto as "Gavampati,"[72] whose typescript manuscript is my main source of reference.[73]

Although Shorto does not claim an early date for the "Gavampati" text in the above translation, he did write elsewhere that the earliest extant copy of the Mon language version of the "Gavampati" may date to 1710,[74] which would make it one of the earliest copies of a Myanmar Mon "history" of themselves written in Mon, assuming the dates attributed to the "Mon Yazawin," *Nidana*, and *Yazadhiyaza Ayedawpon* are correct.

But the date Shorto gives the "Gavampati" seems to be at odds with some of its contents. Internal evidence shows, for example, that English terms such as "Tavoy," "Martaban," and "Rangoon" are used freely. These may have been Shorto's English-language equivalents of the indigenous terms, but elsewhere in the text he faithfully follows the toponyms as they were written in the indigenous language.[75] If the anglicized terms existed in the original of the text he translated, it suggests these sections were probably added during the period following the First Anglo-Burmese War of 1824–1826, when they came into use. In contrast, for example, Captain George Baker's account of Myanmar in 1759 still used the indigenous "Tavay" for Tavoy, suggesting that the "Gavampati" (or these parts of the text with English names) may have been written well after 1710.[76]

For the "etymology" of Tavoy, the "Gavampati" states that "because the Buddha sat down there [cross-legged] the place was first called Th(a)way (which means cross-legged), which became corrupted and it is now called Daway or Tavoy."[77] The word "now" is what, in part, reveals its (anglicized) lateness, for Tavoy is the English term for Taway (Daway), while Taway is Old Burmese and goes back to Pagan-period inscriptions. The text has other late terms, such as "Kambon Jarah within the present domain of Ayuthaya" or "near the limits of Labohapuri, now Lavo."[78]

What is curious and interesting about the miraculous and ascribed Buddhist origins of the Mon in Myanmar in the "Gavampati" is that the Buddha is said to have first gone to and prophesied the establishment of "Kamboja," "the domains of Sukhothai" and "the sovereignty of Ayuthaya." After the Buddha and the twenty thousand *arahats* with the Mahathera Gavampati "flew along the seashore . . . they turned towards the land of the Mons. Then, calling Gavampati forward, the Omniscient One came to Tavoy *which is the boundary of the Mon country* [my emphasis]."[79]

The Buddha, Gavampati, and his *arahats* went to each (future) sacred site in Lower Myanmar and prophesied Pegu's forthcoming appearance, along with historical places such as Mah Tma (Muttama). Then came the standard Buddha and Ananda discourse (although here, Gavampati replaces Ananda) in which the Buddha smiles upon seeing a place, Gavampati asks why, and the Buddha prophecies the future of that place. In this case, he states that a demon that lives there will become king, who will be known by the title of Varoraja, King Wa Row, possessor of a white elephant. From Wareru on, the "Gavampati" more or less follows the narrative of the *Yazadhiyaza Ayedawpon*, from where it probably obtained the information.

The Slapat

Although considered by early twentieth-century scholars to be one of the most important Mon sources, the *Slapat Rajawan Datow Smin Ron* (translated as the

History of Kings) is later than the "Gavampati" (if the date Shorto gave the latter is correct) and is also less a general history (despite the title given it in English) than a source partial to a particular agenda: the record of kings who donated to the Shwedagon Pagoda. The *Slapat* was originally said to have been written in 1766 by a famous Mon monk simply named Acwo,[80] whose translation by Halliday I use here, and whose assessment I have given in *Mists*, although it bears some repeating here as well.

The full title, *Slapat Rajawan Datow Smin Ron,* was actually given to the work by Père W. Schmidt, who first published it in German in 1906, so we do not know what its original title might have been. C. O. Blagden subsequently began an English translation of Schmidt's work, but apparently never completed it, and that manuscript eventually passed on to Robert Halliday, an American missionary. Using both Schmidt's and Blagden's works, along with what he considered to be the best of the Mon manuscript versions, Halliday published his own English translation of it in the *Journal of the Burma Research Society* in 1923.[81]

The manuscript that Schmidt originally used is quite problematic. It was first sent to Blagden in 1892 by an H. L. Eales, who was an official engaged in the census of Myanmar of 1891. Eales, in turn, had obtained it from Maung Dut, "a Talaing" who was employed by the British government as a revenue officer. The latter had acquired it from a Maung Meik of Saingdi (a village near Pegu) who said he had gotten it from his great-grandfather, one Bala Theikti, who had brought it back to Myanmar after a campaign against Thailand during Bodawpaya's reign. That original from Thailand was then said to have been given to a monk of Kokainggyi, but the son of Bala Theikti was said to have made a copy of it prior to the donation. The manuscript Blagden got from Eales was that son's copy, the original having been lost.[82]

Thus, apart from this long and circuitous route that the "most celebrated history" of the Mon in Myanmar has taken, the manuscript is not even an indigenous Myanmar work but taken from Thailand, where it had been written by unknown hands. And when its author "wrote" it, he indicated that he was collating, composing, and restoring the corrupt lettering of a historical work,[83] the version ultimately translated by Halliday. In the text itself, the author refers to having used the *Mahavamsa* and the *Dhatuvamsa,*[84] which is abundantly clear.

The first forty-eight pages of the published and translated work established the standard and mandatory links to the Buddha during the first *kalpa* (cosmic age) when Buddha was Mahasammata, the first king of the world.[85] In a nonlinear narrative that was "interrupted" by many different subjects, events, and individuals, the story moves geographically between Buddha's India and Yangon, until it finally reaches King Asoka's time and his subsequent ascent to *devaloka* (abode of the gods), whereupon Myanmar comes into the picture more prominently.

The *Slapat* also lists the standard seventeen generations of the "kings of Pegu," beginning with Samala and Wimala, who were said to have received the city of Hamsavati from Indra. The list ends with King Tissaraja, the (now) infamous "heretic turned to wrong-doing" who destroyed Buddha images and forbade worship of the Buddha. But a devout maiden refused to be swayed from the worship of the true religion until finally victory was hers with the help of the Buddha. The *Slapat* states that after Tissaraja, "Pegu the city of the Mons became a desolate wilderness . . . [and] became a Burmese province."[86] The latter event is a reference either to the history of the First Pegu Dynasty, after Tabinshwehti of the Toungoo Dynasty took it in 1539, or the Second Pegu/Toungoo Dynasty and its aftermath. It is likely to be the latter, since Tabinshwehti's earlier conquest did not result in the conditions described, while the conquest and destruction of Pegu in 1599 did, when it was burned to the ground and the region became a wasteland for several decades before being reunified by the Second Ava Dynasty of Upper Myanmar. However, the seventeen generations before Pegu has to be fictional, as there is no evidence of any polity or kingdom in Lower Myanmar prior to the late thirteenth century.

The "steadfast Buddhist maiden" sounds as if Queen Shin Saw Bu of Pegu (1453–1472) were the model, while Tissaraja's age of heresy might have been an allusion to the period when the great Hindu Empire of Vijayanagara (fourteenth to seventeenth century) exerted its influence over Lower Myanmar, either directly, via Arakan, or both.[87] Thus, the "dark age" that was said to have followed Tissaraja is probably a reference to the end of the sixteenth and early seventeenth century when Pegu was destroyed. For eyewitness accounts described Lower Myanmar after the 1599 event as a depopulated wasteland without any central authority, ruled by individual warlords, the most famous of whom was the Portuguese adventurer Filipe de Brito y Nicote, also mentioned in the *Slapat* as a major character.[88]

The memory of such devastation in the late sixteenth century probably inspired the eighteenth-century author to use an appropriate Buddhist "dark age" metaphor. To him, a Buddhist monk, periods of disorder and impurity were invariably followed by periods of order and purity. Since the period of order in his view was the rise of Wareru's late thirteenth-century dynasty, a period of disorder had to be created that preceded it; hence, the fictitious seventeen generations from Wimala and Samala to Tissaraja. The *Slapat*'s author had projected backward what was in reality a much later (and remembered) historical period of "darkness" onto an unknown earlier time, thereby making it precede Wareru's period of order and the rise of historical Pegu.

The tradition of Samala and Wimala as founders of Pegu and the seventeen generations of its kings up to Tissaraja probably entered Lower Myanmar, at earliest, only in the sixteenth century, for we find it first in portions of the sixteenth-century *Nidana,* although we do not find it in the 1710 copy of the "Gavampati." Samala and Wimala may also represent the "Indian brothers" in U Kala's and Twinthin's eighteenth-century stories about Thaton.[89] Not only are the brothers said to be traceable to the lists of Chalukya kings and those of Vijayanagara,[90] their legend is not mentioned in Shin Saw Bu's and Dhammazedi's inscriptions, nor in any of the epigraphy of Lower Myanmar. So their myth appears to be a post–First Pegu Dynasty creation that probably emerged only after the fall of the Second Pegu/Toungoo Dynasty in 1599. With the rise of a new dynasty[91] came a new origin myth, this one revealing influences from South India, possibly via Arakan, which in fact destroyed Pegu.

In contrast, the origin myths regarding the "civilizing" of the Mon people (becoming Buddhists) as recorded in Dhammazedi's inscriptions go back mainly to the stories found in the Sinhalese chronicles and the Pali Buddhist texts of Sri Lanka. Great Buddhist kings such as Asoka, Parakramabahu I, and Anawrahta are the models here, while Sona and Uttara and Sirimasoka are also central figures. Neither Wimala and Samala nor Tissaraja are anywhere to be found in records contemporary to the First Pegu Dynasty. Since the *Yazadhiyaza Ayedawpon* was likely composed after Dhammazedi's reign—only after which the Wimala and Samala legend appeared in Myanmar—it also did not contain their account.

In other words, two legendary traditions of Pegu are evident: one clearly Theravada Buddhist and early, that looked toward Upper Myanmar and Buddhist South Asia, and the other Hindu and late, which looked toward South India and Vijayanagara, representative of the Ramannadesa myth and Mon Narrative conflation.

One of the most important features of the *Slapat* is that it was written by a monk whose main interest was the history of the Sandawshin Pagoda (later called the Shwedagon) and the kings (and queen) who patronized it, so that the history of secular rulers per se would have been *only incidental* to the main thrust of the work. In the introduction and at the end, this religious purpose comes out very clearly. As the author put it, this "history of kings was meant to demonstrate the Law of Impermanence, that their power and might, their wealth and grandeur, could not achieve mastery over Death."[92]

Shin Saw Bu, the only woman sovereign in Myanmar's documented history, is a major figure in the *Slapat* and mentioned at length, particularly for her generosity to the Shwedagon Pagoda.[93] So is Dhammazedi, who is given, relatively speaking, a great deal of space in the work for his contributions to the religion and the Shwedagon, whereas Yazadarit, one of the most famous, powerful, and successful kings of the First Pegu Dynasty (at least, in the opinion of both the Burmese chronicles and modern historiography) was not considered such. Instead, his martial abilities were given some attention but not much else. Indeed, in the "Gavampati," he is actually called a demon (*raksa*).[94] In the "Mon Yazawin" he hardly receives one palm leaf of ten lines.

This disregard for such an important historical figure as Yazadarit leads me to conclude that perhaps the Shwedagon Pagoda—which is the centerpiece around which the events and personalities in the *Slapat* pivot—may not have amounted to much during Yazadarit's reign. Not only does the original Shwedagon inscription that commemorates its founding date to the fifteenth century, but the temple was far smaller in its earlier stages (at the time of Yazadarit)—less than a quarter of its current size. Its measurements during Yazadarit's father, Binnya U's, reign was only forty cubits, about seventy-five feet in height, a far cry from today's approximately 360 feet.[95] Had the pagoda been as central to the religion and culture of Lower Myanmar society during Yazadarit's reign, he surely would have donated much more to it. The point here is that the kinds of political events about which secular authors were concerned were simply not as important to the author of the *Slapat.* As for the account on Wareru in the *Slapat,* the putative founder of the first Mon Dynasty in Lower Myanmar and probably where the documentable history of Pegu begins, there is only a long paragraph, half of which is shared by another character.

There is something else regarding the *Slapat* about which the reader should be aware. As stated, the author lived during the mid-eighteenth century, which was a period when Pegu's power had revived after its destruction in 1599, and when it attempted to resurrect the glory days not only of Yazadarit, Shin Saw Bu, and Dhammazedi, but Tabinshwehti and Bayinnaung. The author must have witnessed Pegu's conquest of Ava, ending the Second Ava Dynasty in April of 1752, as well as its short-lived revival, which was to last for only fourteen years before it was once and for all taken by Alaunghpaya in 1757. Note, however, that none of these events led the author to suggest that *ethnicity* was a factor in the history of Pegu's relations with Ava—a Mon-Burman struggle for supremacy, as so often emphasized in colonial historiography. Rather the Buddhist view of impermanence was given the most "agency," around which, his "history" was organized.

Lik Smin Asah

In or about 1825, the *Lik Smin Asah* (The Romance of Prince Asah) was said to have been written. Although the "original Mon version" is lost, its contents were said to have been preserved in Burmese theatrical presentations in the marketplace. These were in verse, so a trader who knew both languages decided to convert the Burmese into Mon. This was then revised by a monk named Nandasara, who put it into better verse. Another person by the name of Nai Ro then "edited" the work further to give it more "clarity." But according to Halliday (who edited the published translation I am using), Nai Ro's editing did not much improve the original; in fact, he added material he thought deserved to be included, and was inconsistent in deciding what to change and keep.

The text is focused on Prince Asah, the son of Samala and nephew of Wimala, said to have founded Pegu and its dynasty at the same time as the Buddha's *parinirvana.* The elder, Samala, and one Vannadevi (sprung from a pumpkin) begets Asah, whose uncle, Wimala, orders Asah's mother to kill him. Instead, she places the child in the mud among the water buffalo, and he is saved by the spirit of the forest who lives nearby, and subsequently entreats and receives Indra's help in the matter.

Asah grows into a man with the water buffalo keepers. He finally emerges as champion of the Mon, the David who defeats Goliath, the giant warrior of the Indians who had the audacity to invade Pegu a second time. The successful defense against that invasion is dated to around the sixth century AD, when most of the Lower Myanmar Delta was probably still not yet formed, and Pegu was eight hundred years away from being mentioned in an original inscription for the first time. Nonetheless, the *Lik Smin Asah* places the Vijayanagara Empire of the fourteenth to seventeenth centuries AD in the same period as the "Burmese of Ava,"[96] which is partially correct. But the main portion of the text seems to be much later than that, as the Wimala and Samala legend itself cannot be found in any of the contemporary sources of the First Pegu Dynasty. The *Yazadhiyaza Ayedawpon* does mention Prince Asah,[97] hence, that portion of the story must have been a later interpolation. As for an invasion, although none by the Vijayanagara Empire can be found in the usual sources, to reiterate, a Persian account did say that Pegu paid tribute to it.[98]

The *Lik Smin Asah* is late, allegorical, didactic, metaphorical, heroic, and just barely historical. The time is certainly ripe for a detailed exegesis by a scholar knowledgeable in both Mon and Burmese and their literature and history.

"Paklat Talaing Chronicle"

Finally, we come to the so-called "Paklat Talaing Chronicle." To reiterate, this is essentially a term by which most (or all) of the above-mentioned sources stitched together haphazardly and published in two volumes in 1910 and 1912 with different titles, are known. They were produced at Pak Lat, a Mon center in Thailand, at the coaxing (and probably financial support) of colonial scholars, administrators, and their cohorts. But the provenances and chronologies of the manuscripts used as a basis for these two published volumes are not entirely unambiguous, and only recently have they been analyzed in any detail, revealing that they have been "edited" rather freely, reflecting contemporary *Thai* sentiments and perspectives.[99] Their value, therefore, is difficult to assess. What I provide below will have to suffice for now.

The original manuscript itself was called "Uppanna Sudhammavati Rajavamsakatha," which, upon publication in 1910 as volume 1, was changed to *Sudhammawati-rajawamsa; Siharajadhiraja-wamsa (Sudhammawati; Gawampati; Rajadhiraj)*.[100] As the changed title shows, two new sections had been added to the original account of Thaton (or Sudhammawati Rajavamsakatha): one on Gavampati (Gawampati), and one on Yazadarit (Rajadhiraj).[101]

The second volume, titled *Nidana Ramadhipati-katha* and published in 1912, is focused on King Dhammazedi (using his formal title, Ramadhipati).[102] H. L. Shorto's original translation of this work has been undergoing new scrutiny in an edition by Christian Bauer.[103] Although the *Nidana* is mainly about Dhammazedi, it also contains a brief account of Thaton particularly its siege and conquest by Anawrahta (probably taken from the 1910 volume), the founding of Pegu, and the legendary "first dynasty." (These components are all found in the "Mon Yazawin" as well, discussed above.) The Thaton account in the *Nidana* is followed by a brief history of Martaban under Wareru, his successors up to Bannya Thau (Shin Saw Bu), much of it likely taken from the *Yazadhiyaza Ayedawpon* and/or the "Mon Yazawin." Halliday states that the sketches in the second volume "differ a good deal from those of the other volume though agreeing with them in the main."[104]

There are other difficulties with these two volumes, not least, their "cut-and-paste" method of compilation. The second volume is said to be particularly difficult to read, as it includes many words not contained in James M. Haswell's Mon "dictionary" of 1874, and whose meanings were not known to many literate Mon people in Myanmar at the time (1912).[105] That might, at first glance, suggest the text can be dated to earlier than 1874.[106] But that view was challenged by W. G. Cooper, who argued that most of the unknown words were actually miscopied ones.[107] In short, the account of Pegu in the "Paklat Talaing Chronicle" has nothing not already found in the other sources discussed above.[108] The subject of the Myanmar Mon chronicles definitely needs a competent (and unbiased) scholar with knowledge of both Burmese and Mon (and perhaps T'ai as well) to untangle properly.

The Buddhist Sources: *Vamsadipani* and *Sasanavamsa*

Apart from the above "secular" sources, there is another genre of literature that is religious. It does not necessarily represent any ethnic group or region of the country, but can reflect a certain "school" of Theravada Buddhism or "sect," which warrants some discussion. The *Vamsadipani* was written in 1799 in Burmese—itself important—by the Mehti Sayadaw (a Vinaya jurist), while the *Sasanavamsa* was written in 1861 in Pali by Pannasami, during the reign of King Mindon.[109] Both are of the *thathanawin* genre (literally, "religious lineage"), thought to go back to a Buddhist literary tradition in Sri Lanka of the twelfth and thirteenth centuries.[110] In contrast is, of course, the *yazawin* tradition (royal lineage) on which most historians have been dependent. Although the former genre of literature privileges religious history in general, their perspective and data can be important nevertheless. They provide some insight into Pegu's rise, development, and decline from a religious perspective. At the same time, these religious histories also depend on "secular" *yazawin* for keeping their chronology straight, although there are anachronisms in them.

One of the interesting features of the *Vamsadipani* (especially when compared with the *Sasanavamsa*) with regard to Pegu's history is that although it mentions most of its important male sovereigns, it totally ignores Shin Saw Bu even though she was a stalwart devotee of the religion. The *Vamsadipani* also includes the story of the usual "founding" heroes (Wimala, Samala, Wareru), and the usual "destroying" villains (Tissaraja, Manuha)[111] that one finds in various works including the mid-eighteenth-century *Slapat*. The origin stories are still laced with "marriages" between demons and humans, metaphor for nonbelievers "seeing the light" with the advent of Theravada Buddhism. One also finds the Shin Arahan and Anawrahta story and their collusion in the conquest of Thaton (obviously taken from U Kala's *Mahayazawingyi* and not found in the *Slapat*). As expected, the *Vamsadipani* is focused on religious justifications for the conquest, but with a twist: the monks of Thaton were "respectfully invited and led back" to more orthodox Pagan,[112] reminiscent of the narrative about the same event in the fourteenth-century sections of the *Maniyadanabon*.

The *Sasanavamsa*, on the other hand, is importantly different.[113] There is not a word about the founding of the kingdom of Pegu with Wimala, Samala, Prince

Asah, the steadfast maiden, and Wareru (although Muttama itself is mentioned).[114] Rather, it focuses on Thaton and its religious development at the hands of Sona and Uttara, missionaries from the Third Council of Asoka, accounts taken from the *Dipavamsa* about the conversion of Suvannabhumi and repeated by King Dhammazedi in his Kalyani Inscriptions of the fifteenth century. This reflects a bias for, and the influence of, the Mahavihara "school" of Sri Lanka and the Pali sources, not those of South India and Lower Myanmar.

But even in the *Sasanavamsa,* the integration between demons and Buddhism is a trope. It is what turned Thaton from barbarism to civilization. (Sometimes, a society "of hunters and fishermen" is the phrase used to connote uncivilized, pre-believer status.) The convention found in U Kala about the conquest of Thaton by Anawrahta is turned around: the king *brings down* to Thaton the orthodox texts, a north–south movement of "civilizing," a direction that, incidentally, is archaeologically, epigraphically, and historically correct. By the time the *Sasanavamsa* mentions Pegu, it speaks only of King Dhammazedi's reign and his famous religious reform, although a "chief queen" of Muttama is mentioned as patron of two famous monks linked to Lower Myanmar's orthodoxy. (Those two monks are probably Dhammazedi and his colleague who rescued Shin Saw Bu from Ava, a story to be more fully told in a subsequent chapter.)

Part of the reason for the differences between the *Sasanavamsa* and the *Vamsadipani* may have to do with subtle tensions concerning the orthodoxy of contesting lineages of the *sangha* in the kingdom as perceived by their authors at the time the works were written: one in 1799 under King Bodawhpaya, and the other under King Mindon in the mid-1860s, both of whose capitals were centered in Upper Myanmar. And although of the same dynasty, the two kings likely patronized one of two major sects then current, each claiming the most direct and purest lineage. Another reason for their differences appears to be the audience each author wished to address. Thus, Lower Myanmar texts of a folksy nature, such as the *Lik Smin Asah,* were clearly not part of the Pali universe to which the author of the *Sasanavamsa* belonged. In contrast, the *Vamsadipani* (written in the vernacular) included such stories, suggesting that the author deliberately wanted to address the non-elite and was aware of the prevailing literature in parts of the kingdom outside his immediate intellectual circles and sociocultural universe. Or, perhaps the author of the *Vamsadipani* knew Lower Myanmar's literature better, read the Mon language (or had access to the translations of Mon works such as the *Lik Smin Asah* and *Slapat*), and was more attuned to things "secular" and the common people than was the author of the *Sasanavamsa.*

Miscellaneous Contemporary European Sources

There are about five firsthand European accounts of the First Pegu Dynasty that I have used. These are the records of Nicolo di Conti, Athanasius Niktin, Ludovico di Varthema, Hieronymo Santo Stefano, and Lewes Vertonmannus. Each varies in historical value and has a particular perspective, although those who stayed longer in Pegu, as one would expect, generally have accounts that are fuller. The merchant of Venice, di Conti, who was also at Ava, had little to say. The Russian, Niktin, followed di Conti nearly half a century later and had a bit more to say, as did Santo Stefano, a Genoese, who also stayed relatively long. The last two were both there during the reign of Bannya Ram, Dhammazedi's successor, as was Varthema, a Bolognese. Lewes Vertonmannus visited Tenasserim about 1503–1504 during the reign of Bannya Ram, of whom he had some kind things to say. But as none of their accounts deals with the origins of Pegu, they will be used where applicable—that is, mainly during the last reign of the First Pegu Dynasty.

Finally, I have used secondary material written in English, but mainly to analyze the "lineage" and evolution of historical writing on the First Pegu Dynasty by modern historians. These amount to about a half dozen works, particularly those of Phayre and Harvey and some of the material on which they depended. Other later secondary sources, such as D. G. E. Hall's *Burma* and Htin Aung's *History of Burma* are also part of that historiography. These English-language sources are particularly useful for demonstrating how hopelessly mired they were in the colonial myths that surrounded Pegu and Lower Myanmar, not to mention their privileging of the Second Pegu/Toungoo Dynasty under Tabinshwehti and Bayinnaung (the sixteenth century) rather than that of Shin Saw Bu and Dhammazedi (the fifteenth century), since the former was far more politically and military accomplished and spectacular than the latter—precisely a reason for my writing part 2.

Conclusion

Compared to the Burmese-language sources for Ava, the Mon sources for Pegu are desperately wanting, in terms of both quantity and quality. The Kingdom of Pegu erected approximately one-seventh the number of epigraphs as the Kingdom of Ava, while producing, at most, two texts of a rather parochial (biographical) nature without any "national" breadth or depth. All other Mon-language texts are late and of a hagiographic nature. In other words, there simply is no comparison between the historiographic traditions of Ava and Pegu, a conclusion that may not sit well with some but must be seriously acknowledged. Nonetheless, those are the "cards" we are dealt, and so must use them as best as we can. Similarly, the indigenous religious texts: although their's is less a regional difference, they had clear biases nonetheless of a religious nature. The European texts have their unique perspectives as well but, on the whole, are factual and without the kinds of subtle biases we are most concerned with. However flawed, all are necessary for the reconstruction of the First Pegu Dynasty and kingdom. The narrative reconstructed in the ensuing chapters, therefore, must be regarded in the context of the nature of the available sources on the Kingdom of Pegu.

11

The Origins of Pegu and Its Founding Fathers

The rise of Pegu in the latter half of the thirteenth century was likely shaped by several "push" and "pull" factors then important in the region. These were long-term patterns that occurred between the eleventh and sixteenth centuries in Southeast Asia, some of which came together only during the second half of the thirteenth century (rather than earlier or later), creating a "conjuncture," in Fernand Braudel's sense, with direct and indirect effects on the making of Pegu.

To the north, of course, was Pagan, whose decline and weakened hold on Lower Myanmar at the end of the thirteenth century allowed it to strike out for independence. On the west of the "new Teng-lung kingdom" was the maritime region of Arakan, inhabited by Arakanese (essentially Burmese) speakers, more often than not controlled by the interior, but increasing its gaze toward both the Bay of Bengal and the interior of Upper Myanmar. Although Arakan had not yet fully integrated the various components that came together subsequently in the sixteenth century as the Kingdom of Mrauk-U, its underpinning maritime and commercial ingredients were already there and operating, which were to affect the history of Pegu subsequently. On the other side of the Gulf of Muttama lay Ayuthaya, dominated by T'ai speakers who had moved from their earlier centers in central Thailand and the agrarian interior to the increasingly blossoming commerce of the coasts. This process was also to have an impact on the rise and development of Pegu.

Toward the south lay many port cities such as Htaway (Tavoy) and Myeik (Mergui) that acted as windows to Pegu's external world. Although Sri Vijaya had long declined in influence and power, its memory and legacy (if not also some of its descendants), had already begun the process of reconstituting itself on the other side of the Straits, first at Temasek, then at Melaka,[1] to become, subsequently, one of the epicenters of maritime commerce in Southeast Asia.

The late thirteenth century was also the period when Islam, closely tied to trade, had been establishing beachheads in parts of Island Southeast Asia such as northern Sumatra, and had begun to make its influence felt in the interior areas, subsequently penetrating as far east as Brunei, Trengganu, and East Java. But as far as Lower Myanmar is concerned, there is little evidence of Islam's direct role in its development at this time, although its influence on Arakan later and the whole of maritime Southeast Asia, is, of course, a most important one.

The late thirteenth and early fourteenth centuries also witnessed the Yuan (Mongol) Dynasty being replaced by the Ming in China, perhaps the greatest maritime power of this age and the next, whose presence in and penetration of Southeast Asian waters was one of the principal factors in bringing about the origins of the Age of Commerce that was to follow a century later.[2] The great empire of Vijayanagara in South India was another rapidly rising power during this time, which would subsequently make, if it had not already made, a significant impact on the commercial and cultural development of maritime Myanmar and Southeast Asia via the Bay of Bengal.[3] Other areas in South and Southeast Asia during the late thirteenth century saw maritime development as well, and surely others about which we are unaware.

Farther east was the synthesis of maritime and inland forces that had materialized in Dai Viet, the "classical" state of Vietnam. Traditional Southeast Asian studies, in the United States and most Western countries, have not conventionally considered Dai Viet a maritime, but a mainland state. More recent research has shown, however, that at its height it was probably as much a maritime polity as it was an inland agrarian one,[4] another "hybrid state" with direct maritime (and overland) links to China, other parts of Southeast Asia, India, and the Mediterranean, while still very much in control of the upstream agricultural resources of the Red River.[5]

Similarly, although the earlier polity in central Java that we call "Early Martaram" appears to have been mainly agrarian initially, by the time its successor in Majapahit emerged and developed in East Java, it too appears to have become (or was rapidly becoming) more like later Dai Viet and Ayuthaya: a hybrid, with one foot in agriculture and another in trade, to the extent that it (Majapahit) became a force to contend with in the seas where Sri Vijaya-Jambi was once dominant.

Despite this growth in the late thirteenth and early fourteenth centuries in the coastal areas of Southeast Asia, historians of early Southeast Asia (particularly those of us enamored with the "mainland" states) have tended to lament this period as a depressed one, since it was thought to have ushered in the "decline" of the great "classical states." Yet, if one regards decline as change, per se, then this age can also be interpreted as one of birth or rebirth. Ava, Pegu, Ayuthaya, Dai Viet, and Melaka, among others, all rose during this period, so that it was characterized as much by "birth" and "rebirth" as it was by "decline" and "death." That makes it a bit more palatable (for some of us) to accept the decline of the great inland agrarian kingdoms as part of a process that generated the birth of newer kingdoms and, in Myanmar, the rebirth and continuation of old societies.

Somewhat earlier in central and mainland Southeast Asia itself, the Mon speakers—longtime inhabitants of what is now Thailand—had been pushed in different directions from what scholars think were their homelands of Dvaravati and Haripunjaya by the migration of T'ai speakers. One of the places they moved to (from Haripunjaya, but apparently not from Dvaravati) was west into Lower Myanmar. Other "push" factors included conflicts with the Khmers of Angkor and deadly outbreaks of disease thought to have affected Haripunjaya.

By the late eleventh century, a large number of Mon speakers had probably settled in Lower Myanmar. For the first time, inscriptions written in Old Mon and erected by Upper Myanmar king Kyanzittha are found there, celebrating his expansion into the heart of Lower Myanmar. The earliest of these is dated to 1093, suggesting that there was likely a sizeable number of Mon speakers already inhabiting the region by that time; why else would he use the language? And by the very early twelfth century (perhaps 1102 AD), Mon speakers were mentioned at Pagan for the first time participating in state ceremonies of integration.

Along with the "push" factors were also "pull" factors. The Kingdom of Pagan had been growing steadily since the ninth century: ideologically, militarily, politically, and economically. Its economic growth expanded during the eleventh century, accelerating after the twelfth and thirteenth centuries, stimulated by the booming temple-construction industry, which not only increased the population of skilled craftsmen but ultimately also the general population of Pagan. This directly enhanced the increase and development of new agricultural lands, the economic basis for the Kingdom of Pagan. And although the continuous demand for labor was met initially by conquest, economic and social incentives soon replaced it with voluntary emigration.

Good, well-irrigated land was given to those who became crown cultivators, and tax and corvee exemptions were granted as incentives to those who worked for the religion, while relatively high salaries were given to skilled craftsmen. Labor in Pagan was paid, normally in cash (silver, gold, copper, and perhaps lead) as well as kind (*padi*, rights to *padi*, horses, elephants, boats, draught animals, and other such valuables). Pagan's temple-construction industry was also socioculturally important (and attractive), which, along with jobs, became additional magnets not only for the recruitment of new people to Upper Myanmar but also for their retention.

One of the routes to Pagan from other places in the region was via Lower Myanmar, so that the latter, once a frontier region of few people, had become, by the twelfth and thirteenth centuries, a staging area for the movement of people farther upriver and inland, or alternatively, for their own settlement on the coasts, working in trade and commerce. Both the "push" and "pull" factors had turned the once sparsely populated frontier area of Lower Myanmar into a demographically (and hence, economically) viable and vibrant region.

These long-term patterns were affected by more short-term, immediate events. In or about 1281, the T'ai "kingdom" of Lanna led by King Mangrai conquered what was probably the last major center of the Mon in Thailand, Haripunjaya. This surely led to another large migration of Mon speakers into Lower Myanmar, where there was already a sociocultural network of communities with a similar culture speaking the same language to welcome them. If so, that event may have finally enabled the Mon speakers of Lower Myanmar, now with the requisite demographic "critical mass," to forge a polity of their own shortly thereafter in Muttama.

Helping that development was Pagan's losing its hold on the coastal areas of Lower Myanmar, in large part caused by long-term structural problems inherent in its system, already discussed in part 1. More immediately, it also had to do with the first two Mongol invasions of Upper Myanmar, which occurred during the last several decades of the thirteenth century. Although neither one was successful, the Mongols' destabilizing presence and frightful image nevertheless exacerbated and accelerated the internal, structural weaknesses of Pagan, which in turn had a direct impact on the making of Pegu. And it is to this first, independent kingdom in Lower Myanmar, the "new Teng-lung kingdom" of the Chinese, that we now turn.

Wareru, Muttama, and the "New Teng-lung Kingdom": The First Phase

Both remote and immediate factors helped shape the rise of the first independent dynasty of Lower Myanmar, known in local sources as the Wareru Dynasty, said to be founded in 1287 by one Magadu, also known by his regnal names of Wagaru, Wareru, Waru, and Warow. The dynasty and the "kingdom" he created grew powerful and confident enough that in a little more than a decade, in 1298, it sought and obtained recognition from China as an independent polity in Southeast Asia. Called the "new Teng-lung kingdom" by the Chinese, it was centered at Muttama (Martaban), a city built earlier as part of Pagan's administrative apparatus when it expanded to the coasts in the late twelfth century.

Although Pagan was not entirely effete in Lower Myanmar—quelling a rebellion there as late as 1296—it was clearly on a downward spiral, on which Muttama and Lower Myanmar in general capitalized. Around the time that Muttama received recognition from China as an independent kingdom, Ram Kamhaeng, the king of Sukhotai, had died, leaving the kingdom without strong leadership and releasing some pressure from that direction on Muttama. Two years later, Upper Myanmar (for the third time) was invaded by the Mongols, and although this raid was also unsuccessful, it nonetheless contributed to Pagan's continued decentralization for several more decades. All these factors allowed the untrammeled growth of an independent Lower Myanmar in the late thirteenth and early fourteenth centuries.

MAGADU: "FOUNDER" OF THE FIRST PEGU DYNASTY

Much of the story concerning Magadu comes from the *Yazadhiyaza Ayedawpon.* It begins with the standard legitimating devices and obligatory links to the Buddha and (in this case, instead of Ananda) the Arahant Gavampati. Immediately thereafter, the *Ayedawpon* turns to Muttama, which was, it claims, founded by King Narapatisithu of Pagan.[6] After building it, the king left a *myosa* (governor) by the name of Aleinmma and returned to Pagan. Thus, the earliest extant history of the Mon in Myanmar whose original source is thought to have been Mon attributes the founding of their first political center in the country to a Burmese king of Pagan, a statement significant in itself.

The account in the *Yazadhiyaza Ayedawpon* about Muttama's rise is corroborated by the best contemporary and original inscriptions we have. Not only does Muttama as a place-name first appear in Old Burmese in an original inscription of 1176, during Narapatisithu's reign (1173–1210), its emergence also coincides with the chronology and extent of Pagan's expansion into, and pacification of, Lower Myanmar. The expansion begun earlier in the mid-eleventh century by his predecessors Aniruddha, Kyanzittha, and Alaungsithu, by Narapatisithu's reign Pagan had reached the Tenasserim Peninsular as far as Mergui, the southernmost major city of present-day Myanmar.

It is also precisely during the same period (1298 to be exact) that the Yuan source noted in the previous chapter called the *Zhi-yuan Zhengmian Lu* reported the presence of a "new Teng-lung kingdom" in Lower Myanmar *for the first time.* Muttama had sent an embassy to China requesting recognition, thereby attesting that it was by then independent of (or seeking independence from) Pagan. That Muttama as a toponym in the Mon language does not appear until the early fourteenth century, around the same time that Pegu began to emerge as a discreet Lower Myanmar kingdom, also attests to the general chronology of its development.

The *Yazadhiyaza Ayedawpon* then switches from these mainly historical accounts to Buddhist legitimation once again, this time, in the form of a Buddha prophecy. It states that at the place where Muttama was built resided a demon by the name of Sumana,[7] who at first wanted to battle the Buddha. Eventually, however, the demon "saw the light" and provided for the Buddha's needs, and treated him with courtesy and respect. The Buddha then prophesied that in time, the demon, after changing his nature and becoming human, would take the name Magadu and become lord of the white elephant at a place called Takawwun.

Thus, the story of Muttama and Sumana receiving the all-important Buddha prophecy—a prerequisite for any legitimate Buddhist capital and its dynasty—was clearly an allegory for the conversion of the Lower Myanmar inhabitants to Theravada Buddhism. At the same time, it generally corresponds to what we know about the development of Muttama and Lower Myanmar: there simply is no evidence of an independent kingdom or polity in Lower Myanmar until Magadu's.

The *Yazadhiyaza Ayedawpon*'s statement about this transformation from "demonhood" to "humanity" was probably not new, and appears to have been already part of an earlier written tradition. There are two Old Mon inscriptions, called the Trap and Pandit, now located at Thaton and most likely erected in the fourteenth century during King Yazadarit's reign. They refer to a Raksa Pura (City of Demons) along with the name of a king that is extremely close to Magadu (or Makata, his brother), so that this Raksa Pura is surely a reference to Muttama rather than Thaton, as convention has it. (Thaton did not yet exist in epigraphy or archaeology, while the Raksa, likely a reference to Magadu, could also be to Yazadarit, who reigned later.)[8]

Subsequently, King Dhammazedi of Pegu, a successor of Yazadarit, continued this notion of transformation from nonbeliever to believer status using demon-hood as metaphor.[9] But he did not attribute it to Magadu, mainly because the latter did not yet exist in the country's historiography: the *Yazadhiyaza Ayedawpon* where Magadu first appears had not yet been compiled. In that transformation from demon-hood to humanity, which Dhammazedi attributes to all of Lower Myanmar, he considers Asoka, Parakramabahu I, and Anawrahta to be primary agents. In particular, Dhammazedi used the story of Sona and Uttara's mission from the Third Buddhist Council of Asoka to Suvannabhumi to effect that transformation from demon-hood to humanity.

By 1710, the Mon text called the "Gavampati," described in the previous chapter,[10] continued the tradition of the *Yazadhiyaza Ayedawpon,* wherein Magadu's demon origins were not yet forgotten. But by the time the celebrated *Slapat* was written in the mid-eighteenth century, Magadu was no longer a demon. It records that "King Warow . . . had become lord of a white elephant and was king over in Martaban."[11] Thus, sometime between the early and mid-eighteenth century, when Lower Myanmar (for the second time) rose to prominence briefly (between 1740 and 1754), Magadu's demon origins had been expunged from the Mon records. Perhaps by then also the Mon of Lower Myanmar had been Theravada Buddhists long enough that they no longer needed any such legitimation myths.

In the *Zinme Yazawin* (Chronicle of Chiang Mai) and the *Yazadhiyaza Ayedawpon,* the "dynasty" of Muttama began with a union between Magadu of Lower Myanmar and the daughter of the "king of Sukhotai." Although the former chronicle was written in Myanmar in Burmese, it "privileged" the Siamese perspective nonetheless by making King Mangrai demand and receive a princess from Lower Myanmar rather than the other way around (where Magadu eloped with the daughter of the king of Sukhotai).[12] There is, of course, not a hint of his "demon" origins; rather, the focus was on Chiang Mai and King Mangrai's role in providing Pegu with royal stock.

In the *Yodaya Yazawin* (Chronicle of Ayuthaya), written in Burmese in Myanmar, with a copying date of 1845, the Magadu story is also too close to the one found in the *Yazadhiyaza Ayedawpon* to be coincidental. And here as well, his demon status had long been expunged. He is referred to as "a native of Takawwun village in Mottama township and of Mon lineage."[13] In fact, with the exception of his demon origins, the entire account of Magadu in the *Yodaya Yazawin* appears to have followed the *Yazadhiyaza Ayedawpon.*

What is interesting is that the *Yodaya Yazawin,* meant to be a history of Ayuthaya, included Magadu's story at all. Why is he even a part of Ayuthaya's narrative? The reason, I think, is the close relationship that might have existed between Phra Ruang, king of Sukhotai at the time, and Magadu, his son-in-law by elopement (?). But there must have been some assumption on the part of the authors of the *Yodaya Yazawin* that Muttama (as well as Sukhotai) were part of Ayuthaya's origins and (subsequent) dominions, and therefore, their early history and "kings" were linked. It seems as if the writers of the *Yodaya Yazawin* had the *Yazadhiyaza Ayedawpon* in front of them.

By the time Phayre published his history in 1883, Magadu's demon origins had been totally forgotten, and he was now a full-fledged human and founder of the first Mon dynasty of Lower Myanmar. The probable reason Phayre did not mention Magadu's demon status was that he might not have used the *Yazadhiyaza Ayedawpon,* and although he did admit that he used the *Slapat,* Magadu's demon status had been expunged in that text by then. Harvey, however, did list the *Yazadhiyaza Ayedawpon* in his bibliography, although his work also failed to mention Magadu's demon origins, perhaps because he considered it "superstition" and not history. He also seemed to have preferred the "Paklat Talaing Chronicle," in which Magadu's supernatural origins had long been expunged.

When Magadu reached a certain age, continued the *Yazadhiyaza Ayedawpon,* he became the merchant leader of about thirty others who traded with Sukhotai. On his journey there, another omen appeared, which was interpreted by a sage that Magadu would leave commerce and become a king within the year. At Sukhotai, he was promoted to keeper of the royal elephants for the king, rising fairly high in the system. He also fell in love with the king's daughter, and while the king was away fighting the "Java Kalas" (Java South Asians, or Java Indians), apparently on the coastal areas of what is now Thailand, Magadu eloped with his daughter and, with a load of gold and silver, many retainers and warriors, went back to Takawwun, his hometown in Lower Myanmar. There, Magadu was said to have treated his people well. (This part of Magadu's story appears nearly verbatim in the *Yodaya Yazawin,* and, after the death of Phra Ruang, Magadu's story also ends.)[14] (The elopement story is found in some of the northern T'ai chronicles written in or around the early sixteenth century, so it should be considered a trope for certain kinds of events rather than historical.)

As his power grew—in part probably as a result of Mon refugees migrating from Haripunjaya around 1281 when it was conquered by T'ai king Mangrai—Magadu planned to take Muttama and oust its governor, a descendant of King Narapatisithu's original appointee. By cleverly manipulating the governor's carnal desires for his own beautiful sister, Magadu established closer contacts with him, eventually killing him. Again, the details of the story itself may or may not be historical; the author might have been making a statement about *tanha* (desire).

The *Yazadhiyaza Ayedawpon* gives *sakkaraj* 643 (1281) as the date Magadu seized Muttama and killed its governor, the same date as the conquest of Haripunjaya by Mangrai.[15] This is corroborated by U Kala[16] and the much later *Hmannan,* which had one sentence on "Wariru": that he killed Aleinma in *sakkaraj* 643 (1281 AD).[17] Twinthin's *Yazawinthit,* however, dates the event to 1284,[18] the year the Mongols first invaded the Pagan kingdom. The latter date makes more sense, since the flight of refugees from Haripunjaya in 1281 would have needed some time to have an effect on the demographic (hence, political) situation in Lower Myanmar. Also, since Pagan would have been preoccupied with the Mongols in 1284, it would have created the opportunity for Magadu to seize Muttama and declare its independence from Upper Myanmar without repercussions. Indeed, as noted, between 1284 and about 1289, not a single religious donation was recorded at Pagan, suggesting a period of crisis at the capital.

Magadu subsequently consecrated Muttama as a proper royal city with the seven requisites, implying that it alone was the legitimate center of Lower Myanmar. Part of the ritual included erecting the "auspicious posts" of the city; under each, a pregnant woman was said to have been crushed,[19] a practice that only in nineteenth-century Upper Myanmar came to be known as the *myosade.* The *Yazadhiyaza Ayedawpon* states that her stomach burst when one of the city's posts was dropped on it, releasing eight snakes, seven of which died immediately, while one moved to the west and died there. That omen was read by the wise men, who declared that this dynasty would have eight kings, seven of whom would die in the city while the last one would go west and rule from there, "foretelling" the move to Pegu by Magadu's dynasty.

On his ascension at Muttama, Magadu adopted the regnal name of Waru, short for Suwaru, "descended from the sky," but most popularly known as Wareru. The *Yazadhiyaza Ayedawpon* claims that during that same year, Wareru was said to have ordered the compilation of the famous code of civil law called the "Waru Dhammathat," ostensibly written in Mon by a group of learned men.[20] (There are many problems with this assertion, discussed below.) Without explaining how one ascribes a particular ethnicity to demons, the *Ayedawpon* then claimed that Wareru's father was Mon.[21] In T'ai sources, his ethnic background is more ambiguous: he is sometimes Shan and sometimes Mon. There may have been good political reasons for claiming that he was Shan by T'ai speakers, and equally good reasons for the *Yazadhiyaza Ayedawpon* making him Mon.

Although Magadu's ethnic background, either as allegory or as history, is not an issue in the origins of Pegu, colonial historians have tended to prefer his Shan ancestry. Phayre wrote that he was "a merchant of [Shan] race [who] acquired wealth and authority." Harvey wrote that he was a "Shan pedlar [*sic*] born at Donwun in Thaton district, [who] took service in the elephant stables of the chief of Sukhotai . . . became Captain of the Guard, [and subsequently] eloped with the chief's daughter and some kindred spirits from the Guard, [to] . . . set up at his native village."[22] And since D. G. E. Hall based much of his indigenous precolonial history of Myanmar on both Phayre and Harvey's works, it is not surprising to find these accounts also repeated in his *Burma.* In a chapter titled "The Mon Hegemony," the account of Wareru is nearly a verbatim of Harvey's. It stated that Wareru "is said to have been a Shan pedlar born at Donwun in Thaton district. He took service with the ruler of Sukhotai, became Captain of the Guard, eloped with his chief's daughter and ran away to seek his fortune in Myanmar."[23]

Pagan had governors administering parts of Lower Myanmar since the mid-eleventh century, so that while Wareru had wrested Muttama away from the Pagan-appointed governor by the late thirteenth century, according to the *Yazadhiyaza Ayedawpon,* the Burmese chronicles, and the *Slapat,* Pegu was still governed by a Pagan governor named Tayaphya. The *Slapat* recorded that Tayaphya was the third generation of governors originally sent from Pagan, successor to "Akhamaman" and "Kakkhaya."[24] (The chronology suggested by the *Slapat* is consistent with the first unequivocal mention in epigraphs of Pegu as a city by then.) By the last several years of the 1280s, however, both Tayaphya and Wareru, probably aware of Pagan's problems with the Mongols, and anticipating that Pagan would not send troops down to Lower Myanmar for minor reasons, formed a marriage alliance whereby they exchanged daughters and made them their respective consorts.

However, that strike for autonomy by Tayaphya in allying with Wareru triggered an unexpected military response from Pagan. According to the *Yazadhiyaza Ayedawpon,* King Narathihapade of Pagan sent minister Yazathingyan with an army to quell it.[25] The Burmese chronicles claim this punitive mission occurred around 1287, during the last year of King Narathihapade's reign. The nineteenth-century *Hmannan* records it as a successful event, whereby Muttama once again fell under Pagan's control but was left under a local governor, perhaps Wareru, since other sources state that Wareru continued to rule. Indeed, Wareru's retention of his position at Muttama may be the outcome of a divide-and-rule policy by Pagan to split up the two, for soon, Tayaphya and Wareru were fighting each other.

Tayaphya is said to have made use of *kala bayingyi* ("Indian" or "South Asian feringi") musketeers against Wareru (although the statement is probably an anachronism, as both the term "feringi" and the presence of firearms may be too early for the date of the events claimed). But he was unsuccessful, and Wareru captured him. His life was spared, however, since Tayaphya was, after all, father of one of Wareru's wives. Instead Tayaphya was taken to Muttama, while his fief, Pegu, was placed under a governor who was a vassal of Sukhotai's king, suggesting that perhaps the latter was also involved in these events. The *Yazadhiyaza Ayedawpon*'s account appears to be historical, especially since the Ram Kamhaeng inscription of 1292 claimed Pegu (Hansabati) as one of its vassal cities.[26]

Subsequently, Tayaphya made another unsuccessful attempt on Wareru's life, so was finally executed, following a rather dramatic scene. His queen, Wareru's daughter, tied her hair to Tayaphya's, challenging the executioner to carry out his duties. After some surgical separation of the two, Tayaphya was finally killed without harming a strand of the daughter's hair. The interesting thing about this story is that whereas the *Yazadhiyaza Ayedawpon* was quite matter-of-fact about the relationship between Wareru and Tayaphya, the *Slapat,* written much later, and by a Mon monk with certain didactic purposes in mind (and also perhaps some ethnic identity issues), turned it into a fight between Wareru's (Mon) compassion and honor against Tayaphya's (Burmese) treachery and dishonor.

In 1293, the Buddha's prophecy that Sumana, the demon, will one day become "lord of the white elephant" was realized when the king of Sukhotai sent Wareru a white elephant, legitimating his role as a *cakkavatti.* When Wareru received such recognition from the king of Sukhotai, King Kyawswa of Pagan, son and successor of Narathihapade, must have regarded it as a challenge to his authority and sphere of influence. He sent a force down in 1296 to "quell rebellion" in the region around Dala. The general leading that force, Anantajeyyapikram, returned to Pagan after retaking Dala and erected an inscription in Pagan to commemorate his victory and announce his subsequent religious donation, whose costs were financed by his "reward from battle" he received from the king.[27]

But Muttama itself was apparently not taken,[28] for, as shown above, in 1298 Wareru and his kingdom received formal recognition from China as an independent "new Teng-lung kingdom." Pagan, by then, probably could not do much, as it was once again (and for the third time) being harassed by the Mongols. That allowed Lower Myanmar to strike out for autonomy once and for all and finally rid itself of Upper Myanmar control.

Wareru was said to have been murdered in 1301 by Tayaphya's sons (his own grandsons) while he was in the toilet. The *Yazadhiyaza Ayedawpon* gives this eulogy: he ascended the throne at age thirty-nine, reigned for twenty-two years, and died at the age of sixty-one. It then stated in verse (which rhymed in Burmese), "Do not leave the roots behind when you cut down rattan cane and do not keep the son near you when you have killed his father."[29] The grandsons who assassinated Wareru did not succeed to the throne, for the ministers hunted them down and had them killed. The judgment of the *Ayedawpon* regarding Wareru as king was favorable, saying that he "ruled with justice and brought benefits to this people."[30]

THE PROBLEM OF THE *WAGARU DHAMMATHAT*

One of the earliest sources attributed to the thirteenth century and the beginning of the First Pegu Dynasty is the *Wagaru Dhammathat.* The long-held convention in Myanmar studies is that it was compiled during Wareru's reign in the late thirteenth century, while his capital was still at Muttama. It was considered by at least two historians to be "the earliest surviving lawbook in Burma," making it Wareru's "chief monument today. . . . The collection was made at [his] command, by monks from the writings of earlier Mon scholars preserved in the monasteries of his kingdom."[31]

These statements, made by Harvey and Hall, were not based on original research but on Emil Forchhammer's assessment of that *Dhammathat.* He had published a work titled *King Wagaru's Manu Dhammasattham. Text, Translation, and Notes* in 1885, based on a copy of a manuscript by that name dated to 1707 and written in Pali-Burmese *nissaya.*[32] (In effect, the latter is a running translation, where each phrase in Pali is followed by one in Burmese.) The first part of Forchhammer's publication is an English translation of the manuscript, followed by the actual text.

The contention by Forchhammer here was that written, codified civil law in the country began with Wagaru. If true, this manuscript should be admissible as evidence to reconstruct his dynasty's legal system, or at least describe its laws. But a closer analysis of its only surviving copy compels us to be more cautious and reject it as a thirteenth-century product.

First, it is not clear what the provenance of this manuscript really is. Its ending paragraph (196), which normally describes the particulars regarding the text, is not unambiguous. Forchhammer's English translation of that paragraph states, "I, Thera Buddhaghosa by name, being desirous of promoting the interests of the religion, shall proceed carefully, according to the letter or as handed down, to translate King Wagaru's dhammathat from the Talaing language into Burmese.... The transcribing of King Waru's Dhammathat was finished before sunset on Tuesday, the 6th of the waxing moon Thadingyut, in the year 1069 (B.E. = 1707 A.D.)."[33] This sounds as if one person, Buddhaghosa, were doing the translating and transcribing.

Christian Lammerts, who wrote his PhD on the Burmese *dhammathats* at Cornell, read the same Pali sections of the *nissaya* for me in the following manner: "I, [Buddhaghosa by name], desiring the prosperity of the Sasana, shall translate into Brahma-*bhasa,* without faults [by the letters], the *dhammasat* of King Varu, *which was written* [by Buddhaghosa] *in Ramanna-bhasa* [my emphases]."[34]

This reading creates several problems regarding Forchhammer's interpretation. First, it suggests *two* persons, at least one of them named Buddhaghosa (if not both) were involved: one who wrote the Varu's *Dhammathat* (presumably) earlier, and one who did the translation into Brahma-*bhasa.* Lammerts' reading of the Pali-Burmese text separates the "dhammasat of King Varu" *written* [by Buddhaghosa] "in Ramanna-bhasa" from the one that was *translated* by another Buddhaghosa. Forchhammer's version has only *one* person doing both the translating and the transcribing, all in 1707, not distinguishing between them. (The presence of more than one Buddhaghosa poses no problems; it is a common title for accomplished monks in Myanmar.)[35]

A second problem that needs further analysis is that neither the terms "Talaing" nor "Burmese" used by Forchhammer is contained in the manuscript itself; only Ramanna-*bhasa* and Brahma-*bhasa,* as Lammerts has it. Forchhammer had substituted the word "Talaing" for the term "Ramanna-*bhasa,*" clearly because the word "Talaing" was the convention of his day for the Mon language and people, even if etymologically and historically incorrect. The problem arises, however, when he also substitutes the word "Burmese" for "Brahma-*bhasa,*" so that the whole sentence is interpreted to mean that the manuscript was being translated *from* the Ramanna language *into* Burmese.[36]

Literally, however, Brahma-*bhasa* means "Brahma language" and is not ordinarily a reference to Burmese, as confirmed by a well-known scholar of Burmese,[37] but to Sanskrit/Pali. Notwithstanding, and regardless of what "Brahma-*bhasa*" means, because we have the end product in hand, we know what the translator meant by Brahma-*bhasa:* it was *not* a reference to Burmese only but to the Pali-Burmese *nissaya* of the text.

Besides, the Burmese part of the *nissaya* in paragraph 196 does not say the manuscript was translated *from* Ramanna-*bhasa into* Brahma-*bhasa.* Rather, it states that "by means of [*phyin*] the Ramanna language" and "by means of [*phyin*] the Brahma language, I, Buddhaghosa by name... shall perform it [*pyu pay*]." If by "performing it" he meant translation, then *by means of both* the Ramanna language and the Brahma language, the Pali-Burmese *nissaya* (which is in effect a translation) was being created. In other words, both Ramanna-*bhasa* and Brahma-*bhasa together* were used to construct the *nissaya;* it was not *from* one *to* the other.

But there is also a third activity mentioned by the person who wrote the last two sentences of the manuscript. According to my own reading of the Pali-Burmese, he made it clear that "on Tuesday, before sunset, the sixth waxing day of the month of Thatinkyut, Sakkaraj 1069 [1707] [he] *finished copying* [my emphasis] King Wagaru's dhammathat."[38] This means the manuscript was only being *copied* in 1707.

From the evidence available and above analysis, then, what seemed to have happened is the following. The *Wagaru Dhammathat,* first written in Ramanna-*bhasa* by a Buddhaghosa, was subsequently translated (as *nissaya*) using *both* Brahma-*bhasa* and Ramanna-*bhasa* by a second Buddhaghosa (or unnamed person), to be finally copied down in 1707. It was a three-stage process: one written, one translated, and one copied.

A fourth—and the most important problem for us regarding the purpose of this chapter—is the date when the original *Wagaru Dhammathat* was written ostensibly "in Ramanna-*bhasa.*" There is nothing in the 1707 copy to suggest that it goes back to the thirteenth century and Wareru's dynasty. The Buddhaghosa most famous in Myanmar's history is the one who lived during the reign of either King Dhammazedi or King Bayinnaung. Indeed, the *contents* of the *Dhammathat* itself—the abbreviations used, the words themselves (along with their spelling), and their tone markers (note that Mon is not a tonal language)—all indicate that the text is a compilation much later than the thirteenth century, assuming the copying was accurate.

For example, the use of signs for denoting *kyats* (as in the "$" sign before a numeral denoting dollars) is a numeral with a circle on top of it, used throughout the text. This is late usage (still used today) and not found in original Burmese or Mon inscriptions of the thirteenth century in either Upper or Lower Myanmar that I am aware of. Similarly, the spelling for the word *hpaya* (lord, monk, the Buddha) is not spelled the way it was in the thirteenth century (as *purha,* or variants of it). The tone markers also suggest much later usage: the *visagara* (two dots identical to a English colon that follow a word) is used throughout this manuscript to denote the "high" tone, a regularity that is not found in original Pagan, Ava, or First Pegu inscriptions,[39] particularly those dated to the thirteenth century, when this *dhammathat* was said to have been compiled. The spelling for *kyun* is also late, written as *akyin kyun.* The word for "at" (*nhuik*) was always spelled out during the thirteenth century, whereas its symbol (such as "e.g." for "for example" or "i.e." for "that is") is a relatively modern development, used throughout this manuscript. These are just a few examples to suggest that the original compilation of the Forchhammer manuscript was not likely to have been done in the thirteenth century, but much later.

A fifth problem is that simply because the name Waru is part of the title of this *dhammathat* does not mean it was written during his reign or that he was responsible for it, no more than the title *Manu* (found on many *dhammathats* in Myanmar including this one) means the text actually goes back to the original mythical Manu of India (and "his" *Laws of Manu*). Such an interpretation takes these kinds of formal titles too literally, especially when such practices are meant to enhance the prestige of the manuscripts by giving them some antiquity and classical credentials.

Also surprising, neither the name Wagaru, or its aliases (Magadu, Wareru, Waru), nor the writing of a *dhammathat*, especially by him, is mentioned in any contemporary record of either Muttama or the First Pegu Dynasty, which traced its lineage to Wagaru. It is especially noteworthy that the Kalyani Inscriptions of King Dhammazedi—a public, legitimating document—never once mentioned it. If such an important feat had been accomplished by the dynasty's ascribed founder, why would its members not publicize it? (In fact, the first time the statement that Wareru had the *dhammathat* compiled appears in the *Yazadhiyaza Ayedawpon*, over three hundred years later!)

Most important, the Forchhammer thesis ignores the best primary evidence available on the chronology of codified civil law in the country. The first original and contemporary evidence concerning written codified civil (and criminal) law can be found in the Old Burmese inscriptions of thirteenth-century Pagan,[40] which precedes this (1707) copy of the *Wagaru Dhammathat* by nearly five centuries! Indeed, the *Pitakat Thamaing* (history of texts) whose latest version dates to the nineteenth century, states that the first *dhammathat* in Myanmar, the *Pyumin Dhammathat*, precedes even Pagan's version by several hundred years, but we do not need to go back that far to make the case.

Apart from such problems of evidence, there is also simple logic that renders such a thesis doubtful. Wareru was, after all, a "demon" (a metaphor for a nonbeliever) prior to becoming a human peddler of merchandise, only later to become the lord of Muttama, the center of a recently emerged, small polity whose stature is unknown. To suggest that he and his kingdom were the first in the entire country to accomplish such an important feat, when they were preceded by over a millennium by much more accomplished kings and polities, demonstrated to have been qualitatively and quantitatively superior in many ways (including legal matters where both a civil and criminal written code and judicial system existed), privileges him and his society well beyond what is reasonable.

Giving Wareru (and the Mon) such agency is nearly all Forchhammer's work, from which Hall's and Harvey's statements on this particular issue were derived. Indeed, this whole line of thinking that privileged the Mon of Lower Myanmar despite evidence and logic to the contrary is very much part and parcel of the Mon Paradigm, in whose development Forchhammer was an early and important player.[41] In nearly everything else he has written, Forchhammer has demonstrated an obvious bias for the Mon of Myanmar and their alleged antiquity. Not only were they "his people" but also the sentimental favorites of most colonial authors.[42] Indeed, as demonstrated, the Mon Paradigm dominated early Myanmar scholarship profoundly, and Forchhammer's work was right at the center of it.

As early as the 1940s, J. S. Furnivall was already skeptical of Forchhammer's thesis. He wrote:

> If originally compiled under Wagaru, it [the *Wagaru Dhammathat*] had been current among the Mons for some 250 years, yet it seems to have little Talaing colouring. One would have expected it, if current for so long, to have been adapted by the Mons. . . . Moreover at the time of Wagaru and for the next 200 years Pegu was barbarous and anarchic, and an unlikely home for a code of law. It seems permissible to suspect then that the . . . tradition of its early origin among the Mons needs stronger evidence than is at present forthcoming.[43]

Admittedly, this topic of the *Wagaru Dhammathat* needs more primary research, better documentation, and more debate in Myanmar studies than it has had. Hopefully, the small group of Myanmar scholars who have been conducting serious research on the history of the Burmese *dhammathat* during the past several decades will clarify these kinds of problems and issues for the rest of us.[44] Presently, however, there is neither original evidence nor convincing analysis to support the notion that the *Wagaru Dhammathat* represented state and society during the kingdom of Muttama in the late thirteenth century, especially its earlier years when Wareru was its leader. However the problem may ultimately be resolved; in the present study, the assertion that the *Wagaru Dhammathat* was the first written civil code in Myanmar is considered untenable. I am therefore reluctant to use it as a source for reconstructing Wareru's reign, and will relegate it instead to later colonial hagiography instead of Lower Myanmar Mon history.

Returning to the end of Wareru's reign, Phayre and the *Yazadhiyaza Ayedawpon* state that Khunloa (perhaps the T'ai rendition of the Mon Khun Lau), younger brother of Wareru (also named Makata in the *Yazadhiyaza Ayedawpon* and possibly in the Trap and Pandit inscriptions),[45] succeeded to the throne. The *Ayedawpon* chastised him as being careless, neglecting the city's defenses and ultimately losing the confidence of the people. Eventually, he was killed, dying young, at the age of thirty-three, after reigning fourteen years. Khunloa was followed by approximately five successors to the throne; all genealogically "legitimate" to some degree via marriage or birth, thereby fulfilling the omen regarding seven of the eight snakes mentioned above. Some reigned for only a few days, while others somewhat longer. The general picture one gets from the *Yazadhiyaza Ayedawpon* on this period is that there were simply too many contenders to the throne at the time, and no one leader was strong enough to unite all the important fortified cities of Lower Myanmar under one umbrella.

By the late thirteenth and early fourteenth centuries, Lower Myanmar's fortunes, as well as its elite political relationships, had grown closer to Sukhotai, Chiang Mai, and Ayuthaya, both as contestants and allies. There was far more military and political jockeying for position between Lower Myanmar and the T'ai states than with Upper Myanmar, all of which comes out clearly in the *Yazadhiyaza Ayedawpon*'s narrative on Wareru and his descendants.

In time, the northern T'ai chronicles came to identify Muttama as the main port through which a renewed Theravada orthodoxy from Sri Lanka arrived, to reform and rejuvenate the decaying or decadent *sangha* of Thailand in the late thirteenth and early fourteenth centuries. (That may be one of the reasons that the T'ai claimed Wareru as one of their own.) This vaunted role of Muttama appears to be recognized also by T'ai inscriptions.[46]

Thus, while Muttama's "uncivilized" status was needed by the *Yazadhiyaza Ayedawpon* for legitimating Wareru's dynasty and Pegu subsequently, it was apparently not a concern of the T'ai authors, for that rationalization is not found in the T'ai sources. They also did not, as a result, adopt the tradition that Lower Myanmar was Suvannabhumi, to where Sona and Uttara was said to have first arrived with Theravada orthodoxy. Instead, Suvannabhumi was perceived to have been Chiang Mai.[47] With regard to this, the *Ayedawpon* agrees explicitly, in effect also rejecting Dhammazedi's (and later Mon) claims that Lower Myanmar was Suvannabhumi, and by implication, the orthodoxy brought by Sona and Uttara.

But why would the *Yazadhiyaza Ayedawpon,* written relatively shortly after Dhammazedi's reign, not accept his claim that Suvannabhumi was Lower Myanmar, and its implications for the antiquity of Ramannadesa? Part of the reason, it appears, is that there probably were some doctrinal tensions between Dhammazedi's *sangha* and that of the king under whom the *Ayedawpon* was written. It also suggests some Upper Myanmar influence in the composition of the *Yazadhiyaza Ayedawpon,* for why would any self-respecting son of Lower Myanmar reject his own region to be Suvannabhumi? It also suggests some T'ai influence in the *Yazadhiyaza Ayedawpon.*

Perhaps it was also personal for the authors of the work. After all, Dhammazedi had shed his robe to become king, which may not have sat well with the authors, who did not particularly approve of certain types of clergy who hid behind their robes. Also, the Second Pegu/Toungoo Dynasty, especially under Bayinnaung, when the *Yazadhiyaza Ayedawpon* is conventionally thought to have been written, was quite a secular-minded court, and one wonders how its ministers credited with the work might have judged kings such as Dhammazedi, who on the one hand rejected the cloth for the throne, yet on the other piously purified the *sangha* as being impure for political and economic reasons.

In any case, during this time of Pegu's development (early fourteenth century), Upper Myanmar more often than not left Lower Myanmar alone, since it was itself in the process of reuniting its disparate forces into an integrated entity under the First Ava Dynasty. That would have to wait several more decades, however, so Lower Myanmar had the time and opportunity to forge a united polity without interference from its inland, agrarian competitor. That too would have to wait, at least until the center was finally moved from Muttama (under the shadows of a rapidly expanding and powerful Ayuthaya) to Pegu, a more secure place militarily, and better located to capitalize on the link with Upper Myanmar's agricultural resources and the burgeoning trade in Southeast Asian waters. Ironically, however, that move also made Pegu more vulnerable to attack from Ava and the interior of Myanmar than Muttama had been.

Binnya U and Pegu: The Second Phase

Finally, Binnya U (the eighth snake) succeeded to the throne (1353–1385), taking the title Lord of the White Elephant. The narrative on him is sizeable, in fact, more than that given to Wareru, the "founder" himself. Binnya U is also mentioned in the two major Burmese chronicles, but only when he attacked Ava in 1373, not when he ascended the throne at Pegu.[48] In Lower Myanmar, he is mentioned as king and grandfather of Queen Shin Saw Bu in one of her inscriptions dated to 1455.[49]

Binnya U initially retained Muttama as the capital of his kingdom. But three years after he ascended the throne, forces from Chiang Mai attacked. This was ostensibly called "the Shan invasion" by the people of Lower Myanmar, which was successfully repelled by natural and supernatural forces, one of which was the power of the white elephant given to Wareru earlier by the king of Sukhotai, still in the possession of his family. To enhance the prestige and power of his kingdom, Binnya U subsequently sent a mission to Sri Lanka, requesting some bodily relics of the Buddha. This was granted, and the relics were enshrined on a mountain peak from which the white elephant had magically defeated the forces from Chiang Mai.

The reason for Chiang Mai's interest in Muttama appears to be mainly economic, located strategically as it was with direct ocean access to the Gulf of Muttama and the Bay of Bengal on the West and the Straits of Melaka and the waters of Island Southeast Asia on its south. From there, of course, the trade routes led to the South China Sea. That was the kind of direct access that Chiang Mai did not have, especially with Ayuthaya blocking the way to the coasts within Siam itself. One domestic opponent of Binnya U requested Chiang Mai's support and, in return, promised to give him ten *viss* of gold (each *viss* equals about 3.75 pounds) from the port duties of Muttama if the city fell to him.[50] Chiang Mai complied, revealing how military, economic, and political motives, not common ethnic identity, were the main concerns. But Binnya U made a counteroffer to the lord of Chiang Mai, proposing a marriage alliance between him and Binnya U's daughter, making them relatives. (The pact also included five young male elephants as "dowry.") Chiang Mai, probably looking at the long-term benefits of this pact, agreed.

Despite this new ally, because of continued subterfuge by his domestic opponents, Binnya U finally moved his capital to its final place, Pegu. According to the *Yazadhiyaza Ayedawpon,* Pegu had regressed, from its "former" (mythical) stature as royal capital after the legendary Samala-Wimala dynasty ended with the "bad king" Tissa, until Binnya U made it into a royal capital (*Yazahtani*) in 1349.[51] As noted above, Pegu was not a new city but an already established and important governorship under the Kingdom of Pagan long before this event. The history of Lower Myanmar suggests that by the end of the thirteenth and beginning of the fourteenth century, there were at least two premier centers there (Muttama and Pegu) whose population may have been predominantly

Mon speakers. (Thaton, might have been a possible third, but does not appear in original epigraphy until the late fifteenth century.)

In hindsight, Binnya U's move to Pegu from Muttama proved to be a blessing. Muttama was too close to the passes to and from Ayuthaya, which was developing into a major power in the region by then. In fact, Ayuthaya would later claim Tenasserim, Maulamyaing (Moulmein), and Muttama under its domain. Pegu was far enough from Ayuthaya to be well defended, protected by numerous major streams and at least one large river (the Thanlyin) between it and Anyuthaya, and was rapidly growing as a major urban center and valuable port city of Lower Myanmar when it became the capital. This early tension and competition between the deltas of the Irrawaddy and the Chao Phaya for control of the Gulf of Muttama and coastal Tenasserim, the Kra Isthmus, and the upper reaches of the Malay Peninsula was a harbinger of things to come, and would play itself out fully only two hundred years later when Pegu, under the Second Pegu/Toungoo) Dynasty, conquered Ayuthaya twice within a span of a decade.

Unfortunately, Pegu's problems were not only external with Ayuthaya and the T'ai. Ultimately, the decisive ones were internal, and lay essentially with Binnya U's own kinfolk. Not only was there a large pool of legitimate contenders to the throne, but each had been given a fief to govern so that each had a demographic, economic, and a military base of his/her own. That encouraged the forming of self-interested alliances with one another or with more distant powers, as both Upper Myanmar and Thailand were periodically drawn into the internal politics of Lower Myanmar.

Yet, what made one a "legitimate" (de jure) king of Pegu was not simply de facto success, but making sure that one's genealogy (and thereby also that of one's offspring) could be linked via the chief queen to the original "demon" Sumana, alias Magadu. The system set the stage for the large, legitimate pool of contenders for the throne to regularly contest it. Much of this struggle was also personal and involved the standard uncle-nephew conflicts, cousin-cousin competition, and of course, the intrigue by queens and princesses who wanted their offspring to succeed to the throne. Geo-economically, it involved the trade revenues of the premier cities of Lower Myanmar at the time: Pegu, Dagon, Myaungmya, Muttama, and Pathein (Bassein).

From those struggles—whose narrative is long and complicated, amounting to about forty printed pages—would emerge Binnya U's eldest son, a brash young man who had married his half-sister and fled to Dagon (today's Yangon), making it his center, eventually to become the source of many court intrigues. Indeed, the author of the *Yazadhiyaza Ayedawpon* placed his own personal opinions into the mouth of the prince's father, the king, by having him say that his son, then named Bannya Nwe, was "harsh and cruel," without any consideration for his father, and that he "will not be compatible with the people," so "should not become king" in the future.[52] This reflected the authors' perspective as ministers loyal to the reigning king rather than to the usurper. As it turns out, Bannya Nwe became one of the most successful kings of the First Pegu Dynasty, without whom the dynasty probably would not have survived much beyond Binnya U.

Symbolically as well, Binnya U suffered, for the white elephant given to Wareru by the king of Sukhotai died during his reign, along with an invaluable and extremely important chief minister who had served him. All the people of the country mourned for both when they died, and the eulogy given to the white elephant by the *Yazadhiyaza Ayedawpon* is extremely interesting. It is virtually the same as that given to other kings of the dynasty, not only citing the usual date of "ascension," years of "reign," age at death, so on, but also using the correct verbs, nouns, and classifiers reserved for royalty.[53]

Several pages of omens and prophecies were recounted, many in Burmese rhyme schemes created (or at least found early) at Ava, all of which were interpreted to validate the future ascension of the prince, Bannya Nwe. Each of these was first given in Mon, after which, wrote the authors, "this is its translation in the Myanma language," and the verse was reproduced in Burmese[54] (which helps confirm the contention that the original was probably written in Mon). But the fact that these omens and prophecies were even needed suggests that Bannya Nwe's ascension was not considered entirely legitimate in the eyes of the authors responsible for producing the *Yazadhiyaza Ayedawpon* (or in the eyes of the authors of the manuscript they translated).

After Bannya Nwe's father's long illness, which in part triggered these struggles, and subsequent (natural) death, Prince Bannya Nwe allied himself with some of his brothers and "feringy [Portuguese?] gunners,"[55] and eventually succeeded in seizing Pegu in 1385, which was held by other kinfolk. The prince was the famous Yazadhiyaza (king of kings), more popularly known as Yazadarit, whose story is the focus of the *Yazadhiyaza Ayedawpon* and the next chapter.

Yazadarit the Unifier

Prince Bannya Nwe, crowned king "on the spot" as Yazadarit[1] (1383–1423), was to become one of the most politically and militarily competent leaders of Pegu. The account of his crowning "on the spot" where an "earlier" Mon hero, Atha (Asah) was said to have defeated a Hindu giant,[2] is probably part of his ex post facto legitimation narrative, for, as noted in earlier chapters, the story of Asah was not written down until about 1825, so this portion of the *Yazadhiyaza Ayedawpon* was likely a later interpolation.

In contrast, the most well-known and (ostensibly) respected Mon history, the *Slapat,* along with the "Gavampati," both remembered him as a "demon." The authors of these two texts had either confused his story with that of Magadu, or did, in fact, feel that the appellation was deserved. There was obviously also some borrowing from various Mon and Burmese sources, not only in terms of this particular statement about his being a "demon," but also in terms of other events, allegories, and symbolisms, as we shall see.

To reiterate, the *Slapat* was more concerned with the patronage record of the Shwedagon Pagoda by Pegu's kings—how much gold, land, and people they donated to its upkeep—than with their military or administrative abilities. And although Yazadarit was not stingy, especially given the priorities of state at the time, the *Slapat* was comparing him to his successors, particularly Shin Saw Bu and Dhammazedi, who had benefited from Yazadarit's rule. Hence, from our (Western) perspective, although Yazadarit may have been a "good" or (at least) competent king, from the *Slapat*'s perspective, he was neither.

The Early Years

The *Yazadhiyaza Ayedawpon* gives the date of Yazadarit's formal ascension to the throne in 1383 AD, on the twelfth waxing day of the moon in the month of Dabodwe (January).[3] This creates some minor problems, for it means he was crowned prior to taking Pegu in 1385, and therefore could not have been "crowned king on the spot" when he took Pegu, as Harvey asserted.

Once in power, he was said not to have executed his opponents, as "customary" (perhaps, expected), although some probably deserved it, according to the political values held then at court. This was especially true of the Mahadevi, chief queen and elder sister of his father (Yazadarit's aunt), who took care of him as a child but plotted against him later when he rose to power. Even after he spared her life, she was said to have said of Yazadarit: "So, he is still there, the sight of him is like grit in my eyes."[4] The only one of note that Yazadarit executed was his opportunistic and unscrupulous vassal, Smim Maru, but he also announced he would execute the minister of his father, Tein Nge.[5] But the minister's query as to why, Yazadarit's answer, and the minister's response have become a standard moral aphorism, a stock dialogue that is meant to be taken as didactic, much like Pagan's Queen Saw's famous admonishment of King Narathihapade for his behavior. In the *Yazadhiyaza Ayedawpon,* it is a statement about the value of wise ministers, often the only stable pillars of the court during constant, destabilizing intrigues, and about how kings should be just and fair in their judgment of ministers who are there only to serve the king and state. (Of course, the *Yazadhiyaza Ayedawpon* was written by a group of "wise men" likely to have been ministers.)

When ordered to be executed by Yazadarit, so the story goes, Minister Tein Nge said that his only crime was being "a servant of your father, the king."

> I pay court only to a king who wears a white umbrella, not to one who is without this emblem of kingship. If you should take umbrage . . . [at] this and have me executed, I lose nothing more than my life . . . [but] the underpinnings of good administration would be uprooted for good. People would point out my fate as an example of losing one's life and leaving one's wife destitute for being loyal only to a crowned king and omitting to make overtures like offering advice to a pretender who later becomes king. Such attitudes are . . . anathema to good administration and will destroy your peace of mind. The citizenry and ecclesiastics as well will suffer should such attitudes become prevalent in a country.[6]

The king was speechless after this reply, noted the *Yazadhiyaza Ayedawpon,* and reinstated the minister with all his fiefs and title.

As at Ava, and Myanmar's history in general, upon the ascension of a monarch, his most trusted vassals or those who had a hand in his ascension were rewarded with titles and fiefs. Even Mahadevi, whose eyes stung when she saw Yazadarit, was given Dagon (Yangon) as fief, in deference, said the *Yazadhiyaza Ayedawpon,* for what she had done for the king when he was a child. The action, of course, also enhanced Yazadarit's stature, for it was considered a magnanimous gesture that reflected the compassion of a buddha. Yet, it also provided her with the wherewithal to rebel.

But Lauk Hpya, Yazadarit's uncle and lord of Myaungmya, a major town in the western part of the Lower Myanmar Delta, refused to give allegiance to Yazadarit, confirming once again the well-established theme of uncle-nephew struggles. Instead, he sent envoys to the court of Ava submitting to Minkyiswa Sawkai, then king of Ava. Lauk Hpya suggested that before Yazadarit has time to consolidate his domain, Ava should attack by land, while he would attack by water. And in the standard "macro" used by the Burmese chronicles, Lauk Hpya told Minkyiswa, "You can have the inner core, just give me the outer shell."[7] Lauk Hpya knew full well that Ava was just waiting for an opportunity to take the coasts, which Upper Myanmar had not controlled since the Pagan Dynasty was on its last legs, when it retook Dala in 1296.

U Kala's perspective, from Upper Myanmar and in hindsight after nearly four hundred years regarding this particular incident, is importantly different. First, there is much more in the message sent by Lauk Hpya to Minkyiswa Sawkai that revealed nuances not found in the *Yazadhiyaza Ayedawpon.* Second, U Kala also viewed Yazadarit as a usurper, whereas (understandably) the *Yazadhiyaza Ayedawpon* does not, although there are instances in which his legitimacy is questioned. But these are done mainly prior to his ascension, affirming the principle of "retroactive karma."

On the other hand, there are other points of agreement so close to each other in the two narratives that it is quite obvious certain stories were taken verbatim by U Kala from the *Yazadhiyaza Ayedawpon.*[8] For instance, even the name of Yazadarit's elephant, Adaraung, who "lost its tail," was recorded by both accounts. As noted in the previous chapter, it is very likely that U Kala used the *Yazadhiyaza Ayedawpon* in his account of Yazadarit, which commanded over one hundred printed pages, longer than what the author gave most Burmese kings.

After Yazadarit's uncle's offer to Ava, Minkyiswa Sawkai was said to have mobilized his men and, with various lords of different important cities, marched along "the Tharawaddy route," down the valley of the Irrawaddy. According to the *Ayedawpon,* his commanders were the king's son and the lords of Kukhan, Sagaing, and Salin, all south of Ava in the Dry Zone. Another force went down the Sittaung River valley, the Toungoo route; it included Hsinphyushin, lord of Rakhaing (Arakan, at the time, a vassal of Ava), along with the lords of Taungdwin, Taung-ngu, Pandaya, and Myede. With this list, the *Yazadhiyaza Ayedawpon* in effect confirmed the extent of Ava's hegemony during Minkyiswa Sawkai's reign as described by U Kala.

The author of the *Ayedawpon* wrote that as Yazadarit's force marched out, monks climbed the Thinbaw pagoda to get a better view of the battle,[9] no doubt a stab at those clergy who were not following the rules of the *Vinaya* against such worldly "spectator sports." The authors of the text were a secular, practical, "this-world" oriented group of scholars and clearly not awestruck by everyone in saffron robes.

Finally, after several stalemates and mishaps, Minkyiswa Sawkai had to retreat to Ava, as he lost many elephants, horses, and men that fell into Yazadarit's hands. Following the successful defense of his realm, Yazadarit flaunted his victory by sending presents containing bolts of velvet, felt, and cotton cloth, along with gold and silver, to Minkyiswa Sawkai, with a not-too-subtle message saying that, because the latter on his last visit had "departed so quickly," he did not have time to offer these presents. Minkyiswa Sawkai did not appreciate the innuendo about his quick and easy defeat obvious in the language of "this young Mon,"[10] so the presents were returned. For such personal slights and insults, the enmity between Upper and Lower Myanmar continued throughout the reigns of these two kings.

The main geopolitical problem for both Yazadarit and any Upper Myanmar attacker was the terrain in Lower Myanmar. It was difficult moving from east to west; indeed, it was easier to move upriver to Ava (and vice versa) than to move from Pegu to Myaungmya, just south of Bassein and far closer than Ava was. The delta there has nine major tributaries with sizeable widths and strong currents as they debouch into the Gulf of Muttama, along with dozens of large streams. Bassein had been the major port for traffic to and from South Asia and points west during both the Pagan and the early part of the "Early Modern" period. Whereas, on Pegu's east, although there were not as many difficult streams to traverse to reach important cities like Muttama, the cities themselves were nearly all walled and therefore formidable obstacles. Although that geographic context favored Pegu's defenses vis á vis Ava, it was also to remain a mitigating factor to unifying Lower Myanmar by Pegu subsequently.

Yazadarit knew that the terrain was as much an obstacle to Ava as it was to his own desire to unify Lower Myanmar. Thus, after successfully defending against Ava, he spent much time focusing on consolidating the region's main centers of power: Muttama, Maulamyaing, Pathein, Dagon, and Myaungmya. He was successful, but it took incredible discipline, military skill, and political will to do it, leaving his successors, particularly Shin Saw Bu and Dhammazedi, with a kingdom that was far less fractious and reasonably well integrated and wealthy. This was lost on the religiously oriented chroniclers, such as the author of the *Slapat*, who did not consider Yazadarit an exemplary king, claiming he did little for the religion. In fact, however, he did not neglect the religion; he was simply so overwhelmed with consolidating his realm that he could not devote the amount of time and resources to the religion that Shin Saw Bu and Dhammazedi, who would enjoy the peace and stability that was the result of Yazadarit's labors, could.

In this process of consolidation, most of it occurring during the last two decades of the 1300s, not only did Yazadarit have to contend with Ava in the north—which, at a moment's notice, could be at his doorstep (it reportedly took only about five days by express war boat from Ava to Yangon where crews were changed at intervals along the river)—but also, more serious in some ways, his own kinfolk were constantly vying for the throne. By 1388, Yazadarit had taken Muttama, strategically and economically a most important city of Lower Myanmar.[11] With Muttama came Maulamyaing (Moulmein), just across the Thanlyin (Salween) River, both sides controlling its mouth to the Gulf of Muttama, thence to points south and east to the rest of Island Southeast Asia, and west to the Bay of Bengal and India.

By the early 1390s, Yazadarit's famous general Byataza took Myaungmya, held by Yazadarit's uncle and most potent enemy, Lauk Phya, who had engineered the war with Ava. Yazadarit showed mercy and, instead of executing him, consigned him to be a *paya kyun* (pagoda servant) for the Shwedagon Pagoda for the rest of his life. More important than Myaungmya was Pathein (Bassein) port nearby, which controlled the traffic west to east from the Bay of Bengal to Myanmar. It was given to another of Yazadarit's able generals, Thilawa.[12] Most, if not all, the walled towns in between these two west-east poles (Pathein and Muttama) were also taken and given as fiefs to the king's supporters. In effect, Yazadarit had all of the cities and towns in Lower Myanmar that mattered by 1390.

The king celebrated this integration of Lower Myanmar by giving his weight in gold to the Shwemawdaw Pagoda at Pegu, contrary to what the later *Slapat* had to say about Yazadarit's lack of largesse regarding the religion. (The *Slapat,* of course, was primarily a record of donations made to the Shwedagon, not the Shwemawdaw, its "rival" in sacredness in Lower Myanmar.) Yazadarit built up the latter pagoda with pavilions and other accouterments, along with forty satellite *stupas.* In the traditional manner, he fed over a thousand monks for seven days, giving each five hundred *viss* of copper. At the time, the king was only twenty-three years old.[13] His kingdom of Hanthawaddy was likened to the abode of the *nats,* a phrase reminiscent of those found in Pagan and Ava inscriptions. It was not all hyperbole, however, for even competitor Ayuthaya recognized Pegu's growth, power, and stability, sending an "elephant fit for a king." It was received by a royal escort of five ministers, one hundred elephants, and five thousand soldiers. Chiang Mai also was involved in Pegu's affairs, perhaps to counterbalance Ayuthaya's influence.

At the death of the old chief queen, a new chief queen of Yazadarit was consecrated. She was the daughter of a man named Sitrepain who was the son of another named Bannya The, who, dissatisfied with the king of Chiang Mai, Maharat (Mahayaza), had left his service to serve Binnya U, Yazadarit's father. (The author of the *Yazadhiyaza Ayedawpon* went through an elaborate genealogy to legitimize this new chief queen.) Ayuthaya and Chiang Mai were certainly concerned with the affairs of Pegu.

But such consolidation of his power and kingdom only made competition for his position more intense at home, as Yazadarit continued to contend with members of his own royal family. At the same time, as he consolidated his power, he was able to neutralize or eliminate his enemies. His elder sister, whose eyes felt like they had grit in them whenever she saw him, finally took poison and died after she was hounded by Yazadarit for everything she had, including her fief of Tala, opposite Dagon (modern Rangoon) which he had given her in the first place.[14] In order to offset such demerit, and in the manner of righteous kings of the country (*dhammaraja*), prisoners were pardoned from death row. And as already noted above, the life of his treasonous uncle was spared by allowing him to live out the rest of his life serving the Shwedagon Pagoda.[15]

Kingship also meant he had the very unpleasant "duty" of being tough on his own son. Bawlawkyantaw was accused, probably by a jealous competitor whose path to the throne was cut off by him, of "sharpening his elephant tusks" and honing his martial skills. Remembering his own history as a young lad of sixteen who took the throne by force, Yazadarit had to believe that his son might do the same. And after a tearful story in which the prince insisted that he was innocent of any plot against his father (he was only practicing his martial skills as a prince should), and after saying his prayers at the Shwemawdaw Pagoda, Bawlawkyantaw was executed.[16]

Then came the opportunity Yazadarit had been waiting for: Minkyiswa Sawkai of Upper Myanmar died in 1400. The *Ayedawpon* states that Yazadarit "raised his fist in jubilation when he heard of this."[17] Minkyiswa Sawkai's son and heir became king, but was assassinated the same year, ostensibly because he was insane, at least according to the *Ayedawpon*. The younger brother of Sawkai succeeded to the throne as Mingaung the First, who had a long and prosperous reign until 1423. And with his ascension began a relationship with Yazadarit that was fodder for dramatic literature. But not yet, for with the death of Minkyiswa Sawkai, it was time to test Ava's strength. Yazadarit formed a huge armada—it reportedly had four thousand vessels, including rafts carrying elephants and horses[18]—and set out for Ava. Pegu had grown in economic and political power in Lower Myanmar from the development of trade on the coasts of Southeast Asia earlier with South India, the arrival of Islam in Southeast Asian waters, and the rise and development of Ayuthaya and Melaka and the growth of the Ming in maritime affairs.

The narrative (taken from U Kala and the *Ayedawpon*) stated that Yazadarit attacked Pyi, riding on his royal barge named the *Karaweik*.[19] But he did not succeed (wrote U Kala) because of the guns his opponents had. Although able to defend Pyi successfully, the forces of its governor were not as proficient on water as Yazadarit's were, so Yazadarit decided to bypass Pyi and forge ahead to Ava instead. However, he left his daughter, Princess Talamikyaw, who had become ill, near Pyi in a stockade, protected by some of his troops. This simple act was to have grave consequences in the history between Ava and Pegu for many years to come.

Ava placed all the riverine towns under alert as Yazadarit went up the Irrawaddy all the way to Pagan, then stopped and worshiped at the pagodas. But he went past Ava to Tagaung, far in the north, did the same there and, on his return downriver, stopped at Sagaing (across from Ava) to worship at another famous pagoda. He then simply weighed anchor in the middle of the Irrawaddy and did nothing.[20] Puzzled, Mingaung asked the summoned ministers and advisers how to get Yazadarit to leave; none of them said a word and remained silent. Finally, one of them named Sakyothu (Pinya Thukyo in the *Yazadhiyaza Ayedawpon*), well versed in the *Tipitakas* and horoscopes, said he could preach to Yazadarit so that he would "see the light" and, hopefully, leave. The king gave his approval, and when Sakyothu met with Yazadarit, he instructed the latter in various Buddhist doctrines and beliefs that are more or less common knowledge among Buddhists but were made to appear as new and surprising to Yazadarit.

The dialogue between the two allowed U Kala an occasion to have the Ava monk "civilize" the king of Pegu in terms of Buddhism and, in the process, claim (implicitly) that Ava, after all, has for long been a Buddha-prophesied city, not just any ordinary site like "modern" Pegu that only recently emerged. The monk also gave Yazadarit information regarding the strength of the kingdom, naming the major towns in both the northern and southern divisions under its authority, including the riverine towns along the Irrawaddy that stretched from the Dry Zone to the coasts, altogether numbering fifty-three walled cities under Ava.[21]

Yazadarit then said that he had come initially with the intention of attacking this kingdom of the Myanma. But since he had now heard the teachings, he would return home. He then broke up five of his golden barges and erected a *zayat* (rest house) with their materials for a nearby pagoda. He also fed one hundred monks and donated myriad things such as betel nuts and chiles, after which he descended the river.[22] This whole episode made Yazadarit appear uncivilized, with little or no knowledge of state diplomacy or basic tenets of Buddhism, particularly about the doctrines regarding greed and longing. The Ava monk told Yazadarit that "clearly you need a mentor." The outcome of this exchange was, in the chronicles' view, Yazadarit's "seeing the light."[23] Both chronicles euphemized the event as a sort of religious awakening for Yazadarit and an illustration of the general role monks played in bringing peace to warring kings. The incident also allowed the insertion of a didactic literary device that preached the positive consequences of Buddhist doctrine on human activity. Yazadarit's building of monasteries in Upper Myanmar and, later on his way down, at Pagan, were also statements about power and their "markers," following the practice of earlier Pagan kings who built temples in areas they could roam at will, rationalized by the notion of *dharmavijaya*,[24] or righteous conquest.

Mingaung set fire to the *zayat* built by Yazadarit, who, on his way downriver, saw the smoke and said, "My good deed is being set afire." He wanted to turn around and attack Ava but was dissuaded by his generals, who said the demerit accrues to the one who has set fire to the good deed.[25] If you need to fight, they persuaded him, we will attack those villages close to Pyi. Mingaung was sobered by the event, for it had demonstrated Pegu's power. He said, "They came all the way here and returned without breaking one sword or lance. If they ever come again, it will be a crisis." So he gave orders to two generals to give chase, which they did, and when Yazadarit stopped at Sale to take back a Buddha image allegedly taken during the reign of Anawrahta in the eleventh century from "Talaing Pran" (Talaing Kingdom), Ava's troops caught up with him and "many Talaing" were killed, although Yazadarit himself made it back to Pegu.[26] His daughter, however, whom he had left at a stockade near Pyi on his way up to Ava, was captured by Ava's forces and presented to Mingaung, who gave her (as princess designate) to his son and crown prince, Minye Thihathu. Yazadarit went on a rampage, executing the one responsible for guarding her (who had fled) and ravaging nearby walled towns until they all submitted.

The relations between Yazadarit and Mingaung were more or less a stalemate after these events upriver. They sent each other expensive presents; Pegu giving Ava two elephants with gold howdahs, one hundred horses, one thousand Chinese *paso* (men's sarongs) and rugs, while Ava gave Pegu five male and five female elephants with gold howdahs on each. After these preliminary ceremonies were held among the generals, the kings met personally at a famous pagoda. There, they exchanged white umbrellas and betel boxes, and negotiated the boundaries between the two kingdoms. The *Ayedawpon* states that the two kings demarcated their territories with Tapindarang as the western border and Thapaka the eastern, while upstream was the territory of Ava, and downstream the territory of Pegu.[27] Yazadarit then said that he would "maintain a garrison in the stockade named Baranasi in Talehsi" and requested Mingaung "to bear with it until he retired that garrison. [For] this was only to impress the neighboring kings," he said, and assured Mingaung that "it would not be held with a strong force."[28] Mingaung agreed, and they parted on cordial terms.

But they did not remain that way, as Ava accused Pegu of not honoring the pact. In the former's attempt to chastise Pegu, Chiang Mai's help was sought for its strategic position at Pegu's "back." Ava requested the latter with promises of "the choicest of women, horses and elephants to your heart's content."[29] Arakan was needed by Ava to provide the opposite pincher move, so it too was involved. Thus, the political and military relations between Ava and Pegu often drew both Arakan and Chiang Mai into it. That meant Pegu had to have Bassein as a buffer against attack from Arakan while intriguing with (or hoping that) the Shan principalities on Ava's north would keep it busy in that direction.

Eventually, Ava sent a large force in 1403, said (by the *Yazadhiyaza Ayedawpon*) to be 150,000 strong, with six thousand cavalry and five hundred elephantry. It included Shan levies recently taken at Bhamo, which marched on Pegu via the Toungoo route down the Sittaung River valley. Yazadarit also prepared to defend Lower Myanmar with eighty thousand troops, over two hundred "jousting elephants and over five hundred young male and female elephants." His knowledge of tidal waters and their ability to surprise people unfamiliar with them was used to his fullest advantage, which caused considerable damage, especially to Ava's Shan troops. He also used guerilla tactics to deplete food and other supplies that Mingaung needed, slowly demoralizing his enemy without doing much fighting on a large scale, something Ava wanted, being superior in numbers. Eventually, Mingaung had to sue for peace and return to Ava.[30]

Occasionally, Ava got the upper hand, particularly when Minyekyawswa, Mingaung's young son of seventeen, commanded his troops. During the first decade of the fifteenth century, Ava took parts of Lower Myanmar, including the stockaded towns in the heart of Yazadarit's kingdom: Tala, Dagon (Yangon), and Thanlyin (Syriam). But even with that kind of advantage, Yazadarit proved a formidable foe. He would ally himself with the Shan chiefs, particularly of Hsenwi, which would send Mingaung back to defend Ava, having to leave Lower Myanmar in the hands of his selected governors, who, one by one, invariably lost to Yazadarit.

The campaigns between Ava and Pegu continued well into the first two decades of the fifteenth century. Most of the causes, if the chronicles are to be believed, were mainly personal. Yazadarit had Mingaung's daughter and had made her his queen, possibly a deliberate, provocative action, which ate at Mingaung, for he had given Yazadarit's daughter, whom he had captured, to the crown prince rather than keeping her for himself. Even Yazadarit's own minister chastised him on this matter, saying that "My lord and the Burmese are constantly at war which has caused suffering among the people from year to year, and the root cause of this is because my lord has taken the King of Ava's daughter . . . to wife after her capture. . . . This has embarrassed her father greatly causing this unending strife. If she had been wed with one of the princes her father would not be so furious and his anger would have gradually subsided."[31]

Crown Prince Minyekyawswa's enthusiasm for wanting to battle Pegu also seemed to have been personal; he was reputed to have said that he would not be content until he ate Yazadarit's flesh, figuratively speaking.[32] Reckless and full of bravado, he finally overextended himself and was wounded and captured by Yazadarit. Yazadarit treated him as a worthy opponent and honorable warrior, and offered medicine for his wounds and promised to return him to Ava or, if he wished, to make him crown prince and marry him to his daughter. But the prince replied, "I will not take your medicine . . . since I will never become someone's vassal, death I deem to be more honorable than to go on living."

What is important to note here is that not once did the author of the *Yazadhiyaza Ayedawpon* use the *ethnicity* of the Mon in Minyekyawswa's refusal to become Yazadarit's crown prince: it was a matter of *vassalage.* And so, said the Mon chronicle, "refusing to take medicine, Minyekyawswa died at the stroke of the third quarter of the night." The ministers, charged with his burial, cremated him, and then placed his bones in the center of a splendid temple.[33]

Apart from the personal agendas and personalities of the main characters, the various lords of strategic cities who served the respective crowns had their own personal interests as well, allying with whomever best served them, while the *sawbwa* of Upper Myanmar and the T'ai powers at Chiang Mai could be persuaded by monetary and other rewards to support one side or the other as the occasion may dictate. Finally the wars abated when Mingaung captured one of Yazadarit's sons, Bannya Set, so that neither king had the upper hand any longer. The *Yazadhiyaza Ayedawpon* stated that thereafter Mingaung turned to doing meritorious work, "sponsoring the building of pagodas and monasteries, engaging in charitable deeds and observing the precepts. Four or five years later, he passed away."

This account of Mingaung in the *Yazadhiyaza Ayedawpon* is similar to that recorded by U Kala, particularly the sentiment Yazadarit was said to have felt with regard to the loss of a worthy adversary. The *Yazadhiyaza Ayedawpon* states that "on hearing the news [of Mingaung's death], Razadarit mused how they had spent years fighting each other and now that Mingaung was no more . . . the inexorable law of impermanence . . . [had] led Mingaung away, leaving him alone to ponder on its significance."[34] Contrast this to the time Yazadarit pumped his fist in the air when he heard of Minkyiswa Sawkai's death earlier.

When Yazadarit's bevy of queens heard the news, they teased him, saying, "Mingaung is your brother as well as your father-in-law [since Yazadarit had married Mingaung's daughter]. Now that he is gone, why don't you march to Ava and take his queens, concubines, the whole lot?"[35] Yazadarit parried their taunting and retorted that he was now too old for war. From now on, he would bear the burden of nurturing them with one shoulder, while supporting the progress of meritorious work with the other. From that day, Yazadarit, "no longer indulged in preparation for war but turned his attention toward the building of religious edifices, the replication of scriptures, in charity, observance of the precepts and religious meditation."[36] Two years later, he died of a wound suffered from a hunting accident.

Apart from the personal nature of the tension between these two kings that dominated the relations between Ava and Pegu, there must have been other, larger factors that the chronicles did not mention; after all, they were *yazawin* whose main purpose was to record the genealogy of kings. One of these factors, surely, was the lucrative revenues of Lower Myanmar, desired and sorely needed by Ava, as its landed wealth was not only already limited when it emerged, but thereafter continued to flow into the *sangha* as it developed.

But such factors were seldom mentioned in these *yazawin*, except inadvertently. When the lord of Bassein and chief minister of Yazadarit, Tein Nge, was reluctant to surrender the town to Ava as demanded by the Ava generals, he said that the town was full of wealthy merchants from whom he received a large amount of revenues.[37] When it was finally captured, "wealthy persons by ancestry, Indians, Mussulman and citizens gave tributary gifts of gold, silver, rich cloth, velvet, felt, caulking material and red morinda dye" to the Ava generals to prevent the looting and sacking of the town.[38] In another case, Chiang Mai's help was obtained by promising a small part of Muttama's trade revenues. In yet another case, Arakan's lucrative trade with the rest of the Bay of Bengal was mentioned as part of the reason both Ava and Pegu wanted it under their hegemony.

Whatever the factors, not once did the issue of Burman-Mon ethnicity as casus belli ever come up implicitly or explicitly between the two centers, as conventional colonial historiography has it. Ethnicity was probably not considered a matter of concern for either of the two chroniclers. Rather, the crucial issue appears to have been geopolitical and economic competition between the commercial coasts and the agrarian interior, along with the personalities of their leaders. Thus after Minyekyawswa died and the control of Ava's forces was left in the hands of his generals, Yazadarit's chief minister, Tein Nge, suggested playing the "cultural/regional card" with the lord of Salin, one of Ava's generals, for he "hails from Myaungmya" in Lower Myanmar. The suggestion was clear: even though he held a fief under Ava, his cultural and regional loyalties, not ethnic identity, were thought to have been important. So a message was sent by Yazadarit to the lord of Salin that attempted to exploit the latter's presumed regional sentiments. "Bassein and Myaungmya count as your ancestral home and if you accept my suzerainty I will give you any one of these fiefdoms you fancy."

The reply by the lord of Salin is instructive with regard to the point being made here; namely, that loyalty was personal, and often preempted parochial and regional (and certainly ethnic) considerations: "I have no yearnings for either Bassein or Myaungmya for I have drunk water from [Upper] Myanmar." When his reply was reported to Yazadarit, he said, "[the lord of Salin] is as steady as they come."[39]

It is true, of course, that the chroniclers sometimes used ethnicity in the dialogue of their characters to dramatize an event or sensationalize their narrative, but this was used more in a self-deprecating manner against one's *own* ethnicity, than against that of one's opponent. Once, when Yazadarit was in trouble with the advance of Ava's forces, one of his sons tried to minimize the situation to assuage the king, who turned to his son and said, "Do you know my predicament, you imbecile of a Mon?"[40]

At the end of the *Yazadhiyaza Ayedawpon,* the reader is confronted with the usual didactic conclusion. Although Yazadarit was a mighty king, he "could not withstand Death's assault. . . . [He] was dragged willy-nilly to the realm of Death. Living beings without exception cannot escape from its clutches unless one has attained the knowledge of the right path and the perception of its fruition. That is why everyone should try to attain the knowledge of the right path and perception of its fruition which are like the celestial thunderbolt and the supernatural weapons which can keep Death's hordes at bay."[41]

Then the *Yazadhiyaza Ayedawpon* provided Yazadarit's horoscope, so crucial in the culture of the country regardless of ethnicity:

> On the 6th waxing day of the moon of Dabodwe [January-February] 711 [1349 AD], with the Sun in Cancer, Mercury in Virgo, Mars in Pisces, the Moon in Leo and Saturn in Scorpio, with the latter horoscope he was born as Basum Bansak. Later he was named Bannya Nwai. After he became king, he assumed the name of Rajadhiraja. Subsequently, only after he killed his son Bawlawkyantaw . . . he assumed the name of Sactasum.[42] In sakkaraj 745 [1383 AD], on the 3rd waxing day of the moon, Thursday, he went to Dagum town and rebelled. That same year, in the month of Dabodwe, 2nd waxing day, Thursday, he became king. In sakkaraj 783 [1421 AD], he reached impermanence. . . . Following the words of men of learning, so that these victorious campaigns can become models of precedence, the composition of these men of learning was done.[43]

Thus ends the *Yazadhiyaza Ayedawpon,* comprising 360 pages of modern printed Burmese text.

In contrast, and most interesting, the later *Slapat* gives a single paragraph to the entire life of Yazadarit. It stated, "The son of Bana U, Siharaja by name, when at the age of sixteen years, rebelled against his father. When his father was no more, he became king. This king because he had made friends with enemies, had gained a knowledge [*sic*] of the customs of war. This king as he went on his kingly duties in whatsoever way he turned there was no one who dared strive with him. Because he was great in war always, he had no opportunity to enshrine pagodas. He could only make offerings. This king was also called Rajadhirat. He did not attain to a great age. Becoming king in 745 [1383 AD], he reigned thirty-eight years. Having reached the age of fifty-four years, he reached impermanence in 783 [1421 AD]."[44]

Written by a monk whose priorities were religious, the *Slapat* judged Yazadarit according to those priorities. Even his adversaries at Ava honored him better, mentioning him several times on imperishable stone inscriptions.[45] There are no original and contemporary sources to indicate the extent of Pegu at the

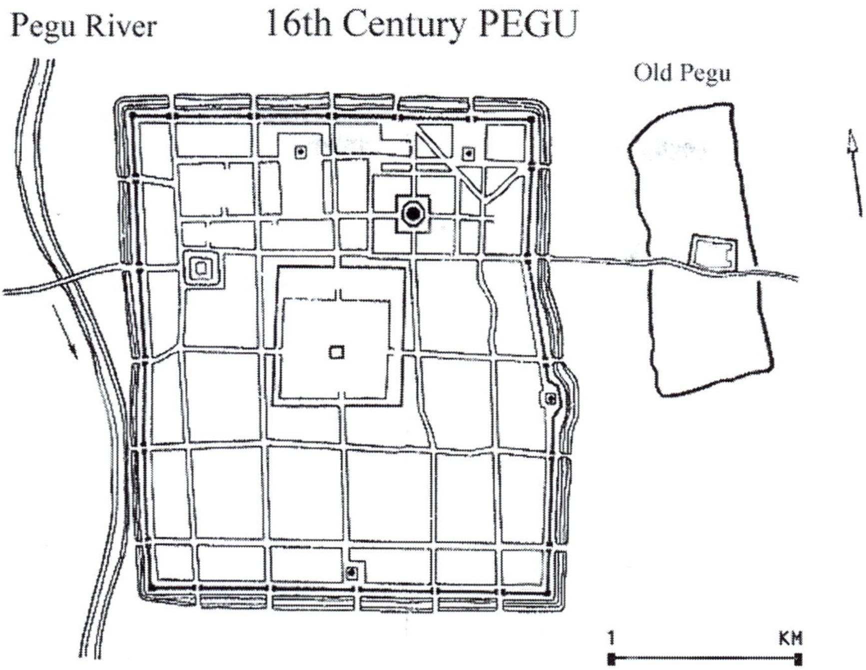

Figure 4. Old and New Pegu

time of Yazadarit's death, so figure 4 is provided, for it represents both "old Pegu" (of Yazadarit) and "new Pegu" (of probably Dhammazedi or his successors).[46]

Yazadarit's Successors

There is some discrepancy in the sources with regard to the immediate successor of Yazadarit. But most agree that he was succeeded by his eldest son, Bannya Dhamma Yaza (1423–1426).[47] His two younger brothers known (in Phayre's work) as "Binya Ran" and "Binya Keng," governors of Dala and Dagon, fearing for their safety, decided on a pact between them for their protection against their older brother. However, a deal must have been struck between Bannya Ram ("Binya Ran" of Phayre) and the king, for the former was made heir apparent in return for breaking with Binya Keng, who then went to the king of Ava for support. But things did not work out between them, and Binya Keng eventually decided to come back into the fold of Pegu. That gave Bannya Ram the upper hand, and he persuaded Binya Keng to relinquish his fief of Dala and instead take Muttama, himself taking Dala, thereby controlling the most important towns in the western region: Tharawaddy, Pathein, and Dala that guarded the common invasion route from Ava. When the king of Ava marched on Pegu again, Bannya Ram offered a marriage alliance instead, offering his sister Princess Saw Bome (later Shin Saw Bu) to the king of Ava. When this offer was accepted, she was said to have been consecrated queen at Pegu first, only after which she returned to Ava with its king.

When the eldest brother, the king, died (after only three years), apparently poisoned by one of his queens, Bannya Ram ascended the throne (1426–1446). His younger brother he kept as governor of Muttama, and although far enough from the throne, it nonetheless gave him sole access to that city's lucrative commercial revenues. After eighteen years, the younger brother died and was replaced by his sister as governor of Muttama, who was married off to an official of high rank.

Bannya Ram was said to have been more conciliatory and used diplomacy with Ava instead of military confrontation, marrying one of the daughters offered by the king of Ava. As a result, there was no war between the two, Pegu was prosperous, and the king was said to have been beloved by his subjects. Like most monarchs of Pegu, he patronized the two greatest shrines in Lower Myanmar, the Shwedagon and the Shwemawdaw. He died in 1446. Compared to Yazadarit, none of his immediate successors was able to match his accomplishments, yet the *Slapat* gave each more sentences than Yazadarit received, mainly for their meritorious deeds performed.

Bannya Waru (Bana Barow in the *Slapat*), 1446–1450, son of Shin Saw Bu by her first husband, ascended the throne, confirmed by a contemporary inscription as one of Yazadarit's successors.[48] He is said to have been the grandson of Yazadarit by the *Slapat* and nephew of Bannya Ram. He was especially known for being concerned with peace, morality, and stability in his kingdom, establishing law and order, and meting out royal justice. All this was said to have encouraged ethical behavior among the citizenry, so that from his time on, recorded the *Slapat*, "there were no thieves and robbers at all. It was not necessary to stay out the stair [draw up the staircase after dark] to close the door. . . . If a thing was forgotten in any place, no one dared pick it up. One could come back and get it where it was. Town and village was [*sic*] always upright and true."[49]

The *Slapat* also recounted how the king once disguised himself as a commoner and went out riding. On one occasion, his horse collided with a potter who was carrying pots on his head, who stumbled, fell, and broke his pots. The potter admonished the king, not knowing who he was, saying, "You ride so often and yet you do not look out for people. You have broken my pots. Suppose I go and make my appeal to his Majesty Bana Barow, do you think you will save your life? Hearing what the hawker said, laughingly and without anger, he borrowed money from someone and paid the man the price of his pots. There was never any king among all the kings who reigned in Pegu that did such good deeds as this king did."[50] The *Slapat* continued to say that "he took great delight in the three gems. . . . As to the Rangoon [*sic*] hair relic pagoda . . . *which had not been completed* [my emphasis], he built up again until the bell was finished."[51] (From this king's name and character, especially his record regarding the law, one wonders if Bannya Waru rather than Wareru was really the one responsible for the

Wagaru Dhammathat?)[52] If it were a product of Pegu, then Bannya Waru is a better candidate for the *Wagaru* [Wareru] *Dhammathat.*

His successor (1450–1453), nephew of Yazadarit, named Dasaraja in the *Slapat,* received as much space in the *Slapat* as did Yazadarit. He "bore the name of Bana Kandau (Bannyakyan in Harvey), but because his slaves took the kingdom, he was called Dasaraja," and reigned only three years. (His historicity is confirmed by contemporary inscriptions.)[53] The reason for receiving accolades despite his short reign was that he accomplished much in terms of the Shwedagon pagoda. The *Slapat* stated, as it "was not yet finished, from the bell he built it up to a finish at the umbrella, and put on its crown."[54] The Shwedagon Pagoda inscription confirms the *Slapat*'s account of the temple's newness: "what his Majesty's mother . . . had built was finished. When it had been finished His Majesty Bana Ken Dau . . . had it plastered, erected the spire (and) set up the umbrella."[55] Thus, contrary to current belief and national legend, the primary evidence demonstrates that it was only prior to his own reign starting in 1450 that the Shwedagon was actually built. This king was twenty-five years of age when he assumed the throne, "and reigned three years until he was twenty-eight. In the year 825 [1463 AD], Bannya Kendau passed away and returned to the devalokas."[56]

He was followed by another nonentity named Mamohtau who, according to the *Slapat,* had been separated from his mother as a child, and therefore called the "orphan king." As he reigned for only seven months, said the *Slapat,* he "had no opportunity of enshrining the relic chambers of the pagodas."[57] He was said to have had a very "cruel disposition" and was an "adulterer."[58] Despite that, he himself had no male heirs, and allegedly put to death all male members of royalty, leaving no male descendant of Yazadarit, so the ministers raised Shin Saw Bu, Yazadarit's daughter, as sovereign. And with her and her successors, Pegu finally reached its "golden age," the focus of the next chapter. But Pegu would not have enjoyed the peace and stability that came with Shin Saw Bu and Dhammazedi had it not been for Yazadarit and his youthful daring, military acumen, political sensibilities, and ruthless single-mindedness. Some credit should also go to the diplomatic and even-tempered Bannya Ram and the "justice-loving" Bannya Barow (Waru).

13

The Golden Years at Pegu
Shin Saw Bu, Dhammazedi, and Bannya Ram

Considered the "golden years of Pegu" by colonial historians, the fifteenth century was undoubtedly the zenith for the Kingdom of Pegu, particularly in terms of peace, religious activity, security, wealth, and exemplary leadership. One could almost call this period of time the "lull before the storm," for soon thereafter, it was ignominiously conquered by an upstart, "upstream" center called Toungoo. But before all that happened, these years contributed much to the history and historiography of Myanmar (figure 5).

All the inscriptions of Pegu confirm the existence of nearly all the kings of the First Pegu Dynasty mentioned in the Mon and Burmese chronicles, particularly the important and famous ones who are the subject of this chapter. Some of their kinship relations are also confirmed, as are many of their regnal years. This is most evident in the Shwẹdagon Pagoda inscription, which recounted the monarchs that donated to it, in the process providing a list from Binnya U to Dhammazedi.[1] However, as noted, since the total number of Mon inscriptions recovered during the First Pegu Dynasty palls in comparison with the Old Burmese ones recorded during the post-Pagan and Ava periods in Upper Myanmar, the same kind of analysis that I have done regarding Ava's leaders in part 1 of this book cannot be done for Pegu.

Thus, for example, although informative, only about three inscriptions have been discovered so far in Lower Myanmar that can be unequivocally identified as belonging to Shin Saw Bu, in addition to those erected by others such as Dhammazedi that happen to mention her. She is, of course, recalled in a contemporary inscription of Ava, where both her Mon title, Bannya Thau, and her popular Burmese name, Shin Saw Bu, were used.[2] Most of the Mon inscriptions found at Pegu city belong to Dhammazedi, especially his long Kalyani Inscriptions comprising ten stones that record a kingdom-wide reform of the *sangha*, along with more than a dozen inscriptions he erected at Pegu. Indeed, an unprecedented number of original epigraphs and other sources for reconstructing his reign exist, compared with others in his dynasty and most dynasties of Myanmar. We have much more on, and by, him, for instance, than we have on a far more famous king, Anawrahta of Pagan. There are other useable inscriptions of Lower Myanmar, but their provenance and identity are ambiguous, so caution must be used with these.

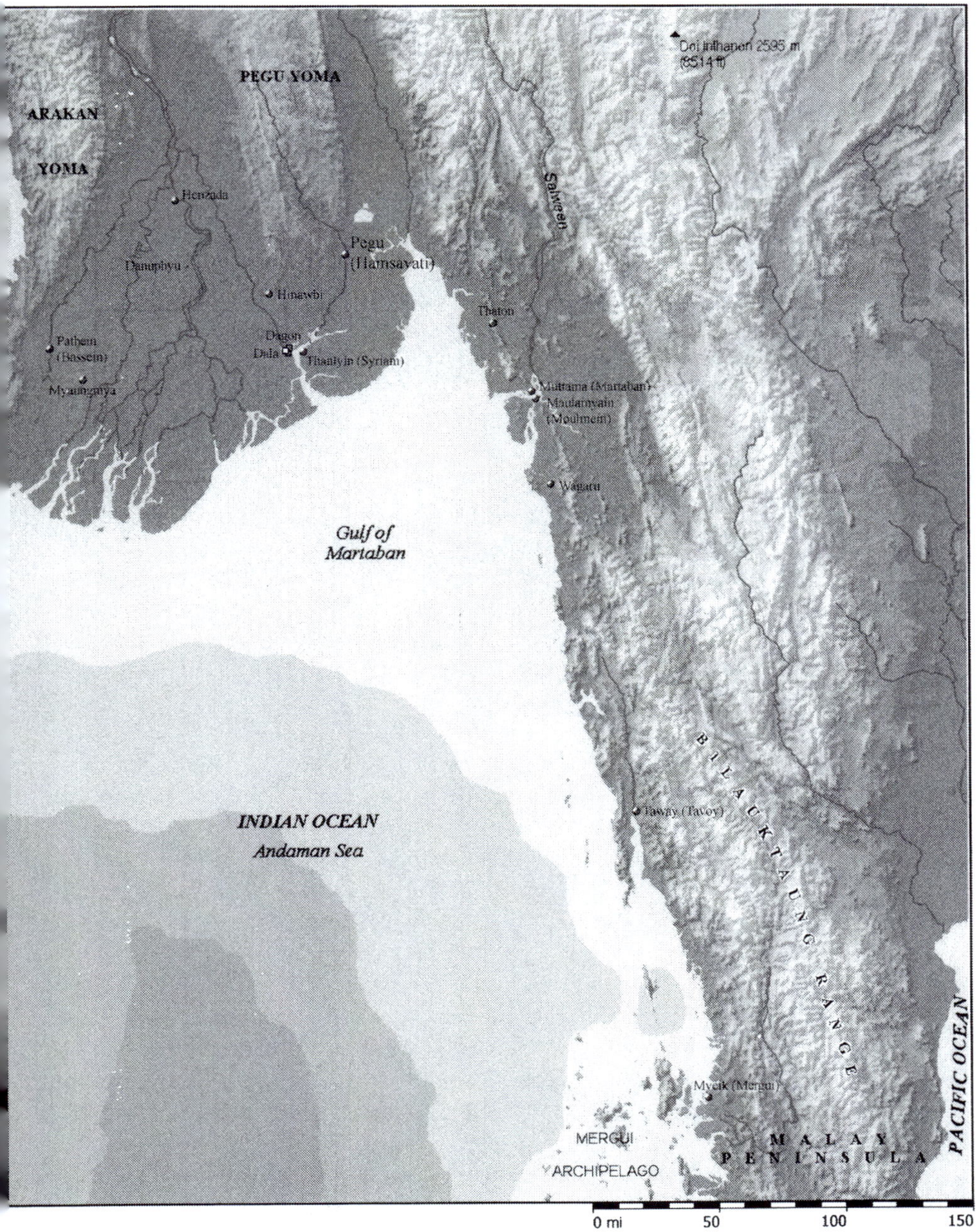

Figure 5. Kingdom of Pegu at its height

As for later chronicle accounts, more information is available on Shin Saw Bu in Burmese written in Upper Myanmar than the Mon language *Slapat*, which gives her one page (although considerable for that work), focused on her religious virtues. But it is more than compensated by the "Paklat Talaing Chronicle" which is as much nationalistic hagiography as it is serious history. Although Dhammazedi commands also about a page in the *Slapat*, there is a sizeable amount in the late "Paklat Talaing Chronicle" on him, also of a hagiographic nature.

There is far less information about the third major king of this "golden age" of the First Pegu Dynasty, Bannya Ram. He is given some space in the *Slapat*, while some unidentified post-Dhammazedi inscriptions at Pegu written in royal style might have belonged to him, although they do not mention him explicitly. He is also recalled in the accounts of several Western visitors who came to Pegu during his reign. But until a serious scholar who knows both Mon and Burmese attends to these needs and does not simply glorify the history of the Mon in Myanmar, what I present here must suffice.

Apart from these primary sources, there are some secondary popular works, and a few in relatively reliable compilations such as the *Myanma Swe Son Kyan* (*Encyclopedia Birmanica*) in Burmese, which has information on important monarchs. Master's theses on some of them also exist in Mandalay, Yangon, and Dagon Universities, but I have not been able to access them, although that is not a major drawback, as they should have used the same primary sources that I did.

Shin Saw Bu (1453–1470/1472?)[3]

Shin Saw Bu's life is not without some drama, controversy, and mystery. There is consensus that she was daughter of the chief queen of Yazadarit[4] and that her birth was on a Wednesday in the month of Tabaung (answering to March) in Burmese year 757 (or 1395 AD), which appears to be historical. She was said to have married a nephew of Yazadarit, Bannya Bye, around 1415, with whom she had two sons and a daughter.[5] However, the next several years, after her husband died, are controversial in fact as well as interpretation.

In part, the controversy arises because of the different perspectives and agendas of the sources, but also because her experience during those years is the stuff from which romantic adventure stories are made. These include her exile to Ava while she was still a young princess; her marriage to either the crown prince or king of Ava; her popularity at Ava as a queen who was given the Burmese title Shin Saw Bu ("her short ladyship," a reference to her physical stature, not her temperament); and finally her rescue by, and daring escape downstream to, Pegu with two monks,[6] one of whom, named Mahapitakadhara at the time, later succeeded her as King Dhammazedi. What follows is her story as far as I can reconstruct from indigenous and other sources.

Around 1422 or 1423, when the major western cities of the kingdom of Pegu were being besieged by the armies of Ava, Prince Bannya Ram, son of Yazadarit and brother of Shin Saw Bu, struck a deal with Ava's generals that offered his sister to the king of Ava in a marriage alliance. At the time of that event, Shin

Saw Bu was widowed, and was either twenty-eight or twenty-nine years old. At Ava, she became a popular queen, receiving the affectionate Burmese title Shin Saw Bu, as noted above, with which she was thereafter known in Burmese history until today. (Even a road in Yangon is named after her—Shin Saw Bu Lan—which, under colonial rule, was called Windsor Road.) After she had lived in Ava for six or seven years, she planned to escape to Pegu. Feigning a potentially fatal illness, she persuaded the king of Ava, Mohnyin Mintaya, to allow two monks from Pegu (then residing and studying at Sagaing, across the river from Ava) to attend to her spiritual needs.

Although U Kala did not go into great detail with regard to this particular episode, according to parts of the "Paklat Talaing Chronicle," the two monks apparently stole past the guards on their way out with Shin Saw Bu hiding in a trunk carried by them, covered with monks' robes said to have been gifts from her to them, thereby making the Burmese guards look like fools and the Mon monks, super secret agents.[7]

Once outside the city walls, they all escaped downstream by boat via a prearranged route. When it was discovered the next morning that she had disappeared, Ava sent five ministers with five war boats after her. But they were unsuccessful, for she and the two monks hid by day and moved only at night. The "Paklat Talaing Chronicle" records that "they continued all the way to the Pegu border. When their pursuers reported upon returning to Ava that they had scoured the country as far as the frontier without seeing any sign of their quarry, the King of Ava simply said: 'The lady was not contented here and has taken refuge in her own country. It is as she wished.'" "Once across the border" the monk who was to become Dhammazedi "sent a letter to the captains [of Pegu] telling them what had happened."[8] When the escapees reached the capital, she was greeted with great pomp and ceremony by its people, especially (by now) King Bannya Ram, her younger brother, who had given her to the king of Ava in exchange for ending an earlier siege.[9]

Shin Saw Bu's marriage alliance to the king of Ava is dated by U Kala to 1423 and her escape from Ava to 1429.[10] This means she was twenty-eight when exiled (if her birth date of 1395 is correct) and stayed for only six years at Ava, returning to Pegu at age thirty-four. Twinthin's *Myanma Yazawinthit* has it slightly different. It puts the year of Shin Saw Bu's marriage alliance a year earlier, in 1422, but her escape is dated to the same year as U Kala's, in 1429.[11] That puts her Ava stay at seven rather than six years. However, Twinthin wrote that she was already twenty-nine when she was married to the king of Ava, not twenty-eight,[12] so that she would have been thirty-six (not thirty-four as U Kala has it) when she returned. Harvey has her returning from Ava at age thirty-five in 1430, one year after the dates given by U Kala and Twinthin.

In contrast, and rather interestingly, the *Slapat* does not mention her exile to Ava at all! Moreover, it begins her reign in 1463 at age fifty-eight, and places her death in 1470 at age sixty-five,[13] giving her only seven years of reign. Harvey dates her ascension to 1453 (ten years earlier), but also gives her only seven years of reign, for she was said to have unofficially given up her throne to Dhammazedi to manage, not ending her reign officially until 1472. Harvey and the *Slapat* also differed on her age at ascension (fifty-two and fifty-eight respectively).[14] Thus, the main discrepancy between the *Slapat* and Harvey regarding Shin Saw Bu as sovereign is the date of her ascension, and her age at, and year of, death.

Despite these differences, the above four sources are generally close on the following dates and years. Shin Saw Bu was likely born in 1395, sent to Ava in 1422 (or 1423) at age twenty-eight (or twenty-nine), remained there for six (or seven) years until 1429 (or 1430), returned, and finally succeeded to the throne in 1453 (or 1463), at age fifty-two (or fifty-eight), ending her reign in 1470 (or 1472) at age sixty-five or seventy-eight.

Quite different in terms of both narrative and perspective, is the "Paklat Talaing Chronicle." It claimed that Shin Saw Bu was already "queen" of Pegu at age twenty and ruled for eight years *before* being "captured" and sent to Ava to become chief queen of Minyehswagyi. (There was no such king at Ava.) The "Paklat" also stated that she remained at Ava for twenty-two years and escaped only by 1444 or 1445, returning to Pegu at age fifty, without providing the date of her ascension or death. The "Paklat" also pushed her successor, Dhammazedi's ascension, to 1587,[15] over a hundred years too late and well after Pegu was already taken by Tabinshwehti of the Toungoo Dynasty. From all the above calculations and ones I have made of these sources, it is clear the authors of the "Paklat" did not bother with even a basic analysis of their own math, and did not consider the information they had with any seriousness.

Why was there this disregard by the authors of the "Paklat Talaing Chronicle" for "impossible" or inconsistent information, and their cavalier attitude for obvious discrepancies between their work and those of the others? I contend it was in large part because the "Paklat" compilers had a more compelling and modern agenda to pursue, which, in their view, the earlier *Slapat* had failed to promote. One of these was a "we are victims" theme (suggested to them by at least one colonial scholar, Emil Forchhammer) and quite obvious in the "Paklat." Thus, for example, Shin Saw Bu's marriage alliance and exile to Ava was depicted as a forced "capture" and, to use their own words, a "rape of the Queen" by Ava's king,[16] a statement not found anywhere else, nor is it supported by the events as recounted in every other source that mentioned the event.

The "Paklat Talaing Chronicle" also effused some of the nationalistic sentiments of the twentieth century, often stirred up by colonial administrators, scholars, and missionaries such as Robert Halliday, G. W. Cooper, and Dr. Frankfurter, among others. These sentiments were later "confirmed" and perpetuated by twentieth- and twenty-first-century academics who gushed over the Mon as the "Greeks of Southeast Asia," ignominiously conquered by the "less civilized" Burmans, T'ai, and Khmers. Following Forchhammer, the theme of the Mon as "downtrodden victims" of the Burmese, particularly, was manipulated to the utmost by the "Paklat Talaing Chronicle" in the Shin Saw Bu story.[17] Her mythology (and that of the Mon in general as "victims") continued into the twentieth-century separatist goals of the Mon in Thailand, who attempted to portray their history as one of long resistance to Burmese rule, much like Vietnam's image of itself as long-time resister of Chinese imperialism, which still resonates today. It appears, then, that concerns of modern ethnic nationalism have shaped Shin Saw Bu's most recent account.

The "Paklat Talaing Chronicle" had also sanitized and embellished Shin Saw Bu's relationship with Dhammazedi, perhaps to explain the suspicions aroused for their having spent several days and nights together during their escape, much fodder for suggesting a physical relationship between them. That she was given to Ava by her younger brother as part of a truce and marriage alliance between Ava and Pegu during a siege by Ava, which had the upper hand, also needed some sanitizing, hence the "rape" interpretation. And because both Shin Saw Bu and Dhammazedi became, ex post facto, famous and celebrated sovereigns of Pegu, while neither was in line for the throne (or in Dhammazedi's case, even royalty), their characters needed some pro forma sanitization and legitimation in any case.

That legitimation was in part secured by the use of certain auspicious and ominous events. One of these is the famous story of Dhammazedi's robe and its "flight." Before changing into his robe after bathing, it was picked up by a "prodigious wind," which set it down "on the topmost point of the Queen's palace," signifying his destiny to become king. While clear in its political implications, the story also suggested in no uncertain (Freudian) terms their physical relationship, stoking the rumors about it rather than assuaging them.[18] Another auspicious event had to do with two vultures circling Dhammazedi's monastery clockwise while he was still a monk, alighting outside his window, on the northeast, and facing him. He sent a pupil to fetch meat to give to the vultures, and as soon as they had eaten it, they "cried out in Pali" a phrase from which "he knew for certain that he would be king."[19]

One of the methods used by the "Paklat Talaing Chronicle" to rationalize the closeness between Shin Saw Bu and Dhammazedi was to make it appear as if it were a mother-son relationship. They did this by stating that she adopted him as her legal son, although he was only seven years her junior.[20] In reality, however, most sources state that he was her son-in-law, having married Shin Saw Bu's daughter, which therefore explains the use of the word "son" from her perspective. In the inscriptions, they are sometimes referred to as "mother and son," or as "royal mother and royal son."[21]

Thus, although some of these differences can be chalked up to mistakes made in the copying process (as all are copies of one kind or another), in especially the *Slapat* there is a particular religious perspective that reflects the author's priorities. As it was written by a monk, he held the queen in high regard for her religious activities, recording that she was "great in faith and self-sacrifice. Kings of the eight directions sent messengers with presents without intermission." And that "she accomplished a great many meritorious works, first in regard to pagodas great and small, and also in respect to monks who have undertaken the burden of study and the burden of contemplation. She built many monasteries and made them over to the monks. She made offerings without number [incalculable] all the time."[22]

At the same time, the author of the *Slapat* elided the story leading up to her exile at Ava, her years there, and her dramatic escape, although the author must have known of it if he had read U Kala, as he apparently did. It may be that the innuendos that arose later regarding her relationship with Dhammazedi during the escape may not have sat well with the author of the *Slapat.* Moreover, his work was focused on the history of the Shwedagon Pagoda, so he was interested only, or mainly, in her behavior as queen as it pertained to supporting Buddhism and, specifically, her patronage of that particular shrine. And because she did that in quite extravagant fashion, she was held in high esteem. Her Ava story would have just compromised her otherwise stellar religious record.

Still, she commanded only one page in the *Slapat,* and did not get an entire treatise of her own as Yazadarit did (at least none that we know of). To be sure, that paucity is not totally out of character for the *Slapat*; even someone as accomplished as Yazadarit was allotted only one short paragraph in it. The reason for this, to reiterate, was Yazadarit's alleged lack of generosity to the Shwedagon—at least, not as much as the author of the *Slapat* would have liked.[23] The main criterion for the *Slapat*'s praise of kings and queens, then, was the degree to which they patronized the religion, while their other (secular) accomplishments were considered incidental.

Apart from these kinds of perspectives is another with historiographic implications: the Burmese chronicles simply had more information on her than did the Mon histories, so that some of the earliest and fullest narratives regarding her life, reign, and even her title, by which everyone knew her, are in the Burmese language. She commanded several pages in U Kala's early eighteenth-century *Mahayazawingyi.* Twinthin's late eighteenth-century *Myanma Yazawinthit* devoted more than two pages to her story and called her the "Mon Princess" when not using her title. The erudite author even reproduced a poem by the famous literary figure of Ava, Shin Maha Rahtasara, in which she is referred to as Shin Maharattathara.[24]

Why would the story of the only woman sovereign in the country's history to which the Pegu Mon could rightly lay claim not attract the attention of its own historians except as "victim"? Was it not as important to them as it was to the Burmese historians (and to us in the twenty-first century)? If it were not that important to the Mon of Lower Myanmar at the time, what does that say about *our* writing of *their* history using *our* notions of what is important? Is it even a legitimate historiographic task?

U Kala's account of Shin Saw Bu is the earliest we have, while the *Slapat* was written nearly a century later, so that the latter probably borrowed much from the former, suggesting that the author of the *Slapat* not only had access to U Kala's history but must have known Burmese.[25] He recorded that Shin Saw Bu was known as "Takhan Cau Pho," that is, Shin (Ladyship) Saw Pu (short), as noted above, a Burmese title given to her while queen at Ava and by which she is thereafter known in the country. The *Slapat* also stated that only later was she called by her Mon royal title, Bannya Thau. That, however, is not entirely correct, for, as noted above, a 1444 royal inscription at Ava, nine years before she was consecrated sovereign at Pegu, referred to her as Bannya Thau. Even her brother, who was king of Pegu at the time, was mentioned by his Mon title in the Ava inscriptions.[26] All this shows there was some knowledge of each other's kingdoms, at least, of each other's royalty, with due respect given.

In terms of her story in the contemporary inscriptions, those erected at Pegu are much fuller, as one would expect. There are two (what appear to be) royal Mon inscriptions in Lower Myanmar dated to 1455 and 1462 that are likely to be hers. Although the donor's name is not recorded, they fall within her reign, and she is mentioned by name in the third person. In terms of style and content, they reveal Ava influences, down to the specific curses at the end targeted at those who violate her good deed. After all, she was part of Ava's royalty, similarly inclined in their quest for merit and making donations that followed a particular, standard format.[27]

Another Mon inscription dated to her reign, also without identifying who the donor was—although clearly a member of royalty—records an incredible amount of money and goods donated, which only a sovereign could have afforded. Some lines are flaked off, but in many places the donated items and costs remain legible. These include some 2,100 *viss* of silver (7,875 pounds) and another five hundred *viss* (1,875 pounds) of something else (perhaps gold?). Then another 17,083 *viss* of silver (64,061.25 pounds) is recorded as being donated, along with 1,720 robes and many other household items for the monks. Also given were 4,503 *viss* (3.75 pounds per *viss*) of black pepper and 24,620 *viss* of "Indian pepper" (hot chiles?), which, the record stated, comes to 29,123 *viss* on an annual basis. Then to another group of monks, 15,154 in all, many more of the same or similar items were donated.[28] And, as noted above, there is at least one inscription in Old Burmese that corroborates her presence and stature.[29]

There is some consensus among most of the sources regarding the final years of Shin Saw Bu's life, even if her age at, and the date of, her death differed slightly from one source to the next. After reigning seven years, wrote the *Slapat* (nineteen, according to Harvey), Shin Saw Bu

> handed over the government to the monk, Dhammazeti, who was viceroy. Then her Majesty Bana Thau went away down to Rangoon [*sic*]. She had them build and enlarge the Rangoon [*sic*] pagoda platform. Her majesty also put on a crown. Her Majesty went on the scales and made them take her own weight in gold, twenty-five *viss* [about ninety-four pounds],[30] and beating it out into leaf, cover the pagoda from the dome to the umbrella and down to the bottom. . . . She had them cast a bronze bell of one thousand seven hundred *viss* [6,375 pounds] weight. She had them pave the Rangoon [sic] pagoda platform with paving stones. Stone posts were put all round the pagoda, and stone lamps were put all round. . . . [Then came] a day when her Majesty Bana Thau grew sick, and wishing to contemplate the Rangoon [*sic*] hair relics which glowed and glistened, she opened her eyes and having attained tranquility, she passed away and returned to the devalokas . . . in the year 832 [1470 AD] . . . [at age sixty-five].[31]

Perhaps the most sympathetic assessment of her by an outsider can be found in G. E. Harvey's statement: "Daughter, sister, wife, and mother of kings, she ruled well, leaving behind so gracious a memory on earth that four hundred years later the Talaings could think of no fairer thing to say of Queen Victoria than to call her Shinsawbu reincarnate."[32]

Dhammazedi (Ramadhipati Sri Paramamahadhammarajadhiraja)[33]

Dhammazedi (1472–1492)[34] was one of the most important monarchs of the First Pegu Dynasty and has come to be regarded as one of the country's exemplary kings. Although he is best known for his kingdom-wide religious reform and patronage of Theravada Buddhism in Lower Myanmar, he could not have accomplished what he did had he also not been politically minded and astute. One of the advantages he had was his broader vision of the kingdom, partly because he spent some time at Pagan and Ava during his earlier career as a monk and was not just a Pegu product. His background enabled him to be realistic about Upper Myanmar while being aware of the tremendous place religion played in the whole country, economically, politically, and socially. That background was what gave him the kind of broader vision not found among some of his predecessors and successors.

The story begins with the issue of monk-turned-king. That transformation needed some rationalization and justification. At the beginning of his account in the "Paklat Talaing Chronicle," he was said to have agonized over his actions about Shin Saw Bu's rescue, for this sort of political activity was strictly forbidden to monks; not to mention murder, as he was said to have killed the other monk who had helped rescue the queen, subsequently, when he became king. Such secular activities by one who was much celebrated for his knowledge of the scriptures had to be rationalized. Consequently, the authors of the "Paklat Talaing Chronicle," probably also monks, provided the alleged scriptural basis for Dhammazedi's actions by having him think out loud in the following way:[35]

> for me to assist in the escape of a woman taken in war would be a major violation of the Sikkhapada. On the other hand, if I were to renounce my cloth and become a layman it is unlikely that I should be admitted to the palace [at Ava, in order to rescue her]. But if I were to put off my robe and be reordained as a novice, I could wear the cloth without making a fraudulent claim to monastic status, and not being bound by the monastic vows, I could take all necessary means to resolve this contingency. For the office of fraudulently representing oneself to be a monk consists in saying that one is one, taking part in corporate acts of a chapter, and causing laymen to maintain one with their gifts.[36]

The last point regarding the legality of lay gifts to properly ordained monks especially, needed to be addressed, for Dhammazedi became famous for his *sasana* reform in which that issue was central,[37] not to mention the clearly political and personal reasons for his actions, even if changing his status to that of a novice technically rationalized those actions.

Also important was another disingenuous rationalization concerning his lay behavior while still a monk, placed at the very beginning of the section on his rise to kingship.[38] It was clearly meant to legitimate Dhammazedi's reign ex post facto, for a monk to have been carrying on such covert, commando-like military activities could not be condoned by authors who were also monks. So, just before Dhammazedi died, the authors once again put thoughts into his mind, making him regret becoming a king in the first place, nevertheless finding some scriptural justification for it. He was said to have thought:

> I greatly regret having been obliged to abandon the state of a monk who shall know transcendental happiness, and become king. . . . Moreover, because I was induced to turn my face towards worldly success the life of the abbot of the Klan Duiw Monastery came to an end; that also I greatly regret. And I greatly regret that Minye Kyawzwa, the eldest son of my bosom should have met his death as a result of my heedless and foolishly unconsidered words. I greatly regret also the fault which accrues to me from deposing all the monks in the kingdom [a reference to his *sasana* reform], though admittedly I gained merit when I raised them again afterwards. The sinful sum of these four causes of my regret I have greatly to fear; then let me wash it away.[39]

Dhammazedi atoned for all that, of course, by doing much meritorious work, which the "Paklat Talaing Chronicle" described and listed in great detail, much of it confirmed by his inscriptions. But for his alleged murder of his comrade in arms in the queen's rescue from Ava, nothing was said.

Phayre's sources state that when Dhammazedi ascended the throne, the nobles were discontented, as he had no hereditary right. But when they saw how well he ruled the country, they were reconciled to him. They went on to say that "he is celebrated in the history of Pegu for his great wisdom. Numerous instances are given of the difficult questions which he solved, and the decisions he gave in various legal suits. Embassies came to him from China, Siam, Ava, Han (?), and Ceylon. He was earnest in religion. He made no wars, but extended the boundary of his kingdom east of the Than-lwin [Salween], establishing the district of Mhaing-lun-gyi. His subjects believed that he could make gold."[40]

And although, like Shin Saw Bu, Dhammazedi also commands only about one page in the *Slapat,* there are over twenty-seven pages in the late "Paklat Talaing Chronicle" on him. That raises some interesting questions regarding the latter source. It means that between the mid-eighteenth century when the *Slapat* was thought to have been compiled, and 1910–1912, after colonial historians and scholars urged the Abbott of the Krun Cinn monastery in Pak Lat, Thailand, to publish these two volumes, approximately twenty-seven pages had been added to the corpus of literature on Dhammazedi that had not existed hitherto.

The question that immediately springs to mind is how and why did the record of the king in the Mon sources expand from one page in the mid-eighteenth-century *Slapat* to approximately twenty-seven in the "Paklat Talaing Chronicle" of the early twentieth? What happened? Did new information suddenly appear out of nowhere? Were forgotten and mislaid manuscripts suddenly (and conveniently) recovered from obscure monasteries? Or, was Dhammazedi's reign being viewed in an entirely new and different context that required some invention and new interpretations? That, in turn, raises some issues regarding the antiquity and credibility of the "Paklat Talaing Chronicle" in terms of its other components, such as the *Yazadhiyaza Ayedawpon,* which Nai Pan Hla (and others) had contended was part of the "Paklat Talaing Chronicle."

The answer becomes clearer when the sources on the king are scrutinized more carefully. To reiterate, the most complete corpus of Myanmar Mon sources is represented by the "Paklat Talaing Chronicle." Its original title, the *Nidana Ramadhipati-katha* was changed upon binding to the *Rajawamsa Dhammaceti Mahapitakadhara* ("History of Dhammaceti Mahapitakadhara") published in 1912. In it is the section on Dhammazedi (the above mentioned twenty-seven pages), even though the title implies that the whole volume is about him. Those twenty-seven pages are largely hagiography. Some appear to be historically based, some seem to be either local and regional folk tales or didactic stories taken from various classical sources such as the *Mahabharata,* and perhaps even the *Ramayana,* but certainly the *Jatakas* stories are recognizable. Others are said to have been taken from Burmese theatrical presentations representing Dhammazedi and Shin Saw Bu as husband and wife.

The *Nidana Ramadhipati-katha* was written well after Dhammazedi's reign, some of it obviously inserted even after the *Slapat* was compiled in the eighteenth century. In one place, for example, Dhammazedi had to astutely deal with "the Mughals," who of course, had not yet appeared in India during his reign, and were not to become a great power for another two centuries. In another place, Prince Asah, hero of the *Lik Smin Asah,* is mentioned as a model prince of ancient times, when, as noted several times, the original Mon text of that work was not written down until 1825.[41] And finally, there are obvious historical anachronisms. Syriam, rather than Pegu, was considered to have been the primary port of embarkation and disembarkation in the *Nidana Ramadhipati-katha.*[42] Yet, Pegu had not yet lost that place to Syriam during Dhammazedi's reign, retaining its position as the port par excellence of Lower Myanmar for another century. Only after that, when the Pegu River began to silt up and Pegu as a center was destroyed by Arakan in 1599, did Syriam rise to replace it. The author was actually describing a situation during *his* life, not one during Dhammazedi's reign.

Another curiosity is that neither U Kala's *Mahayazawingyi* nor Twinthin's *Myanma Yazawinthit* made a fuss about or gave Dhammazedi much space in their histories; indeed, they excluded the early years of his (Wareru) dynasty at Muttama entirely, perhaps considering it illegitimate. Wareru was mentioned once tangentially, while Dhammazedi was referred to briefly when he rescued Shin Saw Bu.

Part of the reason for this neglect might be that the Muttama phase of the First Pegu Dynasty was not directly connected to the history of the Burmese state, which was, after all, Twinthin's focus, as revealed by his original title *Myanma Yazawinthit* (New History of Myanma, or New History of the Myanma

[People]). As for U Kala, although he did not focus on the state in Myanma as Twinthin did, his *Mahayazawingyi* (Great History of Kings) may have left out the Wareru Dynasty because he did not consider its ancestry (demons) to be legitimate royalty.

Yet, a king such as Yazadarit commanded considerable prolixity in both of the above chronicles even though he came from the same dynasty as Wareru. Part of the reason for that might be that much priority was given to kings who were accomplished in political affairs and state development activities, a *kammaraja,* in the Burmese scheme of things. Both Twinthin and U Kala were writing in the "Early Modern" period, which had, by then, experienced several hundred years of the outside world, especially the Western world, in domestic events. And even if the two chronicles ultimately used religion to legitimate society and judge monarchs by that particular criterion, they also had secular concerns. And Yazadarit's record met such concerns: he was a major contender with the kings of Ava and a worthy opponent of theirs during most of his reign, had married Ava royalty, and was "taught" the correct doctrines of Theravada Buddhism as practiced in Ava. He was very much like an Ava king.

Dhammazedi, on the other hand, was not only a monk-turned-king, without any royal pedigree, which must have met with some disapproval from both U Kala and Twinthin; he also did not appear to have had a remarkable record in state development, one with "national" consequences that Yazadarit had. In contrast to the little attention given to Dhammazedi by these Burmese chronicles written in the eighteen century, since then he has received far more space and become far more famous in the modern historiography of Myanmar. Not coincidentally, that began when colonial historians found his Kalyani Inscriptions, translated and published them in 1893, whose information seemed to fit their proclivities and assumptions about the role of their favorite ethnic group (the Mon speakers) in the history of the country. In other words, the "agency" given to Dhammazedi is, in large part, a result of modern historiography and its biases.[43]

But it is not all our doing: the sixteenth-century sections of the *Nidana Ramadhipati-katha* depicted Dhammazedi as the just judge, a most knowledgeable and intelligent monk, a wise king, and most important, a great patron of Buddhism. It was one of his principal monks, taking the famous name Buddhaghosa, who was said to have translated the so-called *Wagaru Dhammathat* into Burmese.[44] Dhammazedi himself also had a legal impact, as attested by his judicial rulings (called *pyatton*) with the authority of legal precedents, while Pegu during Dhammazedi's reign was said to have been a place where the rule of law prevailed. (Perhaps Dhammazedi is a better candidate for the compilation of the *Wagaru Dhammathat* than Wareru, although, as we have seen, one of Dhammazedi's successors, Bannya Ram, might deserve that honor even more.)

Dhammazedi received a bit more attention in the religious histories of Myanmar such as the *Sasanavamsa,* even though they were written much later in the nineteenth century and from an Upper Myanmar perspective of what was considered, at the time, religious orthodoxy.[45] But this attention was more negative than positive, for it considered Lower Myanmar's *sangha* less orthodox—even if its lineage went back to the same source as Upper Myanmar's *sangha* (the Third Buddhist Council of Asoka)—because it was thought to have become corrupted with British rule there, paying less and less attention to the *Vinaya* and ignoring the edicts of the *thatthanabaing* (head of the church) issued from Upper Myanmar.

Among these sources, Dhammazedi's own Kalyani Inscriptions, consisting of ten stones in Middle Mon and Pali that recorded his most accomplished act as a Buddhist king—a kingdom-wide reform of the *sangha*—are perhaps the most reliable in terms of contemporary information on his life and thought. However, they are also Dhammazedi's record of self-legitimation, along with that of his kingdom and his *sangha*. The Kalyani Inscriptions are certainly the source of many myths in the historiography of Lower Myanmar, including the most revered pagoda there today, the Shwedagon.[46]

Nonetheless, Dhammazedi's reform as recorded on the Kalyani stones preserved the actual processes and procedures in the Mahavihara tradition of Sri Lanka that continues until today. His chosen monks were sent there to be reordained in that tradition, the only one considered orthodox by Theravada Buddhists. They returned as the highest-ranking members of the order, and then proceeded to reordain the rest of the clergy at home. That shifted the balance of power within the *sangha* by making his monks the most senior, along with additional economic ramifications that enhanced the resources the state had lost to the *sangha* over many years, a complicated issue dealt with elsewhere.[47] The reform also had the effect of unifying the various, often fissiparous, sects, reducing what was once an unwieldy *sangha* to a more controllable size. But not surprisingly, the authors of the *Nidana Ramadhipati-katha* did not see his reform in that way. Rather, they saw it as behavior accruing demerit rather than merit, as shown above in one of Dhammazedi's "regretful acts" that he wanted to atone.

He was also said to have sent missions to Bodhgaya—the most sacred of Buddhist pilgrimage sites, where Gautama reached enlightenment—as most of Myanmar's leaders were wont to do, including Prime Minister U Nu after independence in 1948.[48] Such accounts recorded in the Kalyani Inscriptions explicitly compared Dhammazedi's prestige to that of earlier Upper Myanmar Pagan kings, especially Anawrahta, Kyanzittha, and Narapatisithu, but *not* to Yazadarit and Shin Saw Bu of Pegu, his own direct predecessors who belonged to the same ethno-linguistic group and dynastic family. Part of the reason for this may have been to rationalize his nonroyal status by celebrating notions of legitimate kingship that were more universal in their Buddhist underpinnings than those founded on genealogical criteria alone. Thus, he presented himself as part of the lineage of certain Pagan kings—even if they were considered Burmese and belonged to Upper Myanmar—for it was their qualifications as Buddhist kings in a larger ecumene that mattered most, not their ethnicity or genealogy. To Dhammazedi, religio-political concerns almost always preempted ethnic and regional ones. It was later colonial scholarship that gave "agency" to reified ethnicity and led Myanmar scholarship down a perilous (ethnic) path for many decades thereafter—some of it never finding its way out.

In spite of his reform measures, which attempted to reduce the size and wealth of the *sangha* to more controllable proportions, in the end, Dhammazedi donated the most to the *sangha* among Pegu's kings anyway, whose record is reproduced in a long list in the "Paklat Talaing Chronicle," some of it confirmed by his inscriptions. He was said to have built

> [the] shrine of the Four Buddhas. On the four sides of it he put up covered approach ways extending 1,000 cubits from the eastern portal and the same distance from the . . . [other ones]. He made gifts to all the clergy in the kingdom, for every abbot a bed and for every monk a couch, together with a set of the eight necessaries, robes, umbrella, almsbowl, and the rest. He built a pulpit in the ordination hall at the shrine and heard sermons there. . . . He enlarged the Shwe Dagon and provided a new *hti* and finial as well as gilding it from the ground up, and dedicated four captains of . . . [*paya kyun*] with 100 . . . to each staircase, besides 100 . . . to tend the offerings, together with land for its upkeep and land for the precinct. He did as much at the Shwemawdaw. He restored all the ruined pagodas and made good various image halls and images. He built monasteries without number [incalculable], such as the Mahajayarama Cave-temple group, with 40 [?] constituent monasteries, to which he dedicated 200 parcels of land (?) and 10,000 . . . [*paya kyun*]; the Nandarama, with 40 constituent monasteries, to which 50 . . . [*paya kyun*] and 500 measures of land were dedicated; the Vijjarama, the Asokarama, and the Pabbarama, all with 40 constituent monasteries, to which he made similar allocations; the Veluvana, with 100 monasteries, to which 300 . . . [*paya kyun*] and 500 measures of land were dedicated; and the Mat, with 100 monasteries also, to which he dedicated 500 . . . [*paya kyun*] and 1,000 measures of land. . . . Then he handed over the government of the kingdom to his heir apparent, the Uparaja, and shaving his head put on the robes of a lay brother, keeping the sabbath rule and teaching the monks daily; nor did he again meddle with affairs of state.[49]

The whole tenor of his reign exuded piety, spiritualism, and cultural advancement, and less military and political achievement, although those were not ignored. In fact, and to reiterate, Dhammazedi's notion of Ramannadesa, the "realm of the Rman" (the "Camelot" of the Myanmar Mon) was created precisely to counteract Ava's state ideology of the "realm of the Myanma." He was surely aware of the political advantages of having a secular unifying ideology formed around a distinct ethno-linguistic identity, especially since the religion used to attain unity was common to both kingdoms.

Dhammazedi lived to a ripe old age of eighty (although the *Vamsadipani* puts it at seventy-five).[50] Phayre wrote that he "died after a prosperous reign of thirty-one years" in 853 (1491 AD, although Harvey puts it in 1492).[51] "He received the funeral honours of a Tsekya-wati (Chakrawai-ti), or universal monarch, and a pagoda was built over his bones, which was crowned and gilded all over, as if it were an object of worship."[52] Both early and modern historians are responsible for the hagiography and historiography of Dhammazedi current today.

Bannya Ram

According to Phayre and the *Nidana Ramadhipati-katha,* Dhammazedi was succeeded by his son and heir apparent, Bannya Ram, in 1491 (or 1492, following Harvey). The king was the grandson of Shin Saw Bu, named after her brother, and known for his gentleness. Yet, some claim Bannya Ram conducted a "massacre of the kinsmen" to protect his position. This information was probably taken from the *Slapat,* where it is recorded that "he at once had all the royal offspring put to death."[53]

In contrast is the *Nidana Ramadhipati-katha,* well-sanitized by the time it was published in the twentieth century, where no such thing is recorded, although it did mention cases of abusing power. Thus, for example, Bannya Ram, desiring a princess already married to another prince, offered him four princesses in return for his. There were other instances of court intrigue, of course, where this prince or that queen was jailed on suspicion of rebellion and put to death.

One of the most vivid descriptions of pomp and power—whether pomp was for power, or power for pomp, as the late Clifford Geertz liked to put it—was Bannya Ram's coronation ceremony. I quote here at length from Shorto's translation because of the marvelous pageantry that must have inspired much awe and wonder for those watching it. If nothing else, the literary achievements attained by Pegu's scribes by this time, as attested by this description, are worth noting.

> On Thursday, the 9th waxing of Asadha, 857 [1495 AD], Cancer being in the ascendant, the King mounted his chariot of state to go and worship at the Shwemadaw. The arrangements were more sumptuous than can be told. Covered stands were erected east of the high ground, from the entrance to the pagoda to the city gate, hung from the gable-horns to the floor with awnings, floral tracery, yak's-hair tassels, and swags of flowers. Trellises had been put up on either side of the road and adorned with hanging banners, flagpoles, and sugarcane plantains, and along the route burnt lamps and incense, lanterns and perfume.
>
> When the time came for the procession of the chariot of state—it was like a chariot of the gods with its gilded superstructure—the King, accoutred with the five articles of the regalia, stepped into it, with Queen Agga-sirimayadevi on his right and Queen Maharajadevi on his left; both of them gallantly arrayed as for coronation. Virgins splendidly garbed fanned them with yak's-tail whisks, standing two before, two behind, and two on either side, and four white umbrellas shaded the vehicle, which was drawn by two teams of eight fine horses with gold-mounted harness. 400 respectable citizens, appropriately resplendent in waistcloths of cloth of gold with girdles and trousers, with bracelets and golden flowers stuck in their hair and ears, and having bathed in scented water before tying sashes of eight-figured cloth about their

waists, laid hold of scarlet ropes which were also attached to the chariot. The charioteers in festal array, with shoulder belts and hair ornaments, walked at the crested fore-end of the shaftpole leading the teams.

Before, behind, and on either side went royal concubines in groups of six, splendidly arrayed, holding yak's-tail whisks and peacock-feather fans. The ministers, captains, and chiefs, accoutred like the charioteers, took station round the King in the order of their precedence. The golden sword and the jewelled goad were carried in front with the white and gold and pearl umbrellas. On either side and in front of the chariot, nobles, ministers, and captains, some wearing waistcloths of cloth and gold and dignified with shoulder belts, walked with the queens, and before them musicians of every kind, playing Mughal drums and Haw drums, *jatuin* drums and Indian drums, reedhorns, horns, and trumpets, conchs, flutes, *le nay*, ken and mouth-organs, went on with a thunder calculated to drown even the surf of the ocean.

In front of them dancers and dancing-girls with small drums, and then men with bamboo clappers, beat out a rhythm as they danced. Further ahead mouth-organ players postured, behind the banners, guidons, streamers of welcome, and great garlands; and at the head of all marched detachments of the four corps of the army.

Behind the chariot of state, a multitude of hanging banners, lamps, and yak's-hair tassels like a forest of sal trees in spring bobbed round the King's riding elephant with its jewelled golden harness and lances and the cow elephant with the jewelled gold drum. Then came Queen Atuladevi's palanquin attended by chiefs bearing the coronation regalia, and her gilt open litter with the household [*kyun*] following it among the blare of horns and trumpets. Next to more drums and horns and trumpets came the palanquin of Queen Rajadevi, attended by chiefs bearing white umbrellas and followed by her household [*kyun*] and train, and then the other ladies of the Household [*kyun*] and train, and then the other ladies of the Household under red canopies decorated with myrobalans. Beyond the stands countless braziers burned to prepare food. The rear of the procession was brought up by the elephants, their riders carrying golden shields, and further detachments of the four corps of the army.

After the King had worshipped, he left the Shwemadaw and lodged in a gilt pavilion in the city. Next morning, the day being Friday, the 11th waxing of Vaishakha, 857, Aries being in the ascendant in the middle third, he entered a five-tiered pavilion, where he bathed, then with his two noble queens went across to the tiring-house. When he was robed, he entered another pavilion with a spire of seven tiers, its doors and niches adorned with tracery which glittered with gold and silver, there to be consecrated king.

Sitting in the pavilion, which would have put a mansion of the gods to shame, he set out four lines of lamps about the statue of Asah triumphant on the Seven-cubit Ground. Then he took his place on the throne with its jewelled cords, and was invested with the fivefold regalia of scarlet: the white umbrella, the diadem, the two-edge sword, the yak's-tail whisk, and the slippers. Then the plate of the Thousand Streams, with its myriad holes, was

> brought in by eight brahmins of noble family and immaculate conduct, in fair clean garments. They took hold of the right-voluted conchs which were suspended from their shoulders on golden chains, and to a burst of sound from the instruments and the shouts of those present like the sound of the sea, the King was consecrated.
>
> After his consecration he was blessed by monks of good standing and the brahmins inscribed (his title) on a plate of gold. Prince Baram sat in the place of honour to this right and Prince Naw Khwan in that to his left, while his brothers-in-law, who had married Dhammaceti's daughters, sat next to them; the ministers and captains allotted places to all the chiefs. The coronation feast lasted for seven days and seven nights.[54]

Another display of pomp and power in 1501 deserves mention as well. At that time, the king went up to Pagan, ostensibly to worship at the Shwezigon, one of the most sacred pagodas in the land for the hair relics of the Buddha said to be enshrined therein. On this occasion as well, the king's power and status were displayed by a large resplendent naval force, surely designed to awe not only his uncle, who was lord of Pyi, located right on the river path to Pagan, but also his upstream rival, Ava, along with all the people on the way. The authors who described it wrote that "the arrangements were more sumptuous than can be told; we describe them to the best of our ability."[55] And sumptuous they certainly were, as the description is even more magnificent than that of his coronation ceremony, especially as this occasion occurred on the mighty Irrawaddy River, the banks of which must have been packed to overflowing with the people of the kingdom, as the long train of gilt ceremonial barges and hundreds of finely carved and majestically designed war boats slowly moved against the current.

But what might interest historians most about the journey all the way to Pagan to worship at the Shwezigon is that it was even done at all, as if part of the legitimation of a Lower Myanmar Mon king required paying homage to an Upper Myanmar temple. The Shwezigon is attributed to Burmese king Anawrahta approximately six hundred years earlier in the Dry Zone of Upper Myanmar, the heartland of the Burmese speakers, yet apparently continued to be considered one of the palladia of state that had to be acknowledged, even by kings of Lower Myanmar centered at (then) maritime Pegu. Unless, of course, the whole event was meant to taunt Pyi and Ava that Pegu could go up the Irrawaddy anytime with impunity. Neither possibility needs to vitiate possible religious motives, especially as the temple was believed to contain genuine hair relics of the Buddha, making such visits virtually compulsory for any monarch aspiring to cakkavatti status. But whether political or religious, the event demonstrates that the country's overall Buddhist culture was a *shared one,* preempting, and rendering less important, other forms of localism, including ethnic identity.

European sources also seem to confirm Bannya Ram's power and wealth at Pegu. Nicolo di Conti writes of the city as a very populous one, twelve miles in circumference (see figure 4).[56] By this he obviously meant the entire city, including both the inner, walled royal section and the houses outside it, as satellite photography (and personal visits) confirm. Niktin, the Russian who followed di Conti, noted in 1496 that Pegu was "no inconsiderable Port, principally inhabited by Indian Dervishes" who dealt in *manik, iakrut,* and *kyrpuk,* which he said were products of Pegu. This remark is extremely important with regard to the issue of who the "Talaing" were, for here he makes clear Pegu was inhabited by "Indians" (Dervishes=Muslims?), about whom he was presumably familiar. It lends further credence to the conclusion that the people of Lower Myanmar consisted of not only Mon speakers but also those of varied ethnic and cultural backgrounds—hence, the term *kun-lun* used for them (and other coastal peoples of Southeast Asia in general) by the Chinese. Santo Stefano described Bannya Ram as having more than "ten thousand elephants" and an abundance of rubies "and many other precious stones."

Varthema was also there during Bannya Ram's reign. He described Pegu as "being on the mainland" and "near to the sea. On the left hand of this, that is, towards the East [actually West], there is a very beautiful river by which many ships go and come. This city is walled and has good houses and Palaces built of stone with lime." He acknowledges the king as being "extremely powerful in men, both foot and horse, and has with him more than a thousand Christians. [I presume these were Portuguese gunners.] And he gives to each, for pay, six golden *pardai* per month, and his expenses." Varthema also mentions the many "great Moorish merchants" and "all kinds of spices. We lodged in the house of a Moorish merchant, and we told him where we came from, and that we had many corals to sell, and saffron, and much figured velvet, and many knives. The said merchant, understanding that we had this kind of merchandise, was greatly pleased. This country is most abundant in everything which is produced in India, but no grain [wheat?] grows there. They have rice here in great abundance. Their laws, manner of living, dress, and customs, are the same as at Calicut, and they are a warlike people, although they have no artillery."[57]

Varthema's account of his meeting with the king provides further clues as to some of the sources of the monarch's wealth. During the course of the conversation, the king had a box brought out,

> which was two palms in length, worked all round in gold, and was full of rubies within and without. And when he had opened it, there were six separate divisions, all full of different rubies; and he placed it before us, telling us that we should take what we wished. [And then he] took a good handful of rubies from each of the divisions of the said casket, and gave them to him [Varthema's companion]. Their value was estimated at 100,000 ducats. Wherefore, by this he may be considered to be the most liberal King in the world, and every year he has an income of about one million in gold, and he gives all his income to his soldiers.

Varthema recorded that the king "wears more rubies on him than the value of a very large city; and he wears them on all his toes. And on his legs he wears certain great rings of gold, all full of the most beautiful rubies; also on his arms, and his fingers are full. His ears hang down half a palm, through the great weight of the many jewels he wears there, so that seeing the person of the King by a light at night, he shines so much that he appears to be a sun."[58]

Thus, to a considerable degree, Pegu's wealth must have been based on trade with Ava's interior products—such as rubies and rice but also lac, wax, ivory, horn, lead, tin, long pepper, and nypper vine—in exchange for the silver and gold that Pegu received in return, much of which likely ended up on Ava's pagodas. Harvey wrote that part of Pegu's wealth stemmed from its role as a port of trade, to where many nonlocal products from other regions of Southeast Asia and the world were brought: "pepper from Achin in Sumatra, camphor from Borneo, scented woods and porcelain from China." There was apparently no local coinage according to Harvey, but sometimes goods were weighed against the *ganza,* an alloy of lead and brass of specified weight stamped by merchants.[59] In short, not only did Pegu's wealth stem from its role as an entrepôt for the Bay of Bengal trade in western Mainland Southeast Asia, but it was also the conduit for its interior products, becoming the most reliable supplier of food for Melaka—the Hong Kong and Singapore of yesteryear.[60]

Lewes Vertonmannus visited Tenasserim about 1503–1504, during the reign of Bannya Ram, of whom he says, "The King useth not such pomp and magnificence as doth the King of Calicut, but is of such humanity and affability that a child may come to his presence and speak with him."[61] There is little else that he recorded. Eight years after Varthema, Ruy Nunez d'Acunha, the "Ambassador of Albuquerque," travelled to the court of Bannya Ram. A treaty was signed at Muttama in 1519 between the king and an Anthony Correa (who represented the Portuguese), demonstrating that Muttama and Tenasserim must have been under Pegu still. The account is told by the Portuguese historian Manuel Faria y Sousa.[62]

Despite the king's stature outside his court, inside were some real problems centered around the usual suspects: the king's nephew and his followers. The problems apparently involved prince Minye Kyawswa (a Burmese title given to him by Dhammazedi) and others who would benefit from his premature ascension. Finally, in 1526, after a long reign of thirty-four years, in which there was no war with Ava or any of his regional governorships, the king died of an illness that the chronicle called *javara.*[63]

The *Nidana Ramadhipati-katha* then lists the king's works of merit. He too had donated much to the religion. He not only crowned the Shwedagon with a new finial, he also erected the distinctive circle of *stupas* around it, rarely found elsewhere except at the Shwemawdaw. He enlarged and added to the height of many other *stupas* around his kingdom, cast bronze bells and Buddha images (one weighing fifteen thousand *viss,* about 56,250 pounds), built several large monasteries, endowed them with land and labor, and also held public festivities that he called "Brahmanical rites" on behalf of the court Brahmins, their families, and followers.[64]

The *Slapat* gives Bannya Ram more sentences than it did even Yazadarit. Again, the reason was his contribution to the religion as measured by his works of merit. It was said he

> had regard to the ten objects, and had real joy in almsgiving. His heart also was given over to liberality to . . . [*kyun*], followers, companions, ministers, military officers, and nobility. He also humbled himself before the three gems and did them great service. In the year 854 [1492 AD], on the thirteenth of the light half of the month Pausha, he built a palace. . . . When his Majesty reached the age of forty-eight, he built forty-eight little pagodas on the base [of the Shwedagon]. He again enlarged the great base, and made offerings in golden almsbowls with golden litters every day. He had eight men hang a golden bell as an offering. . . . [He] reigned thirty-five years till he was eighty-one years of age. In the year 888 [1526 AD], his Majesty, Bana Ram passed away and returned to the devalokas.[65]

He was succeeded by his son and heir apparent, Rajadhipati, at midmorning, who mysteriously died that same afternoon. (The *Slapat* leaves him out of the list of kings entirely, as does Harvey.) Three days later, sixteen-year-old Daka Rat Pi (1526–1538)—Harvey's Takayutpi and Phayre's Takarwultbi—the last of Wagaru's line, succeeded to the throne. The *Slapat* acknowledges his piety by recording that he was a "ruler of much faith and self-sacrifice . . . sensible of the benefits of the three gems." He was also said to have done "many meritorious works in pagodas, temples, and preaching halls. For the . . . [Yangon] hair relic pagoda he . . . consecrated a chain of gold adorned with sapphires and many different kinds of precious stones, and put it on the dome of the pagoda. His Majesty gave as an offering to the pagoda a royal tusker elephant, with two young ones, a silver almsbowl, and eight men." Then, surmised the *Slapat*, "If this king had had Sammapayoga, he might have lived to the age of 85 years, and might have ruled the realm. Thus have the wise men spoken," suggesting the existence of an earlier account on which the *Slapat* was based. But "because he had not Sammapayoga he reached only the age of twenty-eight and had to give up his life in a jungle place. He was sixteen years of age when he began to reign, and was king for twelve years until he reached the age of twenty-eight. In the year 900 [1538 AD], he passed away, and returned to the devaloks." The *Slapat* concluded that the king "never looked at a book, took no heed of good practice, but only sported with elephants and horses in jungle bush, and searched for shellfish and crabs. He was like a deaf and dumb person."[66]

In 1539, after two tries, the city of Pegu was taken by King Tabinshwehti of newly arisen Toungoo, which lay at the edge of the Dry Zone in the Sittaung River valley. Once again, the Dry Zone had conquered the center of the coastal maritime region to reestablish Dry Zone Paramountcy, a historical pattern that had, for more than a millennium, been the rule. This time, however, the conquerors remained in Lower Myanmar, making Pegu their capital. Although short-lived, the Second Pegu/Toungoo Dynasty and kingdom of sixteenth-century Myanmar was the most extensive in its history, a subject dealt with in detail elsewhere by an eminent historian of Myanmar.[67]

Harvey considers the years 1423 to 1539 "the happiest years in the annals of Pegu."[68] As he was referring to the end of the First Pegu kingdom, he may be correct. It was certainly a period with relatively little protracted warfare, of relative peace and unity, and a time when most of its kings focused on patronizing the religion with the gold and silver they acquired from the growing trade in Southeast Asia. Consequently, Harvey anointed this decade and a half to have been "the golden age of Lower Burma," and even "if few traces remain, that is because it was a simple civilisation."[69] Not only was it a simple civilization, it was the *first* civilization in, and generated by, Lower Myanmar. And unlike Pagan, there was no long-term pattern of structural decline at Pegu, for it was gone almost as suddenly as it had come.

The Historical Legacy of the First Pegu Dynasty

Determining historical legacies is a subjective matter, depending on what one considers important. Historical legacies, moreover, are often viewed as necessarily positive, celebrating accomplishments, usually of "winners," when in fact they can also be negative, of "losers" decrying their failures. However one interprets it, claiming legacies needs convincing evidence. Whatever we think might be important, in order to demonstrate that the Kingdom of Pegu did in fact have an impact in some significant and unique way (negative or positive) on the subsequent history of the country or region, empirical evidence must be produced.

Admittedly, methodologies in some disciplines make it easier to prove certain contentions than those in others. Legacies of a political, religious, linguistic, or literary nature are demonstrable, hence, can be more convincingly affirmed or refuted than (say) those of an art historical nature, where analysis can be extremely tautological and subjective. But even more difficult than art history are categories that the Annales School refers to as "mentalities": intangible and abstract concepts presumably held by the society in question.

One of these abstract mentalities that Pegu left as a legacy is the notion of a pan-Mon community in the term "Ramannadesa," "the realm of the Rman," created by Dhammazedi in the late fifteenth century. Although not perpetuated by his immediate successors—it died after his reign ended—it was later resurrected by colonial scholars and officials and, subsequently, embraced by other scholars of Myanmar, indigenous and foreign. Regardless of the way the notion of the "realm of the Rman" may have evolved, it is at root still a historiographic legacy regarding an "imagined community" that is still very much with us.

In this chapter, I focus on the provable, concrete legacies of the First Pegu kingdom, asking whether or not its history did in fact produce individuals and events that led to the establishment of institutions and ideas longer lasting than itself, with consequences for the country's history as a whole, particularly on the state (as both history and state are the focus of this book). But I will also ask how the intangible mentalities—the ideas produced by Pegu—affected its historiography with long-lasting consequences for posterity's understanding (and misunderstanding) of that kingdom.

Before answering these questions, we should realize from the outset that it is far more difficult to assess Pegu's legacy than Ava's. As stated several times, there is much more information about the latter, in terms of both primary and secondary sources, even though both kingdoms endured for nearly the same amount of time: approximately two hundred years each.[1] During that period of time, whereas the post-Pagan and Ava periods produced approximately 431 Old Burmese inscriptions, at least two "chronicles," and dozens of literary works in both prose and verse, the First Pegu Dynasty managed to produce practically no verse of national stature, and only about fifty-seven Middle Mon inscriptions, some of which are undated, partly legible, or of unknown provenance. And the only two "historical" sources written about (not by) the First Pegu Dynasty—the *Nidana* and *Yazadhiyaza Ayedawpon*—were later products. Everything else written about Lower Myanmar and the First Pegu Dynasty discussed herein—the *Nidana,* the *Slapat,* the *Lak Smin Asah,* the "Mon Chronicle," and the "Paklat Talaing Chronicle"—was done centuries later, dating from the eighteenth to the first two decades of the twentieth century, and all of them are at least partly hagiographic in nature. There is some pertinent information about Pegu's Pali production in the *thathanawin* (religiographic) tradition, and although useful, neither the *Vamsadipani* nor the *Sasanavamsa* was written by the Mon of Pegu; both were produced in Upper Myanmar, and both are late.[2]

Perhaps one of the more important caveats in terms of Pegu's legacy is that whatever potential some of it might have had in Myanmar's history, it was quickly eclipsed by the achievements of the Second Pegu/Toungoo Dynasty that replaced it. Conventionally called the First Toungoo Dynasty in Western historiography, it conquered and made Pegu its capital in the first half of the sixteenth century, whence it went on to military accomplishments never before attained in Myanmar or Mainland Southeast Asian history.[3] When observers of Myanmar refer to Pegu, they invariably mean this dynasty of Tabinshwehti and Bayinnaung, not the one ruled by Shin Saw Bu and Dhammazedi.

Nonetheless, I will make an attempt to assess the significance of the First Pegu Dynasty in light of what has been gleaned from the sources we have at our disposal and have analyzed in the preceding chapters. Although the First Pegu Dynasty was important to Myanmar's history (and perhaps Southeast Asia's as well) in a few select ways, the image of Myanmar crafted during the most recent two decades of the twentieth and twenty-first centuries virtually guarantees that its imagined role will surpass its actual historical one.

Ethno-linguistic and Sociocultural Legacies?

One of the conventions about Pegu and its mythology is that it was a unique, "ethnic" Mon kingdom, thereby setting it apart from the Burmese landscape. Notwithstanding the myriad problems of reifying ethnicity (and here, of reifying an ethnic kingdom), it is probably true nonetheless that (1) Pegu's royalty and leadership were composed mainly of, or most of them identified themselves as, Mon speakers; (2) that the dominant segment of the population in the kingdom was probably composed of people whose mother tongue was Middle Mon; and (3) that the language of state, and perhaps also the lingua franca of society, was Middle Mon, even though the society at large was quite mixed.

Admittedly, there have been cases in history—such as Kandyan Sri Lanka and Yuan China (among others)—where the language of the rulers and their subjects were not the same. In Myanmar, however, for the most part, the rulers appear to have spoken and written in the same language as the majority of the people they ruled, so that there was a common lingua franca of state and society, even if various ethno-linguistic groups lived, worked, and spoke their own languages in that same society. One could make the same case for other areas of Southeast Asia as well, so that we are fairly justified in saying that Dai Viet was "Vietnamese," Ayuthaya was "T'ai," Angkor "Khmer," and Mataram/Majapahit "Javanese," as long as we are speaking of language.

Even assuming that we are correct in claiming that language is culture, the problem here is referring to kingdoms in ethnic terms, as colonial historians did. When they wrote that Pagan was Burmese, and Pegu, Mon, not only did they mean that these kingdoms were composed of and led by Burmese and Mon speakers, but they also implied that somehow the kingdom had assumed the same "ethnic characteristics" attributed to their people—"introspective" Mon and "prosaic" Burmans.[4] One can imagine the kinds of problems these sorts of assumptions and projections, based on reified ethnicity, can lead to. Are we to assume that Pegu, as a kingdom, was "introspective" and Pagan, "prosaic"? This is precisely my reason for discarding ethnic labels for communities and (especially) political entities such as kingdoms, whenever possible, and using geopolitical and economic ones instead: inland agrarian Ava and maritime trade-centered Pegu.

Notwithstanding, and even if the First Pegu Dynasty was important historically as the first-ever independent kingdom in Lower Myanmar led by Mon speakers, how else was this ethno-linguistic feature a "legacy" that affected the country's history? The Mon language had little (if any) importance in the shaping of the national language; at least none that primary evidence has demonstrated. To be sure, there probably was some linguistic borrowing between Ava and Pegu, but nothing that could be considered a legacy. In fact, most, if not nearly all of the most important and complex vocabulary regarding (say) conceptions of the cosmos, time, space, the state, society, salvation, and so on, found in original Pegu inscriptions, had been part of the vocabulary of Upper Myanmar society for centuries, having arrived there much earlier from India and/or Sri Lanka.

The same can be said regarding the religious literature of Pegu of this period. The texts that encompassed, defined, discussed, analyzed, circumscribed, and preserved the above-mentioned conceptions and their vocabulary—mainly found in the Buddhist *Tripitakas,* the *Jatakas,* and the *Rajavamsa* tradition—were already known at Pagan several hundred years earlier and at Sri Ksetra during the Pyu period even earlier. Not surprisingly then, Upper Myanmar already exhibited the manifestations of that literary foundation found in art, architecture, iconography, and conceptions of state and king well before the First Pegu Dynasty emerged in the late thirteenth century.

In terms of vernacular literature as well—that is, texts written in Middle Mon—the First Pegu Dynasty produced little or nothing in either verse or prose that can be considered "national" legacies; at least we have no record of it. None of today's major verse forms or the most eminent figures of Myanmar's literature described in an earlier chapter has been attributed to the First Pegu Dynasty; rather, it is to Ava that that honor belongs.[5]

Even the verse found scattered here and there in the much later *Yazadhiyaza Ayedawpon* follows the four syllabic and "climbing" (or "descending") rhyme schemes of Burmese verse that was ubiquitous at Ava,[6] found not only in the dozens of literary works produced during that period but in many of its inscriptions as well. Nor did Pegu develop any original genre of prose literature that could be considered a national model to be considered a "legacy."

One cannot find any Middle Mon inscriptions of the First Pegu Dynasty written in verse either, even ones erected by royalty. All were written in straightforward prose. In contrast, many Ava inscriptions were written either almost entirely in verse or in a mixture of verse and prose, in which case, at certain poignant points in the prose, verse breaks out, to later return to prose. Probably the best example of an inscription found written nearly totally in verse at Ava is Shin Thilawuntha's long inscription of nearly fifty-four lines (and that, on just one face of the stone), commemorating the building of his monastery called the Yadanabeikman Kyaung in 1509 at Sagaing.[7] Although Thilawuntha is an exceptional figure, verse erected by fairly ordinary people can also be found in the inscriptions of Ava, while Pegu left no record of religious texts considered exemplary by literary scholars of Myanmar, even from Dhammazedi's reign.

What, then, does the evidence have to say about Pegu's ethno-linguistic and/or sociocultural legacy? With the small population of Mon speakers in the country (approximately 2 percent in modern times), the earlier development and long domination by Burmese state and society starting at Pagan and continuing for another eight hundred years until today, the problematic nature of Pegu's sparse sources, and the brevity of the First Kingdom and Dynasty of Pegu, I am afraid its ethno-linguistic and/or sociocultural legacy for the country as a whole is minimal.[8] It is hardly comparable to Ava's, and certainly nowhere close to Pagan's—precisely one of the reasons the Mon Paradigm had to be invented in the first place to mitigate the reality of that impoverishment.

Pegu's Contribution to Religion and Its Art

The two monarchs most renowned for their contributions to the Theravada Buddhism of Lower Myanmar, and the country as well, were Shin Saw Bu and Dhammazedi. The queen and the Shwedagon Pagoda are virtually synonymous, for the temple as it exists today is mainly the result of her work: the height, the base and platform, the stone and marble circumambulatory, the oil lamps surrounding the base of the *anda,* the *hti* (finial), and much of the endowed land and labor. It was not until her reign that the Shwedagon as we know it today materialized, even if its legendary origins take it back much further. As shown in an earlier chapter, she spent much on the economic bases of the Shwedagon, and in general, on the religion and *sangha* that ensured their survival to this day.

Dhammazedi's role, although also exemplary in terms of financial support, was importantly different from Shin Saw Bu's. His dual expertise as king and monk went a long way toward achieving this: Dhammazedi knew his religion but also his politics.[9] The success of his kingdom-wide *sasana* reform had enormous religious, political, and economic importance. It established his stature as an exemplary reformer-king. Although this image was largely self-proclaimed, nonetheless, he is often associated by other writers with Asoka and Parakramabahu I of Sri Lanka, as well as kings Anawrahta and Narapatisithu of Pagan, who were as exemplary in their own kingdom-wide reformations. That stature placed him on a pantheon of reformist kings of Myanmar, at least from the perspective of modern historians.

His *sasana* reform must have been effective—at least it established a lasting precedent—for it was emulated by others subsequently. King Thalun of the Second Ava Dynasty initiated a similar reform in the seventeenth century, as did King Mindon, who convened the Fifth Buddhist Council in the mid nineteenth century. This trend continued among leaders of the modern state: U Nu convened the Sixth Buddhist Council in 1954–1956, and U Ne Win promulgated the *sasana* reforms of 1980.

Dhammazedi's purification of the *sangha* not only attempted to reestablish the orthodoxy of his *sangha* along the doctrines and procedures practiced by the Mahavihara school of Sri Lanka, but also linked the origins of his *sangha* to two of Theravada's most famous missionaries—Sona and Uttara—so that the lineage of his *sangha* was traced to the perceived pinnacle of Theravada orthodoxy, the Third Buddhist Council of Asoka. Thereafter, Dhammazedi's *sangha* offered what appears to have been a viable option to Upper Myanmar's stature and monopoly as the fount of Theravada Buddhism in the country at the time.

These reforms and other public religious activities of Dhammazedi helped enhance the reputation of the Kingdom of Pegu thereafter as an exemplary center for the Sri Lankan brand of Theravada Buddhism in Southeast Asia. Never before in Myanmar's history had the image of Lower Myanmar attained such heights of religious orthodoxy or stature that theretofore only Upper Myanmar had enjoyed. The Kalyani *sima* (ordination hall) built by Dhammazedi, where most of these activities took place, became virtually synonymous with religious reform, in the way the Shwedagon became synonymous with religious sacrality.

Both Shin Saw Bu and Dhammazedi's patronage of the religion set high standards, in terms of exemplary religious zeal and actual financial support as models for posterity to emulate. To be sure, patronage of the religion was not new, but part of a long-established pattern; a long line of monarchs preceded them, many of whose patronage, in both absolute and relative economic terms, actually surpassed theirs.[10] Nonetheless, their religious legacy was very important, and it went beyond Pegu's religion per se into its religious art.

One of the most sacred sites in the country, perceived as holding eight hairs of the Lord Buddha—the Shwedagon Pagoda at Yangon—is arguably without equal today, and remains the major religious contribution of the First Pegu Dynasty. Not only did Shin Saw Bu build up the physical structure of the

Shwedagon to nearly what it is today and endow it with lands that still remain tax-exempt, but Dhammazedi's account of the pagoda's origins placed it back at the Buddha's time.[11] Thus, despite the pagoda's actual history that dates it to not much earlier than the fifteenth century, the belief regarding its crucial link to a sacred time and a sacred place will forever be ingrained in the hearts and minds of the people, in both Upper and Lower Myanmar. It is true, of course, that although the elongated styles of the Shwedagon (and also the Shwemawdaw of Pegu) likely reached their pinnacle at Pegu, they had prototypes at eleventh-century Pagan in the Shwesandaw and Shwezigon, and later at Ava (Sagaing), in the Htupayon.[12]

Along with the Shwedagon, the Shwemawdaw is also considered extremely sacred, housing (two) hair relics of the Buddha. Although legend gives this pagoda a much earlier date as well, its current version most likely goes back only to the First Pegu Dynasty. The Shwethalyaung (reclining Buddha), the largest in precolonial Southeast Asia at over 180 feet long and fifty feet high, is also said to be a product of the First Pegu Dynasty, even if its date is a point of debate.

Dhammazedi is also said to have erected the Ajapala Pagoda, but in terms of style, it is rather nondescript.[13] This monument and another called the Shwegugyi, also thought to have been built by Dhammazedi, were meant to commemorate some of the better-known episodes in the life of the Buddha. The latter is a "replica" of the Mahabodhi temple at Bodhgaya, where the Buddha was said to have attained enlightenment, incorporating the "seven stations" theme into its plans, denoting the seven weeks the Buddha remained at Bodhgaya.[14]

Some have asserted that Dhammazedi's Shwegugyi is unique (along with another at Lanna) in the Buddhist world outside of Bodhgaya in its use of the "seven stations" theme. Yet, centuries earlier at Pagan, King Nadaungmya (1210–1234) was said to have built the Mahabodhi temple, which not only included the "seven stations," but also is much closer visually (as well as in size, shape, and design) to the original than the Pegu version. In fact, I would be surprised if Dhammazedi, who studied in Upper Myanmar for approximately seven years, was not familiar with this temple and inspired by it, reproducing it at Pegu subsequently.

Moreover, Pegu's royal temples were mainly (if not exclusively) solid *stupas* whose domestic origins go back to seventh-century Sri Ksetra or earlier, while its more immediate prototypes go back at least to the beginning of the eleventh century at Pagan. As for the *stupa*-temple, which virtually defines Pagan's sui generis religious architecture, Pegu neither duplicated it nor reproduced it, lacking the expertise, the money, or both.

In terms of monumental religious iconography, even the colossal Kyak Pan Buddhas at Pegu, probably erected during King Dhammazedi's reign[15] (and probably one of a kind for the time and place), actually reflect a standard motif long known at Pagan, perhaps best illustrated by the Ananda temple with its four Theravada Buddhas of this *kalpa* arranged "back-to-back" and facing their respective cardinal directions. In other forms of religious (and perhaps even secular) art as well, the First Pegu Dynasty appears to have contributed very little.

Consequently, there is no such thing in Myanmar studies as a "Pegu style" of painting, sculpture, iconography, or religious architecture that can be attributed to that dynasty and period, whereas we *can* say that there is a distinct "Pagan style" or "Ava style" of painting, sculpture, iconography, and religious architecture. Similarly, we can say there is an Angkorian, Sukhotai, or Ayuthaya style. To be sure, art historians can probably point to works of art from Lower Myanmar during that period that *look different* from their counterparts produced in Upper Myanmar and other regions, and label it "Pegu style." But difference alone does not a style make. No one can, or has yet, demonstrated with securely dated primary evidence, that what the First Pegu Dynasty produced was so distinctive an art style that it became part of the "national" mélange.

The above raises one of the most serious methodological problems in the discipline of art history (especially for historians): that is, the attempt to establish chronology by using style alone. Especially in the case of Lower Myanmar, attributing its art to the First Pegu Dynasty is almost all stylistic speculation of a tautological nature, as most of its remains are not securely dated, or dated at all. Even the Shwegugyi Pagoda noted above has no date or name of donor (other than "lord of the white elephant"), so that its attribution to Dhammazedi is conjecture even if likely. Art historians must go beyond style alone to show that what they consider "Pegu art" is in fact dated to the First Pegu kingdom by contemporary records, rather than simply designating it as such because it is found there in "ancient times" or looks like what they have already declared to be "Pegu style," a self-fulfilling analysis.

There appear to be several practical reasons for Pegu's deficiency in contributing to Myanmar's art history compared with (say) Sri Ksetra or Pagan. First, the kingdom is relatively new and emerged relatively late. By the time it was in fact a bona fide kingdom in the mid- to late fourteenth century, Upper Myanmar's Pyu and Burmese cultures had already produced, for nearly a millennium, much of the artistic legacy of the country. In addition, although we know less about the Pyu, certainly Pagan was far grander, immensely more powerful, larger and wealthier, much better populated, and had nearly four hundred years to accomplish what it did, whereas the First Pegu Dynasty not only arrived late but constituted a total of approximately only two hundred years when it ended. Thus, Lower Myanmar had neither the human and material resources nor the time it needed to produce much distinctive art.

Indeed, by the time Pegu became a viable kingdom with a monarchy and capital, stable enough to even start thinking about producing works of art with a local style—that is, by Binnya U's reign in the mid-fourteenth century—it was almost totally preoccupied with affairs of state focused on survival. By the reign of Yazadarit, Pegu's concerns lay with the growth and development of the state as a regional power. Thereafter, Pegu was under constant pressure, mainly from Upper Myanmar's Ava, but also from internal forces within its own royal family, not to mention external powers on its east such as Ayuthaya, so that most of its life was spent in defending itself or attempting to unify its fissiparous components. Indeed, it is only because patronage of the religion was invariably linked with state legitimation that construction of temples and other such religious works at the "national" level were constructed at all during this time. Indeed, it is precisely because the reigns of Shin Saw Bu and Dhammazedi gave Pegu the stability and peace that it was able to produce the kinds of religious architecture (such as the Shwedagon and Shwethalyaung) that could be considered "national" legacies.

In other words, the First Pegu Dynasty did not contribute something entirely unique to the art history of Myanmar as far as I know; at best, it preserved and maintained the heritage of Upper Myanmar. To be sure, Pegu did enhance the design and grace of Upper Myanmar's solid *stupa* style so that it became more elongated, best illustrated by the Shwedagon Pagoda at Yangon and the Shwemawdaw at Pegu, thereafter reproduced nearly everywhere in the country. And as noted above, Pegu probably also produced the Shwethalyaung (reclining Buddha), the largest in Southeast Asia until recently, which stands out as the example par excellence of that motif. However, none of these is entirely unique, as their prototypes preceded them at Pagan by several centuries, and even earlier in Sri Lanka.

Until art historians of Myanmar make a better distinction between myth and history regarding the country's religious art and architecture, and stop feeding "the legend that was Lower Myanmar," little progress will be made in this field where the methodology is already dependent on rather subjective criteria.

The Economic Legacy of Pegu/Lower Myanmar

The economic significance of the First Pegu Dynasty in the totality of Myanmar's history is probably more important than is generally acknowledged. Although that might seem obvious from Pegu's location near the coasts at the time, what it did specifically, and when, is a question that has not been raised and still needs to be established with primary evidence. Even more important than that is what the First Pegu Dynasty did in terms of laying the foundations for the Second Pegu/Toungoo Dynasty's achievements, which had tremendous historical consequences not only for Myanmar but also for the rest of western and central Mainland Southeast Asia.

During the early phase of the First Pegu Dynasty, when its center was at Muttama, it appears to have controlled the kingdom's trade toward the east and south, while one of its fiefs, Pathein, controlled the west. Pegu itself controlled both ports for most of its life (although interrupted by Ayuthaya off and on), as well as the northbound trade to the interior of Myanmar and beyond. Perhaps the reign of Bannya Ram best exemplified this pattern as described in a previous chapter. This trade subsequently became a regional (Lower Myanmar) pattern that continues today with the recent creation of a deep-water harbor at Dawei (Tavoy), one of Pegu's old port cities.

Also important but less tangible, and perhaps for the first time in early Myanmar's history, trade and commerce of the coasts became a viable option to the agriculture of the interior in the maintenance of the state. Before then, it had been the inland, upriver agrarian environment that led to state formation and its growth and development. But by the fifteenth century, Upper Myanmar had some serious competition in the trade and commerce of Pegu and Muttama, enhanced by their growth in Southeast Asian waters, especially with the advent of the Ming in China, Vijayanagara in South India, Java and Melaka in Island Southeast Asia, and, subsequently, the Spanish in the Philippines and the Portuguese nearly everywhere in the region. With much of Upper Myanmar's good irrigated land regularly and perpetually sequestered in tax-exempt *sangha* hands, there was also a need for cash, particularly silver, most of which was likely supplied by Lower Myanmar, the main reason for Ava's continued attempts to control that region.

And although the following needs to be quantified properly, the First Pegu Dynasty had quite clearly laid the economic foundations and infrastructural wherewithal for Toungoo—an agrarian, Dry Zone polity—to conquer and shift its center of gravity to Lower Myanmar and, in important ways, to *its* way of life. One could argue that part of the economic significance of the First Pegu Dynasty lay in providing the mental and material foundations for the political and military achievements of the Second Pegu/Toungoo Dynasty. The empire of Tabinshwehti and Bayinnaung, which conquered most of western and central Mainland Southeast Asia during the "Age of Commerce"—and the effects it wrought in that region—owed its Lower Myanmar, coastal, and commercial origins, along with a new weltanschauung, to the First Pegu Dynasty of Yazadarit, Shin Saw Bu, and Dhammazedi.

Yet, the Second Pegu/Toungoo Dynasty's stay in Lower Myanmar was short-lived (1539–1599)—a mere sixty years—after which its leaders once more returned to the agrarian "heartland" and to its way of life, although somewhat ambivalently, for they deliberately left ajar the country's "backdoor" that faced the coasts. And although the country's leaders never voluntarily made Lower Myanmar its center again—Yangon, as capital, was *inherited* from the British—there was a time during the Second Ava Dynasty that they seriously considered it and almost returned to the coasts, but for some serendipitous events.

Even today, although the Dry Zone remains the country's "heartland," to which the new capital moved back in 2005–2006, and agriculture continues to be its prevalent socioeconomic lifestyle,[16] the growth of maritime South, Southeast, and East Asia today (not to mention the current interests shown by the West for the region), continues to make Lower Myanmar (and today's Yangon) a viable economic option, at least to supplement the interior's agricultural and natural resources. And that legacy clearly belonged to the First Kingdom of Pegu.

Pegu's Political Legacy

Notwithstanding the supernatural origins attributed to Wareru by the Mon texts for what were obvious symbolic and allegorical reasons, the consensus among historians is that Wareru was a historical figure. Whether he was Shan or Mon is actually a false issue, raised by mainly colonial historians, for reified ethnicity had little or nothing to do with the actual making of history in Myanmar or, for that matter, Southeast Asia. That Wareru established the first, independent kingdom in the history of Lower Myanmar at Muttama, which subsequently led to the development of the First Pegu Dynasty at Pegu, seems plausible enough,[17] surely a legacy of some importance. But even without providing that lineage for Pegu, Muttama as a port city was important in its own right, affecting the history not only of Pagan and Ava, but also, thereafter, of the country in general. In that sense, Wareru's political contribution to the country's history lay in making Muttama a major regional center that continues today.

The subsequent establishment of economic, political, diplomatic, and perhaps even cultural ties with polities on Muttama's east (such as Sukhotai), have not been conspicuous in the historiography of Myanmar, and perhaps also bear additional research from the Thai side. If nothing else, it placed Muttama and the Tenasserim Peninsular in the orbit of Siam, the Isthmus of Kra, and the Straits of Melaka in a more significantly structural way that was to pay huge dividends later with the Portuguese, and thereafter, the English as well.

Binnya U, as the founder of, and first ruler at, the new capital of Pegu, should have been given more credit for the dynasty and kingdom's political and economic development and subsequent establishment than he has so far received either from Mon or Burmese historians.[18] Part of the reason is that his reign has been overshadowed by that of his son and more famous successor, Yazadarit. But in fact, Binnya U's reign of approximately thirty-two years is no insignificant accomplishment, particularly given the period of time in which he ruled and the embryonic nature of his dynasty. Moving his political center from Muttama to Pegu showed sound judgment and some vision, for the new location was militarily and economically advantageous. It was more easily defensible against attacks from the east, and it could take better advantage of the path of commerce that the region was experiencing from all sides at the time. By doing so, Binnya U provided the wherewithal not only for establishing a more viable and secure monarchy but for ensuring its future growth and development, which Yazadarit was fortunate enough to inherit intact.

At the same time, without Yazadarit, the First Pegu Dynasty might have collapsed altogether. The rest of the candidates for the throne after Binnya U's death appear to have had little or no vision beyond their own narrow interests, so that the kingdom could easily have disintegrated into regional loci of power centered in the major towns of Muttama, Dagon, Pathein, Myaungmya, and Pegu, and thus have become easy prey for Ava. But it was Yazadarit's military acumen, political shrewdness, often ruthless single-mindedness, and strong personality that enabled him to unify and preserve what his father had begun. Without Yazadarit, it is almost certain that there would not have been much of a First Pegu kingdom left for posterity. And he accomplished this despite fierce and constant opposition from within his own family, most notably his uncle, the lord of Myaungmya, and his elder sister, the lady of Dagon.

Indeed, such were his military accomplishments and political stature that three hundred years later, the authors of the *Yazadhiyaza Ayedawpon* allotted the equivalent of approximately three hundred printed pages to his story, while five hundred years after Yazadarit ruled, U Kala, writing from Upper Myanmar and from that perspective, gave him the equivalent of over one hundred printed pages in his chronicle, as much as (if not more than) he gave any single Burmese king, including famous ones like Anawrahta and Kyanzittha.

Yet, six hundred years after Yazadarit's reign, a Mon monk who belonged to the same region, ethno-linguistic group, and culture as Yazadarit wrote a "history of kings" (*Slapat*)—really a misnomer, as the contents of his work were more concerned with the record of patronage to the Shwedagon Pagoda—which gave Yazadarit *one paragraph.* Thus, to reiterate, determining legacies often depends on one's opinion of what is considered important. To this monk, political and military accomplishments were only incidental to a leader's religious accomplishments.

This difference in perspective of measuring leadership is not simply the result of distance to the subject in terms of time, but is also one of ideology: in this case, religious ideology. Yazadarit's historical legacy was much better recognized and appreciated by those who wrote "secular" history than by one whose sole concern was with religious patronage. In terms of the former, Yazadarit was being assessed according to his administrative, military, and political accomplishments, whereas in terms of the latter, by his religious largesse. But, and notably, in no case of which I am aware was reified ethnicity a factor in making those judgments.

Apart from his public persona and hints about his private and personal character, Yazadarit's leadership can be best assessed by his actions. Had he not successfully developed the powerful Lower Myanmar kingdom that he did when he did, and had not his military and political talents time and again prevented Ava from taking Pegu, Ava might have reestablished what, in effect, was another Pagan, stretching its dominions from the northern reaches of the country to the coasts. And had Ava become another Pagan, Thohanbwa would probably not have taken it in 1526–1527, so that Toungoo could not have broken away to forge an independent kingdom and dynasty.

That, in turn, would have directly affected the rise and development of the great Second Pegu/Toungoo Dynasty, along with everything its existence generated. There would have been no Tabinshwehti, no Bayinnaung, no conquest of central Mainland Southeast Asia, especially of Ayuthaya. Particularly had Ayuthaya been allowed to continue its development without interruption, its history (and Myanmar's) in central Mainland Southeast Asia in the Early Modern period would have been quite different. Of course, the political relations between Myanmar and Syam subsequently would have also been quite different. But that did not happen. It was largely Yazadarit who provided the First Pegu Dynasty with the wherewithal to mature and grow that allowed the Second Pegu Dynasty to do what it did in the Early Modern period.

Yazadarit also established the foundations on which his most notable successors, Shin Saw Bu and Dhammazedi, built their legacies. Both were also politically important and unique in Myanmar's history. Whereas, to reiterate, she is the country's only documented woman sovereign,[19] he is the country's first and only ex-monk to have shed his saffron robe to take the throne.[20] At the same time, we must be cautious lest our assessment of Shin Saw Bu be influenced by our twenty-first-century "gender-sensitive" values and famous female leaders, rather than those of her own time and culture. While we might celebrate her role today, she was never exalted as the first woman sovereign in the country by records contemporary to, or immediately succeeding, her. Rather, she was venerated for her lavish patronage of the religion, and then, only after a long period of time had elapsed. Neither did she inspire, nor set a precedent for, the emergence of another woman sovereign in her own or any succeeding dynasty, despite the important role queens normally played in an essentially male-dominated court during the country's monarchical period. We should not, therefore, exaggerate this exception as if it were a pattern or prevailing value in Myanmar's history.

Only very recently, and only within the context of late twentieth-century politics, has Shin Saw Bu's role as the only woman sovereign in the country's history prompted a discussion of women leaders with national stature, particularly Aung San Suu Kyi.[21] But the association between Shin Saw Bu and Suu Kyi is politically motivated, narrowly self-serving, and contextually anachronistic, for other than their gender and lineage to fathers who were national leaders, there is no other similarity between the two in terms of their histories, visions, priorities, or behaviors. Thus, although one might be tempted to posit a "gender legacy" for Pegu because of Shin Saw Bu, she *is* an exception; no other woman sovereign ever ascended the throne again. Of course, one could argue that her example nonetheless established a precedent that others, especially in more recent times, could emulate. But is this because of Shin Saw Bu, or is it because of the changes in attitude wrought by the modern world? As much as we might like to claim a "gender legacy" for Pegu because of Shin Saw Bu, I am afraid it would be somewhat specious.

If anything, Upper Myanmar had many queens whose role influenced the country's history (for better or for worse)—Queen Saw of Pagan, Lady of the Tazaung of Ava, Queen Supayalat of Mandalay—than Pegu's queens did. This is neither to support nor criticize the conventional role attributed to women in Burmese society, so praised in English-language literature, but simply to state that although Shin Saw Bu's place in history is exemplary and indeed a legacy attributable to the First Pegu Dynasty, it may or may not have contributed to the important role of women in Myanmar's history.

Nonetheless, Shin Saw Bu's reign is notable in other ways, and probably *because* she was the first woman sovereign in the country's history. Her reign saw little bloodshed. Much of the reason for the peace between Ava and Pegu during her reign may have been the result of her personal knowledge of, and relations with, members of the court of Ava. While exiled there, she learned its ways, was a well-liked and prominent queen, and accepted with grace her given Burmese name Shin Saw Bu (which impugned only her height), a name by which she is best known thereafter by both Mon and Burmese. While sovereign at

Pegu, she provided no reason for discord with Ava, focused as she was on religious activity. As noted above, the size and scale of the Shwedagon Pagoda as we know it today, one of the most holy of shrines in the country, is largely the result of her rebuilding its base, platform, and numerous other parts. It was her religious devotion that inspired the populace, not her martial or administrative abilities.

Similarly with Dhammazedi and his rise to kingship: it was a unique event in the country's history for an established bona fide monk, well versed in the scriptures, to shed the saffron robe to become king without possessing any royal credentials—except by marriage to Shin Saw Bu's daughter, not altogether an illegitimate path. Other princes destined to be king, more often than not, spent years in the royal monasteries as monks or novices; that is nothing new in Theravada Buddhist Southeast Asia. Yet, to actually renounce the robe as a prominent monk to become king is rather unique, at least in Myanmar's history. His reign also saw little significant confrontations with Ava, focused as it was on internal religious affairs.

But Dhammazedi's legacy went well beyond that, affecting both the political and academic legacy of the country at the national level. His creation of the notion of Ramannadesa, the "realm of the Rman," was the first (and only) secular countervailing ideology produced by Lower Myanmar that challenged the long prevailing notion of a Myanma Pyi, "the realm of the Myanma." Not that there could not have existed a sense of "Mon-ness" among individuals, families, villages, or other such communities in Lower Myanmar; there probably was. But there is no original evidence that a "national" identity on a scale beyond these local situations existed except for Dhammazedi's vision of a Ramannadesa. But, to reiterate: the notion of Ramannadesa as a political idea did not go beyond Dhammazedi's reign. None of his successors (one of whom was only a teenager) mentioned it even once. It is therefore unlikely that such a novel and "national" concept, especially when not embraced and championed by leadership, trickled down to the masses, whose interests would have been more local and immediate.

Whatever the reasons may have been, a major historical event occurred that prevented this vision of Ramannadesa from resurfacing, even if Dhammazedi's successors had embraced it. That was the conquest of Pegu in 1539 by Tabinshwehti, who belonged to an Upper Myanmar Dry Zone "Burmese" polity (Toungoo) that had been growing rapidly during the past several decades into a formidable power. With Tabinshwehti's conquest of Pegu, the notion (and fact) of a "realm of the Myanma" was reestablished in Lower Myanmar that rendered Dhammazedi's "realm of the Rman" effete. After all, the former was the prevailing concept for approximately six hundred years, which had only temporarily dissipated in Lower Myanmar with Pegu's rise and development.

Thus, the conquest of Pegu not only reinstated Upper Myanmar control and its predominantly Burmese culture over Lower Myanmar, it also shattered any chance of Dhammazedi's vision of a "realm of the Rman" to resurface. It remained forgotten for nearly another four centuries, until it was finally resurrected in the nineteenth and twentieth centuries, and then, only in the academic and political arenas, not as a populous idea. Dhammazedi never imagined that his dream of a united and peaceful "realm of the Rman" would someday become the rationale for British military designs on Lower Myanmar, for separatist movements, and for academics to use as an issue to support them. Nonetheless, these were, even if inadvertent, legacies of Dhammazedi.

What is clear is that the Mon speakers themselves did not revive it; it was done *on their behalf* by colonial officials and scholars and missionaries for their own narrow reasons. Indeed, even by the mid-twentieth century, the notion of Ramannadesa remained confined to a very small, elite academic (and sometimes) administrative group working for and with the colonial powers. And it remained there in academia, for the most part, where it became "gospel" that haunted early Myanmar and Southeast Asian studies for over a hundred years thereafter.

But subsequently, the political implications of the idea of Ramannadesa materialized with the advent of Mon nationalism in Myanmar during the first several decades of the twentieth century. Indeed, it was in conjunction with Mon nationalism that a new Mon language history was compiled: The "Paklat Talaing Chronicle" mentioned throughout these chapters. Only then did Dhammazedi's fifteenth-century notion of an ancient and glorious "realm of the Rman" begin to trickle down to the larger population of Mon speakers living in Lower Myanmar and Thailand. Yet the publication of these volumes was elite-generated and externally funded, supported by colonial officials and scholars and American missionaries whose privileging of ethnic minorities not only "confirmed" their sentimentalities about the Mon being the "Greeks of Southeast Asia," but also served their political and military agenda of divide and rule.[22]

Today, the notion of an ancient and glorious Ramannadesa is being revived as justification for creating a separate Mon nation within Myanmar with academic support. But it is an "imagined community," to use the late Ben Anderson's famous phrase, with little or no basis in fact. As a result, for the notion to survive, another component had been added: an ideology of victimization exploited by Mon activists, who for all practical purposes are culturally Thai, with their academic and political cohorts living mainly in Thailand.

Thus, despite the fact that Ramannadesa has been thoroughly exposed as myth and hagiography, instead of being relegated to the dustbin of myths and legends, it has been unfortunately revived to defend and provide a forum for the political agenda of modern Mon nationalists and separatists, and supported by academics whose own careers were teetering on the brink of the same dustbin, having depended heavily (or totally) on that legend. Only time will tell if the First Pegu Dynasty's historiographic legacy continues beyond the current generation of Myanmar historians. But for now, it has already made its mark.

Conclusion

It is clear that the historical legacy of the First Kingdom of Pegu is a mixed one. Its ethno-linguistic and sociocultural legacy was short-lived and relatively weak. Its religious legacy—in terms of select features—had more far-reaching and permanent consequences, especially the Shwedagon Pagoda, whose basic style, although derivative and not original, has stood the test of time. But its religious art as a whole was quite ordinary and not exemplary. Its economic legacy, which provided a new mentality regarding the outside world and the maritime regions, promises to be most long-lasting, while its political legacy, particularly in terms of some of its exemplary leaders, may well be one that could match Ava's. And finally, as shown, its historiographic and academic legacy is still with us.

Conclusion

An "Upstream-Downstream" Dualism: Time, Space, and Type in Myanmar's History

The relationship between Ava and Pegu was a symbiotic dualism formed around the elements of time, space, and type.[1] Not only was Ava a reformulation of something old and Pegu the genesis of something new, but one was located in the agrarian Dry Zone while the other was on the commercial coasts, so that each was historically and materially, and in terms of general character, distinct. Whereas the Kingdom of Ava was essentially the resurrection of an old kingdom—Pagan writ small—Pegu was a new kingdom composed of new leaders, people, and cultures. Ava was a familiar, Upper Myanmar polity: the same material environment and demographic base; the same economic, social, and political institutions; the same language, writing system, cosmology, and culture. Pegu, on the other hand, was a new (and the first) independent kingdom that emerged in coastal and commercial Lower Myanmar, led by newcomers from what later became Thailand—the Mon speakers.

Yet, because both were built on the same foundations established earlier by the "Pyu" and Pagan kingdoms, both had certain common elements. They shared virtually the same religion and thought system; certain social customs, values, and mores; familiar political and administrative principles; a common, if contested, history; and certainly the same writing system. These dissimilarities did not produce a *binary* situation (as convention has it) of two irreconcilably antagonistic ethnic entities (Burman and Mon), rather, they created a *dualism* of geopolitical and cultural differences, whose energy and dynamism came from the tension derived from precisely those differences. In fact, Ava and Pegu's relationship not only epitomized Southeast Asia's "upstream-downstream"[2] paradigm, common throughout much of its history, it also continues today in Naypyidaw and Yangon as stated in the introduction. The following analyses describe this relationship as it went through the various periods in Myanmar history, beginning with the Ava period.

The "Upstream-Downstream" Dualism in the Fifteenth Century

The fifteenth-century dualism between Ava and Pegu, representing two dissimilar geo-economic, demographic, and cultural regions, created as much centrifugal as centripetal energy, creating an equilibrium that characterized the period. Equilibrium, of course, need not imply harmony, so that however tumultuous their relationship may have been at times, overall, the status quo was maintained.

What favored equilibrium, in general, is that the real competitors of the agrarian states in Southeast Asia were not their maritime counterparts but other agrarian states like them (such as Pagan and Angkor).[3] Similarly, the maritime states rarely destroyed their inland, agrarian "upstream" neighbors, but went after each other instead (or those more like them)—the Cholas and Sri Vijaya, Pegu and Arakan, Pegu and Ayuthaya, Champa and Dai Viet.

The reason for this modus vivendi between dissimilar states is that they needed each other in the most important ways. One of these was economic, especially with regard to Ava and Pegu in the fifteenth century. Luxury goods and other imported and maritime specialties were exchanged for the basic products of the interior, particularly rice. The famous rice lands of Pegu, in terms of size and scale, did not yet exist—most were not developed until the nineteenth century—so that Lower Myanmar was quite dependent on Upper Myanmar for much of its annual *padi* needs for both consumption and export. The interior also provided products that grew well only or mainly under Dry Zone conditions, such as the large variety of pulses (peanut, soybean, sesamum) important in the peoples' diets, along with sugar (cane and palm) and other foodstuffs for exchange for luxury items and coastal tropical products. This "upstream-downstream" reciprocal exchange system was, of course, facilitated by the country's main north–south artery, the Irrawaddy—represented by the cover of this book—where a well-established infrastructure had been operational since early historic (if not also prehistoric) times.

This "economy of need," in turn, shaped Ava and Pegu's political and military relationship, which was also a modus vivendi in both their interests. Unless Pegu were willing and able to conquer the Dry Zone, keep it, and maintain its agricultural economy along with its infrastructure—and it was not—it had little choice but to preserve the status quo. As for Ava, despite political and military behavior that suggests designs to control the maritime areas, it could not, and so ended up preserving the status quo as well.

Indeed, the history of Ava and Pegu's half-hearted attempts of attacking each other, invariably culminating in public and sensational peace accords held at famous religious sites; officially marking boundaries at places that were already recognized as the limits of their respective domains anyway; forging marriage alliances with each other to cultivate familiarity and create kinship ties; knowingly and deliberately harboring each other's dissidents, more as a means of keeping each other off-balance than inflicting any kind of permanent damage; and even endorsing each other's front-runner candidates for succession to preserve stability demonstrate that both wanted to maintain the status quo. In other words, the history of their political and military relationship does not suggest any genuine desire to eliminate, but only to counterbalance, each other.

Demographically too, they depended on each other's ability to attract labor in labor-scarce early Southeast Asia. Emigration appears to have occurred at both ends: hill peoples were moving down into the great plains of the Dry Zone for the benefits of "civilization" (religion, literacy, art, mainstream culture) as well as for material and sociopolitical benefits (rice, jobs, status, power), while Lower Myanmar's commercial economy also appears to have attracted people to it from overseas and other parts of central Mainland Southeast Asia.

As Ava was an agrarian state with a land-based army, it needed more labor than did Pegu, whose viability was contingent on the size and scale of its maritime commercial operations along with a strong navy. Part of Pegu's excess labor therefore likely migrated to Ava. There, sophisticated irrigation infrastructure based on perennial rivers and streams ordinarily produced a predictable annual surplus, while its continuous temple-construction industry provided well-paying jobs for the services of skilled artisans and craftsmen, which kept dozens of other, related industries humming. All this tended to *encourage* voluntary migration to both places. There is no contemporary evidence to suggest that under normal conditions people *fled* the centers of the lowland valleys to the hills for "political freedom," as has been implied. Instead, it was the other way around: those from the hills most often gravitated toward the lowland centers, for mainly material reasons. Centers in early Southeast Asia tended to attract rather than repel people.

One of the most cordial, cooperative, and nonviolent areas of this dualistic relationship was in the sphere of religion. Although Ava's claim to preeminence in Theravada Buddhism outstripped what Pegu could muster, Shin Saw Bu's record of religious activities and King Dhammazedi's religious reforms were, nevertheless, reason enough for respect and perhaps even envy at Ava. And while Shin Saw Bu's reconstruction of the Shwedagon Pagoda surely attracted pilgrims from Upper Myanmar, Dhammazedi also publicly invoked famous Upper Myanmar kings as exemplary models to emulate.

Such accord was not ideologically difficult for either kingdom, as both believed they had received their Theravada Buddhism from the same source—Sri Lanka—even if each traced the specific lineage of its *sangha* to different religious exemplars who were eminent figures in Asoka's Third Buddhist Council, considered by both to have been the model of orthodoxy in the Buddhist world. Thus, as we saw in a previous chapter, when two famous monks returned from Sri Lanka in the fifteenth century, even during a period of antagonism between the two kingdoms, the decision (by the monks) to accept Ava's invitation to reside there rather than at Pegu was honored by Pegu's king, who, with great pomp and ceremony, escorted them to Pyi, the accepted border town between the two kingdoms. In the sphere of religion, the "upstream-downstream" relationship was more than dualistic: it was singular.

Preserving the political status quo and sharing the same conceptual system, however, does not mean Ava and Pegu's "character" or views of the outside world were the same; in fact, they were importantly dissimilar, the result mainly of their respective material environments and the priorities each engendered. While Ava as a society appears to have been more provincial and homogeneous, Pegu society seems to have been more cosmopolitan and heterogeneous. The reasons may have been cultural to a certain extent, but more likely they were geopolitical; certainly (reified) ethnicity had nothing to do with it. As Pegu's economy was dependent on international and regional commerce, it had to be acutely aware of, and concerned with, external political and economic trends and patterns in India, China, and the rest of Southeast Asia; its survival depended on that awareness of the outside world. Hence, it was more flexible, adaptable, and willing to change, with a more outward-looking view.

Ava's worldview, on the other hand, was nearly the opposite. Its lifestyle and concerns were focused on the domestic environment: the maintenance of irrigation works and cultivated lands, control over its precious stones and interior products, and the retention of its valuable population of cultivators. As a result, Ava was far more cognizant of local rainfall patterns, agricultural yields, the need to maintain its agricultural infrastructure (especially its irrigation canals and weirs), and the need to ensure that members of its population (especially cultivators) remained in their socio-legal categories, than they were of (say) Muslim invasions of North India or the rise of the Ming in China. In other words, the commercial and political affairs of the outside world were not, ordinarily, high priorities for Ava. In that sense, one could say that Ava was predominantly inward-looking, with *less* (not *no*) need for the outside world.

Besides, Ava's outside world—its "front door" (and in general, also Myanmar's throughout most of its history)—faced north toward China, not the coast, which was (historically) its "back door" and "frontier," through which certain luxury goods, ideas, technologies, and cultures of maritime Southeast Asia (and beyond) entered. The maritime regions of Myanmar were Ava's eyes and ears, to a certain extent, but not its heart. That was the Dry Zone—the interior of the "house."

To this "upstream-downstream" dualism must be added a third, complicating component—the hills—so that one might call the whole situation a "tripartism." These hill regions were the "interstices" of the Ava-Pegu dualism. But that does not mean they were unimportant; rather, they constituted a distinct, geo-economic, political, and demographic component of the whole, with a discrete cultural and ethno-linguistic space with which Ava (especially) interacted. In fact, for Ava (less than for Pegu), especially during the fifteenth century, these hill regions were nearly as important as the maritime coasts, and in terms of demographic and political concerns at particular times, even more so.

The hills replenished the labor pool of the plains in both the agricultural and military sectors, while much of the time, they acted as a buffer that blocked the traditional (northern) paths of invasion by others. And when their elite intermarried with Ava royalty, they forged some of the more lasting political alliances, whose offspring in time came to be regarded as members of the Burmese court. For Pegu, however, the hill regions were for the most part only of secondary and tertiary concern. Thus, even if the main "dualism" was between Ava and Pegu, the overall scenario was a "tripartism."

But as this study is focused on the "upstream-downstream" paradigm rather than the tripartite situation, the latter was not dealt with here, especially because it is not possible to do so accurately. There are virtually no primary sources on, from, or about the interstices, especially during the Early Modern period. Much of what we know about it is based on either late colonial ethnographies or information derived from Ava (and Chinese) sources, and so reflects the perspectives of centers. Nonetheless, it would be fair to say at this juncture that even though the "upstream-downstream" relationship between Upper and Lower Myanmar during the fifteenth century was probably more important, in the long run the relationship between the Dry Zone and the hills may actually turn out to have been nearly as significant. One need only look at the far longer and stronger ties the Shan speakers have had with the Burmese speakers of the Dry Zone to better appreciate that. As the largest minority group in Myanmar, with about 9 percent of the current population (with millions more in Thailand), their future relationship with the majority Burmese speakers is also bound to be more important.

Yet—and to reiterate—such a conclusion has been difficult to accept. For nearly two centuries, convention in Myanmar studies depicted the Mon of Lower Myanmar not only as the sine qua non and conveyors of civilization to all of Myanmar (as the "Greeks of Southeast Asia"), but also as the ultimate "victims" of majority "ethnic cleansing," both highly emotional sentiments and shown to be largely (if not totally) erroneous.[4]

The Dualism and the Age of Commerce in the Early Sixteenth Century

By the sixteenth century, Southeast Asia was said to have been well introduced to, and participating in, the Age of Commerce, part of a worldwide phenomenon with important repercussions on the region, especially the maritime areas. And since both Ava and Pegu had emerged and developed during the previous century, when the foundations of the Age of Commerce were just being laid in the region, it raises the question of whether or not there was a cause-and-effect relationship between their emergence and these foundations, or between the "Age" and the dualism itself. Did the developments that eventually led to the Age of Commerce also contribute to the rise and development of Ava and Pegu during the fifteenth century? At least, to what extent was the Age of Commerce a factor in the operation of this dualistic relationship?

Although it is tempting to cast a wide net with a thesis as broad as the Age of Commerce, the Myanmar evidence shows that neither the origins of Ava and Pegu nor the substance of their relationship had much to do with the commercial developments in maritime South and Southeast Asia of the sixteenth century. Ava's rise began as early as the first decade of the fourteenth century and was very much a local, Upper Myanmar affair, having to do with Pagan's decline, the Mongol attacks, and the influx of new people into that area—the Shan. Similarly with the origins of the First Pegu Dynasty: its origins in the last quarter of the thirteenth century with Wagaru had more to do with Pagan's decline and consequent loss of control over Lower Myanmar than with whatever might have been happening in the maritime, coastal world. And if that coastal world were a factor, the situation itself was more local, extending to the Bay of Bengal perhaps, Gulf of Muttama certainly, and possibly to the Straits of Malacca. Indeed, strictly speaking, the "long sixteenth century" of the Age of Commerce had just begun by the time both Ava and Pegu had declined, or were on their deathbeds.

That it was more a local affair also applies to Arakan's general development in Western Myanmar, although the Age of Commerce was more likely to have been a factor in the rise of Mrauk-U, Arakan's capital during the mid-sixteenth century. To be sure, Arakan's development as an independent region of Arakanese (essentially Burmese) speakers was based on older inland agrarian foundations and pre–Age of Commerce trade within the Bay of Bengal and coasts of Myanmar. Arakan had been under Pagan's and, later, Ava's political hegemony during their period of dominance. Even when Mrauk-U, the new center of the Arakanese kingdom (which seemed to have been in part a child of the Age of Commerce) rose by the middle of the sixteenth century, that occurred only after both Ava and Pegu had already declined, allowing it to move more easily into the power vacuum created. Thus, preexisting domestic, geopolitical, and economic reasons were more significant in the rise of all three kingdoms—Ava, Pegu, and Mrauk-U—than were "international" factors characteristic of the famous Age of Commerce.

To be sure, if Ava and Pegu's (and to a certain extent, Arakan's) origins were unrelated (or only marginally related) to the Age of Commerce, Toungoo's conquest of Pegu in 1539 and its decision to make Pegu its capital (instead of returning to Dry Zone Toungoo) certainly appears to have been related to the famous age. Neither decision was based on whim; both events can be interpreted as exploiting the burgeoning of trade and commerce of Lower Myanmar in the sixteenth century. Subsequently, Pegu was strong enough to take Upper Myanmar and reunify the country by midcentury, thereby making it the first time in Myanmar's history that the capital of the unified country lay on the coasts. (That was not to be repeated for another three hundred years or more until Yangon, as Rangoon, was made capital under the British.)

Sixteenth-century Pegu went on to conquer western and central Mainland Southeast Asia, taking Ayuthaya twice and even Vien Chiang, the center of the kingdom that was to become Laos. Surely, such ambitious and risky activities never before attempted by, and uncharacteristic of, Myanmar, even under the powerful Pagan kingdom, were motivated by goals more pertinent to the economic growth of Pegu's rival centers in a larger Southeast Asia maritime region as a result of the Age of Commerce, than by internal, inland agrarian concerns. One could say, then, that the Age of Commerce was a factor in the decision by the leaders of Toungoo to move to, and remain in, Pegu, making it their capital and asserting its power over its eastern neighbors in ways that no dynasty of Myanmar had ever done theretofore.

Similarly, Pegu's about-face decision to leave Lower Myanmar subsequently has been attributed to the decline of the Age of Commerce. It was said to have created a watershed in seventeenth-century Southeast Asia that drove Myanmar's leadership inward. That theory, however, has been called into question and seen good debate already.[5] Therefore, I will not add to it, except to say that, here as well, internal domestic factors appear to have been more important and directly linked to the decision by the country's leadership to return to the "heartland" than was the decline of the Age of Commerce per se.

More specifically, when, in 1599, Pegu was sacked by Mrauk-U and finished off by a resurgent Ayuthaya—two similar and competing polities like Pegu—no central authority was left in Lower Myanmar, turning it into a desolate and anarchic wasteland dominated by warlords, including a Portuguese adventurer, a situation symptomatic of the heterogeneity of the place as well as the decentralized conditions of the age. Some of Pegu's population was taken to Arakan and Thailand, while many likely migrated to Upper Myanmar, where the bulk of the country's Burmese-speaking population was located. Thus, domestic center collapse rather than distant "international" economic downturns elsewhere was responsible for the seventeenth-century "watershed" in Lower Myanmar.

Another reason the Second Pegu/Toungoo Dynasty declined was its overextension; the size of its population and military and human resources could not have sustained for long the huge area it had conquered. Indeed, that overreach on the east, exposing its western flank, was what allowed Arakan to subsequently sack Pegu. These kinds of internal factors seemed to have been more directly responsible for Pegu's inability to maintain its empire and power than the larger economic decline of the Age of Commerce, although it might have played a part indirectly.

In addition, succession in Myanmar was usually contested within the structure of the monarchy, which invariably involved princes and princesses, ministers and advisers, old queens and new queens, personal vendettas and jealousies. That enduring factor surely contributed to the fall of the Second Pegu/Toungoo Dynasty, which had little or nothing to do with regional or worldwide economic conditions, although scarcer economic resources to distribute among the elite must have heightened internal contests.

Related to this dwindling of economic resources, and more directly a factor in the decline of the center, was likely the flow of taxable wealth to the tax-exempt *sangha*, for, as an inexorable feature of merit-making and political and social legitimacy in Myanmar, it was continuous, and created regular and periodic economic problems for the state with political repercussions. Thus, a worldwide or a regional economic downturn of the Age of Commerce (if that began at the end of the sixteenth century) could have reduced the share of wealth ordinarily allotted to more secular clients of the monarchy, thereby exacerbating internal political problems. All these (and other) domestic factors were what first weakened the Second Pegu/Toungoo Dynasty, only thereafter was it affected by the larger, regional economic downturn, allowing little but richer Mrauk-U and an aggrieved but wealthier Ayuthaya to provide the coup de grace to a domestic fait accompli.

Long-term structural and immediate internal domestic factors have almost always tended to preempt short-term, external ones in Myanmar history in any case. Indeed, one could argue that there was no economic downturn in *Upper*

Myanmar at all, but an "upturn" that went against the grain of what may have been happening in the rest of the maritime world. There, a prince of the Second Pegu/Toungoo Dynasty whose fief was located in a strategic town (Nyaungyan), almost immediately reformulated the old, creating another Dry Zone dynasty out of the existing human and material resources, subsequently making the old city of Ava its capital. The dynasty is known in indigenous historiography as the Second Inwa (Ava) Dynasty, although, to reiterate, it is called the "Later" and "Restored" Toungoo Dynasty by Western historians. One should regard the rise of this Second Ava Dynasty as a reintegration of the state, part of an oscillation between disintegration and integration that is a regular feature of Myanmar's history, lasting well into modern times.[6]

When viewed in the longue dureé, the return of the state to Upper Myanmar's agrarian Dry Zone after a mere sixty years in commercial Lower Myanmar highlights an important "autonomous" pattern in the history of the country that I have called Dry Zone Paramountcy elsewhere. With the exception of the Second Pegu/Toungoo Dynasty, which was the first and only precolonial capital of a unified Myanmar to be located in Lower Myanmar, all of the other (five) dynasties in Myanmar's history were located in the interior agrarian Dry Zone. And the reasons for that were also clearly internal. After all, the Dry Zone was where (a) the majority of the country's population resided; (b) the bulk of the country's food supplies and most of its agricultural (especially rice) lands were located; (c) the majority of its most sacred shrines stood; (d) the most renowned of its literature, art, and music masters lived and worked; (e) and where the most spectacular and awe inspiring remains of its origins (Pagan) lay. To all this was (and still is) a deep psychological connection. These kinds of domestic factors, not ephemeral, external ones (even if important) were responsible for such recurring patterns as Dry Zone Paramountcy in the history of Myanmar.

In short, the decline of the Second Pegu/Toungoo Dynasty and the subsequent return of the country's leadership to the inland agrarian heartland to create the Second Ava Dynasty had little or nothing to do with the decline of the Age of Commerce; it was in large measure caused by domestic factors.

The Dualism during the Second Ava Period: Seventeenth and Eighteenth Centuries

After consolidating its demographic, political, and economic resources in Upper Myanmar, the Second Ava Dynasty (1600–1752) began the reunification of the rest of the country by reestablishing its authority over Lower Myanmar during much of the first half of the eighteenth century.[7] As nothing resembling a kingdom had arisen there from the ashes of 1599, the situation was no longer an equal, two-kingdom, "upstream-downstream" dualism. Upper Myanmar had resurrected Dry Zone Paramountcy, and the country began to look as if it were once again under the Pagan kingdom.

But toward the end of the first half of the eighteenth century, a combination of external and internal factors enabled Pegu, which had been placed under an

Upper Myanmar governor, to rebel. After some internal struggles among several Lower Myanmar contenders, a leader with a Mon royal title reasserted Pegu's independence one more time. By midcentury it had capitalized on several Upper Myanmar problems, eventually taking Ava in 1752. But rather than remaining there, Pegu's leaders decided to leave a governor at Ava and return to Lower Myanmar instead, taking back the entire court, including the royal family, its leading monks, scholars, ministers, books, and records.

This situation could have resurrected the two-kingdom dualism of earlier years, as Pegu began to look as if it might become a new dynasty. But it did not have time even to create a second generation of leaders, for a headman by the name of Aung Zeya rallied the Upper Myanmar human and material forces to reformulate what became the last (Konbaung) dynasty of Myanmar. Working out of Shwebo, his capital in the great Mu Valley, he retook Ava in 1755, and within two years had also taken Pegu. Known later as Alaungphaya, he reunited the country under an Upper Myanmar dynasty, and once again reestablished Dry Zone Paramountcy for the fourth time since the Pyu of the first millennium. That was to last for over a hundred years, until the reappearance of the same kinds of economic and political forces that had led to the growth and development of Lower Myanmar earlier in the fifteenth century with the Malay, Ming, South Indians, and Portuguese. This time, however, it was with the much more powerful British, who were not about to accept the subordinate, Lower Myanmar, role in this dualism.

The Dualism under the British: 1886–1942

Britain conquered Myanmar in three phases, beginning with the maritime areas of Arakan and Tenasserim (along with Assam) in the period between 1824 and 1826, followed in 1852 with most of the rest of the Irrawaddy Delta including Pegu, and finally annexing the entire country in 1885–1886. That ended Dry Zone Paramountcy for at least another half century and resurrected a new kind of "upstream-downstream" relationship.[8]

Crucial in this was making Yangon the de facto capital of the new colony rather than Mandalay, which had enjoyed that role during the Konbaung Dynasty. Neither domestic priorities nor the sentiment of the people (implicit or explicit) was considered by Britain in making Yangon capital. It appears to have been a deliberate rejection of the traditional heartland for obvious economic, political, and military reasons. But by so doing, Britain inadvertently resurrected the "upstream-downstream" relationship; only this time, it was no longer a symbiotic, near-equal, two-kingdom dualism. Although in a geopolitical sense it was similar to Pegu under the Second Pegu/Toungoo Dynasty—when the entire country was ruled from Lower Myanmar—this time it was importantly different.

Under the British, the country's capital conveyed and represented another kind of "newness" with serious (and negative) implications for the country's "oldness." Whereas earlier, "oldness" and "newness" were synthesized into a dualism, this "newness" of the downstream region was not only synonymous with modernity, it also associated the "oldness" of the upstream region with backwardness and barbarism. The contrast, satirized in modern Burmese literature,[9] was not only realized in the new political and economic system's avenues for upward mobility, such as English-language–based education, but was also expressed in the mundane details of the world represented by British Rangoon: manners, dress, food, writing system, elite culture, and language of state. In other words, the image of what was "civilized," and where this civilization lay, had been reversed.

The new (colonial) image of Rangoon was clearly not shared by the majority of the Burmese-speaking population. Not only did the new image represent a very tiny minority, it was also considered by the majority to belong to a hopelessly colonized "collaborator class" of Anglo-Burmese, whose mind-set was more Western than indigenous. Rangoon looked, smelled, sounded, and acted like a colonial city. It did not represent or function as the exemplary center of a traditional "theatre state," the preeminent *mandala* of a "galactic polity." Rather, its purpose was to facilitate the colonial export economy for the benefit of the colonizer and its clients. That role and perception persisted well beyond independence in 1948, as Yangon remained an unnatural, manufactured capital of the country for over another half century.

The Dualism Today: Naypyidaw and Yangon

Uncannily similar to the Second Pegu/Toungoo Dynasty, whose center remained in Lower Myanmar for only sixty years, Yangon remained capital of independent Myanmar also for nearly sixty years (1948–2006), after which the center moved back to the heartland when Naypyidaw became capital. Returning to the interior was entirely predictable;[10] it came as no surprise to those knowledgeable about the country, as the call of the agrarian interior has been a compelling siren for approximately two thousand years.

Psychological, cultural, religious, historical, political, economic, and strategic factors—tangible as well as intangible, symbolic as well as practical—were responsible for this move back into the heartland. And the choice of building the new capital next to Pyinmana is also not difficult to understand; it has always been historically and symbolically important. Not only was Pyinmana a prized *myosa*-ship under the monarchy, it was also the town from where the Burma National Army (BNA) as a unit led by Aung San first turned against the Japanese in World War II. The day the BNA marched out of Yangon—March 27, 1945—to effect this about-face has been commemorated as Armed Forces Day, when the army began the sequence of events that it claims eventually led to the independence of the country. But perhaps even more important in the longue dureé of Myanmar history, by returning the capital to the "heartland," Dry Zone Paramountcy was also reestablished after a lapse of nearly 120 years, with little to suggest that this will be reversed in the near future.

While it could be argued that Dry Zone Paramountcy may seem less significant now than it used to be because of the growth in economic and demographic importance of coastal and a more market-oriented Myanmar, when scrutinized carefully, Upper Myanmar, rather than losing, has maintained (indeed, increased) its advantages. Most important, Naypyidaw retains control of the country's political and military power, along with the most important natural resources, found mostly in Upper Myanmar—oil, jade, rubies, marble, teak, tungsten, manganese, tin, zinc, copper, lead—as well as a far more diversified land-form and habitat. Man-made resources also favor Upper Myanmar—hydroelectric power, civilian and military infrastructure (roads, bridges, military bases, the country's largest runway at the Mandalay airport)—while huge amounts of overland trade is conducted between Upper Myanmar and its northeastern and northwestern neighbors, India and China. Dry Zone Paramountcy is not just a vestige of the past; it has regained its importance as a basis for controlling the country.

It is true that the bulk of the country's rice production had shifted to Lower Myanmar by the late 1930s. It is also true that places like Tavoy on the coast are now being developed as deep-water ports, while others on the coasts of Western Myanmar and the Bay of Bengal are also being developed for various purposes, including establishing transport links to India and to the interior of Myanmar. And it appears that Yangon has retained its (colonial and post-independence) function as the doorway to the many intellectual and social trends and patterns of the international world.

Especially today, Yangon exudes a sense of new beginnings, youth, modernity, westernization, adaptability, and some political recklessness (as well as the problems these things bring, such as impossible traffic jams), whereas Naypyidaw, in contrast, conveys a sense of modernity but within tradition, select liberalism but within conservatism, apparent newness but within certain oldness, studied political risk-taking but within a circumscribing cautiousness. In other ways too, the interior has not plunged headlong into the abyss of newness; Upper Myanmar still claims to possess the best of what is considered traditional culture: art, music, dance, puppet theatre, food, politesse, learning, religious behavior. In other words, while acquiescing to Lower Myanmar the role of the country's representative of things current and "global," the interior Dry Zone still holds most of the advantages it once did in ancient times.

To be sure, the role and function of the old Southeast Asian capitals as centers of nearly everything—religion, politics, economy, society, and culture as expressed in the "theatre state"—is now mostly gone. Yet, the demise of such a multitasking center has resurrected the upstream-downstream dualism. Although this time, not as two independent kingdoms duplicating similar functions, but as integrated parts of the same nation exercising some genuine division of labor. In that sense—that is, a single polity whose center is in the Dry Zone—Myanmar in the twenty-first century is more like Pagan was in the thirteenth than Ava and Pegu were in the fifteenth, Second Pegu/Toungoo in the sixteenth, or Yangon in the late nineteenth and twentieth centuries.

And precisely because the integrative ideologies and instruments of the "theatre state" can no longer hold state and society together as they once did, new ideas and practices have taken their place. The most obvious idea is nationalism, along with the structure of the nation-state—components still important and pertinent today. Admittedly, although the nation-state has fostered as much disintegration as integration, nonetheless the latter seems to have the upper hand for now. Religion and language have always been and continue to be integrators also, at least more often than not. They will probably continue to be, if they do not become fodder for disintegration. Geography poses increasingly less of a problem, with the huge infrastructural developments accomplished during the past quarter century, along with modern technology that has made the country "smaller." The growing market economy in many sectors of society promises to play an integrative role as well, provided wealth is evenly distributed. And finally, the modern political system has never been more inclusive, de facto as well as de jure. With its multiparty principles written into the new constitution of 2008, its efficacy has been confirmed by the elections of 2010, the by-elections of 2012, and the most recent elections of 2015 and their implementation in April of 2016. These events have also demonstrated that the smooth passage of power is indeed possible, heretofore a bane in Burmese society for centuries. The country has committed itself structurally and ideologically too deeply now to turn the clock back in any fundamentally significant way.

Perhaps the most important behavior that still needs to change is the persistence and embeddedness of patron-client relations. Although it served precolonial Burmese society very well for centuries, and in many ways saved postcolonial society from total disintegration, horizontal ties must continue to be built that might eventually "undermine" and perhaps marginalize and minimize the vertical (fissiparous) ones, at least in the administrative and political spheres. But neither the notion nor practice of patron-clientelism is likely to disappear soon or completely, especially in the social sphere. Yet, in order to become an effective, twenty-first-century society, Myanmar must address this issue, even if some of its traits that have made Burmese society so human (and attractive) are eliminated.

In Myanmar, rarely is the past discarded; it is continuously "added on," making the country today a multilayered hybrid of old and new. It is true that "downstreamers" may genuinely desire to discard some of the baggage of the past, especially in economic and political ways, and may wish to enjoy living on (what they consider) the cutting edge of modern society. Modernity, its moneymaking opportunities, and its new technologies are all attractive—notwithstanding the strain on the old infrastructure that we are currently witnessing, especially in Yangon.

However, these same "downstreamers" may not want to eliminate certain components of their culture and society that they feel define Burmeseness, which has been preserved mainly by the "upstreamers." These components rest on, among other things, maintaining the country's largely agrarian character, keeping the religion "orthodox," and ensuring that the political system remain fairly centralized and society relatively conservative and quiet, even though all these may mean being "left behind" by the rest of the world, technologically. So once again, we have a dualism of differences within a single whole attempting to work things out, not two binary and adversarial entities struggling to separate.

In this long, historic relationship between the country's "upstream and downstream" regions, both oldness and newness had been accommodated, but oldness seemed to have been the preferred value for most of Myanmar's people most of the time. It has been favored over newness for a variety of complex reasons, not least because one's identity was linked not only to the country's cherished traditions but also to the predominant way of life for the majority of the population—agriculture. The desire for familiar continuity almost always seemed to have preempted the desire for unfamiliar change. Not that change per se was (or is) perceived as anathema; but genuine structural change implies transformation of a socioeconomic, religious, cultural, and political nature that is too difficult to bear and uncomfortable to fathom psychologically for most of the people most of the time. But we shall see if this sentiment remains viable beyond the next several decades, as the current reforms become part of the national psyche and sociopolitical fabric.

Sources and Romanization

1. Michael Aung-Thwin, *The Mists of Ramanna: The Legend That Was Lower Burma* (Honolulu: University of Hawai'i Press, 2005); Michael Aung-Thwin, *Myth and History in the Historiography of Burma: Paradigms, Primary Sources and Prejudices* (Athens: Ohio University Press, 1998). I am aware of the new so-called Sawlu inscription found at Myittha, whose data is contested and, to date, has little bearing on this book.

2. A "new" urbanized area was recently said to have been "discovered" in Lower Myanmar. Although interesting, speculations that the site may be as early as the time of Asoka must await scientifically produced dates and conclusive epigraphic and archaeological evidence (see http://m.irrawaddy.com/multimedia-burma/106916.html).

Introduction

1. I use mainly "Myanmar" throughout this work without implying anything political. But as a Burmese speaker, I should note that using the term "Myanmar" as a noun sounds awkward, since it is an adjective and needs another Burmese word following it. The *notion* of "Myanmar" (or more correctly, "Myanma") changes with the historical context, so is not a fixed one. For an elaboration of the subject, see Michael Aung-Thwin, "Mranma Pran: When Context Encounters Notion," *Journal of Southeast Asian Studies* 39, no. 2 (2008): 193–217; as well as Michael Aung-Thwin and Maitrii Aung-Thwin, *A History of Myanmar since Ancient Times: Traditions and Transformations* (London: Reaktion Books, 2013), preface.

2. This is the date given in the *Yazadhiyaza Ayedawpon* (p. 36) when Pegu became capital, hence different from the date given to Binnya U, its first king, who had moved from Muttama to Pegu to make it his capital.

3. The term "Toungoo kingdom" (or "Toungoo Dynasty") is a creation of Western historiography and does not exist in indigenous histories as such. For reasons explicated below, I prefer to call it the "Second Pegu/Toungoo kingdom" (or dynasty) but have used "Toungoo" here since that name and entity is more familiar to scholars of Myanmar. Henceforth, it will be called the "Second Pegu/Toungoo" kingdom or dynasty.

4. Michael Aung-Thwin, *Pagan: The Origins of Modern Burma* (Honolulu: University of Hawai'i Press, 1985). This period has also been called the "Charter Era" by Victor B. Lieberman.

5. The length of the dynasty depends on how one counts and what is considered the "Toungoo Dynasty."

6. Victor B. Lieberman, *Burmese Administrative Cycles: Anarchy and Conquest, c. 1580–1760* (Princeton, NJ: Princeton University Press, 1984).

7. I am aware of the large amount of scholarship during the past several decades in the field of European history that has successfully rectified some of the negative images of the "medieval" world as a "dark age." For a basic and excellent introduction to the subject, one should consult Brian Tierney's *The Middle Ages* (New York: McGraw-Hill, 1992). But that kind of scholarship has yet to influence Myanmar studies.

8. Michael Aung-Thwin, "A Tale of Two Kingdoms: Ava and Pegu in the Fifteenth Century," *Journal of Southeast Asian Studies* 42, no. 1 (2011): 1–16.

9. Michael Aung-Thwin, "The Myth of the 'Three Shan Brothers' and the Ava Period in Burmese History," *Journal of Asian Studies* 55, no. 4 (1996): 881–901.

10. James C. Scott, *The Art of Not Being Governed: An Anarchist History of Upland Southeast Asia* (New Haven, CT: Yale University Press, 2009).

11. For a thoroughly penetrating review of Scott's study, *The Art of Not Being Governed*, see Victor B. Lieberman's review in "A Zone of Refuge in Southeast Asia? Reconceptualizing Interior Spaces," *Journal of Global History* 5 (2010): 333–346. See also my own assessment of the same in "Debate: A Non-State Approach," Reviews by Michael R. Dove, Hjorleifur Jonsson, and Michael Aung-Thwin of *The Art of Not Being Governed: An Anarchist History of Upland Southeast Asia* by James C. Scott. *Bijdragen tot de Taal-, Land- en Volkenkunde* 167, no. 1 (2011): 95–99.

12. I start my calculations from the first several years of the first decade of the fourteenth century, when King Kyawswa of Pagan was killed by the famous "Three Brothers" and the Kingdom of Pagan finally lost control of both Upper and Lower Myanmar, not from the official date of the founding of Ava in 1364.

13. Anthony Reid, *Southeast Asia in the Age of Commerce: 1450–1680*, vol. 1 (New Haven, CT: Yale University Press, 1988).

14. To be sure, there are published studies of select topics in the histories of Ava and Pegu, such as Jon Fernquest's "Min-gyi-nyo, the Shan Invasions of Ava (1524–27), and the Beginnings of Expansionary Warfare in Toungoo Burma: 1486–1539," *SOAS Bulletin of Burma Research* 3, no. 2 (Autumn 2005), 284–395; and his "Rajadhirat's Mask of Command: Military Leadership in Burma (c. 1348–1421)," *SOAS Bulletin of Burma Research* 4, no. 1 (Spring 2006): 3–29. But no book-length study of each kingdom and their relationship that has used original and contemporary sources has been published in English or Burmese heretofore.

15. D. G. E. Hall, *Burma* (London: Hutchinson's University Library, 1950); G. E. Harvey, *A History of Burma: From the Earliest Times to 10 March 1824: The Beginning of the English Conquest* (London: Frank Cass, 1925); and Sir Arthur Phayre, *History of Burma, including Burma proper, Pegu, Taungu, Tenasserim, and Arakan* (London: Trübner & Co., 1883). Phayre and Harvey's works were generally based on U Kala's *Mahayazawingyi* [Great Royal Chronicle] (Yangon: Hanthawaddy Press, 1960) and U Tin Shein, ed., *Hmannan Mahayazawindawgyi* [Great Royal Chronicle of the Palace of Mirrors] (Yangon: Pyi Gyi Man Taing Piktakat Press, 1967), while Hall depended on Harvey and Phayre for his perspective on indigenous history.

16. I know of no published or unpublished work, in English or Burmese, that has challenged the conventional (and current) historiography of the First Ava and First Pegu Dynasties.

17. Harry J. Benda, "The Structure of Southeast Asian History: Some Preliminary Observations," *Journal of Southeast Asian History* 3 (1962): 106–138.

18. Most, if not all, historians of Southeast Asia working on this era see the period as being transformative. One of the most recent studies, by Barbara Watson Andaya and Leonard Y. Andaya, titled *A History of Early Modern Southeast Asia, 1400–1830* (Cambridge: Cambridge University Press, 2015), chapter 3 particularly, makes that point. There are other individual studies that agree with the above assessment, but perhaps one representative work will suffice. It is *A New History of Southeast Asia*, ed. M. C. Ricklefs (Singapore, Houndmills: 2010), chapters 5, 6, and 7, which explicitly referred to the "Early Modern" period as one of transformation. With regard to Myanmar itself, one of the few scholars cognizant of the larger issues, the late Andrew Huxley, argued that Myanmar was already "Early Modern" in terms of law (see his "Mon Studies during the Nineteenth-Century: The Admiration That Destroys," manuscript, p. 3). This was subsequently published as Huxley, "Mon Studies and Professor Forch-

hammer: The Admiration That Destroys," *Zeitschrift der Deutschen Morenlandischen Gesellschaft* 162, no. 2 (2012): 391–410. He reiterated his argument in "The Pali Legal Tradition: Theft from Vinaya to Dhammathat," that was submitted at the time to the *Journal of the Pali Text Society*, p. 9.

19. Admittedly, I am not much involved in the conversation among historians immersed in the "Early Modern" period and its many complicated issues. But I have some reservations about depicting this era as all transformative. This is elaborated in a paper presented at the Third Congress of the Asian Association of World Historians, held at the Nanyang Technological University, Singapore, May 29–31, 2015.

20. And even here, it is not certain that these periods were not added on later as part of the publisher's organizational scheme.

21. Because *yazawin* is derived from Pali and considered elitist, the word *thamaing* became the politically correct and more suitable word for both "history" and "historiography" during the Socialist period of the 1960s.

22. John Smail, "On the Possibility of an Autonomous History of Modern Southeast Asia," *Journal of Southeast Asian History* 2, no. 2 (1961): 72–102.

23. Although John Smail's "autonomous" history may seem passé, senior historians in the field of Southeast Asian history have only recently begun publishing histories with such a perspective. Yet, more recent generation of Southeast Asian historians often unfamiliar with these older works, nonetheless raise nearly identical issues and problems as if they were totally new. For a recent discussion on that subject, see Michael Aung-Thwin, "A New/Old Look at 'Classical' and 'Post-Classical' Southeast Asia/Burma," in Michael Aung-Thwin and K. R. Hall, *New Perspectives on the History and Historiography of Southeast Asia: Continuing Explorations* (New York: Routledge, 2011), pp. 25–55; and Michael Aung-Thwin, "Continuing, Re-emerging, and Emerging Trends in Southeast Asian History," *TRaNS: Trans-Regional and -National Studies of Southeast Asia* 1, no. 1 (January 2013): 87–104.

24. Here, I am thinking of the type of work by James C. Scott cited earlier in this chapter (*The Art of Not Being Governed*), particularly his description of Zomia, which is highly anachronistic, "acontextual" and "ahistorical."

25. I extrapolate from the distinction between rural and urban made by the late Paul Wheatley in his *Nagara and Commandery: Origins of the Southeast Asian Urban Traditions* (Chicago: University of Chicago, Department of Geography, 1983).

26. See the late F. K. Lehman's "Ethnic Categories in Burma and the Theory of Social Systems," in *Southeast Asian Tribes, Minorities, and Nations*, ed. Peter Kunstadter (Princeton, NJ: Princeton University Press, 1967); also, see Victor B. Lieberman, "Ethnic Politics in Eighteenth-Century Burma," *Modern Asian Studies* 12, no. 3 (1978): 455–482; and Robert H. Taylor, "Perceptions of Ethnicity in the Politics of Burma," *Southeast Asian Journal of Social Sciences* 10, no. 1 (1982): 7–22.

27. Michael Aung-Thwin, *The Mists of Ramanna: The Legend That Was Lower Burma* (Honolulu: University of Hawai'i Press, 2005).

28. Donald M. Stadtner, "The Mon of Lower Burma," *Journal of the Siam Society* 96 (2008): 193–215, is a recent example.

29. Noted Pali scholar Emil Forchhammer was one of the most famous and influential in this line of thinking. The case is detailed in Aung-Thwin's *Mists*, chapter 11, pp. 268–269, and subsequently supported by the research of the late Andrew Huxley, in his "Mon Studies and Professor Forchhammer."

30. *She Haung Myanma Kyauksa Mya* [Ancient Burmese Stone Inscriptions] (hereafter *SMK*), ed. U Nyeing Maung, 5 vols., Archaeological Department, Myanmar (Yangon: Sapebeikman, 1972–1996); and, for Pegu, *She Haung Mon Kyauksa Paung Chok* [Collection of

Ancient Mon Stone Inscriptions] (hereafter *MKPC*), ed. U Chit Thein (Yangon: Ministry of Culture, 1965).

31. Pe Maung Tin, *Myanma Sape Thamaing* [History of Burmese Literature] (Yangon: Khettara Press, 1977); U Kyaw Dun, ed., *Myanma Sa Nyunbaung Kyan* [Anthology of Burmese Literature], 5 vols. (Rangoon: Superintendent Government Press, 1961); and Saw Lu [alias U Saw Tun], *Pagan Khit Myanma Sa* [Burmese Literature of the Pagan Period], 3 vols. (Yangon: Sapebeikman Press, 1996).

32. One good example of a collection of such records is J. S. Furnivall and Pe Maung Tin, eds., *Zambudipa Okhsaung Kyan* (Yangon: Burma Research Society, 1960).

33. I am, of course, referring to "secular" *yazawin*, that is, "*rajavamsa*," not religious ones with the same suffix (*vamsa*).

34. Marc Bloch, *Feudal Society*, trans. L. A. Manyon, 2 vols. (Chicago: University of Chicago Press, 1970).

1. Prelude to Ava

1. Aung-Thwin, *Pagan.*

2. Emmanuel LeRoy Ladurie, *The Mind and Method of the Historian* (Chicago: University of Chicago Press, 1981). It is also likely that another historian of the Annales School, Fernand Braudel, in *On History*, trans. Sarah Matthews (Chicago: University of Chicago Press, 1980), would include his notion of the longue dureé.

3. For details, see Aung-Thwin, *Pagan*, chapter 8.

4. Although Victor Lieberman includes climate change in his *Strange Parallels: Southeast Asia in Global Context, c. 800–1830* (Cambridge: Cambridge University Press, 2003), a more recent and focused analysis can be found in his "Charter State Collapse in Southeast Asia, ca. 1250–1400, as a Problem in Regional and World History," *American Historical Review* 116, no. 4 (2011): 937–963. There is another old theory that attributed the decline of Pagan to the assumed deforestation of the area, as much wood would have been needed to fire the millions of kiln-fired bricks to build the nearly three thousand Pagan period temples. But J. C. MacKenzie's theory, as argued in "Climate in Burmese History," *Journal of the Burma Research Society* 3, pt. 1 (1913): 40–46, had long been disproved, largely because there is scientific evidence that the area around Pagan was never forested to begin with, and that the materials needed for firing the bricks came from elsewhere outside the capital and its environs.

5. One of the best published examples of Roland Fletcher's work is "The Dynamics of Angkor and Its Landscape," in *Old Myths and New Approaches: Interpreting Ancient Religious Sites in Southeast Asia*, ed. Alexandra Haendel (Clayton, Victoria: Monash University Publishing, 2012), pp. 42–62. But he has also given many lectures on the subject that includes the most up-to-date findings regarding the issue, so perhaps one of these saved online might be even more helpful. See, for example, http://www.iias.nl/event/greater-angkor-growth-and-demise-giant-low-density-agrarian-city. See also Brendan M. Buckley et al., "Monsoon Extremes and Society over the Past Millennium on Mainland Southeast Asia," *Quaternary Science Reviews* 95 (2014): 1–19.

6. As this chapter is meant only as a preamble to the rise of Ava, and confined largely to human activities during the Pagan period rather than natural causes within the broader region of Southeast Asia, climate change as a factor in the decline of the state in Southeast Asia is well beyond the scope of this manuscript, which in any case, I must leave to scholars far more competent than I.

7. Aung-Thwin, *Myth and History*, chapter 3.

8. For a stimulating argument about the historiographic significance of crises in history, see Ladurie, *The Mind and Method of the Historian.*

9. Uncannily, the kinds of decentralized conditions from which Pagan itself had emerged in the mid-ninth century seemed to have reappeared. At that time, the Pyu kingdom, conspicuously rich in material treasures in the form of religious buildings and magnificent cities was also invaded by the Kingdom of Nanzhao, now Yunnan and its environs. Although on a different scale, by a different group of invaders, and at a different time, the thirteenth- and fourteenth-century Mongol attacks of the Pagan kingdom, even though they never reached the capital as convention has it, nevertheless resulted in fear and anarchy at the center, leaving a power vacuum there.

10. Aung-Thwin, *Myth and History,* pp. 68, 186, n. 86.

11. A clear distinction has not yet been demonstrated by historians between this Sihasu (Thihathu) of Prome and another with the same name, the youngest of the famous Three Brothers.

12. In a 1378 AD inscription of Ava, he is still remembered as the "Tala Sukri" (Headman of Tala) who became king. See *SMK,* vol. 4, p. 173.

13. *SMK,* vol. 3, p. 173. However, Twinthintaikwun Mahasithu's *Twinthin Myanma Yazawinthit* [Twinthin's New Chronicle of Myanma], ed. U Myint Swe, vol. 1 (Yangon: Mingala Pon Hneit Taik, 1968), p. 159, states that this occurred in 1286.

14. *SMK,* vol. 3, p. 158, lines 4–5. This stone is dated to 1292, so it had to have been referring to the invasion of 1287 rather than the one in 1300–1301.

15. U Kala, *Mahayazawingyi,* vol. 1, p. 316, shows that Athinkhaya, eldest of the Three Brothers, held Myin Saing; the second eldest, Yazathingyan, had Mekkhaya; and Thihathu, the youngest, Pinle.

16. Aung-Thwin, "Myth of the 'Three Shan Brothers.'"

17. *SMK,* vol. 3, p. 179.

18. According to G. H. Luce, "The Early *Syam* in Burma's History," *Journal of the Siam Society* 46 (1958): 151, he was the husband of Saw U, the granddaughter of Thonlula, chief queen of Tayopye's father.

19. In December of 1297, when Kyawswa poured the "royal water" of consecration for the dedication of a monastery, Athinkhaya was again at his side. It was only much later, when Kyawswa demanded loyalty from Athinkhaya against his own brothers that his support finally ended. This can be found in a contemporary Chinese manuscript entitled *"Zhi-yuan Zhengmian Lu,"* p. 10, translated for me by Professor Sun Laichen (hereafter *ZZL*).

20. *SMK,* vol. 3, p. 196, line 18.

21. *ZZL,* p. 8, has 1297. It is on page 673 of Edouard Huber's version of apparently the same text, which he titled the *"Houang Yuan tcheng Mien tou."* See Huber, "La Fin De La Dynastie De Pagan," *Bulletin de l'Ecole française d'Extrême-Orient* 9, no. 9 (1909): 633–680.

22. Yi-Sein Chen, "The Chinese Inscription at Pagan," *Bulletin of the Burma Historical Commission* 1, no. 2 (1960): 154; and G. H. Luce, "The Early *Syam* in Burma's History: A Supplement," *Journal of the Siam Society* 47 (1959): 88, which he took from the section on "Mien" in the *Yuan Shih,* chapter 210.

23. Aung-Thwin, *Myth and History,* chapter 4.

24. Luce, "Early *Syam,*" (1958), p. 156; Huber, "La Fin De La Dynastie," p. 672; and *ZZL,* p. 9, which has this to say: "Ever since [you] submitted to the Great Yuan it costs us too much."

25. Aung-Thwin, *Myth and History,* pp. 98–101. My 1998 interpretation was subsequently supported by Tun Aung Chain in 2004 in his article, titled "The Deposition of Kyawzwa: A Reconsideration of the Inscriptional Evidence," in *Broken Glass: Pieces of Myanmar History* (Yangon: SEMEO, 2004), pp. 45–49.

26. I cite the original Yuan source in *Myth and History*, p. 108.

27. Dr. Than Tun, "History of Burma: A.D. 1300–1400," *Journal of the Burma Research Society* 42, no. 2 (1959): 123; *SMK*, vol. 3, dated to *sakkaraj* 672 (AD 1310).

28. U Kala, *Mahayazawingyi*, vol. 1, p. 317. There should be a royal monastery on the list as well; perhaps it was combined with the royal *stupa*.

29. Ibid., p. 319.

2. The Ava Convention

1. When I use terms such as "Shan" or "Burman," I am referring to the ethno-linguistic groups represented by those terms, as identified by the groups themselves as well as by others.

2. Recent works on the Shan of Myanmar by its own historians do not raise such issues and are disappointingly unoriginal. This is particularly true of Sai Aung Tun's *History of the Shan State from Its Origins to 1962* (Chiang Mai: Silkworm Books, 2009). Although voluminous, it essentially regurgitates the standard published English-language accounts, including the erroneous contention that Ava was Shan, with hardly a single innovative insight that contributes to the Shan historiography of Myanmar or indication that he had kept up with the scholarly literature in the field.

3. See Aung-Thwin, *Myth and History*, chapter 5.

4. As shown in *Myth and History*, p. 124, Phayre had confused the Three Brothers of the thirteenth century with the three Shan *sawbwas* who ruled Ava *after* 1527 when the city was finally taken—over two hundred years later.

5. Aung-Thwin, *Myth and History*, pp. 125–126.

6. Even after Phayre had published his work in 1883, several years later, in 1888 when the *Pitakat Thamaing* (essentially the "national bibliography") was compiled by a minister in charge of the royal library at Mandalay, the Three Brothers remained as they appeared in indigenous historiography as the "three royal brothers," demonstrating further that the myth existed only in the English-language historiography of Myanmar. See Mingyi Maha Thiri Zeyathu's edition of the *Pitakat Taw Thamaing* ["History" or "Account" of the Royal Library], 2nd ed. (Yangon: Tipitaka Nikaya Thathana Committee, 1989), pp. 316–318.

7. Note that we are speaking of language, not "race." Moreover, if the late Pete (Alton) Becker, a "linguistic anthropologist," is correct in saying that language *is* culture, then culturally, Ava was also Burmese.

8. Harvey, *History of Burma*; Htin Aung, *History of Burma* (New York: Columbia University Press, 1967); Hall, *Burma*; and Sao Saimong Mangrai, ed., *The Padaeng Chronicle and the Jengtung State Chronicle Translated* (Ann Arbor: University of Michigan, Center for South and Southeast Asian Studies, 1981).

9. However, both the Karen and Kachin used the title. See E. R. Leach, *Political Systems of Highland Burma: A Study of Kachin Social Structure* (Boston: Beacon Press, 1970).

10. The palace belonging to the *sawbwa* of Nyaungshwe, for example, was obviously a copy of Mandalay's, even to the extent of delineating auspicious positions for the residence of kings, princes, queens; the names and number of thrones; the style and function of regalia, so on.

11. Here, I am not speaking of origins that go back to the Neolithic; I am speaking only of such influences during the Pagan and Ava periods.

12. Harvey, *History of Burma*, pp. 73, 153.

13. Hall, *Burma*, p. 32.

14. Sao Saimong Mangrai, *The Shan States and the British Annexation* (Ithaca, NY: Cornell University Southeast Asia Program, 1965), p. 49.

15. The alleged link between Thadominbya and one of the Three Brothers was made by the chronicles to legitimate Ava; it had nothing to do with the Ava Convention's attempts to tie their (alleged) ethnicities.

16. Aung-Thwin, *Myth and History*, p. 124.

17. My brief survey (in the early 1970s) of his papers at St. Anthony's College, Oxford, stored in several metal cabinets, showed few Burmese works; most were already translated in long, handwritten ledgers of one of the Burmese chronicles.

18. I met him at an informal occasion in Ithaca while I was still an undergraduate at Doane College, Crete, Nebraska. He was teaching at Cornell on the Cornell-SOAS exchange program as visiting professor.

19. The 226 years reflects the views of the Ava Convention, obtained by ending the Pagan period in 1301 AD, when the Three Brothers took actual control of Upper Myanmar, and 1527, when a Shan *sawbwa* did in fact take Ava.

20. Than Tun, "History of Burma"; and Tin Hla Thaw, "History of Burma: A.D. 1400–1500," *Journal of the Burma Research Society* 42, no. 2 (1959): 135–151.

21. Mingyi Maha Thiri Zeyathu, *Pitakat Taw Thamaing*, on p. 320, continued this notion of sacred city found in the chronicles well into the late nineteenth century. Upon recording the poem called *Min Set Linka* (poem on royal lineage), the three Ava *sawbwas* were very much part of the poem's rhyme and rhythm scheme dealing with Burmese kings. In fact, the number of kings who reigned during the life of the city was given at the end of the poem as two notable and essential facts: thirty (kings) and 388 (years) respectively. Both the thirty kings and the 388 years represent the period from 1364, when Ava was founded, to its destruction in 1752, when the life of the city ended, despite the vicissitudes in terms of the lineage of kings. In other words, the dynasty was being defined by the life of the city, not the other way around.

22. Robert Halliday's translation, "Slapat Rajawan Datow Smin Ron" [History of Kings], in the *Journal of the Burma Research Society* 13, nos. 1 and 2 (1923): 58, states that "When Daka Rat Pi [Takayutpi] was no more, Paran Man Soaithi [Tabinshwehti], his Burmese Majesty became king of Hamsavati." The narrative continues as if he was just another king in the same dynasty.

23. Admittedly, the later dates privileged political events rather than "ethnic dynasties," so that whatever criterion one uses—political or reified ethnicity—it will not be neutral.

24. Paul J. Bennett, "The 'Fall of Pagan': Continuity and Change in 14th Century Burma," in *Conference under the Tamarind Tree: Three Essays in Burmese History* (New Haven, CT: Yale University Southeast Asia Monograph Series, 1971), pp. 3–53.

25. Victor B. Lieberman, *Burmese Administrative Cycles*, p. 15, and "Reinterpreting Burmese History," *Comparative Studies in Society and History* 29 (1987): 172. This notion of a politically fragmented Ava period continued for at least two more decades. See Jon Fernquest's "Min-gyi-nyo, the Shan Invasions of Ava," p. 285.

26. Aung-Thwin, *Pagan*, pp. 196–197, and n. 9, pp. 242–243.

27. Aung-Thwin, "Myth of the 'Three Shan Brothers.'"

28. See the reviews by John Badgley in the *Journal of Southeast Asian Studies* 30, no. 2 (September 1999): 364–365; Benedicte Brac de la Perriere's in *Journal of Asian Studies* 60, no. 1 (February 2001): 286–288; and Martin Stuart-Fox in *Journal of the Economic and Social History of the Orient* 44, no. 1 (2001): 88–90. Other senior scholars in the field, such as the late Andrew Huxley, also accepted my conclusions, although in an informal, online discourse.

29. Most obvious is Sai Aung Tun's *History of the Shan State*. Another is Aye Chan's "Burma: Shan Domination in the Ava Period (c. AD 1310–1555)," *Journal of the Siam Society* 94 (2006): 26–50. Although not as cavalier about new research as the former, and recognizing at least some of the problems in the "Ava is Shan" thesis, nonetheless, the work as a whole shows basic

misunderstanding of the most important historiographic issues and problems of the Ava Convention.

30. Aung-Thwin, "A Tale of Two Kingdoms."

31. Aung-Thwin, "Those Men in Saffron Robes," *Journal of Burma Studies* 17, no. 2 (2013): 305–306.

32. Taylor, "Perceptions of Ethnicity."

33. Lieberman, "Ethnic Politics."

34. This number includes all inscriptions of the entire period from 1302 to 1527 as calculated in U Nyeing Maung's *SMK*.

35. Emmanuel LeRoy Ladurie, *The Mind and Method of the Historian*, chapter 1, "History that Stands Still," pp. 1–25.

3. Ava's Founding Fathers

1. *SMK*, vol. 4, pp. 121–122, puts his death in 1344. The *Zatatawpon Yazawin* [Chronicle of Royal Horoscopes], ed. U Hla Tin (Yangon: Ministry of Culture, 1960), places his reign as beginning in 1342.

2. Than Tun, "History of Burma," p. 124.

3. Ibid., p. 125.

4. U Kala, *Mahayazawingyi*, vol. 1, p. 336. The word *akhun* (outer shell, or peelings) is also the word for tax, with the suggesting that taxation is less onerous and taken from the "outer shell," while *ahsan* (the inner core; the fruit itself, so to speak) is what belongs to the people. The word *hsan*, not surprisingly, is also the word for uncooked rice.

5. U Kala, *Mahayazawingyi*, vol. 1, pp. 341–342.

6. Than Tun, "History of Burma," p. 128.

7. U Kala, *Mahayazawingyi*, vol. 1, p. 345. The *Maniyadanabon* was more delicate. It said, "Nga Nu, I do not wish that my wife, Saw Onma, should become the wife of any other man; you must go and deal with her." Shin Sandalinka, *The Maniyadanabon of Shin Sandalinka*, trans. L. E. Bagshawe (Ithaca, NY: Cornell University Southeast Asia Program, 1981), p. 26.

8. This shows that his given name was Sawkai, not Swasawkai, as often stated erroneously, so that his title "Minkyiswa Sawkai" meant "Sawkai, the Exalted King," not "Great king Swasawkai."

9. U Kala, *Mahayazawingyi*, vol. 1, p. 345.

10. *Zatatawpon*, p. 46; and also Shin Thilawuntha, *Yazawinkyaw* [Celebrated Chronicle], ed. Pe Maung Tin (Yangon: Burma Research Society, n.d.), p. 79. The discrepancy is the result of the way the years were counted: the *Zatatawpon* and the *Yazawinkyaw* started counting from Minkyiswa Sawkai's year at Pinya, while U Kala began when he ascended the throne.

11. The story differs in Sandalinka, *Maniyadanabon*, p. 27.

12. U Kala, *Mahayazawingyi*, vol. 1, p. 349–350. For example, he gave his elder daughter Saw Umma to a descendant of Yazathingyan, one of the Three Brothers, and gave them Taungbyongyi as fief. He gave Yamethin to another relative and Pyi to his elder brother. To a trusted follower, Pyan Khyi, he gave Toungoo, and to another, he gave Taungdwingyi. He gave Pagan to a Sithu, Talop to Rajathu, and to Thinkathu, he gave Sagu. Nyaungyan was given to Bhayakyaw, while Pakhangyi went to one Tayaphya.

13. Several articles related to Arakan in a recent special issue of the *Journal of Burma Studies* (19, no. 2, 2015) have raised questions and contributed new ideas to serious issues concerning interpretations and data in the study of Arakan, in part dedicated to the memory and scholarship of Pamela Gutman, who was a pioneer in that field from my generation of Myanmar scholars.

14. The word refers to someone not attached to the crown or *sangha*.

15. The story varies. In Sandalinka's *Maniyadanabon*, p. 1, it was a building on the dam that contained a statue of a woman and seemed to him to be a *nat* and had to do with King Anawrahta, not Alaungsithu, and with the former's lover, not the sons and daughters of Linzin and Ayuthaya.

16. According to Tet Htoot, "The Nature of the Burmese Chronicles," in *Historians of South East Asia*, ed. D.G.E. Hall (London, Oxford University Press, 1961), p. 53, Min Yaza was said to have written the "Zambu Kungya Hpo Yaza Mu Haung." However, the surviving copy of that manuscript, housed in the British Library and catalogued as number 3447, part six, is not what it is said to be. Upon careful scrutiny of its microfilm and digital copies, this palm-leaf *mss* (an 1825 copy) is clearly the *Zatatawpon*, heretofore attributed, in Myanmar studies, to an unknown author. Although the issue is beyond the scope of this book, my current research suggests that the author of the *Zatatawpon* may well be none other than Min Yaza himself. He is also said to have been responsible for the source on which Sandalinka's *Maniyadanabon* is based.

17. Sandalinka, *Maniyadanabon*, pp. xx.

18. Sandalinka, *Maniyadanabon*, p. viii. *Shaukhton* can also be translated as "precedents."

19. U Kala, *Mahayazawingyi*, vol. 1, p. 365.

20. Ibid., p. 367.

21. Ibid., p. 369. However, the editors of the published version of U Kala stated that they had corrected the original, allegedly "misspelled" phrase, which they contend was actually "Talaing Thale" not "Talaing kale," although acknowledging that the *Yazadarit Ayedawpon* also had "Talaing kale." See Amatki Bannya Dala, *Yazadhiyaza Ayedawpon*, 3rd ed. (Yangon: Swesa Press, 1974).

22. U Kala, *Mahayazawingyi*, vol. 1, pp. 370–371. These figures are likely exaggerated, although the strategy probably reflects a standard and well-known approach.

23. Sandalinka, *Maniyadanabon*, p. 31.

24. The published pages run from 346 to 384, and the manuscript sections cover pages 419 to 461.

25. Than Tun, "History of Burma," p. 131.

26. In the case of at least one king who G. H. Luce thought was fictitious and therefore deliberately omitted in his list of kings, the numeral given to the next king with the same title falls short by one Roman numeral when I later discovered that the king omitted was indeed historical. Not only did it skew everyone else's research that followed Luce's but the wrong Roman numeral had to be explained every time these two kings were mentioned.

27. Thilawuntha, *Yazawinkyaw*, p. 79; *Zatatawpon*, p. 46; U Kala, *Mahayazawingyi*, p. 385.

28. U Kala, *Mahayazawingyi*, vol. 1, p. 386.

4. The Consolidation of Ava

1. *SMK*, vol.4, p. 221, line 12b. Tin Hla Thaw, in his "History of Burma," p. 136, wrote that the inscription was a reference to Prancey Noratha (Pyin Si Noyahta) who ascended the throne at age twenty-eight, citing Charles Duroiselle's edition of *A List of Inscriptions Found in Burma* (Rangoon: Superintendent, Government Printing, 1921), pp. 124–125. The original inscription reproduced in *SMK* cited above does not mention any Prancey Noratha, but an Aniruddha Man Co, which Thin Hla Thaw may have assumed to be the same as Prancey Noratha, as "Noratha" is a shortened, Burmese version of the Sanskrit "Aniruddha." The *Zatatawpon* dates the ascension of this person to 1401, although U Kala puts it in 1400 (*Mahayazawingyi*, vol. 1, p. 386).

2. *SMK*, vol. 4, p. 220; Tin Hla Thaw, "History," p. 138. Note that the word "Talaing" was not a reference to the Mon then (or since then, except in colonial historiography), but to the mix of people in Lower Myanmar.

3. *SMK*, vol. 4, p. 220.

4. U Kala, *Mahayazawingyi*, vol. 1, p. 390. Previous cities mentioned were Pinya, Yamethin, Badon, Dipeyin, Taungdwin, Salin, Wadi, Nyaungyan, Talok, Pagan, Sinku, Siputaya, and Pauk Maying.

5. Tin Hla Thaw, "History," p. 138.

6. Ibid., p. 136.

7. Ibid., p. 137.

8. *SMK*, vol. 4, p. 229.

9. U Kala, *Mahayazawingyi*, vol. 1, p. 394. Even by U Kala's time, then, the word *kyun* did not mean "slave" as so often asserted in Myanmar's modern historiography, but a "client," "subject," or "vassal" of the king, similar to the kind of political and social status that the term *samurai* had in Japan, a topic to be discussed more thoroughly in a following chapter.

10. It took approximately four nights and five days from Ava to the coasts by express boat that changed crews at intervals, but eleven days by forced march on land. This was the time given by U Kala, but partially confirmed by Cox (and perhaps also Symes), who visited in the late eighteenth century.

11. U Kala, *Mahayazawingyi*, vol. 1, p. 407.

12. Michael Aung-Thwin, "Prophecies, Omens, and Dialogue: Tools of the Trade in Burmese Historiography," in *Historical Essays in Honor of Kenneth R. Rossman*, ed. Kent Newmyer (Lincoln: University of Nebraska Press, 1980), pp. 171–185.

13. U Kala, *Mahayazawingyi*, vol. 1, pp. 409–410.

14. Since the earliest extant copy of these parts of the *Zambu* may exist in the *Maniyadanabon* of the late eighteenth-century—well after U Kala's work was written—it suggests U Kala had an earlier version of the *Zambu* from which he obtained his information.

15. U Kala, *Mahayazawingyi*, vol. 1, p. 390.

16. Ibid., p. 416.

17. Ibid., p. 417. In modern times, the word *naingnan* means "nation," so "dominion" may be more appropriate here (during U Kala's time), hence, my translation of the word earlier during the Pagan period as "conquered territory." Nevertheless, either translation raises issues regarding the "modernity" (or Western origins) of the concept of political boundaries based on territory.

18. Ibid., p. 428.

19. Ibid., p. 427.

20. *SMK*, vol. 5, p. 35.

21. I am not sure to what extent this is colonial myth-making by Robert Halliday; see his "Slapat," p. 52.

22. Ibid.

23. U Kala, *Mahayazawingyi*, vol. 2, p. 36.

24. Twinthintaikwun, *Twinthin Myanma Yazawinthit*, vol. 1, p. 320, also suggests that Yazadarit actually killed him.

25. U Kala, *Mahayazawingyi*, vol. 2, p. 46. Amatkyi Bannya Dala, *Yazadhiyaza Ayedawpon*, 3rd ed. (Yangon: Swesa Press, 1974), which I use here, concurs with this sequence of events, but other late copies of the same text had the reverse, whereby Yazadarit died first, then Mingaung followed.

26. I suspect the wooden stockade is the inner citadel protecting the palace, outside of which is the brick-walled city, a typical arrangement of royal cities in Myanmar since first century BC Beikthano.

27. Tin Hla Thaw, "History," p. 138, who cites the Sagaing Zedihla Inscription.

28. U Kala, *Mahayazawingyi*, vol. 2, p. 47.

29. *Zatatawpon*, p. 46.

30. Twinthintaikwun, *Twinthin Myanma Yazawinthit*, vol. 1, p. 329.

31. This is the story as told by U Kala, which the later *Hmannan* followed almost verbatim, with some additional detail in the *Yazawinthit*, p. 334. However, neither Harvey's (*History of Burma*) nor Phayre's (*History of Burma*) is the same, although they also depended on these chronicles. Harvey writes that "the *sawbwa* hid in the wood with a bow near where the king was making a canal at Aungbinle in Mandalay district, and shot him dead" (p. 96). Phayre writes, "The king had been induced to go outside the city to direct the excavation of a canal. He was suddenly attacked by a band of armed men and wounded by an arrow. He escaped and fled to Monyin where he died soon after" (p. 82). It is not clear where they got their versions.

32. *Zatatawpon*, p. 46, says 1426.

33. Ibid.

34. Tin Hla Thaw, "History," p. 139.

35. Ibid., p. 139.

36. U Kala, *Mahayazawingyi*, vol. 2, p. 59.

37. Ibid., p. 61. All of these concerns and place-names were also important during Pagan times. "Ban Khyi Chay Tuik," for example, was spelled "Plan Khiy Chay Tuik" during Pagan times but is the same place.

38. There is not a single authentic peasant rebellion in precolonial Burmese history that I know of; all were elite contests, usually princes fighting for the throne and on the whole using hereditary crown soldiers, not peasant armies, since there was none.

39. The only other one, whose history is not known or documented, is the shadowy Kuvera of Arakan.

40. The *Yazawinthit* records that they were from Myanmar, returning from Sri Lanka.

41. U Kala, *Mahayazawingyi*, vol. 2, p. 69. My calculations are based on Pagan period prices, and even assuming that the costs for building these temples had not risen in Ava, they were enormous.

42. Tin Hla Thaw, "History," p. 140; *SMK*, vol. 5, p. 22.

43. U Kala, *Mahayazawingyi*, vol. 2, pp. 68–69.

44. Tin Hla Thaw, "History," p. 141; *SMK*, vol. 5, p. 4.

45. This statement alone makes clear the most important criteria for legitimate kingship: son or brother of the king. As stated numerous times, most of the succession struggles in Burmese history have been between uncles and nephews.

46. U Kala, *Mahayazawingyi*, vol. 2, p. 74.

47. Tin Hla Thaw, "History," p. 141; *SMK*, vol. 5, p. 26.

48. Tin Hla Thaw, "History," pp. 142–143.

49. Ibid., p. 149; *SMK*, vol. 5, p. 4.

5. The Fifteenth Century and the Apogee of Ava

1. *SMK*, vol. 5, pp. 34–38; *Zatatawpon*, p. 46, has a date of 1441.

2. *SMK*, vol. 5, pp. 21–35.

3. U Kala, *Mahayazawingyi*, vol. 2, pp. 75–76.

4. *SMK*, vol. 5, pp. 21–33.

5. Tin Hla Thaw, "History," p. 142.

6. Ibid.

7. U Kala, *Mahayazawingyi*, vol. 2, p. 77.

8. Tin Hla Thaw, "History," p. 144.

9. *SMK*, vol. 5, p. 35.

10. *SMK*, vol. 1, "supplement," p. 43; Tin Hla Thaw, "History," p. 143, translates *nuinnum* as "empire," whereas I think "dominion" might be a better choice.

11. *SMK*, vol. 1, "supplement," pp. 43–45; Tin Hla Thaw, "History," pp. 143–144, states this occurred the next year, in 1449.

12. According to Luce, "Chin Hills," in *Journal of the Burma Research Society* 42 (i): 26, he is apparently "General Wang Chi of the Ming Dynasty," cited by Tin Hla Thaw, "History," p. 143.

13. The editors state that it was not today's Mandalay, but another Mandalay farther north.

14. U Kala, *Mahayazawingyi*, vol. 2; p. 80.

15. Banna Kyam is mentioned in Narapati's 1444 inscription. *SMK*, vol. 5, p. 35.

16. Each *viss* equals three pounds, two ounces avoirdupois.

17. U Kala, *Mahayazawingyi*, vol. 2, p. 80.

18. Ibid., p. 87.

19. He was actually the king's younger brother.

20. *SMK*, vol. 5, p. 65.

21. *Zatatawpon*, p. 46.

22. U Kala, *Mahayazawingyi*, vol. 2, p. 88; *SMK*, vol. 5, p. 65.

23. Tin Hla Thaw, "History," p. 144, stated that the event dates to 1456. But the inscription on which this appears is dated to 1444, although it is on the reverse side of the dated side and could have been added later. See *SMK*, vol. 5, p. 42. U Nyein Maung, editor and compiler of *SMK*, dates it to 1444.

24. U Kala, *Mahayazawingyi*, vol. 2, p. 88.

25. Not today's Dipeyin, on the road to Mandalay from Monywa, but up the Mu River valley, southwest of Ye-U.

26. U Kala, *Mahayazawingyi*, vol. 2, p. 94.

27. Ibid., p. 100.

28. There is some confusion with regard to Mahathihathuya and his successor. Tin Hla Thaw ("History," p. 145) added one king between Mahathihathuya and his successor Dutiya Mingaung (Mingaung the Second), with the royal title of Siri Sudhammarajadipati. But this was the title taken by Dutiya Mingaung upon ascension, not that of someone else. Also, Tin Hla Thaw provided no dates for the end of Mahathihathuya's reign and the beginning of this Siri Sudhammarajadipati, nor was any information provided for the number of years each reigned. The *Zatatawpon*, on the other hand, is clear on this point (p. 47): Mahathihathuya was succeeded by Dutiya Mingaung in 1479, so that the former reigned for twelve years.

29. Tin Hla Thaw, "History," p. 145, dates his ascension to 1482. But the inscription only mentions him; it did not give his ascension date. See *SMK*, vol. 5, p. 68.

30. This means some *myosa* lived at their fiefs.

31. *Zatatawpon*, p. 47. Tin Hla Thaw, "History," p. 145, confirms the date with the Tada-u Shinbinthalyaung pagoda inscription.

6. Ava

1. Even married couples appeared to have had separate legal titles to their individual property, as suggested by one donor who stipulated that the donation included property that was both "my own and my wife's own."

2. The theoretical basis for this is Karl Polanyi (et al.) and his various works, particularly Polanyi et al., *Trade and Market in the Early Empires* (Glencoe, IL: Free Press, 1957).

3. This is precisely what happened in France between the fourteenth and seventeenth century, as Emmanuel LeRoy Ladurie's *Mind and Method* attests.

4. Even today in Myanmar, the recent rise in the wealth of certain classes of business entrepreneurs notwithstanding, civil servants (in effect, functional descendants of *kyun-daw* and *ahmudan*) continue to enjoy the stability and predictability of reliable (even if small) pensions, salary raises, priority on access to living quarters, and sizeable discounts (up to 50 percent) on gasoline, rice, and other items of substance.

5. This would not contradict the use of a clay cup, which was broken at the conclusion of the ritual as described earlier, for the use of a golden cup by the king probably signified the rank and stature of the donor.

6. *SMK*, vol. 5, pp. 99–107.

7. I personally witnessed this procedure for ensuring that the "tops" of trees and the "bottoms" of trees were correctly used in their proper directions even as recently as 2007 when Anawrahta's palace at Pagan was being reconstructed! Tradition is not easily discarded.

8. A recent article in Andrew Huxley's memory by Christian Lammerts provides a good summary of the late scholar's work, along with Huxley's own in various publications included in the bibliography. See Christian Lammerts, "Andrew Huxley: Legal Historian of Burma and Southeast Asia," *Journal of Burma Studies* 19, no. 2 (December 2015): 267–273.

9. For a thorough discussion of this topic regarding both Dhammavilasa and the *Dhammavilasa Dhammathat*, one should consult Dietrich Christian Lammerts' "The Dhammavilasa Dhammathat: A Critical Historiography, Analysis, and Translation of the Text" (master's thesis, Cornell University, January 2005). Subsequently, Lammerts published an article that focused on the authorship of the *Dhammavilasa Dhammathat*, where he raised several important questions about the jurist as well as the work. See "The Authorship of the *Dhammavilasa Dhammathat*," in *Myanmar Historical Commission Conference Proceedings*, part 2, edited by the Golden Jubilee Publication Committee (Yangon: Myanmar Historical Commission, 2005), pp. 190–214.

10. Aung-Thwin, *Pagan*, pp. 120–123.

11. Ibid., p. 120.

7. The Last Decades and the Decline of Ava

1. A synopsis of the Second Ava Dynasty is given in Michael Aung-Thwin and Maitrii Aung-Thwin's *A History of Myanmar*, chapters 6 and 7. That history is given in detail by Victor Lieberman's *Burmese Administrative Cycles*.

2. Of course, the number of inscriptions and the amount of wealth given do not necessarily correspond on a one-to-one basis.

3. I have been compiling a database on such information since my dissertation was completed in 1976. Subsequent technology, such as spreadsheet programs and other database software, has made the tasks of filing and making calculations much easier, faster, and more accurate. Admittedly, the entered data is only as good as my reading of the inscriptions, which is what has taken the longest. I now have a complete database of all known donative and other inscriptions from the Pagan period to the end of the Ava period (and beyond).

4. The large total for silver and gold rests mainly on one inscription, which records a seven-figure amount donated by the king in 1444. However, the numeral given in the inscription for both gold and silver does not correspond to the (Pali) word *lakh* given in the written narrative. So the discrepancy is between one hundred thousand and one million. I have consulted other scholars who read Old Burmese, and their reading for the numeral in the inscription is the same as mine: that is, seven figures with six zeros. The option we have,

therefore, is this: the numeral as given is correct, or the written narrative (*lakh*) is correct. Neither is ipso facto extraordinary. Sun Laichen's study of the gem trade during the Ming period shows that much Chinese silver was used to pay for Myanmar gems, so that the larger figure is not all that unreasonable. (See his "Shan Gems, Chinese Silver and the Rise of Shan Principalities in Northern Burma, c. 1450–1527," in *Southeast Asia in the Fifteenth Century: The China Factor*, ed. Geoff Wade and Sun Laichen (Singapore: National University of Singapore Press, 2010), pp. 169–196. Yet, it is not uncommon for inscriptions to write out in the narrative the amount represented by the numerals given, in the same way modern checks require both the numerals and their corresponding value in letters, either for accuracy or to prevent fraud. I am open to further scrutiny regarding this discrepancy on the amount of silver and gold donated by Narapati the Great. But other than this one particular item, the rest of the donation is not problematic.

5. Of course there are *copies* of originals that were struck later, such as during Bodawhpaya's reign, but they are irrelevant to this discussion.

6. Part of the reason for this sparseness regarding land and labor endowments is that when the capital of the Myanmar state moved to Pegu under Tabinshwehti and Bayinnaung, much of the money was spent on secular concerns (such as Bayinnaung's palace) as well. In addition, it appears that cash was more often used for religious donations than were endowments of land and labor, since the latter were far scarcer, especially in Lower Myanmar, than the former. That has been amply documented by foreign visitors' accounts, which not only comment on the wealth of the king, but also reflect on the power of the state at the time.

7. Frank J. Sulloway, *Born to Rebel: Birth Order, Family Dynamics, and Creative Lives*, 1st ed. (New York: Pantheon Books, 1996).

8. By "true" peasant rebellion, I mean rebellions led by peasant leaders for peasant causes (such as heavy taxation) against the state or its representatives, not by princes against the throne as the ultimate prize.

9. Laichen, "Shan Gems." Indeed, I would argue that one of the reasons for Yuan (Mongol) interest in Pagan in the first place is precisely the gem trade, over which the Burmese king had a monopoly, which the Mongols were attempting to break.

10. This conquest of Ava was the third time, since the first millennium AD with the "Pyu," that the decline of central power in the Dry Zone of Upper Myanmar was directly affected by the north, providing additional support for my contention that the north had always been the "front door" of Myanmar politically and militarily, something that remains true today.

11. Tin Hla Thaw, "History," p. 146. U Kala, *Mahayazawingyi*, vol. 2, pp. 110–111. It is not included in *SMK*, vol. 5.

12. Perhaps at the time the word meant "obsequious."

13. *SMK*, vol. 5, pp. 99–107.

14. Laichen, "Shan Gems," p. 185.

15. U Kala, *Mahayazawingyi*, vol. 2, p. 118.

16. Ibid., p. 131.

17. *Zatatawpon*, p. 44. Because this section of the manuscript follows one dated to 1746 AD and shows some incoherence in it (as if some sentences were missing), I suspect it is a later addition.

18. Whereas the *Zatatawpon* ended the Second Ava period only when the last king of the Second Ava Dynasty, Mahadhammayazadipati, was deposed and taken to Pegu, U Kala ended his work with the previous king, Taninganwei (1714–1733), who reigned while U Kala wrote (U Kala, *Mahayazawingyi*, vol. 3, p. 397). U Kala ended the narrative in 1729 when the crown prince was named. As there appears to be no rhyme or reason for this particular ending, we can presume U Kala must have died around that time. His criterion for the organization and

writing of history had been true to the name *yazawin* (from *rajavamsa,* royal lineage or genealogy), whether they were Shan, Burmese, or Mon.

19. Harvey, *History of Burma,* p. 107, dates this to 1527, whereas both U Kala and the *Zatatawpon* date it to 1526.

20. U Kala, *Mahayazawingyi,* vol. 2, p. 132.

21. Ibid., pp. 135–136.

22. Ibid., p. 138.

23. Ibid., p. 139.

24. By 1538, Tabinshwehti, son of the lord of Toungoo, Mahasiri Jeyyasura (Minkyo Nyo), had taken Pegu, well realizing its commercial importance during this "long sixteenth century," as Tony Reid calls it.

25. Sun Laichen, "Ming-Southeast Asian Overland Interactions, 1368–1644" (PhD diss., University of Michigan, 2000); and also Victor Lieberman's "Europeans, Trade, and the Unification of Burma, c. 1540–1620," *Oriens Extremus* 17, no. 2 (1980): 203–226.

26. U Kala, *Mahayazawingyi,* vol. 2, p. 132.

27. The word *naingnan* is probably best translated for that period as "dominion." Now, of course, it means "nation."

8. Ava's Legacy in Myanmar's History

1. Only a very few studies refer to Ava's art and architecture. For instance, Nina Oshegowa's *Kunst in Burma* (Leipzig: E.A. Seemann, 1988), and U Aye Myint's *Burmese Design through Drawings,* ed. Sone Simatrang, trans. U Thanoe (Bangkok: Silpakorn University and the Toyota Foundation, 1993), are two worth mentioning.

2. *Yothe,* or string puppetry, although probably begun in the Pagan period, is mentioned in the mid-fifteenth-century inscriptions of Ava. An unequivocal record (perhaps the first) on puppet theatre is found in an inscription at the Htupayon Pagoda at Sagaing in 1444, cited numerous times throughout this book. Subsequently, the famous Shin Maharattathara described puppets in his poems around 1484. He also mentioned the public fascination with string puppets during the commemoration ceremony on the completion of a pagoda at Tada-U in 1499. According to Daw Ma Ma Naing, who specializes in current *yothe* production, the poet above once wrote that "many [people] sat on trees and scaffolds, poles and platforms and also rooftops nearby. He mentioned that they would not go home at sunrise, when the puppet show was in its finale." However, puppets were used not only for entertainment. "Marionettes were a means of making people aware of current events, a medium for educating the audience in literature, history and religion, a display of life style and customs. At the same time, they functioned as a mouthpiece for the people in the days of royalty" (Zon Pann Pwint, "Marionettes Enjoy Revival," *Myanmar Times,* September 1–7, 2008, pp. 1–2).

3. Hla Pe, *Burma: Literature, Historiography, Scholarship, Language, Life, and Buddhism* (Singapore: Institute of Southeast Asian Studies, 1985).

4. Mabel Haynes Bode, *The Pali Literature of Burma* (London: Royal Asiatic Society, 1909), pp. 14–30.

5. G. H. Luce, *Old Burma-Early Pagan,* vol. 1 (Locust Valley, NY: J. J. Augustin, 1969–1970), pp. 87–88.

6. U Kyaw Dun, *Myanma*; Hla Pe, *Burma*; Saw Lu [alias U Saw Tun], *Pagan Khit Myanma Sa*; and Pe Maung Tin, *Myanma Sape Thamaing.* A *parabuik* written in 1879 focused on four of the most famous of these literary giants: Shin Maharattathara, Shin Tezawthara, Shin Aggathamadhi, and Shin Thilawuntha. It was published subsequently as *Shin Ratthathara, Shin Tezawthara, Shin Aggathamadhi, Shin Thilawuntha Ahttuppatti* [The Lives of Shin

Rattathara, Shin Tezawthara, Shin Aggathamadhi, Shin Thilawuntha], comp. Mingyi Maha Thirizeyathu (U Yan) (Yangon: Sapebeikman Press, 1974). There are many secondary sources on the subject of Burmese literature in English that one can find in the *Journal of the Burma Research Society* that I have not mentioned here. My point here is not so much a review of the field—which will require another book-length manuscript—but as much as possible to document Ava's legacy in literature with primary sources (or those who used the primary sources).

7. *SMK*, vol. 5, pp. 90–97.

8. That conclusion assumes the earliest sections of the *Zatatawpon* was not written by Min Yaza, although as noted in an earlier chapter, I am of the opinion they were. If so, that would make it the earliest extant "chronicle" in the Burmese language rather than Thilawuntha's *Yazawinkyaw* as convention has it. The date given to the *Yazawinkyaw* is also puzzling, for the text itself puts its completion at 1520, although the author was said by some to have lived only up to 1518.

9. See U Po Byu's "Shin Uttamagyaw and his Tawla, A Nature Poem: I-IX," on the subject, *Journal of the Burma Research Society* 1917, pt. 2–3; 1918, pt. 1–2; 1919, pt. 1–2; and 1920, pt. 1.

10. Once again, this contradicts the supposed linear and progressive manner in which Theravada Buddhist orthodoxy is said to have "moved"—from less to more—automatically "making" the Konbaung period the most orthodox in Myanmar history.

11. Harvey, *History of Burma*, p. 107.

12. I owe much of the information on Burmese literature to the scholars noted, particularly an early, unpublished manuscript by Anna Allott, John Okell, and Dr. Hla Pe titled "Burmese Literature," n.d., 43 pages.

13. Hla Pe, *Burma*, p. 9.

14. Thibaut d'Hubert's recent article, "The Lord of the White Elephant: Interpreting the Islamicate Epigraphic, Numismatic, and Literary Material from the Mrauk U Period of Arakan (ca. 1430–1784)" in the *Journal of Burma Studies* 19, no. 2 (2015): 341–359, raises the important issue of a "complex literate environment of the kingdom's upper social strata" (p. 342) so that one should be cognizant of a perspective that belongs to the "dominant archive" being used. In this case, Adu Min Nyo's "dominant archive" is, of course, Burmese.

15. This poem is translated by John Okell in Hla Pe, *Burma*, p. 9.

16. Po Byu, "Shin Uttamagyaw," p. 262.

17. Mingyi Maha Thiri Zeyathu, *Pitakat Taw Thamaing*, pp. 70, 278.

18. For an example of what is considered a Pagan period *lanka* (*linga*) see Pe Maung Tin's "Anantathuriya's Death Song I" and "II," *Journal of the Burma Research Society* 9, no. 3 (1919): 153–155; and 10, no. 1 (1920): 27.

19. If the *thachin* were a Pagan creation, the suggestion by some that it was a Thai product, the result of two Burmese conquests of Ayuthaya in the sixteenth-century is untenable.

20. This particular genre of source material is being studied by established legal scholars such as the late Andrew Huxley along with Ryuji Okudaira, as well as a younger generation, such as Christian Lammerts. Although a lot more needs to be done on the subject of law, their work is at the forefront. Andrew Huxley, particularly, in his many publications had been untangling the conventions and myths surrounding the primacy given to Mon *dhammathat*. Ryuji Okudaira's "The Burmese Dhammathat," in *Laws of South-East Asia: The Pre-Modern Texts*, ed. M. B. Hooker (Singapore: Singapore National Printers, 1986), pp. 23–142, is a major contribution, as is Dietrich Christian Lammerts' "The Dhammavilasa Dhammatat" (master's thesis, Cornell University, January 2005).

21. Aung-Thwin, *Pagan*, chapter 7, although Christian Lammerts' "Narratives of Buddhist Legislation: Textual Authority and Legal Heterodoxy in Seventeenth through Nineteenth

Century Burma," *Journal of Southeast Asian Studies* 44, no. 1 (February 2013): 118–144, raises some interesting and important questions about that text.

22. *SMK*, vol. 5, p. *gha* and 127–129.

23. Shin Aggathamadhi, for example, fled to and wrote at Shwebo. One of his poems lamented the fall of Ava in an intense, emotional way. It is reproduced in Pe Maung Tin's *Myanma Sape Thamaing*, pp. 129–138.

24. Hall, *Burma*, p. 31.

25. Mingyi Maha Thiri Zeyathu, *Pitakat Taw Thamaing*, pp. 277–278, 284, 286, 288.

26. There is some discrepancy here as to whether he fled to Toungoo or to Prome. Pe Maung Tin, *Myanma Sape Thamaing*, pp. 155–156.

27. The reason for the emphasis is the oft-repeated notion that many Asian societies preferred white skin to brown skin. If so, it is probably the result of much later colonialism and emulation of the "master"; it is not a sentiment found (especially) at fifteenth-century Ava, as this poem testifies.

28. The translation is by John Okell, in Hla Pe, *Burma*.

29. Pe Maung Tin, *Myanma Sape Thamaing*, pp. 140–141.

30. It was also at Ava that a woman, Yaweshinhtwe, wrote *angyin* verse on the fifty-five hairstyles of women at court.

31. I have nothing published to cite with regard to this statement, as he was one of my advisers at Michigan who very often made that assertion.

32. The British had the whole country approximately from Annexation in 1886 to the retreat of the British Burma in 1942 when the Japanese invaded.

33. The only exception was the First Pegu Dynasty, which shared that role with the First Ava Dynasty, both legacies of Pagan.

34. It is only very recently that alternative visions are being offered by dissenting groups, and even then, many of them are financed and supported politically and ideologically by external interests.

35. Some of their famous leaders remembered in late chronicles are also mentioned by name in contemporary Ava epigraphy.

36. Of the forty-plus inscriptions at the Mrauk-U museum that I scrutinized, nearly all were written in perfect Pagan Old Burmese, while a few were in Sanskrit.

37. Thibaut d'Hubert's "The Lord of the White Elephant," in the special issue of the *Journal of Burma Studies* 19, no. 2 (2015), includes a wide variety of historical sources on Arakan.

38. These are the sixty years when Pegu was capital under the Second Pegu/Toungoo Dynasty.

9. The Pegu Convention

1. The "Mon Narrative" refers to the standard corpus of Mon-language sources about the "history" of the Mon in Lower Myanmar written after King Dhammazedi's reign, to be individually discussed in the next chapter. The latest and largest of this compendium is best represented by the two-volume work published at Pak Lat, Thailand, in 1910 and 1912 that Harvey has coined the "Paklat Talaing Chronicle." The first was originally called the "Uppanna Sudhammavati Rajavamsakatha," but upon binding, was retitled as *Sudhammawati-rajawamsa; Siharajadhiraja-wamsa (Sudhammawati; Gawampati; Rajadhiraj)*, ed. Phra Candacanto (Pak Lat, Thailand, 1910) and the second, the *Nidana Ramadhipati-katha*, ed. Phra Candakanto (Pak Lat, Siam, 1912). The late H. L. Shorto translated most of the two volumes into English, which is still not yet published, copies of which were kindly given to me by Professor Victor Lieberman, for which I am truly grateful. The first of these translations contains a section on

Gavampati that represents pages twenty-six to ninety-nine of the first (1910) published volume. The second typewritten translation is much more substantive, which Shorto titled "Translation by Prof. H. L. Shorto, SOAS of Pages 34–44 and 6–264 of the Second of Two Volumes of Historical Texts Issued from Paklat: Nidana Ramadhipati-katha (or as on Binding Rajawamsa Dhammaceti Mahapitakadhara), ed. Phra Candakanto (Pak Lat, Siam, 1912)." There is a newer edition of the second translation of Shorto by Christian Bauer with the help of Pat McCormick called the "Nidana Ramadhipati-katha (The Pak Lat Chronicles, Volume II)," also in manuscript form as of this writing. When I refer to the "Paklat Talaing Chronicle" in this book, I am speaking about the two unpublished translations by Shorto.

2. For a thorough and detailed discussion regarding the myth of Ramannadesa, see Aung-Thwin, *Mists of Ramanna.* However, I'm afraid that the myth continues to be perpetuated today by Myanmar archaeologists unfamiliar with the latest scholarship on the country's history, so that the May 2016 report to SEAMEO by Kyaw U Lwin at Bangkok still insists that Lower Myanmar was Mon back in the fourth century AD. For a preliminary and brief discussion of the myth, see Michael Aung-Thwin, "Lower Burma and Bago in the History of Burma," in *The Maritime Frontier of Burma: Exploring Political, Cultural and Commercial Interaction in the Indian Ocean World, 1200–1800,* eds. Jos Gommans and Jacques Leider (Leiden: Koninklijke Nederlandse Akademie van Wetenschappen, 2002), pp. 25–57. The bulk of the discussion on Pegu will be contained in the present chapter as will the issue of its attributed ethnicity, which was basically part of ex post facto legitimization.

3. The word "Rman" was the fifteenth-century, Middle Mon ethnonym for the term "Mon," which had yet to appear. The earlier term for Rman was "Rmen."

4. The analysis as well as the arguments can be found in Aung-Thwin, *Mists,* chapter 3.

5. Although some might object to my use of the late Ben Anderson's concept here, it is actually quite appropriate and functions in an almost identical way.

6. Late Burmese-language chronicles had used the term "Ramanna" as a reference to Lower Myanmar, but not in the way Dhammazedi had envisioned it in "the Realm of the Rman."

7. Michael Symes introduced that notion in *Journal of his Second Embassy to the Court of Ava in 1802* (London: George Allen & Unwin Ltd., 1955). In it, he wrote, "Much of Burmese civilization, including Hinayana Buddhism, had come to them from the Mons, whose *independent kingdom* [my emphasis] with its capital at Thaton had been conquered by King Anawrahta in the middle of the eleventh century A.D. and incorporated in the empire of Pagan." This, of course, is totally erroneous, as demonstrated in Aung-Thwin, *Mists,* p. 284.

8. Aung-Thwin, *Mists,* pp. 282–284.

9. G. H. Luce, for example, the central proponent of the Mon Paradigm, was married to Pe Maung Tin's sister, both of whom were of Mon background, as were many others involved in early Myanmar scholarship.

10. This was an invitation by the University of Leiden to attend a conference and submit a paper on Lower Myanmar's significance in the history of the Bay of Bengal. I could not attend the conference but submitted the paper, which was published as "Lower Burma and Bago in the History of Burma."

11. Immediately recognizing *Mists* as very important to the historiography of early Myanmar (as a specialist on the country's history) was Victor B. Lieberman who reviewed it as "Excising the 'Mon Paradigm' from Burmese Historiography," *Journal of Southeast Asian Studies* 38, no. 2 (2007): 377–383. Also pertinent would be the late Andrew Huxley's manuscript, which he had shared with me prior to its publication, titled "Mon Studies and Professor Forchhammer," p. 2, independently confirming what I had written, although calling it the "Mon priority"—that is, the giving of "agency" to the Mon by scholars like Forchhammer.

12. Robert Brown's review of *Mists* is typical of this. See his "*The Mists of Rāmañña: The Legend That Was Lower Burma* by Michael A. Aung-Thwin," *Journal of Asian Studies* 67, no. 1 (February 2008): 340–344.

13. Skirting the issue of original evidence in Old Mon or Old Burmese languages not supporting the existence of a Mon kingdom in Lower Myanmar prior to Pagan, is Donald Stadtner's "The Mon of Lower Burma," *Journal of the Siam Society* 96 (2008): 193–215.

14. By "Myanmafication," I am not referring to the "natural" (historical) integration of minority groups into mainstream Myanmar culture over the centuries, but to the recent political and activist contention that the process was deliberate "ethnic cleansing" on the part of the majority.

15. Michael Aung-Thwin, "Parochial Universalism, Democracy Jihad, and the Orientalist Image of Burma: The New Evangelism," *Pacific Affairs* 74 (2001/2002): 483–505.

16. Personal correspondence with Associate Professor of History Maitrii Aung-Thwin, National University of Singapore, March 29, 2007.

17. Critiquing reified ethnicity by American academics is itself not new, going back at least to the 1960s with certain anthropologists and continued by historians and political scientists, as noted in an earlier chapter. The issue I am raising here is the use of reified ethnicity as a criterion for organizing history into ethnic periods as well as seeing it as a causal factor in the making of Burmese history.

18. It is a relatively easy task to conduct a search for the word Ramanya, Ramanna, or Ramannadesa in the relevant sources as most, if not all, are now in English translation and digitized, in one form or another. None of the major works comprising the Mon Narrative mentions the term, although the original manuscript title of the *Nidāna* (to be discussed in detail in the next chapter) is said by H. L. Shorto to have been "Ramaññ'-uppatti-dipaka." But that is all.

19. The *Lik Smin Asah* best represents the Hamsavati (Pegu) legend and its links with Vijayanagara. See Robert Halliday's translation and edition, *Lik Smin Asah: The Story of the Founding of Pegu and a Subsequent Invasion from South India with English Translation, Notes, and Vocabulary of Undefined Words* (Rangoon: American Baptist Mission Press, 1923), pp. 66–73. It is a late (1825) Mon-language work that was translated from, and said to have been preserved in, a Burmese theatrical play. See Aung-Thwin, *Mists*, pp. 99–100.

20. Robert Halliday, "Slapat Rajawan Datow Smin Ron" [History of Kings], *Journal of the Burma Research Society* 13, nos. 1 and 2 (1923): 9–31; 33–67.

21. Although we cannot be certain to what extent Phayre's "Talaing Annals" are the same as the above-mentioned Mon sources, he seemed to have been aware of, and perhaps even used, the *Slapat*. Although he does not mention the *Slapat* by name, he does cite its author in the preface of his *History* (vii) by stating that he used "a history of Pegu in the Mun language by Hsaya dau Athwa, a Talaing Buddhist monk, which was translated into Burmese." For an overview of the kinds of sources Phayre used, and the articles he published before he wrote his *History*, one should consult Patricia M. Herbert's "The Sir Arthur Phayre Collection of Burmese Manuscripts," *British Library Journal* 1, no. 1 (1975): 62–70.

22. Phayre had erroneously attributed the term Ramannadesa to Rama and therefore to much later Hindu influences.

23. The Pegu Project was an attempt to garner Lower Myanmar Mon to help British designs on taking the whole country. See Aung-Thwin, *Mists*, pp. 263–264.

24. Haripunjaya is not mentioned at all, while Dvaravati is mentioned twice only (and then, not as the homeland of the Mon but as a nondescript place). This issue was preliminarily discussed in Aung-Thwin, *Mists*, p. 102.

25. This conclusion can be found in Gerald Diflfoth's work on Dvaravati Old Mon, titled *The Dvaravati Old Mon Language and Nyah Kur* (Bangkok: Chulalongkorn University Print House, 1984), whose importance in this interpretation is assessed in greater detail in Aung-Thwin, *Mists*, p. 163.

26. Aung-Thwin, *Mists*, p. 103, note 112.

27. Personal interviews with people who claimed to be of "Mon background" (both in Myanmar and overseas) leads me to this conclusion.

28. Phayre, *History*, pp. 24–32.

29. Ibid., chapter 3, pp. 24–32.

30. In Burmese tradition, it is dated to 544 BC.

31. This is found in Halliday's "Slapat," p. 52.

32. Historically, this would be sometime in the mid-fourteenth century when Hamsavati was made capital by Binnya U after he moved it from Muttama. *Hamsa* is sometimes defined in Burma studies as a "brahmani duck" or goose. It is, of course, also Brahma's vehicle.

33. Phayre, *History*, p. 30, note 1.

34. The earliest extant version of the two blind brothers who founded Sri Ksetra is probably the *Zatatawpon Yazawin*'s account (pp. 35–36), the early sections of which are dated to the late thirteenth century, although later hands have continued to add to it until the nineteenth century. But another early chronicle, the *Yazawinkyaw* (Thilawuntha, p. 77), dated to the Ava period, does not mention the two blind brothers. Instead, it begins the story with Dwattabaung, son of the elder brother.

35. Halliday, "Slapat," p. 51.

36. Phayre, *History*, p. 31.

37. Aung-Thwin, *Mists*, pp. 98–99.

38. Nilakanta Sastri, *A History of South India*, 3rd. ed. (London: Oxford University Press, 1955), p. 245. Phayre's "Talaing Annals" also recount commerce and contacts with Vijayanagara, but during the mid-fifteenth century. See Sir Arthur Phayre, "On the History of Pegu," *Journal of the Asiatic Society of Bengal* 42, no. 2 (1873): 121.

39. Aung-Thwin, *Mists*, p. 90.

40. Halliday, *Lik Smin Asah*, p. 80.

41. Both Harvey and Hall consider Wareru to be historical: Harvey, *History of Burma*, p. 110, and Hall, *Burma*, p. 34.

42. The reasons for the sequence given by traditional Lower Myanmar historiography are complicated and convoluted, but if the reader wishes to examine them, they can be found in Aung-Thwin, *Mists*, pp. 101–103.

43. For Muttama, see *SMK*, vol. 1, pp. 65–69. *Original* Old Burmese inscriptions first mention Pegu only by 1212 and 1266 (as Payku), when it was still a governorship under the Kingdom of Pagan. It was also known as "Hansabati" (that is, "Hamsavati," its Sanskrit name) in Ram Kamhaeng's inscription of 1292. The "Zambu Kungya . . ." British Library manuscript cited in an earlier chapter shows that Pegu was founded in 1276 (leaf 97). For Thaton (Pali Sadhuim), which does not appear until 1479, see Luce, *Old Burma*, vol. 2, inset entitled "Ramanna Desa"; and Aung-Thwin, *Mists*, p. 59.

44. It is possible, and one can argue that Pegu was mentioned in epigraphy earlier, in 1086. But this particular inscription is a copy, not an original, so that in terms of original epigraphy, Muttama still precedes Pegu.

45. We can still see road signs using the term Ussa Pegu.

46. The etymology of the word "Talaing" is, of course, not known for certain, although all scholars of Myanmar agree that during the Pagan period, the word was a reference to the

people living in Lower Myanmar *in general*, including but not exclusively the Mon. It is somewhat like the Chinese term *kun-lun*, which refers to the coastal people of Southeast Asia rather than to any particular ethno-linguistic group.

47. Aung-Thwin, *Mists*, chapter 2.

48. Because the inscription that mentions Pegu, dated to 1086 AD, is a copy, not an original, I prefer the date of 1212 noted above, as its inscription is an original making the date more reliable (see *SMK*, vol. 1, p. 326).

49. For the complete list of the urban areas created by Pagan, see the chart in Aung-Thwin, *Mists*, p. 59. The inscription in which most of these names appear is King Narapatisithu's of 1196 AD (see *SMK*, vol. 1, pp. 65–69). See also Luce, *Old Burma*, vol. 1, pp. 26–27.

50. Although Anthony Reid's famous phrase limited the "age of commerce" to the post-fifteenth century mostly, I see a similar phenomenon occurring earlier during these centuries with similar economic and political consequences.

10. Sources for the Reconstruction of Pegu

1. U. Chit Thein, *She Haung Mon Kyauksa Paung Chok*, 1965 (hereafter abbreviated as *MKPC*). These numbers reflect the way U Chit Thein had organized the work, so that each face is counted as a separate inscription.

2. The Kalyani Inscriptions can be found in vol. 3, part 2, while the others, in vol. 4, part 1, of *Epigraphia Birmanica*.

3. Since the Mon inscriptions are written in the Burmese script, I can read them. But I don't know the language, so have depended on the Burmese translation of them found in part 2 of the U Chit Thein work.

4. In addition to one Mon inscription found in the early 1970s of no consequence to this study, another inscription was recently discovered in Myittha, Kyaukse (in 2013), that has resulted in some controversy and erroneous reporting in the newspapers. It is thought to belong to the queen of King Sawlu, Anawrahta's son, although it is popularly known as "King Sawlu's Inscription." On one face, it contains what is thought to be Old Mon written in Pagan script as well as another language about which the scholars are not in agreement. There is neither a clear date on the stone nor is the dating system that was used obvious. And even if the date tentatively attributed to it as the eleventh century by one scholar is correct, it does not alter the dearth of Mon inscriptions for the study of Pegu.

5. Kyanzittha's use of Old Mon is an issue, with a literature all its own, but is beyond the scope of this book. See Aung-Thwin, *Mists*, pp. 246–247.

6. As noted, the Kalyani Inscriptions are not included in this corpus, and although there is a bell inscription erected at Pagan in the mid-sixteenth century by King Bayinnaung in Middle Mon, it does not belong to the First Pegu Dynasty but the one that followed, and so is not considered a record contemporary to our current enterprise.

7. Of course, compared to the study of Sri Vijaya by O. W. Wolters, who had only about eight Old Malay inscriptions to work with, the Pegu corpus seems abundant.

8. *MKPC*, vol. 2, p. 100.

9. Ibid., p. 6.

10. These terms reveal notions of kingship at both Pagan and Ava (see Aung-Thwin, *Pagan*, chapter 3). Note, however, that the last term (*kammaraja*) is not a Buddhist but a modern Western social science term of analysis, probably first coined by Robert Heine-Geldern in his *Conceptions of State and Kingship in Southeast Asia* (Ithaca, NY: Southeast Asia Program, Cornell University, 1956).

11. *MKPC*, vol. 2, plate 85.

12. I am thankful to Professor Sun Laichen, not only for introducing me to this text but for also translating it for me. It is extremely valuable for the last few decades of the Pagan kingdom as well, as shown in Aung-Thwin, *Myth and History*. With regard to Lower Myanmar in the present study, particularly Muttama's situation, it contains a very brief but extremely important sentence. For a more complete assessment of this source, see Aung-Thwin, *Mists*, pp. 55–56 and their notes.

13. All the analysis and evidence for this topic have been provided in Aung-Thwin, *Mists*, chapter 3.

14. Wheatley, *Nagara*, p. 221; Phayre, *History*, p. 28; Luce, *Old Burma*, vol. 1, p. 21. See Aung-Thwin, *Mists*, chapter 11, for the full discussion.

15. Sun Laichen translates these as "Wu-la-he" and "Wu-du-lu-xin-he."

16. See the bibliography of Geok Yian Goh's dissertation called "Cakkravatiy Anuruddha and the Buddhist Oikoumene: Historical Narratives of Kingship and Religious Networks in Burma, Northern Thailand, and Sri Lanka (11th–14th Centuries)" (PhD diss., Department of History, University of Hawai'i, 2007). The microfilm copy of the manuscript itself can be found in the *List of Microfilms Deposited in the Centre for East Asian Cultural Studies. Burma. Part 8* (Tokyo: Toyo Bunko, 1976). It was succeeded by Thu Nandar's edition, titled *The Catalogue of Materials on Myanmar History in Microfilms Deposited in the Center for East Asian Cultural Studies*, vol. 1 (Tokyo: Tokyo University of Foreign Studies, 2004).

17. Aung-Thwin, *Mists*, pp. 123–124; U Tet Htoot, "Nature of the Burmese Chronicles," pp. 50–62.

18. *Zatatawpon*, p. 41.

19. Ibid., p. 44.

20. There is some controversy here, however, as the document itself states it was completed by 1520, which postdates Thilawuntha's death.

21. The *Yazawinkyaw* mentions the existence of earlier Burmese chronicles on Prome, Pagan, Pinya, and Ava.

22. It is catalogued as reels 85–86 in the *List of Microfilms*, p. 25.

23. H. L. Shorto, "A Mon Genealogy of Kings: Observations on the Nidana Arambhakatha," in *Historians of South East Asia*, ed. D. G. E. Hall (London: Oxford University Press, 1961), p. 64.

24. Aung-Thwin, *Mists*, 133–135.

25. The "Paklat Talaing Chronicle" is called the *Rajavamsa Katha* by several Mon scholars today.

26. Shorto, "Mon Genealogy of Kings," pp. 63–72.

27. Ibid., p. 65.

28. Ibid., p. 64.

29. Ibid., p. 65.

30. Ibid., pp. 64–65.

31. The romantic aspect of the relationship between Shin Saw Bu and Dhammazedi is apparently found in later Burmese theatrical presentations, not in the chronicles. See J. A. Stewart, "Excavation and Exploration in Pegu," *Journal of the Burma Research Society* 7, no. 1 (1917): 14–25.

32. Shorto, "Mon Genealogy of Kings," p. 64.

33. Generally, the whole word *ayedawpon* has a more precise meaning than just "story." It suggests some sort of "crisis" or "struggle."

34. Nai Pan Hla, *Yazadhiyaza Ayedawpon Kyan* (Yangon: Thein Than U Press, 1977), pp. 9–10. See also his "Yazadarit Ayedawpon Kyan nhin Mon Thichin Mya" [The Yazadarit Ayedawpon Treatise and Mon Songs], *Journal of the Burma Research Society* 56, no. 1 (1973): 99–126. Nai Pan Hla may have been reacting to the preface of the published version of the *Yaza-*

dhiyaza Ayedawpon edited by Zawgyi, which states that Bannya Dala *translated* the Mon-language chronicle with the name *Yazadhiyaza* already on it, giving it the title *Yazadhiyaza Ayedawpon* at completion. But this whole theory is fraught with problems, not least because Zawgyi's source for his conclusion is none other than Nai Pan Hla's own 1977 Burmese translation of the Mon version, which Zawgyi apparently thought was the original Mon manuscript.

35. Indeed, Nai Pan Hla himself admitted in his translation of the *Yazadhiyaza Ayedawpon Kyan* (pp. 11–12) (from Mon into Burmese) that he took the Mon version from the 1910 Pak Lat publication. See a more detailed analysis of this issue in Aung-Thwin, *Mists*, pp. 134–135.

36. We find this statement in *Twinthintaik Wun, Mahasithu U Htun Nyo, Mahayazawinthit (Nyaung Yan Set)*, ed. U Thein Hlaing (Yangon: Universities Historical Research Department, 1997), preface (pp. *kho* and kho:).

37. Thu Nandar, *Catalogue of Materials*, pp. 9–10, 33.

38. Most of the two leaves that King Yazadarit commanded in this "Mon Yazawin" are also taken up not by his story but by the moral aphorism of his father's minister, whom Yazadarit had sentenced to death, but retracted after the minister's eloquent plea.

39. See R. Halliday, trans., *Slapat Rajawan Datow Smin Ron: A History of Kings with Text, Translation, and Notes* (Rangoon: Burma Research Society, 1923), p. 10.

40. Bannya Dala, *Yazadhiyaza Ayedawpon*, p. *hsa*.

41. Twinthintaikwun, *Twinthin Myanma Yazawinthit*, vol. 1, p. 156, footnote 2.

42. Ibid., p. 466.

43. *Yazadhiyaza Ayedawpon Kyan*, ed. Ko Shwe Thein Min (Yangon: Pan Shwe Pyi Sa Auk Taik, 2012), p. 390. One of these twelve palm-leaf manuscripts was found in the library of the eminent scholar and administrator, the Kinwun Mingyi who served Kings Thibaw and Mindon of the last Burmese dynasty. The one that the minister copied himself is dated to 1864: that is, the time the copying was completed. Fortunately, the Kinwun Mingyi remembered to place his own "end statement" at the end of his copy, which stated that "in *Sakkaraj* 1226 [AD 1864] . . . the copying of the *Yazadhiyaza Ayedawpon* was finished." It is this version that Ko Shwe Thein Min has edited and published, whose Burmese text, however, is virtually the same as the one published earlier by Zwe Sa Press that I use in this book.

44. My thanks to U Saw Tun, retired from Northern Illinois University, for alerting me to this work.

45. See the introduction to his edition of the *Yazadhiyaza Ayedawpon Kyan* (pp. 1–13), where Ko Shwe Thein Min convincingly lays out his case. One of the factors that had led other scholars astray is that the much respected "national bibliography," the *Pitakat Taw Thamaing* (p. 292, item no. 2033) states that Bannya Dala was the editor/compiler of the original *Yazadhiyaza Ayedawpon*, which most scholars (including myself) had accepted as true.

46. Bannya Dala, *Yazadhiyaza Ayedawpon*, p. 360.

47. John Okell, personal correspondence, June, 2014.

48. Correspondence with Dr. Than Than Win, March 21, 2008, and again, June 2, 2014. Her later translation differed a bit but the gist remained the same.

49. U San Lwin, trans., "The Campaigns of Razadarit-Binnya Dala," p. 154 (manuscript). This translation is hereafter cited as "Campaigns," which was subsequently published as San Lwin, trans., and Sunait Chutintaranond, ed., *The Campaigns of Razadarit, by Binnya Dala* (Bangkok: Institute of Asian Studies, 2007). I have not had access to that work but only to the original translation by San Lwin. My thanks to Jon Fernquest for supplying me with this valuable piece of scholarship.

50. Correspondence with Pat McCormick, July 1, 2014. His dissertation, titled "Mon Histories: Between Translation and Retelling," University of Washington, 2010, is likely to be one of the most valuable studies regarding the subject.

51. *Yazadhiyaza Ayedawpon*, ed. Ko Shwe Thein Min, pp. 1–13.

52. U Kala, *Mahayazawingyi*, p. *nga* (in the editor's preface).

53. One of these was the account of the last years of Yazadarit and Mingaung I, which were nearly identical except the accolades were reversed.

54. Halliday, *Lik Smin Asah*, p. vi.

55. One finds Prince Asah's name in the *Yazadhiyaza Ayedawpon* on page 128.

56. San Lwin, "Campaigns," p. 104.

57. In U Kala's *Mahayazawingyi*, it can be found in vol. 1, pp. 438–439. In Twinthintaikwun's *Twinthin Myanma Yazawinthit*, not written until the very late eighteenth century, it is found in vol. 1, pp. 280–282. In the *Yazadhiyaza Ayedawpon*, the story can be found on pp. 232–234. In the latter work, there is a "footnote" in which the author states, "in the Mon chronicle, it is said to be the Southern Queen, in the Yazawingyi [i.e., U Kala's], she is the daughter of Atwin Thinmhu, and in the Yazapon [another perhaps "earlier" chronicle], not believing the Queen, she was dethroned" instead. This suggests that the Burmese-language *Yazadhiyaza Ayedawpon* that survives may be a translation of an earlier Mon manuscript, unless the reference ("Mon chronicle") means the chronicle *about* the Mon rather than a reference to the title itself.

58. Aung-Thwin *Mists*, pp. 123–124, and p. 361, note 88.

59. Sandalinka, *Maniyadanabon*, pp. 84–85.

60. Sandalinka, *Maniyadanabon*, p. xix.

61. San Lwin, "Campaigns," pp. 113, 118. However, I cannot find the word "the enemy" in the published version of the *Yazadhiyaza Ayedawpon* that I am using, just "those who defended the ramparts" (p. 252); and on another occasion (p. 266), the word "enemy" is also not found, just implied. The published version of the *Yazadhiyaza Ayedawpon* may have changed what had been in the original palm-leaf version that San Lwin used, or his translation was loose, as it was still a draft.

62. Shorto, "Mon Geneaology of Kings," pp. 69–72. This, of course, raises the question of whether or not U Kala read Mon or was referring to the Burmese-language *Yazadhiyaza Ayedawpon*.

63. Counting just the major works listed in *Pitakat Taw Thamaing*, the nineteenth-century annotated bibliography, the Burmese-language texts on various subjects numbered well over two thousand, the "histories" themselves, over seventy-four. At most, the *total* number of works written in Mon that has survived comes to fewer than half a dozen, some of them near-duplicates. The *Pitakat Taw Thamaing* was written in 1888 by the head librarian of the court, whose more than 2,040 entries is a very interesting glimpse of the kinds of subjects being written and read, at least at the court. His table of contents is organized by both author and title of the work, with many cross-references making it easy for the reader to find what he or she wants. He also has extensive expository pages on certain select categories, such as *dhammathat* and *yazawin*. I use the reprinted version of 1989, recompiled by Mingyi Maha Thiyi Zeyathu.

64. This becomes most poignant for ministers like Bannya Dala (especially if he did have a hand in the translation of the work), for although a trusted adviser of King Bayinnaung, he fell out of royal favor toward the end, and was exiled to a remote village (now in Thailand) to die there a nonentity.

65. This is the number given by the Toyo Bunko catalogue. But the cover of the manuscript itself has "133 A" and "134" written on it. I am not certain to what those numbers refer, although they look like catalogue numbers. Note also that this reference is to the original catalogue (*List of Microfilms*), not the newer one redone by Thu Nandar (*Catalogue of Materials*).

66. It is no. 2017 in the *Pitakat Taw Thamaing*.

67. "Mwan Rajawan" (Mon Yazawin) manuscript, last leaf (*ghe*). In *List of Microfilms*.

68. Aung-Thwin, *Mists*, pp. 85, 145–146.

69. J. A. Stewart, "Note on Some Authorities for the History of Burma," *Journal of the Burma Research Society* 13, no. 2 (1923): 69–76.

70. Pe Maung Tin, "Burma Manuscripts in the British Museum," *Journal of the Burma Research Society* 14, no. 3 (1924): 221–246 (here p. 233). Phayre's collection of manuscripts in the British Library covers numbers OR 3403–3480 only. See Patricia Herbert's work, "The Sir Arthur Phayre Collection of Burmese Manuscripts," *British Library Journal* 1, no. 1 (1975): 62–70. My thanks to Daw San San May at the British Library for providing me with some of this information.

71. U Kala, *Mahayazawingyi*, vol. 1, page *nga*.

72. Hereafter, I cite this under Shorto, "Gavampati" (ms). One should not confuse this unpublished translation by Shorto with his article called the "The Gavampati Tradition in Burma," in *R. C. Majumdar Felicitation Volume*, ed. H. B. Sarkar (Calcutta: Firma K. L. Mukhopadhyay, 1970).

73. As noted in the previous chapter, the section on Gavampati can be found in the *Sudhammawati-rajawamsa; Siharajadhiraja-wamsa (Sudhammawati; Gawampati; Rajadhiraj)*, ed. Phra Candacanto (Pak Lat, Thailand, 1910), pp. 26–99.

74. Shorto, "Gavampati Tradition in Burma" p. 18.

75. Shorto, "Gavampati" (ms), pp. 1, 2–3, 9–10.

76. *Reprint from Dalrymple's Oriental Repertory, 1791–7 of Portions Relating to Burma* (Rangoon: Government Printing, 1926), p. 12.

77. Shorto, "Gavampati" (ms), p. 3. The statement that Tavoy is the "boundary of the Mon country" supports my contention that the Mon arrived only *after* the Burmese speakers were already inhabiting the region, for we find Burmese speakers both north and south of Tavoy and the Mon speakers. Clearly, they had driven a wedge into a Burmese-speaking area, at whose southern boundary lies Tavoy, where the people speak a version of Burmese very close to the version spoken north of it. Also, the word *thaway* (from where the anglicized Tavoy is derived) is Old Burmese, not Mon, and found in the inscriptions of Pagan (*SMK*, vol. 1, p. 345, among others). In short, Mon sources themselves help verify the lateness of their own emergence in the region.

78. Shorto, "Gavampati" (ms), p. 3.

79. This confirms my argument in *Mists* that Tavoy was the southernmost point, and Pegu the northernmost point, of the Mon "wedge" that split the already present Burmese column, further demonstrating the lateness of the Mon arrival in Lower Myanmar.

80. Charles Otto Blagden, "The Chronicles of Pegu: A Text in the Mon Language," *Journal of the Royal Asiatic Society* (1907): 367–374 (here p. 369).

81. There is some confusion on this issue as well. In his book, *The Talaings* (Rangoon: Superintendent, Government Printing, Burma, 1917), p. 129, Halliday stated that Schmidt's title was *A History of Pegu in the Mon Language*, but on pp. 9–10 of the preface to his translation of the *Slapat* ("Slapat"), Halliday calls it "Slapat Rajawan Datow Smin Ron."

82. For a description and analysis of this manuscript, see Blagden, "Chronicles of Pegu": 367–374.

83. Halliday, "Slapat," p. 34.

84. Ibid., pp. 34, 38.

85. The author confuses Mahasammata with Mahasammanta, p. 34.

86. Halliday, "Slapat," p. 51.

87. Richard M. Eaton, "Locating Arakan in Time, Space, and Historical Scholarship," in *The Maritime Frontier of Burma: Exploring Political, Cultural and Commercial Interaction in the Indian Ocean World, 1200–1800*, eds. Jos Gommans and Jacques Leider (Amsterdam: Koninklijke Nederlandse Akademie van Wetenschapen and KITLV Press, 2002), pp. 225–231.

88. Quotes by Jesuits visiting Lower Burma at the time can be found in Harvey, *History of Burma*, pp. 183–184.

89. U Kala, *Mahayazawingyi*, vol. 1, pp. 246–247.

90. Phayre, *History*, p. 30. However, I have not been able to find them among the dynastic lists provided by Sastri's *History of South India*.

91. By the very end of the sixteenth century, the Second Pegu (Toungoo) Dynasty had rapidly declined in power, but its rulers had already developed plans for returning to the agrarian Dry Zone well in advance of its destruction. One might notice that the Mon texts consider two separate dynasties as one: Yazadarit's fourteenth- to fifteenth-century dynasty, of which Dhammazedi was a part, and Bayinnaung's Toungoo Dynasty, which established Pegu as its center in the mid-sixteenth century. The reason is that Pegu, as Buddha-prophesied city, was the important criterion for defining a dynasty, while lineage was secondary.

92. Halliday, "Slapat," p. 66.

93. Ibid., p. 55. She was said to have given her weight in gold, which, with her crown on, was twenty-five *viss*, not quite ninety pounds, making her a slight woman indeed.

94. Shorto, "Gavampati" (ms), p. 14–15. This is very interesting, as the Trap and Pandit inscriptions, probably erected by Yazadarit, are the only ones to mention a Raksapura.

95. Halliday, "Slapat," p. 52.

96. Halliday, *Lik Smin Asah*, p. 143.

97. Bannya Dala, *Yazadhiyaza Ayedawpon*, p. 128.

98. Sastri, *History of South India*, p. 245.

99. Personal correspondence with Dr. Patrick McCormick.

100. One should also be aware that this same volume has another title: *Pathama Sudhammavati Gavampati, Rajadhiraj*. For this, see Charles Duroiselle, "Talaing Nissayas," *Journal of the Burma Research Society* 3, no. 2 (1913): 103–145.

101. These additions are my own assessment, given the title.

102. As noted in the previous chapter, upon binding, this work was retitled the *Rajawansa Dhammaceti Mahapitakadhara*.

103. My thanks to Dr. Pat McCormick for sending me Bauer's edition, along with the drafts that included his (McCormick's) input.

104. Halliday, *The Talaings*, p. 130, and *Lik Smin Asah*, vii, note.

105. In assessing the *Lik Smin Asah*, Halliday describes how this happened, and I suspect it occurred in many other cases as well. It was not only a matter of people not knowing the older vocabulary, so that new words were substituted for the old ones without a secure knowledge of the former's meaning, or of making careless "typos," but was also a deliberate attempt to rewrite what was currently thought to be the "truth" or an attempt to "improve" on the prose or verse of the older version. Sometimes, Halliday writes, long insertions were made, obscure words omitted with better-known ones taking their place, and there was a "manifest desire on the whole to make the text plainer" (*Lik Smin Asah*, p. v).

106. Duroiselle, "Talaing Nissayas," p. 105.

107. W. G. Cooper, "A Note on Talaing Nissaya and Vocabulary," *Journal of the Burma Research Society* 4, no. 2 (1914): 126.

108. Indeed, this is confirmed by Pat McCormick, who stated that the *Nidana* and the so-called "Paklat Talaing Chronicle" are one and the same (personal correspondence, June 6, 2014).

109. Patrick Arthur Pranke, "The 'Treatise on the Lineage of Elders' (*Vamsadipani*): Monastic Reform and the Writing of Buddhist History in Eighteenth-Century Burma," PhD diss., University of Michigan, 2004, pp. v–vi.

110. Pranke, "'Treatise,'" p. vii.

111. Ibid., pp. 145–146, 167–169, 172.

112. Ibid., p. 146.

113. Paññasami, *Sasanavamsa* [History of the Religion], trans. Bimala Churn Law (London: Pali Text Society, 1952), pp. 40–53.

114. This convinces me even more of the lateness of the *Lik Smin Asah* (1825), in which these characters and their story are paramount. There is also no reason Pannasami should have known about this folktale, sitting in Upper Myanmar among the educated elite, and even if he did, there is no reason to believe he knew the Mon language in which it was written.

11. The Origins of Pegu and Its Founding Fathers

1. O. W. Wolters, *The Fall of Srivijaya in Malay History* (Ithaca, NY: Cornell University Press, 1970); Leonard Y. Andaya, *Leaves of the Same Tree: Trade and Ethnicity in the Straits of Melaka* (Honolulu: University of Hawai'i Press, 2008); and Kernial Singh Sandhu, Paul Wheatley, and Ton Abdul Aziz bin Mat, *Melaka: The Transformation of a Malay Capital, c. 1400–1980* (Kuala Lumpur: Oxford University Press, 1983). John Miksic, however, argues that Temasek (modern Singapore) preceded Melaka in succeeding Sri Vijaya. See his *Singapore and the Silk Road of the Sea: 1300–1800* (Singapore: National University of Singapore Press and the National Museum of Singapore Press, 2013).

2. Anthony Reid, *Southeast Asia in the Age of Commerce, 1450–1680*, Volume One: *The Lands below the Winds* (New Haven, CT: Yale University Press, 1988).

3. Jos Gommans and Jacques Leider, eds., *The Maritime Frontier of Burma: Exploring Political, Cultural, and Commercial Interaction in the Indian Ocean World, 1200–1800* (Leiden: Koninklijke Nederlandse Akademie van Wetenschappen, KITLV Press, 2002).

4. John K. Whitmore, "The Rise of the Coast: Trade, State and Culture in Early Đai Viêt," *Journal of Southeast Asian Studies* 37, no. 1 (2006): 103–122.

5. Michael Aung-Thwin, "A New/Old Look at 'Classical' and 'Post-Classical' Southeast Asia/Burma," in *New Perspectives on the History and Historiography of Southeast Asia: Continuing Explorations*, eds. Michael Aung-Thwin and K. R. Hall (London Routledge, 2011), pp. 25–55.

6. Note that, instead, the "Mon Yazawin" attributes this founding to earlier Pagan king Alaungsithu, and thereby contributes to the esoteric "controversy" between Narapatisithu and Alaungsithu, a running debate that saw many palm-leaf sentences in the nineteenth-century *Hmannan Yazawin.*

7. Bannya Dala, *Yazadhiyaza Ayedawpon*, p. 4.

8. Aung-Thwin, *Mists,* chapter 4, has the full argument. Interestingly enough, there is an "Ogre Island" offshore of Muttama.

9. In fact, Dhammazedi does not mention Magadu; his seems to have been a different historical tradition.

10. Shorto, "Gavampati" (ms), p. 12–13.

11. Halliday, "Slapat," p. 54.

12. Sithu Gamani Thingyan, *Zinme Yazawin* (Chronicle of Chiang Mai), trans. Thaw Kaung and Ni Ni Myint, ed. Tun Aung Chain (Yangon: Universities Historical Research Centre, 2003), pp. 6–9. Although the narrative refers to what appears to be a later Lower Myanmar king, Sutasoma, King Mangrai's alliance with Lower Myanmar occurred in the late thirteenth century, and makes much more sense if the "exchange" of princesses were a reference to Magadu's story. The translated manuscript has no copying date but is said to have belonged to the *sawbwa* of Onbaung (p. iv) supplemented by another with a copying date of 1762 (p. iii).

13. Bannya Dala, *Yazadhiyaza Ayedawpon,* pp. 4–7; and Tun Aung Chain, ed. and trans., *Chronicle of Ayutthaya: A Translation of the Yodaya Yazawin* (Yangon: Myanmar Historical

Commission, 2005), p. 9. Recently, U Thaw Kaung (and Ni Ni Yin) published a "complete" version of this work in Burmese—the above translation by U Tun Aung Chain omitted the appendices—as *Yodaya Yazawin* (Yangon: Department of Historical Research and National Library, 2014). The work is ostensibly compiled from the testimonies of the numerous people taken from Ayuthaya after its conquest in 1767 by the Burmese, although the name of the compiler is not known. The copy of the manuscript discovered in the 1970s is dated to before 1886, but the story has become quite complicated, needing much more than a footnote here. See U Thaw Kaung's pages *khu* to *gu* and Chris Baker's "Before Ayutthaya Fell: Economic Life in an Industrious Society: Note on the Testimonies and the Description of Ayutthaya," *Journal of the Siam Society* 99 (2011): 72–80.

14. Tun Aung Chain, *Chronicle of Ayutthaya*, p. 13.

15. Bannya Dala, *Yazadhiyaza Ayedawpon*, p. 10.

16. U Kala, *Mahayazawingyi*, vol. 1, p. 298.

17. U Tin Shein, ed. *Hmannan Mahayazawindawgyi* [Great Royal Chronicle of the Palace of Mirrors]. 3 vols. (Yangon: Pyi Gyi Man Taing Piktakat Press, 1967), vol. 1, p. 351.

18. Twinthintaikwun, *Twinthin Myanma Yazawinthit*, vol. 1, p. 156. The chronicles had probably confused a more recent governor for Aleinma, the one appointed by Narapatisithu, for it would have made him ten when he was appointed and nearly ninety years old when he was ousted.

19. Bannya Dala, *Yazadhiyaza Ayedawpon*, p. 11.

20. Ibid., p. 10.

21. Ibid., p. 5.

22. Phayre, *History*, p. 65; Harvey, *History of Burma*, pp. 110–111.

23. Hall, *Burma*, p. 34.

24. Halliday, "Slapat," p. 51.

25. Bannya Dala, *Yazadhiyaza Ayedawpon*, p. 12.

26. Provided it was not a forgery. However, I concur with the late David Wyatt's assessment, and that of the late Bill Gedney, and some of the best Thai scholars, such as Anthony Diller, that this inscription was not a late forgery.

27. *SMK*, vol. 3, p. 196, lines 18–19.

28. Since the *Yazadhiyaza Ayedawpon* is said to be a translation of the "Mon Yazawin," it means, essentially, that the latter must have had older information on at least Narathihapade and Yazathingyan, not to mention Narapatisithu who built Muttama (mentioned earlier).

29. Bannya Dala, *Yazadhiyaza Ayedawpon*, p. 17. Of course, it rhymes in Burmese, not in English.

30. San Lwin, "Campaigns," p. 6.

31. Harvey, *History of Burma*, p. 111; Hall, *Burma*, p. 34. Hall cited Harvey and Harvey cited Forchhammer.

32. Emil Forchhammer, ed. and trans., *King Wagaru's Manu Dhammasattham. Text, Translation, and Notes* (Rangoon: Government Press, 1885) (hereafter cited as Forchhammer, *Wagaru Dhammathat*).

33. Forchhammer, *Wagaru Dhammathat*, p. 39.

34. Personal communication.

35. Harvey, *History of Burma*, p. 120, wrote that the most famous Buddhaghosa in Myanmar was the one who lived during King Dhammazedi's reign.

36. Another Burmese language expert, Dr. Than Than Win, translates the above paragraph in the following way: "I am an elder whose name is Buddha Ghawtha [Buddhagosha] and since I desire the benefit of the (*sasana*) religion, I am going to inscribe King Waru's Dhammathat in the Mon language into the language of Brahma. You, the wise judges, make a decision/your

decisions (You, the wise judges, decide) relying on the word for word translation. King Waru finished transcribing the Dhammathat on Tuesday, the 6th day of the rising moon of the month of Thadingyut, Sakaraja 1069."

37. John Okell, whom I also consulted, wrote, "I agree with you that deriving Mranma from Brahma is highly implausible." Personal correspondence, April 2, 2006.

38. That the manuscript was only *copied* in 1707 is very clear. See paragraph 196, Forchhammer, *Wagaru Dhammathat,* p. 71.

39. There is only one exception. In an inscription of Pagan dated 1219 AD, what appears to be the *visagara* (which looks like the English colon) is quite clear. But it is not at all clear that it was a tone marker, so its function is unknown. And it is not found thereafter until much later. Pe Maung Tin's "Dictionary Jottings: Philological Features of the Inscriptions," *Journal of the Burma Research Society* 19, no. 3 (1929): 78–79, explains the late use of some tone markers.

40. Aung-Thwin, *Pagan,* chapter 6. See also Okudaira's "Burmese Dhammathat," pp. 26–29.

41. Huxley, "Mon Studies and Professor Forchhammer," 391–410. He makes a strong case that questions Forchhammer's knowledge of Pali and other credentials.

42. Aung-Thwin, *Mists,* chapter 11.

43. J. S. Furnivall's "Manu in Burma: Some Burmese *Dhammathats,*" *Journal of the Burma Research Society* 30, no. 2 (1940): 351–370, especially footnote 3, p. 356.

44. The three scholars most active on the subject of Burmese *dhammathats* are Ryuji Okudaira, Christian Lammerts, and the late Andrew Huxley, whose works are listed in the bibliography.

45. Aung-Thwin, *Mists,* p. 107.

46. Prasert Na Nagara and Alexander B. Griswold, *Epigraphic and Historical Studies* (Bangkok: Historical Society, 1992).

47. For epigraphic support of Suvannabhumi being in Thailand, see also David K. Wyatt, "Relics, Oaths and Politics in Thirteenth-Century Siam," *Journal of Southeast Asian Studies* 32, no. 1 (2001): 3–65.

48. Twinthintaikwun, *Twinthin Myanma Yazawinthit,* vol. 1, p. 213; U Kala, *Mahayazawingyi,* vol. 1, p. 361, has it in 1370.

49. *MKPC,* vol. 2, p. 60.

50. Bannya Dala, *Yazadhiyaza Ayedawpon,* p. 32.

51. Ibid., p. 36. This suggests the Wimala-Samala legend was already in existence by the sixteenth century when the *Yazadhiyaza Ayedawpon* was written, or it was a later interpolation.

52. Bannya Dala, *Yazadhiyaza Ayedawpon,* p. 40.

53. Ibid., p. 26.

54. Ibid., pp. 62–65.

55. I am not certain the Portuguese were there that early.

12. Yazadarit the Unifier

1. Harvey, *History of Burma,* p. 113.

2. Bannya Dala, *Yazadhiyaza Ayedawpon,* p. 128.

3. Ibid., p. 130. Harvey puts it in 1385 (*History of Burma,* p. 113) and Phayre, also in 1385 (*History,* p. 68). Neither cites any source, another reason I do not think either used the *Yazadhiyaza Ayedawpon.*

4. Bannya Dala, *Yazadhiyaza Ayedawpon,* p. 130.

5. In Harvey, he is called Deinmaniyut and is not mentioned at all in Phayre, whereas in Bannya Dala, *Yazadhiyaza Ayedawpon* (pp. 130–131), he is clearly called Minister Tein Nge. In San

Lwin's translation, this minister is also called Deinmaniyut ("Campaigns," p. 59). Later in the *Yazadhiyaza Ayedawpon* (p. 217) he is finally called Teinmaniyut.

6. I have used San Lwin's translation ("Campaigns," p. 60), for its accurate recapturing of the dialogue. The original is in Bannya Dala, *Yazadhiyaza Ayedawpon,* p. 131.

7. Bannya Dala, *Yazadhiyaza Ayedawpon,* p. 133.

8. By that I mean U Kala probably borrowed from the *Yazadhiyaza Ayedawpon* originally. Then when the *Yazadhiyaza Ayedawpon* was recopied later, after U Kala had written his work, it would turn around and borrow information from U Kala. Thus, a chronologically earlier text when recopied later would sometimes incorporate what the later text had written. So, a text that is considered earlier (such as the *Yazadhiyaza Ayedawpon*) is not necessarily the source of even an identical piece of information found in what is considered a later text (such as U Kala's) if we have only their copies to deal with.

9. Bannya Dala, *Yazadhiyaza Ayedawpon,* p. 135.

10. San Lwin, "Campaigns," translates the phrase as "this young Talaing" when the original Burmese text had "this young Mon." Indeed, throughout his work, San Lwin translates the word "Mon" as "Talaing," apparently having imbibed the Mon Paradigm and colonial historiography's erroneous contention that "Talaing" was an exclusive reference to the word "Mon." But as we know now, the word "Talaing" cannot be found in any record in Myanmar written in the Mon language; it was not part of their vocabulary for themselves. Today, when asked, all Burmese that I have interviewed who are unaware of colonial historiography always contend that the word "Talaing" is a reference to a *mixture* of ethnic groups, sort of like the word Creole, but most often a reference to a mixture of Karen and some other group, perhaps South Indian. There is some hint of this in the Ming sources that often refer to the people in Lower Burma as *k'ulah,* obviously taken from the Burmese *kula* [*kala*], an early reference to South Asians (or those who looked like them), not a general designation for "foreigner," as so often reported in later colonial works. It certainly is not a reference to the Portuguese, as Harper correctly argues. Thus, it seems likely that this Lower Burma kingdom or polity that emerged in the late thirteenth century, which clearly included a large number of South Asians and their offspring, consisted of people ethnically and/or culturally distinct from those in Upper Myanmar (at least in the perspective of the Chinese).

11. Bannya Dala, *Yazadhiyaza Ayedawpon,* p. 147.

12. Ibid., p. 161.

13. Bannya Dala, *Yazadhiyaza Ayedawpon,* has 1410 (p. 163). But San Lwin amended the date in his translation which he said is based on the actual "palm leaf manuscript" (see San Lwin, "Campaigns," p. 74).

14. Bannya Dala, *Yazadhiyaza Ayedawpon,* p. 162.

15. Ibid., p. 162. There is some inconsistency here, since earlier Lauk Phya was said to have become a *hpaya kyun* (pagoda servant).

16. Ibid., pp. 163–164.

17. San Lwin, "Campaigns," p. 78; Bannya Dala, *Yazadhiyaza Ayedawpon,* p. 170.

18. Bannya Dala, *Yazadhiyaza Ayedawpon,* p. 170.

19. It is the name of a popular restaurant in Yangon today that sits on the royal lakes. It is also shaped like a *karaweik,* mythical bird.

20. The account by U Kala and the *Yazadhiyaza Ayedawpon* here are slightly different, but not on the major points.

21. U Kala, *Mahayazawingyi,* vol. 1, p. 401.

22. Ibid., p. 403. The issue of chillies in Southeast Asia this early—prior to the Spanish ships that sailed from the Americas to Asia—has been contested and is a topic for another manuscript.

23. Bannya Dala, *Yazadhiyaza Ayedawpon,* p. 181.

24. It may hark back to Indian kings performing the *asvamedha.*

25. Even this dialogue was nearly verbatim in Bannya Dala, *Yazadhiyaza Ayedawpon,* p. 181, although the advice was given by the monk, not the generals.

26. These were U Kala's words, not those in the *Yazadhiyaza Ayedawpon,* since Mon do not call themselves "Talaing." (Neither does anyone else except Western historians or those influenced by their historiography.)

27. Bannya Dala, *Yazadhiyaza Ayedawpon,* p. 197.

28. Ibid., p. 197. San Lwin, "Campaigns," p. 90.

29. San Lwin, "Campaigns," p. 90; Bannya Dala, *Yazadhiyaza Ayedawpon,* p. 198.

30. If one wanted to study battle formations, strategies, and structures of both Ava's and Pegu's armies, the *Yazadhiyaza Ayedawpon* is an important source of information.

31. San Lwin, "Campaigns," p. 151.

32. Bannya Dala, *Yazadhiyaza Ayedawpon,* p. 290.

33. San Lwin, "Campaigns," p. 148; Bannya Dala, *Yazadhiyaza Ayedawpon,* pp. 345–346. The sentence can also be read as "the splendid Kyat Tale pagoda" rather than "the middle of a splendid temple."

34. San Lwin, "Campaigns," p. 152; Bannya Dala, *Yazadhiyaza Ayedawpon,* p. 356. In Nai Pan Hla's translation of the *Yazadhiyaza Ayedawpon,* Yazadarit died first, followed shortly by Mingaung. But clearly, all the chronicle evidence we have goes against this.

35. San Lwin, "Campaigns," pp. 152–153; Bannya Dala, *Yazadhiyaza Ayedawpon,* p. 357.

36. Bannya Dala, *Yazadhiyaza Ayedawpon,* pp. 357–358.

37. San Lwin, "Campaigns," p. 135.

38. Ibid., p. 137.

39. Ibid., pp. 149–150.

40. Ibid., p. 121.

41. Ibid., p. 153; Bannya Dala, *Yazadhiyaza Ayedawpon,* p. 359.

42. Bannya Dala, *Yazadhiyaza Ayedawpon,* p. 359. "Sactasum" refers to a king in a *Jataka* story who killed his son.

43. Bannya Dala, *Yazadhiyaza Ayedawpon,* p. 360.

44. Halliday, "Slapat," p. 52.

45. *SMK,* vol. 5, pp. 47, 59, 69.

46. Although "new Pegu" is usually attributed to Bayinnaung of the next dynasty, the reports by European visitors clearly indicate that it was already built by one of Yazadarit's successors.

47. Phayre, *History,* p. 81, and "History of Pegu," p. 120. San Lwin's translation gives 783 (1421 AD) as the date for Yazadarit's death, so what happened in between his death and the ascension of his successor is unknown, although some sort of "civil war" in the struggle for the throne is likely. Harvey suggests such a scenario (*History of Burma,* pp. 115–116).

48. *Epigraphia Birmanica,* vol. 4, p. 42.

49. Halliday, "Slapat," p. 53.

50. Ibid., p. 54.

51. Ibid., pp. 54–55. In part, this explains why Yazadarit was not well received in the *Slapat,* whose author was concerned mainly with the kings who patronized the Shwedagon, which was probably just being built or was not even built yet by Yazadarit's reign, so he had no occasion to donate to it.

52. Phayre, "History of Pegu," p. 121.

53. *Epigraphia Birmanica,* vol. 4, p. 42.

54. Halliday, "Slapat," p. 55.

55. *Epigraphia Birmanica,* vol. 4, p. 42.

56. Halliday, "Slapat," p. 55.
57. Ibid.
58. Ibid.

13. The Golden Years at Pegu

1. *MKPC*, vol. 2, p. 80.
2. *SMK*, vol. 5, p. 35.
3. Harvey, *History of Burma*, p. 117, gives her these official regnal years, and although I am not sure where he got those dates, they come closest to my analysis discussed below. These years add up to nineteen, but in fact she actually ruled only for about seven, leaving the rest to her crown prince, Dhammazedi, as she was ill and had moved to Dagon (Yangon).
4. Halliday, "Slapat," p. 55.
5. "Shin Saw Bu" by one M. T. [could be Pe Maung Tin], who provided a loose translation of the Burmese note by Saya Thein (of Hmawbi) on the queen, states that she had one son and two daughters instead. See Saya Thein, "Bago Hanthawaddy Myo go Min aphyit nhin so san daw mu thaw Shin Saw Bu akyaung" ["Account of Shin Saw Bu Who Reigned as King in Hanthawaddy (Pegu)"], *Journal of the Burma Research Society* 1, no. 2 (1911): 10–16.
6. The "Paklat Talaing Chronicle" stated there were five monks altogether, making a valid chapter for ordination.
7. H. L. Shorto, "Translation," pp. 2–3.
8. Shorto, "Translation," p. 4.
9. The account of this is in Twinthin's *Twinthin Myanma Yazawinthit*, vol. 1, p. 332.
10. U Kala, *Mahayazawingyi*, pp. 50, 60.
11. Twinthintaikwun, *Twinthin Myanma Yazawinthit*, vol. 1, pp. 332, 345. Phayre's sources in "History of Pegu" agreed, p. 120.
12. Twinthintaikwun, *Twinthin Myanma Yazawinthit*, vol. 1, p. 333.
13. Halliday, "Slapat," pp. 55–56.
14. Ibid., p. 56; Harvey, *History of Burma*, p. 117. There are other versions of Shin Saw Bu's regnal dates written by more "modern" authors, such as Saya Thein cited above, which agree with Harvey's in certain respects but also with the *Slapat* in others.
15. Shorto, "Translation," p. 7.
16. Shorto, "Translation," p. 3. Bauer's edition of the same work confirms Shorto's translation, p. 26.
17. For the creation of this myth, see Aung-Thwin, *Mists*, chapter 11.
18. Saya Thein of Hmawbi wrote in "Account of Shin Saw Bu" (noted above) that Burmese plays often depicted Shin Saw Bu and Dhammazedi as husband and wife, something he was attempting to correct.
19. Shorto, "Translation," p. 5.
20. Halliday, "Slapat," p. 57, states that he was fifty-one when he shed the robe and became Viceroy, which occurred when Shin Saw Bu became queen in 1463 when she was fifty-eight. But the "Paklat Talaing Chronicle" has him fourteen years her junior. See Shorto, "Translation," p. 26.
21. *Epigraphia Birmanica*, vol. 4, p. 42; and *MKPC*, vol. 2, p. 80. Of course, there is a wide range of people who can fit as "mother" and "son" in Southeast Asian society; it need not have been a genetic relationship.
22. Halliday, "Slapat," p. 55.
23. Ibid., pp. 55–56.
24. Twinthintaikwun, *Twinthin Myanma Yazawinthit*, vol. 1, p. 333.
25. Halliday, "Slapat," p. 55.

26. *SMK,* vol. 5, pp. 34–37.

27. *MKPC,* vol. 2, pp. 60–61, nos. 62 and 63.

28. Ibid., pp. 61–63, no. 64. I have no way to judge whether or not these figures of silver and gold are exaggerated, but the number of robes and weight of black and "Indian" pepper does not seem unreasonable.

29. *SMK,* vol. 5, p. 35.

30. Her small stature and light weight would give some credence to the escape story where she was able to fit into a trunk carried by two men.

31. Halliday, "Slapat," p. 56. As noted above, Harvey has 1472 for her death (*History of Burma,* p. 117).

32. Harvey, *History of Burma,* p. 117.

33. The title varies a bit from inscription to inscription.

34. Harvey, *History of Burma,* p. 118. An inscription has him ascending the throne only in 1475, although that sounds like the date of formal coronation, which invariably postdates de facto ascension. See *MKPC,* vol. 2, p. 65.

35. Shorto, "Translation," p. 3.

36. Ibid.

37. Michael Aung-Thwin, "The Role of *Sasana* Reform in Burmese History, Economic Dimensions of a Religious Purification," *Journal of Asian Studies* 38, no. 4 (1979): 671–688.

38. Shorto, "Translation," pp. 1–2.

39. Ibid., pp. 24–25.

40. Phayre, *History,* p. 122.

41. Halliday, *Lik Smin Asah,* "Introduction."

42. Shorto, "Translation," p. 17.

43. Phayre's account of Dhammazedi in his *History,* written over ten years before the Kalyani Inscriptions were read, translated, and published, gave him only a sentence and a paragraph, whereas in Harvey's account, written after the inscriptions were discovered and published, the king had risen not only in stature and "agency," but verbiage as well.

44. Harvey, *History of Burma,* p. 120.

45. Paññasami, *Sasanavamsa,* pp. 48–52.

46. See Aung-Thwin, *Mists,* for the mythology concerning the erroneous antiquity of Ramannadesa and much of the sacred sites and relics it was said to have contained. Indeed, the legend regarding the antiquity of the holiest and most sacred site there, the Shwedagon, was begun by Dhammazedi's immediate predecessors; it cannot be demonstrated to have preceded Yazadarit's reign by much, if at all.

47. Aung-Thwin, "*Sasana* reform."

48. U Nu, *Saturday's Son* (New Haven and London: Yale University Press, 1975), p. 274.

49. Shorto, "Translation," p. 25. One should be reminded that the English word "slave" in Shorto's translation is not only an anachronistic "etymology" but an incorrect representation of the institution itself, already discussed at length in part 1. Hence, I have substituted his word "slave" with the indigenous term *kywan* (or *kyun*), as contained in the source itself.

50. Pranke, "Treatise," p. 187; Harvey, *History of Burma,* p. 120, like Arthur Phayre, also has age eighty.

51. Harvey, *History of Burma,* p. 120, puts it in 1492.

52. Phayre, "History of Pegu," p. 122.

53. Halliday, "Slapat," p. 57.

54. Shorto, "Translation," pp. 28–30. I have not attempted to correct anything here as Shorto's English is one of a kind, and he may have spelled and used words that are not commonly known.

55. Ibid., p. 30.

56. According to Kennon Breazeale in his "Editorial Introduction to Nicolò di Conti's Account," Conti did not write about his extensive travels. Our knowledge of him has been filtered through the works of two men to whom he recounted his adventures. A Spanish nobleman, Pero Tafur, was visiting the seashore near the monastery at Mount Sinai in 1437 when Conti arrived there, on his way back to Europe from Asia. Conti was accompanied by his wife, whom he had met and married in India, and by his four children, who were born in the course of his travels. Tafur travelled with the Conti family by caravan to Cairo and then set out for Crete. The wife and two children died in an epidemic in Egypt, and Conti returned with his remaining children to Venice, his native town. In 1439 he went to Florence during a papal visit to that city, and at that time he related the stories of his travels to the papal secretary, Giovanni Francesco Poggio Bracciolini. See ("The Itinerary of Ludovico di Varthema of Bologna from 1502 to 1508," *SOAS Bulletin of Burma Research* 2, no. 2 (Autumn 2004).

57. "Itinerary of Ludovico di Varthema of Bologna," 120. The reference to Calicut, of course, confirms the view that Lower Myanmar was inhabited by various groups from numerous parts of South India.

58. V. C. Scott O'Connor, *Mandalay and Other cities of the Past in Burma* (London: Hutchinson & Co., 1907, reprint 1987), pp. 360–364. Some of the quotes and their sources can also be found in Harvey, *History of Burma*, pp. 120–122.

59. Ibid., p. 122.

60. Ken Breazeale, historian of Southeast Asia with considerable knowledge about the European sources of this era, said that "the very large number of contemporary [European] sources convey the impression that Pegu was the most important and most reliable source" of food, especially for Melaka (personal correspondence, Wednesday, April 6, 2016).

61. Stewart, "Note," 72.

62. O'Connor, *Mandalay and Other Cities*, pp. 366–367.

63. Shorto, "Translation," p. 44.

64. Ibid., p. 43.

65. Halliday, "Slapat," p. 57.

66. Ibid., pp. 57–58.

67. Lieberman, *Burmese Administrative Cycles.*

68. Harvey, *History of Burma*, p. 121.

69. Ibid.

14. The Historical Legacy of the First Pegu Dynasty

1. The number of years depends, of course, on when one starts counting. In both, I include the foundations to their emergence, so that for Ava, I begin with the first decade of the fourteenth, and for Pegu, the last decade of the thirteenth century.

2. For an excellent analysis of this tradition within the context of Burmese Buddhist historiography, see Pat Pranke's translation of the *Vamsadipani* ("Treatise"). The *Sasanavamsa* (Paññasami), p. 53, also lists several Pali works attributed to Pegu.

3. The one that comes closest is the Khmer empire centered at Angkor, whose scale nearly equaled that of Pegu's.

4. G. H. Luce explicitly wrote that Burmans were "prosaic" while the Mon were more "introspective," while Harvey is well known for writing about the "barbarous" Shan.

5. In none of the works of Dr. Hla Pe, Pe Maung Tin, John Okell, Anna Allott, U Saw Tun [Saw Lu], or U Kyaw Dun have I seen Burmese verse attributed to Mon verse and documented with an original, dated source.

6. For example, see Bannya Dala, *Yazadhiyaza Ayedawpon,* pp. 43, 85, 88, 98.

7. *SMK,* vol. 5, pp. 90–97.

8. One of the few colonial scholars to go against the grain of the Mon Paradigm was B. R. Pearn in his *A History of Rangoon* (Rangoon: American Baptist Mission Press, 1939), who had little positive to say of Mon contributions to the country's material culture.

9. Aung-Thwin, "*Sasana* Reform."

10. There is no comparison in terms of quality and quantity, in terms of relative and even absolute wealth, between Shin Saw Bu and Dhammazedi's patronage and that of many Pagan and Ava kings who preceded them.

11. Aung-Thwin, *Mists,* chapter 3.

12. Ibid., chapter 9.

13. For Dhammazedi's Mon inscription that records this, see *MKPC,* vol. 1, pp. 130–138, and for the Burmese translation, see part 2, pp. 67–70. It has also been translated into English in *Epigraphia Birmanica,* vol. 4, pt. 1, pp. 1–16.

14. See Alexander Griswold, "The Holy Land Transported," in *Paranavitana Felicitation Volume* (Colombo, Ceylon: M.D. Gunasena, 1965), pp. 173–221, for the general trend; also U Aung Thaw, *Historical Sites in Burma* (Rangoon: Ministry of Culture, 1972), p. 109, for the best Myanmar example.

15. *Epigraphia Birmanica,* vol. 4, p. 57.

16. Over 75 percent of the country's wealth is derived from the agricultural sector, while nearly 80 percent of its labor is in agriculture-related occupations.

17. Even if a case can be made for automatically associating reified ethnicity with a political entity, his ethnic background (once he became human) is, as noted in earlier chapters, said to have been both Mon and Shan.

18. Although the *Yazadhiyaza Ayedawpon* gives him considerable attention, it does it within the context of Yazadarit's role, while U Kala just barely mentions his name in a different context.

19. Indeed, one inscription of Pegu referred to her as "bayin ma" (female king), as well as the usual "mi baya" (queen) (*MKPC,* vol. 2, p. 96).

20. It is true that a woman by the name of Kuvera was said to have reigned in Arakan as sovereign, but the story has not been documented.

21. Shah Paung, "Leading Ladies," *The Irrawaddy* 13, no. 9 (September 2005): n.p.

22. Aung-Thwin, *Mists,* chapters 11 and 12.

Conclusion

1. This chapter draws on two of my earlier publications about Ava and Pegu: "Lower Burma and Bago in the History of Burma," in *The Maritime Frontier of Burma: Exploring Political, Cultural and Commercial Interaction in the Indian Ocean World, 1200–1800,* ed. Jos Gommans and Jacques Leider (Leiden: Koninklijke Nederlandse Akademie van Wetenschappen, KITLV Press, 2002), and its sequel, called "A Tale of Two Kingdoms: Ava and Pegu in the Fifteenth Century," *Journal of Southeast Asian Studies* 42, no. 1 (2011): 1–16.

2. I take the "upstream-downstream" phrase from Ben Bronson's article on that subject. See Ben Bronson, "Exchange at the Upstream and Downstream Ends: Notes toward a Functional Model of the Coastal State in Southeast Asia," in *Economic Exchange and Social Interaction in Southeast Asia: Perspectives from Prehistory, History and Ethnography,* ed. K. L. Hutterer (Ann Arbor: University of Michigan, Center for South and Southeast Asian Studies, Papers on South and Southeast Asia 13, 1977), pp. 39–52.

3. Michael Aung-Thwin, "Spirals in Burmese and Early Southeast Asian History," *Journal of Interdisciplinary History* 21, no. 4 (1991): 575–602.

4. Aung-Thwin, *Mists.*

5. For a discussion on this issue, see Victor B. Lieberman's "An Age of Commerce in Southeast Asia? Problems of Regional Coherence—A Review Article," *Journal of Asian Studies* 54, no. 3 (1995): 796–807.

6. I see this event as one of reintegration in an oscillating process rather than the new phase in a linear and progressively increasing integrative process that is suggested by Victor Lieberman in *Strange Parallels: Southeast Asia in Global Context, c. 800–1830* (Cambridge: Cambridge University Press, 2003). Such oscillation continued well into the twenty and twenty-first centuries. See Aung-Thwin and Aung-Thwin's *A History of Myanmar*, chapter 12.

7. For this period in Myanmar's history, the most detailed account is that of Victor Lieberman's *Burmese Administrative Cycles.*

8. I use 1942 as the date for the effective end of British rule when the Japanese and Myanmar's nationalist forces destroyed the old colonial order. Of course, the number of years depends on how one counts the British colonial period. It can begin with 1824–1826 and the First Anglo-Burmese War, ending in 1948 and formal independence, or with 1885–1886 and the annexation of the country, ending with 1942, when the Japanese invaded. I am using the latter.

9. Hla Pe, *Burma*. See also the "Introduction" in Ma Ma Lay's *Blood Bond*, trans. Than Than Win, ed. Michael Aung-Thwin, University of Hawai'i Center for Southeast Asian Studies Translation Series (Honolulu: University of Hawai'i Center for Southeast Asian Studies, 2004).

10. Michael Aung-Thwin, "Principles and Patterns of the Precolonial Burmese State," in *Tradition and Modernity in Myanmar: Proceedings of an International Conference held in Berlin from May 7th to May 9th, 1993*, eds. Uta Gartner and Jens Lorenz (Berlin: Humboldt-University zu Berlin, 1994), p. 37.

BIBLIOGRAPHY

Adu Minyo. *Yakhaing Minthami Egyin* [Lullaby of the Arakan Princess]. Yangon: Hanthawaddy Press, 1965.

Andaya, Barbara Watson, and Leonard Y. Andaya. *A History of Early Modern Southeast Asia, 1400–1830.* Cambridge: Cambridge University Press, 2015.

Andaya, Leonard Y. *Leaves of the Same Tree: Trade and Ethnicity in the Straits of Melaka.* Honolulu: University of Hawai'i Press, 2008.

Aung Myint, U. "The City of Ketumati (Toungoo)." *Myanma Thamaing Thutethana Sasaung* [Myanmar Historical Research Journal] 3 (1998): 27–45.

Aung Thaw, U. *Historical Sites in Burma.* Rangoon: Ministry of Culture, 1972.

Aung-Thwin, Michael. "Burmese Historiography-Chronicles (Yazawin)." In *Making History: A Global Encyclopedia of Historical Writing,* edited by D. R. Woolf, pp. 119–122. New York: Garland, 1997.

———. "Continuing, Re-Emerging, and Emerging Trends in Southeast Asian History." *TRaNS: Trans-Regional and -National Studies of Southeast Asia* 1, no. 1 (January 2013): 87–104.

———. "Debate: A Non-State Approach." Reviews by Michael R. Dove, Hjorleifur Jonsson, and Michael Aung-Thwin of *The Art of Not Being Governed: An Anarchist History of Upland Southeast Asia* by James C. Scott. *Bijdragen tot de Taal-, Land- en Volkenkunde* 167, no. 1 (2011): 95–99.

———. "Hmannan Mahayazawindawgyi [the Great Royal Chronicle of the Glass Palace]." In *Making History: A Global Encyclopedia of Historical Writing,* edited by D. R. Woolf, pp. 417–419. New York: Garland, 1998.

———. "The Legend That Was Lower Burma." *International Conference on Texts and Contexts.* Yangon: Universities Historical Research Centre, 2001.

———. "Lower Burma and Bago in the History of Burma." In *The Maritime Frontier of Burma: Exploring Political, Cultural and Commercial Interaction in the Indian Ocean World, 1200–1800,* edited by Jos Gommans and Jacques Leider. Leiden: Koninklijke Nederlandse Akademie van Wetenschappen, 2002.

———. *The Mists of Ramanna: The Legend That Was Lower Burma.* Honolulu: University of Hawai'i, 2005.

———. "Mranma Pran: When Context Encounters Notion." *Journal of Southeast Asian Studies* 39, no. 2 (2008): 193–217.

———. *Myth and History in the Historiography of Early Burma: Paradigms, Primary Sources, and Prejudices.* Athens: Ohio University Press, 1998.

———. "The Myth of the 'Three Shan Brothers' and the Ava Period in Burmese History." *Journal of Asian Studies* 55, no. 4 (1996): 881–901.

———. "A New/Old Look at 'Classical' and 'Post-Classical' Southeast Asia/Burma." In *New Perspectives on the History and Historiography of Southeast Asia: Continuing Explorations,* edited by Michael Aung-Thwin and K. R. Hall, pp. 25–55. London: Routledge, 2011.

———. *Pagan: The Origins of Modern Burma.* Honolulu: University of Hawai'i Press, 1985.

———. "Parochial Universalism, Democracy Jihad, and the Orientalist Image of Burma: The New Evangelism." *Pacific Affairs* 74 (2001/2002): 483–505.

———. "Principles and Patterns of the Precolonial Burmese State." In *Tradition and Modernity in Myanmar: Proceedings of an International Conference held in Berlin from May 7th to May 9th, 1993,* edited by Uta Gartner and Jens Lorenz, pp. 15–44. Berlin: Humboldt-University zu Berlin, 1994.

———. "Prophecies, Omens, and Dialogue: Tools of the Trade in Burmese Historiography." In *Historical Essays in Honor of Kenneth R. Rossman,* edited by Kent Newmyer, pp. 171–185. Lincoln: University of Nebraska Press, 1980.

———. "The Role of *Sasana* Reform in Burmese History, Economic Dimensions of a Religious Purification." *Journal of Asian Studies* 38, no. 4 (1979): 671–688.

———. "Spirals in Burmese and Early Southeast Asian History." *Journal of Interdisciplinary History* 21, no. 4 (1991): 575–602.

———. "A Tale of Two Kingdoms: Ava and Pegu in the Fifteenth Century." *Journal of Southeast Asian Studies* 42, no. 1 (2011): 1–16.

———. "Those Men in Saffron Robes." *Journal of Burma Studies* 17, no. 2 (2013): 243–334.

Aung-Thwin, Michael, and Kenneth R. Hall, eds. *New Perspectives on the History and Historiography of Southeast Asia: Continuing Explorations.* New York: Routledge, 2011.

Aung-Thwin, Michael, and Maitrii Aung-Thwin. *A History of Myanmar since Ancient Times: Traditions and Transformations.* 2nd ed., updated and expanded. London: Reaktion Books, 2013.

Aye Chan. "Burma: Shan Domination in the Ava Period (c. AD 1310–1555)." *Journal of the Siam Society* 94 (2006): 26–50.

Aye Myint, U. *Burmese Design through Drawings.* Edited by Sone Simatrang. Translated by U Thanoe. Bangkok: Silpakorn University and the Toyota Foundation, 1993.

Badgley, John. Book Review. *Journal of Southeast Asian Studies* 30, no. 2 (September 1999): 364–365.

Baker, Chris. "Before Ayutthaya Fell: Economic Life in an Industrious Society: Note on the Testimonies and the Description of Ayutthaya. *Journal of the Siam Society* 99 (2011): 72–80.

Bannya Dala, Amatkyi. *Yazadhiyaza Ayedawpon.* 3rd ed. Yangon: Swesa Press, 1974.

Bauer, Christian. "Nidana Ramadhipati-katha (The Pak Lat Chronicles, Volume II)." Manuscript.

The Biographies of Shin Ratthathara, Shin Tezawthaya, Shin Aggathamadhi, Shin Thilawuntha. Yangon: Sapebeikman, 1974.

Blagden, Charles Otto. "The Chronicles of Pegu: A Text in the Mon Language." *Journal of the Royal Asiatic Society* (1907): 367–374.

Bloch, Marc. *Feudal Society.* Translated by L. A. Manyon. 2 vols. Chicago: University of Chicago Press, 1970.

Bode, Mabel Haynes. *The Pali Literature of Burma.* London: Royal Asiatic Society, 1909.

Braudel, Fernand. *On History.* Translated by Sarah Matthews. Chicago: University of Chicago Press, 1980.

Bronson, B. "Exchange at the Upstream and Downstream Ends: Notes toward a Functional Model of the Coastal State in Southeast Asia." In *Economic Exchange and Social Interaction in Southeast Asia: Perspectives from Prehistory, History and Ethnography,* edited by K. L. Hutterer, pp. 39–52. Ann Arbor: University of Michigan Center for South and Southeast Asian Studies, Papers on South and Southeast Asia 13, 1977.

Brown, Robert. "Review: *The Mists of Rāmañña: The Legend That Was Lower Burma* by Michael A. Aung-Thwin." *Journal of Asian Studies* 67, no. 1 (February 2008): 340–344.

Buckley, Brendan M., Roland Fletcher, Shi-Yu Simon Wang, Brian Zottoli, and Christophe Pottier. "Monsoon Extremes and Society over the Past Millennium on Mainland Southeast Asia." *Quaternary Science Reviews* 95 (2014): 1–19.

The Burma Historical Commission. *Pagán Minsasu Thutethana Lokngan* [Research Project on the Collection of Pagán Ink Inscriptions]. Yangon: Ministry of Culture, 1964.
The Burney Papers. Edited by David K. Wyatt. Westmead, UK: Gregg International, 1971.
Chen, Yi-Sein. "The Chinese Inscription at Pagan." *Bulletin of the Burma Historical Commission* 1, no. 2 (1960).
Chevilliot, E. "I.O. Library [India Office], Catalogue of Burmese MSS" (handwritten).
Chit Thein, U., trans. and ed. *She Haung Mon Kyauksa Paung Chok* [MKPC]. Yangon: Ministry of Culture, 1965.
Chronicle of Ayutthaya: A Translation of the Yodaya Yazawin. Translated by Tun Aung Chain. Yangon: Ministry of Education, Union of Myanmar, 2005.
Cooper, W. G. "A Note on Talaing Nissaya and Vocabulary." *Journal of the Burma Research Society* 4, no. 2 (1914): 126.
de la Perriere, Benedicte Brac. Book Review. *Journal of Asian Studies* 60, no. 1 (February 2001): 286–288.
d'Hubert, Thibaut. "The Lord of the White Elephant: Interpreting the Islamicate Epigraphic, Numismatic, and Literary Material from the Mrauk U Period of Arakan (ca. 1430–1784)." *Journal of Burma Studies* 19, no. 2 (2015): 341–359.
Diflfoth, Gerald. *The Dvaravati Old Mon Language and Nyah Kur.* Bangkok: Chulalongkorn University Print House, 1984.
Duroiselle, Charles, ed. *A List of Inscriptions Found in Burma.* Archaeological Survey of Burma, edited by Charles Duroiselle. Rangoon: Office of the Superintendent, Government Printing, 1921.
———. "Mon Inscriptions." *Epigraphia Birmanica Being Lithic and Other Inscriptions of Burma* 1, no. 2 (1960): 69–168.
———. "Talaing Nissayas," *Journal of the Burma Research Society* 3, no. 2 (1913): 103–145.
Eaton, Richard M. "Locating Arakan in Time, Space, and Historical Scholarship." In *The Maritime Frontier of Burma: Exploring Political, Cultural and Commercial Interaction in the Indian Ocean World, 1200–1800*, edited by Jos Gommans and Jacques Leider, pp. 225–231. Amsterdam: Koninklijke Nederlandse Akademie van Wetenschapen and KITLV Press, 2002.
Epigraphia Birmanica: Being Lithic and Other Inscriptions of Burma. Edited by Charles Duroiselle. Vol. 3, Archaeological Survey of Burma. Rangoon: Government Printing and Stationery, 1923.
Epigraphia Birmanica: Being Lithic and Other Inscriptions of Burma. Edited by U Mya. Vol. 4, part 1, Archaeological Survey of Burma. Rangoon: Superintendent, Government Printing and Stationery, 1934.
Epigraphia Birmanica: Being Lithic and Other Inscriptions of Burma. Edited by Charles Duroiselle. Vol. 1, part 2. Archaeological Survey of Burma. Rangoon: Superintendent, Government Printing and Stationery, 1920.
Fernquest, Jon. "Min-gyi-nyo, the Shan Invasions of Ava (1524–27), and the Beginnings of Expansionary Warfare in Toungoo Burma: 1486–1539." *SOAS Bulletin of Burma Research* 3, no. 2 (Autumn 2005): 284–395.
———. "Rajadhirat's Mask of Command: Military Leadership in Burma (c. 1348–1421). *SOAS Bulletin of Burma Research* 4, no. 1 (Spring 2006): 3–29.
Forchhammer, Emil, ed. *King Wagaru's Manu Dhammasattham. Text, Translation, and Notes.* Rangoon: Government Press, 1885.
Furnivall, J. S. "Manu in Burma: Some Burmese *Dhammathats.*" *Journal of the Burma Research Society* 30, no. 2 (1940): 351–370.

Furnivall, J. S., and Pe Maung Tin, eds. *Zambudipa Okhsaung Kyan.* Yangon: Burma Research Society, 1960.

Goh, Geok Yian. "Cakkravatiy Anuruddha and the Buddhist Oikoumene: Historical Narratives of Kingship and Religious Networks in Burma, Northern Thailand, and Sri Lanka (11th–14th Centuries)." PhD diss., University of Hawai'i, 2007.

Gommans, Jos, and Jacques Leider, eds. *The Maritime Frontier of Burma: Exploring Political, Cultural and Commercial Interaction in the Indian Ocean World, 1200–1800.* Leiden: Koninklijke Nederlandse Akademie van Wetenschappen, 2002.

Government of India. "The Kalyani Inscriptions Erected by King Dhammaceti at Pegu in 1476 D.C. [*sic*]." In *Archaeological Survey of India*, edited by Archaeology Survey of India. Rangoon: Government Printing and Stationery, 1892.

Griswold, Alexander. "The Holy Land Transported." In *Paranavitana Felicitation Volume*, pp. 173–221. Colombo, Ceylon: M.D. Gunasena, 1965.

Hall, D. G. E. *Burma.* London: Hutchinson's University Library, 1950.

Halliday, Robert, ed. *Lik Smin Asah: The Story of the Founding of Pegu and a Subsequent Invasion from South India with English Translation, Notes, and Vocabulary of Undefined Words.* Rangoon: American Baptist Mission Press, 1923.

———. "Slapat Rajawan Datow Smin Ron" [History of Kings]. *Journal of the Burma Research Society* 13, nos. 1 and 2 (1923): 9–31; 33–67.

———. *The Talaings.* Rangoon: Superintendent Government Printing, Burma, 1917.

Harvey, G. E. *A History of Burma: From the Earliest Times to 10 March 1824: The Beginning of the English Conquest.* London: Frank Cass, 1925.

Heine-Geldern, Robert. *Conceptions of State and Kingship in Southeast Asia.* Ithaca, NY: Cornell University Southeast Asia Program Department of Far Eastern Studies, 1956.

Herbert, Patricia M. "The Sir Arthur Phayre Collection of Burmese Manuscripts." *British Library Journal* 1, no. 1 (1975): 62–70.

Hla Pe. *Burma: Literature, Historiography, Scholarship, Language, Life, and Buddhism.* Singapore: Institute of Southeast Asian Studies, 1985.

Hla Tin, U., ed. *Zatatawpon Yazawin* [Chronicle of Royal Horoscopes]. Yangon: Ministry of Culture, 1960.

Htin Aung, Dr. *Burmese History before 1287: A Defence of the Chronicles.* Oxford: The Asoka Society, 1970.

———. *History of Burma.* New York: Columbia University Press, 1967.

Huber, Edouard. "La Fin De La Dynastie De Pagan." *Bulletin de l'Ecole française d'Extrême-Orient* 9, no. 9 (1909): 633–680.

Huxley, Andrew. "Mon Studies and Professor Forchhammer: The Admiration That Destroys." *Zeitschrift der Deutschen Morenlandischen Gesellschaft* 162, no. 2 (2012): 391–410.

———. "Pre-Colonial Burmese Law: Conical Hat and Shoulder Bag." *25 Int'l Institute of Asian Studies Online News* (2001), http://www.iias.nl/iiasn/25/theme/25T7.html.

"The Itinerary of Ludovico di Varthema of Bologna from 1502 to 1508." *SOAS Bulletin of Burma Research* 2, no. 2 (Autumn 2004).

Kala, U. *Mahayazawingyi* [Great Royal Chronicle]. Edited by Saya Pwa. 3 vols., vol. 1. Yangon: Hanthawaddy Press, 1960.

Kirichenko, Alexey. "From Ava to Mandalay: Toward Charting the Development of Burmese *Yazawin* Traditions." *Journal of Burma Studies* 13 (2009): 1–75.

Kyan Daw, and Yi Yi, Dr. "Shwedagon Zedi Taw Gyi Hma Kye Ok Mya, Apaing (1) [Copper Plates from the Shwedagon Zedi, Part (1)]. *Myanma Thamaing Thutethana Sasaung* [Myanmar Historical Research Journal] 1 (1995): 195–211.

Kyaw Dun, U., ed. *Myanma Sa Nyunbaung Kyan* [Anthology of Burmese Literature]. 5 vols. Rangoon: Superintendent Government Press, 1961.

Ladurie, Emmanuel LeRoy. *The Mind and Method of the Historian.* Chicago: University of Chicago Press, 1981.

Laichen, Sun. *Chinese Historical Sources on Burma: A Bibliography of Primary and Secondary Works.* DeKalb: Center for Southeast Asian Studies Northern Illinois University, 1997.

———. "Ming-Southeast Asian Overland Interactions, 1368–1644." PhD diss., University of Michigan, 2000.

———. "Shan Gems, Chinese Silver and the Rise of Shan Principalities in Northern Burma, c. 1450–1527." In *Southeast Asia in the Fifteenth Century: The China Factor,* edited by Geoff Wade and Sun Laichen, pp. 169–196. Singapore: National University of Singapore, 2010.

Lammerts, Christian. "Andrew Huxley: Legal Historian of Burma and Southeast Asia." *Journal of Burma Studies* 19, no. 2 (December 2015): 267–273.

———. "The Authorship of the *Dhammavilasa Dhammathat.*" In *Myanmar Historical Commission Conference Proceedings,* part 2, edited by the Golden Jubilee Publication Committee, 190–214. Yangon: Myanmar Historical Commission, 2005.

———. "The Dhammavilasa Dhammathat: A Critical Historiography, Analysis, and Translation of the Text." Master's thesis, Cornell University, January 2005.

———. "Narratives of Buddhist Legislation: Textual Authority and Legal Heterodoxy in Seventeenth through Nineteenth Century Burma." *Journal of Southeast Asian Studies* 44, no. 1 (February 2013): 118–144.

Leach, E. R. *Political Systems of Highland Burma: A Study of Kachin Social Structure.* Boston: Beacon Press, 1970.

Lehman, F. K. "Ethnic Categories in Burma and the Theory of Social Systems." In *Southeast Asian Tribes, Minorities, and Nations,* edited by Peter Kunstadter. Princeton, NJ: Princeton University Press, 1967.

Lieberman, Victor B. "An Age of Commerce in Southeast Asia? Problems of Regional Coherence—A Review Article." *Journal of Asian Studies* 54, no. 3 (1995): 796–807.

———. *Burmese Administrative Cycles: Anarchy and Conquest, c. 1580–1760.* Princeton, NJ: Princeton University Press, 1984.

———. "Charter State Collapse in Southeast Asia, ca. 1250–1400, as a Problem in Regional and World History." *American Historical Review* 116, no. 4 (2011): 937–963.

———. "Ethnic Politics in Eighteenth-Century Burma." *Modern Asian Studies* 12, no. 3 (1978): 455–482.

———. "Europeans, Trade, and the Unification of Burma, c. 1540–1620," *Oriens Extremus* 17, no. 2 (1980): 203–226.

———. "Excising the 'Mon Paradigm' from Burmese Historiography." *Journal of Southeast Asian Studies* 38, no. 2 (2007): 377–383.

———. "How Reliable Is U Kala's Burmese Chronicle? Some New Comparisons." *Journal of Southeast Asian Studies* 17, no. 2 (1986): 236–255.

———. "Local Integration and Eurasian Analogies: Structuring Southeast Asian History, c. 1350–c.1830." *Modern Asian Studies* 27, no. 3 (1993): 475–572.

———. "A New Look at the Sasanavamsa." *Bulletin of the School of Oriental and African Studies* 39 (1976): 137–149.

———. "Provincial Reforms in Taung-ngu Burma." *Bulletin of the School of Oriental and African Studies* 43, no. 3 (1980): 548–569.

———. "Reinterpreting Burmese History." *Comparative Studies in Society and History* 29 (1987): 162–194.

———. *Strange Parallels: Southeast Asia in Global Context, c. 800–1830.* Cambridge: Cambridge University Press, 2003.

———. "A Zone of Refuge in Southeast Asia? Reconceptualizing Interior Spaces." *Journal of Global History* 5 (2010): 333–346.

List of Microfilms Deposited in the Centre for East Asian Cultural Studies. Burma. Part 8. Tokyo: Toyo Bunko, 1976.

Luce, G. H. "The Early *Syam* in Burma's History." *Journal of the Siam Society* 46 (1958): 123–214.

———. "The Early *Syam* in Burma's History: A Supplement." *Journal of the Siam Society* 47, no. 1 (1959): 59–101.

———. *Old Burma-Early Pagan.* 3 Vols. Locust Valley, NY: J. J. Augustin, 1969–1970.

Luce, G. H., et al. *Inscriptions of Burma.* London: Oxford University Press, H. Milford, 1934.

Ma Ma Lay. *Blood Bond.* Translated by Than Than Win. Edited by Michael Aung-Thwin. University of Hawai'i Center for Southeast Asian Studies Translation Series. Honolulu: University of Hawai'i Center for Southeast Asian Studies, 2004.

Maung Maung. *The Story of Wunzin Min Yaza.* Yangon: Tain Lon Zambu Press, 1912.

McCormick, Patrick. "Mon Histories: Between Translation and Retelling." PhD diss., University of Washington, 2010.

———. "Writing a Singular Past: Mon History and 'Modern' Historiography in Burma." *SOJOURN: Journal of Social Issues in Southeast Asia* 29, no. 2 (2014): 300–331.

Miksic, John. *Singapore and the Silk Road of the Sea: 1300–1800.* Singapore: National University of Singapore Press and the National Museum of Singapore Press, 2013.

Mingyi Maha Thiri Zeyathu, ed. *Pitakat Taw Thamaing.* Yangon: Tipitaka Nikaya Thathana Committee, 1989.

MKPC (see *She Haung Mon Kyauksa Paung Chok* or Chit Thein, U.)

Mon Yazawin (see Mwan Rajawan)

Mwan Rajawan (Mon Yazawin) [microfilm copy in the Toyo Bunko]. *List of Microfilms Deposited in the Centre for East Asian Cultural Studies. Burma. Part 8.* Tokyo, 1976.

Mya, Thiripyanchi U. *She Haung Ok Khwek Yokpwa Sintutaw Mya: Votive Tablets of Burma.* Part 1. Yangon: Archaeological Survey of Burma, 1961.

Myanma Swe Son Kyan [Encyclopedia Myanmar]. 1998–1999.

Nagara, Prasert Na, and Alexander B. Griswold. *Epigraphic and Historical Studies.* Bangkok: Historical Society, 1992.

Nai Pan Hla. "Yazadarit Ayedawpon Kyan nhin Mon Thichin Mya" [The Yazadarit Ayedawpon Treatise and Mon Songs], *Journal of the Burma Research Society* 56 no. 1 (1973): 99–126.

———. *Yazadhiyaza Ayedawpon Kyan.* Yangon: Thein Than U Press, 1977.

A New History of Southeast Asia. Edited by M. C. Ricklefs. Singapore: Houndmills, 2010.

Nidana Ramadhipati-katha. Edited by Phra Candakanto. Pak Lat, Siam, 1912.

Nu, U. *Saturday's Son.* New Haven and London: Yale University Press, 1975.

Nyein Maung, ed. *She Haung Myanma Kyauksa Mya* [Ancient Burmese Stone Inscriptions]. Vols. 1–5. Yangon: Sapebeikman, 1972–1996.

O'Connor, V. C. Scott. *Mandalay and Other Cities of the Past in Burma.* London: Hutchinson & Co., 1907 (Reprint 1987).

Okudaira, Ryuji. "The Burmese Dhammathat." In *Laws of South-East Asia: The Pre-Modern Texts,* edited by M. B. Hooker, pp. 23–142. Singapore: Singapore National Printers, 1986.

Onkyi, Daw. "Narapati Sagaing Htupayon Kyauksa [The Sagaing Htupayon Inscription of Narapati]." *Myanma Thamaing Thutethana Sasaung* [Myanmar Historical Research Journal] 5 (2000): 73–97.

Oshegowa, Nina. *Kunst in Burma.* Leipzig: E. A. Seemann, 1988.

Paikhu Yazawin [Pegu Chronicle]. National Library. Yangon.

Paññasami. *Sasanavamsa* [History of the Religion]. Translated by Bimala Churn Law. London: Pali Text Society, 1952.

Parker, Edward Harper. *Burma: With Special Reference to her Relations with China.* Rangoon: Rangoon Gazette Press, 1893.

Pearn, B. R. *A History of Rangoon.* Rangoon: American Baptist Mission Press, 1939.

Pe Maung Tin. "Anantathuriya's Death Song I." *Journal of the Burma Research Society* 9, no. 3 (1919): 153–155.

———. "Anantathuriya's Death Song II." *Journal of the Burma Research Society* 10, no. 1 (1920): 27.

———"Burmese Manuscripts in the British Museum," *Journal of the Burma Research Society* 14, no. 3 (1924): 221–246.

———. "Dictionary Jottings: Philological Features of the Inscriptions." *Journal of the Burma Research Society* 19, no. 3 (1929): 78–79.

———. *Myanma Sape Thamaing* [History of Burmese Literature]. Yangon: Burma Research Society, 1977.

———. "Phonetics in a Passport." *Journal of the Burma Research Society* 12, no. 2 (1922): 127–132.

Phayre, A. P. *History of Burma, including Burma proper, Pegu, Taungu, Tenasserim, and Arakan.* London: Trübner & Co., 1883.

———. "On the History of Pegu." *Journal of the Asiatic Society of Bengal* 42, no. 2 (1873): 121–159.

Po Byu, U. "Shin Uttamagyaw and His Tawla, A Nature Poem: I-IX." *Journal of the Burma Research Society* 1917, pt. 2–3; 1918, pt. 1–2, 1919, pt. 1–2, and 1920, pt. 1.

Polanyi, Karl, C. M. Arensberg, and H. W. Pearson. *Trade and Market in the Early Empires.* Glencoe, IL: Free Press, 1957.

Pranke, Patrick Arthur. "The 'Treatise on the Lineage of Elders' (*Vamsadipani*): Monastic Reform and the Writing of Buddhist History in Eighteenth-Century Burma." PhD diss., University of Michigan, 2004.

Preliminary Report of the Kyoto University Scientific Survey to Burma 1974. Kyoto: Kyoto University, 1976.

Pugam Yazawin [Chronicle of Pagan]. National Library. Yangon.

Reid, Anthony. *Southeast Asia in the Age of Commerce, 1450–1680.* Volume One: *The Lands Below the Winds.* New Haven, CT: Yale University Press, 1988.

Reprint from Dalrymple's Oriental Repertory, 1791–7 of Portions Relating to Burma. Rangoon: Government Printing, 1926.

Sai Aung Tun. *History of the Shan State from Its Origins to 1962.* Chiang Mai: Silkworm Books, 2009.

Sandalinka, Shin. *The Maniyadanabon of Shin Sandalinka.* Translated by L. E. Bagshawe. Vol. 115. Cornell University Southeast Asia Program Data Papers. Ithaca, NY: Cornell University Southeast Asia Program 1981.

Sandhu, Kernial Singh, and Paul Wheatley, eds., with Ton Abdul Aziz bin Mat. *Melaka: The Transformation of a Malay capital, c. 1400–1980.* Kuala Lumpur: Oxford University Press, 1983.

San Lwin, U., trans. "The Campaigns of Razadarit-Binnya Dala." Manuscript.

San Lwin, trans., and Sunait Chutintaranond, ed. *The Campaigns of Razadarit, by Binnya Dala.* Bangkok: Institute of Asian Studies, 2007.

Sao Saimong Mangrai, ed. *The Padaeng Chronicle and the Jengtung State Chronicle Translated.* Ann Arbor: University of Michigan, Center for South and Southeast Asian Studies, 1981.

——. *The Shan States and the British Annexation.* Vol. 57. *Southeast Asia Program Data Paper.* Ithaca, NY: Cornell University Southeast Asia Program, 1965.

Sastri, Nilakanta. *A History of South India.* 3rd ed. London: Oxford University Press, 1966.

Saw Lu [alias U Saw Tun]. *Pagan Khit Myanma Sa* [Burmese Literature of the Pagan Period]. 3 vols. Yangon: Sapebeikman Press, 1996.

Saya Thein. "Bago Hanthawaddy Myo go Min aphyit nhin so san daw muthaw Shin Saw Bu akyaung [Account of Shin Saw Bu who reigned as King in Hanthawaddy (Pegu)], *Journal of the Burma Research Society* 1, no. 2 (1911): 10–16.

Scott, James C. *The Art of Not Being Governed: An Anarchist History of Upland Southeast Asia.* New Haven, CT: Yale University Press, 2009.

Sears, Laurie J., ed. *Autonomous Histories, Particular Truths: Essays in Honor of John R. W. Smail.* Madison: University of Wisconsin Center for Southeast Asian Studies, 1993.

Shaffer, Lynda. *Maritime Southeast Asia to 1500: Sources and Studies in World History.* Armonk, NY: M.E. Sharpe, 1996.

Shah Paung, "Leading Ladies." *The Irrawaddy* 13, no. 9 (September 2005): n.p.

She Haung Mon Kyauksa Paung Chok [MKPC] [Collection of Ancient Mon Stone Inscriptions]. Translated and edited by U Chit Thein. Yangon: Ministry of Culture, 1965.

She Haung Myanma Kyauksa Mya [SMK] [Ancient Burmese Stone Inscriptions]. Vols. 1–5. Edited by Nyeing Maung. Yangon: Sapebeikman, 1972–1996.

She Khit Myanma Sa Kabya Mya: Burmese Classical Poems Selected and Translated. New York: Rangoon Gazette Limited, n.d.

Shorto, H. L. "The Dewatau Sotapan: A Mon Prototype of the 37 Nats." *Bulletin of the School of Oriental and African Studies* 30 (1967): 132–133.

——. *A Dictionary of Modern Spoken Mon.* London: Oxford University Press, 1962.

——. *A Dictionary of the Mon Inscriptions from the Sixth to the Sixteenth Centuries.* London: Oxford University Press, 1971.

——. "The Gavampati Tradition in Burma." *R. C. Majumdar Felicitation Volume.* Edited by H. B. Sarkar. Calcutta: Firma K. L. Mukhopadhyay, 1970.

——. "A Mon Genealogy of Kings: Observations on the Nidana Arambhakatha." In *Historians of South East Asia,* edited by D. G. E. Hall. London: Oxford University Press, 1961.

——. "Nidāna Rāmādhipatī-kathā (The Pak Lạt Chronicles, Volume II)." Edited by Christian Bauer. Manuscript.

——. "Translation by Prof. H.L. Shorto, SOAS of Pages 34–44 and 6–264 of the Second of Two Volumes of Historical Texts Issued from Paklat: Nidana Ramadhipati-katha (or as on Binding Rajawamsa Dhammaceti Mahapitakadhara), ed. Phra Candakanto (Pak Lat, Siam: 1912)." Manuscript.

Sithu Gamani Thingyan. *Zinme Yazawin* (Chronicle of Chiang Mai). Translated by Thaw Kaung and Ni Ni Myint. Edited by Tun Aung Chain. Yangon: Universities Historical Research Centre, 2003.

Skilling, P. Dvaravati. "Recent Revelations and Research." In *Dedications to Her Royal Highness Princess Galyani Vadhana Krom Luang Naradhiwas Rajanagarindra on Her 80th Birthday,* edited by C. Baker, pp. 87–112. Bangkok: The Siam Society, 2003.

Smail, John, W. "On the Possibility of an Autonomous History of Modern Southeast Asia." *Journal of Southeast Asian History* 2, no. 2 (1961): 72–102.

SMK (see *She Haung Myanma Kyauksa Mya* or Nyeing Maung)

Spellman, J. W. "The Symbolic Significance of the Number Twelve in Ancient India." *Journal of Asian Studies* 22, no. 1 (1962): 79–88.

Spencer, G. "Temple Money-Lending and Livestock Redistribution in Early Tanjore." *Indian Economic and Historical Review* 5 (1968): 277–293.

Spiro, Melford E. *Buddhism and Society: A Great Tradition and Its Burmese Vicissitudes.* Berkeley: University of California Press, 1982.
Stadtner, Donald M. "The Mon of Lower Burma." *Journal of the Siam Society* 96 (2008): 193–215.
Stewart, J. A. "Excavation and Exploration in Pegu." *Journal of the Burma Research Society* 7, no. 1 (1917): 14–25.
———. "Note on Some Authorities for the History of Burma." *Journal of the Burma Research Society* 13, no. 2 (1923): 69–76.
Stuart-Fox, Martin. "Book Review." *Journal of the Economic and Social History of the Orient* 44, no. 1 (2001): 88–90.
Sudhammawati-rajawamsa; Siharajadhiraja-wamsa (Sudhammawati; Gawampati; Rajadhiraj). Edited by Phra Candacanto. Pak Lat, Thailand, 1910.
Sulloway, Frank J. *Born to Rebel: Birth Order, Family Dynamics, and Creative Lives.* 1st ed. New York: Pantheon Books, 1996.
Symes, M. *An Account of an Embassy to the Kingdom of Ava, Sent by the Governor-General of India, in the Year 1795.* London: W. Bulmer, 1800.
———. *Journal of His Second Embassy to the Court of Ava in 1802.* London: George Allen & Unwin Ltd., 1955.
Taung Ngu Yazawin [Chronicle of Taung-ngu]. Tokyo: Toyo Bunko, 1976.
Taw Sein Ko. "The Linguistic Affinities of the Pyu Language." *Journal of the Burma Research Society* 5, no. 2 (1915): 102–110.
———. *Lithic and Other Inscriptions of Burma.* Rangoon: Superintendent of Government Printing, 1972.
———. "A Preliminary Study of the Kalyani Inscriptions of Dhammacheti, 1476 A.D." *Indian Antiquary* 22 (1893): 29–53, 85–89, 150–159, 206–218, 236–243.
Taylor, Robert H. "Do States Make Nations?" *Southeast Asia Research* 13, no. 3: 261–286.
———. "Perceptions of Ethnicity in the Politics of Burma." *Southeast Asian Journal of Social Sciences* 10, no. 1 (1982): 7–22.
———. *The State in Myanmar.* Honolulu: University of Hawai'i Press, 2009.
Tet Htoot, U. "The Nature of the Burmese Chronicles." In *Historians of Southeast Asia,* edited by D. G. E. Hall, pp. 50–62. London: Oxford University Press, 1961.
Tha Myat, Thiripyanchi U. *Mon Myanma Ekaya Thamaing* [History of Mon-Myanma Alphabet]. Yangon: Ministry of Culture, 1956.
———. *Myazedi Khaw Gubyauk Kyi Pyu Kyauksa* [The So-Called Myazedi Pyu Inscription of the Gubyauk Kyi]. Rangoon: Democracy Publishing Co. Ltd., 1958.
———. *Pyu Phat Ca* [Pyu Reader]. Rangoon: U Hla Din, 1963.
Than Tun, Dr. "Administration under King Thalun (1629–1648)." *Journal of the Burma Research Society* 51, no. 2 (1968): 173–188.
———. "History of Burma: A.D. 1300–1400." *Journal of the Burma Research Society* 42, no. 2 (1959): 119–133.
———. "History of Shwegyin Nikaya (Shwegyin Sect in the Order of Buddhist Monks) in Burma." *Shiroku* 3, no. 16 (1983): 15–25.
———. *Khit Haung Myanma Yazawin* [History of Ancient Myanma]. Yangon: Maha Dagon Publishers, 1969.
———. *Myanma Thamaing Mye Pon Mya* [Maps of Burmese History]. Yangon: Myanmar Historical Commission, 2005.
———, ed. *The Royal Orders of Burma, A.D. 1598–1885.* Kyoto: Center for Southeast Asian Studies, Kyoto University, 1983.
Thein Hlaing, U, ed. *Twinthintaik Wun, Mahasithu U Htun Nyo, Mahayazawinthit (Nyaung Yan Set).* Yangon: Universities Historical Research Department, 1997.

Thet Tin, U. *Shwemawdaw Thamaing* [History of the Shwemawdaw]. Yangon: Burma Translation Society, 1955.

Thilawuntha, Shin. *Yazawinkyaw* [Celebrated Chronicle]. Yangon: Burma Research Society, n.d.

Thu Nandar. *The Catalogue of Materials on Myanmar History in Microfilms Deposited in the Center for East Asian Cultural Studies.* Vol. 1. Tokyo: Tokyo University of Foreign Studies, 2004.

Tierney, Brian. *The Middle Ages.* New York: McGraw-Hill, 1992.

Tin Hla Thaw. "History of Burma: A.D. 1400–1500." *Journal of the Burma Research Society* 42, no. 2 (1959): 135–151.

Tin Shein, U, ed. *Hmannan Mahayazawindawgyi* [Great Royal Chronicle of the Palace of Mirrors]. 3 vols. Yangon: Pyi Gyi Man Taing Piktakat Press, 1967.

Toe Hla, Dr. "Money-Lending and Contractual 'Thet-Kayits': A Socio-Economic Pattern of the Later Kon-Baung Period, 1819–1885." PhD diss., Northern Illinois University, 1987.

Trager, F. N., and W. J. Koenig with the assistance of Yi Yi. *Burmese Sit-táans 1764–1826: Records of Rural Life and Administration.* Tucson, AZ: Association for Asian Studies, 1979.

Tun Aung Chain, ed. and trans. "The Deposition of Kyawzwa: A Reconsideration of the Inscriptional Evidence." In *Broken Glass: Pieces of Myanmar History*, pp. 45–49. Yangon: SEMEO Regional Centre for History and Tradition, 2004.

Tun Nyein, U. "Maunggun Gold Plates." *Epigraphia Indica* 5, no. 4 (1889–1899): 101–102.

Twinthin Mahasithu, *Mahayazawinthit.* Yangon: Daw Myint Myint Press, 1998.

Twinthintaikwun Mahasithu, *Twinthin Myanma Yazawinthit* [Twinthin's New Chronicle of Myanma]. Edited by U Myint Swe. Vol. 1. Yangon: Mingala Pon Hneik Taik, 1968.

Vickery, Michael. *Champa Revised.* Singapore: National University of Singapore, 2004.

Wales, H. G. Q. "Anuruddha and the Thaton Tradition." *Journal of the Royal Asiatic Society* 3–4 (1947): 152–156.

———. "Dvaravati in South-East Asian Cultural History." *Journal of the Royal Asiatic Society* 1–2 (1966): 40–52.

———. *Early Burma-Old Siam.* London: Bernard Quaritch Ltd., 1973.

Wheatley, Paul. *Nagara and Commandery: Origins of the Southeast Asian Urban Traditions.* Chicago: University of Chicago Department of Geography, 1983.

Whitmore, John K. "The Rise of the Coast: Trade, State and Culture in Early Đai Viêt." *Journal of Southeast Asian Studies* 37, no. 1 (2006): 103–122.

Wisseman Christie, J. "The Medieval Tamil-language Inscriptions in Southeast Asia and China." *Journal of Southeast Asian Studies* 29, no. 2 (1998): 239–268.

Wolters, O. W. *The Fall of Srivijaya in Malay History.* Ithaca, NY: Cornell University Press, 1970.

Woodman, Dorothy. *The Making of Burma.* London: Cresset Press, 1962.

Wyatt, David K., and W. Arunrat. *The Chiang Mai Chronicle.* Chiang Mai: Silkworm Books, 1998.

———. *The Crystal Sands: The Chronicles of Nagara Sri Dharrmaraja.* Ithaca, NY: Cornell University Southeast Asia Program Department of Asian Studies, 1975.

———. "Relics, Oaths and Politics in Thirteenth-Century Siam." *Journal of Southeast Asian Studies* 32, no. 1 (2001): 3–65.

Yadanatheinga Konbaungmyoti Mintayagyi Ameindaw [Edicts of the Great King Who Built Yadanatheingy]. London: India Office Library Burmese Manuscripts, n.d.

Yatana Thikha Myo Thamaing [Account of Yatana Thikha Town]. Yangon: Sapebeikman, 1976.

Yazadhiyaza Ayedawpon Kyan. Edited by Ko Shwe Thein Min, Yangon: Pan Shwe Pyi Sa Auk Taik, 2012.

Yi Yi, Dr. "Additional Burmese Historical Sources 1752–76." *Naingnan Thamaing Thutethana Sasaung* [Researches in Burmese History] 3 (1979): 103–120.

———. "Kongbaung khit sittan mya" [Revenue Inquests of the Kongbaung Period]. *Journal of the Burma Research Society* 49 (1966): 71–127.

———. *Myanma Naingnan Akhye Ane 1714–1752* [Conditions in Burma 1714–1752]. Yangon: Myanma Thamaing U Si Htana, 1973.

Zatatawpon Yazawin [Chronicle of Royal Horoscopes]. Edited by U Hla Tin. Yangon: Ministry of Culture, Union of Myanmar, 1960.

Zhi-yuan Zhengmian Lu [ZZL]. Translated by Sun Lai Chen. Manuscript.

Zon Pann Pwint. "Marionettes Enjoy Revival." *Myanmar Times*, September 1–7, 2008, pp. 1–2.

INDEX

About the Author

MICHAEL A. AUNG-THWIN is professor of Asian studies at the University of Hawai'i at Mānoa, having previously taught at Elmira College in upstate New York and Northern Illinois University in DeKalb, Illinois. He obtained his MA at the University of Illinois at Urbana-Champaign and his PhD at the University of Michigan in Ann Arbor. Publication of this book will form a "trilogy" from the University of Hawai'i Press, which also published his *Pagan: The Origins of Modern Burma* (1985) and *The Mists of Ramañña: The Legend That Was Lower Burma* (2005). Born in Myanmar, the author has returned to the country dozens of times in the past two decades and recently coauthored a general text, *A History of Myanmar since Ancient Times: Traditions and Transformations* (2013), with his son Maitrii Aung-Thwin of the National University of Singapore. His many articles and other books also deal mainly with Myanmar, mostly of the precolonial period.